The Guide to the American Revolutionary War In the Deep South and on the Frontier

The Guide to the American Revolutionary War in the Deep South and on the Frontier

Battles, Raids, and Skirmishes

Norman Desmarais

Busca, Inc.
Ithaca, New York

Busca, Inc.
P.O. Box 854
Ithaca, NY 14851
Ph: 607-546-4247
Fax: 607-546-4248
E-mail: info@buscainc.com
www.buscainc.com

BUSCA

BUSCA = SEARCH

*E
230
S7
D47
2013
C. 2*

First Edition

Printed in the United States of America

ISBN: 978-1-934934-07-4

Publisher's Cataloging-In-Publication Data
(Prepared by The Donohue Group, Inc.)

Desmarais, Norman.
   The guide to the American Revolutionary War in the Deep South and on the Frontier : battles, raids, and skirmishes / Norman Desmarais. -- 1st ed.

   p. : ill., maps ; cm. -- (Battlegrounds of freedom ; [7])

   Includes bibliographical references and index.
   ISBN: 978-1-934934-07-4

   1. United States--History--Revolution, 1775-1783--Battlefields--Southern States. 2. United States--History--Revolution, 1775-1783--Battlefields--West (U.S.) 3. Southern States--History, Military--18th century. 4. West (U.S.)--History, Military--18th century. 5. United States--History--Revolution, 1775-1783--Campaigns--Southern States. 6. United States--History--Revolution, 1775-1783--Campaigns--West (U.S.) I. Title.

E230.5.S7 D47 2013
973.3/3

All maps Copyright © 2013 DeLorme (www.delorme.com) Street Atlas USA®. Reprinted with permission.

Photography: author unless otherwise noted
Front cover photo: *Council of war. Reconstructed Fort Randolph, Point Pleasant, WV. Courtesy of Ed Lowe. ©EDLO Images. Used with permission.*

Composition: P.S. We Type ◆ Set ◆ Edit

The author has made every effort to ensure the accuracy of the information in this book. Neither the publisher nor the author is responsible for typographical mistakes, other errors, or information that has become outdated since the book went to press.

This volume is part of the BATTLEGROUNDS OF FREEDOM series.

To the men and women of our armed forces who go in harm's way to preserve the freedoms our ancestors have secured for us.

CONTENTS

Please see the Busca website **www.buscainc.com** for more Resources on the volumes by
Norman Desmarais including complete chronological and alphabetical lists of battles,
raids, and skirmishes; a complete Bibliography for all sources used and cited in the cre-
ation of these volumes; and photos.

LIST OF ILLUSTRATIONS

Maps

Photos

ACKNOWLEDGMENTS

I would like to express my gratitude to Jack Montgomery, acquisitions librarian at the University of Western Kentucky, Bowling Green, for igniting the spark to write this book, for his encouragement through the project and for introducing me to Connie Mills, the Kentucky Library Coordinator at the Kentucky Library and Museum. Michael Cooper, my publisher fanned the flame, nurtured the idea and brought it to fruition.

I also wish to thank Providence College for providing research and faculty development funds as well as time to pursue research. That research began with one sabbatical and extended beyond two others. The staffs at the Phillips Memorial Library of Providence College and the other academic libraries in Rhode Island were very helpful in obtaining and providing much research material.

David Loiterstein, Marketing Manager at Readex, also deserves my gratitude. He arranged for me to review the Early American Imprints Series I: Evans, 1639–1800 and the Early American Newspapers Series I, 1690–1876 and Series II, 1758–1900. The review periods coincided with important stages in my research. This undoubtedly made for better, more thorough, reviews, and it provided me with access to a wealth of primary sources that opened new avenues of research.

The members of the Brigade of the American Revolution (B.A.R.), the Continental Line and the British Brigade generously give of themselves to help recreate the era of the American War of Independence. Some of these people work at musea or at historical sites. Some are members of their town historical societies or even historians for their city or town. Many are amateur historians who know a great deal about the Revolutionary War in their area. They provided enormous insight into events and the location of sites. Special thanks go to Bob Winowitch and David Clemens who guided me around Long Island to ensure that I visited all the relevant sites there. They also provided historical material and referred me to important sources for further information.

Other B.A.R. members, including Todd Braisted, Todd Harburn, Lawrence McDonald, and VivianLea Solek read portions of the manuscript, suggested corrections and/or identified sources of additional information.

Many of the photographs were taken at various re-enactments. Without the efforts of the members of the B.A.R., these photos would not have been possible. Paul Bazin, Ed Lowe, Daniel O'Connell, Todd Harburn and Bob Kashary deserve credit for providing additional photographs.

There is a certain serendipity to research. During the 225th anniversary re-enactment of the march to Yorktown, Virginia, as the troops crossed the Hudson River in whale boats, I overheard B.A.R. member Daniel Hess talking about an engagement in which one of his ancestors had fought. I had been trying to locate documentation for that event, so I asked him about it after disembarking. He later sent me a copy of his ancestor's pension application, which not only described the event that I had been trying to document but also identified two other events unknown to me.

DeLorme's Street Atlas USA software was very valuable in creating and annotating all the maps. GPS devices are useful for locating known places with addresses. They are not so useful for getting to a general location such as a particular hill or field. Maps are more useful for this purpose, but it takes a specially trained eye to identify changes in terrain that may cover earthworks or fortifications. The late Marshall Sloat had such an eye and I am grateful to him for accompanying me on some research trips, as both a companion and a navigator. He helped me locate landmarks, monuments and other physical features that would elude the common person. He also helped document the visits with photographs.

Edward Ayres, Historian for the Jamestown-Yorktown Foundation, based at the Yorktown Victory Center in Yorktown, Virginia provided valuable assistance in locating Revolutionary War era maps.

John A. Robertson has done a yeoman's job in creating interactive maps to complement this series. The maps can be viewed as a Google or Yahoo cartographic or topographical map with cartographic, aerial or hybrid views. Google Earth maps can be zoomed to a variety of detail levels. Below an altitude of 200 feet, the maps turn to ground level view and allow taking a virtual tour of the landscape with a 360-degree view. One can toggle easily between aerial and ground level views. There's also a facility to add place marks or create polygons to modify the map to one's liking, add images, record a tour or show sunlight across the landscape. A ruler makes it easy to measure distance between locations. Google Earth also has many photos that can be viewed with a single mouse click. These can sometimes provide a virtual tour of the better-known sites.

Moving the cursor over each marker on the map displays the abbreviation for the state and the location name. Clicking on the marker reveals the dates of the action(s) there in mmddyy format along with an abbreviation for the volume that covers them and the page numbers. There's also an option to enter one's address or zip code to get driving directions. The maps can be accessed at **http://gaz.jrshelby.com/desmarais/**.

I wish to extend special thanks to my wife, Barbara, for her patience and support during the long periods of research and writing. She also accompanied me on many research trips and read maps and gave me directions as we drove to sites. She visited more forts and battlefields than she cares to remember.

Mark Hurwitz proofread the entire text and provided valuable feedback and suggestions. He also wrote the foreword. June Fritchman kindly offered some help with corrections and revisions of prior manuscripts in this series.

FOREWORD

by
Mark Hurwitz
Commander
Brigade of the American Revolution

To paraphrase Historian Geoffrey C. Ward, "the American War for Independence was fought from the walls of Quebec to the swamps of Florida, from Boston, to the Mississippi River." Now, if a shot was fired in anger, Norman Desmarais has documented it in this landmark study and guide, *The Guide to the American Revolutionary War.* It is a worthy successor to his *Battlegrounds of Freedom* (2005).

This comprehensive guide to the famous and unknown sites is groundbreaking. Beyond Lexington, Concord, Trenton, Brandywine, Saratoga, Monmouth, and Yorktown, Norman has fretted out the smaller actions and skirmishes which make up the eight year conflict, 1775–1783. Amazingly, Norman has found sites where settlers were scalped on the frontier to ships exchanging cannon fire on the high seas.

Norman Desmarais's passion for history comes as no surprise to me. After corresponding with Mr. Desmarais on an earlier multimedia CD-ROM project (*The American Revolution.*—American Journey: History in Your Hands series.—Woodbridge, CT: Primary Source Media, 1996), I finally got to meet him in November, 1995, when he attended a Brigade of the American Revolution (B.A.R.) event at Fort Lee Historic Park, Fort Lee, NJ. At that time, I had the opportunity to introduce him to Carl Becker, Commander of the 2nd Rhode Island Regiment, from his native state. Carl recruited him on the spot, and Norman, the academic historian, began his career as a re-enactor.

Becoming a "living historian" allows one to have laboratory to work in, wearing the uniforms, feeling the sweat, handling the weapons, experiencing the linear tactics, hearing the field music, smelling the smoke, which gives real perspective to the study of this period of history. This experience even goes beyond the "Staff Rides" of historic battlefields that the U.S. Army conducts with its officers.

The B.A.R. and the 2nd R.I. Regiment gave Norman the opportunity to visit many of the historic battle sites and get to see them "from the inside" and with the eye of a common soldier. This travel fueled his love for research and launched his encyclopedic study of Revolutionary War battle sites covering all of North America.

As a re-enactor, I have been studying the American War of Independence for nearly 35 years. Reading Desmarais's manuscript, I made discoveries both near and far.

- ◆ Being brought up and currently residing in my hometown of Springfield, NJ, I knew of the famous Battle of Springfield, June 23rd, 1780. Norman's research uncovered the following precursor, among many other actions there: "The militia killed and wounded 8 or 10 Waldeckers near Springfield on Sunday morning, January 19, 1777. They captured the rest of the party, 39 or 40, including 2 officers without suffering any casualties." (*The Pennsylvania Evening Post,* January 23, 1777)
- ◆ Meanwhile he found, west of the Mississippi: "St. Louis, Missouri—A small marker at 4th & Walnut Streets in downtown St. Louis which commemorates

the action that occurred on May 26, 1780." Desmarais's detailed entry then illuminates this unique action.

♦ Then at the end of the War for Independence, Savage Point, GA (Savage Point is located at a bend in the Ogeechee River at Richmond Hill State Park.): "Gen. Wayne suffered 5 men and horses killed and 8 wounded. He captured a British standard, 127 horses, and a number of packs." (*The Pennsylvania Packet or the General Advertiser.* 11:924 (August 15, 1782) p. 3)

I hope that readers can use this guide to find for themselves that history truly "happened here" as they travel the breadth of America and Canada.

PREFACE

The Guide to the American Revolutionary War in the Deep South and on the Frontier: Battles, Raids, and Skirmishes is the final volume of this geographic history of the American War of Independence. The idea for the project came at a re-enactment of a 225th anniversary event when I overheard some of my fellow interpreters commenting about the several events on the calendar that summer that they knew nothing about. There had been no guidebooks published about the Revolutionary War since the nation's bicentennial in 1975. Moreover, those guidebooks and most of the history textbooks only cover the major, better-known battles such as Lexington and Concord, Bunker Hill, Trenton and Princeton, Saratoga, Camden, Guilford Courthouse and Yorktown.

Battlegrounds of Freedom: A Historical Guide to the Battlefields of the War of American Independence[1] served the purpose of an overview. It covered all the major battles and several of the minor ones, along with the winter encampments at Morristown and Valley Forge. It also included a chapter on re-enacting to make it distinctive from other guidebooks. The success of that volume encouraged me to continue the project.

This continuation of the *Battlegrounds of Freedom* series covers the battles and, much more specifically, the raids and skirmishes of the Revolutionary War, many of which do not get covered even in the most detailed history books. The series intends to provide comprehensive, if not exhaustive, coverage of the military engagements of the American War of Independence. It also aims to serve as a guide to the sites and the military engagements. It does not intend to cover specifically naval battles, but it does include naval actions in which one of the parties was land-based. British ships fired frequently on shore installations, ship-building industries, towns, houses or troops on land. Such actions usually provoked a hostile response, even if a weak one. These minor clashes also illustrate the dangers faced by coastal residents and by troops moving within sight of enemy ships. Actions on inland lakes or bays are considered along with land actions as are attacks on enemy watering parties or other landing parties.

The work also covers engagements between French or Spanish troops and Crown forces as well as raids by Native Americans instigated or led either by British officers and agents or by Congressional forces. It does not attempt to cover raids on the cabins of western settlers that would have occurred regardless of the war, even though the residents retaliated.

Francis B. Heitman's *Historical Register of Officers of the Continental Army during the War of the Revolution, April 1775 to December 1783*[2] provides an alphabetical list of 420 engagements. This list seems to have been adopted as the U.S. Army's official list of battles and actions. Howard Henry Peckham's *The Toll of Independence: Engagements & Battle Casualties of the American Revolution*[3] expands this list to 1,330 military engagements and 220 naval engagements. He gives a brief description of the actions arranged chronologically, but his concern is primarily to tally the casualties. My research started with Peckham's work for the list of engagements, as his is comparatively the most extensive.

The multiple *Guide to the American Revolutionary War* volumes almost triple the number of engagements (almost 4,000) found in Peckham. They correct some of the entries and provide documentary references. The lack of primary source materials makes some actions very difficult to discover and document. The problem is most evident in "neutral territory," such as Elizabethtown, New Jersey, and Staten Island, New York, where conflict pretty much became part of everyday life. Sometimes, military actions occurred in several places during the same expedition or as part of a multi-pronged effort. Rather than repeat a narrative in several different places, we refer the reader to the main or a related account through *See* and *See also* references. However, each volume of the series is intended to be self-contained as much as possible with respect to the others.

Mark Mayo Boatner's *Encyclopedia of the American Revolution*[4] and his *Landmarks of the American Revolution: A Guide to Locating and Knowing What Happened at the Sites of Independence*[5] have long been considered the Bible for Revolutionary War aficionados and re-enactors. These works appeared in a new edition in 2007.[6] This is an excellent source to begin research on the Revolutionary War together with *The Encyclopedia of the American Revolutionary War: A Political, Social, and Military History.*[7]

Organization

Each volume in the *Battlegrounds of Freedom* series covers its respective states affected by the war and each location where an engagement occurred. It follows a hybrid geographical/chronological approach to accommodate various audiences: readers interested in American history, re-enactors, tourists and visitors. The states are arranged from north to south and east to west. Within each state, the engagements appear chronologically. Locations with multiple engagements also appear chronologically so readers can follow the text as a historical sequence or "story" of a site before proceeding to the next one. For example, the treatment of the events at Augusta, Georgia covers engagements dating from (January 29, 1779; February 3, 1779; February 14, 1779; September 14–18, 1780; May 22 to June 5, 1781) before proceeding to Fort Henderson (Spirit Creek) (January 30, 1779). Cross references have been added as necessary.

The text identifies the location of the sites as best as can be determined, provides the historical background to understand what happened there, indicates what the visitor can expect to see there and identifies any interpretive aids. It is not meant to replace the guides produced for specific sites and available at visitor centers. These guides usually provide more details about the features of a particular site. Also, monographs devoted to specific engagements or campaigns will be more detailed than what we can present here.

Strategic Objectives

The presence of large numbers of troops in an area gave residents cause for concern. The soldiers were always short of food and constantly searching for provisions. It took a lot of food to feed an army. While troops were allotted daily rations, they rarely received their full allocation.

A soldier's typical weekly ration would consist of:
- 7 pounds of beef or 4 pounds of pork
- 7 pounds of bread or flour sufficient to bake it
- 3 pints of peas or beans
- ½ pound of rice
- ¼ pound of butter[8]

This would translate to the following weekly rations for an army of 1,000 men:
- 3½ tons of beef or 2 tons of pork
- 3½ tons of bread or flour sufficient to bake it
- 94 bushels of peas or beans
- 1¾ tons of rice
- 250 pounds of butter

The threat of a foraging expedition caused residents to hide their cattle and the expedition usually elicited an attack from the enemy. As one side tried to obtain food and supplies, the other tried to prevent them from doing so or to re-capture the stolen goods along with the enemy's baggage and supplies. While most of these actions were militarily insignificant, they often had the effect of reducing both forces. Crown forces were harder to replace because they usually had to come from overseas.

Military objectives not only included the capture of enemy forts, strongholds and armies but also the control of important crossroads, rivers and ferries. The rivers were the 18th-century highways and made travel and transportation much quicker than the unpaved roads. Controlling these strategic points either facilitated or blocked troop movements and supply lines.

Nomenclature

The two sides in the American War of Independence are generally referred to as the British and the Americans. However, this is a gross oversimplification. While it is a convenient way to refer to both sides, it is often inaccurate, particularly when discussing engagements in the South where most of the actions were between militia units or armed mobs with very few, if any, regular soldiers. For example, Major Patrick Ferguson was the only British soldier at the Battle of Kings Mountain (South Carolina). Many actions in the South seem to have been occasions for people to settle grudges with their neighbors in feuds that resemble that between the Hatfields and the McCoys. In a sense, the war in the South was very much a civil war. In other areas, it took on the nature of a world war.

Moreover, the provincials were British citizens—at least until they declared their independence on July 4, 1776. Prior to that date, the provincials believed their grievances were with Parliament and not the King. Most of the citizens did not favor independence but rather hoped for redress of their grievances and the re-establishment of relations with Parliament. However, when King George III sided with Parliament and declared the colonies in rebellion on August 23, 1775, the provincials realized that their hopes were dashed. After the news reached the colonies on October 31, 1775, they began to see independence as their only recourse.

The Declaration of Independence made a definite break between England and her American colonies, but it took a while for those ideas to become widely accepted. In fact, it took 18 months after the outbreak of the war to enunciate that objective; and it took eight years to win the war that secured the independence of the United States of America. Even though England officially recognized the new country with the signing of the Treaty of Paris in 1783, it often continued to act as though it still controlled the colonies. This was one of the factors that led to the War of 1812.

While the provincials called themselves Americans, to refer only to those who favored independence as Americans is too broad, as they were less than a majority of the population. Although all the provincials were British citizens until the signing of the Declaration of Independence and their effective independence at the end of the war, to refer to them as Americans confuses a political position with hegemony. That would be comparable to referring to Republicans or Democrats as Americans, implying that the other party is not American. Similarly, to refer to them as Patriots implies that those who remained loyal to the King were less patriotic when they fought to maintain life as they knew it.

Consequently, we refer to the supporters of independence as Rebels, Whigs, or Congressional troops. We also distinguish between the local militias and the regular soldiers of the Continental Army ("Continentals") as narratives allow further distinction. We also refer to Allied forces to designate joint efforts by Congressional forces and their foreign allies, primarily French and Spanish.

Similarly, the "British" armies were more complex than just English troops. They certainly consisted of Irish, Scot and Welsh troops. We sometimes refer to them by regiment, e.g. 71st Highlanders, Black Watch, Royal Welch Fusiliers, when individual regiments are prominent in an engagement. They are also referred to generically as Regulars or Redcoats. (Some derogatory references call them lobsterbacks or bloodybacks because of the flesh wounds from whipping—a common form of punishment at the time.)

While British troops are often called Redcoats, not all wore red coats. The artillerymen wore dark blue coats. While some of the dragoons wore red, others such as Tarleton's Legion, wore green coats. There are instances where the two sides confused each other because of the similarity of the coats. For example, Major General Henry "Light-Horse Harry" Lee (1756–1818) and his legion tried to surprise Lieutenant Colonel Banastre Tarleton (1744–1833) on the morning of February 25, 1781. The front of Lee's Legion encountered two mounted Loyalists who mistook them for Tarleton's Legion. The Loyalists were taken to General Lee who took advantage of their mistake by posing as Tarleton. He learned that Colonel John Pyle had recruited about 400 Loyalists and that they were on their way to join Tarleton. Lee and his men continued the ruse, surrounded the Loyalists and captured them all, depriving General Charles Cornwallis of badly needed troops at Yorktown.

Loyalist troops were issued both red and green uniforms with a wide variety of facings. Those who wore the green coats were sometimes referred to as Green Coats or simply as the Greens. Some authors refer to the Loyalists as Tories, a term which has taken on derogatory significance.

Moreover, King George III, who was of German origin, arranged to reinforce his armies with large numbers of German troops. They wore coats of various shades of blue, as well as green with red facings. Many of these soldiers came from the provinces of Hesse Hanau and Hesse Kassel and became known as Hessians. Other regiments were known by their provinces of origin (e.g., Braunschweiger or Brunswick and Waldeck) or by the name of their commander (von Lossberg, von Donop, etc.).

We use the terms Crown forces, King's troops, Royal Navy to refer to these combined forces or the regiment name, commanding officer, or group designation (e.g. Hessians, Loyalists) to be more specific.

People of color fought on both sides. We use the currently politically correct terminology of African Americans, even though not all of them came from Africa, and Native Americans as the generic terms. We also use the specific tribal name, if known: Iroquois, Mohawk, Oneida, Cherokee, etc. Mulattoes referred to people of mixed race. Quotations retain the terminology used by the original writer.

The Native American tribes tended to support the Crown because they realized that the settlers coveted their land and presented a greater threat than the British Army. Great Britain had fewer troops in the West (west of the Appalachians) than in the East (along the East Coast and east of the Appalachians), so it needed their support. More than 1,200 Delawares, Shawnees and Mingoes lived in the Ohio valley. North of them, 300 Wyandots, Hurons and 600 Ottawas and thousands of Chippewas inhabited southern Michigan and the shores of Lake Erie. Several hundred Potawatomis extended toward the southern end of Lake Michigan. The area north and east of Fort Pitt was occupied by the Senecas and several hundred Miamis lived along the Maumeee and upper Wabash rivers. The Weas, Piankeshaws, Kickapoos and other tribes settled on the Wabash and west toward the Mississippi, while an unknown number of Foxes, Sauks and Mascoutens lived beyond the Great Lakes.

The Native American tribes were unreliable and not great assets as combatants. Sometimes, they were even a liability. For example, the murder of Jane McCrea by her Native American escorts during the Saratoga campaign brought new recruits to the Congressional forces and deterred Loyalists from actively supporting the Crown troops. British commanders often found it impossible to determine whether the Native Americans would fight and for how long. When they did fight, they usually did so in small groups and for limited periods. They were also often divided by rivalries among themselves, easily frightened by any show of strength and usually unwilling to leave their families for long campaigns. Without the support of the Native Americans, however, Crown forces had no hope of controlling the West. The Crown forces provided the tribes with gifts every year to insure their continued support. These gifts included a large supply of ammunition and clothing as well as gifts for the chief warriors.[9]

Nobody knows how many provincials remained loyal to King George III during the American War of Independence. Many history books credit John Adams with estimating that one-third of the population favored the Revolution, one-third were against it and another third leaned to whichever side happened to control the area. The quotation reads:

> I should say that full one-third were averse to the revolution. These, retaining that overweening fondness, in which they had been educated, for the English, could not cordially like the French; indeed, they most heartily detested them. An opposite third conceived a hatred of the English, and gave themselves up to an enthusiastic gratitude to France. The middle third, composed principally of the yeomanry, the soundest part of the nation, and always averse to war, were rather lukewarm both to England and France.[10]

On another occasion, Mr. Adams noted that the colonies had been nearly "unanimous" in their opposition to the Stamp Act in 1765 but, by 1775, the British had "seduced and deluded nearly one third of the people of the colonies."[11]

In the first quotation, Ray Raphael[12] notes that Adams was writing about the political sentiments of Americans toward the conflict between England and France in 1797, but the two quotations somehow blended together in popular historiography to refer to the American War of Independence. So Adams has become the definitive contemporary source on the political allegiance of the period.

Conventions and Parts of This Book

Cognizant that one may begin a tour anywhere, the first occurrence of a person's name in a section identifies him or her as completely as possible with the full form of the name with birth and death dates, if known. Some readers will probably find this awkward or cumbersome as they read several sections. We hope that those who consult a specific section will find this helpful.

Most chapters begin with a map of the sites in that state to facilitate orientation, and additional maps face the beginning of their respective sections. Some chapters with many actions are subdivided north to south and east to west, and these divisions are reflected with references to their respective maps. These maps have pointers to engagement locations and are printed on regular paper like the photos.

Engagements are then listed chronologically within their subdivisions along with the corresponding map. Locations with multiple engagements group those events in chronological order under the same heading to provide a historical sequence or "story" of a site before proceeding to the next one. Cross references have been added as necessary.

Each site begins with the name of the city or town (or the most commonly known name of the engagement) and the name (and alternate names) of the battle or action. The location names are followed by the dates, in parentheses, of significant actions discussed in the text. Specially formatted text identifies the location of the site, indicates what the visitor can expect to see and identifies any interpretive aids. Historical background to understand what happened at a site follows. In any case, this book does not mean to replace more-detailed tourist guides for specific sites that are available at visitor centers.

Events are marked with a bullet character (★) for easy identification and to dispel confusion.

Travelers should take care to map their route for most efficient travel as many sites are not along main roads. Sometimes, one must backtrack to visit a place thoroughly. Travelers should also be aware that some locations in a particular state may be farther than other locations in a neighboring state. Consulting maps allows the visitor to proceed from one location to another with the least amount of backtracking. It also offers options for side trips as desired. Consult the maps and the appendices at the publisher's web site (**www.buscainc.com**) to see how battle sites are grouped and keyed to major cities or locations. Interactive maps for this series are also available at **http://gaz .jrshelby.com/desmarais/**.

One of the appendices gives a chronological list of battles, actions and skirmishes. History books often present events in purely chronological order. However, that is not a good approach for a guidebook to follow, as events can occur simultaneously great distances apart. For example, the powder alarm in Williamsburg, Virginia occurred on the same day as the battles of Lexington and Concord in Massachusetts. The web site also features a comprehensive state-by-state alphabetical list of locations where actions (battles, raids or skirmishes) took place.

Other books take a thematic approach, covering campaigns or specific themes like the war on the frontier. This technique, while more focused, often ignores information relevant to a site that properly belongs to another theme. For example, a theme covering Major General John Burgoyne's (1722–1792) campaign of 1777 may not cover the capture of Fort Ticonderoga in 1775 or its role in the Seven Years War (also known as the French and Indian War).

The many photographs, with descriptive captions and keyed to the text, are important for identifying details of historic buildings, monuments, battlefields and equipment. Many of the photos are of battle and event re-enactments. All photos, except otherwise identified, are by the author. Full-color photos of some of the images in this and other volumes are on the publisher's web site (**www.buscainc.com**).

Another feature that modern readers and visitors will find useful are URLs for web sites of various parks and tourist organizations. These URLs are correlated with various battle sites and sometimes events. Visitors may want to consult these web sites ahead of time for important, updated information on special events, hours, fees, etc. These URLs were active and accurate at the time this book went to press.

The Glossary provides definitions for some 18th-century military and historical terms. There are also scholarly reference Notes for sources used in this book and an

Index. The full Bibliography of the sources consulted for the *Battlegrounds of Freedom* series is on the publisher's web site (**www.buscainc.com**).

Most of the sites described in this book are reconstructions or restorations. Many buildings were damaged during the War of Independence or fell into disrepair over the years. They were refurbished, for the most part, for the nation's bicentennial in 1975–1976. Battlefield fortifications were sometimes destroyed after a battle so they could not be re-used by the enemy at a later time. For example, the hornworks and siege trenches at Yorktown, Virginia were destroyed after the surrender of General Charles Cornwallis so the Crown forces could not re-use them for a subsequent assault. They were, however, rebuilt and used again during the War of Rebellion (Civil War). There are many houses and structures still standing that demonstrate what life was like in the 18th century. Only those related to the battles are covered.

Many of the sites have been obliterated by urban development and have nothing to see or visit. Houses and other construction have supplanted them. One battlefield is covered by a shopping mall; another has been submerged under a man-made lake; others were destroyed by high-rise apartment or office buildings. Many are remembered only with a roadside marker. Some don't even have that.

Many sites have little importance to the outcome of the war. Some actions were mere skirmishes or raids lasting only a few minutes. For example, some actions consisted of a single volley. After one of the forces fired, it fled. Yet, some important events, such as the capture of Fort Kaskaskia by George Rogers Clark in Illinois and the capture of Fort Ticonderoga by Benedict Arnold, Ethan Allen and the Green Mountain Boys were effected without firing a single shot. The battle at Black Mingo Creek, South Carolina lasted only 15 minutes. Other engagements, particularly those involving Lieutenant Colonel Francis Marion, known as the Swamp Fox, were fought in the swamps of South Carolina and are hard to find.

Some sites remain undeveloped and virtually ignored. This is not necessarily bad. While erosion, neglect and plant or tree growth slowly undermine earthworks, they do significantly less damage than the rapid deterioration resulting from bikers and walkers.

One cannot easily cover all the sites of the American War of Independence. However, one can visit all the sites and events that affected the outcome of the war. One can also visit enough locally significant spots to get an understanding of what the war was like for the people of that region. This book tries to cover the extant battle sites and hopes to serve as a companion on the voyage of discovery.

Norman Desmarais
normd@providence.edu

THE DEEP SOUTH

1
GEORGIA

Georgia was a British buffer between the Spanish in the south and the French in the west. It differed considerably from the other colonies in several respects:

1. It entered the Revolutionary movement later than the other colonies. This is partly because it had been a pet colony of Parliament and received more benefits in Royal salaries and other Crown expenditures than it paid in taxes.
2. The British relied on their Native American allies extensively in the backcountry.
3. The Whigs engaged in persistent factional infighting.
4. The Royal government was restored in a large part of its territory.
5. Many Georgians viewed the war as much a fight for Native American lands as a war against Great Britain.

When the *Georgia Gazette* called for the election of delegates to a provincial congress, only five of the colony's 12 parishes responded. They selected delegates to attend the Second Continental Congress in January 1775, but the men declined to go because they could not claim to represent a unified colony. However, that mood changed in May 1775 when news arrived of the outbreak of hostilities in Lexington and Concord, Massachusetts. The news was accompanied by an erroneous, but widely believed, report that the British instigated an uprising of Native Americans.

Ten parishes then sent delegates to the Second Provincial Congress in Savannah, the capitol of the colony, in July 1775. Georgia joined the other 12 colonies in adopting the Continental Association, passed the previous October, which banned trade with Britain. It also established an executive body, the Council of Safety, and authorized local committees to enforce the Continental Association. The committeemen called themselves the Sons of Liberty and used violence to intimidate those who disagreed with them.

When British warships arrived off the coast of Georgia on Thursday, January 18, 1776, to free merchant vessels laden with rice that the Associators had impounded, the people feared an invasion.[1]

The British evacuated Philadelphia, Pennsylvania in June 1778, partly because they needed to supply troops for operations in the Caribbean and Florida. General Henry Clinton (1730–1795) sent 5,000 troops to St. Lucia in the West Indies in November 1778, and another 3,000 under Lieutenant Colonel Archibald Campbell (1739–1791) to join Major General Augustine Prevost (1723–1786) in St. Augustine, Florida.

By moving south, the British were closer to the West Indies where the fleet could protect their interests and guard against the French. The Loyalists were also more numerous in the South, especially in the Carolinas and Georgia. The King's ministers hoped to bring the southern states into the fold one by one and, from bases there, to strangle the recalcitrant North. A small British force operating from Florida quickly overran thinly populated Georgia in the winter of 1778–1779.

Georgia supplied 2,679 men to the Continental Army.

The Georgia Historical Society (501 Whitaker Street, Savannah (phone: 912-651-2125; website: **www.georgiahistory.com**) serves as the state's main authority on Georgia's history. It houses a museum and archives, sells a variety of publications, and manages the state's historical markers. The Georgia Department of Archives

> and History (5800 Jonesboro Road, Morrow, GA 30260 (678-364-3700)) also has
> responsibility for some historic sites.

See the map of northern Georgia.

Fort Dartmouth (Feb. 1776)

According to Thomas Brown (1744–1814), Fort Charlotte, South Carolina, was the
only stronghold of any consequence in the interior, and it was highly vulnerable to a
siege. On the Georgia side just north of Fort Charlotte was Fort Dartmouth on the
Broad River. Thomas Waters (ca. 1738–after 1810) had been promoted to captain and
given command of the small fort on the Georgia side of the Savannah River in August
1775. Fort Dartmouth held a garrison of 25 rangers stationed primarily as a defense
from Native American raids. As part of an assessment of the Augusta area, Thomas
Brown told East Florida Governor Patrick Tonyn (1725–1804) that Waters had previously surrendered the fort under pressure from the local Liberty Boys.

Brown was not certain of the loyalty of Captain Waters because Waters had surrendered the fort to a band of Liberty Boys (in February 1776?). The Georgia Council of
Safety then ordered them to give the fort back to the Rangers, so the fort was once more
under Waters's command.

Other than these two backcountry posts, the town of Augusta was defenseless, or,
to use Brown's expression, Augusta was "very accessible to the Creek Indians to whom
it lays quite exposed." There were about a hundred houses in Augusta, several of them
stockaded (as the Reverend Tennent had described the previous September). The fall of
Augusta would "distress the rebels beyond measure," Brown believed, and would open
the Savannah River to the friends of the Royal government.[2]

Cherokee war of 1776

Tawsee(?) or Tassee (April 1, 1776)

Tetome (April 1776)

Unnamed (April 4, 1776)

Caue(?) (April 5, 1776)

Early (April 7(?), 1776)

Estatoe (Aug. 8, 1776)

Eustustee, or Ustisti (Aug. 11, 1776)

Frog Town (Oct. 2, 1776)

Little Echota (Oct. 2, 1776)

Nacoochee Valley (Oct. 2, 1776)

> Tawsee was on the southern shore of the Tugaloo River east of where route US 123
> (Toccoa Highway) crosses it in Toccoa.
>   Tetome was about 1.7 miles west of Tawsee and just west of route US 123 (Toc-
> coa Highway) in Toccoa.
>   The unnamed town was about 5 miles southeast of Tawsee and is now under
> Hartwell Lake.
>   Caue was about 3.4 miles farther southeast, also under Hartwell Lake.

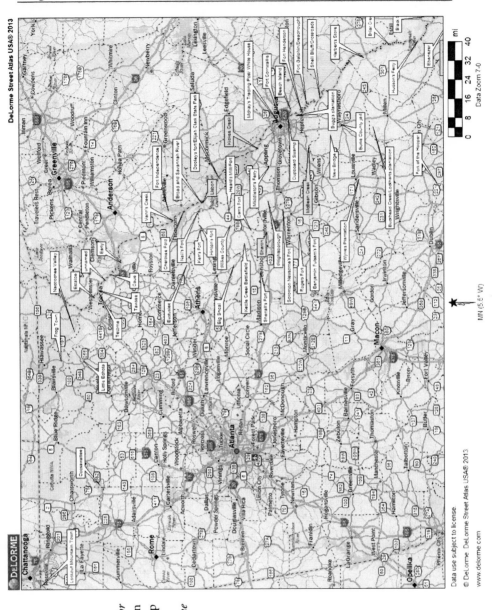

Northern Georgia: Map for The Guide to the American Revolutionary War in the Deep South and on the Frontier © 2013 DeLorme (www.delorme.com) Street Atlas USA®

> Early, also under Hartwell Lake, was another 6.5 miles southeast.
>
> Estatoe was on the south shore of the Tugaloo River about 3.6 miles northwest of Tawsee. There were several Cherokee towns with this name. This one should not be confused with the one in North Carolina.
>
> Eustustee or Ustisti was about a mile north of Carlton, on the north side of Fork Creek.
>
> Frog Town, Little Echota and Nacoochee Valley were Cherokee Valley Towns. Frog Town was located along the Hiawassee River, possibly about 7.5 miles south of Hiawassee. Little Echota was located on the Chattahoochee River, possibly in what is now Helen. Nacoochee Valley was probably located along the western shore of what is now Nacoohe Lake. These sites are all within the boundaries of the Chattahoochee-Oconee National Forests.

Colonel Samuel Jack (ca. 1742–1807) went on a rampage burning Cherokee towns in April 1776. He started at Tawsee or Tassee and Tetome, probably on Monday, April 1. He then proceeded southeast to burn an unnamed town on Thursday, April 4. The following day, he burned Caue, followed by Early about April 7.

Bands of Cherokees and Loyalists retaliated by attacking settlements in South Carolina and Tennessee in June 1776. The governments of South Carolina, Georgia, North Carolina, and Virginia quickly organized punitive expeditions. Colonel Samuel Jack was one of the first to respond and had his men in the field by July.

★ Colonel Andrew Williamson (ca. 1730–1786) marched into northwestern South Carolina with 1800 troops and some Catawba scouts in August, burning Cherokee villages along the way. His men burned Estatoe on Thursday, August 8, 1776 and Eustustee or Ustisti on August 11. Williamson went from South Carolina into Western North Carolina to rendezvous with General Griffith Rutherford (ca. 1731–1800). There, he rested and reorganized his troops before marching to Cherokee Middle Towns in September.[3] See **Tennessee, Cherokee Campaign of 1776** pp. 230–238.

★ General Griffith Rutherford (ca. 1731–1800) sent Colonel Thomas Sumter (1734–1832) and a detachment to Frog Town about Wednesday, October 2, 1776. They burned and destroyed the Cherokee town along with Little Echota and Nacoochee Valley. They then returned to the army at Chota before marching to Keowee Old Towns on the Tugaloo River.[4] See **Tennessee, Cherokee Campaign of 1776** pp. 230–238.

Coosawattee (1780)
Lookout Mountain Town (1780)

> The Chicamaugas moved down the Tennessee River to the foot of Lookout Mountain and built the "Five Lower Towns". They were Lookout Town (near present Tiftonia, Tennessee); Crow Town (near present Stevenson, Alabama); Long Island (near present Bridgeport, Alabama); Runningwater (near present Haletown, Tennessee); and Nickajack (near present Shellmound, Tennessee).
>
> Coosawattee, also called Coosawattee Old Fields, was established in 1774 on the Coosawattee River in Ellijay. It is now under Carter Lake.
>
> Lookout Mountain Town was in northwest Georgia near the Tennessee border and about 13 miles east of the Alabama border. It was a short distance south of routes GA 189 (GA 157 N|Scenic Highway) and GA 157 (Mc Farland Road).

Colonel John Sevier's (1745–1815) men burned Coosawattee and Lookout Mountain Town in late November or early December 1780 as they marched toward Tennessee to destroy the Cherokee villages there.[5] See **Tennessee Cherokee Campaign of 1780** pp. 246–249.

Near juncture of Broad and Savannah rivers (July 12, 1776)

> The junction of the Broad and Savannah rivers is at J. Strom Thurmond Lake, west of Willington, Mount Carmel and Sumter National Forest.

Colonel Elijah Clarke (1733–1799) led his Georgia militiamen in an attack on some Cherokees near the juncture of the Broad and Savannah rivers on Friday, July 12, 1776. They killed four Cherokees but lost three killed and four wounded.[6]

Big Shoals, Oconee River (July 22, 1776; May 1781)
Long Creek
Coweta Ambush
Oconee River (April 2, 1782)

> Big Shoals, also known as Long Creek or Dry Fork of Long Creek, was probably near the mouth of the Dry Fork of Long Creek. Dry Fork Creek merges into Long Creek which, in turn, merges into the Ogeechee River. Sources say the skirmish occurred near the Oconee River. As it seems there is no Long Creek that merges with the Oconee River, it's possible that Long Creek was on the Ogeechee River. There's another location known as Big Shoals, currently called Barnet Shoals, on the Oconee River approximately 16 miles west of the source of Dry Fork Creek. Older sources date the action as occurring in 1776. Some modern sources date it in 1777.
> Captain Thomas Dooley's detachment of Continental troops was camped on Dry Fork Creek and the Creeks ambushed them between the camp and Big Shoals.[7]

A party of about 50 Creeks or Cowetas stole seven horses from Captain Thomas Dooley's (d. 1776) 1st Georgia Continental Regiment and a unit of 20 Virginia militiamen stationed at Long Creek. Dooley, on the way to join a Continental brigade, pursued them on foot. He found the horses and took possession of them. On his way back, he was ambushed at Big Shoals in Wilkes County, near the Oconee River, about 7 AM on Monday, July 22, 1776.

Dooley was shot in the leg early in the skirmish. He encouraged his men to continue fighting and set an example by firing his rifle twice at the enemy after he had been wounded. When the Creeks discovered that the commanding officer had fallen, they rushed out from the cane swamp to capture him.

Lieutenant John Cunningham (1750–1829), who was second in command, ordered a retreat. Dooley called to his men not to abandon him. The last man who saw Dooley said that he was trying to defend himself with the butt of his weapon, even though he was unable to stand. The Continentals lost nine men killed in the action. Dooley and three other wounded men were captured and murdered.[8]

★ Major Anderson of South Carolina and a detachment of Colonel Elijah Clarke's (1733–1799) men skirmished with some Native Americans and Loyalists near Big Shoals in May 1781. They killed two Native Americans and one Loyalist and took two

Loyalists prisoners and hanged them from a hickory tree at the lower end of the Big Shoals. The Whigs lost Captain Holloway (1737–1781).[9]

★ Colonel Robert Anderson (Andersen) (d. 1813), of South Carolina, received intelligence that a body of Loyalists, Cherokees and Creeks planned an attack against the frontier. He informed Colonel Elijah Clarke (1733–1799), of Georgia, and they decided to rendezvous at Freeman's fort on the north side of the Broad River in present-day Elbert County on Monday, April 1, 1782. Clarke and 100 Georgians arrived at that location and joined Anderson's 300 Carolinians. They crossed the Oconee River early the next morning. One of the scouting parties commanded by Captain George Barber (1743–1822) (one report referred to him as Captain "Black") stumbled into the main body of Native Americans who were unaware of the presence of the Whig force. They pursued Barber's party as they retreated. Colonel Clarke advanced to meet Barber's party and the Native Americans scattered in confusion. The Whigs killed about a dozen Native Americans in the ensuing fight and captured two Loyalist guides whom they hanged on the bank of the Oconee River. The Whigs lost only one man killed.[10]

Waynesboro
Burke County Jail (Jan. 26, 1779)
Fuzzel's Place
Burke County (May–June 1779)
Buckhead Creek (Aug. 3, 1779 or Aug. 14, 1779 or Aug. 24, 1779)
Lockhart's Plantation
Burke County (1780)

> The Burke County jail was 20 miles southeast of Augusta near what is now Waynesboro. It was the political center for the newly created Burke County, formerly St. George Parish. The February 18, 1779 issue of *The* (Charleston) *South-Carolina & American General Gazette* published an account of the action here under the heading Letter from Camp at Fuzzel's place in Georgia, 27 January 1779. This may have led some people to name the engagement Fuzzel's Place.
>   The incident at Buckhead Creek or Lockhart's plantation is sometimes dated August 14, 1779 or August 24, 1779. Lockhart's plantation was in the Big Buckhead Creek community, probably about 13 miles south of the Burke County jail.

The East Florida Rangers led the advance of Lieutenant Colonel Archibald Campbell's (1739–1791) army as they marched toward Augusta in January 1779. They planned to join forces with the backcountry Loyalists and Native Americans there. The Burke County Militia mustered at the Burke County jail to stop them.

Major General Augustine Prevost (1723–1786) ordered Colonel Thomas Brown (1750–1825) and his Rangers to rescue several Loyalists held in the jail, even though he did not think much of Brown and his Rangers. Lieutenant Colonel Campbell wrote that Brown's detachment "was composed of a mere Rabble of undisciplined Freebooters" and disagreed with Prevost about attacking the Burke County jail. He wrote "the Rebels who were numerous in that Quarter would either unite in force sufficient to repel Colonel Brown's Detachment . . . or they would retire to the back Country before it was in my Power to get sufficiently into their Rear, to cut off their Retreat." However, as Prevost outranked Campbell, the operation proceeded as planned.

Lieutenant Colonel James Ingram (ca. 1749–1795), of the Richmond County Militia, met with the Whig leaders at the Burke County jail while Colonel Benjamin Few (1744– or 1763–1815) and Major John Twiggs (1750–1816) brought in reinforcements. Even though Ingram knew that Prevost's force of 3,000 men prepared to engage his 120 militiamen, he did not post any pickets Monday night, January 25, 1779.

Brown positioned his men to storm the jail and courthouse buildings the following morning. They were to attack when the Whig militiamen fired their morning gun. Colonel Brown, Colonel Daniel McGirth (d. ca. 1789) and 230 mounted Loyalists attacked the Whigs at the log jail early in the morning while the men inside were still sleeping. The rangers executed a "very sudden and violent" attack from three sides. The sleeping militiamen were quickly aroused. About half of them fled, were captured or were killed. The others, boarded up inside the log building, exchanged a "warm fire." The Loyalists made several assaults on the building but withdrew after a 45-minute fight, leaving three men dead on the ground and seven more wounded and captured. Colonel Brown's arm was shattered and Colonel John Thomas had his upper lip shot away. The Whigs lost five men killed and nine wounded. Brown's forces left the jail and rejoined Campbell's column the next day. The Burke County Militia withdrew from the jail and joined forces with Colonel Samuel Elbert's (1740–1788) army and withdrew to Augusta.[11]

★ Colonel John Dooly (ca. 1742–1780) and Lieutenant Colonel Elijah Clarke (1733–1799) patrolled the Georgia frontier to guard against Native American attacks while Major General Benjamin Lincoln (1733–1810) operated against British Major General Augustine Prevost (1723–1786) in South Carolina in the late spring of 1779. Colonel John Jones (1728–1793) and Colonel John Twiggs (1750–1816) of the 4th Regiment of Georgia Militia, and Colonel Benjamin Few (b. 1744) or (1763–1815) of the 2nd battalion of the 2nd (Richmond County) Regiment of Georgia Militia shadowed the British outposts, cutting off their supplies from the surrounding countryside.

Colonel Few took his battalion of about 150 men on a raid through Burke County in May. He reported:

> Georgia. Richmond County. Sir. I am just returned with the Militia of this Battalion from a Rout[e] which we have taken through the lower part of Burke County in Order to Disperse some parties of the Enemy that was there Embodering against us, which we had the good fortune to Do effectually, and took their Lieut Colo [Joseph] Marshall and Major Howell and Capt. Wood prisoners with many others that was Inimical to us. We also Defeated a small party of the Florida Scout, made three of them Prisoners, And took six of their Horses and Saddles and Other plunder, so that I Don't Think any number of the County will Again Attempt to take up arms Against us, as many of them seem convenced of their Error and have again promised their Allegiance to the United States of America, and I would still wish to exercise every power that I possess against our Common Enemy And will therefore inform you my present Situation and Strength and beg that you would give me such Directions as you think will be most productive of Publick good.
>
> The Battalion which I Command at this time Consists of About 150 effective Men, tho we had more than twice that number before the Enemy Distress'd us here.
>
> If the Accounts which we have had is true I Sincerely Congratulate you on Your Success and beg that you would Favour me with A line or two of Confirmation.
> I am Sir with much Respect Your Most Obdt Servant
>
> Benjamin Few
> General Lincoln[12]

★ Colonel Daniel McGirth (d. ca. 1789) and his Loyalists began to pillage the western Georgia settlements in the summer of 1779. Some Creeks and Loyalists arrived at Savannah about Tuesday, August 3rd with instructions not to kill the women and children. They returned two days later with five scalps and three female prisoners which they delivered to Colonel Thomas Brown (1750–1825) at Ebenezer.

Colonel John Twiggs (1750–1816) mustered 150 Georgia militiamen and some troopers of the 1st Regiment Continental Light Dragoons under Lieutenant Colonel John Jameson (1758–1842). They overtook and surprised McGirth and 30 or 40 of his raiders at Isaac Lockhart's plantation on Buckhead Creek in Burke County on Tuesday, August 3rd or Saturday, August 14, 1779 or Tuesday, August 24, 1779.

Twiggs placed his best mounted men in front and ordered the charge. The skirmish lasted about 15 minutes, without much effect. McGirth escaped into a nearby swamp. As he retreated, Twiggs's men killed nine Loyalists, wounded nine others, and captured four along with 23 horses and 15 stands of arms. McGirth was shot in the thigh and was bleeding so badly that he was falsely reported as having been killed. Thanks to his fast horse, he escaped into a nearby swamp. Twiggs had one private and three horses killed and one of his dragoon captains mortally wounded.[13]

★ Colonel John Dooly (ca. 1742–1780) killed two men, Corker (either ensign Edward Corker or John Corker) and Webb in a skirmish in Burke County in 1780. The following day, Colonel John Twiggs (1750–1816) attacked a party of Colonel Daniel Mc-Girth's (d. ca. 1789) men who had plundered and burned several houses. Twiggs's men killed three Loyalists, captured five, and retook their plunder.[14]

Washington

Kettle Creek (Nov. 1778; Feb. 14, 1779; Jan. 3, 1782; after May 6, 1782)

The Kettle Creek Battlefield (**www.kudcom.com/www/att05.html**) is on Warhill Road off Route GA 44 (Greensboro Road) west of Washington. From Washington, take route GA 44 (Greensboro Road) west for 6.8 miles, turn right at the state historical marker for Kettle Creek Battleground after 1.2 miles, then turn left for 1.2 miles and take a final left on a dirt road for 1.6 miles to a stone obelisk.

The road leading to the battleground ends at the hill marked with a 20-foot-high stone obelisk. The monument, erected in 1930, commemorates the battle. Two memorial stones honor John Shank (1761–1835) and John Lindsey, two soldiers of the American War of Independence. Colonel Andrew Pickens and his men camped near here the night before they attacked Colonel John Boyd's (d. 1779) men, but the exact site of the camp is unknown. There are no markers explaining the action or describing the battlefield.

The South Carolina militiamen established a station, a blockhouse (see Photo GA-1), on Kettle Creek in 1776 and named it for Robert McNabb (1730–1778) who served as a private in Captain Robert Carr's (d. 1779) company of Wilkes County Militia from September 15 to October 15, 1778. Native Americans attacked McNabb's fort and destroyed it in November 1778. Most accounts say McNabb was killed in the attack. Others say that he and his family survived and rebuilt the fort and that he was killed on Monday, January 3, 1782 when a party of Creeks ambushed and killed him and a party of his men at the rebuilt fort.[15]

★ In the battle of Kettle Creek, Colonel Andrew Pickens (1739–1817) and about 300 South Carolina and Georgia militiamen ambushed a group of 700 North Carolina Loyalists, who were plundering their way through South Carolina on their way to enlist in

GA-1. *Blockhouse of Fort King George at Darien, GA. The small openings, loopholes, are for firing muskets. Larger loopholes would accommodate cannons.*

the British Army at Augusta. The new recruits would have increased Loyalist opposition in the area.

Colonel John Boyd (d. 1779) left Savannah shortly after January 10, 1779 to rally the Loyalists in the South Carolina backcountry. Reports place him deep in the Georgia backcountry by January 24, seeking guides into South Carolina. He managed to raise a force of Loyalists in Anson County, North Carolina, near the South Carolina line. He and Major John Spurgin (d. 1779) and 350 recruits broke camp near present-day Spartanburg, South Carolina on Friday, February 5 and marched across South Carolina. Colonel John Moore (1758–1836) joined them along the way with 250 other North Carolina Loyalists, bringing their ranks to about 600 men. Robert DeMond (b. 1889), writing from the Loyalist perspective, reported that Boyd and his men "lived off the land as they pursued their march." Benson John Lossing (1813–1891), writing from the Whig point of view, stated that "like plundering banditti, they appropriated every species of property to their own use, abused the inhabitants, and wantonly butchered several who opposed their rapacious demands."[16]

Colonel Andrew Pickens received a message telling him of Boyd's proximity, so he ended his siege of Lieutenant Colonel Andrew Hamilton's (1741–1835) Loyalists at **Carr's Fort** (see pp. 32–34). He recrossed the Savannah River near Fort Charlotte, close to the junction of the Broad and Savannah rivers and pursued Boyd west from Ninety Six, South Carolina toward the river crossing at Cherokee Ford, 10 miles north of Fort Charlotte where eight Whig militiamen in a redoubt armed with two swivel guns (see Photo GA-2) prevented Boyd from crossing. When Captain James Little (1737–1807) arrived from the Georgia side of the ford with 40 Georgia militiamen, they made "the canoe whiz till they got over" to reinforce the blockhouse. Boyd moved 5 miles upriver to occupy the high ground opposite the mouth of Vanns Creek (see pp. 30–32). He

GA-2. Swivel gun mounted on a tree stump. The mount allows it to rotate in any direction.

and his 600 Loyalists crossed the river on rafts, swimming their horses alongside on February 11. Captain Little and his Georgia militiamen, together with Captains Robert Anderson (1741–1812), William Baskin (1737–1794), John Miller (1746–1832), and Joseph Pickens and their South Carolina militiamen, totaling about 100 men, attacked Boyd's force as they were landing on the Georgia side of the Savannah River. Boyd's force outnumbered Captain Little's men and drove them back. He then continued his march toward Augusta.

Colonel Andrew Pickens, meanwhile, moved upstream on the Carolina side and made a complete circle, crossing the Savannah River behind Boyd. He followed Boyd down the Georgia side. Unaware that Pickens was right behind him, Boyd camped on the north side of Kettle Creek, less than a mile from Carr's Fort, near where the creek joins the Savannah River. On Sunday morning, February 14, 1779, as the horses were grazing and the Loyalists were having breakfast, Pickens attacked with about 340 men. Colonel John Dooly commanded the right, Colonel Pickens the center, and Colonel Elijah Clarke (1733–1799) the left.

A first surprise assault took the hilltop. The Loyalist pickets fired and fell back into camp. Boyd quickly rallied about 100 of his men behind a fence but was forced to retreat when his left was outflanked. Boyd quickly reorganized his disordered troops and resumed fighting. Colonel Elijah Clarke (1733–1799) and more than 50 men "gained the action" by rushing through a creek and taking the opposite hill despite being heavily outnumbered.

The bitter fight went on for about an hour or two when Boyd fell with two mortal wounds. The Whigs responded with coordinated flank attacks that enabled them to cross the creek and attack the Loyalists from the rear. The inexperienced troops failed to complete the maneuver, and Pickens had to bear the brunt of the enemy fire. The Whigs forced the Loyalists to retreat across the creek. The battle lasted another half hour before the Loyalists surrendered.

The Whigs suffered nine dead and 23 wounded but they killed about 40 men and wounded or captured another 75. Boyd died of wounds that night. The Whigs recaptured 26 of their own men and brought charges of treason against 70 Loyalists. A Special Court of General Sessions held at Ninety Six convicted all the prisoners of high treason. The victors hanged five of the leaders and pardoned the rest. Southern militiamen were not inclined to have mercy on those who sided with the Crown forces because the British encouraged African-American slaves to run away from their masters and employed them on fatigue duties in British camps.

About 270 of Boyd's North Carolinians proceeded to Augusta to join Lieutenant Colonel John Hamilton's (d. 1817) Loyalists. They formed the North Carolina Royal Volunteers, under Lieutenant Colonel John Moore, and the South Carolina Royal Volunteers (later the 2nd Battalion of the South Carolina Royalists Regiment). The victory at Kettle Creek checked the string of British victories to regain control of Georgia, strengthened the desire for independence in the colony, and lowered the morale of the Loyalists in the interior of Georgia and South Carolina. It also encouraged Whig militiamen to join the forces assembled at Purrysburg under Major General Benjamin Lincoln (1733–1810).

Lincoln decided to recover Georgia but attempts to do so in February and March 1779 failed. A stronger effort in April caused Major General Augustine Prevost (1723–1786) to move to Charleston, South Carolina in May, and Lincoln withdrew from Georgia. Neither side gained much ground in these engagements, and the Whigs suffered much heavier losses.[17]

★ Colonel Josiah Dunn (1735–1783), commander of the 2nd (Upper) Battalion of the 2nd (Richmond County) Regiment, Georgia Militia, was killed in a night skirmish at the confluence of Kettle Creek and the Little River after May 6, 1782.[18]

Wilkes County

Ogeechee River (Dec. 12, 1773; March 20, 1780)

Wilkes County (July 1779; early Aug. 1781; Sept. 1, 1781; Nov. 6, 1781; May 23, 1782; May 25, 1782)

Sherrall's Fort (Jan. 14, 1774)

Lisbon (1776)

Deer Creek

Fulsam's Creek

Benjamin Fulsam's Fort (1777)

Ambush of Fulsam's Company, Ceded Lands (Aug. 1778)

Nail's Fort (Aug. and Nov. 1778)

Poplar (or Camp) Creek of the Ogeechee River

Rogers Fort (spring 1779)

Solomon Newsome's Fort (March 22, 1779)

Wrightsborough (March 1781)

Ceded Lands (March 1781)

Heard's Mill/Fort (May 1781; Sept. 10, 1781)

Hinton's Fort (April 30 or May 1, 1782)

Wilkes County, also known as the Ceded Lands, was named to honor John Wilkes who had championed colonists' issues in the British House of Commons prior to the

American War of Independence. It was one of the original counties created from Native American lands in 1773. It was later divided many times to form modern Wilkes, and all or part of Elbert, Hart, Madison, Oglethorpe, Taliaferro, Warren, and Lincoln counties.

Sherrall's or Sherrill's Fort was on the North Fork of the Ogeechee River, 4 miles from the head of the Ogeechee River. It was about 1.1 miles south-southwest of Union Point.

Lisbon is on the western shore of J. Strom Thurmond Reservoir, at the end of Mallorysville Lisbon Road off route GA 79 (Elberton Highway) in Tignall.

Benjamin Fulsam's or Fulsom's Fort was near the junction of Long Creek and the Ogeechee River in Warrenton, about 0.5 miles north of where route GA 16 (Macon Highway) crosses the Ogeechee in Jewell.

Nail's Fort was at Deer Creek, on the north side of the Broad River, about 26 miles from the river's mouth. Some Revolutionary War pensioners claimed that this fort was at the head of the Broad River; but they probably meant at the fork.

Rogers Fort was probably where route CR 165 (Hamburg State Park Road) passes through the community of Mayfield in Sparta.

Solomon Newsome's Fort was on the south side of Briar Creek in Warrenton. It was about 0.7 miles northeast of the intersection of route GA 80 (Washington Highway) and Brier Creek Road.

Wrightsborough is in McDuffie County on Wrightsboro Road, about 3.5 miles west of route US 78 (GA 10|GA 17|Washington Road).

Heard's Mill/Fort was located on Stephen Heard's property at the mouth of Anderson's Mill Creek, a tributary of Fishing Creek. It was probably located near where route GA 17 Tignall Road crosses Anderson's Mill Creek about 1.5 miles south of Tignall and about 7.75 miles north of Washington. Wilkes County had another Heard's Fort which was located several miles southeast of Stephen Heard's Fort. John Heard's Fort was built at the confluence of Anderson's Mill Creek and Fishing Creek. This fort was constructed near the beginning of the American Revolution. It was briefly occupied by Loyalists in 1779 and 1780.[19]

William White's house was at the head of the Ogeechee River.

Hinton's fort was on the east bank of Chickasaw Creek, near its mouth.

A band of Creeks killed William White, his wife, two sons and three daughters, ranging in age from 4 to 17 years old, at their home on the north fork of the Ogeechee River on Christmas day 1773. This incident was the beginning of a series of Creek raids that temporarily halted the settlement of the Ceded Lands.[20]

★ A band of Native Americans attacked Sherrall's or Sherrill's fort on January 14, 1774 and killed William Sherrall (d. 1774), four white settlers and two black slaves.[21]

★ Colonel Elijah Clarke (1733–1799), of the Wilkes County Militia, led a wagon train transporting supplies from "Jacob Patterson's & Richer Moore's" to Fort James, to protect those supplies from the Native Americans in 1776. A band of Native Americans attacked them as they passed near a fort in the area which later became Lisbon. Clarke and two of his men were wounded and three others were killed. The Native Americans had about the same number of casualties. Both forces withdrew. Captain William Pulliam (1748–1829) set out to pursue the attackers and skirmished with them north of the Broad River.[22]

★ Several hundred Creek warriors operated along the Georgia frontier during July and August of 1778. Two of George Galphin's nephews, David Holmes and Edmund Barnard (b. 1743 or 1756), joined the Loyalists and led parties from the Lower Chattahoochee towns of Red Ground (Ekanachatte), Neal's Landing (on the eastern shore of Seminole Lake, about 2 miles north of the Florida border) and Miscaque toward St. Augustine. They had already crossed the Swanee River when they learned that the Whig forces had withdrawn from their expedition against East Florida, so they also turned back.

The Upper Creeks refused to follow Captain David Taitt, British Deputy Superintendent of Indian Affairs, deciding to attack the Georgia and Carolina frontiers on their own. One war party ambushed Captain Benjamin Fulsam or Fulsom (d. 1778), of North Carolina, and his company near his fort on Fulsom's Creek in the Ceded Lands in 1778. They caught the militiamen outside Fulsam's fort and killed Captain Fulsam and seven of his men. The warriors then destroyed several plantations, driving the inhabitants away. They destroyed the fort in March 1779, along with Well's and Rogers forts. They used the ruins as a camp until they learned that Colonel Andrew Pickens (1739–1817) and Captain John Dooly (ca. 1742–1780) were approaching with a large party of Georgia and South Carolina militiamen; so they withdrew.[23]

★ Several hundred warriors from Eufalees, Apalachee Old Fields and other lower Chattahoochee towns went into the Ceded Lands above the Broad River on Sunday, August 9, 1778. They massacred a number of the inhabitants and destroyed the settlements on the River. The (Charleston) *South Carolina and American General Gazette* reported:

> . . . (T)he Indians have killed from 20 to 30 of the inhabitants, men, women, and children; carried off many horses, and killed many cattle and hogs, besides having also burnt and laid waste to the greatest part of the settlements on Broad River, and done some damage on Ogeechie.

Both Georgia and South Carolina called out the frontier militia. The 1st Battalion Georgia Continentals marched quickly from Savannah to the northwest, and the light dragoons posted at Ebenezer were ordered to Augusta. However, the Cherokees were warned in late August that the Whigs were preparing a counteroffensive, and the Creek raids stopped.[24]

★ Joseph Nail (Neal) moved from Virginia to Wilkes County, Georgia before the war and built a fort at Deer Creek, on the north side of the Broad River, to protect his family against Creek attacks. The Creeks attacked Wilkes County in August 1778 and killed 20 settlers but could not capture the fort. Colonel Andrew Williamson (ca. 1730–1786) and 500 South Carolina militiamen came to Georgia in August 1778 to protect the frontier in the event of other attacks.[25]

★ The Creeks attacked Nail's Fort a second time in November 1778 and burned it. Nail rebuilt the fort in the same spot.[26]

★ Colonel Benjamin Few (b. 1744) or (1763–1815) was sent into the Georgia backcountry in early July 1779 to protect the inhabitants from a possible uprising. He attacked and defeated a Native American war party of 70 warriors in Wilkes County, killing seven, wounding two, and taking two prisoners.[27]

★ Drury Rogers (1737–1791) built his fort below the mouths of Poplar Land or Camp Creeks on the Ogeechee River. A band of Native Americans led by Captain David Taitt, British Deputy Superintendent of Indian Affairs, attacked and destroyed this fort in the spring of 1779 after its garrison had fled.[28]

★ Captain Solomon Newsome, lieutenants Bentley (d. 1779) and Alexander and five other Whigs ran into a Creek ambush near Briar Creek in Wilkes (present-day Warren) County on Monday, March 22, 1779. The Creeks killed Bentley and a private and captured Captain Newsome. The other five escaped without their horses or supplies. Captain Newsome later escaped from the Creeks commanded by Captain David Taitt, British Deputy Superintendent of Indian Affairs. He reached his fort, on the south side of Briar Creek, in time to warn the garrison of the approach of the Native Americans who attacked that same night. As the militiamen were forewarned, they were prepared for the attack and repulsed the warriors.[29]

★ Colonel Andrew Pickens (1739–1817) and part of his South Carolina regiment joined Colonel John Twiggs (1750–1816) and Captain Joshua Inman's troop of horsemen about Monday, March 20, 1780. The band of about 300 men marched down the Ogeechee River intending to surprise Colonel Daniel McGirth (d. ca. 1789). They killed several of McGirth's men and captured three or four others, but McGirth himself escaped.[30]

★ Governor Sir James Wright (1714–1785) claimed a party of about 60 Whigs entered the Ceded Lands in March 1781 and murdered 11 people in their houses, some as they lay in their beds. He added that a party of seven armed rebels shot Major Andrew Moon (d. 1781) of the Augusta Regiment of Loyalist Militia. Major Moon realized their intentions and turned sideways as the attackers fired. One bullet grazed his chest. Another broke his arm. He died at his home in March 1781, probably from his wounds.

The Loyalists also claimed that the Whigs plundered the village of Wrightsborough. "Burnt Foot" Brown [Colonel Thomas Brown (1750–1825)] sent Colonel James Grierson (d.1781) and 100 Loyalist militiamen to Wrightsborough to catch the raiders. He also sent Major Henry Williams to the Broad River with another 100 men on a similar mission. The *Royal Georgia Gazette* in Savannah reported:

> A set of the most barbarous Wretches that ever infected any country, amounting some say to 200, others 250, lately crossed the Savannah from the northward, surprized and murdered several Loyalists at Wrightsborough and on the Ceded Lands, stripping their families of the necessities of life.[31]

★ A band of Native Americans and Loyalists went to Heard's Mill in May 1781. They killed five Whigs. Every able-bodied Whig went in pursuit of them.[32]

★ Bands of Loyalists, including Colonel Thomas Waters (ca. 1738–after 1810) and the Tillets [Giles (1750–1815), James (b. 1766), and Samuel (1720–1799)] operated in the Georgia backcountry along with Native American war parties before the Whigs captured Fort Cornwallis and retook Augusta. Captain George Barber (1743–1822) was ordered to protect the Whig forts and disperse these raiders.

The Loyalists captured Freeman's fort on the north side of the Broad River in the Ceded Lands near the site of what is now Mallorysville in Elbert County in early August of 1781. *The Royal Gazette* gave the following account:

> Captain Cane, of Col. [Thomas] Waters' regiment of the Georgia [Loyalist] militia about five weeks ago, with a party of 15 men surprised Freeman's Fort in the New Purchase in Georgia with a garrison of 18 Rebels, killed one, took the rest prisoners, and burned and destroyed the fort, stores and a block-house. . . .[33]

★ James Tillet (b. 1766) and a few Loyalist militiamen and Native Americans attacked a detachment of about 20 Whigs on Clarke's Creek in the Ceded Lands, near present-day Clarke's Station Baptist Church, at the end of August 1781. Tillet claimed he killed 18 of them; the other two escaped. The Whigs reported that Tillet and his raiders attacked and captured two small forts on the Broad River and murdered 18 men, women, and children, taking prisoner "such of the women as were able to bear the fatigues of a rapid march" and compelling them "to endure all the difficulties of a savage life."[34]

★ Giles Tillet (1750–1815) and a few Loyalists met a party of Whigs between the Broad and Savannah rivers in the Ceded Lands about Saturday, September 1, 1781. Tillet claimed his men killed eight Whigs without suffering any losses.[35]

★ Captain Samuel Tillet (1720–1799) and five Loyalists attacked a band of Whigs at Heard's Mill about Monday, September 10, 1781. They killed three Whigs, drove the others from their post, and seized 28 horses and four slaves belonging to Savannah Loyalists. They also "disarmed 16 Rebels at different places on the ceded lands."[36]

★ Colonel Elijah Clarke (1733–1799) led his militiamen against some Native American towns in Wilkes County on Tuesday, November 6, 1781. They killed 40 Native Americans and two white men and captured 40 prisoners, including two whites. They burned several towns and some "villages and plantations," destroying 1,000 bushels of corn and "a large quantity of provisions." Some of the Native Americans fled into the mountains and were pursued. Clarke's men "killed some and found some hundred bushels of Corn, which they had hid."[37]

★ Creek warriors attacked a blockhouse (see photo GA-1) in Wilkes County on Friday, May 23, 1782. They kept up a fire for a considerable time before withdrawing. They killed six cattle and every valuable horse. Captain George Barber (1743–1822) pursued the Creeks to the South Fork of the Oconee.

★ Another party of Creeks murdered and scalped a Mrs. Rose two days later near a station in the fork of the Broad and Savannah rivers. It appeared as if they meant to storm the fort, but the four men defending the fort sallied forth, surprised the attackers and drove them off. Major George Dooly (d. 1821) mustered a party at the murder site before daybreak and pursued the Creeks. However, as he did not have enough horses, he was forced to return.

Captain George Barber fell in with the Creeks on his return and skirmished with them. He drove them off, took all their provisions and retook the scalp. The Creeks escaped through large Cain Swamp.

Ezekiel Cloud's (1762–1850) version of the raid states that it occurred about the last of April or first of May 1782. The raiders attacked Hinton's fort near the mouth of Chickasaw Creek and kept up their fire for about two hours. They killed five milk cows and cut out their forequarters before withdrawing. Captain George Barber raised a party of 20 volunteers from the vicinity around Jeremiah Cloud's blockhouse, about 4 miles distant from the forest, and set out in pursuit. They chased the raiders into the Creek Nation but were unable to catch them after nearly three days.

One of Barber's men shot at a deer for food. This alerted the Creeks, to their presence. Barber then left the trail and headed north in search of Creek camps. He found the trail that ran from the Creek Nation to the white settlements and followed it. He set up his camp along the shore of a creek for the night. The Creeks apparently heard the shot at the deer and followed Barber's men and stole their horses during the night, as the horses were out grazing.

When Barber's men returned to the settlements, they skirmished with yet another Creek war party. The Creeks withdrew about a half mile into a swamp. Barber's men found 12 packs on the battleground. One of them contained the scalp of a white woman whom the Creeks had killed on the Wilkes County frontier. Barber's men reported they had wounded one of the Creeks.[38]

Augusta
Fort Cornwallis and Fort Grierson
McKay's Trading Post, White House (Jan. 29, 1779; Feb. 3, 1779; Feb. 14, 1779; Sept. 14–18, 1780; May 22 to June 5, 1781)
Weatherford's Raid (March 9, 1782)

Andrew McLean, a Scot and associate of Robert Mackay (1772–1816), owned McKay's Trading Post, better known as the White House, but he did not reside there. McKay's Trading Post was a strongly fortified stone building on an elevation known as Garden Hill. It was about 300 yards west of the Savannah River, about midway between Riverwatch Parkway (GA 104) and Goodrich Street, about 100 yards north of Kendrick Place and about 2 miles northwest of Fort Cornwallis.

Fort Cornwallis and Fort Grierson were in Augusta. The site of Fort Cornwallis is at 6th and Reynolds Streets. The fort was built by James Oglethorpe in 1735 as protection for traders on the Savannah River. Named Fort Augusta, after the Princess of Wales, it was renamed Fort Cornwallis in the Congressional forces' attack on Augusta in September 1780. Fort Cornwallis was torn down in 1786. The approximate location of Fort Grierson, the temporary British stronghold commanded by Colonel James Grierson (d. 1781), is 11th and Reynolds Streets, a mile west of Fort Cornwallis.

St. Paul's Church marks the site of Fort Cornwallis. It is the fourth one to do so. When this church was first built in 1750, it stood "under the curtain of the fort." A Celtic cross behind the church marks the site of Fort Augusta. One of James Oglethorpe's cannons stands at the foot of the cross. There are no apparent remains of Fort Cornwallis.

There is a marker for the site of the Maham tower a few feet off Reynolds Street on 8th Street. The site, formerly the Cotton Exchange building, now houses the Georgia Bank & Trust.

Augusta was a strategic gateway into the Georgia upcountry and, hence, was of great importance to the British. Rev. William Tennent described the place on September 7, 1775:

> Every valuable house in Augusta is surrounded by a strong wooden fortification, formed of three inch plank, in deep grooves of upright posts, not less than ten or twelve feet high. These forts are differently constructed; some have large strong pentagonal flankers at each corner, in which from twenty to forty men each may fight. The flankers have two stories, and on the upper floor are mounted a number of three-pounders. Others have demi-flankers projected from the middle of each side to answer the same purpose. These buildings serve, in times of peace, for chair-houses and other offices, but, in war, render the inhabitants secure in the midst of savages.[39]

Lieutenant Colonel Archibald Campbell (1739–1791) captured Augusta on Friday, January 29, 1779 with virtually no opposition and no casualties. Cheering Loyalists welcomed him and some 1100 inhabitants took the oath of allegiance over the next few days. The Crown forces held the fort until February 1780, when Continental pressure across the Savannah River forced them to abandon it.

After Lieutenant Colonel Archibald Campbell (1739–1791) captured Augusta on January 29, 1779, both armies watched each other across the Savannah River. Colonel Campbell could not attack Colonel Andrew Williamson's (ca. 1730–1786) forces because he had no boats to cross the river. Williamson could not attack because he was waiting for Brigadier General John Ashe's (1720–1781) reinforcements.

★ While Lieutenant Colonel Archibald Campbell (1739–1791) had four flatboats constructed, each capable of carrying 70 men and 16 rowers, small groups of Colonel Andrew Williamson's (ca. 1730–1786) troops would cross the Savannah River occasionally to plunder the British, harass their camp or reconnoiter. Lieutenant William Butler (1759–1821), of Brigadier General Andrew Pickens's (1739–1817) militia, led one of these patrols on Wednesday, February 3, 1779.

Sergeant MacAllister (d. 1779), of the 71st Highlander light infantry, was standing guard at the house of Major Andrew Moore (1752–1821) who was taken prisoner when Colonel Campbell captured Augusta. Major Moore was unable to get across the river, was captured and requested that a guard be placed on his house as a courtesy to his wife and family. Such safe guards were a normal procedure which both sides were supposed to respect.

As Lieutenant Butler's patrol passed by the house where Sergeant MacAllister was standing guard, MacAllister mistook them for Loyalists and called out to them. When he realized his mistake, he charged with his bayonet (see Photo GA-3) but was shot by Lieutenant Butler. Williamson described a militiaman named Vessels as "A Mad Crazy Fellow, who acted As a guide to the party; cut and Mangled the body in a shocking and Barbarious manner before it was perceived what he was doing." Williamson had Vessels arrested and sent in irons to Major General Benjamin Lincoln (1733–1810) at Purrysburg, South Carolina. Lincoln released Vessels who claimed the British had cut his son to pieces.

GA-3. Bayonet charge. Reenactors portraying a Continental unit execute a bayonet charge at reconstructed Fort Randolph, Point Pleasant, WV. The man in the second line has no bayonet, so he "clubs" his musket to use it as a club. Courtesy of Ed Lowe. ©EDLO Images. Used with permission.

Rumors spread that the militiamen had only wounded MacAllister and that Butler's entire patrol "cruelly cut with Hatchets" as he lay there bleeding. Major William
"Bloody Bill" Cunningham (d. 1787) later killed Butler's father in retaliation, and the
71st Highlanders took their revenge for Sergeant MacAllister's death at the Battle of
Briar Creek on March 3, 1779.[40]

★ The Crown forces evacuated Augusta about 1 AM on Sunday, February 14, 1779
after destroying the flatboats which they had constructed to cross the Savannah River.
Lieutenant Colonel Archibald Campbell (1739–1791) left his wounded in the care of
Brigadier General Andrew Williamson (ca. 1730–1786), an indication that his retreat
was sudden and unexpected.

General Williamson immediately ordered Colonel LeRoy Hammond (1728–1789)
and Lieutenant Colonel John McIntosh (1755–1826) and a detachment of 200 mounted Continentals to follow the Crown forces withdrawing down to Savannah and to
harass their flanks and rear. The Continentals finished crossing their horses about 10 PM
and marched about 3 miles, then stopped to feed and refresh the horses and allow the
men to get some sleep.

Large bodies of Loyalists got together and more than 600 crossed the Savannah River,
intending to join the Crown forces. However, Colonel Andrew Pickens (1739–1817)
marched up the Broad River with a strong force to intercept them and to prevent them
from joining forces.[41]

First Siege

★ Lieutenant Colonel Thomas Alexander Brown (1744–1814), British superintendent
of Indian Affairs in the Southern Department, headed north from St. Augustine, Florida
with a force of East Florida Rangers, together with Lieutenant Colonel James Grierson
(d.1781) and 250 Creek warriors, to reclaim Augusta for the King. He reached Augusta
in early June 1780. He sent a message demanding Colonel John Dooly (ca. 1742–1780)
to surrender the last remaining armed Whigs in Georgia. Brown also dispatched William Manson (b. 1744) into Wilkes County to administer the oath of allegiance to the
inhabitants. Colonel Dooly, fearing retaliation against family members, surrendered his
400 militiamen to Manson on a ridge overlooking the later site of Washington, Wilkes
County, on Monday, June 5, 1780. The Crown forces now controlled all of Georgia.

General Charles Cornwallis (1738–1805) had drawn all of his available forces to his
headquarters near Camden, South Carolina in late summer 1780. Colonel Elijah Clarke
(1733–1799) saw an opportunity to recapture the Georgia upcountry from the British.
He and Lieutenant Colonel James McCall (1741–1781) were returning to Augusta from
a recruiting expedition in the area of Ninety Six, South Carolina in early September
1780. They hoped to raise a force of 1000 men—more than sufficient to destroy the
small Loyalist garrison at Augusta—but McCall could only muster 80 men and Clarke
350. They rendezvoused at Soap or Sope Creek in Georgia, 40 miles northwest of Augusta. Colonel Clarke's forces were inadequate to recapture Augusta, but he did not want
to abandon his plan. When they approached Augusta undetected on Thursday morning,
September 14, 1780, they divided into three groups. Lieutenant Colonel McCall commanded the right, Major Samuel Taylor commanded the left and Colonel Clarke took
the center.

Major Taylor moved into a Native American camp near Hawk's Creek in the west by
accident. After some firing, the Native Americans retreated to Augusta where they joined
Captain Andrew Johnston's (d. 1780) King's Rangers at McKay's Trading Post, known

as the White House, located a mile and a half northwest of the town. Major Taylor advanced and took possession of the post.[42]

When Major Taylor attacked the house, Colonel Thomas Brown (1750–1825) mobilized his men to reinforce Captain Johnston, led a counter-attack and was wounded. He also sent dispatch riders, by two routes, to alert Colonel John Harris Cruger (1738–1807) at Ninety Six, South Carolina, of the situation at Augusta. Colonel Brown's command consisted of 250 men from several corps but mostly Florida Rangers, 250 Creeks, and 50 Cherokees.

Clarke's and McCall's troops caught the rest of the garrison by surprise and they captured Forts Cornwallis and Grierson without much resistance. Clarke took 70 Loyalists and all the Native American men prisoners, placed them under guard, and headed to assist Taylor. As Clarke's forces arrived, Brown and his men took shelter at the White House, located about 80 yards from the river. Both sides continued firing from 11 AM until night, but the Loyalists were not dislodged. The Native Americans retreated behind the river banks. When the firing finally stopped at the end of the day, Clarke posted guards to keep the enemy in place. Lieutenant Colonel Brown fortified the house during night by filling earth between the spaces in the weatherboards and ceiling and closing up the windows with the floor boards.

The Whigs brought up a 6- and a 4-pounder the next morning, but they did not have proper carriages, so the field pieces were of little use. Moreover, Captain William Martin (1745–1780) of South Carolina, the only qualified artillerist present, was fatally wounded early in the day. Small arms fire continued throughout the day and still failed to dislodge the Loyalists. Clarke was unaware, though, that Brown had been shot through both thighs early in the engagement and that he and other wounded men were in much suffering. Yet, they refused to surrender. Clarke also cut off the enemy's water supply early that morning when they drove a band of Cherokees from the river bank. Lieutenant Colonel Henry "Light-Horse Harry" Lee (1756–1818) recounted how Brown and his men survived:

> To remedy this menacing evil, Colonel Browne ordered all the earthen vessels in the store to be taken, in which the urine was preserved; and when cold, it was served out with much economy to the troops, himself taking the first draught. Disregarding the torture of a wound in his leg, which had become much swollen from exertion, he continued booted at the head of his small gallant band, directing his defence, and animating his troops by his presence and example.[43]

One of Brown's dispatch riders arrived at Colonel Cruger's headquarters early in the morning of September 15th. That night, 50 Cherokees crossed the river by canoe to reinforce the Loyalists. Clarke demanded Brown's surrender again on the morning of September 17th but Brown refused. Another summons was sent that afternoon, saying that Brown would be held personally responsible for the consequences of his failure to submit. Brown rejected the request again.[44]

The 300 Loyalists and 400 Creeks and Cherokees withstood the Whig attacks for four days, but the Whigs were not strong enough to take the post by assault. Colonel Clarke's scouts notified him, on the evening of the 17th, that Colonel Cruger and 500 British Regulars and Loyalist militiamen were approaching. They arrived on the opposite side of the river at 8 AM on Monday, September 18, 1780. Many of Clarke's men had returned home or gone to visit friends and families around Augusta, so his force was quite reduced in strength.

Clarke raised the siege and retreated about 10 AM. He lost about 60 men killed and wounded in the engagement. He left in such a hurry, to avoid being caught, that he left his wounded. Captain Asby (d. 1780) and 28 others, including the wounded, were captured and executed. Captain Asby and 12 of the wounded prisoners were hanged on the staircase of the White House so Colonel Brown, lying there wounded, could see them die. The Native Americans scalped the victims and threw them in the river. Several other prisoners were also hanged.

The remaining prisoners were handed over to the Creeks and Cherokees who formed a circle with the prisoners in the center. Some were scalped before being struck by weapons of war. Others were thrown into the fire and roasted to death. Clarke's adjutant, Major James Carter (1750–1780), was mortally wounded at the White House door, trying to prevent the Loyalists from gaining possession of it. His fellow soldiers braved great risks and brought him to Mrs. Elizabeth Hobson Bugg's (ca. 1727–1799) plantation where he died a few days later. The Crown forces lost at least two officers (Captain Andrew Johnston and Ensign Silcox of the Florida Rangers) and about 70 Creeks and Cherokees killed. Colonel Clarke paroled the officers and soldiers who had been captured, but they disregarded their parole and took up their arms immediately after Clarke retreated.

See also **Bugg's Plantation** pp. 34–35.

Clarke's men dispersed after this engagement and planned to meet at the end of September. About 300 men and 400 women and children gathered. They began a march of almost 200 miles through the mountains to avoid the enemy. They arrived at the Watauga and Nolichucky rivers in Tennessee on Wednesday, October 11th, starving and forlorn.[45]

Lieutenant Colonel Cruger agreed with Governor James Wright on the need to retaliate for Clarke's attack on Augusta. He decided to "lay Waste and destroy the whole Territory" of the Ceded Lands (Wilkes County). Colonel Cruger destroyed 100 plantations, the forts in the area, and what had been the Whig courthouse. He arrested more than 60 men and imprisoned them for having assisted Clarke and turned others over to the Creeks and Cherokees to be tortured and murdered.

Second Siege

★ Whig Lieutenant Colonel Micajah Williamson (1744–1795) led a detachment that marched toward Augusta on Monday, April 16, 1781. Captain Stephen Johnson and his company of Effingham County militiamen and Colonel John Baker (1750–1830) and his militiamen from the southern part of Georgia joined him there. Colonel Josiah Dunn (1735–1783) and Jared Irwin (1750–1818) also arrived with a few men from Burke County. Colonel LeRoy Hammond (1728–1789) and Major James Jackson (1757–1806) also joined them with the South Carolina militiamen in the vicinity of Augusta. The combined force of about 1,300 militiamen invested Augusta. After almost four weeks of fruitless siege, as the militiamen were planning to return home, Major Jackson reminded them of enemy cruelties and the necessity of staying in the fight. The militiamen stayed. Brigadier General Elijah Clarke (1733–1799) arrived on May 15 with 100 men, took command and raised the Whigs' morale.

Major Philip Dill (d. 1782) raised a force of Loyalist militiamen and marched to break the siege. Clarke sent Colonel Isaac Shelby (1750–1826) and a detachment of mountainmen along with Captain Patrick ("Paddy") Carr's (1761–1820) Georgians to oppose Major Dill's Loyalists which they did at Walker's Bridge on Briar Creek.

See **New Bridge** p. 30.

General Clarke had no artillery for the siege, so he took an old 4-pounder the British had abandoned and had it mounted and placed it in a battery about 400 yards from Fort

Grierson. A blacksmith forged projectiles for the piece; but the Whigs fired it sparingly, due to the short supply of gunpowder.

Clarke sent an express to Brigadier General Andrew Pickens (1739–1817) who, with 400 men from Anderson's Regiment, was acting as a blocking force between Augusta and Ninety Six. Although the Native Americans continued raiding the Georgia and South Carolina frontier, Pickens sent some of his men to Clarke and notified Major General Nathanael Greene (1742–1786) of his situation. General Greene promised his assistance and sent Lieutenant Colonel Henry "Light-Horse Harry" Lee's (1756–1818) Legion (composed of horse troops and companies of infantrymen) and Major Pinketham Eaton's (d. 1781) North Carolina Militia to support Pickens and Clarke while his main army moved against Ninety Six.

Pickens and Lee decided to attack Fort Grierson, named for Colonel James Grierson (d. 1781), the commander of the garrison located half a mile west of Fort Cornwallis in the center of Augusta. They intended to intercept the Loyalists before they could reach Fort Cornwallis. Fort Grierson, the smaller of the two forts guarding the town, had a garrison of only 80 Georgia militiamen and two pieces of artillery.

General Pickens and Colonel Elijah Clarke (1733–1799) would attack from the northwest, while Major James Jackson's North Carolina Continentals and the militiamen would go down the river to attack from the northeast. Lee's infantry and artillery were on the south side to support Major Pinketham Eaton and his North Carolinians. Major Joseph Eggleston (1754–1811) and Lee's Legion waited in ambush between the two forts and blocked the northern approaches to Fort Cornwallis. The troops, half of them carrying axes, marched toward Fort Grierson on Wednesday, May 23, 1781.

The three infantry detachments advanced simultaneously against Fort Cornwallis garrisoned by Colonel Thomas Brown (1750–1825) and 330 Loyalist militiamen and 300 Creek warriors. They encountered little resistance. The Loyalists fled into Fort Grierson. The North Carolina Continentals waded across the shallow gully and began to chop the stockade. Lieutenant Colonel Brown sallied forth from Fort Cornwallis with part of his garrison and two field pieces; but, when he saw Lee's ambush, he returned to Fort Cornwallis and bombarded Lee with his artillery.

Realizing the futility of resistance, Colonel Grierson ordered the gates open and had his men rush to the safety of the larger Fort Cornwallis a mile away. Clarke's men offered stiff resistance, killing 30 and wounding or capturing another 45 and capturing two artillery pieces. The Loyalists wounded Major Eaton in the thigh and then executed him with his own sword. Colonel Grierson, the commander, was taken prisoner and shot by an unknown Georgian, according to the Richmond County Historical Society. Benson Lossing identifies him as Captain Samuel Alexander (1733–1790 or 1757–1817) of the Georgia militia.

General Pickens then began to concentrate on Fort Cornwallis. Unable to take Fort Cornwallis by storm, the militiamen began a siege and started digging siege trenches. The Crown forces mounted two sorties and drove the men from the trenches in fierce, hand-to-hand fighting. The Whigs decided to build a Maham tower (see Photo GA-4) (at what is now the corner of 8th and Reynolds Streets). The tower, made of logs and filled with earth, had an embrasure (see Photo GA-5) at the top that accommodated a 6-pounder, allowing the militiamen to deliver deadly cannon and musket fire from it into the fort. The height of the Maham tower constructed at Augusta is unknown, but it was tall enough to dominate the interior of Fort Cornwallis which was just two modern blocks away.

GA-4. Maham tower at the Ninety Six National Historic Site. The tower is made of logs tapering slightly to the summit. Riflemen in the top could fire into a stockade, redoubt or fort. The remains of the zigzag trenches are visible at the base of the tower in the foreground.

GA-5. Embrasures are openings in a wall for guns. These embrasures are in an earthen wall and are part of the Grand French Battery at Yorktown, Virginia.

The defenders tried unsuccessfully to drive off the builders with fire from their two heaviest guns and to destroy the Maham tower. Brown refused a second request to surrender on May 31 and the following morning. The Whigs began a cannonade with a captured 6-pounder they had mounted in the Maham tower the previous night. They were joined by small arms fire, and riflemen drove the Loyalist gun crews from their pieces. The 6-pounder also destroyed the two cannons that had been firing at the tower.

Brown agreed to consider a conditional surrender on June 4, as the Whigs prepared for a final assault. However, as that day was the King's birthday, negotiations were put off until the following day. The Loyalists laid down their arms on June 6, 1781 and a guard marched them off to be paroled in Savannah. Whig casualties totaled 40 men. Crown forces lost about 52 officers and men killed and 334 were made prisoners. The day after the surrender, Lee set out to join Greene at Ninety Six, the only British post remaining in the interior of Georgia and the Carolinas. The capture of Augusta won the support of the Georgia backcountry for the Whig cause.[46]

★ Sir Patrick Houstoun (ca. 1745–1785) and David Douglass (1755–1839), a Whig who took the oath of allegiance and was commissioned as major in the Volunteers of Augusta, deserted to the Whigs on February 20, 1782 as did a large number of the first and second de Lancey battalion, probably because some of the officers lost their rank and pay when the Georgia Loyalists were combined with the King's Rangers.

The defections stung Cornet Martin Weatherford who took a detachment of seven Volunteers of Augusta and set out from Savannah on Saturday, March 2, 1782. They headed to Augusta where they arrived at dusk the following Tuesday, March 5. They intended to wait until dark to make their appearance. However, an African-American who had accompanied them deserted. Cornet Weatherford was afraid that the deserter might give the alarm. The Loyalists immediately moved through Brigadier General "Mad Anthony" Wayne's (1745–1796) lines and headed to the house of former Whig governor Glasscock, where they found Mr. William Glasscock (1729–1793), Captain Alexander Daniel Cutchbert and Mr. David Douglass. They took Captain Anthony Cutchbert (1751–1832) and Mr. Douglass prisoners. The desertion of the African-American prevented the Loyalists from capturing Governor Alexander Martin (1740–1807) who resided about a mile from Glasscock's. After traveling a few miles with his prisoners, Cornet Weatherford dismissed them on parole.

★ On his return from Augusta, Cornet Martin Weatherford fell in with a militia scout of six men at a house near Briar Creek. He disarmed them all and paroled them together with some others he met on his route, a total of 14. He executed Colonel Josiah Dunn (d. 1782) and Captain "Paddy" Carr (d. 1782). The small raiding party returned on Tuesday morning without any losses and with considerable booty of horses and arms.[47]

Fort Henderson (Spirit Creek) (Jan. 30, 1779)

McBean's Creek (Jan. 30, 1779)

Cupboard Swamp (Jan. 31, 1779)

Near Spirit Creek (Sept. 8, 1781)

Fork of the Hooper (Dec. 3, 1781)

McBean's Swamp (Dec. 13, 1781)

William Faden's 1780 map places Fort Henderson on Spirit Creek about 11 miles south-southeast of Augusta.[48]

> Cupboard Swamp, now known as Phinizy Swamp, is located in the present wetlands between Gordon Highway [route US 1 (US 25|US 78|US 278)] and route I-520 (Bobby Jones Expressway|GA 232|GA 415) at the Bend of the River, a little below Moore's Bluff southeast of Augusta.[49]
>
> The Fork of the Hooper River is about 40 miles west-southwest of Ogeechee, about 0.5 miles south of the intersection of route GA 56 and Norristown Covena Road in Swainsboro.
>
> McBean's Swamp is near Fort Henderson southwest of Augusta.

Lieutenant Colonel Archibald Campbell (1739–1791) decided to rest his men after a 9-mile march on Friday, January 29, 1779, before proceeding to Augusta. He sent Colonel John Maitland (1732–1779) with Captain Sir James Gardiner Baird's (ca. 1760–1830) light infantry, two 3-pounders and the East Florida Rangers to Telfair's Plantation at 10 PM. There, they would be on the north side of McBean's Creek about a mile behind the Georgia militia under Colonel Samuel Elbert (1740–1788), Colonel John Twiggs (1750–1816), and Colonels William Few (1748–1828) and Benjamin Few (b. 1744) or (1763–1815). The rest of Campbell's force began to move toward McBean's Creek at 2 AM and marched the 7 miles by 4 AM. They waited for Maitland to fire his two cannons at daybreak, giving them the signal that his troops were at the hill.

The 71st Regiment formed a line across the road, placing a 6-pounder on each flank and a howitzer in the middle. They advanced at dawn but found the militiamen had abandoned their camp "so sudden, that their pots with Beef and Pork were left standing on Fires just lighted up, and the Water scarcely heated." Two of Lieutenant Colonel Thomas Alexander Brown's (1744–1814) East Florida Rangers stumbled into the camp half an hour before Colonel Maitland was supposed to fire his guns, eliminating the element of surprise.

The British captured a few of Elbert's Georgians who tried to escape through a swamp. They fired grapeshot into "suspicious Parts of the Swamp without dislodging any of the Rebels." Ninety slaves from George Galphin's (1709–1780) plantation joined the Crown forces. Colonel Campbell promised to return the slaves if Galphin would surrender Campbell's brother-in-law and information about Colonel Elbert's force at Augusta. Galphin provided the information, but only after Augusta fell.

Colonel Campbell left the light infantrymen and the East Florida Rangers at McBean's Creek to rest after their long night march. The 71st Highlanders, the New York Volunteers and the Georgia dragoons pursued Elbert's Georgians. Campbell's men caught up with the militiamen at Spirit Creek in the early evening.

Elbert had left 200 men at Fort Henderson, a small stockade on the other side of Spirit Creek. Campbell fired his howitzer and two 6-pounders at the fort from a distance of 300 yards. The Georgians abandoned the post after 10 minutes, leaving a few dead behind. A company of the 71st Highlanders crossed Spirit Creek and captured the fort.

The Crown light infantrymen and the East Florida Rangers at McBean's Creek heard the cannon fire and ran to the fight. Colonel Elbert's Georgia militiamen attacked them and inflicted about 20 casualties and captured the rest.

Campbell's forces rested at the fort that night. Warned that Colonel Archibald Lytle (1730–1790) reinforced Elbert's Georgians with 200 North Carolina riflemen, Colonel Campbell's men marched 3 miles to a location known as Cupboard Swamp. They arrived at 9 AM on Monday, January 31, 1781 and spotted some of Elbert's men on horseback.

Elbert's men fired some shots at them with their carbines then rode away. They then set up an ambush but Elbert's main force had withdrawn at 8 o'clock that morning.

Brigadier General Andrew Williamson (ca. 1730–1786) took possession of the ferry boats so the Crown forces could not pursue the Georgians across the Savannah River. Campbell's forces marched 12 more miles and captured Augusta without incident. The Loyalists came out of hiding and greeted them with cheering.[50]

★ John Goodgame (1744–1781), William Simmons, and one Honeycut plotted to murder Lieutenant Colonel James Jackson (1757–1806) in mid-August 1781. They also planned to seize Nathan Brownson (1742–1796), the new governor, and as many members of the Executive Council as they could and take them to Savannah. The conspirators sent a message to Lieutenant Colonel Alured Clarke (1745–1832) outlining their plans. Clarke responded by ordering Captain Benjamin Brantley and 45 men to the outskirts of Augusta, where they joined the conspirators during the night.

However, David Davis, Colonel Jackson's servant, learned of the plot and warned his master. Colonel Jackson mustered his Georgia Legion, both cavalry and infantry, and arrested the three ringleaders and 17 others. A court martial convicted them. The three leaders were hanged and the others were pardoned after showing "apparent penitence."

Captain Brantley's men marched as far as Spirit Creek, about 10 miles below Augusta, on Saturday, September 8, 1781. They skirmished with a small party of Whigs, consisting of a lieutenant and seven privates, about 1.5 miles from Brigadier General John Twiggs's (1750–1816) camp at Spirit Creek. When Captain Brantley learned that the plot had failed, he retreated to Savannah.[51]

★ Two Creeks informed Brigadier General John Twiggs (1750–1816) in Augusta that a party of Chickamaugas and some traders were trying to go to Savannah for trade goods or other supplies. General Twiggs mustered all the militiamen he could—72 officers and men—and rode out to intercept the Chickamaugas on Saturday, December 1, 1781. They found the Chickamaugas at the Fork of the Hooper River, about 40 miles west-southwest of Ogeechee at daybreak on December 3rd and attacked immediately. They soon overwhelmed the Chickamaugas, killing 20 of them and 12 white traders. They captured seven women and two children, including the daughter of Oconnostota, and seized 199 horses, 15,000 pounds of deer skins, and 1,500 beaver pelts. Twiggs lost 12 men, one-sixth of his force.

★ Benjamin Brantley and eight of Brigadier General John Twiggs's (1750–1816) riflemen mistakenly ambushed a group of fellow Georgians near McBean's Swamp on Thursday December 13, 1781. They killed the president of the council in Augusta and another man.[52]

Middleton's Ferry (Feb. 9, 1779)
Herbert's Store (Feb. 18, 1779)
Thomas's Plantation (Feb. 22, 1779)

Middleton's Ferry was 17 miles northwest of Augusta at Appling, probably where route US 221 (GA 47|Ray Owens Road|Appling Harlem Highway) crosses Kiokee Creek.

James Herbert's Store was on the Savannah River about 45 miles southeast of Augusta.

James Thomas's plantation was on Belchers Mill Creek, or Mill Creek, about 7 miles northeast of Brooklet.

Captain Moses Wheatley or Whitley and 40 East Florida Rangers were sent to guard Middleton's Ferry while Captain Robert Phillips (d. 1782) and 20 South Carolina Royalists went to Brownsborough, 10 miles further up river, to observe any movements of Congressional troops. These small posts were a prime target for Lieutenant Colonel Leonard Marbury (1750–1796) and his Georgia Regiment of Horse Rangers who actively pursued anybody they suspected of loyalty to the King.

Colonel Marbury was headed to the Burke County Jail with 20 prisoners that he captured at Middleton's Ferry on Tuesday, February 9, 1779 when he learned that Lieutenant Colonel Archibald Campbell (1739–1791) had detached Lieutenant Colonel John Thomas, Jr. (1751–1819) and 150 Burke County Loyalist militiamen to intercept him and rescue the prisoners. Marbury rode to Thomas's house to surprise him instead. When he arrived at Thomas's house on Monday, February 22nd, he found Captain Williams and an advance party of four men. He took all of them prisoners.[52a]

★ Lieutenant Colonel Archibald Campbell's (1739–1791) army left Boggy Gut Creek on Wednesday, February 17, 1779 and marched to Odom's Ferry where they built a bridge of rafts to cross over to the north side of Briar Creek. There, they built a redoubt to block any pursuit by Continental Brigadier General John Ashe (1720–1781) and to wait for any survivors of the battle at Kettle Creek which occurred three days earlier. General Ashe sent Colonels LeRoy Hammond (1728–1789), John McIntosh (1755–1826) and John Twiggs (1750–1816) to harass Colonel Campbell's lines. They passed in front of the British position at Odom's Creek to burn the bridges along the south side of Briar Creek.

★ General Andrew Williamson (ca. 1730–1786) took a position on the Carolina side of the river near Augusta. He retained his militia and some of the Georgia militia and sent Lieutenant Colonel Leonard Marbury (1750–1796) with 50 dragoons and some militiamen to take a post near Brownsborough, in Richmond County. Lieutenant Colonel John McIntosh (1755–1826) mustered some Richmond County militiamen and headed down river behind the Crown forces at Augusta. They surprised one of their outposts consisting of 70 men at Herbert's store on Thursday, February 18, 1779. They killed four and took 10 prisoners, including three British officers, and captured 200 horses from Colonel Campbell's retreating army.

★ On his way back to camp, Colonel LeRoy Hammond (1728–1789) captured a captain in the Georgia Loyalist militia and 10 of his men who were on their way to guard Middleton's Ferry. Hammond's men arrived back at camp on Wednesday night without any loss.

★ Captain Moses Wheatley or Whitley and lieutenants McKenzie and John Hall (of the 44th Regiment and a native of South Carolina) led a reconnoitering party of 20 of the King's Rangers toward Brownsborough to determine if any Whig forces were gathering in that area. Lieutenant Colonel Leonard Marbury's (1750–1796) spies reported Wheatley's position and strength. Marbury sent Captain John Cooper (1751–1819) and 12 dragoons to attack Captain Wheatley's rear while Marbury advanced on his front. Cooper arrived at his destination much sooner than expected and charged Wheatley and his party while they were stopped to cook dinner. Completely surprised, the Rangers surrendered without resistance.[53]

★ Lieutenant Colonel Leonard Marbury (1750–1796) then continued to Brownsborough where his men charged Captain Robert Phillips's (d. 1782) men as they entered their camp. However, Phillips had taken proper security precautions and reacted quickly, killing two Georgians and driving the rest back. He then pursued Marbury's Rangers and captured 10 of them and some of their provisions.[54]

Louisville
Rocky Comfort Creek Settlement
Rocky Comfort Creek (March 22, 1779)
Wylie's Plantation (March 1781)

> Wylie's Plantation was located in the Rocky Comfort Creek Settlement, located at the confluence of Rocky Comfort Creek and the Ogeechee River about 1.5 miles southwest of Louisville, Georgia.

When the Crown forces entered South Carolina, they encouraged the Creeks to attack the Georgia and South Carolina settlements all the way to Augusta. South Carolina Loyalists wore a red cross and a sprig of pine on their hats to identify themselves so that the Creeks would not harm them.

When Captain David Taitt, British Deputy Superintendent of Indian Affairs, crossed the Ogeechee River with 120 Creeks and Cherokees led by Alexander McGillivray, also known as Hoboi-Hili-Miko (1750–1793) and Chief Guristersigo ("the Magnificent") (1752–1782) in early March 1779, General Andrew Williamson (ca. 1730–1786) sent colonels Joseph William Pickens (1737–1781), LeRoy Hammond (1728–1789), and Thomas Dooley to destroy them. As the Crown forces had already withdrawn from Augusta, Captain Taitt and his party did not find any forces to support. When they learned that the Carolinians were hunting them, the Creeks refused to proceed and went their own way. Some headed toward Briar Creek and captured Captain Solomon Newsome of the Georgia militia who managed to escape and return to his fort on the south side of Briar Creek, ahead of his captors, to warn the garrison. When the Creeks attacked the fort that night, the militiamen were prepared and drove them off.

Colonel LeRoy Hammond and some of Colonel Pickens's militiamen ran into some Creeks at Rocky Comfort Creek on Monday, March 22, 1779 (or Sunday, March 28). They killed eight and took six prisoners, including three white men. They had only one casualty, Major Francis Ross (1743–1779) who was mortally wounded in the stomach. He died three days later.[55]

★ Lieutenant James Kennedy and a few of his men attacked some Loyalists at the plantation of "Old James Wylie, in the district of Rocky Creek" in March 1781. The Loyalists, thinking they were outnumbered, fled through the "old fields" but counterattacked when they realized they outnumbered the attackers. They forced Kennedy and his men to withdraw. Both sides lost at least one man killed.[56]

Savannah River near Augusta (Dec. 1780)
Upper Three Runs

Captain Joseph Vince's (1745–1811) company of Captain James McKay's Regiment fought some Loyalists commanded by one Elsey at the Upper Three Runs in December

1780. The Whigs routed Elsey and killed nine of his men while only having one of their own wounded.

Another band of Loyalists, commanded by one Franklin, had three men killed in another engagement soon afterward. The Whigs had one man killed.[57]

New Bridge (May 1, 1781)

> New Bridge was located at the present-day Walker's Bridge where Story Mill Road crosses Briar Creek, about 25 miles south of Augusta and about 4 miles north of the Burke County Jail.

An epidemic of smallpox hit the camp of the Wilkes County Militia after the fight at Beattie's Mill, South Carolina on March 21, 1781. Colonel Elijah Clarke (1733–1799) was struck and Lieutenant Colonel James McCall (1741–1781) died from it. Lieutenant Colonel Micajah Williamson (1744–1795) assumed command until Colonel Clarke recovered. The militia units of colonels Williamson, John Baker (1750–1830), and LeRoy Hammond (1728–1789) joined forces on Monday, April 16, 1781 and placed Augusta under siege. Colonel Williamson made his camp within 1200 yards of forts Cornwallis and Grierson but Colonel Thomas Brown (1750–1825) did not attack them because he did not know the size of the Georgia force. Colonel Clarke recovered from smallpox and arrived with 100 new recruits to assume command in May.

Major Philip Dill mustered Loyalists from St. George and St. Matthew Parish to march to Augusta to lift the siege. Clarke sent some of his North Carolina militiamen under Captain Moses Shelby (1760–1828) and Georgia troops under Captain Patrick ("Paddy") Carr (1761–1820) to intercept them before they arrived in Augusta. Both forces met at New Bridge on Briar Creek on Tuesday, May 1, 1781. The militiamen drove off the Loyalists, killing and wounding several. Captain Moses Shelby was wounded.[58]

Kiokee Creek (Feb. 6, 1779)

> This event occurred at the Savannah River near Kiokee Creek about 13 miles north of Augusta.

There were several forts on the frontier about 50 miles from Augusta which had been built for protection in case of Native American raids. When Lieutenant Colonel Archibald Campbell (1739–1791) was told that they were ready to surrender to the British, he sent Captain Andrew Hamilton to accept their surrender. Captain John Dooly (ca. 1742–1780) learned of Hamilton's mission and set out with 100 Georgia Whigs to attack Hamilton in Wilkes County. Hamilton learned of the advance and ambushed Dooly and his men as they crossed the Savannah River about 13 miles north of Augusta, near Kiokee Creek on Saturday, February 6, 1779. Hamilton drove the Georgians back to the South Carolina side of the river.[59]

Fort Independence (ca. Feb. 7, 1779)
Cherokee Ford (Feb. 10, 1779)
Vanns Creek (Feb. 12, 1779)

> Cherokee Ford and Vanns Creek are in eastern Elbert County. Cherokee Ford was an important crossing of the Savannah River between Georgia and South Carolina. It played a significant role in the American War of Independence, as many military

units used it, particularly prior to the Battle of Kettle Creek (February 14, 1779) and the occupation of Augusta by the Crown forces. The site was located on the Savannah River south of Vanns Creek in Elbert County and approximately 70 miles north of Augusta. It is now under the Richard B. Russell Reservoir. It was near where the railroad crosses the lake about 600 yards north of route 72.

Cherokee Ford was one of the few places on the upper Savannah River that could be crossed without a boat. A fort known as McGowan's Blockhouse, on the South Carolina side, defended the area as early as 1778. It was north of the Pacolet River on the waters of Goucher Creek and was well fortified and well stocked with military supplies. When the British occupied Augusta in January 1779, Lieutenant Colonel Archibald Campbell (1739–1791) and his small army awaited reinforcements as he expected South Carolina Whigs to try to retake the town. He believed the Congressional forces on the opposite side of the Savannah River greatly outnumbered his own.

Fort Independence was located about 3.6 miles due northeast of McGowan's blockhouse, on the western shore of Richard B. Russell Lake in Iva, South Carolina. One source claims this action happened on February 10th in concert with a nearby skirmish known as Vanns Creek. Another source claims it happened on February 12th.

Colonel Andrew Pickens (1739–1817) called for Captain Robert Anderson (d. 1813) to bring reinforcements before he left Carr's Fort in Georgia for South Carolina. Captain Anderson's men were ordered to patrol the Savannah River to prevent the Loyalist forces from crossing it.

Colonel John Boyd (d. 1779) was marching south toward Georgia with 600 to 800 North Carolina Loyalist militiamen. He intended to take his recruits to the British post at Augusta. Along the way, a band of about 500 of Colonel Boyd's men captured the Whig outpost at Broad Mouth Creek and burned Fort Independence around Wednesday, February 7, 1779.

★ Colonel John Boyd (d. 1779) and his men arrived at Cherokee Ford [near Captain James Little's (1737–1807) home] on Wednesday, February 10, 1779. Captain Robert Anderson (d. 1813) had been monitoring Boyd's movements near the Savannah River and garrisoned McGowan's (McGowin's) blockhouse (see Photo GA-1), located on a hill overlooking the ford, and commanding the crossing. (A high ridge along the river allowed travelers to avoid the low swampy river bottoms and many huge rocks formed a natural and partially manmade bridge across this shallow area in the river.) Lieutenant Thomas Shanklin (1725–1829) [also identified as Ramsey (1741–1813) or Calhoun (1722–1786)] and eight South Carolina militiamen were ordered to oppose Boyd and prevent his force from crossing into Georgia. They had two swivel guns (see Photo GA-2).

When the Loyalists arrived at Cherokee Ford, Colonel Boyd demanded that Lieutenant Shanklin surrender the fort and allow the Loyalists to cross into Georgia. Even though he had received reinforcements of 40 Wilkes County militiamen under Captain James Little (1737–1807), Shanklin's force was still outnumbered by almost 100 to one. Yet, he refused both requests. One account says that the fort responded with a cannon shot. Another says that a man in the blockhouse by the name of Alexander McCopin had a blunderbuss (see Photo GA-6) and that the men prepared a round from their own shot bags and powder horns. McCopin loaded it and fired it at the enemy. Meanwhile, Captain Little sent a dispatch to Captain Anderson to apprise him of the situation at Cherokee Ford and to request assistance.

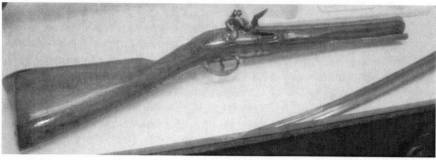

GA-6. Blunderbuss. A blunderbuss, or musquetoon, is used to fire shot with a scattering effect at close range. It is highly effective for clearing a narrow passage, door of a house or staircase, or in boarding a ship. This is a photo of Ethan Allen's blunderbuss at the Fort Ticonderoga museum.

Colonel Boyd did not want to take any unnecessary casualties, so he decided not to attack the blockhouse and marched northward to search for an easier, undefended crossing of the Savannah River. He proceeded approximately 5 miles north to the South Carolina side of the mouth of Vanns Creek. He divided his men into small groups. They built rafts to transport their baggage and swam across with their horses under sharp fire from Captain Anderson's South Carolina militiamen and Captain James Little's Georgia militiamen.

Captains Robert Anderson (Andersen) (d. 1813), William Baskin (1737–1794), John Miller (1756–1804), and Joseph William Pickens (1737–1781) arrived at Cherokee Ford with about 80 South Carolina militiamen. The reinforcements and the 50 men already stationed there marched north, hoping to prevent Boyd's forces from crossing Vanns Creek. They arrived as the Loyalists were still crossing the river on Friday, February 12th. Most of the Loyalists were on the Georgia side when Anderson began his attack. The low ground and the cane brakes along the riverbank shielded many of Boyd's men, some of whom crossed the river and attacked Anderson from behind. Caught between two overwhelming forces, Anderson retreated to Cherokee Ford. He lost one man killed, 15 wounded, and 18 captured, including captains Baskin and Miller. Boyd acknowledged losing 100 men killed, wounded and missing, most of them deserters, in the battle which lasted over an hour.

Anderson rejoined Brigadier General Andrew Pickens's (1739–1817) main force which had crossed from South Carolina into Georgia at Cedar Shoals. Reinforced by Anderson's retreating men, Pickens had about 400 men to confront Boyd and the Loyalists as they proceeded toward Augusta. Pickens caught up with Boyd and defeated him at Kettle Creek on Saturday, February 14th. The actions at Vann's and Kettle creeks reduced Boyd's force by about half.[60]

Carr's Fort (Feb. 10, 1779)

The stockade known as Carr's Fort after Captain Robert Carr (d. 1779) of the Wilkes County Militia, was located at "the fork" of Beaverdam Creek and the Little River in Wilkes County, just west of the Savannah River and about 6 miles south of Washington. Andrew Pickens later described Carr's fort as "an old Stockade fort, full of little old cabins & very dry." It was the site of several fights with Creek warriors in

1778 and 1779. The Creeks robbed and killed Captain Carr in the latter fight. Carr's Fort should not be confused with Kerr's Fort which was 14 miles from the mouth of the Broad River at the mouth of Long Creek in Elberton.[61]

Archaeologists from the LAMAR Institute which focuses on researching, locating, identifying, and interpreting fortifications and battlefields of the Colonial, Revolutionary War, War of 1812, and the Civil War periods, discovered the site of Carr's Fort in early 2013. They plan to publish a complete report on the Carr's Fort Battlefield project in early 2014.

When the British occupied Georgia in 1778, Lieutenant Colonel Archibald Campbell (1739–1791) sent Captain John Hamilton (d. 1817), a North Carolina Loyalist, to administer the oath of loyalty to the Crown to the settlers in Wilkes County. Captain Dugald Campbell and 80 Loyalists accompanied him and garrisoned Carr's Fort.

Colonel John Dooly (ca. 1742–1780) and Lieutenant Colonel Elijah Clarke (1733–1799) took their 100 militiamen into South Carolina. The militiamen skirmished with Captain Hamilton's Loyalists about 30 miles up the Savannah River from Augusta. Dooly crossed the Savannah River into Georgia, but Hamilton drove him back. Colonel Andrew Pickens (1739–1817) joined Dooly in South Carolina with his Upper Ninety Six Regiment of militiamen. Dooly now commanded about 350 men who crossed the Savannah at Cowen's Ferry, about 3 miles above Hamilton's camp on Wednesday night, February 10, 1779. They marched to attack him the following morning; but Hamilton, unaware of any danger, went to visit the forts in the country and to administer the oath of allegiance to the inhabitants he encountered.

Pickens pursued Hamilton to Carr's Fort which he imagined would be his first destination. The main body would advance quickly and attack the enemy in the rear. Pickens's men were so close to the enemy's rear when they arrived at the fort that the Loyalists shot their own last man as he entered the gate, "supposing him to be one of the enemy." Both sides exchanged a brisk fire but with little effect. The Loyalists' musket fire commanded the spring, so when Pickens decided on a siege, he had to cut off the water supply. If he could gain possession of a new log building near the fort, he could accomplish his objective as it commanded the spring. Captain William Freeman (1751–1822) and about 40 men from his company quickly crossed the open exposure under enemy fire and gained control of the building.

Early in the evening, they captured the enemy's horses, accoutrements and baggage and secured all escape routes. A request to surrender was refused in the afternoon as was a request for the women and children to leave the fort. The building occupied by Captain William Freeman and his men not only commanded the spring, it also overlooked the huts within the fort so they could easily fire at the occupants. The attackers thought the besieged could only hold out for about 24 hours without food or water. However, Colonel Pickens received a letter from his brother, Captain Joseph William Pickens (1737–1781), informing him that Colonel John Boyd and 700 to 800 North Carolina Loyalists were traveling through South Carolina to enlist in the British Army at Augusta.

Some volunteers wanted to set fire to the fort at different places, at the same time, to force an immediate surrender; but Pickens decided against the proposal because of the distress it would cause to the families living inside the fort. Pickens abandoned the siege, leaving Hamilton in possession of the fort without horses or baggage. Hamilton retreated to Wrightsborough where he stayed for a few days before proceeding to Augusta.

His report stated his losses at nine killed and three wounded. Pickens lost five killed and seven wounded.

Pickens left Carr's fort, crossed the Savannah River near Fort Charlotte, and headed toward Long Cane where he expected to find reinforcements to ambush the Loyalists at the Battle of Kettle Creek.[62]

The Crossroads, Beech Island (March 21, 1779; March 31, 1779)
Shell Bluff

Beech Island is on the Savannah River about 8 miles southeast of Augusta. The Crossroads may have been located at present Shell Bluff, about 24 miles south of Augusta.

Loyalist Major Henry Sharp (d. 1779), pursued by Lieutenant Colonel Leonard Marbury (1750–1796), decided to stop running and attacked Marbury's camp at The Crossroads on Beech Island on Sunday, March 21, 1779. Both sides suffered several casualties in the indecisive action. Sharp retreated and Marbury's troops continued pursuing him.

Colonel John Thomas, Jr.'s (1751–1819) Loyalist militiamen tried to ambush Marbury but his advance guard was captured in the attempt. Marbury then moved to join forces with Lieutenant Colonel Ely Kershaw (1743–1780) and his South Carolina militiamen, but he and 30 of his men were surrounded in the northern part of Burke County and captured.

★ Lieutenant Colonel Ely Kershaw (1743–1780), reinforced by Lieutenant Colonel John Twiggs (1750–1816) and his Burke County militia, set out to attack the Burke County jail, the Loyalist headquarters. The Loyalist militia under Major Henry Sharp (d. 1779) and Major John Spurgin (d. 1779) attacked Kershaw's camp at The Crossroads at 8 PM on Wednesday night March 31, 1779. Both sides numbered about 200 men. The battle soon became a sabre fight that endured for two hours in the woods. Most of the militiamen fled, but the 60 who remained managed to push the Loyalists back 2 miles to the Burke County jail, near the main body of Crown forces at Briar Creek.

They suffered only a few casualties: one man shot in the arm, another in the hip and one man mortally wounded in the hand when his gun exploded. The Loyalists lost 20 men killed, including Major Spurgin found dead on the field and Major Sharp, mortally wounded in the chest and his hand shot off, and seven captured.[63]

Beech Island, Savannah River (May 1, 1781)
Bugg's Plantation (May 2, 1781)

Bugg's Plantation is also known as New Savannah. It was about 8.3 miles due south-southeast of Augusta, on the west bank of the Savannah River and east of the east-west runway at Bush Field.

After the engagement at New Bridge (see p. 30), Captain Moses Shelby (1760–1828) and Captain Patrick ("Paddy") Carr (1761–1820) returned to Colonel Elijah Clarke's (1733–1799) militia at Beech Island. Colonel Thomas Brown (1750–1825) learned that the militiamen were on the island and sent a force out to eliminate them. A detachment of Loyalists and Native Americans went to the island in canoes on Tuesday, May 1, 1781, but Clarke, notified of their plan, escaped after his pickets were killed.[64]

★ The following day, Colonel Elijah Clarke (1733–1799) sent Captain Moses Shelby (1760–1828) and Captain Patrick ("Paddy") Carr (1761–1820) to intercept the Loyalists who killed the sentries on Beech Island. They found the Loyalists at Edmund Bugg's plantation and killed or wounded several of them. The others fled to Augusta. Mrs. Bugg refused the Loyalists permission to bury their dead on her plantation, forcing the wounded to move them into South Carolina. Some of Captain Carr's men decided that the prisoners were not working fast enough in removing the bodies, so they killed some of the Native American prisoners which made the others work faster. The militia suffered no losses at all in the skirmish.[65]

See also **Beech Island** in *The Guide to the American Revolutionary War in South Carolina*.

Lincoln County
Dooly's (Dooley) Fort (Aug. 1780)

> Dooly's Fort is located in Elijah Clarke State Park in Lincoln County.

Colonel John Dooly (ca. 1742–1780) surrendered his Georgia regiment to Major William Manson (b. 1744) at Dooly's Fort on Monday, June 5, 1780, less than a month after the surrender of Charleston, South Carolina (May 12). Dooly's house on the Savannah River, known as Lee's Old Place or Dooly's Fort, consisted of a plantation, a fort and a ferry.

Captain William Corker and a party of Loyalists killed Dooly in front of his family in August 1780. Dooly was considered a prisoner of war on parole so his murder was against the rules of war. Captain George Dooly (d. 1821) assumed command of his brother's regiment and executed several Loyalists in retaliation.[66]

Silver Bluff, near Jackson, Aiken County, South Carolina
Silver Bluff
Sam Moore's Raid (Aug.–Dec. 1777)
Fort Galphin/Fort Dreadnought (May 21, 1781)

> The home of George Galphin (1709–1780), Deputy Superintendent of Indian Affairs, was turned into a small stockaded place which the Whigs called Fort Galphin and the Crown forces, who occupied it for most of the war, called Fort Dreadnought, suggesting it was invincible. This site is actually in South Carolina, but it is more relevant to Georgia than to South Carolina. It was on the north side of the Savannah River about 12 miles south of Augusta on Silver Bluff. To get there, from the junction of routes SC 5 (Main Street) and SC 62 (South Silverton Street) in Jackson, South Carolina, drive northwest on route SC 5 for 2.2 miles to the junction with CR 315, an unimproved road (Bluff Landing Road). Turn left and follow that road west for 2.3 miles to the Savannah River at Silver Bluff. Fort Galphin/Dreadnought was about 100 yards south of Silver Bluff.

Lieutenant Samuel Moore (1711–1788) and a band of East Florida militiamen left St. Augustine, Florida in August 1777 to capture or kill George Galphin (1709–1780), Deputy Superintendent of Indian Affairs, and to destroy his house and store at Silver Bluff. When he reached the Canoochee River, Moore sent a detachment to search for Galphin and Captain Benjamin Porter. Captain Porter and his 20 Georgia Continentals were escorting a band of Native American ambassadors to Ogeechee Old Town where they would transfer them to Lieutenant Colonel Daniel McMurphy (1737–1819) and his Georgia militiamen. Captain John Gerrard (d. 1777), of the 3rd Georgia Continental Battalion, accompanied them. He operated the ferry on the Savannah River near Shell Bluff, so he was familiar with the surrounding territory. Galphin remained at his home at Silver Bluff.

Captain Porter's detachment was only 7 miles from Silver Bluff when 16 of Moore's Rangers ambushed them. The Continentals and the Native Americans fled, leaving Captain Gerrard. Captain Gerrard bore some resemblance to George Galphin, so Moore's men mistook him for Galphin and killed him.

Colonel Samuel Elbert (1740–1788) received news of the ambush and immediately set out to intercept Moore's raiders with 80 men of the 2nd Georgia Continental Battalion. They marched 60 miles, 12 of them through a dense swamp, but failed to catch Moore's men. Lieutenant Colonel John Baker (1750–1830) and Colonel James Screven (1744–1778) also tried unsuccessfully to intercept Moore at the Florida border.

★ A detachment of volunteers and draftees left Savannah in the middle of September 1777 to join the efforts of searching for the Loyalists along the Altamaha River. Colonel Screven and his 80 men found 30 to 40 of Moore's raiders on Thursday, September 25 near Fountain Neck on the north side of the Altamaha River. Screven's men killed one or two Rangers and captured some cattle, horses, and saddles. They also recovered 1,867 Continental dollars which Moore's men had taken from Captain Gerrard's body at their earlier ambush of Porter's detachment.

★ Georgia Whigs received reports, in October of 1777, that Lieutenant Samuel Moore's (1711–1788) men were still in the area along the south side of the Ogeechee River. One report stated that they had rendezvoused in a fork of the Canoochee River. Colonel Elbert ordered Colonel James Screven (1744–1778) to move his force to the Canoochee River. He instructed Screven to have his men wear a white piece of paper or linen as a cockade in their hats, since "the enemy commonly have red in their hats. . . ." As a further precaution, to avoid a conflict between friendly forces, the first party of Screven's men that saw the other would give a loud "hem." The other party, if friendly, would answer by clapping their hands together twice.

★ The Whigs received a report, in December 1777, that Lieutenant Samuel Moore's (1711–1788) men were forming small parties along the Ogeechee River. One of these parties was reportedly bringing a Mrs. Love, said to be the wife of one of the Rangers, back to East Florida. The Rangers supposedly used a canebrake about half a mile above Bowden's place, on the south side of the Canoochee River, as one of their camps. Colonel Samuel Elbert (1740–1788) ordered Colonel Joseph Habersham (1751–1815) to march his men across the Canoochee toward the Ohoopee in pursuit of the Rangers. The Whigs were once again ordered to wear white cockades in their hats to avoid confusion.[67]

★ Two Loyalist companies garrisoned Fort Galphin in May 1781, during the final days of the siege of Augusta. Colonel Elijah Clarke's (1733–1799) forces strengthened with each passing day. One of these new arrivals was Brigadier General Andrew Pickens (1739–1817) who brought about 400 men from Colonels Robert Anderson's (Andersen) (d. 1813) regiment. Pickens immediately invested two forts across the river near Augusta to cut off assistance to Fort Galphin at Silver Bluff. He also requested Major General Nathanael Greene (1742–1786) for aid.

General Greene sent Lieutenant Colonel Henry "Light-Horse Harry" Lee (1756–1818) and his Legion, consisting of three companies of cavalry under captains Joseph Eggleston (1754–1811), Ferdinand O'Neal or O'Neale, and James Armstrong (1728–1800) and three companies of infantry commanded by captains Patrick Carnes, Jacob Rudulph (1744–1795), and Levin Handy (1754–1799). He also had some of Brigadier General Thomas Sumter's (1734–1832) men and part of a battalion of North Carolina militiamen.

Lee was moving rapidly toward Augusta because General Greene feared that Colonel John Harris Cruger (1738–1807) might withdraw his garrison from Ninety Six and join Colonel Thomas Brown (1750–1825) at Augusta when he learned of Lord Francis Rawdon's (1754–1826) retreat after the battle of Camden (April 21, 1781). One of Rawdon's messages intercepted from Camden expressed his desire for Cruger to do just that.

Lee had his dragoons and infantrymen share the horses and covered the 75 miles from Fort Granby in less than three days. Along the way, Lee learned that Cruger was strengthening his fortifications, preparing for a siege. Some of Clarke's militiamen had attacked several boats bringing the king's annual gifts to the Cherokees and Creeks and forced them into port at Fort Galphin (Dreadnought) where the fort's heavy guns overlooking the river kept them at bay. As he approached Augusta, Captain Neal informed Lee that the annual king's present had recently arrived at Fort Galphin for temporary storage. This was a considerable quantity of material, including weapons. Lee wanted to capture these supplies or prevent them from going to the Native Americans.

Lee sent some of his Legion, reinforced by Major John Rudulph and parts of two Georgia and South Carolina militia regiments, to help Clarke capture Fort Galphin. They hastened to the fort, mounting the infantrymen behind the dragoons, with the artillery to follow later. They arrived at Fort Galphin the next morning, Monday, May 21, 1781, and found the stockaded farmhouse garrisoned by two companies of Colonel Thomas Brown's Loyalist militia. They hid in a pine grove, along an open field surrounding the fort, and prepared for the assault. Rudulph and Clarke, knowing that the Crown forces in the garrison held the local militia in contempt, sent a small force in front of the fort to feign an attack and make a hasty retreat, as a decoy, while most of the Continentals hid.

When the fort's defenders rushed out to pursue Rudulph's bait, Clarke's militiamen and Lee's regulars rushed through the open gates, surprising the enemy soldiers inside and capturing them. Major Rudulph chased the first group back, quickly surrounding and subduing them with little opposition. Clarke and Rudulph killed three or four defenders, wounded a few others, and captured 126 prisoners, including 70 British Regulars who would be sorely missed in the defense of Augusta. A few escaped into the woods. The attackers lost only one man who died of sun stroke. They also captured a large store of blankets, clothing, small arms, ammunition, rum, salt, medicines and other articles.

Lee then reassembled his troops, crossed the river and headed to Augusta that evening to join Pickens for an attack on Fort Cornwallis and Fort Grierson two days later. With the Continentals in control of the fort, British reinforcements in Augusta could not reach Ninety-Six, Major General Nathanael Greene's (1742–1786) next objective. Lee was now free to march on Savannah.

Cherokee Campaign of 1782 see Tennessee.

Near Sharon (May 24, 1782)

Sharon is about 10 miles south of the Kettle Creek battlefield.

Some Cherokees under a British officer attacked Brigadier General "Mad Anthony" Wayne's (1745–1796) camp of Pennsylvania Continentals near Sharon Friday night, May 24, 1782. They killed six Continentals and wounded about eight, but they lost about 20 killed.[68]

Georgia frontier (mid-July 1782)

Colonel Elijah Clarke (1733–1799) and his militia encountered some Cherokees and Loyalists moving east from the Georgia frontier to obtain supplies from the British in mid-July 1782. He defeated them and killed several.[69]

Bell's Creek (Dec. 5, 1782)

Bell's Creek was near Fort Henderson southwest of Augusta.

A Congressional galley shelled (see Photo GA-7) a British camp at Bell's Creek on Thursday, December 5, 1782.[70]

GA-7. Shots and shells. Round shot (cannonball) is used for battering an obstacle such as a fort wall or ship's hull. The ball can be heated (hot shot) to embed in a ship's hull and set it on fire. Grape and canister shots are fired against troops. Chain, bar, sliding bar and star shots are used against vessels to destroy the rigging and immobilize a vessel. A shell, also called a bomb, is a hollow metal ball filled with gunpowder. It has a large touch-hole for a slow-burning fuse which is held in place by pieces of wood and fastened with a cement made of quicklime, ashes, brick dust and steel filings worked together with glutinous water.

Savannah and vicinity
See the map of southern Georgia and Florida.

Savannah (May 11, 1775; Sept. 3 to Oct. 28, 1779; Sept. 17, 1779; Sept. 22, 1779; Sept. 24, 1779; Oct. 9, 1779; March 22, 1782; April 5, 1782; May 2 or 3, 1782; May 15, 1782)

Cockspur Island, Beaufort County (July 9, 1775; Feb. 11, 1776; March 1, 1776; April 12, 13, 1776; May 12–13, 1776)

Savannah Harbor (Jan. 12, 1776; March 3, 1776; March 11, 1776)

Savannah River (Feb. 11, 1776; March 11, 1776)

Hutchinson Island, Battle of the Rice Boats (March 3–6, 1776)

Savannah Bar (March 12, 1776)

Tybee Island (March 25, 1776)

Yamacraw Bluff (Yammacraw) (Savannah) (March 4, 1776)

Wilmington Island (Sept. 12, 1776)

Morgan's Fort, Ogeechee River (July 31, 1777; March 1779)

Ogeechee Road (Feb. 1778; Feb. 1780; May 21, 1782; June 24, 1782)

Ogeechee River (June 22, 1778; July 12, 1781; late May 1782)

Salter's Island, Four Mile Point, Savannah River (Dec. 28, 1778)

Brewton Hill (Girardeau's Plantation) (Dec. 29, 1778)

Abercorn Creek (March 20, 1779)

Black Swamp (April 22, 1779)

Yemassee Bluff (April 23, 1779)

Hickory Hill (Butler's Plantation) (June 28, 1779)

Ebenezer (July 21, 1779; March 1782; June 23, 1782) (also known as the Three Sisters)

Savannah Coast (Sept. 6, 1779)

Ogeechee Ferry (Harris's Bridge, Brown's Defeat) (Sept. 19, 1779; March 25, 1780; April 4, 1780; Feb. 1, 1782; May 20, 1782)

Savage Point (Oct. 1, 1779)

McGillivray's Plantation (Oct. 16, 1779)

Tybee Lighthouse (Jan. 17–27, 1780)

Sir James Wright's Plantation at Ogeechee (March 25, 1780)

Inland Waterway (Savannah River), near Savannah (Sept. 23, 1781)

Indian Old Fields, near Ogeechee Ferry (Nov. 2, 1781)

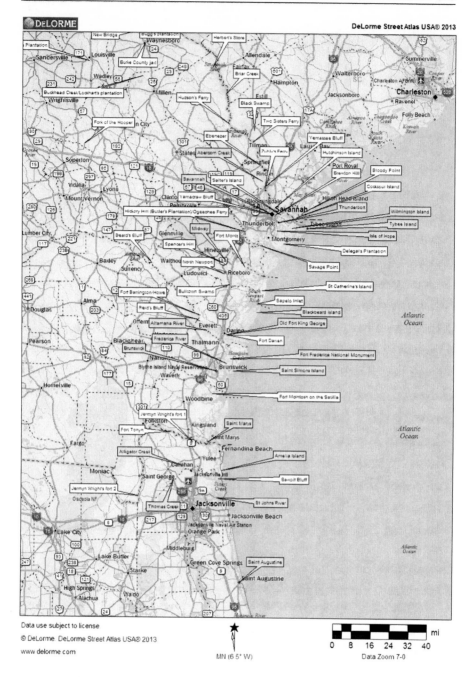

Southern Georgia and Florida: Map for The Guide to the American Revolutionary War in the Deep South and on the Frontier
© 2013 DeLorme (www.delorme.com) Street Atlas USA®

White House on the Ogeechee (Nov. 2, 1781)
St. Andrew Parish (first week of Feb. 1782)
Hutchinson Island (Feb. 26, 1782)
Tybee Roads (May 1, 1782; Jan. 30, 1783)
Baillou's Causeway (May 21, 1782)
Isle of Hope (April 3, 1782)
Snider's (April 14, 1782)

Cockspur Island, at the mouth of the Savannah River, was also called Long Island. It was known as Peeper Island during colonial times and got the name Cockspur for the shape of its reef.

Bloody Point is on the southeast end of Daufuskie Island at the entrance to the Savannah River and north of Tybee Island. Tybee Lighthouse is on Tybee Island near Fort Screven, almost at the end of General George Marshall Boulevard.

Hutchinson Island is located in the Savannah River east of the historic downtown of Savannah. It has been developed as a convention complex and residential neighborhoods. Captain William McGillivray's plantation was on Hutchinson Island.

Tybee Island is at the mouth of the Savannah River.

Yamacraw Bluff was on what is now West Bay Street, in Savannah, between Bull Street and Whitaker Street near City Hall. A marker denotes the site. The Yamacraw built their village in the area of Fahm Street, two blocks south of West Bay Street and 0.2 miles east of route US 17 (GA 25A|GA SPUR 404). When James Edward Oglethorpe (1696–1785) established the town of Savannah in 1733, he fortified Yamacraw Bluff with five cannons. Georgia was governed by a Provincial Congress and a Council of Safety, both controlled by the Whigs in 1775. The colony boycotted British goods and the citizens of Savannah refused to trade with the British soldiers in the 1770s.

The Savannah History Museum, in the converted passenger terminal of the Central of Georgia Railway on Martin Luther King, Jr. Boulevard at Louisville Road, is located on Spring Hill. A marker near the entrance to the building highlights the Continental and French attack on the Spring Hill Redoubt (see Photo GA-8), after a three-week siege, on October 9, 1779. In 2003, the City of Savannah purchased the site of the battlefield, across Louisville Road, from the Norfolk Southern Railway, successor of the Central of Georgia Railway. The city, together with the Coastal Heritage Society, removed the tracks and did an archaeological study of the site in August 2005. They built a redoubt as a memorial a "safe distance" from the archaeological site and dedicated the new Battlefield Memorial Park on October 9, 2007. A 1911 Sons of the American Revolution plaque sits directly on top of the original location of the Spring Hill Redoubt which archaeologists identified in 2005. The swamps and wooded marshes through which the militia units got entangled have been filled and converted to industrial use. The causeway over which the attackers advanced no longer exists.

Louisville Road and Jones Street mark the location of the fortifications where the important actions occurred. The strong western line of defenses of the Crown

GA-8. Spring Hill redoubt (reconstructed), Savannah, GA

forces ran along Martin Luther King, Jr. Boulevard, previously known as West Broad Street. Their southern line of defenses ran through Madison Square (Bull Street and East Macon Street). The French gathered for the final attack at the old Jewish burial ground [at Cohen Street and Spruce Street off route US 17A (GA 25A|GA 404 Spur|West Boundary Street) six blocks southwest of the museum. Spruce Street has been reclaimed and grassed over as part of Battlefield Memorial Park.

Admiral Comte Jean-Baptiste-Charles-Henri-Hector d'Estaing was wounded twice trying to rally his men during the third assault against the western line. Count Casimir Pulaski was fatally shot in the thigh with grape shot in the same area as he rode forward to rally the troops. Sergeant William Jasper (ca. 1750–1779) was also killed in the assault as he rescued the colors of his 2nd South Carolina Regiment. A bronze plaque in Madison Square honors the dead and wounded. The sculpture in the center of the square memorializes Sergeant Jasper and the bas relief panels represent three episodes of his career: the ramparts of Fort Sullivan near Charleston, South Carolina, where Jasper replaced the flag under heavy fire (see **Fort Sullivan** in *The Guide to the American Revolutionary War in South Carolina*); the liberation of prisoners at what is now called Jasper Springs near Savannah (see **New Ebenezer** pp. 45, 58–59); and his last moments in the attack of October 9, 1779. A monument in Monterey Square (Bull Street and East Wayne Street) honors Pulaski.

General Nathanael Greene, who died at Mulberry Grove Plantation near Savannah on June 19, 1786 and was buried in the Graham vault at the Colonial Park Cemetery until 1901, has been re-interred with his son, George Washington Greene, beneath the Nathanael Greene monument in Johnson Square (see Photo GA-9) (Bull Street and East Saint Julian Street). Major General Marie Jean Paul Joseph du Motier Marquis de Lafayette laid the cornerstone on March 21, 1825.

A monument to the Chasseurs Volontaires (see Photo GA-10), called the Fontanges Legion after its French commander, Major General Vicomte François de Fontanges (1740–1822), is located in Franklin Square at Montgomery Street and West Saint Julian Street. It includes young men who would become famous in the Haitian revolution.

GA-9. Nathanael Greene monument in Johnson Square (Bull Street and East Saint Julian Street, Savannah) marks the grave of General Nathanael Greene and his son, George Washington Greene. The Marquis de Lafayette laid the cornerstone on March 21, 1825.

Wilmington Island is west of Tybee Island and east of the Wilmington River. The actual site of the action here is unknown as there is no official record of a battle being fought on the island. However, there was some fighting on the northern part of the island as several old bayonets and small cannon balls have been plowed up in a field near Camp Walleila, a Girl Scout camp.

GA-10. Fontanges Legion monument, located in Franklin Square at Montgomery Street and West Saint Julian Street, Savannah, commemorates the Chasseurs Volontaires, called the Fontanges Legion. The regiment included young men who would become famous in the Haitian revolution. The drummer boy commemorates 12-year-old Henri Christophe, future king of Haiti who was wounded at the battle of Savannah. Photo courtesy of Paul Bazin.

Route US 17 (GA 25|Ogeechee Road) runs south from Savannah to the Ogeechee River. The Ogeechee Ferry was 15 miles south of Savannah where route US 17 (GA 25|Ogeechee Road) crosses the Ogeechee River near Hickory Hill (Butler's plantation). Morgan's Fort was probably near the Ogeechee Ferry. The White House and Indian Old Fields were also near the Ogeechee Ferry.

Savage Point is located at a bend in the Ogeechee River at Richmond Hill State Park.

Sir James Wright's plantation was near the Georgetown section of Savannah, east of exit 94 off Interstate 95, west of route US 17 (GA 25|Ogeechee Road) and north of route GA 204|Abercorn Street.

Salter's Island was about 3 miles downstream from the city of Savannah. It is the site of Fort Jackson (1 Fort Jackson Road), the oldest standing fort in Georgia and named for Colonel James Jackson (1757–1806).

Brewton Hill (John Girardeau's plantation, Fair Lawn) was located on the Savannah River about half a mile east of downtown Savannah in an industrialized section of the town. It was later the site of Confederate Fort Boggs. The site is now the Savannah Golf Club.

Tattnall's house (Fair Lawn plantation) was approximately at what is now the intersection of East Taylor and East Broad Streets.

Nobody knows for sure where the Black Swamp camp was located. It was probably about 2.5 miles south of Garnett. James Owenby's (Ownby or Ownbey) (1761–1850) pension application gives us the best idea. He stated "That he marched from there to South Carolina and joined the Army under the command of Genl Lincoln [Benjamin Lincoln] at Purrysburg. From there he was marched up the [Savannah] River to a place called the Two Sisters Ferry where he remained for some time and then marched 8 miles further up the River to a place called the Black Swamp where he remained until discharged on the 10th of April 1779. . . ."[71]

Yemassee Bluff was a strategic point that commanded Abercorn Creek and Zubly's Ferry. Abercorn Creek is west of the Savannah River in Rincon, at the Savannah National Wildlife Refuge.

Hickory Hill, James Butler's 1,500 acre plantation, was on the south side of the Ogeechee River, about 13 miles south-southwest of Savannah.

New Ebenezer was located approximately 20 miles northwest of Savannah on the Savannah River, at the terminus of route GA 275 (Ebenezer Road). The Jerusalem Church (built 1769) is the oldest church building in the state and the only building remaining from the colonial town. It is the most prominent and important historic structure on the site which also has two other historic buildings. Jerusalem Church and several portions of the town's original fortifications are intact. The church was used as a hospital, stable and commissary. Modern parishioners complain that paint will no longer adhere to the church's interior walls because the British hung salted meat against them. Bullet holes on the exterior of the building are supposedly remnants of British boredom.

The Two Sisters Ferry was across the Savannah River from Ebenezer. What is called the Three Sisters Ferry was most likely the Two Sisters Ferry. It was probably about 10 miles upriver from Ebenezer. The troops were stationed at the Two Sisters Ferry to observe Crown troop movements at Ebenezer, on the opposite side of the Savannah River from the ferry, until the arrival of Major General John Ashe.[72]

Georgia's founder, James Edward Oglethorpe (1696–1785) planned the New Ebenezer settlement as a military post but the German Salzbergers who settled here in the 1740s were non-violent. They accepted their military responsibilities very reluctantly. The town changed hands several times during the American War of Independence. It declined after the war, which damaged buildings and property, and never recovered.

New Ebenezer was an important stronghold for the Whigs from the beginning of the American War of Independence until the Crown forces landed at Savannah in November 1778. It also served as a collection point for Congressional soldiers captured in the area. However, as in most towns in the colonies, there were portions of the population that remained loyal to the Crown.

Captain Jacob Walthour fortified the town with a series of earthworks in March 1776. The town served as a supply depot from March 1776 until November 1778. A variety of munitions, food and other supplies were stored here. The powder magazine held about 7,000 pounds of gunpowder and was expanded in November 1778 to receive munitions being evacuated from Savannah. The guard was increased from 12 to 17 men at this time. After the surrender of Savannah, the Crown forces soon occupied New Ebenezer. The Loyalist sympathizers welcomed them, including Rev. Triebner the pastor of Jerusalem Church.

St. Andrew Parish was in what is now Liberty and McIntosh counties, south of Savannah. It included the towns of Midway, Sunbury and Darien.

Baillou's causeway was on what is now Basin Road in southwestern Savannah. It was about 0.6 miles north of the Kings Ferry Bridge over the Ogeechee River. The southern end of Basin Road meets route US 17 (SR 25|Ogeechee Road) about 200 yards northeast of the bridge. The causeway was about 0.5 miles north of that junction.

Isle of Hope is about 7 miles south-southeast of Savannah.

John Gotlieb Snider's (Schneider) house was on the west bank of the Savannah River, about 1.75 miles south of Zubly's Ferry.

Savannah, the largest town and port in Georgia, was the key to controlling the colony. When news of the outbreak of hostilities in Lexington and Concord, Massachusetts arrived in early May 1775, the Georgia Liberty Boys sprang into action immediately and seized 600 pounds of powder from the provincial magazine in Savannah on Thursday, May 11, 1775.[73]

Governor Sir James Wright (1714–1785) heard rumors of an attempt to kidnap him; so, in early June, he ordered Captain Samuel Elbert's (1740–1788) grenadier company to protect him. However, the officers of the company refused to turn out. They "threw down their commissions," and declared they would fight in defense of their liberties.[74]

★ Captain Richard Maitland's HM Armed Schooner *Phillipa* sailed from London bound for Georgia with 16,000 pounds of gunpowder on May 2, 1775. The Association of Georgia learned of the *Phillipa*'s anticipated arrival "by intercepted letters." The Georgia Liberty Boys' Captain Samuel Elbert (1740–1788) and Lieutenant Joseph Habersham (1751–1815) together with General John Barnwell (1748–1800), Captain John Joyner and Tunis Tebout, Liberty Boys from Beaufort, South Carolina, agreed to capture the *Phillipa*. They moved to Bloody Point, Daufuskie Island, with 40 men in two barges, in early July, to guard the inlet to the Savannah River and await the *Phillippa*'s arrival, intending to seize her cargo of gunpowder.

Lieutenant William Grant anchored the HM Schooner *St. John* conspicuously in Tybee Roads to ensure the *Phillippa*'s safe arrival. The Georgia Council of Safety had the schooner *Elizabeth* fitted with 10 6-pound carriage guns and 12 swivel guns (see photo GA-11) and renamed her the *Liberty*. The *Liberty* departed from Bloody Point along with the two barges to meet the *Phillipa*. Apparently outgunned, the *St. John* sailed away. The Liberty Boys met the *Phillippa* about 4 leagues from the Tybee Bar on Friday, July 9th. As the pilot was guiding the *Phillippa* to the Bar, the *Liberty* closed on her and fired two musket shots at her. That night, the *Liberty* anchored beside the *Phillippa*.

The next day, the *Phillippa* was ordered to anchor off Cockspur Island. The South Carolina militiamen on the island rowed out to her, surrounded her and inspected her papers. They then took her powder and "seven hundredweight of leaden bullets" and all the bar-lead, sheet-lead and arms they mistakenly believed were destined to be traded with the Native Americans to keep them loyal. In reality, the *Phillipa*'s cargo was a private consignment of powder directed to merchants at Charleston, South Carolina; St. Augustine, Florida and Savannah, Georgia. The Liberty Boys sent 7,000 pounds of powder to Charleston and the Georgians kept the remaining 9,000 pounds. Later, South Carolina urged Georgia to send 5,025 pounds of this gunpowder to the Congress in Philadelphia for the Continental Army. The Liberty Boys later released the *Phillipa* and Captain Maitland set sail with a cargo for Jamaica.[75]

★ Captain Peter Rainier's (1741–1808) long-awaited ship *Polly* arrived off Tybee Island on Friday, September 15, 1775 with a cargo of 250 barrels of gunpowder intended as the king's annual present to the Native Americans. The Liberty Boys seized the *Polly* and removed the gunpowder and 50 muskets intended for the light infantry company.

GA-11. Whaleboat with swivel gun. Reproduction of a whaleboat with a 1½ pound swivel gun.

They brought the powder and weapons to Savannah "in Great Triumph." Some sources give the date of the *Polly*'s arrival as Sunday, September 17. However, the *Georgia Gazette* for Wednesday, September 20, 1775, stated that this vessel arrived at Tybee from London on "Friday [September 15]."[76]

★ Colonel Lachlan McIntosh (1727–1806), convinced that the British intended to take Savannah and restore Sir James Wright (1714–1785) to power, placed guards at likely landing sites and set up ambushes on the roads leading to the city. This action placed a heavy burden on the already overextended forces and reduced the number of troops available to guard the waterfront. The Council of Safety went into emergency session and renewed the Continental Association on the day it was due to expire. The Council also ordered McIntosh to make sure only authorized vessels left port and that all others had their rudders and rigging removed.[77]

1776

★ The British fleet that had left Charleston, South Carolina, in January 1776 made the mouth of the Savannah River its base of operations, threatening any nearby vessels. Nine Rebel volunteers burned three British ships and damaged six others in Savannah Harbor on Friday, January 12, 1776.[78]

★ The HM sloop of war *Tamar* and several other ships arrived off the coast of Tybee Island to secure fresh provisions on Saturday, January 13, 1776. Three more warships, including the *Raven*, arrived on the 18th and brought reinforcements that Governor Sir James Wright (1714–1785) had requested when the Rebels had seized control of Georgia the previous June. The island served as a haven for Loyalists fleeing from Savannah. One of these refugees was the Royal Governor himself.

Joseph Habersham (1751–1815) and the Georgia Council of Safety had Governor
Wright and other royal officials arrested at "Government House" on the site of the Telfair house (on the east side of State Street at Barnard Street in Telfair Square) on January
18th. He placed the royal officials under house arrest in response to the arrival of the
British ships. Governor Wright pleaded unsuccessfully with his captors to remain loyal
to the government. He told them that they could not resist the British Army and Royal
Navy and that he could ensure the town's safety. Dr. William Read was present at Government House that day and recorded:

> The regiment of riflemen were encamped at the west end of the Government House,
> and the men would frequently fire their rifles at the house (a wooden house) not-
> withstanding his [Dr. Read's] remonstrances to the contrary, and the orders of
> Samuel Elbert, now nominated as General. Dr. R. got one of his mother's servants
> to carry in a slip of paper, warning the inmates to lay down on the floor for safety
> against the rifle balls. Sir James' two daughters Sarah . . ., and Bella . . ., were in the
> house, and all of his Majesty's members of Council. At length these Western soldiers
> became tired of the service, and talked of breaking in and destroying the prison-
> ers; Dr. Read's anxiety became extreme. He saw that the parole was broken by the
> violence of these riflemen, as a parole implies safety and protection to the prisoners.
> He advised Sir James to fly, and advised, by a slip of paper, the manner of getting
> clear, convinced that if he was out of the way the remaining prisoners would be more
> mercifully and leniently dealt with; and thus it happened. . . ."[79]

★ More ships and 200 troops arrived in February. Governor Sir James Wright (1714–
1785) and several of his councilors broke their paroles and managed to escape Sunday
night, February 11, 1776, during a storm. They took refuge on the HMS *Scarborough*,
anchored at Cockspur Island at the mouth of the Savannah River. The Whigs feared
that the British warships in the vicinity might raid along the Georgia coast or try to trade
in Savannah. Would the British force the town to defy the Continental Congress and to
trade with them or would they use military force to take what they wanted?

The town prepared to defend itself. The inhabitants fortified the town as much as
possible and the government called out the militia. Samuel Elbert (1740–1788) was
placed in command and Lieutenant Colonel Stephen Drayton (1736–1810) and Major
Joseph Habersham (1751–1815) were appointed his subordinate officers. The Georgia
militia erected two 18-pounders on 40-foot high Yamacraw Bluff in Savannah, allowing
them to rake, with artillery fire, any ship coming near them. They also sank a vessel in
the narrow part of the channel leading to Savannah, preventing any large force from
reaching the town.[80]

★ When the Georgia Assembly refused to answer his letters, Governor Sir James Wright
(1714–1785) authorized the troops to advance on Savannah where 20 captured British
merchant ships full of rice were located. If the British Regulars could recapture these
ships, they would be able to supply their army under siege in Boston.

Major John Maitland's (1732–1779) Royal Marines landed on Cockspur Island on
Friday, March 1, 1776 in an attempt to capture the rice ships. They skirmished with the
militiamen there. The marines had four wounded while the militiamen only had one
wounded.[81]

★ Captain Andrew Barkley, commander of the British naval squadron, pleaded with
Savannah's Whig government to prevent military conflict and asked the town to trade
freely with his fleet, but the Council prepared to burn the city rather than to submit to
royal authority. They restructured the military leadership, mainly for political reasons.
They appointed Colonel Lachlan McIntosh (1727–1806) to command, with Colonel

Samuel Elbert (1740–1788) and Major Joseph Habersham (1751–1815) as adjutants. McIntosh was frustrated that he didn't have sufficient authority, as he had to deal with both the Provincial Congress and the Continental Congress.

Captain Barkley, badly in need of resupplying his ships and unable to secure provisions around Tybee Island, decided to try to capture some of the more than 20 merchant ships anchored at Hutchinson Island just north of the town. They were laden with a large supply of rice and a variety of goods.

Meanwhile, Colonel Lachlan McIntosh mustered 20 to 30 Continentals, 300 to 400 Georgia militiamen, 153 South Carolina militiamen and a company of Creek warriors to defend the town and its harbor. He expected the squadron to maneuver around the island to attack Savannah from the north. He sent a detachment of about 300 men to Yamacraw, a village about a quarter of a mile up river, to try to prevent a landing. They set up a battery of three 4-pounders and waited. He also sent Colonel Archibald Bulloch (1731–1777) and 150 men opposite Brewton's plantation to prevent a landing on Hutchinson Island. The British "paraded" their ships for a few days within gunshot of the sentinels who were ordered not to fire unless they were fired upon first or if the enemy attempted to land.

The HM Armed Vessel *Cherokee* sent all her marines on board the HM Schooner *Hinchinbrook* and sailed up the Back River toward Savannah in company with the HM Sloops *St. John* and *East Florida,* the transport *Symmetry* and three schooners on Saturday afternoon, March 2, 1776. They sailed a few miles below Savannah where the Whigs had sunk a boat in an attempt to block the channel. Colonel Bulloch's militiamen disobeyed orders and fired several shots at the British vessels but missed. The Bluff Battery fired on the vessels frequently. The *Cherokee* fired a gun and gave the signal to weigh anchor at 11 PM when she heard several guns fired up the river.[82]

The schooner *Hinchinbrook* and the sloop *St. John*, each with 8 or 10 guns, sailed up the river and entered the passage behind Hutchinson Island to cover the British landing instead of attacking the town. They were interested in the rice boats at the upper end of Hutchinson Island and not Savannah. They were attacked by two companies of riflemen. A smart engagement continued for most of the day until the tide went out and the vessels went aground.

Majors James Grant (1720–1806) and John Maitland (1732–1779) landed some 300 troops consisting of the 40th Regiment of Foot and a detachment of Marines, with some howitzers and field pieces on the island in the middle of the night. They moved quickly across the swampy island to board the rice boats which had been ordered to have their rudders and rigging removed to prevent their capture. But the orders were not carried out. The troops worked their way to the boats undetected and boarded them about 4 AM. They found that they still had their rudders and rigging and were ready to sail, even though they were ordered to have been removed two days earlier.[83]

★ Colonel Lachlan McIntosh (1727–1806) and his men arrived on Hutchinson Island the following morning, March 3, to destroy the rigging and cripple the ships. The soldiers surprised and captured them. That same morning, the *Hinchinbrook* and *St. John* sailed around the island to reconnoiter the captured rice boats. The *Cherokee* sent a boat to assist the *Hinchinbrook* and *St. John* at 6 AM. Colonel McIntosh, thinking the ships were finally going to attack the town, ordered his men to fire on them. They fired several guns from Yamacraw Bluff and from the town at 10 AM.

Several guns and volleys of small arms were fired from the town that afternoon. The two vessels struggled against the river current and the sporadic fire from shore and managed to pull up alongside the captured vessels that afternoon. A ship on fire was observed near the town at 5 PM along with three other vessels in flames. They proved to be British merchant ships which the Whigs destroyed. The Whigs killed or wounded six British. McIntosh lost two killed and three wounded.

As the sailors prepared to escape with their prizes, McIntosh received intelligence about the capture of the rice vessels. He sent two unarmed officers to Hutchinson Island to negotiate with the British but they were promptly taken prisoner. One of them was Captain Joseph Rice who commanded a boat of observation. He went aboard one of the ships about 9 PM. Two Rebel sailors, who claimed they came on shore for clothes, reported that the British troops were on board the ship and that Captain Rice had been captured.[84]

A small unarmed party was ordered to go alongside the vessels to ask for Mr. Rice to confirm the previous intelligence, but they were also taken prisoners. The vessel fired two 4-pounders directly into the British vessels. The little 3-gun battery opened fire and the British returned fire. The engagement continued very smartly from 12 to 4 PM with ball, langrage and small arms from both sides, without touching a single Rebel; but several British soldiers were seen falling.[85]

★ When Colonel Lachlan McIntosh (1727–1806) received news of the capture of his delegates, he ordered his batteries to resume firing on the British ships. Both sides exchanged fire for several hours but with little effect. When the townspeople heard the news of the imprisonment of McIntosh's unarmed officers, they became outraged and many demanded that the militia attack. But McIntosh could not find enough boats to get his men across the river to the island.

When a second attempt at negotiation for the prisoners failed, McIntosh tried to burn the British boats and their prizes. He sent a fireship upriver toward the British position about 4 PM, but the fireship was too large and ran aground. A second, smaller sloop arrived at the target and ignited two of the rice boats, but the British managed to slip down river, taking 10 rice boats with them. The soldiers who were left on the island fled northward under the shot of riflemen and langrage. Many ran in the marsh in great confusion, fearing the riflemen who were out of range. They proceeded to the east side of the island where they were picked up. The British then sailed away with the 10 rice boats. Majors James Grant (1720–1806) and John Maitland (1732–1779) called for a cessation of hostilities and promised to withdraw to Tybee and not molest the Georgians again.[86]

★ The engagements continued on Skidaway and Cockspur Islands. The Georgians ended the day with six killed and two white men and one Native American slightly wounded. The British acknowledged six casualties. Their transports removed 1,600 barrels of rice. Savannah was unharmed. Several members of Governor Sir James Wright's (1714–1785) governing council were soon arrested and used to exchange for the Whig prisoners held by the British. After the prisoner exchange, the British sailed away with Wright and most of the royal officials. The rule of the Royal government ended in Georgia.[87]

★ The HM Armed Vessel *Cherokee* came abreast of the Whig guardhouse at Savannah at 7 AM on Monday, March 4, 1776 and fired a broadside at it along with the transport *Whitby*. The cannonade continued until 8 o'clock.[88]

★ The deposed Royal Governor, Sir James Wright (1714–1785), launched a raid with British naval forces against Savannah on Thursday, March 7, 1776. They captured 11 merchant ships carrying rice and posed a direct threat to the city. The Whigs counterattacked by setting fire to two merchant ships and, on the waning tide, floated them down the river to the British troop transport.

★ Colonel Stephen Bull (1734–1779) learned of the attack on Savannah and left Purrysburgh, South Carolina with 400 South Carolina militiamen on Monday, March 11, 1776. He proceeded down the Savannah River and landed on Hutchinson Island where he fired on some of "the King's troops" forcing them to withdraw, abandoning two field pieces but taking 10 of the rice-laden merchant ships with them.

The HM Armed Vessel *Cherokee* and a transport sailed up the Savannah River to help the British vessels withdraw, but the captains of those vessels threw about 2,000 pounds of rice overboard and sailed out of range of Colonel Bull's floating artillery.[89]

★ When Captain George Bunner's brigantine *Georgia Packet*, en route from Philadelphia to Savannah with a cargo of flour, bread, beer and rum, arrived off the Savannah Bar on Tuesday, March 12, 1776, she was captured by the HM Sloop *Raven*. A party of militiamen tried to retake her but lost about two killed, five wounded and four captured.[90]

★ Colonel Archibald Bulloch (1731–1777) and a raiding party of about 50 Creeks and Georgia militiamen, who were painted like Creeks, went to Tybee Island in an attempt to capture Sir James Wright (1714–1785). They did not find Wright, who had returned to his ship, but they did find a party of six British marines from the transport *Symmetry*. They accompanied 12 laborers who went to the island to cut wood and to procure water. Bulloch's men attacked about 1 PM Monday, March 25, 1776. They engaged in a "brisk fire" that killed one marine and wounded another. A shipwright named Nicholas was shot through the head. They captured one marine (who later escaped) and several Loyalists. They also set fire to three Loyalists' houses. The HM Schooner *Hinchinbrook* fired two shots to alarm the ships. Captain Edward Thornbrough (1754–1834) sent armed boats and a company of marines from the HM Sloop *Tamar*, moored in the Savannah River off Cockspur Island, to Tybee to evacuate any Loyalists.

The Royal Navy ships near the island fired three broadsides at the Georgians and then sent a landing party on shore. The Georgians kept up constant rifle fire, forcing the relief party to move out of range. The relief party burned two houses on the island. Shortly after this, all but two of the British vessels left the Savannah River.[91]

About 1:30 PM, Colonel Bulloch's raiding party attacked a small party of six unarmed marines from Captain John Ferguson's HM Armed Vessel *Cherokee,* sent to the island with 12 slaves to cut wood and get water. They shot one man through the head and captured the 12 African American slaves and one white man who later escaped. The marines removed the wounded and any Loyalists. The militiamen suffered no harm. The *Cherokee* came close to shore, fired three broadsides at the Rebels, dispersed them, and landed several men under a heavy fire. The landing party re-embarked and the *Cherokee* sailed out of range.[92]

★ Captain John Ferguson's HM Armed Vessel *Cherokee* and Captain John Stanhope's HM Sloop *Raven* cut off the Rebels who attacked the British on Cockspur Island on Friday, April 12, 1776. They concluded the action the next day, killing one, wounding two and capturing 15.

★ A raiding party of Georgians attacked the British post on Cockspur Island at 11 o'clock on Sunday, May 12, 1776 and attempted to capture "a White Man a Pilot & some Negroes." They were discovered approaching the post and were fired upon. When one man was killed, the others retreated toward their boats to escape. The HM Sloop *Raven* and the HM Armed Vessel *Cherokee* sent sailors to the west end of the island in three boats to cut off any escape. They captured one of the boats with three wounded Georgians in it. The prisoners told the British sailors of an armed schooner that was waiting for them up the Savannah River at Four Mile Point.

Sailors from the *Raven* and *Cherokee* sailed up the Savannah River in a pinnace (see Photo GA-12) and two boats at 1 AM on May 13th to find the armed schooner, armed with six swivel guns (see Photo GA-11) and six organs. (An organ contains several barrels of small arms, fixed upon one stock so as to be all fired together.) Two other boats were assigned to guard Cockspur Island during the attack. The sailors easily captured the armed schooner because Captain John Brown (1743–1830) and his eight-man crew thought the British sailors were part of the returning raiding party. The schooner was sailed back to Cockspur Island. The British captured three other men from the raid at 11 o'clock as they tried to get up the river.[93]

★ The Crown privateer *Governor Tonyn* sailed into DeFoskey Creek on Wednesday morning, August 14, 1776. A number of Whigs on shore fired several volleys of musketry at her. She returned fire with several guns.[94]

★ A band of marauders, thought to be Loyalists, left Cockspur Island and surprised two Continental guards posted on Wilmington Island on Wednesday, September 11, 1776. Colonel Samuel Elbert (1740–1788) expected them to return the following night "to plunder the other Part of the Island, where a Sergeant and six Privates from the Georgia Battalion" were posted. He sent Lieutenant Isaac Hicks (1758–1826), of the 2nd Georgia Battalion, with a detachment of 25 men (10 privates from the 1st Georgia Battalion, two from the 2nd Georgia Battalion, and 12 privates and one sergeant from the 3rd Regiment (Rangers) South Carolina Continentals to reinforce the post.

GA-12. Pinnace (left) of the HMS Victory. A pinnace was a 28-foot boat used to convey the captain or officers ashore or to other ships. It was generally rowed by eight oarsmen but could be rowed by four.

Lieutenant Hicks and his detachment reached Wilmington Island early the following morning and found 11 blacks and five whites "busy in carrying off their Booty."
They fired and killed two or three in the first volley. A general engagement ensued. The
Whigs killed two blacks and captured one black and four whites. The fifth white escaped
"very much wounded." Lieutenant Hicks lost two men killed. Captain Robert Good-
wyn (b. ca. 1740) expected the raiders to return to Wilmington Island, so he brought a
detachment of the 3rd South Carolina to assist Lieutenant Hicks. However, the raiders
returned by another route.[95]

1777

A party of Creeks crossed the Ogeechee River near Morgan's Fort during the night of
Thursday, July 31, 1777. They broke down the door of Samuel Delk's house and rushed
in. Samuel Delk was not at home. The Creeks killed and scalped his wife and four children. They also took his eldest daughter, a girl of 14, captive. Another son, 15-year-old
David, would have suffered the same fate had his mother not sent him to a spring for
water just before the attack. Lieutenants James Little (1737–1807) and Samuel Alexander (1757–1817) or his younger brother James (1760–1798), led a party in pursuit of
the Creeks. They pursued for about 40 miles until the raiders split up and the Georgians
lost their trail.[96]

1778

★ Brigadier General Andrew Pickens (1739–1817) and a force of 500 men ambushed
approximately 800 Creeks, led by a British agent, on the Ogeechee Road as they proceeded to Augusta in February 1778. The Creeks scattered but Pickens overtook their
rear guard and captured a principal chief. The engagement prevented reinforcements
from relieving the Crown forces at Augusta.

★ Colonel Samuel Elbert (1740–1788) and his army crossed the Altamaha River on
Wednesday, May 27, 1778 and camped at Reid's Bluff. Major General Robert Howe
(1732–1786) requested 300 slaves from Georgia to cut a road but only 56 arrived to
help the two brigades. The poorly equipped Continental regiments had no tents or
camp equipment. The Georgia militia competed with them for supplies and often intercepted shipments for their own use.

★ The Continentals marched to Spring Branch on Sunday, June 14, 1778. Governor
John Houstoun (1744–1796) promised Major General Robert Howe (1732–1786) that
the Georgia militia would march in three or four days to rendezvous with the Continental troops. The army skirmished with the East Florida Rangers on Wednesday, June
17, 1778 and captured one man and eight horses. General Howe's main army joined
Colonel Samuel Elbert's (1740–1788) troops two days later on the Great Satilla River
but Colonel Andrew Williamson's (ca. 1730–1786) South Carolina militia had not arrived.

★ Lieutenant Colonel Thomas Alexander Brown (1744–1814 sent Captain James
Moore (d. 1778) and some East Florida Rangers to collect horses on the Satilla and
then, with 76 Rangers and some Native Americans, to join a group of Loyalists. The
combined force would circle behind Major General Robert Howe's (1732–1786) force
and attack the rear. Some of Moore's men deserted at the Ogeechee River and informed
the local militia about Moore's location. The militia ambushed the Rangers near Augusta on Monday, June 22, 1778. They killed nine and captured Captain Moore and 20
of his men. Moore was then shot to death.

General Howe's army crossed the Satilla River on 50- by 14-foot rafts on June 23rd. The Georgia militia had arrived within a few miles of his army on June 28th. However, when some of them tried to assist the Continentals, Governor John Houstoun (1744–1796) had them arrested for marching without orders. When Houstoun finally arrived, he refused to place his militia under the command of a Continental officer. Neither commander would yield to the other.[97]

See **Florida, The Battle of Alligator Bridge** pp. 116–120.

★ The British evacuated Philadelphia, Pennsylvania in June 1778, partly because they needed to supply troops for operations in the Caribbean and Florida. General Henry Clinton (1730–1795) sent Major General James Grant (1720–1806) and 5,000 troops to St. Lucia in the West Indies in November 1778. Lieutenant Colonel Archibald Campbell (1739–1791) sailed from New York with another 3,000 aboard approximately 50 ships on November 12 to join Major General Augusine Prevost (1723–1786) in St. Augustine, Florida, intending to capture Georgia back from the Whigs. Brigadier General John Campbell (d. 1806) and 1,300 men were sent to Pensacola, Florida to conquer the Spanish colony there. General Prevost planned to march north from Florida to meet Campbell, but he was delayed.

By moving south, the British were closer to the West Indies where the fleet could protect their interests and guard against the French. The Loyalists were also more numerous in the South, especially in the Carolinas and Georgia. The king's ministers hoped to bring the southern colonies into the fold one by one and, from bases there, to strangle the recalcitrant North. A small British force operating from Florida quickly overran thinly populated Georgia in the winter of 1778–1779.

Lieutenant Colonel Campbell's force encountered a heavy gale which damaged several ships and forced the fleet to return to Staten Island. They sailed again on Friday, November 27, but privateers attacked some of the ships shortly after leaving. Another storm separated some of the vessels from the main fleet which were presumed lost until they arrived off the Georgia coast the following Friday, December 4. William Haslem deserted from his transport and swam ashore. He gave Governor John Houstoun (1744–1796) a detailed description of the invasion forces and their mission.[98]

Several vessels were destroyed and a number of men drowned along the way. The weather drove 10 ships toward the coastline of Charleston, South Carolina on Friday, December 17, 1778. The South Carolina militiamen lit signal fires to alert the people that the British fleet was coming.

Major General Robert Howe (1732–1786), of North Carolina, was some 30 miles south of Savannah at Sunbury, where he had gone to defend the area, when Major General Augusine Prevost marched north into Liberty County. When he received news of the arrival of the British ships off the Georgia coast, Howe ordered his galleys north to cover Tybee Roads and Warsaw Sound and instructed them to withdraw to Augustine Creek if they should be outgunned. He left Major Joseph Lane (1740–1801) and a force of 200 Continentals and a few militiamen at Sunbury while he returned to Savannah where he arrived about Sunday, December 12. Howe immediately ordered his deputy quartermaster general to report the number, size and location of all the boats in public service. He also requested reports on the state of the public stores in the departments of the deputy quartermaster general, the deputy clothier general and the commissaries of purchases and issues and on the readiness of the regimental surgeons and the Georgia Continental Artillery.

British Commodore Hyde Parker's (1742–1782) fleet sailed directly to Savannah and arrived early Wednesday morning, December 23rd. The British did not know that two Georgia Continental galleys were Savannah's strongest defense at the time. The *Alert, Vigilant, Keppel, Greenwich* and 34 transports that were able to get over the Savannah Bar sailed past the Port Royal lighthouse and up the Savannah River. When they reached Four Mile Point, they came under fire from the two Georgia galleys under the command of Commodore Oliver Bowen (1742–1800). The lack of wind and the tide forced the lead ship, the *Vigilant*, to sail toward the galleys. Commodore Bowen's vessels fired at the British for two hours but with little effect. When the *Vigilant* was in position to fire her 24-pounders, Bowen retreated up the river. This engagement delayed the Crown forces for the day. That night, they could see the Continental campfires burning to the northwest of Girardeau's plantation.[99]

The rest of the fleet assembled at the anchorage off Cockspur Point at the mouth of the Savannah River and anchored on December 24th. A grenadier in the Grenadier Regiment von Trümbach, aboard one of the British transports, reported that the British fleet "raised white flags as if we were French." Two British warships then "entered the harbor posing as friends and sailed as far as . . . 'the Mud Hole,' and dropped anchor" and remained there without any interference from the Whigs. [The "Mud Hole" was "Five Fathom Hole" in the Savannah River, a quarantine station opposite the Whig battery on Salter's Island known as the "Mud Fort" (later the site of Fort Jackson)].[100]

Lieutenant Colonel Campbell decided to strike immediately, before Howe's expected reinforcements arrived. He sent Captain Sir James Gardiner Baird's (ca. 1760–1830) light infantry company ashore, at John Girardeau's plantation at Brewton Hill, on Friday night, December 25 to "pick up some of the Inhabitants" who could provide intelligence of the strength and position of the Continental forces. The troops returned the next morning with "a White Overseer and a Black named Peter." The two told Campbell that Savannah was defended by 1,200 Continentals and 600 militiamen with 10 pieces of artillery and that three galleys guarded the river approaches to the town. In reality, General Robert Howe had only 672 Georgia and South Carolina Continentals and about 150 Georgia militiamen. About one-fourth of his men were ill and many were too feeble to endure strenuous combat.

The two ships at Five Fathom Hole suddenly raised British flags after Christmas. Both sides exchanged heavy fire as the British fleet sailed up to Savannah and landed during the night of December 25.

Lieutenant Colonel Campbell decided to land at Girardeau's plantation and try to capture the town in a surprise attack. He disembarked his army of 3,500 at Brewton Hill, the usual name for John Girardeau's plantation, on Tuesday, December 29, 1778. [The British called it Sheridoe's plantation, a corruption of Girardeau. The site of the plantation is located on the Savannah River about half a mile east of downtown Savannah in an industrialized section of the town.] The army consisted of two battalions of Brigadier General Simon Fraser's (1737–1777) Highlanders (71st Regiment of Foot), two Hessian units of Woellworth and Wissenbach, and four Loyalist battalions comprised of mostly New York Loyalists (American Volunteers), and a detachment of artillery. The Loyalist units included deserters of Irish descent from the Continental Army. There were so many deserters who switched sides that Lieutenant Colonel Lord Francis Rawdon (1754–1826) formed an entire battalion of them in Philadelphia and called them the Volunteers of Ireland.[101]

The old entrenchments at Savannah were in disrepair, so General Howe sent out fatigue detachments to construct small defensive works below Tattnall's fence in front of Fair Lawn plantation (approximately at what is now the intersection of Taylor and East Broad Streets) the night before the British assault. He deployed his troops in front of the old works on the eastern side of the city. His main force was positioned at Tattnall's house to cover the Tybee Road that led from the British landing site. His line extended from the fort in the Trustees' Garden on his left (northeast shoulder of the city), southward along Savannah's eastern bluff to his headquarters at Tattnall's house on his right. He placed Colonel George Walton's (1749–1804) Georgia Continentals on the left and the South Carolina Continentals on the right. He positioned two guns of the Continental artillery in the center and one on each flank on the edge of swamps and waited for the British to attack.[102]

A group of about 50 South Carolina Continentals under Captain John Carraway Smith occupied Girardeau's plantation buildings at the crest of Brewton's Hill. They knocked planks out of the walls to shoot at the enemy and waited for the British light infantry to come within 100 yards before firing. A volley killed Captain Charles Cameron (d. 1778) of the 71st Highlanders, and three of his men. The light infantrymen dislodged the South Carolinians who rushed out the back doors or jumped out the windows to escape. They secured the high ground and later bayoneted (see Photo GA-3) the wounded Continentals in the streets and squares of Savannah to avenge Captain Cameron.

The Continental artillery began firing round or solid shot at long range toward the flatboats landing the British troops. However, they were too far away to be effective. Lieutenant Colonel Campbell halted his men on open ground along a rail fence on Governor James Wright's (1714–1785) plantation, about 1,000 yards in front of Howe's main force. A small, wooden bridge on the road between Savannah and Thunderbolt separated the two forces. It was in flames and General Howe's riflemen had advanced to cover it to prevent the British from extinguishing the fire.

General Howe withdrew his troops to the vicinity of the Fair Lawn plantation and Brewton Hill plantation. They formed along the road, with two regiments of South Carolina Continentals, 100 Georgia militiamen and an artillery piece on the right flank. The line ran from the road down to wooded swampland alongside and was anchored on the left by Colonel Samuel Elbert's (1740–1788) Georgia militia and a field piece. A trench extended along the entire line and there were two other artillery pieces placed in the middle of the road.

Colonel Campbell induced Quamino (Quamina, Quash, or Quosh) Dolly, one of Sir James Wright's elderly slaves at Fair Lawn "to conduct the Troops, by a private Path through the Swamp, upon the Right of the Americans" for a small reward. Dolly told them about a gully that would lead the troops through and then around to attack Howe's right flank from the rear.

Captain Sir James Gardiner Baird's (ca. 1760–1830) light infantry company advanced up the road within sight of General Howe's line. As General Howe expected a frontal assault and waited for the attack, Colonel Campbell attacked Howe's left to conceal Baird's 350 light infantrymen and Loyalists who plodded through the swamps to strike Howe's right flank. Howe's artillery opened fire but got no response. Then, Baird's party emerged from the swamp about half a mile south of Colonel George Walton's (1749–1804) position. They quickly moved to about 70 or 80 yards in front of Walton, formed a line two men deep and suddenly struck the right flank, catching them by surprise. Major

Joseph Woodruff's (1739–1799) artillery fired "four or five times with round shot at the distance of 150 paces" but with little effect. They spiked their guns and ran.

Baird's men raced up the Ogeechee Road toward McGillivray's Gate at Spring Hill to cut off the retreat while Colonel Campbell's main body made a frontal assault. With the enemy attacking from every direction at once, General Howe ordered a retreat. The South Carolina Continentals led the withdrawal, followed by the artillery and then the Georgia Continentals. The 71st Highlanders quickly crossed the marshy rivulet near the town and reached the fort at Trustees' Garden. The Savannah militiamen ran out. They were surrounded by the Highlanders, grounded their weapons and surrendered.

As the Georgia Continentals approached the cemetery (now known as the Colonial Cemetery), Colonel Elbert realized that the British were on his flank and in his front. He ordered his light infantry to attack in an attempt to break through the weakest point. He then ordered his men to form an open column of platoons. When they got behind the cemetery, Elbert saw there was a proper distance between the sections and ordered his men to change formation to files. British shells (see Photo GA-7) began to break the formation into a disorganized mass.

The Congressional forces began to fall back in complete confusion and then fled into the swamps in a panic. Most of the retreating soldiers on the right flank managed to escape, but those on the left had to cross a deep tidal creek, Musgrove Creek, as the tide was high. Many drowned or were captured. Campbell then occupied Savannah, arresting suspected Rebels, looting and burning their homes, while the British fleet moved upriver to take the boats docked at the town's wharves. The Whigs lost more than half of their forces: 83 men dead (battle casualties and drownings) and 453 (including 38 officers) captured. The Crown forces had only seven battle deaths and 19 wounded. They also captured three ships, three brigs, and eight smaller vessels in the harbor and one stand of colors, 48 cannons, 23 mortars (see Photo GA-13), 94 barrels of powder in the town as well as the fort, with all its stores, and the capital of Georgia.

GA-13. Mortar used for firing shells (also known as bombs) in a high arc over fortifications, particularly to get behind walls and other high obstacles that cannons cannot reach. The shell often detonates in the air, raining metal fragments with high velocity on the fort's occupants.

The British thought that the easy capture of Savannah would let them expand their occupation into a center of loyalism. After General Prevost arrived from Florida with another 1,000 men, Lieutenant Colonel Campbell went up the Savannah River to recruit Loyalist volunteers. About 1,400 Loyalists joined Campbell at Augusta; but, on February 14, at the Battle of Kettle Creek (see pp. 10–13), the Whig militia ambushed another 700 on their way to enlist. News that Major General Benjamin Lincoln (1733–1810) was coming with an army of more than 1,500 men convinced the Crown forces to withdraw to Savannah.[103]

The January 26, 1779 issue of *The Charlestown Gazette* published the intriguing report that Colonel James Ingram (ca. 1749–1795), "an aid de camp of Gen. Lincoln's, at the head of a detachment of Continental troops, had crossed the Savannah river and erected the American standard." However, Major General Benjamin Lincoln's (1733–1810) papers make no mention of Colonel Ingram's appointment as an aide-de-camp or that he was sent to Georgia in command of a detachment of Continental troops.[104]

1779

★ Lieutenant Colonel Archibald Campbell (1739–1791) made New Ebenezer his headquarters as he prepared to subdue the northern interior of Georgia. Campbell left New Ebenezer on January 24, 1779 with approximately 1,000 soldiers and headed north toward Augusta. After a brief occupation of Augusta, Campbell returned to New Ebenezer a month later on February 24, 1779.

Campbell's secretary, Ensign John Wilson, was a capable engineer who began to strengthen the town's fortifications in January 1779 to protect the Crown troops from the militia forces occupying Purrysburg, South Carolina, just across and downstream from New Ebenezer. They constructed new redoubts and posted additional artillery to defend this important link in the chain of communications between the Georgia upcountry and British headquarters in Savannah. The improvements included a series of redoubts connected by palisade lines (see Photo GA-14) that completely encompassed the town and the mouth of Ebenezer Creek. The 2nd battalion of the 71st Regiment of Highlanders became a permanent guard to occupy the strategic village.

GA-14. *Palisade is a fence of pales or stakes, pointed at the top, and set firmly in the ground in a close row with others to form an enclosure or defense*

When the British decided to abandon the post, they burned the magazine and withdrew in early September 1779. Major General Benjamin Lincoln (1733–1810), General Lachlan McIntosh and a large army of nearly 5,000 men camped briefly at New Ebenezer soon afterward, as they prepared to move on British-held Savannah. They were having considerable trouble attempting to cross at Zubly's Ferry, so they camped outside New Ebenezer as they commandeered boats and made rafts to make the slow crossing of the Savannah River.

★ The armed sloop *Greenwich* and a British galley were sighted a little above Abercorn Creek, near Purrysburgh, South Carolina on Friday, March 19, 1779. The South Carolina galleys *Congress* and *Lee* and a sloop, left Purrysburgh at midnight to investigate the sighting. All the South Carolina vessels ran aground before they had sailed 2 miles. It was almost daylight when they were refloated. Despite having lost the element of surprise, they decided to attack anyway.

Meanwhile, an armed flatboat joined the British squadron which had constructed a battery on the south side of the Savannah. When the Carolina fleet got within 250 yards of the British squadron, the *Congress* ran aground again and came under fire at 10 AM. The engagement continued until 1 PM when the Carolinians decided to abandon the attack after losing 40 men killed and wounded, including their commander.[105]

★ Lieutenant Colonel John Thomas, Jr. (1751–1819) and Major Henry Sharp (d. 1779) tried to muster the Loyalist militia at the Burke County jail in March 1779, after the engagement at Briar Creek. Lieutenant Colonel Thomas Alexander Brown's (1744–1814) East Florida Rangers were supposed to join them but withdrew to Paris Mills when they learned Colonel LeRoy Hammond's (1728–1789) regiment was approaching. Major Sharp and his Georgia light dragoons captured Fort Morgan, a Whig outpost on the Ogeechee River in March 1779. Lieutenant Colonel Leonard Marbury (1750–1796) and Colonel Matthew Singleton (1722–1787) then pursued Major Sharp and his Loyalists.[106]

★ Lieutenant Colonel William Henderson (1748–1787) and a company of 40 men of the 6th South Carolina Regiment guarded Yemassee Bluff, near Black Swamp, on Thursday night, April 22, 1779, when a party of about 30 or 40 Loyalists, disguised as Native Americans, crossed the river at Yemassee and attacked a small guard post of six men there the following morning. The Loyalist attack was a complete surprise because neither the guard post nor any of the 6th Regiment ever fired a shot. The South Carolinians, though surprised, ran off the attackers without firing a shot and pursued them into the swamp. Brigadier General Thomas Sumter (1734–1832) was certain that no Native Americans were involved because all the raiders knew how to use the bayonet.

Colonel Henderson sent for the rest of the regiment "but could not come up with them." The raiders burned Captain Joachim Hartstone's house where the rest of the guards were sleeping. Hartstone was a rice planter who lived at Great Swamp on the road from Purrysburg to the Coosawhatchie Bridge. The raiders murdered and scalped an old African American woman but Hartstone and his family escaped. The Carolinians abandoned their position but returned after the raiders had gone.

Some Hessian deserters informed the Whigs that there were about 50 Native American warriors stationed in the swamps opposite Purrysburg to prevent desertions from the British Army. A party of Native Americans crossed the river a little below Purrysburg a short time later, but one of the Continental picket guards drove them back.

Lieutenant Colonel Alexander McIntosh (1732–1780) and 100 men of the 5th South Carolina Regiment reinforced the post at Black Swamp. Brigadier General William

Moultrie (1730–1805) requested that the governor send an additional 20 Catawbas to Black Swamp to counter the Loyalist raids. Colonel McIntosh abandoned the post on April 28 when Major General Augustine Prevost (1723–1786) landed 300 men at Purrysburgh.[107]

★ Colonel John Twiggs (1750–1816), Colonel John Baker and 70 Georgia militiamen marched down the south side of the Great Ogeechee River and halted on the plantation of Mr. James Butler, called Hickory Hill. On Monday, June 28, 1779, he received information that three militia guides were accompanying Captain John K. Muller and 40 mounted grenadiers (see Photo GA-15) of the 60th Royal American Regiment to attack him.

Colonel Twiggs sent Major John Cooper (1751–1819), of Marbury's dragoons, and Captain Joshua Inman to meet the enemy with about 30 to 35 men. (The others had gone foraging). They laid some brushwood in their front to serve as an abatis (see Photo GA-16) and formed across a rice dam which Captain Muller and his men had to cross. When the Loyalists approached, the Georgians shot several dragoons out of their saddles in the first volley.

GA-15. Members of the Brigade of the American Revolution portraying British grenadiers. This photo depicts Scottish Highlanders wearing red regimental coats with black facings, bearskin helmets, and a blue and green tartan kilt. Grenadiers were members of an elite unit selected on the basis of exceptional height and ability.

The Crown troops dismounted and formed by a fence. Captain Muller was shot through the thigh and supported himself with his sword as he encouraged his men to charge. A musket ball soon passed through his arm and lodged in his body. Lieutenant Swanson, his second in command, was wounded a few moments later.

Colonel Twiggs took advantage of the confusion in the British ranks and ordered 10 men to cut off the British retreat while the others mounted the enemy's horses and set out in pursuit. After "an irregular fire for ten minutes" the Crown troops retreated into the second ambush. Colonel Twiggs captured the entire detachment of two officers and 30 privates, except for the three militia guides who fled when the first shots were fired. The British lost seven killed, 10 wounded and 28 captured. The three guides were the only ones to escape. The Whigs had only two men wounded: Colonel Joseph Maybank (1735–1783) and Captain Aquilla Whitaker (1755–1824) and Lieutenant John Carswell (1760–1817) captured. The wounded were brought to Savannah, where the nearest surgeon was located. Captain Muller died of his wounds two hours after the conflict.[108]

★ Major General Benjamin Lincoln (1733–1810) ordered "the Georgia troops, Captain Joseph Newman's (1740–1804) company of horse" and Sergeant William Jasper's (ca. 1750–1779) Georgia troops "to harass and perplex the enemy in that state" in July 1779. After the capture of Savannah, the Crown forces established a hospital at Ebenezer

GA-16. Abatis is a defensive mechanism made of sharpened branches pointing out from a fortification at an angle toward the enemy to slow or disrupt an assault. Modern armies use barbed wire for the same purpose. The branches in this photo are not sharpened so as not to injure anybody.

and Sergeant Jasper's brother served in the Crown forces there. Sergeant Jasper decided to visit his brother who was very surprised to see him. Sergeant Jasper lied and told him that he was no longer a soldier and that he no longer found any encouragement in fighting for his country. After a stay of three days, he returned to report to his commander everything he had seen.

Encouraged to go back to Ebenezer, Jasper returned a few weeks later with Sergeant John Newton (1757–1787). They were both welcomed in the camp and stayed for several days. When a small party of Congressional prisoners was brought into camp, Sergeant Jasper's brother told him that the prisoners were on their way to Savannah to be hanged. The wife and child of one of the prisoners was with them. Jasper and Newton decided to rescue them.

Jasper and Newton waited until the guards marched away from the post. They went in a different direction from that of the prisoners and tried to intercept the party but found it impossible to catch up to them. Jasper thought the guards would stop at a spring 2 miles from Savannah, so he and Newton headed there. They arrived before the British guards did on Wednesday, July 21, 1779, and laid in ambush. When the British arrived at the spring, they grounded their arms and half of the guards led the prisoners to the well to drink while the mother and child rested on the side of the road. Jasper and Newton struck when two of the guards rested their muskets against a tree to fill their canteens. They grabbed the muskets, shot the two guards, clubbed the muskets (see Photo GA-3) and charged the other guards, knocking down two more and grabbing their muskets. The remaining guards surrendered and the prisoners were released. Sergeant Jasper hurried his party across the Savannah River.[109]

★ A French fleet and army of 4,450 under Admiral Comte Jean-Baptiste-Charles-Henri-Hector d'Estaing (1729–1794) arrived off Savannah on Wednesday, September

1, 1779. Major General Benjamin Lincoln (1733–1810) and Brigadier General Casimir Pulaski (1747–1779) joined them with over 2,100 men. The three divisions [d'Estaing's; General Arthur, Count de Dillon's (1750–1794) and Colonel Louis Marc Antoine Vicomte de Noailles's (1756–1804)] of the French army encamped east of the Ogeechee Road and the Continental troops camped to the left of the French all the way to McGillivray's Plantation on the Savannah River.

★ The British sent out patrols to determine the location of Admiral Comte Jean-Baptiste-Charles-Henri-Hector d'Estaing's (1729–1794) fleet as it approached Georgia. The HMS *Rose* went out of Savannah on Friday, September 3, 1779 to investigate a report of several large ships. She returned with news that the French ships were near the coast.

The 74-gun ship of the line *Magnifique* (see Photo GA-17) captured the sloop *Polly* and her crew on Monday, September 6th. Five French sailors boarded the *Polly* but that night a gale blew her away from the French fleet toward Tybee. The French sailors, unaware of their location, sailed the *Polly* up the Georgia coast. The English prisoners on board added to the confusion by telling their captors that the Savannah River was the entrance to Charleston, South Carolina.

The crew sailed the *Polly* in the mouth of the river and anchored, whereupon she was captured. The sailors informed their captors that the French fleet consisted of the 74-gun *Magnifique*, the 64-gun *Sphinx*, two frigates, a schooner, and a cutter, all bound to Boston for masts and spars.[110]

★ After news of Major General John Burgoyne's (1732–1792) surrender at Saratoga, New York, in October 1777, the French signed both a Treaty of Amity and Commerce

GA-17. French frigate

and a Treaty of Alliance with the United States. Admiral Comte Jean-Baptiste-Charles-Henri-Hector d'Estaing (1729–1794) sailed north from the Caribbean with a fleet of 33 warships (totaling more than 2,000 guns) and 4,000 troops. He sailed into Charleston Harbor on Friday, September 3, 1779 and arrived off the coast of Georgia the following day when a British lookout sighted five French men-of-war and several sloops and schooners approaching Tybee Island.

The *Paris Gazette* reported that the troops landed there consisted of 2,979 "Europeans" and 545 "Colored: Volunteer Chasseurs, Mulattoes, and Negroes, newly raised at St. Domingo." The Volunteer Chasseurs, called the Fontanges Legion after its French commander [Major General Vicomte François de Fontanges (1740–1822)], included young men who would become famous in the Haitian revolution, such as Pierre Astrel (b. 1753), Pierre Auba (b. 1750), Louis Jacques Beauvais (b. 1756), Jean-Baptiste Mars Belley (1747?–1805), Martial Besse (b. 1758), Guillaume Bleck (b. 1745), Pierre Cangé (b. 1756), Jean-Baptiste Chavannes (1755–1791), Pierre Faubert (b. 1752), Laurent Férou (b. 1765), Jean-Louis Froumentaine (b. 1752), Barthélemy-Médor Icard (b. 1753), Gédéon Jourdan (b. 1757), Jean-Pierre Lambert (b. 1728), Jean-Baptiste Léveillé (b. 1753), Christophe Mornet (b. 1739), Pierre Obas, Luc-Vincent Olivier (b. 1753), Pierre Pinchinat (b. 1746), Jean Piverger (b. 1748), André Rigaud (1761–1811), Césaire Savary (b. 1756), Pierre Tessier (b. 1756), Jérome Thoby (b. 1753), Jean-Louis Villate (1751–1802), and Henri Christophe (1757–1820), future king of Haiti (see Photo GA-10). Christophe was 12 years old at Savannah. He volunteered as a freeborn infantryman and served as orderly to a French naval officer.

Upon learning about the arrival of the French fleet, Major General Augustine Prevost (1723–1786) ordered all his troops posted outside Savannah to prepare to come join him in Savannah. Captain James Moncrieff (1744–1793), of the British engineers, sailed down the river on Wednesday, September 8, with 100 men and a howitzer to strengthen the outposts and batteries at Tybee. The schooner *Rattlesnake* followed them with three officers and 50 men. Captain Moncrieff burned the fort on the 10th and returned to Savannah with the garrison.[111]

D'Estaing's fleet captured the 50-gun *Experiment*, the frigate *Ariel*, and two store ships carrying the £30,000 payroll for the Savannah garrison along with Brigadier General George Garth (d. 1819) who was on his way to take command of the British forces in Georgia. The French off-loaded their heavy cannons and mortars (see Photo GA-13) at Thunderbolt and Causton's Bluff on Saturday, September 11. The heavy rains slowed their progress, as they had to haul the heavy guns about 5 miles from the landing sites. The French troops began landing at Beaulieu, on the Vernon River, that night. They unloaded more artillery that had to be dragged about 15 miles to their emplacements. Meanwhile, the British in Savannah continued to build fascines (see Photo GA-18) for their defenses. They sank six British ships in the river to block the French.

Major General Benjamin Lincoln (1733–1810) hurried south with 600 Continentals, Count Casimir Pulaski's (1747–1779) 200 legionnaires and 750 militiamen to join d'Estaing. He reached Cherokee Hill, just west of Savannah on September 15. The following day, d'Estaing demanded that General Prevost surrender the city, but he gave Prevost 24 hours to consider the terms. This gave Prevost enough time to strengthen his defenses and receive reinforcements of Colonel John Maitland (1732–1779) and 800 Regulars from the garrison at Beaufort, South Carolina, after a remarkable forced march through swamps, marshes, and streams. Colonel John Harris Cruger (1738–1807) was on his way from Sunbury with the 1st Battalion of de Lancey's Brigade.

GA-18. Fascines are long bundles of sticks tied together, used in building earthworks and in strengthening ramparts. The fascines are in the foreground of this photo. The middle ground shows gabions, which are cylindrical baskets made of wicker and filled with earth for use in building fortifications.

D'Estaing got upset as the Redcoats dug their trenches. He sent Prevost a letter saying, "I am informed that you continue intrenching yourself. It is a Matter of very little Importance to me, however for Form's sake, I must desire that you will desist." With his total manpower raised to 3,250 plus a considerable number of militiamen and armed slaves, Prevost declined to surrender. Unfortunately, the Franco-American force had to hurry its attack because d'Estaing was unwilling to risk his fleet in a position dangerously exposed to hurricanes, remembering his experience at Rhode Island where he was caught in one. Moreover, his sailors were dying of scurvy at the rate of 35 a day.

★ Captain William Campbell (d. 1779) and 200 British light infantrymen made a sortie on Friday morning, September 17, 1779 to attack a covering party of about 200 French at a battery near the barracks. They were repulsed and pursued into their redoubts with the loss of 53 men killed, including Captain Campbell and two other officers, and nearly 100 wounded. The French lost about 26 men killed and 84 wounded, including 10 officers. The French were so eager and impetuous that, instead of waiting for the enemy, they leapt out of their trench, attacked and pursued them with the bayonet (see Photo GA-3) until the cannon from the British redoubts galled them and inflicted their greatest loss.[112]

★ On Friday evening, September 17, 1779, "the guns for the retreat were fired an hour earlier than usual as a signal that hostilities were resumed."[113]

★ Brigadier General Casimir Pulaski (1747–1779) and his legion, along with Colonel Peter Horry (1747–1815) and some of the 1st Regiment Continental Light Dragoons, went in pursuit of Colonel Daniel McGirth (d. ca. 1789) on Saturday, September 18, 1779. The Continentals trailed McGirth's Loyalists as they drove a large number of "horses, cattle and Negroes to St. Augustine." Pulaski ordered his dragoons to remain near the Ogeechee Ferry, about 15 miles south of Savannah, to intercept any provisions. Meanwhile, he overtook McGirth's party near the Ogeechee Ferry and captured 50 men along with some livestock and slaves. Pulaski returned to the ferry the next day, gathered his dragoons and returned to camp.[114]

★ Major General Augustine Prevost (1723–1786) chose the Spring Hill Redoubt (see Photo GA-8), off the town's southwest corner, as the strongest point of his defense. At 9 PM Wednesday evening, September 22, 1779, M. de Guillaume, lieutenant of grenadiers in the regiment of Guadeloupe, of the Viscount de Noailles's division, attempted to capture an advance enemy post at Thunderbolt Bluff on St. Augustine Creek, 5 miles southeast of the city, with 50 picked men. Disregarding the Viscount de Noailles's instructions, they rushed head-on, attacking, with full force, a post which should have been captured by surprise. The Viscount de Noailles, following closely to support him, saw that success was impossible and ordered a retreat. The Crown forces repulsed the French with a lively fire of artillery and musketry that killed six men and wounded several others.

★ The following day, the Allied armies completely invested Savannah. The siege of the 2,500 British Regulars and Loyalists under Major General Augustine Prevost (1723–1786) lasted until Monday, October 18, 1779. The allied forces began digging siege trenches on September 23rd and installed cannons by October 3rd.

★ General Prevost had the barracks in the center of his lines pulled down on Monday, September 27th to erect a great battery. A British sortie against the French trenches on Friday, September 24, 1779 cost the attackers four killed and 15 wounded, but they killed and wounded 70 Frenchmen. French artillery in siege lines began to bombard (see Photo GA-7) the town on Monday, October 4, 1779.[115]

★ A force of Georgia Continentals prevented Lieutenant James French and a detachment of 111 Crown troops from reaching Savannah on Friday night, October 1, 1779. The Crown troops, including a detachment of sick and wounded of de Lancey's Brigade from the Sunbury garrison, had sailed into the Ogeechee River to escape the French fleet and camped on Savage Point, about 15 to 20 miles south of Savannah. In addition to de Lancey's invalids, Lieutenant French had command of five vessels—four of them fully armed. The largest mounted 14 guns and was manned by 40 seamen.

Colonel John White, his servant, Captain Augustus Christian Georg Elholm (d. 1799), a sergeant and three privates were on patrol. They lit fires in the woods around Lieutenant French's camp to make it appear that a whole army was bivouacked there. They then rode around the camp shouting out orders to fictitious units, deceiving the Loyalists into thinking they were surrounded by a larger force. Colonel White demanded the Loyalists to surrender and told Lieutenant French that his army so hated the Loyalists that they would slaughter the prisoners if they saw them. Colonel White told Lieutenant French that he would protect his prisoners from the concealed Continental Army and order three guides—half of White's force—to escort the 150 prisoners. Lieutenant French quickly surrendered along with the privateer sloops and a schooner carrying a shipment of salt. Colonel White took them prisoners, along with Colonel Moses Kirkland (1730–1787), of the South Carolina Loyalist Militia, and 130 stands of arms. He then mustered local militiamen who took charge of the prisoners and escorted them to Savannah. The men also burned the five British vessels.

Colonel Kirkland was much despised by the Whigs and had been General Henry Clinton's (1730–1795) advisor during the planning of the Southern Campaign that resulted in the capture of Savannah. The Whigs bound him and his son in irons and placed them on board a galley which the British later captured. Kirkland rejoined the Crown forces in Savannah.[116]

★ Early Monday morning, October 4, 1779, allied gunners fired the first shots of a bombardment (see Photo GA-7), hoping to weaken enemy resistance. A furious bombardment by land and sea from 10 mortars and 54 pieces of heavy artillery continued for seven days but killed only a few men. Some drunken French gunners hit their own lines. After being reprimanded, they resumed firing "with more vivacity than precision." The cannonade failed to produce the desired result.

When d'Estaing learned, on October 8th, that bad weather was approaching and the assault trenches would not be completed until 10 days later, he abandoned plans to make a systematic approach by regular parallels and prepared for an immediate attack. Major General Benjamin Lincoln (1733–1810), in charge of some 5,000 troops agreed somewhat grudgingly.

★ The Allies planned to make a coordinated attack against the Spring Hill Redoubt at 4 AM on Saturday, October 9, 1779. Brigadier General Isaac Huger (1743–1797) would lead 500 South Carolina and Georgia militiamen in a diversionary attack against Cruger's Redoubt on the White Bluff Road and break through their defenses if possible.

The Crown defenses included the armed brig *Germain* in the Savannah River (near the foot of West Broad Street) which could deliver enfilade fire along the allies' northwest flank. This ship covered the Sailors' Battery (roughly at the present intersection of West Oglethorpe Avenue and Martin Luther King Jr. Boulevard (West Broad Street), so named because it was armed by sailors manning a 9-pounder. The Sailors' Battery covered the Spring Hill Redoubt (now the intersection of Louisville Road and West Broad Street) where Prevost expected the main assault. A line of earthworks and smaller redoubts connected these main posts and a thick swamp protected the western front. A fourth redoubt was located where the brick Continental barracks had been demolished overnight to erect the battery that covered White Bluff Road leading from Savannah to the south. A fifth redoubt was at Trustees' Garden at the northeast corner of the British line.

The French under General Arthur Count de Dillon (1750–1794) would emerge from a swamp in a secondary assault against the Sailors' Battery on the British right flank. However, Dillon's men got lost and the Crown forces, in strongly entrenched positions, repelled the attack in what was essentially a Bunker Hill in reverse. The allies suffered staggering losses. British grenadiers (see Photo GA-15) of the 60th Regiment and marines charged. Fierce hand-to-hand fighting threw the allies into confusion and finally into flight. After the repulsion of other thrusts, Lincoln gave up. The Fontanges Legion, stationed as a reserve in the rear guard, prevented the annihilation of the allied force. Brigadier General Count Casimir Pulaski (1747–1779) led his 200 legionnaires in a cavalry assault that resulted in his death. Martial Besse and Henri Christophe were slightly wounded and returned to Saint Domingue (now Haiti).

Eighteen years later, General Besse visited the United States on official business. He disembarked at Charleston, South Carolina "dressed in the uniform of his grade." Authorities forced him to post a bond as required by South Carolina law for all incoming blacks. When the French consul in Charleston protested that General Besse was a representative of his government and that he was wounded at the siege of Savannah, the bond was remitted.

The French and American allies mounted a direct assault on the Crown forces who were aided by hundreds of "armed blacks" gathered from the countryside to build redoubts, mount cannon, and serve as guides and spies. Their "incessant and cheerful labours, in rearing those numerous defenses which were completed with so much expedition as to astonish the besiegers, ought not to be forgotten in a history of this memorable siege." They fought a long and bloody battle in the ditch outside the Spring Hill Redoubt, trying to get to the top. The Continentals managed to gain the parapet and planted the South Carolina Crescent and the French colors on it, but they were immediately knocked down. The allies made three attempts to place their colors on the parapet and the Crown forces tore them down each time. Count d'Estaing's standard bearer was shot down and d'Estaing was wounded in the arm trying to reorganize the French forces. When Lieutenant Gray (d. 1779), the Continental standard bearer was killed, Sergeant William Jasper (ca. 1750–1779) supported the colors until he was mortally wounded.

None of the French grenadiers managed to get inside the redoubt and many were killed with the bayonet. Le Vicomte de Castries reported that the captain of the volunteers from Martinique or Guadeloupe and three-quarters of the company were killed in the trenches and the corps of riflemen was almost completely destroyed. "In less than half an hour more than 2,500 men were killed on the spot." D'Estaing was wounded a second time with a shot through the leg. Colonel Lachlan McIntosh (1727–1806) asked him for instructions and was told to circle left so as not to interfere with the French reorganization. This diverted the column into Yamacraw Swamp, where its left flank came under fire from the *Germain* until the end of the battle.

The Congressional forces lost about 444 men, including 80 dead in the ditch and 93 more between it and the abatis. The French sustained approximately 650 officers and men wounded. We don't know the Crown losses, but they range from approximately 55 to 155 men. Most authorities accept the figure of about 40 killed and 63 wounded.

The French army departed the area and boarded their ships on October 20, 1779. D'Estaing then sailed away to the West Indies. General Lincoln marched his army back to Charleston, which would fall the next year. The second attempt at Franco-American co-operation ended in much the same atmosphere of bitterness and disillusion as the first. As in Rhode Island, this affair displayed poor coordination between the Americans and the French. Each allied commander disliked his counterpart and departed Savannah with a mutual distrust. American and French coordination and cooperation would improve at the Battle of Yorktown in 1781.

The allied defeat at Savannah confirmed the British as masters of Georgia and paved the way for the offensive that would capture Charleston and most of South Carolina the following year. The British would later evacuate Savannah on July 11, 1782.[117]

★ Mr. Gillivray's plantation, guarded by "armed negroes" (most likely the Negro Cavalry Company) was the scene of a great deal of skirmishing on Saturday, October 16, 1779. Congressional troops attacked the African American Loyalists but were driven back "from the Buildings on the Plantation into the Woods." The defenders ran out of ammunition and were obliged to retreat. They lost one man killed and three wounded but they captured "two Rebel Dragoons and eight Horses, and killed two Rebels." A British account notes:

> Saturday, the 16th, in the afternoon there was a "great deal of skirmishing on Mr. Gillivray's plantation, betwixt some Negroes and a Party of Rebels and the latter were several Times driven from the Buildings on the Plantation into the Woods. Want of Ammunition, however, obliged the Blacks to retreat in the Evening, with the loss of one killed, and three of four wounded. The Enemy Loss is not known. There was very little firing this Night from the French, who had sent off all their Cannon except two."[118]

1780

Major General Benjamin Lincoln (1733–1810) ordered Commodore Abraham Whipple (1733–1819) south from Massachusetts with four Continental ships to aid in the defense of Charleston, South Carolina. The squadron consisted of the frigates *Queen of France* and *Boston* and the sloops *Providence* and *Ranger*. The ships passed through a heavy gale northeast of Bermuda and arrived in Charleston on Thursday, December 23, 1779 after a voyage of 27 days. The gale damaged the *Queen of France* so much that a "jury of carpenters" condemned her.

The *Ranger* and the *Providence* were ordered to patrol between Cape Romain, South Carolina and St. Augustine, Florida on Monday, January 17, 1780 to scout for any British transports approaching Charleston. The two ships were becalmed outside the harbor for three days when they spotted a brig in the fog outside the bar to Charleston harbor on the 23rd. They decoyed the captain of the Royal Navy brig into thinking that the Tybee River was the entrance to the Savannah River. The brig followed the *Ranger* and the *Providence* into the harbor and was captured with 17 reinforcements for the New York Volunteers aboard. She was renamed the *General Lincoln*. A British ship captured the *Eagle*, the *Ranger*'s tender, just outside the harbor three days later.[119]

★ Commodore Whipple put out to sea at dawn on Monday, January 24, 1780 and headed south to search for any British navy vessels. He spotted two sloops and a brig off of the Tybee Lighthouse and quickly captured them with a few infantrymen, 40 light dragoons of the British Legion and the Bucks County Light Dragoons, seven or eight officers, and an equal number of passengers aboard. A gale off Cape Hatteras blew the ships off course and they had to throw two horses and the gear for 40 more horses overboard. When Commodore Whipple saw the British fleet on the horizon, he quickly returned to Charleston to alert General Lincoln. The Royal Navy chased two ships on another reconnaissance mission back into Charleston harbor on Thursday, January 27th.[120]

★ Colonels Andrew Pickens (1739–1817) and John Twiggs (1750–1816) joined forces to raid Savannah in February 1780. They engaged Loyalists in several skirmishes at the Ogeechee River before a group of British soldiers arrived, crossed the river, and attacked them. The British then recrossed the river and withdrew.

In one of the skirmishes, Captain Thomas Dooley lost two men killed [Edward or John Corker (d. 1780) and Webb (d. 1780)]. The next day, Colonel Twiggs attacked a party of Colonel Daniel McGirth's (d. ca. 1789) men who had plundered and burned several houses. He retook the property, killed three Loyalists and took five of them prisoners.[121]

See also **Dooly's Fort** p. 35.

★ A detachment of New York Volunteers rode out of Savannah on patrol and was ambushed by Colonels Andrew Pickens (1739–1817) and John Twiggs (1750–1816) and a party of about 300 mounted militiamen on Saturday, March 25, 1780. Most of the militiamen were armed with rifles but a few acted as saber-wielding cavalrymen. The riflemen pinned down the New York Volunteers until the King's Rangers came to their rescue. Pickens's militiamen retreated after plundering and burning Royal Governor Sir James Wright's (1714–1785) rice plantation at Ogeechee. They burned seven of his barns which contained 350 barrels of rice, preventing British collection parties from taking it to Savannah. The Whigs then raided James Butler's plantation, about 2 miles away, and shot four of his slaves and wounded three more.Major General Augustine Prevost (1723–1786) sent Colonel Daniel McGirth (d. ca. 1789) and his light horsemen to search for the militiamen; but the Loyalists were worse than the raiders and provoked much resentment from the civilian population.[122]

★ Major General Augustine Prevost (1723–1786) sent Captain Conklin (d. 1780) with the 1st battalion of Dulaney's corps, consisting of two subalterns and 64 men, to the Ogeechee River to disperse the militiamen in that region. They marched from Savannah at 3 AM on Tuesday, April 4, 1780 and arrived at the Ogeechee ferry about 10. There, some slaves informed Captain Conklin of the number and position of the militiamen. After the Crown forces crossed the Ogeechee, Captain Conklin ordered his ensign and 15 men to file off to the left so as to come upon the militia's right flank.

Colonels Andrew Pickens (1739–1817) and John Twiggs (1750–1816) observed the enemy as they were crossing the river and watched their motions, aware of their plan. They ordered the main body of militiamen to conceal themselves from the enemy's view. They held an advantageous position from which they cut off the Loyalists' right flank. Captain Shadrack Inman (d. 1780) and 20 mounted militiamen appeared in the open to decoy the Loyalists into advancing. They planned to draw the Loyalists into close action and cut off their retreat route.

Pickens and Twiggs took their positions on the flanks and waited for the enemy to approach. They did so with apparent confidence. Captain Inman attacked prematurely, compelling the flanks to engage before the enemy got off the causeway. Captain Conklin was mortally wounded early in the skirmish. Lieutenant Roney assumed command and resorted to the bayonet. He made a desperate charge (see Photo GA-3) and was also wounded. Captain Inman's dragoons pressed the ensign's detachment and compelled them to retreat through the swamp in a rice field where the cavalrymen could not pursue them.

The Loyalists regrouped and carried the wounded to the boats, keeping up a retreating fire until they reached the river. The Loyalists lost two privates killed and seven wounded, including the first and second officers in the command. Captain Conklin died the next morning.[123]

★ Privateer Captain Anthony and his crew of 20 headed up the Ogeechee River to capture a schooner and her cargo of rice during the night of Thursday, July 12, 1781. They captured the schooner, but British Captain Roger (?) Scallan's galley intercepted them before they could get her out to the sea. Anthony lost one man killed and another wounded. He escaped to the shore and rejoined his privateer the following night.[124]

★ Colonel John Twiggs (1750–1816) returned to Georgia after the battle of Blackstock's plantation, South Carolina (Monday, November 20, 1780) to sever communications between Savannah and the British posts at the Great Ogeechee ferry and Sunbury. He sent Lieutenant Colonel James Jackson (1757–1806) with 390 militiamen and Continentals, consisting of Stallings's dragoons, Captain James McKay's riflemen, Captain John Grant's (d. 1781) volunteers and Captain Patrick Carr's Volunteer Dragoons and the Georgia Legion to attack the British post known as the White House at Great Ogeechee Ferry.

They marched from Colonel Twiggs's camp on Monday, October 29, 1781. They arrived at the White House on Friday, November 2. Colonel Jackson encountered a scouting party of Captain William Johnston's (d. 1850) King's Rangers at the White House or Indian Old Fields, near the Ogeechee River Ferry on November 2 and captured two dragoons before they could give the alarm. His prisoners informed him that the British were aware of his intentions even though they did not know his route or that he was already in the vicinity. The British had reinforced the post with about 150 dragoons and 50 to 100 infantrymen in addition to the Loyalist militiamen of the countryside who were divided into three parties about three quarters of a mile from each other.

Captain Johnston was unaware that Jackson had captured his scouts and that Jackson's men were advancing on him in three columns. Captain Patrick ("Paddy") Carr's (1761–1820) troops, one of Colonel James McKay's companies of dragoons and the Georgia Legion were in the center and Colonel McKay's riflemen were on their flanks. Jackson ordered the dragoons to charge through the yard to break any body of horsemen or infantrymen that might be formed. The riflemen were ordered to patrol along each side of the house where the Crown forces had two fortified piazzas. They were also ordered to keep up "a smart fire in case of resistance."

The British took shelter in the house when the dragoons charged. A rifle shot from the house immediately killed Captain Grant who led the riflemen on one of the flanks. His men fled into the swamp with their officers chasing them in a futile attempt to get them to stop. Colonel Jackson's troops attacked so suddenly that Captain Johnston realized it only when the attackers demanded his surrender. He agreed, removed his coat and presented his sword to Colonel Jackson when Captain Carr suddenly killed Captain Thomas Goldsmith (d. 1781), one of Johnston's officers. Captain Johnston, believing that the Whigs would give his men no quarter, raced to the house and ordered his men to retake their weapons and "sell their lives as dear as possible." The action resumed with such energy that Jackson and his men had to retreat, leaving Captain Grant and several of his men dead on the ground and Captain William Bugg of Jackson's militia wounded.

Lieutenant Colonel George Campbell (1732–1799) and his King's American Regiment and a company of the King's Rangers were half a mile away and rode to the fight. They charged into the Georgia militiamen and dispersed them, losing 12 men killed and wounded in close combat.

Jackson's force remained to plunder the Loyalist homes while Captain James McKay rode to Butler's house, a mile from the ferry, where Captain James Howell (1734–1808) and 15 Loyalists were stationed. Although Captain Howell was sick in bed, the Loyalists offered stiff resistance. McKay's party killed five men and captured Howell and five others. The militia had six men killed, seven wounded, and six captured in the engagements.[125]

1781

★ Colonel William Harden's (1743–1785) men continued to harass any British moving between Charleston and Savannah after the battle of Eutaw Springs. A man named Qua piloted a boat down the inland waterway toward Savannah on Friday, September 23, 1781. Captain Palmer of "Lord Charles Greville Montagu's (1741–1784) Regiment and sundry other passengers" were on board. The vessel was ambushed and Captain Palmer's servant was killed before the pilot could surrender. Everyone on board was taken prisoner.[126]

★ Detachments of 182 men from the 7th Regiment (Royal Fusilier) and the light infantry company of the King's American Regiment arrived from Charleston, South Carolina on Saturday, December 22, 1781 to reinforce Lieutenant Colonel George Campbell at Savannah and to protect the town from an anticipated siege. However, this detachment had only one captain and "very few" subalterns.[127]

1782

★ Brigadier General "Mad Anthony" Wayne (1745–1796) crossed the Savannah River at Two Sisters' Ferry on January 12, 1782, with 100 of Colonel Stephen Moylan's (1734–1811) dragoons and a detachment of artillery commanded by Colonel Walton

White (1750–1803) to restore Whig authority in Georgia. Colonel Wade Hampton (1752–1832) with 300 South Carolina mounted infantrymen and Colonel James Jackson (1757–1806) with 170 Georgia militiamen soon joined him. General Wayne needed more men, arms and supplies to accomplish his objective. He requested the governor to create an African-American Regiment but was refused.

Unable to take Savannah with the means at his disposal, Wayne drove the enemy's outposts back into the town, suppressed Loyalist bands and cut off supplies. Lieutenant–Colonel Alured Clark (ca. 1745–1832), commander of Crown forces in Georgia, ordered a scorched-earth policy. As his outposts withdrew, they burned everything they could not carry back into Savannah. Clark also sent out a force to open the way for the Cherokees and Creeks to come help him. Colonel Jackson's Georgia militiamen gave them some stiff resistance. Wayne drove back into British lines any reinforcements sent from Savannah. Wayne's forces could find no supplies there, so he had to bring his supplies and forage from Augusta and South Carolina.

★ Three hundred Creeks approached Wayne's camp, intending to attack the pickets during the night of Saturday, January 22, 1782. They accidentally fell upon the main body at 3 AM. The Continentals drove them off in a fierce fight in which their leader, Guristersigo ("the Magnificent") (1752–1782), and 17 others were killed. General Wayne captured another 12 in the pursuit and executed them at sunrise. British desertions accelerated, especially among the German Loyalist troops.

★ On Sunday morning January 27, 1782, Lieutenant Colonel James McKay and his regiment of rangers were ordered to intercept a band of 26 Creeks marching toward Savannah. McKay and his men disguised themselves as Loyalists and deceived the Creeks, by telling them they were British dragoons. They led the Creeks to Brigadier General "Mad Anthony" Wayne's (1745–1796) camp where they were surrounded and disarmed without a fight. General Wayne tried to convince the Creeks of his peaceable intentions toward them. He turned his captives over to Colonel James Jackson's (1757–1806) Georgia Legion, but they escaped about a week later. Colonel Walton White's (1750–1803) dragoons recaptured some of them.

Brigadier General Alexander Leslie (1740–1794), British commander in the South, was concerned that he could not continue operations and proposed a truce to Major General Nathanael Greene (1742–1786). Colonel Clark and governor Sir James Wright (1714–1785) suggested a truce to General Wayne. The Continental officers saw this as a ploy and continued the siege, which lasted for six months before the British evacuated the city for Charleston on July 10 and 11th. They took 4,000 Loyalists and 5,000 slaves with them. General Wayne entered Savannah as soon as the last Crown troops departed.[128]

★ Major John Habersham (d. 1782) and his men crossed at Ogeechee Ferry about an hour after dark on Wednesday, January 30, 1782 and camped at Sir James Wright's (1714–1785) plantation. They intended to prevent a party of 300 Choctaws from reaching Savannah. Despite a heavy rainfall that continued for two days, Major Habersham marched all day and camped at Holden's. The following morning, Captain Patrick ("Paddy") Carr (1761–1820) reported that his men refused to march any further due to the rain and the condition of the road.

Major Habersham represented himself as being Lieutenant Colonel Thomas Alexander Brown (1744–1814), whose name and reputation were familiar to the Choctaws, and succeeded in getting several Choctaws to join him. However, Lieutenant Oswald and some of the militiamen disobeyed orders and killed several Choctaws. They brought some of them into the woods, tied them to trees, shot and cut them to pieces, claiming they were enemy Chickasaws. The Choctaws gradually realized that Habersham and his men were not British and Habersham's mission fell apart.

★ Lieutenant Oswald's men raided the Scots' settlement in St. Andrew's Parish during the first week of February 1782. They killed 11 Loyalists residing there. Captain Samuel West's men and some of the dragoons decided to leave without permission.[129]

★ Samuel West, now a major commanding a detachment from Carr's Independent Corps and the Liberty County Militia, pursued Colonel Daniel McGirth's (d. ca. 1789) Loyalists on the south side of the Ogeechee River in February 1782. The two parties engaged and at least one Whig, Daniel Danielly (or Dannelly), was wounded.[130]

★ Colonel Hezekiah Williams, commanding 50 Loyalists and Native Americans left Savannah about 11 AM on Wednesday, February 13, 1782 to attack Colonel James Jackson (1757–1806) who was encamped at Cuthbert's sawmill on Hutchinson Island. The Loyalists fired first, wounding two or three of Jackson's men. However, the two forces were separated by an unfordable creek and the bridges had been destroyed. Both sides fired at each other at long range until nearly sundown. Jackson sent a party of infantrymen along the creek bank in an attempt to flank Williams. However, the Loyalists retreated before Jackson's men got into position.[131]

★ In February 1782, there was a considerable quantity of unthreshed rice on Hutchinson Island, opposite Savannah, and a large amount of stacked rice on Royal Governor Sir James Wright's (1714–1785) plantation, about half a mile southeast of Savannah. Brigadier General "Mad Anthony" Wayne (1745–1796) ordered Brigadier General John Barnwell (1748–1800) to burn the rice on Hutchinson Island while Colonel James Jackson (1757–1806) destroyed the rice at Governor Wright's plantation.

Loyalist militia Lieutenant Colonel Andrew De Veaux, Jr. (1758–1812) (also spelled DeVeaux) arrived at Beaufort, South Carolina and destroyed all the boats General Barnwell had collected for this mission. Despite the loss of his boats, General Barnwell could not offer any serious opposition with his small force of 50 men of the St. Helena Volunteer Militia Company. Nor could he execute his orders to destroy the rice; so he ordered his brother, Lieutenant Colonel Edward Barnwell (1757–1808), to take 50 men in boats to cross the river to burn the rice on the island. Barnwell and his men set out at 1:30 AM on Wednesday, February 26, 1782. They planned to land on Hutchinson Island at 2 AM. However, a spy reported their intentions to Lieutenant Colonel De Veaux who sailed to the Back River, between Hutchinson Island and South Carolina, to prevent Barnwell's troops from reaching the rice stores.

The Loyalists ambushed Barnwell's men as they approached Rochester's Ferry. Barnwell lost two men killed and four wounded in the sharp exchange of fire. One of Barnwell's boats went aground as they retreated. Three of the men who could not swim were captured. DeVeaux claimed he destroyed the boats and put the Whigs "to the bayonet."

When the Loyalists ambushed Barnwell's men, General Wayne ordered Jackson and Major Francis Moore (d. 1782) to cover Barnwell's retreat. Jackson's 30 dragoons drove in the British pickets and accomplished their mission "in the presence of the whole British army" and escaped "through a camp of 200 Tories and refugees, who had been inoculated with the Small pox & were altogether at his mercy." Wayne observed that Savannah "was highly illuminated at the expense of Sir James Wright."

General Wayne reported to Major General Nathanael Greene (1742–1786) that, if Barnwell had been successful in destroying the forage on Hutchinson Island, the British cavalry would have been "annihilated." Greene replied, "Your maneuver in the destruction of the enemies forage was capital. How strange to tell that the enemy are hounded with less than one third their numbers."[132]

★ The garrison at Savannah was running low on provisions in March 1782. The Crown forces needed to send heavily armed foraging parties into the countryside to search for food. Brigadier General "Mad Anthony" Wayne (1745–1796) learned, toward the end of March 1782, that the Crown forces were preparing to send out another foraging party. General Wayne's troops attacked the foraging party and some Choctaw warriors 3 miles from Savannah on Friday, March 22, 1782. Wayne's dragoons charged immediately. The Crown troops responded in force but the dragoons pushed them back. As the Crown troops retreated, the Choctaws killed and scalped Major John Habersham (d. 1782), one of the dragoons, in view of "the British officers and troops, who were out in force, but retreated with precipitation." When they returned to Savannah, the lieutenant governor and other British officers led a parade through the streets of Savannah. The Choctaws displayed the scalp they had captured and mangled and disfigured the dragoon's dead body, cutting off the upper lip and nose and chopping up the face. About 300 squaws took part in a day of rejoicing on the green near Fort Prevost (formerly Fort Bulloch or the Garden Battery) that culminated with a dance on Friday, April 5. General Wayne threatened retaliation, stating "we have since taken a Chickasaw chief, . . . we shall hold him, who, with the first British officer that falls into our hands will eventually be sacrificed to the manner of that brave unfortunate dragoon."[133]

★ Captain James Swinney was involved in a conflict with Governor John Adam Treutlen (1726–1782) one night in March 1782 at Ebenezer. Swinney received several wounds in the fight that left Governor Treutlen dead. The Treutlen family claims that five Loyalists rode up to the Treutlen house and demanded that Treutlen come outside. When he refused, the men set fire to the house, forcing Treutlen, his wife and children to come outside. The men seized Treutlen and killed him in full view of his family. However, Loyalist activity in the area was almost non-existent at this time. As Treutlen had married his third wife only a few days earlier, some people think his murderer may have been a jilted suitor. Captain Swinney received a pension from the British for his wounds.[134]

★ After the combined Franco-American forces failed to retake Savannah in December 1779, some 1,500 Crown forces reoccupied New Ebenezer on March 6, 1780 which remained under their control in May of 1781 when 200 Hessians were garrisoned there. New Ebenezer was again firmly under Whig control in April 1782, as Brigadier General "Mad Anthony" Wayne (1745–1796) and his force occupied the town and made it their headquarters. The British made an unsuccessful cavalry and infantry sortie on New Ebenezer in May, in an attempt to remove Wayne from the town (see **Morgan's Fort; Ogeechee River** p. 53).[135]

★ Lieutenant Colonel George Campbell, of the Queen's Rangers, led another foraging party on Tuesday, April 2, 1782. The party consisted of a line of dragoons and about 90 infantrymen, nearly 100 Loyalist militiamen, and all of the Native American warriors in the vicinity of Savannah. They marched about 8 miles into the surrounding territory and returned that same evening with "a quantity of Forrage."[136]

★ A band of armed Whigs, with blackened faces, raided the home of Mrs. Ann Parker at the Isle of Hope in Christ Church Parish during the night of April 3, 1782. A Loyalist report stated that the raiders stole her property, slashed her son, James Parker, with a cutlass and beat and threatened other members of the household. Governor Sir James Wright (1714–1785) offered a reward of £20 for the arrest of the culprits.[137]

★ Major Philip Dill (d. 1782) and a party of 30 Loyalists headed up the Savannah River just before daylight on Sunday, April 14, 1782. They landed at William Knox's (1732–1810) house, and ambushed five of Lieutenant Colonel James Jackson's (1757–1806) dragoons and their guide. Seventeen balls "passed through the house." The Whigs returned fire with one rifle and one pistol and drove off the Loyalists. John Gotlieb Snider (Schneider) (1752–1894) shot and killed Major Dill and one of the dragoons wounded two Loyalists with his pistol.[138]

★ The HMS *Retrieve* sank off Tybee Roads on Wednesday, May 1, 1782. Lieutenant Colonel von Porbeck reported:

> We have had some unusually hot weather for the last ten days. Today we had a very severe thunderstorm, accompanied by a gale which caused a ship to capsize and sink. It had been moored about two English miles off this town. The ship was called *Retrieve*, and was owned at London. She was of 300 tons, had a crew of 35, and 20 cannon, was armed by the Royal Government. She had many presents aboard from the Indies which were lost together with nine sailors who were drowned when she sank.[139]

★ Captain Bryce of the artillery received information about Thursday or Friday, May 2 or 3, 1782, that a party of Loyalists was driving a herd of cattle to Savannah from the South Carolina side of the river. Without waiting for support, Bryce mounted three of his artillerymen and pursued the Loyalists with two or three guides. They fell in with them 4 miles from Savannah and captured three Loyalists and 170 head of cattle.[140]

★ Brigadier General "Mad Anthony" Wayne (1745–1796) received intelligence on Wednesday, May 15, 1782 that the British had assembled a large supply of provisions and 300 to 400 head of cattle and horses at a base on the St. Marys River. The provisions were intended for the garrison in Savannah and for their Native American allies. General Wayne ordered Captain Patrick ("Paddy") Carr (1761–1820) and 50 or 60 of his volunteers to surprise this post and destroy the supplies.[141]

★ Loyalist Governor James Wright (1714–1785), embarrassed by the raids of Colonels Andrew Pickens (1739–1817) and John Twiggs (1750–1816) and the Second Battle of Ogeechee River, dispatched a force of 66 men to halt them. Brigadier General Elijah Clarke (1781–1783) sent out a party of 100 men, consisting of volunteer militiamen and a few regulars under the command of captains James Ingram (ca. 1749–1795) and William Corker, on Sunday, May 19, 1782. They crossed the Great Ogeechee River the next morning and broke into small detachments to collect cattle. They recrossed the Ogeechee with their booty when Lieutenant Colonel James Jackson's Georgia Legion ambushed Captain Ingram's detachment on their way back to Savannah.

Brigadier General "Mad Anthony" Wayne's (1745–1796) scouts observed the movements of the Loyalists and communicated them to the general who decided to take advantage of the thick, low woods through which they must pass. He sent his dragoons to annoy their front and flank. A sharp skirmish ensued. Jackson's 20 dragoons attacked the front guard (Captain Isaac Atwood's (1741–1812) dragoons) and drove it in upon the main body. They then pursued Jackson who gave them another fire and withdrew again. He retreated about 3 miles to Struthers' or Strother's plantation where the Loyalists posted themselves on each side of the road, in a swamp. They fired at the front guard and retreated. General Clarke sent another detachment of 260 infantrymen and 80 dragoons to reinforce Captain Ingram's detachment at Little Ogeechee, 8 miles from Savannah.

General Wayne put his whole force in motion to intercept the enemy's retreat but his men had a difficult time marching across the swampy country, so they did not reach their destination until 10 PM. Wayne ordered Captain Alexander Parker and his 60 infantry-men to take possession of Baillou's causeway. As Captain Parker moved into position, on Tuesday, May 21, 1782, he discovered a small patrol of enemy cavalry in his front. Both parties advanced until they met. When the captain of the dragoons demanded the countersign, the Crown officer, either from confusion or mistake, advanced until it was too late to correct his error. Captain Parker's dragoons captured the officer and 18 dragoons. Only one escaped to alert Lieutenant Colonel Thomas Alexander Brown (1744–1814) whose column was arriving at the causeway.

The dragoons and infantrymen charged the Loyalists about midnight, throwing their cavalry into confusion and pressing upon the columns of infantrymen. The causeway was too narrow for either to act effectively, so the Crown forces fell back without much loss, as General Wayne could not get up in time to press his advantage. They killed five Crown troops and wounded others, including the second in command. General Wayne lost two men killed and three wounded in the van and two men killed and one wounded during the day. He anticipated bringing Brown into a general action the next morning; but Brown had a number of militiamen who knew the country well and guided him through deep swamps to White Bluff where he arrived before daylight and arrived safe in Savannah the next morning.[142]

★ Lieutenant Colonel Stephen Johnson's Effingham County Militia, posted on the Ogeechee River, ambushed Captain Benjamin Brantley's Loyalists as they crossed the river into Effingham at the end of May 1782. The militiamen killed Brantley and any of his men caught in the water and unable to escape. They captured the rest of Brantley's Loyalists and tried them by court-martial for murdering Myrick Davies (1742–1781), the Whig lieutenant governor of Georgia, and Joel Lewis. Several of them were executed in Savannah, on June 4, the King's birthday.[143]

★ Lieutenant Colonel Thomas Alexander Brown (1744–1814) and Chief Emistisiguo (1752–1782) or Emistesego ("the Big Fellow") or Guristersigo ("the Magnificent") (1752–1782) led a party of 300 Creeks and some whites to attack Brigadier General "Mad Anthony" Wayne's (1745–1796) camp at the Three Sisters Ferry on the Ogeechee Road, about 5 miles from Savannah. They advanced through the whole state of Georgia unnoticed, except by two boys who were taken and killed. The Crown forces learned that General Wayne was at the Gibbons plantation near Savannah. There were two plantations with the same name in the area, both owned by widows named Gibbons. A picket guard occupied the "upper Mrs. [Joseph] Gibbons' plantation" 7 miles from Savannah, while General Wayne and his main body occupied the "lower Mrs. [Barack] Gibbons."

Their white guides informed the Crown leaders of General Wayne's position, but they were unaware that he moved every night to avoid surprise. Wayne's main body decamped late Saturday evening, June 22, 1782 and exchanged place with the pickets. They now held the post, at the lower Mrs. Gibbons's plantation, which Chief Emistisiguo planned to attack.

Captain Alexander Parker commanded the artillery, the cavalry and the light infantry of Lieutenant Major Thomas Posey's (d. 1818) regiment placed in the rear of the camp at Mrs. Barack Gibbons's plantation. He posted a guard and chain of sentinels. Major Posey's 7th Virginia Regiment was posted in the front, with a guard and chain of sentinels, a few hundred yards ahead on the road leading by Mrs. Gibbons's to Savannah. The light infantry came up from Savannah to join them. They took their post in the rear of the camp, near the artillery. General Wayne posted only one sentinel from the quarter-guard on the main road to his rear—the very road which Chief Emistisiguo planned to take.

The Creeks emerged from their hiding places in the deep swamps soon after nightfall on the 23rd and advanced in silence. They approached General Wayne's camp about 3 AM on Monday, June 24, 1782 when they halted and prepared for battle. Believing the camp consisted of only a small detachment, Chief Emistisiguo sent a small party to surprise and kill the guard, after which they would signal the main body to press forward. The braves did their duty and the whole force attacked General Wayne's rear, yelling and using their tomahawks, spears, scalping-knives and guns.

General Wayne and Major Posey had wrapped themselves in their cloaks and lay down close to each other. Their men were in a profound sleep. When the alarm roused the officers, they were soon met by Captain Parker who reported that the sudden attack confused his men and requested orders. Colonel Posey ordered the light infantrymen to rally behind the house. He and Captain Parker soon rallied the men and led them in a bayonet charge (see Photo GA-3). Both sides fought hand-to-hand with tomahawks, swords and bayonets. Posey himself had killed one or more of the enemy as well as Sergeant Thompson (d. 1782) of Parker's light infantry. Sergeant Thompson had disobeyed orders and taken off his coat and tied a handkerchief around his head. Even though he was actively engaged in the fight, because of his appearance, Major Posey mistook him for a Creek, in the smoky darkness, and thrust his sword through Sergeant Thompson's body.

The Crown forces drove a light company in the rear of Major Posey's battalion and took possession of two pieces of artillery. Captain Alexander Parker immediately rallied the company placed there to protect those pieces and advanced on the Crown forces along with Captain James Gunn's (1753–1801) 1st Continental Dragoon company despite the heavy fire and hideous yelling from every direction. Major Posey and Major Samuel Findley (1752–1829) charged the Crown forces in flank at the same time.

Major Posey then filed off to the right to rejoin his regiment and led his men in a charge on the enemy's rear that put them to flight. General Wayne filed off to the left with the cavalry and encountered a large body of Creeks. His horse was killed and, sword in hand, he led Captain Parker's infantry and the quarter-guard. They drove the Creeks back toward the cannon where Chief Emistisiguo and some of his warriors tried to capture the guns. The Continentals soon routed the Creeks, mortally wounding Chief Emistisiguo just as he was about to kill Wayne. "After receiving an espontoon (see Photo GA-19) and three bayonets in his body, encouraging his warriors all the while, [Emistisiguo] retired a few paces, composedly laid himself down, and died without a groan or struggle." Chief Emistisiguo was 30 years old, weighed about 220 pounds, and was six feet three inches tall. After his death, the rest of his men fled. The Continentals also killed 14 Creeks and two white men, captured a British standard and 117 pack-horses loaded with pelts. General Wayne suffered five men and horses killed and eight wounded.

General Wayne expected the Creeks and the British to make a combined attack, so he prepared to receive them at the same time as he tried to prevent them from joining forces. He scattered his troops in every direction to pursue the fleeing Creeks. Major Posey headed toward Savannah "to ascertain the situation of the British." When his regiment reached the forks of the road, about a mile from town, he detached a small party to observe the British guards and to determine whether they retained their usual positions. The scouting party soon returned and reported that they did.

A trooper arrived, shortly afterward, with information that he discovered a large body of men less than half a mile to the rear. However, it was too dark for him to distinguish

GA-19. Spontoon. The spontoon is a sergeant's symbol of authority. It can be used as a weapon, but it is more commonly used to line up and manage the troops. The sergeant leading the column is carrying a spontoon.

whether they were Creeks or British. Major Posey marched immediately and ordered the trooper to show him where he discovered the enemy. As they approached, Major Posey saw that they were Creeks standing in a road leading through a large swamp.

While the regiment prepared for battle, about a dozen Creeks advanced about 20 or 30 paces and halted, looking intently, unsure whether the soldiers were British troops or the enemy. Major Posey noticed that the main body had retired and hid in the swamp, so he waved his sword for the few Creeks to advance. As they approached, Major Posey ordered them placed under guard. His troops then searched the swamp for the others but could not find any of them.

Major Posey returned to the forks of the road. General Wayne arrived a short while later with the rest of the troops. "The general appeared in a good humor until he discovered the Indian prisoners, his countenance then changed, and he asked Posey in a very peremptory manner, how he could think of taking those savages prisoners. Posey related the circumstance of the manner in which they were decoyed, and observed that he thought it wrong to put them to death after they became prisoners; he said they should not live, and they were accordingly put to death."[144]

1783

★ Loyalist privateers, captains Manson and Peter Hare (1748–1834), captured several vessels along the southern Georgia coast in January 1783. They took a schooner bound from East Florida to South Carolina. They then captured a vessel sailing from Savannah to Charleston with a cargo of 13 barrels of flour. They also "plundered" several canoes traveling south from Carolina, stealing the provisions they carried and kidnapping the slaves who happened to be aboard.

Manson and Hare sailed their two "whale boats" (see Photo GA-11) into Tybee Roads on Thursday, January 30, 1783. They sent some raiders up the Back River in canoes to kidnap two slaves and a Mr. Allison. The raiders released Allison when they returned down river. Captain John Howell set out in his galley the following day to pursue the raiders but they escaped.[145]

Brunswick County (Feb. 20, 1776)
John Ancrum's Plantation

Brunswick, the county seat of Brunswick County, now Glynn County, is in south-eastern Georgia, south of the Altamaha River. John Ancrum's plantation may have been on the southern part of the peninsula.

A party of Rebels under Captain Dupre routed 50 men from Captain Francis Parry's HMS *Cruizer* who were pillaging John Ancrum's (1724–1799) plantation in Brunswick County on Tuesday, February 20, 1776.[146]

Cherokee Campaign of 1776 (July 1, 1776–May 20, 1777) see **Tennessee.**

Beaverdam Creek (ca. July 25, 1776) see **Beaver Creek, Pennsylvania** in *The Guide to the American Revolutionary War in Pennsylvania, Delaware, Maryland, Virginia and North Carolina.*

Townsend
Fort Barrington/Fort Howe (Oct. 27, 1776; July or Aug. 1777; March 13, 1778; June 4, 1778)

Fort Barrington was a pine and earthen fort built in 1751 to protect the King's Road, the major north-south route across the Altamaha River along the southern frontier of Georgia. It was named for Lieutenant Colonel Josiah (or Jessiah) Barrington and later renamed Fort Howe after General Robert Howe, commander of the Southern Department. It was located 2 miles below town on a bank of the north side of the Altamaha River (see Photo GA-20), near Lower Sansavilla, 20 feet above the 300-yard-wide river.

Fort Barrington was a 70-square foot wooden stockade with 4 bastions (see Photo GA-21), a two-story wooden blockhouse (see Photo GA-1) and a gun on each wall. Many prominent figures on both sides of the American War of Independence served at this important post. The fort was only 13 miles from the coast in a direct line, but it was 30 miles by the winding river. Nothing remains of the fort.[147]

To get to the site of Fort Barrington from Townsend, take Steel Bridge Road south-west from route GA 57 near its intersection with route GA 250/GA 251 (Briardam Road). Proceed for 4.5 miles to the end. Turn left on Old River Road. Go 1.6 miles and turn right (west) onto a local or rural road that ends at Barrington Road, a dirt road, after 1.9 miles. Turn right on Barrington Road and go about a mile to the approximate site of the fort on the east bank of the Altamaha River.

From Darien, take route GA 251 west from route US 17 a short distance north of Darien. At the fork of route GA 251 and Cox Road (about 4.3 miles), bear left and follow Cox Road, which was the Old River Road, for about 5.5 miles to Barrington Road, an unmarked dirt road which branches to the left. Follow Barrington Road for about 3.2 miles to a fork that leads to a boat landing and picnic area. Just off the left

GA-20. *Altamaha River at the site of Fort Barrington*

fork of the road in the woods might be the remains of breastworks. The center of the fort was probably in the camp area there.

A band of Floridians and their Creek allies destroyed the plantation of William Williams, just south of the Altamaha River, on Friday, October 27, 1776. They then crossed the river and attacked Fort Barrington which had been recently occupied and was defended by only 18 men. This party of Creeks is the only one known to be working with the British at this time. It consisted of a Chiaha chief and a hunting party of 18 or 19 warriors. They attacked 40 Georgia Rangers, killed four and wounded two. They then returned safely to East Florida. The South Carolina Horse came to Georgia's assistance, but they arrived too late.

★ The Creeks were divided between pacifists and dissidents. When the Chiaha party's bragging about their exploits encouraged other tribes, the Creeks became more active in December 1776. One party brought Georgia scalps and prisoners to John Stuart (ca. 1710–1779), Superintendent of the Southern Indian Department, at Pensacola, Florida. Tallachie, one of the principal chiefs of the Lower Creeks, assured Governor Patrick Tonyn (1725–1804) that all the Native American tribes would support the British.

General Lachlan McIntosh (1727–1806) received information by Thursday, December 12, 1776 that the Creeks and a large party of horsemen were near the St. Marys River preparing to raid south Georgia. After conferring with Brigadier General Robert Howe (1732–1786), commander of the Southern Department, he ordered Captain William McIntosh (1726–1801) to occupy Fort Barrington, renamed Fort Howe, and to supervise the construction of stockades at Beard's Bluff, the Satilla and the St. Marys.

★ General Robert Howe (1732–1786) directed that all recruits be forwarded to the posts on the Alatamaha River as soon as they were enlisted, as the southern frontier was

GA-21. Bastion is a fortification with a projecting part of a wall to protect the main walls of the fortification. Shown are (top) the northwest bastion of Fort George (Castine, ME) and the entrance to the southwest bastion (lower left of photo) and (bottom) the northeast stone bastion of Fort Ticonderoga.

very exposed. A party of 150 Loyalists and Latchoway Seminoles attacked a group of 20 of these new recruits within 2 miles of Fort Howe in July or August 1777. The recruits were crossing a thick bay swamp when they were attacked and 14 of them killed. Lieutenants John Brown (1736–1803) and Enoch Anderson (1753–1824), in command, escaped with only six of the men.

Colonel James Screven (1744–1778) received the news of the attack the next morning. He mustered the southern militia and summoned Lieutenant Colonel John McIntosh (1755–1826) and his regulars from Darien to bury the dead. They proceeded to the location of the attack where they found the dead, unburied and scalped. Their bodies were ripped open, their intestines scattered about on the ground, and their faces mangled beyond recognition. The attackers had already crossed the river at Reid's Bluff (on the southwest side of the Altamaha River at the point where the modern Wayne-Glynn County lines meet in the river) and were already beyond reach, on their way to St. Augustine, Florida.[148]

★ Major General Augustine Prevost (1723–1786) received intelligence, in February 1778, that the Whigs were preparing for another invasion of Florida, even though a stream of refugees from the South Carolina backcountry strengthened Crown forces in East Florida. Many small parties of five or six men each were reported in Georgia traveling from Carolina into Florida. The Floridians took the initial action while the Continental Congress was discussing plans for the invasion of East Florida with a force under Major General Robert Howe (1732–1786) and Colonel Samuel Elbert (1740–1788).

Lieutenant Colonel Thomas Alexander Brown (1744–1814) and his East Florida Rangers made an increasing number of raids into Georgia from East Florida during the spring of 1778, putting pressure on General Robert Howe to take the offensive. Brown led a party of 100 East Florida Rangers and 10 Creeks against Fort Barrington during the night of Thursday, March 12, 1778 to stop or delay the third expedition against St. Augustine, Florida (see **Florida, St. Augustine** pp. 113–120). They swam across the chilly Altamaha, which was about a quarter of a mile wide near the fort at that time of year, and stormed the fortifications before sunrise, catching the garrison completely off guard and forcing them to surrender. The attackers lost one man killed and four wounded. They killed two, wounded one, and captured the fort and 23 men, two artillery pieces and two swivel guns (see Photo GA-2). The Florida Rangers destroyed the cannon, burned the fort, ran off the cattle and moved south to St. Augustine with their prisoners when they learned that a large force of Georgia Whigs was headed there. Some of the Rangers were sent to Georgia and South Carolina while Colonel Brown withdrew to Fort Tonyn on the St. Marys with the rest.[149]

Major General Prevost thought that the destruction of Fort Howe was not important. Except for a small force downriver from Darien near the coast, the Georgians now had no posts on the St. Marys, the Satilla or the Altamaha rivers. The Florida Rangers could now raid cattle herds with no opposition. This victory, 50 miles behind enemy lines, gave the Florida Rangers a vital link to Loyalists in South Carolina and an advanced position from which they could raid developed areas in the northern part of Georgia. While the Georgia militiamen could stop large groups of Loyalists, they were virtually ineffective against smaller groups. This victory now allowed even large groups to travel the backcountry unopposed.[150]

★ A party of about 16 Native Americans killed and partially scalped a gunsmith named Seeds (d. 1778) on the road between Fort Howe and Reid's Bluff (on the south side of the river 2 miles downstream from Fort Howe) on Thursday morning, June 4, 1778. Major Bernard Romans (ca. 1720–ca. 1784) and Captain George Young of the artillery, who had crossed the Altamaha just 10 minutes after Seeds, found the bodies of the man and his mare. Some privates on a honey-hunting expedition saw the Native Americans, pursued them into a swamp but failed to capture them.[151]

Waverly
Fort McIntosh on the Satilla (Feb. 2–4, 1777; Feb. 18, 1777)
Fort McIntosh (Feb. 17–18, 1777)

Captain Taylor's house on the St. Marys River was fortified and renamed Fort McIntosh for Captain George McIntosh who garrisoned it with a detachment of the 60th

Regiment, known as the "Royal Americans." This may be the same site known as Fort Tonyn in Hilliard, Florida, opposite Greenville, Georgia.

A party of Creeks with the British forces discovered a Rebel fort on the Satilla River, 26 miles from Fort McIntosh on the St. Marys River (probably Fort Tonyn). It was "built of split puncheons . . . the earth thrown up about four feet and secured by small pines from the ditch upwards—the ditch was only begun upon—the flanks and curtain extended about Sixty paces." It was on the north bank of the Satilla River about halfway between the present-day towns of Waycross and Jessup, southwest of Jekyll Island and east of route I-95. It was a stockade made of split puncheons located on rising ground 80 yards from the river's north bank. It was 100 feet square with a bastion (see Photo GA-21) in each corner and a blockhouse (see Photo GA-1) in the center. It was built to protect the King's Road, the major north–south route of the day, and was garrisoned by 50 Continentals under the command of Captain Richard Winn (1750–1818). Period accounts also refer to this fort as "Fort McIntosh" but, to differentiate the two, the one in Waverly is usually called "Fort McIntosh on the Satilla."[152]

East Florida experienced a food shortage late in 1776 and early 1777 as refugees, Native Americans and rangers went to St. Augustine, Florida for protection. They consumed large quantities of food, causing the military stores to run out. They only had 221 barrels of flour, eight barrels of pork, and six tierces (app. 252 gallons) of rice on February 3, 1777. Governor Patrick Tonyn (1725–1804) requested Brigadier General Augustine Prevost (1723–1786) for authorization to conduct a cattle raid in Georgia in early 1777 and to send a detachment of troops to support the Rangers and Creeks. Prevost made all kinds of excuses and refused to cooperate, so Tonyn decided to risk going into Georgia without protection rather than face certain starvation.

Some accounts say that Lieutenant Colonel Thomas Alexander Brown (1744–1814) assembled his Florida Rangers and led them on raids from a base of the St. Marys River. They approached Fort McIntosh, named for General Lachlan McIntosh (1727–1806) and located on the left (northeast) bank of the Satilla River in southern Georgia, on Sunday, February 2, 1777. Colonel Brown advanced with a flag of truce to demand the fort's surrender. Captain Richard Winn (1750–1818) requested an hour to consider the demand. Colonel Brown agreed but, when the time had expired, Winn refused to surrender, fearing the Seminoles would torture and scalp him and his men. The Seminoles set fire to the woods around the fort, giving the signal for the Loyalists to begin the attack. This diversion allowed the East Florida Rangers to advance up the road undetected. The Rangers and Seminoles surrounded the fort, taking cover behind small trees and brush that had not been removed when the fort was built. They also cut off access to the only water supply outside the fort. The defenders of Fort McIntosh ran out of ammunition and provisions in the seven-hour battle that ended at nightfall. They reported four dead and three wounded. The remaining 68 were captured. The attackers lost only one Seminole who was wounded in the neck. The Crown forces continued firing on the fort until the next day. The garrison surrendered after two days. They were all paroled except for two officers who were taken to St. Augustine as hostages.[153]

★ Most accounts say the attack occurred on Tuesday, February 18, 1777. Brigadier General Augustine Prevost (1723–1786) ordered Lieutenant Colonel Lewis Valentine Fuser (d. 1780) to lead a raid with 162 Regulars comprised of 49 men from Captain Patrick Murray's light company of the 4th battalion of the 60th Regiment; 18 grenadiers of the 2nd battalion of the 60th Regiment; 54 men, probably from the 3rd Battalion of the 60th Regiment commanded by Captain George Mcintosh; 17 light infantrymen of the 14th and 16th Regiments; 22 East Florida Rangers from St. Augustine, about 75 Creeks and two interpreters (John Hambly and John Proctor) and Dr. Williams. This was comparable to the entire regular military strength of Georgia at the time.

They headed north from St. Augustine, Florida on the King's Road with a band of Seminoles and a battery of field pieces in February 1777. They passed through Cowford at the St. Johns River, then marched to the St. Marys River where they stopped at Captain William Taylor's house at King's Ferry. They fortified the area and named it Fort McIntosh, probably as a bit of humor, as they were marching to attack the Whig fort in Georgia with the same name. Captain George McIntosh garrisoned the new fort with a detachment of the 60th Regiment. The fort may be the same one later known as Fort Tonyn (see **Florida** pp. 113–120). Lieutenant Colonel Brown's Rangers and Creeks then headed for the southernmost post of the Georgia Whigs, a new stockade fort on the Satilla River.[154]

The Crown forces found 30 tierces (1,260 gallons) of rice 7 miles from Fort McIntosh. Captain Patrick Murray and a party of 50 men of the 60th Regiment (Royal Americans) filled their haversacks and knapsacks with the rice but could only take six tierces (252 gallons). Captain David Squires's Loyalist sloop *Otter* took the remaining 1,008 gallons of rice.

A band of 20 East Florida Rangers, 75 Seminoles and Loyalists were the first to reach Fort McIntosh on the Satilla River on Monday, February 17, 1777. They tried to ambush and capture three Continentals who walked out of the fort to cut wood. One of the Seminoles let out a war whoop. Captain Patrick Murray reported that one of the Seminoles wounded one of the Continentals with his tomahawk as he was filling buckets with water from the creek. A "warm fire from every quarter" broke out, and the Crown forces "kept up a smart fire on the garrison for about five hours."

Captain Richard Winn (1750–1818) of the 3rd Regiment of South Carolina Horse commanded the garrison of 50 men from the 3rd Regiment of South Carolina Continentals and a detachment of about 20 men from the 1st Battalion of Georgia Continentals.

Colonel Brown demanded an unconditional surrender which Captain Winn refused. The Crown forces renewed the attack which continued until late afternoon, inflicting a number of casualties. The wounded suffered greatly as there was no surgeon to treat them. As night approached, the rangers withdrew a short distance, leaving a guard around the fort.

As soon as it was dark, Winn sent an express to Fort Howe on the Altamaha River, about 25 miles to the northeast, requesting assistance. The express arrived about daylight the next day and was told the 40-man garrison could not spare any men.

When Lieutenant Colonel Lewis Valentine Fuser (d. 1780), of the 60th Regiment, learned that Captain Winn had sent a rider to Fort Howe to ask for reinforcements, he and his men set out immediately. They marched all night and joined Brown's rangers the next morning. When Colonel Fuser arrived with 150 Regulars from his camp 20 miles away, he sent a messenger to Captain Winn, asking him to examine the attacking forces formed in a single line in front of the fort. Meanwhile, Lieutenant Colonel Brown ordered the Seminoles not to shoot at any occupants of the fort who were observing the troops.

The attack resumed at 9 AM. Fuser demanded the fort's surrender again at 3 PM. His ammunition nearly exhausted and his provisions insufficient for more than one day, Winn concluded that it was best to make terms while he still had means of defense rather than to be reduced to the necessity of an unconditional surrender.

Colonel Fuser and Captain Winn drew up the articles of capitulation. Winn insisted "that for the further safety of the prisoners against Indian treachery, a complete company of British regulars should escort them to the Altamaha, opposite to Fort Howe, and that the British commander should be responsible for the conduct of the Indians and Florida Rangers toward the prisoners." Fuser refused to agree to this condition, saying that he would only be responsible for the conduct of the British Regulars. Winn broke off the negotiations and returned to the fort to acquaint his men (see cover photo) with the situation. They prepared for a renewal of hostilities when Fuser reopened the negotiations and agreed to Winn's demand.

Captain Winn and Lieutenant Toles marched out and surrendered the garrison about sunset. Lieutenants John Milton (ca. 1740–1817) and William Caldwell (1765–1840) were taken as hostages under the terms of the capitulation and confined in the fort at St. Augustine for nine months, until exchanged. The other prisoners were paroled. After the usual ceremonies, they proceeded about 2 miles in the direction of Fort Howe under an escort. Early in the evening, after they made camp, the Crown officers and soldiers who composed the guard, gradually disappeared and returned to their camp, leaving the prisoners without a guard by 10 PM. Captain Winn suspected that some treachery was imminent for him and his men who were left without protection or means of defense. He roused his men and headed toward Fort Howe through the woods to avoid getting caught by the Seminoles. They traveled 35 miles through bays, swamps, and ponds and reached Fort Howe about 10 o'clock the following morning.

Meanwhile, Lieutenant Colonel Francis Marion (1732–1795) and 107 men of the 2nd and 5th South Carolina Regiments, with four guns of the 4th South Carolina Artillery and two sloops, hurried to reinforce Fort McIntosh, but they arrived too late. When he learned of the surrender, Marion immediately returned to Charleston, South Carolina.

★ Another relief force of about 300 men was ambushed less than 4 miles away when they came under fire from four rangers. They lost six men killed or wounded, halted and made camp.

Colonel Fuser occupied Fort McIntosh, but three days later, he learned that an army was on the march to intercept him. The Crown forces burned Fort McIntosh and proceeded to Fort Howe (formerly Barrington) on the Altamaha River, taking with them 2,000 head of cattle, which had been brought in by the East Florida Rangers. The fort was commanded by Captain Chesley Bostick (1740–1808). General Lachlan McIntosh (1727–1806) concentrated all his available forces to strengthen Fort Howe and Beard's Bluff, the next post up on the Altamaha, to prevent the Crown forces from crossing the Altamaha. The Georgia militiamen relieved the Continental troops who were moved south. General McIntosh only had 109 men from the 1st battalion and the light horse to block the advance. He succeeded in halting the Crown forces at the Altamaha on Sunday, May 4, 1777, losing 12 men and himself wounded. Lieutenant Colonel Fuser turned around and returned to St. Augustine with 2,000 head of cattle and 30 tierces (about 1,260 gallons) of rice collected by the Rangers.[155]

Purrysburgh, South Carolina/Rincon, Georgia
Zubly's Ferry (Jan. 1, 1779)

Purrysburgh, South Carolina, named after Swiss founder Pierre Purry, was about 13 miles north of Savannah. Zubly's Ferry probably crossed the Savannah River in the area where the railroad or route I-95 cross it today.

Lieutenant Colonel Archibald Campbell (1739–1791) continued to move up the Savannah River toward Purrysburgh, South Carolina after the capture of Savannah. When he received information that Congressional forces were taking the slaves of Georgia Loyalists to South Carolina, he gave "a Confidential Mulatto" a musket and "sent him forward with a Number of Negroes to the Bank of the River to call out to the Rebels for God's Sake send over the Boats and save his Master's Slaves from falling into the hands of the King's Troops."

Captain Alexander Campbell (d. 1779) hid his light infantry (71st Highlanders) in the woods on the Georgia side of Zubly's Ferry on Friday, January 1, 1779. The Whigs rowed the ferryboats over to the Georgia side and when they reached the shore, the mulatto fired his musket. The light infantrymen seized the boats. They had no casualties and "rescued" 83 slaves.[156]

Sylvania
Briar Creek (Jan. 26, 1779; March 3, 1779; Aug. 14, 1779; May 2, 1782)
Briar Creek Massacre (Jan. 1781)

> Briar Creek Battleground is at Briar Creek Bridge, East Ogeechee Street, 11 miles east of Sylvania. Turn left to cross the bridge over Briar Creek. A large historical marker has a map showing the movements of the two forces and a lengthy description of the battle. There is no other development at the site except for a causeway running through it. The east bank of the creek is used for camping.

Major General Augustine Prevost's (1723–1786) army faced Major General Benjamin Lincoln's (1733–1810) Continental Army across the Savannah River on Tuesday, January 26, 1779. After the fall of Savannah, the Continentals were trying to retake the colony while the Crown forces were consolidating their hold on it. Although the Crown forces had taken Augusta with little effort, Continental pressure across the river forced them to abandon the city during the night of Saturday, February 13, 1779.

★ Brigadier General John Ashe (1720–1781) crossed the Savannah River with 1,400 men and some 100 Georgia Continentals under the command of Colonel Samuel Elbert (1740–1788). They were on their way to join Brigadier General Andrew Williamson (ca. 1730–1786) and his force of 1,200 men on the South Carolina side of the Savannah River across from Augusta. They arrived on Saturday evening, February 13, 1779. The Crown forces evacuated Augusta that night and completed their withdrawal by sunrise.

General Williamson ordered Colonel LeRoy Hammond (1728–1789) and a party of militiamen, together with Lieutenant Colonel John McIntosh (1755–1826) and a detachment of Continentals, to follow the Crown forces withdrawing down to Savannah and to harass their rear. The 200 mounted Congressional troops finished crossing their horses about 10 PM and marched about 3 miles, then stopped to feed and refresh the horses and allow the men to get some sleep.

They resumed their pursuit at daylight the following day. They found that the Crown troops had destroyed all of the bridges which delayed them. About 11 AM, the Whigs reached the site where the Crown troops had encamped the previous night. Hammond changed his course and took a route through the woods, moving around the Crown force. He arrived at the Briar Creek bridge ahead of the Crown troops. The Whigs camped at Briar Creek while they rebuilt the bridge, but they failed to take adequate defensive precautions. They also awaited reinforcements which they received with the arrival of 207 South Carolinians.

General Prevost saw this as an opportunity to strike. He ordered a small diversionary force out from Savannah to march toward the Continentals while his younger brother, Lieutenant Colonel James Mark Prevost (1736–1781) led a second force of 900 Regulars to circle around the Continentals and come down from the north. Meanwhile, General Ashe had ordered Major Francis Ross (1743–1779), of South Carolina, and 300 horsemen, to reconnoiter the enemy at Hudson's Ferry, near Briar Creek, on Wednesday morning, March 3, 1779. He intended to attack that post as soon as he received reinforcements from General Griffith Rutherford (ca. 1731–1800).

Ross discovered the trail of some of the Crown troops advancing on General Ashe, but he did not think it of any importance, so he did not report it. General Prevost's flanking maneuver caught General Ashe completely by surprise. His troops deployed about 150 yards in front of Ashe's, cornering him against the swamp and the unrepaired bridge around 4 PM. The Whig militiamen fled immediately. Ashe faced annihilation but took no steps to counter the attack. He formed his troops in a column with Colonel Samuel Elbert's (1740–1788) Continentals in front. They advanced and fired three volleys, then shifted to the left which put them in the line of fire of the advancing New Bern Regiment, preventing them from firing. The Edenton Regiment got off course and moved right, creating a gap in the North Carolina Militia line of battle. Crown troops moved into the gap.

The Halifax Regiment on the Continental left broke without firing a shot. Panic quickly spread through the other militia units. The Georgia Continentals continued to fight, almost alone. The Crown troops killed or captured all of them. A Highlander knocked Colonel Elbert down and was about to bayonet him when Elbert gave the Masonic sign of distress and a British officer intervened to spare his life.

Ashe tried to rally his troops, but they fled into the swamps of the Savannah River where many drowned in a desperate attempt to swim across the river. Nearly 200 Continentals were killed or drowned and 11 were wounded. They lost another 200 prisoners, seven guns and many small arms and ammunition, their baggage and colors. The Crown forces lost five men killed and 11 wounded. Soldiers of the 71st Highlanders set fire to the brush along the Savannah River that evening to flush out any Whigs who might still be hiding there. The fire killed many of the wounded. John Dooly (ca. 1742–1780), recently promoted to Colonel, and his Wilkes County militiamen arrived later to bury the dead.

General Ashe was court-martialed for being unprepared to meet the enemy. This terminated his military career. The Battle of Briar Creek destroyed Ashe's force and allowed the Crown forces to reoccupy Augusta, confirming their position in the South and ending General Lincoln's hope of retaking Georgia. The Continentals would not be able to retake Georgia until after the Crown forces left two years later.[157]

★ Some Georgia militiamen under Colonel John Twiggs (1750–1816) and some Virginia cavalrymen under Lieutenant Colonel John Jameson (1758–1842) attacked Colonel Daniel McGirth (d. ca. 1789) and 25 Crown troops at Briar Creek on Saturday, August 14, 1779, killing five and capturing nine. Twiggs had only one man wounded.

★ A party of 30 South Carolina militiamen crossed the Savannah River from South Carolina "for the purpose of plundering the inhabitants of Georgia" in January 1781. After a detachment of British light infantrymen ambushed and defeated them, Lieutenant

Colonel Archibald Campbell (1739–1791) got a false report from the prisoners that Major General Benjamin Lincoln (1733–1810) had moved to Calibogie Sound. Lincoln was still at Purrysburgh waiting for an attack on Charleston.

Campbell left 30 South Carolina Royalists and 20 Georgia dragoons to guard the bridge at Briar Creek. The fortress there had become a formidable defensive position with an abatis (see Photo GA-16) around the houses and loopholes (see Photo GA-1) to fire through. Campbell's messengers encouraged the South Carolina Loyalists to rebel against the Whig authorities and assured them that the Whigs would be defeated easily with their help.

Colonel James Boyd mustered about 800 Loyalists from North and South Carolina west of the Broad River. They marched along the South Carolina frontier toward the Savannah River to join Colonel Campbell in Augusta. A British officer marching with them observed that "most of the elements from Ebenezar to August are in a ruinous, neglected state; two thirds of them deserted, some of their owners following the King's troops others with the Rebels, and both revengefully destroying the property of each other."[158]

★ Colonel Daniel McGirth (d. ca. 1789) vowed to kill everyone who had not sworn allegiance to the King. His band of Loyalists crossed the Savannah River in January 1781 and rode down the South Carolina side of the river. His men murdered 17 inhabitants at Briar Creek and burned the settlement to the ground. The victims included Tarleton Brown's father. His son, in North Carolina, wrote: "Hearing that the British, Tories and Indians had murdered our father and sixteen more of his neighbors, burning to ashes his house and all within it, our mother and sisters escaping to the woods, with little or nothing to support upon, and no male friend to help them, my blood boiled within my veins, and my soul thirsted for vengeance." The raid induced Captain James McKay and Colonel William Harden (1743–1785 to call out their militiamen to search for the Loyalist raiders.[159]

★ Lieutenant James Stallings, of the Georgia Legion, and a young man named Lyons stopped at a house on the north side of Briar Creek to obtain food for their tired horses and for themselves on Thursday, May 2, 1782. Henry Cooper and five of his men attacked the house about 3 PM. Lieutenant Stallings's horse was too exhausted to flee, so he and Lyons abandoned it and ran to the swamps and escaped. The horse they left behind had Brigadier General "Mad Anthony" Wayne's (1745–1796) dispatches in the saddle bags.[160]

★ June 24, 1782 see **New Ebenezer** pp. 45, 58–59.

Hudson's Ferry (July 27, 1781)

Robert Hudson's (1735–1806) Ferry was a very important place in southeastern Georgia in the 18th century, as it was one of only a few crossing points over the Savannah River between the Fall Line and the city of Savannah. Lieutenant Colonel Archibald Campbell (1739–1791) and the 71st Regiment occupied the site, 37 miles upstream from Savannah, during the British Southern Campaign in 1778/1779. Today, Hudson's Ferry is a part of rural Screven County, about 2 miles northwest of the Effingham County line.

Colonel Isaac Shelby (1750–1826) fought a band of Georgia Loyalists at Hudson's Ferry on Friday, July 27, 1781.[161]

St. Catherines Island (April 24, 1776; April 18, 1782)

> St. Catherines Island is about 30 miles south of the Savannah River.

A band of Rebels on St. Catherines Island fired at the boats of Lieutenant Alexander Ellis's (d. 1778) HM Schooner *Hinchinbrook* on Wednesday afternoon, April 24, 1776. The *Hinchinbrook* returned fire with several guns.[162]

★ Captain Donald Cameron discovered a 12-gun Whig privateer sloop near St. Catherines Island on Thursday, April 18, 1782. Captain Cameron attacked part of her crew which had already landed. He forced them to take refuge in their boats under cover of the sloop's guns. When the crew reboarded, the privateer immediately weighed anchor and headed out to sea. The Loyalists had one man wounded. The Whig loss is unknown.[163]

Sapelo Inlet (Jan. 2, 1777)
Sapelo Sound (Aug. 3, 1779)
Blackbeard Island (April 24, 1781)

> Sapelo Inlet is at the mouth of the Sapelo River between St. Catherines Island and Blackbeard Island. Blackbeard Island is part of Sapelo Island.

A small armed vessel came into the Sapelo Inlet on Thursday, January 2, 1777. The Loyalist vessel, commanded by Captain Kebly and outfitted to defend against Whig privateers, was disguised as a trading vessel. The decoy succeeded in getting Captain Woodruff and two of his men off of their row galley *Georgia,* stationed in the inlet, and aboard Kebly's vessel. Meanwhile, other Loyalists from the vessel landed on Sapelo Island (Blackbeard Island) to plunder Mrs. Isabella MacKay's plantation, taking several slaves. The alarm was sounded and the crew of the row galley *Georgia* landed on the island to pursue the raiders. They captured seven of the raiders. Captain Kebly headed out to open sea with a favorable wind and escaped, as the *Georgia* fired at him.[164]

★ As Major General Augustine Prevost's (1723–1786) force was headed to Sunbury, a gale scattered his flotilla on Saturday, January 2, 1779. Some of the troops landed on Little Cumberland Island for several days and survived by eating alligator meat and drinking Madeira wine found on a wrecked ship.

General Prevost detached Major Colin Graham with three companies of the 16th Regiment and Captain Patrick Murray's light infantry company of the 4th Battalion 60th Regiment to seize the rice stores on Broughton Island and then move to Sapelo high bluff, where they were to forage for Mrs. Isabella Mackay's cattle. Ensign Karl Lewis Theodore Schoedde moved up the south bay of Sapelo in the moonlight and captured the guard of seven men. Captain Murray and his party met Schoedde and his prisoners, and they all followed Major Graham by the inland passage.

Captain Murray landed at the Sapelo indigo works. He took Baron Breitenbach (lieutenant in the 4th Battalion, 60th Regiment), Ensign Schoedde and 30 men to the salt depot to search for Whigs. Not finding any, they marched to Mrs. Mackay's house. Ensign Schoedde entered the guardhouse and silently took the guards prisoners. Sergeant Dornseif and two men changed clothes with the prisoners and went up the stairs to the look-out where they "relieved the sentry." Then, they arrested Lieutenant David Montaigut, commander of the Whig detachment (and Mrs. Mackay's son), along with the remainder of his men. Captain Murray and his men then moved on to Sunbury.[165]

★ Captain Samuel Spencer (1739–1794) sailed his South Carolina schooner *Witch* into Sapelo Sound on Tuesday, August 3, 1779 when a British privateer from St. Augustine armed with six guns attacked him. Captain Spencer succeeded in boarding the privateer and capturing her after a 15-minute engagement. That night, some of Spencer's men landed on Sapelo and took Richard Leake (d. 1802) and William Moss (1763–1841) prisoners. They later paroled both men on the south end of Sapelo.[166]

★ Captain John Howell (1756–1830) captured the HMS *Britannia* off the Ogeechee River on Saturday, April 14, 1781. When he was returning with his prize on Tuesday, the 24th, Captain McEvoy and the *Cormorant* pursued Captain Howell and overtook the *Britannia* which struck her colors and dropped anchor. Captain McEvoy sent his boats toward the *Britannia*, but Captain Howell fired at them and slipped anchor. The *Britannia* sailed to the south end of Blackbeard Island where she fought the *Cormorant* until the late afternoon. Captain Howell abandoned the *Britannia* and ordered her burned to avoid a night attack. He pardoned the prisoners he captured on the 14th and left them on the island.[167]

Altamaha River (May 4, 1777; April 12, 1782)
Reid's Bluff (April 10, 1782)
New Hope Plantation (April 11, 1782)

> The mouth of the Altamaha River is north of Fort Frederica and south of Sapelo Inlet. The river runs from the northwest of the state to the southeast.

Colonel Augustine Prevost (1723–1786) was promoted to the rank of brigadier general early in May 1777 and his command was extended to include West Florida. As Colonel Samuel Elbert (1740–1788) and his men headed toward Florida, Governor Patrick Tonyn (1725–1804) summoned the Creeks and asked the governors of South Carolina and Georgia to send some Cherokees. Six weeks after Tonyn's appeal, Prevost wrote to General William Howe (1732–1786) that the Rebels had been baffled and had returned to Georgia, that the Creeks had been rendered unreliable by the work of the Rebel emissaries, and that, in the space of a few days, East Florida "could be invaded either by land or water by an army well supplied with artillery, provisions, &c." He asked permission to enroll a troop of mounted rangers and wanted Colonel John Stuart (ca. 1710–1779), Superintendent of the Southern Indian Department, to find means of protecting the Cherokees who had been recently severely defeated by the combined efforts of Virginians, Carolinians and Georgians and were now threatened with destruction for their loyalty. He thought that the Creeks were already inclined to the Continental side which was evident by the enforced flight of Stuart's agents from the Creek nation after being robbed.[168]

Colonel John Baker led 109 Georgia militiamen in a second expedition against St. Augustine in East Florida. He encountered a band of British-allied Native Americans along the way at the Altamaha River on Sunday, May 4, 1777. He engaged them and had two men wounded in the skirmish.[169] See **Florida** pp. 108–113.

★ A Creek chief named White Fish, from one of the lower towns, escaped from the Whigs during the last week of March 1782 and went to a camp at the forks of the

Canoochee River where he found about 300 warriors encamped. He arrived two hours ahead of Major Francis Moore (d. 1782) and his men who were pursuing him. The warriors murdered several Loyalist guides whom they thought had betrayed them with false information that the road to Savannah was open. White Fish and the other warriors immediately set out for the Altamaha River, intending to return to their own territory.

Brigadier General "Mad Anthony" Wayne (1745–1796) ordered Moore to take up a position where he could block White Fish's band in the event they attempted to go from Frederica to Savannah by water. Moore was also instructed to intercept a band of Choctaws escorting a British shipment of ammunition and presents to the upper Creek country.

Reports of what happened to Major Moore vary. Captain Patrick ("Paddy") Carr (1761–1820), writing from camp at "McDonalds Scotch Settlement" near Darien on April 12, reports that Moore and 28 men set out in boats from some neighboring islands and Rory McIntosh's on Monday, April 8 in search of Loyalists and Native Americans. When they reached the mouth of the Altamaha River, they took some prisoners who informed them where several Native Americans had camped. Moore sent half of his men back with the prisoners and proceeded up the Altamaha with the remaining 14 men.

Moore captured 30 horses at Reid's Bluff and proceeded to a house where he found about 20 Native American warriors and Captain Donald Cameron's Loyalist Rangers. Moore left seven men with the horses, and attempted to make friends with the Native Americans and Loyalists by deceiving them. However, they were wary of him and cocked their muskets. Moore ordered the seven men who were with him to open fire. A "smart firing commenced which lasted upwards of a half [h]our. . . ."As the Native Americans were in a strong log house, Moore's men, who were out in the open, retreated, leaving Major Moore and two others "on the ground." Captain James Nephew (1760–1827) succeeded to the command of the Whigs.

The Whigs retreated across the river in two parties and one of the men drowned. Carr planned to recross the Altamaha with Moore's men on the 13th. They were "all in high spirits & wished to have a opertunity to retaliate for Mores death." An angry Loyalist reported Moore's death in the Savannah newspaper as follows:

> On the 7th of this month ten Creek Indians, having crossed the Alatamaha [sic, Altamaha] on their return to the Nation, fell in with a party of 17 Rebels, under the command of a Continental Major Moore, at Reid's Bluff. Moore came up to them at a log house with his men dressed in red, told them he was a British officer, shook them by the hand, and said he was glad to see them. Supposing that the Indians were now in his power, this perfidious, treacherous, rebel villain, ordered his men to fire upon them, by which one was killed, and four wounded. Rouzed by a sense of their danger, the Indians returned the fire, killed Moore, a Capt. Smith, and two others, and, by an almost incredible exertion, routed the whole party, and drove them into the river, from which 'tis believed few, if any, have escaped."

Hugh McCall reported the incident as follows:

> A party of Indians, passing from Savannah toward the Creek nation, had stolen some horses on the frontier of Liberty county. They were pursued by major Francis Moore, with fifteen men, by whom they were overtaken at Reid's bluff, in a log-house. Moore was close to the house before he discovered the Indians, and in open ground, where he could not commence an attack, except under great disadvantages; therefore he advanced under the pretense that his command consisted of royal militia. He gave his hand to some of the Indians who came to the door, but soon found

he was suspected. He ordered his men to prepare for action: the Indians closed the door, and on the first fire Moore was killed and Smith wounded. Finding that the Indians had a superiority of numbers, and were too well fortified to be dislodged; captain Nephew, who then commanded, was compelled to retreat. Smith could not be carried off, consequently, he was murdered so soon as he fell into the hands of the savages.[170]

★ Captain John Lyons, who had been with Major Francis Moore (d. 1782) at Reid's Bluff, joined Captain Patrick ("Paddy") Carr (1761–1820) at John McDonald's plantation. Together, they set out in pursuit of the Native Americans to get revenge. Captain Carr and 65 mounted militiamen, including Robert Sallette (1750–1790), crossed the Altamaha and marched to New Hope plantation on Thursday, April 11, 1782. They intended to intercept some boats under the charge of Captain Donald Cameron of the King's Rangers. The Whigs killed one of the Loyalists named Hoover (d. 1782) at the house and took their post near the plantation. Captain Cameron received information about the Whigs' intention and landed with eight Rangers and about 30 Cherokees and Creeks. Eight Chocktaws joined him on his march. The Loyalists attacked, routed and pursued the Whigs 2 miles. The Whigs lost many horses and 14 men but none of the Loyalists or Native Americans was harmed.[171]

Saint Simons Island (August 10, 1777)

> Saint Simons Island is at the mouth of the Brunswick River opposite Jekyll Island.

Some boats from a British armed vessel anchored in St. Andrew's Sound, between Cumberland and Jekyll Islands, landed on St. Simons Island on Sunday, August 10, 1777. The crews attacked Captain Arthur Carney's 4th company of the 1st Georgia Regiment. They captured Captain Carney, five citizens and several African Americans and carried them away in the barges along with as much household furniture as they could transport. After his capture, Carney became an active Loyalist and proved himself a great cattle thief.

Colonel Samuel Elbert (1740–1788) ordered various troops of the Continental Light Horse to go from the frontier to Savannah to defend the capital from an expected raid by the Crown forces. However, the light horsemen refused to obey the order, and Elbert blamed their officers, who "have no more authority over them than if they had no commission at all."[172]

Frederica, St. Simons Island harbor (Oct. 1776; April 19, 1778)
Rebecca & Hinchinbrook
Near Frederica (May 1 or 2, 1782)

> Frederica was located on the Frederica River on the western edge of Saint Simons Island about 12 miles from Brunswick. While only about 10 miles in a direct line from Darien, it is considerably farther by road because of all the waterways and wetlands. Fort Frederica (see Photo GA-22) was connected to St. Simons fort on the south end of the island by a 6-mile military road.
>
> The site of the former town is now a national monument administered by the National Park Service. To get there, take the F. J. Torras Causeway from route US 17 to St. Simons Island. At the first traffic light, turn left onto Sea Island Road and proceed 1.5 miles to Frederica Road and turn left at the traffic light. Follow Frederica

GA-22. The ruins of Fort Frederica on St. Simons Island

Road for 2 miles through the traffic circle to the park entrance 300 yards past Christ Church.

William Oldis, a strong Loyalist, attacked Frederica in an armed schooner with 60 men in October 1776. The Loyalists burned part of the settlement and sailed up the Turtle River where they raided Arthur Carney's settlement.[173]

★ The only narrative of the event of April 19, 1778 comes from a letter by Georgia's Colonel Samuel Elbert (1740–1788) to Major General Robert Howe (1732–1786), dated April 19, 1778. The British were in the area of Frederica, in April 1778, searching for the galleys that comprised Georgia's navy. Shipwrights came from Philadelphia to Savannah to build flat-bottomed, oared vessels with a low draught which allowed them to carry heavy loads and to be very maneuverable. These boats were ideal for protecting the inner passage from Florida to Georgia because they were well suited to close fighting in the rivers and channels that larger British vessels could not navigate as easily.

The British made plans to capture some of these galleys for their own use. They had already captured the brigantines *Hatter* and *Rebecca* from South Carolina and the 14-gun brigantine *Hinchinbrook*. These vessels were now located at Frederica and their crews were looking for an opportunity to capture some of Georgia's galleys.

Colonel Samuel Elbert had already marched from Darien to Fort Howe on Friday, April 17, 1778, when he learned that the British boats were moored at Frederica with a captured brig. He formulated a plan to attack them. He boarded his men (three field officers, six captains, 18 subalterns, 24 sergeants, six drummers, two fifers, and 300 Georgia Continentals) aboard the galleys *Washington* under Captain John Hardy (1742–1803), *Lee* under Captain John Braddock (1743–1797), and *Bulloch* under Captain Archibald

Hatcher (1723–1812). Captain George Young commanded an artillery detachment with two field pieces loaded on a flatboat. They departed from Darien on Saturday, April 18, 1778 and landed north of the village of Pikes Bluff, about 1.5 miles north of Frederica. Colonel Elbert left some officers and a few soldiers aboard the boats to protect them while a detachment of 100 men went into Frederica where they captured three marines and two sailors of the *Hinchinbrook*.

The galleys attacked the British vessels about 10 AM the following morning, taking them by surprise. As the British positioned their vessels to defend themselves, the artillery of the galleys "damped the courage" of the British sailors. The large guns on the galleys allowed Elbert's crews to stay out of range of the British guns and still hit their targets. The bar and chain shot (see Photo GA-7) severely damaged the rigging of the *Hinchinbrook* and the *Rebecca*. As the British tried to escape down the Frederica River, they ran aground and abandoned both the *Hinchinbrook* and the *Rebecca*. They escaped with the *Hatter* and sailed to Jekyll Island with rescued crewmen. Although Elbert wanted to continue the attack and capture the *Hatter*, she departed quickly and ended the engagement. Elbert had no casualties. He captured nine of the *Hinchinbrook's* crew and her cargo which included 300 uniforms previously captured in the *Hatter*, off Charleston, that were intended for Colonel Charles Cotesworth Pinckney's (1746–1825) 1st South Carolina Regiment. The action was a significant victory, as it showed how unorthodox tactical fighting by a small state navy could compete with and sometimes defeat a powerful British naval force.

Major General Robert Howe (1732–1786) sent Colonel Andrew Williamson (ca. 1730–1786) and 1,100 militiamen along with 300 1st South Carolina Continentals from Charleston, South Carolina to reinforce Colonel Elbert. General Howe and his army arrived at Fort Howe on Saturday, May 9, 1778 where they remained to await provisions from South Carolina, due to the summer heat. Colonel Pinckney wrote to Brigadier General William Moultrie (1730–1805) about the conditions:

> What can be more cruel than crowding eight, ten, and twelve men into one tent, or oblige those who cannot get in, to sleep in the heavy dews? what is more inconvenient than to have only one camp-kettle to ten, twelve or fifteen men? and in this hot climate to have one small canteen to six or eight men?[174]

★ Captain Patrick ("Paddy") Carr (1761–1820) engaged in a skirmish with about 70 Choctaw warriors near Frederica on Wednesday or Thursday, May 1 or 2, 1782, forcing them to return to their boats.

The same band of Choctaw warriors attempted to cut through to their territory by land the following day. Lieutenant Nicholas Miller, of Colonel James Jackson's (1757–1806) legion, and 12 men waited in ambush for them. When the Choctaws got within 10 yards, Miller's men opened fire and charged with the bayonet (see Photo GA-3), routing them, leaving five dead and many wounded.[175]

Southern Georgia (end of Aug. 1778)

Georgians had anticipated that East Florida Rangers were preparing for an invasion for several months. Major General Robert Howe (1732–1786) expressed his concern to his council of war (see cover photo) at Fort Tonyn in July 1778. He noted enemy movements in Florida, posts that the enemy occupied and other posts which they were trying to secure, and the positions of their armed vessels and men-of-war (see Photo GA-17) were signs of plans for an immediate invasion. He also reported on the number of insurgents who were arming themselves in Georgia and South Carolina and gathering in

East Florida as well as the information that deserters, spies and others brought from St. Augustine, Florida.

A band of East Florida Rangers raided southern Georgia at the end of August 1778. Georgia scouts killed three of the Rangers. However the main invasion did not begin until November.[176]

Liberty County
Battle of Fort Morris

Midway (Nov. 20, 1778; Nov. 24, 1778; Nov. 25, 1778; June 4, 1779; June 27, 1779)

Bulltown Swamp (Nov. 24, 1778)

Spencer's Hill, Midway (Nov. 24, 25, 1778)

Liberty County (Feb. 27, 1780)

St. John's Parish (March 27, 1780)

Sunbury, Liberty County (April 21, 1776; March 28, 1780; Sept. 18, 1781)

Fort George (formerly Fort Morris) (Jan. 9, 1779; June 4, 1781)

The Midway Church (see Photo GA-23) (Congregational) is on route US 17 (GA 25|Ocean Highway|South Coastal Highway 17) next to the Colonial Midway Museum. The church's cemetery (**roadsidegeorgia.com/site/midwaycemetery.html**) is the

GA-23. Midway Church (Congregational) was the Continentals' secondary defense line in the battle of Midway. It is next to the Colonial Midway Museum and the cemetery is the burial place of a number of Whigs, including Brigadier General James Screven.

burial place of a number of Whigs, including Brigadier General James Screven (1744–1778).

A short distance south of the Midway Church, there are at least 7 historical markers, all on the same side of the road—5 of them are near the intersection in front of the church.

Spencer's Hill is about 1.5 miles south of the Midway Church.

Route US 17 crosses Bulltown Swamp (see Photo GA-24) 11 miles south of Midway Church and just north of the route I-95 overpass at exit 17.

The Continental Congress commissioned Fort Morris (see Photo GA-25) in 1776. Slaves built the large earthworks on a bluff overlooking the Midway River. It was Georgia's largest fortification, measuring 275 feet in length along the east (river) side, 191 feet on the northern side, 240 feet on the west and 140 feet on the south. Besides the marshes on three sides, the fort was surrounded by a moat 10 feet deep and 10 feet wide at the bottom and 20 feet wide at the top. It had seven embrasures (see Photo GA-5), each about five feet wide to accommodate 25 guns of various sizes, ranging from 4- to 24-pounders, mounted on platforms. Congressional forces garrisoned the post to protect the port of Sunbury against British forces in both the American War of Independence and the War of 1812.

The Battle of Fort Morris is also known as the Battle of Midway. Fort Morris State Historic Site (**www.cr.nps.gov/goldcres/sites/morris.htm**) is at 2559 Fort Morris Road, 7.9 miles northeast of Midway. At the intersection of routes Interstate-95 and US 84, travel east for 4.6 miles, following signs. Turn left after 2.5 miles, then bear right on a dirt road for 0.6 miles to the fort. Visitors can still see remains of the

GA-24. Bulltown Swamp. Colonel John Baker and some Georgia Continentals and mounted militiamen encountered Lieutenant Colonel James Mark Prevost's army, marching north from Florida, here.

GA-25. Fort Morris, built on a bluff overlooking the Midway River, was Georgia's largest fortification. When Lieutenant Colonel Lewis Valentine Fuser demanded the fort's surrender, Lieutenant Colonel John McIntosh responded: "Come and take it."

breastworks, embrasures, and the moat. They can also take a walking tour or use the picnic facilities. A museum interprets the history of the site.

Sunbury no longer exists. It was a town south of Savannah and a little more than a quarter of a mile south of Fort Morris which protected it. With a population of more than 1,000 people during the American War of Independence, it was the second largest port in Georgia, but it had completely disappeared by the time of the Civil War.

Sunbury was the key for any Congressional force planning to attack St. Augustine, Florida, or for any British unit intending to occupy Savannah. It served as the advance camp for the Congressional forces under Colonel William Moultrie (1730–1805) who planned to attack the Loyalists in East Florida in 1776. However, the heat and malaria began decimating the troops at the rate of 15 a day, causing Colonel Moultrie to return to Charleston, South Carolina.

St. John's Parish was one of three parishes that would eventually make up Liberty County.

Captain Henry Bryne's (d. 1780) HMS *Hind*, anchored off the "Sunbury" River, sent the HM Armed Schooner *Hinchinbrook*, the *Hind*'s tender and boats to a creek near Sunbury on Sunday, April 21, 1776. The crewmen burned a brig that was loading and a ship still under construction as a 20-gun privateer. A party of about 650 or 660 Whigs on St. Catherines Island attacked the British naval force as they returned to the *Hind*. The British retreated into the woods after a half-hour engagement that damaged the tender's hull and sails.[177]

★ General Sir Henry Clinton (1730–1795), in New York, ordered Major General Augustine Prevost (1723–1786) to the St. Marys River to cooperate with Lieutenant Colonel Archibald Campbell's (1739–1791) invasion fleet in mid-October 1778. Late in 1778, the Crown forces decided to invade Georgia from Florida. General Prevost ordered his brother, Lieutenant Colonel James Mark Prevost (1736–1781) and his force of 100 Regulars and 300 Rangers and Native Americans with a 4½-inch coehorn mounted on a Congreve carriage to collect cattle for food for the Crown forces at Midway and Newport for the winter. They arrived in Georgia, north of the Altamaha River, on November 19, 1778.

Lieutenant Colonel Lewis Valentine Fuser (d. 1780) took another force of 500 men (including 250 men of the 60th (Royal Americans) Regiment, accompanied by the armed flat *Thunderer* and two privateers. They landed at Colonel's Island and threatened Sunbury, 15 miles south of Savannah, as a diversion for the cattle raid. The two forces were supposed to rendezvous at Sunbury and then proceed to Savannah to join with Lieutenant Colonel Archibald Campbell's (1739–1791) force of 2,000 men sailing from New York. The Battle of Midway prevented the two forces from joining.

When Lieutenant Colonel Prevost arrived at Midway on Saturday, November 20, 1778, Colonel John White and a group of 100 Continental Army Regulars constructed a small breastwork across the causeway near Midway Meeting House and placed two pieces of light artillery there to block the Crown forces. Brigadier General James Screven (1744–1778) joined Colonel White on November 22 with 20 mounted militiamen. Screven thought their combined force was too small to stop Prevost, so he and White decided to abandon the breastwork and set up an ambush at Mrs. Spencer's Hill, about 1.5 miles south of Midway Meeting House, where thick woods closed on the roadway. Loyalist Lieutenant Colonel Thomas Alexander Brown (1744–1814), of the East Florida Rangers, was familiar with this terrain but grossly overestimated the size of the Congressional forces. He decided to establish an ambush at the same location Screven selected. The Loyalists heard Screven and his men approach. Screven and his aide-de-camp, Lieutenant Thomas Glascock (1756–1810), "inclined to the right to examine the ground" while Colonel White prepared for action.

Glascock advanced to reconnoiter and stumbled into the ambush. Stunned, he called back to Screven. The East Florida Rangers immediately realized his identity and shot Screven 11 times. He was captured and died in captivity two days later. The Rangers' first volley also killed Captain William D. Strother (d. 1778), who accompanied Screven as a volunteer.

Prevost ordered his Regulars to reinforce the Rangers. A shot from a field piece struck Prevost's horse in the neck as it crossed the road. As Prevost fell with his horse, his troops faltered. Major Charles-Noel-François Romand de l'Isle ("De Lisle") (1744–1784), thinking that Prevost had been killed, quickly advanced with his field pieces to capitalize on the confusion. Prevost remounted and the British recovered. The Continentals withdrew to Midway Church and formed a new defense line in the town.

White forged a letter from Colonel Samuel Elbert (1740–1788) which looked like an order to retreat. It also mentioned a large body of cavalry had crossed the Ogeechee River and was coming to attack Prevost from behind. White made sure Prevost received the letter. Meanwhile, Elbert and 200 men marched to the Ogeechee where they met White's retreating force.

As Fuser had not yet arrived at Sunbury, Prevost withdrew, after gathering all the cattle he could find and burning the Congregational church which was used to store arms and ammunition. He also burned almost every dwelling-house, and all the rice and other cereals he could find. He also took 200 slaves, 2,000 head of cattle, horses, and even poultry and plate. He sold his plunder at a public sale on the St. Marys River and received £8,000.

Governor John Houstoun (1744–1796) wrote Henry Laurens (1724–1792), giving the following description of Prevost's destruction:

> [T]heir Savage Warfare beggars Description, and brands their Names, as well as their Cause, with Infamy. Not a House which they came across but was laid in ashes, and the plentiful well Settled Parish of St. John now presents one continued Scene of Horror Ruin & Devastation. Even helpless women & infant Children were thought happy in having escaped with their lives—their Cloathes were refused them.[178]

★ Lieutenant Colonel James Mark Prevost (1736–1781) killed or captured every man he encountered, as he met no opposition until he reached the point where the Savannah to Darien road crossed Bulltown Swamp (see Photo GA-24). His men also plundered and destroyed property all along their line of march, angering the inhabitants of the region. As Colonel John Baker (1750–1830) and some Georgia Continentals and mounted militiamen marched to Midway, on Wednesday, November 24, 1778, with "three days provisions of bacon & biscuit with 40 rounds ammunition each," they encountered Prevost's army, marching north from Florida, at Bulltown Swamp. Colonel Baker chose this spot to delay Prevost's advance and confronted Prevost's forces with his mounted militiamen.

A short skirmish ensued in which one man was killed and Colonel Baker, Captain John Cooper (1751–1819), and William Goulding (d. 1782) were wounded. Colonel Baker's Continentals continued to fight, awaiting Brigadier General James Screven's (1744–1778) reinforcements to arrive and cut off Lieutenant Colonel Prevost's force. Baker and his command retreated after the short skirmish. Prevost then proceeded north to Midway where he encountered more opposition.[179]

★ Both forces engaged in another skirmish later the same day at North Newport bridge (now Riceboro) where route US 17 (GA 25|North Way) crosses over Riceboro Creek. The British killed Charles Carter (d. 1778).[180]

★ Lieutenant Colonel Lewis Valentine Fuser (d. 1780), of the 60th Regiment, delayed by headwinds, arrived at Sunbury on Wednesday, November 25, 1778, after Lieutenant Colonel James Mark Prevost (1736–1781) had already left. He immediately besieged Fort Morris. Expecting the arrival of Colonel Prevost, Fuser wrote to Lieutenant Colonel John McIntosh (1755–1826) who commanded 127 Continentals and some local militiamen at the fort in Sunbury, demanding his surrender:

> Sunbury, Nov. 25, 1778. Eight o'clock in the morning.
>
> Sir,
>
> You cannot be ignorant that four armies are in motion to reduce this province; the one is already under the guns of your fort, and may be joined when I think proper by col. Prevost, who is now at the meeting house. The resistance you can or intend to make, will only bring destruction upon this country. On the contrary, if you deliver me the fort which you command, lay down your arms, and remain neuter until the fate of America is determined, you shall, as well as all the inhabitants of this parish, remain in the peaceable possession of your property. Your answer, which I expect in an hour's time, will determine the fate of this country, whether it is to be laid in ashes or remain as above proposed. I am sir, your most obedient, &c
>
> L. V. Fuser, col. 60th reg. and commander of his majesty's troops in Georgia, on his majesty's service.

[On the outside] P.S. Since this letter is closed, some of your people have been firing scattering shot about the town. I am to inform you, that if a stop is not put to such irregular proceedings, I shall burn a house for every shot so fired.

Major Joseph Lane (1740–1801) brought the letter into the fort and soon returned with the following answer:

Fort Morris, Nov. 25, 1778

Sir,

We acknowledge we are not ignorant that your army is in motion to endeavor to reduce this state. We believe it entirely chimerical that col. Prevost is at the meeting house; but should it be so, we are in no degree apprehensive of danger from a junction of his army with yours. We have no property, compared with the object we contend for, that we value a ruse, and would rather perish in a vigorous defence than accept of your proposals.

We, sir, are fighting the battle of America, and therefore disdain to remain neuter till its fate is determined.—As to surrendering the fort, receive this laconic reply.— COME AND TAKE IT.

Major Lane, whom I send with this letter is directed to satisfy you with respect to the irregular loose firing, mentioned on the back of your letter.—I have the honor to be, sir, your most obedient, &c

John M'Intosh, Lieutenant Colonel (of the Continental troops.

Lieut. Col. L. V. Fuser, of his Britannic majesty's troops in Georgia.

About half past eleven o'clock, A.M. major Lane returned, after having signified to col. Fuser that the loose firing complained of was intended to prevent the British troops from plundering the town: and as to his threatening to burn a house for every shot, the major remonstrated to col. Fuser, that such a proceeding would be rather savage and inhuman; but if he was determined to do it—in order to convince them how little we were to be deterred by such threats, as soon as he burned a house at one end of the town, we would apply a torch to the other, and let the flames meet in the centre by a mutual conflagration.[181]

When Fuser learned that Prevost had withdrawn, he sailed down the coast to Fort Frederica on St. Simons Island. The Georgia Assembly later voted to present Lieutenant Colonel John McIntosh with a sword with the engraving "Come and take it!"

★ A few weeks later, in December 1778, Major General Robert Howe (1732–1786) and 950 men who had marched to Sunbury departed to counter the Crown forces near Savannah. They left Major Joseph Lane (1740–1801) and about 200 Continentals at Sunbury. After the fall of Savannah, General Howe sent an urgent dispatch to Major Lane, on December 29, ordering him to evacuate his post. However, the leading residents of Sunbury successfully entreated Lane to keep his garrison there to protect them.

A gale scattered Major General Augustine Prevost's (1723–1786) flotilla on January 2, 1779. Some of his troops landed on Little Cumberland Island and survived for several days by eating alligator meat and drinking Madeira wine found on a wrecked ship. Others were blown to the Sapelo Inlet (see p. 88). The transport carrying Lieutenant Colonel Isaac Allen (1741–1806) and three companies of New Jersey Volunteers got separated from Campbell's fleet and the troops joined Prevost's force when they returned on Wednesday, January 6, 1779.

Roderick McIntosh (1713–1779), General Lachlan McIntosh's (1727–1806) Loyalist cousin and member of Captain Patrick Murray's light infantry company (4th Battalion 60th Regiment), had been reconnoitering the fort. He sallied out early Tuesday morning, January 6, with his claymore in hand and fortified with liquor, to demand the surrender of Fort Morris. Major Lane knew him and forbade anyone to fire on him in his condition. He opened the gate and invited Mr. McIntosh to take possession but he refused. One of the fort's defenders fired his rifle, striking Rory in the face, under his eyes. Rory stumbled and fell backwards. He recovered immediately and retreated flourishing his sword. Several shots followed. The Whigs ceased firing when Lieutenant Baron Breitenbach and Sergeant Supman of the 4th Battalion Light Infantry ran to Rory's rescue and carried him back.

That same morning, the Whigs turned 23 horses out of the fort. Captain Murray and his men drove in the escort and the horses. Later that day, Prevost arrived with a formidable force of 2,000 men (a detachment of the 16th Regiment, most of the 60th (Royal Americans) Regiment, a small detachment of Royal Artillery, the South Carolina Royalists, the East Florida Rangers, the East Florida Volunteers and some Native Americans). They laid siege to Sunbury and Fort Morris.

Whig galleys in the river fired on the Crown forces when the tide was high and the fort kept up a bombardment. The defenders held out for three days until a brief bombardment (see Photo GA-7) caused the 159 Continentals and 45 militiamen to surrender on January 9. The Congressional forces lost one captain and three privates killed, seven wounded, 24 guns and a large quantity of provisions, while the Crown forces had one man killed and three wounded. The grenadiers (see Photo GA-15) of the 4th Battalion escorted their 193 prisoners along the inland waterway to Savannah. Whig Fort Morris became Loyalist Fort George.[182]

★ Mr. Thomas Young (1764–1848) invited some British officers to dine with him at Belfast on the Midway River on Friday, June 4, 1779 to celebrate the King's birthday. Captain Samuel Spencer (1739–1794), commanding a privateer, decided to surprise and capture the party. He proceeded up the Midway River that evening and landed with 12 of his men between 8 and 9 PM. They entered the house and took Colonel John Harris Cruger (1738–1807), commander of the 1st Battalion de Lancey's Volunteers and of the garrison at Ninety Six, and the British officers at the table prisoners of war.

Captain Spencer intended to capture some slaves, so he kept his prisoners under guard until morning. After taking their paroles, he allowed his prisoners to return to Sunbury. Colonel Cruger was soon exchanged for Colonel John McIntosh (1755–1826) who had been captured at Briar Creek on March 3, 1779.[183]

★ Colonel John Twiggs (1750–1816), Major John Baker (1750–1830) and 30 horsemen proceeded from Augusta toward Sunbury on Sunday, June 27, 1779. Major Baker attacked and defeated Colonel Daniel McGirth (d. ca. 1789) and a party of Georgia Royalists at the White House at Midway Meeting House, killing and wounding several Royalists. Robert Sallette (1750–1790) almost severed Lieutenant Gray's (d. 1779) head from his body with his saber. Sallette was such a dreaded warrior that, on one occasion, an affluent Loyalist, offered a reward of 100 guineas to any person who would bring him Sallette's head. Sallette learned of the offer and placed a pumpkin in a bag which he brought to the Loyalist's house. Pointing to the bag, he told the man that he came to claim the reward of 100 guineas for Sallette's head which he had in the bag. He requested that the money be counted out for him before he delivered the head. When the Loyalist put the money on the table, Sallette pulled off his hat and placed his hand upon his head, saying, "Here is Sallette's head." The Loyalist was so frightened at the response that he ran away, but Sallette brought him to the ground with a well directed shot.

Colonel Baker heard that a number of Continental officers on parole were going to Sunbury, so he headed there and retook seven of them at Mrs. Arthur's place, about

5 miles from Midway Meeting House. Colonel Baker sent the officers and his Royalist prisoners to Canoochie. When he received information that a party left Savannah against him, Colonel Twiggs headed to Mr. James Butler's plantation. Colonel Baker's party captured a number of African Americans, horses and a large quantity of dry goods which they found at Thomas Savage's plantation on the Ogeechee River.[184]

★ A detachment of Congressional troops encountered an enemy party in Liberty County on Sunday, February 27, 1780. They killed four white men and six Native Americans and had only one man slightly wounded.[185]

★ A Whig detachment met a party of Loyalists and Native Americans in St. John's Parish on Monday, March 27, 1780. They engaged in a sharp skirmish, killing four Loyalists and six Native Americans and only had one man slightly wounded.[186]

★ A party of Georgia militiamen routed some Loyalists and Native Americans at Sunbury on Wednesday, March 28, 1780, killing 10 of them.[187]

★ Captain John Howell (1756–1830), a privateer captain, stopped a slave who had been sent out to catch fish on Monday, June 4, 1781. The slave told him that the British officers planned to celebrate the King's birthday that evening at Mr. James Kitchin's house, less than 400 yards from Fort George, formerly Fort Morris and renamed for the king. Captain Howell decided to capture the officers during dinner.

Howell and 12 men approached the fort with muffled oars and landed at Sunbury. They surrounded the Kitchin house at 11 PM and captured the entire party of 12 men, including Colonel Roger Kelsall of the St. John's Parish Militia who had treated Howell badly when he was a prisoner earlier in the war. Howell wanted to take Kelsall out to the river to drown him, but Mrs. Kitchin convinced him to spare Kelsall's life. Captain Howell paroled his prisoners and returned to his privateer.[188]

★ Captain Caldeleugh's British brigantine *Dunmore* sailed from Sunbury for Jamaica on Monday, September 18, 1781. Shortly after the *Dunmore* sailed out of Tybee Roads and crossed the bar, Captain John Howell (1756–1830) and Captain John Braddock (1743–1797), both in schooner-rigged galleys attacked her. Captain Braddock commanded the larger galley—60-feet long with two carriage guns and a number of swivels (see Photo GA-11) and a crew of more than 50. The vessels engaged in a "brisk" fight for four hours, from 10 AM to 2 PM. The crews of both galleys attempted to board the *Dunmore* whose fire forced them to sheer off. Both galleys ran aground but got off to return to the action. The *Dunmore* managed to escape, but she was so damaged that she had to go to the port of Savannah for repairs.

When the *Dunmore* resumed her voyage in October, Captain Howell, aboard the *Sailor's Delight*, was waiting for her with Captain Braddock's galley and Captain George McCumber's (1756–1841) galley *Tyger*. They attacked the *Dunmore* again, but she outsailed them and succeeded in escaping a second time. In the chase, the *Tyger* capsized near Hilton Head Island, spilling 32 men into the sea. Captain Howell picked up 30 of them.[189]

Fort Darien (late 1778–early 1779)

The site of Fort Darien was located on a bluff overlooking the Darien River toward the end (about 1 mile) of what is now route GA 25 Spur (Fort King George Drive). Route GA 25 Spur is about 0.2 miles south of the center of Darien and east of its junction with routes US 17 (GA 25) and GA 99 (North Walton Street), just before the bridge across the Darien River. There are four markers on the northeast bank of the bridge that describe Darien, its port, Fort Darien and nearby Fort King George. Houses and a Visitors Center now occupy the site.

General James Edward Oglethorpe (1696–1785) selected the site of Fort Darien in 1736. This fort, on the first high bluff near the mouth of the Altamaha River and 10 miles from the Atlantic, was built to protect the town of Darien and its port from the Spaniards in Florida. It consisted of two bastions (see Photo GA-21) and two half bastions and mounted several cannons. After the War with Spain, the fort was no longer needed and fell into ruins. It was rebuilt and armed during the American War of Independence to defend the town against the Crown forces.

Another marker in front of the city hall, at the intersection of North Way and Washington Street, notes that Darien was burned by Federal forces on June 11, 1863.

Route GA 25 Spur (Fort King George Drive) leads to McIntosh Road and to a reconstruction of old Fort King George (see Photo GA-1 and Photo GA-26) about 1.25 miles away. Archaeologists excavated the site which included a small blockhouse (see Photo GA-1) about 26 feet square with three floors and a lookout in the gables, officers' quarters and a barracks. A moat and palisades surrounded the fort on three sides, excepting the river side. The fort was occupied by the English-speaking settlers between 1721 and 1727, during which time more than 140 officers and men lost their lives in conflicts with Spanish expeditions. The site also includes a reconstructed Guale Indian village.

Another marker, on route US 17 (GA 25|North Way) where it crosses King Swamp, about 7 miles north of Darien, commemorates Ardoch (see Photo GA-27), the plantation home of the McDonalds, who were Loyalists during the American War of Independence. Charles McDonald (1752–1782) was killed in the presence of his wife and children in a skirmish here and his house was burned. Buddy Sullivan seems to be the only source of this information. He states:

GA-26. *Fort King George (reconstructed) included a small blockhouse, officers' quarters and a barracks. A moat and palisades surrounded the fort on three sides.*

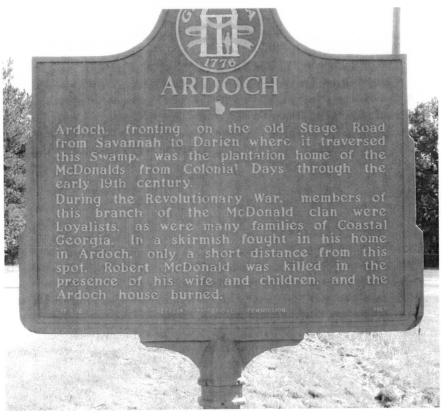

GA-27. *Ardoch marker commemorates the Ardoch plantation where Charles McDonald, a Loyalist, was supposedly killed in the presence of his wife and children.*

Ardoch was a plantation that developed in the center of the District of Darien about halfway between Darien and Sapelo Bridge. Ardoch was not close to any tidal streams or rivers, unusual for the 18th century plantations of the Scots.

Ardoch abutted a large swamp and fronted on the Broad Road which connected Darien and Savannah, roughly paralleling present-day US 17. It was the plantation of Charles and Margaret McDonald until the time of the American Revolution.

In the Revolution this branch of the McDonald clan tried to remain neutral. Charles McDonald was shot and killed in the presence of his family during a skirmish at Ardoch, after which the plantation was looted by renegades.[190]

According to the marker, Captain Patrick ("Paddy") Carr (1761–1820) and Captain Samuel West deserted Brigadier General "Mad Anthony" Wayne's (1745–1796) command in 1782 and plundered St. Andrew's Parish. They murdered 11 Loyalists, including Ardoch's owner, Charles McDonald (1752–1782). McDonald was killed in his own doorway in the presence of his wife and children and the house was burned.

Ludowici
Beard's Bluff (Dec. 28, 1776)

Beard's Bluff is on the Altamaha River at the end of Beard's Bluff Road, which runs along Beard's Creek, in Ludowici. One should not confuse this local or rural road with the Beard's Bluff Road in Odum and Jessup, Georgia on the south side of the Altamaha. The two main roads which intersect in Ludowici (McDonald and Cypress streets have different designations depending on the direction: US 25 (US 301|GA 23|GA 57); US 84 (GA 38|Cypress Street); US 25 (US 84|Cypress Street); and GA 57 (McDonald Street). Take route US 25 (US 301|GA 23|GA 57) northwest and proceed for 14.5 miles to route CR 261. A marker here directs you to turn south (left) onto Beard's Bluff Road. Beard's Bluff is 5 miles down the road.

Beard's Bluff was an important stockade on the Georgia frontier during the American War of Independence. The British encouraged the Native American tribes to attack the colonists. The site, which controlled a crossing, was the scene of frequent skirmishes between the Native Americans and the local militiamen who manned the post.

At the end of 1776, Lieutenant Jeremiah Bugg (1752/1757–1787) commanded a company of 27 Continental light horsemen at Beard's Bluff, about 40 miles north of Fort Howe on the Altamaha River. A band of Native Americans wounded a man outside the "fort or loghouse" late Wednesday evening, December 27, 1776. The lieutenant led 12 men to reconnoiter early the next morning. About 400 yards from the fort, they came under fire from a party of Native Americans concealed in the swamp of Beard's Creek. The Native Americans killed four men and Bugg's horse.

The survivors, who had not fired a single shot, fled to the fort, leaving Lieutenant Bugg to fend for himself. The Native Americans scalped the dead and stuck an arrow into each one. Lieutenant Bugg managed to return to the fort to find his men so panic-stricken that they refused to leave the fort or even to try to maintain their post. After burying their dead, the men all deserted. Lieutenant Bugg managed to persuade only one man to accompany him to Fort Howe to report the attack. General Lachlan McIntosh (1727–1806) ordered Lieutenant Ignatius Few (1750–1777) to march from Savannah with 12 horsemen to relieve Bugg. He then sent Captain Chesley Bostick (1740–1808) and 40 infantrymen.[191]

Georgia coast (Oct. 26, 1779; Nov. 9, 1779; Dec. 8, 1779)

The frigate HMS *Guadeloupe,* bound from Quebec to Georgia, ran into a hurricane Sunday night, October 24, 1779 and was blown into the path of Admiral Comte Jean-Baptiste-Charles-Henri-Hector d'Estaing's (1729–1794) fleet which was leaving Savannah. She narrowly escaped capture by three 74-gun French warships. Captain Samuel Spencer's (1739–1794) brig *Betsey,* loaded with lumber and rice at Sunbury was captured by the *Witch* on her maiden voyage and was escorted to Charleston, South Carolina. She then headed to Cap François, Antigua when she encountered the *Guadeloupe* and the *Roebuck.* Unable to hoist her sails in the gale, which lasted until Tuesday, the 26th, the *Betsey* could not outsail the warships which captured her during the storm.

★ The *Betsey* then fell in with the HMS *Tryal* and *Chance* off the coast of Saint Domingue (about 641 miles east of Nassau and 330 miles north of San Juan, Puerto Rico) on Tuesday, November 9, 1779. She was dismasted and so disabled by the stress of the weather that her captors burned her after taking out the men and some of the most valuable articles.[192]

★ Captain Perouse captured the British privateer *Tiger* on Wednesday, December 8, 1779. The *Tiger* was originally a French privateer commanded by Captain Jacques Baby dit Duperon (1731–1789) and captured by the HMS *Ceres* off the coast of South America in October 1778. Both ships joined the French fleet departing Savannah.[193]

Campbell's Plantation (Feb. 26, 1782)

Lieutenant Ford and a detachment from the 7th Regiment and the King's American Regiment marched to William Campbell's plantation at 10 PM on Tuesday, February 26, 1782. They surprised a party of Whigs, killed three, wounded several, and took four prisoners, some of whom had British protections in their pockets.[194]

Skidaway Island
Delegal's Plantation (July 25, 1782)

Philip Delegal's plantation was at the southeast point of Skidaway Island, about 13 miles southeast of Savannah.

Brigadier General "Mad Anthony" Wayne (1745–1796) ordered Lieutenant Colonel James Jackson (1757–1806) and a few militiamen of his Georgia Legion to occupy a post at Philip Delegal's (ca.1713–1781) plantation on Skidaway Island. They were ordered to oppose Lieutenant Colonel Thomas Brown (1750–1825) and his force of about 500 Regulars, Native Americans and Loyalists who had sailed from Tybee on Wednesday, July 24, 1782 and landed on Skidaway Island. Meanwhile, General Wayne advanced to join him with his light infantry, artillery and cavalry.

Colonel Jackson's men captured an armed British boat with her crew on Thursday, July 25, 1782. However, a superior number of Crown troops, supported by two armed galleys and several large armed vessels destroyed the buildings on Delegal's plantation, forcing them to retreat. Colonel Brown and his men then re-embarked and proceeded to Ossabaw Island, where they remained for some time.[195]

2
FLORIDA

Spain sided with France during the Seven Years War (French and Indian War) (1756–1763) and ceded Florida to Great Britain in exchange for Cuba in the Royal Proclamation of 1763 which ended that war. The British divided the territory into two colonies: East Florida and West Florida. The Apalachicola River divided the two parts and still serves as a county boundary. East Florida occupied most of the present-day state and had its capital at Saint Augustine. West Florida, with its capital at Pensacola, extended westward to the Mississippi and included parts of present-day Alabama, Mississippi and Louisiana (see the chapters on those states).

Many Loyalists from Georgia and South Carolina fled to East Florida during the American War of Independence. Raids and counterraids were common along the East Florida-Georgia border. Spain joined the war in 1779 and captured Mobile (now Alabama) in 1780 and Pensacola in 1781. The British formally returned both East Florida and West Florida to Spain in the Treaty of Paris in 1783.

> The state tourism website (**www.visitflorida.com**) provides a little information about historical landmarks.

See the map of southern Georgia and Florida.

St. Augustine Bar (August 7, 1775)
St. Johns River (August 1775)
St. Augustine (1776, 1777, 1778)

> St. Augustine, the oldest city in the United States, is on the east coast of Florida south of Jacksonville. The Castillo de San Marcos National Monument (see Photo FL-1) is on the Matanzas River, east of the intersection of route FL 1A (South Castillo Drive) and Shenandoah Street. The fort interprets the Spanish fort of the 17th century. The St. Augustine restored Spanish Quarter is a short walk south of the Castillo. The St. Augustine Historical Society is on Charlotte Street.

The South Carolina Sloop *Commerce* got under way at 6 AM on Monday, August 7, 1775 and headed toward the St. Augustine bar. Captain John Hatter saw a sailing vessel at anchor off the bar and approached her. He hailed her and found her to be the brigantine *Betsey*, commanded by Captain Alvere Lofthouse, from London. Captain Hatter sent his sloop to board her. The crew searched the *Betsey* and found 11,000 pounds of gunpowder consigned to the local garrison aboard. The men of the *Commerce* took 111 barrels, one half barrel and 30 small kegs.

The *Betsey* also had 23 men aboard, including 12 soldiers from shore, eight seamen, the captain, two mates and a steward. The *Commerce* had 21 whites and five African Americans. However, Captain Hatter thought it prudent to bribe the men with £100 currency. He also gave the captain a draught for £1,000 for the powder. The men spiked the *Betsey's* two cannons about 11:30 AM and returned to the *Commerce* which passed the St. Johns River at 4 PM.[1]

FL-1. Castillo de San Marcos (St. Augustine) is the oldest fort in the continental United States. It anchored the St. Augustine defense system (city wall, supplementary lines, and outposts at Matanzas Inlet, the St. Johns River and St. Marks. The Castillo replaced the last of nine successive wooden forts which protected the city and Spanish shipping since 1565. Courtesy of Paul Bazin.

★ The Whigs began thinking about capturing St. Augustine as early as the fall of 1775. The British garrison was defended by only 150 soldiers and housed Loyalists from the southern colonies, called refugees. The increasing number of refugees coming to East Florida created a greater need for food. The Florida Rangers (local volunteers) looked to Georgia as a source of supply and stole much of it there. While some of the troops got as far as the St. Johns in September, most never got out of Georgia, putting an end to the expedition. Cattle stealing raids from Florida resumed.

★ Major General Charles Lee (1731–1782) planned an expedition to destroy the Loyalist settlements along the St. Johns River by August 1775. He assembled his forces at Savannah. They consisted of 260 Continentals and a contingent of Virginia and North Carolina militiamen. However, as General Lee made his preparations, the Continental Congress summoned him to Philadelphia. Before leaving, he ordered the Virginia and North Carolina troops to follow him.

First Florida Expedition (1776)

The Continental Congress recommended to the Carolinas and Georgia on Monday, January 1, 1776, that they capture St. Augustine which, by then, had been reinforced with additional British troops:

> Resolved, That the seizing and securing the barracks and castle of St. Augustine will greatly contribute to the safety of these colonies, therefore it is earnestly recommended to the colonies of South Carolina, North Carolina and Georgia to undertake the reduction of St. Augustine, if it be thought practicable. . . .
>
> Resolved, That the first resolution together with copies or extracts of such of the intercepted letters as tend to shew the state of the forts and garrison at St. Augustine be transmitted by express to Henry Middleton and John Rutledge Esqrs members of Congress to be by them laid before the committees directed to meet [at Charleston] in consequence of the above resolution and in case the enterprize be judged practicable that immediate preparations be made by the joint force of the said colonies (viz. South Carolina, North Carolina and Georgia) and the expedition be undertaken without delay at the expence of the united colonies.

Colonel William Moultrie (1730–1805) assumed command of the expedition after the Continental Congress summoned Major General Charles Lee (1731–1782) to Philadelphia. The expedition soon encountered trouble as the troops marched south. The hot summer sun and the swamps of the Ogeechee River made the march very difficult. Fever and camp sicknesses devastated the men as they did not have a medicine chest with them. The death rate climbed to 14 or 15 a day. The expedition reached Sunbury, about 25 miles south of Savannah, and had to turn back, ending the Whigs' first serious attempt to invade Florida.[2]

Second Florida Expedition (April–May 1777)
Nassau River
Sawpit Bluff (May 4, 1777; May 14, 1777)
Battle of Thomas Creek (May 17, 1777)
Amelia Island (May 19, 1777)

The battle of Thomas Creek took place where route US 1 (US 23|FL 115|South Kings Road) crosses Thomas Creek (see Photo FL-2) in Callahan. A historical marker is located on route US 1 (US 23|FL 115|South Kings Road) south of Callahan. It is between the north and southbound high-speed lanes on the south side of the bridge that crosses Thomas Creek at the county line. The battlefield remains undeveloped, much as it was in 1777.[3]

Sawpit Bluff (see Photo FL-3) was near the mouth of the Nassau River, about 1.25 miles south of the confluence of the Intercoastal Waterway and the Nassau River in Jacksonville.

FL-2. Thomas Creek, site of the battle on May 17, 1777

FL-3. Sawpit Bluff, the rendezvous point for Lieutenant Colonel Samuel Elbert's Continentals and Lieutenant Colonel John Baker's Georgia militiamen for the second Florida expedition. It gets its name from George Rolfe's saw mill, which was nearby.

After the failure of the 1776 expedition, Florida Loyalists were not content to remain on the defensive. They organized a retaliatory expedition to invade Georgia early in 1777. Lieutenant Colonel Lewis Valentine Fuser (d. 1780) commanded 500 British Regulars and 100 East Florida Rangers, under Lieutenant Colonel Thomas Alexander Brown (1744–1814) and Colonel Daniel McGirth (d. ca. 1789), a battery of field pieces and about 400 Creeks. They took the King's Road (now State Road Number Four) north from St, Augustine and passed through Cowford. They left Captain George McIntosh, of the 60th Regiment ("Royal Americans") and a garrison of 50 men at the house of Captain Taylor when they reached the St. Marys River. The men fortified the house and named it Fort McIntosh, probably as a bit of humor, as they were marching to attack the Whig fort of that name on the northeast side of the Satilla River.

See below pp. 113–120 and **Georgia, Fort McIntosh on the Satilla** pp. 81–84.

Planning began for a second expedition in 1777. Brigadier General Robert Howe (1732–1786), the new Continental commander, met with Button Gwinnett (1735?–1777) and the members of the Council of Safety in March. They had only 400 troops available and insisted that General Howe provide enough to capture St. Augustine. As Howe was unsure that he could raise sufficient troops for the task, Council president Gwinnett planned the campaign without consulting either Howe or General Lachlan McIntosh (1727–1806), Georgia's Continental commander.

Gwinnett's call for militiamen brought in fewer than 200 men, and he was forced to swallow his pride and request General McIntosh's aid on March 25. McIntosh prepared to march with his Continentals, even though he agreed with General Robert Howe that their available force was too small to accomplish much.

Gwinnett and McIntosh were always at odds—mostly because Gwinnett publicly accused McIntosh's brother of disloyalty. The Georgia Council of Safety recalled both of them to Savannah in mid-April 1777. They settled their feud on May 16, 1777, in a duel at Savannah. McIntosh called Gwinnett a scoundrel and Gwinnett challenged him to a duel. They exchanged shots at a distance of only 12 paces. Both men were wounded in the thigh. Gwinnett died three days later of blood poisoning.

Lieutenant Colonel Samuel Elbert (1740–1788), the new commander of the Congressional forces in Georgia, embarked the 400 Continentals, who were healthy enough to travel, on the morning of Thursday, May 1, 1777. The flotilla the Georgians put together to invade Florida consisted of three row galleys, two armed sloops and some transports carrying 20 cannons—12- to 24-pounders, besides swivels (see Photo GA-2). These troops, which probably consisted of all of the 1st and 2nd Georgia battalions, proceeded at a leisurely pace through the inland waterway to the St. Marys River.

Lieutenant Colonel John Baker (1750–1830), commanding the Georgia Continental Light Horse, led another force overland at the same time. These troops consisted of 109 volunteers from the Georgia militia and those of his light horsemen who had horses. Colonel Thomas Sumter's (1734–1832) South Carolina Horse did not participate in the expedition, as Baker had expected, because General Howe had recalled those troops.

Colonel Baker spent two days getting his troops across the Altamaha River, swollen by spring floods. Native Americans attacked his camp at dawn on Sunday, May 4. The skirmish lasted only a few minutes and left two soldiers wounded: lieutenants Robeson and John Frazer (1756–1825). One Native American was killed. Baker and 40 men pursued the attackers as far as Finhalloway (Penholoway) Creek, about 12 miles from camp, but they could not catch up with them. Baker's force started marching southward the next morning. The only difficulty they faced en route was crossing the Satilla and St. Marys rivers.

An unidentified woman from Amelia Island went aboard the galley *Congress* during the night of May 14 to warn Colonel Elbert that the British had been forewarned of their approach. She also gave them some of the details of their preparations.

Baker's militiamen arrived at the rendezvous location at Sawpit Bluff (see Photo FL-3) at the appointed time on May 12, ahead of the Continentals. Colonel Baker immediately sent out a 40-man detachment to scout the countryside as far as Cowford. The scouts discovered that the Crown forces were aware of the expedition and were preparing a strong resistance.

Lieutenant Colonel Thomas Alexander Brown (1744–1814), about 40 East Florida Rangers and some Native Americans boarded a schooner and an eight-oared boat to reconnoiter Baker's camp. A warrior named the Black Creek Factor led a party of Native Americans who stole 40 horses from Baker's camp during the night of Wednesday, May 14. Baker found the horses the next day, just 4 miles away, hobbled beside a swamp. The Native Americans used the horses as a trap to ambush the militiamen, but the plan failed.

Baker divided his force into three parties. One was ordered to stay in plain view to divert the Native Americans' attention while a smaller group cut the horses loose. Once the horses were free, the third party rushed between the horses and the swamp and drove the animals off. A group of 15 Native Americans pursued Baker's larger force. The militiamen killed one of the warriors but Baker could not persuade his men to sustain a battle and the Native Americans finally gave up the chase. Baker's men returned north on Saturday, May 17, 1777 to a better spot for observation and possible retreat.

★ As Baker searched for easy places to cross the creeks in the area, Major James Mark Prevost (1736–1781) and 300 British Regulars supported by Lieutenant Colonel Thomas Alexander Brown (1744–1814) and 100 Loyalist Florida Rangers and a band of loyal Native Americans marched to George Rolfe's saw mill at Sawpit Bluff, near the mouth of the Nassau River (11 miles due north of the present city of Jacksonville), where they encamped. The Crown forces surprised Baker at Thomas Creek about 10 o'clock Saturday morning, May 17, 1777. Major Prevost organized three columns of 100 men each to attack with fixed bayonets (see Photo GA-3).

Outnumbered four to one, 20 to 30 of Baker's men fled at the first volley. Heavy enemy fire forced Colonel Baker to retreat through the swamp with his remaining 50 men. Many of his men deserted in the swamp. The skirmish lasted about five minutes and Baker was almost captured. One of his men stole Baker's horse and used it to escape. Baker shouted at the rider that he would be shot in the back if he did not stop. The man stopped and he and Baker both escaped.

Baker lost eight men killed (including five massacred by the Native Americans after they surrendered), nine privates and two officers wounded and 31 captured. Captain Ignatius Few (1750–1777) and about 40 militiamen surrendered. The Native Americans killed all but 16 of them. The Native Americans captured Baker's baggage, commission, papers, and the plan of the proposed invasion of East Florida.[4]

★ When the Continentals arrived Sunday night, May 18, their boats could not get through the Amelia Narrows, just south of the St. Marys River. Colonel Elbert dispatched Lieutenant Robert Ward (d. 1777), of the 2nd Regiment, with about 20 men to round up all the inhabitants of Amelia. One of them, William Pryce, escaped in a canoe and gave the alarm.

Elbert detached another party, consisting of a subaltern, a sergeant, and 14 privates of the 1st Regiment, to join Ward's group on the south end of Amelia Island on May 19 because the troops were very short of provisions. Their most important duty was to kill and salt all the beef and hogs they could procure. Ward had specific orders not to mistreat any prisoners he might take, especially women and children.

A group of Loyalist inhabitants fired on his party, killed Lieutenant Ward and badly wounded two of his men. When news of the incident reached Elbert on May 20, he dispatched Lieutenant Jacob Winfrey (1740/50–1784) with orders to burn every house on Amelia Island and to destroy all the stock. He also captured at least seven slaves belonging to a man named Moore.[5]

Colonel Elbert's order book dated May 25, 1777 contains the following comments:

> On the morning of the 19th we were Joined by thirteen Colo. Baker's men, soon after
> by two more, & two Days after by three others, who all agree in the account of that
> unfortunate Gentlemen being attacked on Saturday, the 17th, by a Superior Number
> of Regulars who were assisted by the Florida Scout and a Number of Indians. . . .

Elbert decided that he did not have a strong enough force to capture East Florida; so he abandoned the expedition on May 26 and returned to Georgia, as Baker had already done. The raids from East Florida resumed immediately.

Georgia Loyalists provided the Crown forces in Florida with sufficient information about the size of the expedition for them to take adequate precautions to defend themselves and to send troops to Amelia Island and a detachment of artillery to defend the battery at St. Johns Bluff. They also sent an armed schooner and sloop to defend the inland passage between Amelia Island and the mainland. When Elbert realized the inability to preserve secrecy, he wrote a letter to General McIntosh on May 26, 1777 stating:

I am Just now favored by a Letter from Colo. Screven, wrote at your Desire; I lament the Behavior of Colonel Baker's Men, but it will always be the case where Subordination is wanting; this little Success will make the Enemy very Impudent, particularly the Indians; I think from every Information we can get that the Enemy are at present on their Guard, that little can be done, unless by a formidable Invasion, which I Judge to be rather too much for Georgia to undertake till her Forces are put on a more respectable footing, and therefore would recommend confining our Operations intirely to the defencive till a more favorable opportunity, we have too many Secret Enemies amongst us who Keep up a regular correspondence with our Florida Neighbors, and until they are put a Stop to it will be impossible for us to enter Florida without their having timely notice of our approach.

Major General Augustine Prevost (1723–1786) wrote to General William Howe (1732–1786) on June 14 about the skirmish at Thomas Creek:

Major Prevost grieves much that he had not a small party of that kind with him in his last skirmish with the rebel horse, as few of them could have escaped, having a deep river to pass after they were defeated. The Rangers and Indians who were with him at the time not being looked upon as being under the major's command, when urged by him to pursue, said their horses were too much fatigued. The Indians entirely intent on plunder thought nothing but securing all the horses they could find; and the King's troops, many of them barefoot and overcome with excessive heat, could not attempt to come up with people who fled with all possible swiftness and were on horseback.[6]

★ Governor Patrick Tonyn (1725–1804) intended that Captain John Mowbray with the sloop *Rebecca* and all the armed ships and vessels would sail into Saint Marys, while the troops marched northward scouring the island along their way. He hoped they would make a well concerted attack and defeat the Whigs. He ordered the armed ships *Rebecca* and *Hawke* to sail down the Saint Johns River and anchor outside the bar. He ordered the *Meredith* and the smaller armed vessels to be ready to go out to join them on short notice. However, a windstorm forced the *Rebecca* and the *Hawke* to sea. The *Rebecca* fell in with and engaged a 16-gun brigantine. They fought a brisk running battle dominated by the Whigs. The *Rebecca* silenced their fire for eight minutes and was bearing down upon the brigantine, the crew ready to board, when the brigantine renewed her fire. A shot destroyed the *Rebecca*'s topmast and tore her mainsail, which gave the brigantine the advantage in sailing and an opportunity to escape.

The *Rebecca* engaged to the leeward and the brigantine's decks were very much exposed to her fire. Two men were seen falling, from the tops, dead into the sea. Many others were believed to have been killed and nine wounded. The *Rebecca* returned in too shattered a condition to proceed to Saint Marys. The crew captured two captains and nine privates.

The Georgians tried to get their vessels through the shallow narrows between Amelia Island and the mainland for six days, struggling to move the last few miles into the St. Johns River and threaten St. Augustine. However, the three Georgia galleys under the command of Commodore Oliver Bowen (1742–1800) carried some heavy ordnance. One galley had an 18-pounder in her stern plus swivels (see Photo GA-11). A second galley had one 12-pounder in her bow and another 12-pounder in her stern, plus swivels. The third galley had one 18-pounder in her bow and another 18-pounder in her stern, plus two 9-pounders and four 6-pounders. These galleys were consequently too heavy to proceed through the shallow waters.

Colonel Elbert was unwilling to return to the open ocean in his unseaworthy craft, and he couldn't take a land route. His supply of beef was low, so he decided to return to the Satilla on May 26. When he arrived at Cumberland Island, he could muster only about 300 men, including Baker's Light Horse. So ended the second East Florida expedition.[7]

Third Florida Expedition (April–July 1778)
Fort McIntosh
Cabbage Swamp (June 29, 1778)
Alligator Creek Bridge (June 30, 1778)
Fort Tonyn (July 2, 1778)

Fort Tonyn was a British fort built where the King's Road from St. Augustine crossed the St. Marys River, the official border separating the colonies of Georgia and Florida. Fort Tonyn may have been located on the south bank of the St. Marys River along Lessie Road near Cabbage Swamp, about 1 mile east of Mills Ferry (Kings Ferry). Archaeological investigation in 1975 supports the location of the fort here (Reddick 1976; 20; Bullen 1961; Boatner 1968; Ward 1975). Some researchers locate it on Amelia Island at Fernandina Beach at the site now occupied by Fort Clinch. The fort was occupied by small detachments of Regulars and militiamen as reinforcements arrived.

Nothing remains of Fort McIntosh which was another British fort located south of Mills Ferry on the old Oakland Plantation. This Fort McIntosh should not be confused with the fort of the same name on the Satilla River in Georgia which was garrisoned by Congressional forces. To get to the site from the southwest, take route W CR 108 off US 1 (US 301) in Hilliard. After about half a mile, the road will intersect with route FL 115A (Kings Ferry Road). Follow Kings Ferry Road for about 8 miles. Fort McIntosh may have been located along this road or along Middle Road which is now farms and woodlands.

From the east, take exit 380 off Interstate 95 South (FL 9) and go south on route US 17 (FL 5) to CR 108. Turn right (west) and follow CR 108 for about 7.8 miles to Lessie Road. Turn right (north) on Lessie Road toward Kings Ferry (about 8 miles). Lessie Road crosses Cabbage Swamp about 5.3 miles from CR 108. The swamp is not visible from the road and there are no markers.

Alligator Creek Bridge was in Callahan, on route US 1 (US 23|US 301|FL 15) about a quarter mile northwest of route FL 2 (FL 200|East State Road|Highway A1a) and about 14 miles south of Fort Tonyn. Alligator Creek is a tributary of the Nassau River which it joins near Thomas Creek. A marker on the southeast corner of the modern bridge describes the action. A commercial development occupies the site of the British earthworks here (see Photo FL-4).

Georgia Governor John Houstoun (1744–1796) and his council began planning another expedition against St. Augustine early in 1778. They offered 500 acres of land in East Florida to anyone who could operate between the St. Marys and St. Johns rivers for three months. The offer recruited about 2,000 troops by the end of April. Major General Robert Howe (1732–1786) commanded the Continentals, Governor Houstoun headed the Georgia militia and Colonel Andrew Williamson (ca. 1730–1786) led the South Carolina militia. Commodore Oliver Bowen (1742–1800) commanded the Georgia navy. While Howe and Houstoun argued over who should have overall command of the

FL-4. Alligator Creek marker commemorates the skirmish at Alligator Creek bridge. A commercial development occupies the site of the British earthworks here.

expedition, Bowen refused to take orders from either one until they determined whether the navy was Continental or state.

The Georgia Continentals reached the Midway District by Thursday, April 9, 1778. They were at General McIntosh's plantation on the Altamaha River by Sunday the 12th. General Howe's Continentals were still on the march to Fort Howe, the rendezvous point on the Altamaha, when Colonel Daniel McGirth (d. ca. 1789) led a Loyalist raiding party north into the Midway District. McGirth encountered General Howe's superior force of Continentals along the way and retreated to the St. Marys, alerting the British to the Whig presence.

The Whig forces reached burned-out Fort Howe on Tuesday, April 14 and camped there. Colonel Samuel Elbert's Georgia brigade consisted of the 1st, 2nd, 3rd and 4th Georgia battalions of infantry, a detachment of light horsemen and two companies of artillery. Colonel Charles Cotesworth Pinckney's (1746–1825) South Carolina Continentals consisted of detachments from the 1st, 3rd, and 6th South Carolina Regiments and a detachment of artillery. Major Charles-Noel-François Romand de l'Isle ("De Lisle") commanded the Georgia and Carolina artillery.

Colonel Elbert marched a detachment of three field officers, six captains, 18 subalterns, 24 sergeants, six drummers, two fifers and 300 privates to Darien, Georgia on the 16th where they boarded the galleys *Washington, Lee* and *Bulloch*. Captain George Young's detachment from the 1st Company of Georgia Continental Artillery boarded a flatboat with two field pieces. Colonel Elbert left detachments of men on board the galleys to act as marines while his main force landed near Frederica on St. Simons Island, Georgia.

Elbert sent Lieutenant Colonel Robert Rae and Major Daniel Roberts (1734/5–1779) with about 100 men to enter the town where they captured two sailors and three marines from HMS *Hinchinbrook*. The Continental galleys found three British vessels in Raccoon Gut near Frederica about 5:30 AM on Sunday, April 19. They were the *Hinchinbrook*, the privateer *Rebecca* and the snow *Hope*. The *Hinchinbrook* and *Rebecca* ran aground. They leaned over on their sides as the tide ebbed, exposing their decks to the galleys' fire. Unable to return fire, the crews escaped in their longboats.

Captain John Mowbray tried unsuccessfully to destroy the *Rebecca* before abandoning her. The Continentals captured nine of the *Hinchinbrook*'s crew, Captain Mowbray and all the other crewmen of the *Rebecca* without any casualties. The captured cargo included 130 uniforms originally brought from France by the Marquis de Brétigny and seized from Captain John Hatter's vessel off the Charleston Bar. This Continental victory left the frigate *Galatea* as East Florida's only naval defense.

Colonel Charles Cotesworth Pinckney (1746–1825) formed the Carolina Continental forces into a brigade the following week. A detachment of 30 matrosses from the South Carolina artillery also arrived and joined Major Romand's Georgia Continental artillery. Brigadier General Andrew Williamson (ca. 1730–1786) was on his way to Fort Howe with 800 to 1,200 South Carolina militiamen and Commodore Oliver Bowen of the Georgia Continental Navy commanded the expedition's naval elements. Colonel Elbert's 500 Georgia Continentals had already been encamped at Fort Howe for almost a month. The number of desertions increased, particularly among the soldiers of the 4th Battalion Georgia Continentals, as the unseasonably hot temperatures got hotter.

The Georgia and Carolina brigades finally started breaking camp on Monday, May 25. They crossed the Altamaha and camped at Reid's Bluff on the south side of the river, only 3 miles upstream from Fort Howe, from May 28 to June 6. Heavy rains delayed the crossings and seriously endangered their ammunition. Provisions ran short.

★ Enemy scouting and raiding parties fired on the Congressional forces, keeping them confined. A party of 16 Native American warriors killed and scalped Samuel Seeds (1733–1778), the expedition's armorer, Thursday morning, June 4, as he traveled between Fort Howe and Reid's Bluff.

Sickness devastated the camp. An estimated 300 men had become so ill on June 6 that they were moved out of the camp at Reid's Bluff to Darien, Georgia. Only about 700 Continentals were fit for duty a week later.

★ Whig Lieutenant Colonel Francis Henry Harris's scouting party and Major John Habersham's (d. 1782) mounted volunteers encountered a detachment of East Florida Rangers on the north side of the Satilla River on Wednesday, June 17, 1778. They engaged in a brief skirmish and Harris's men captured eight good horses, five saddles and bridles, their blankets and one Ranger.

★ The Whigs crossed the Satilla River and encamped near Fort McIntosh on the St. Marys on Tuesday, June 23, 1778. They met with no resistance in the crossing and none in taking the deserted Fort Tonyn on the southern bank of the St. Marys. The remaining Georgia and South Carolina Continentals fit for duty crossed the St. Marys on June 28. As the last of the South Carolina Continentals were crossing the St. Marys, Governor Houstoun, Brigadier General James Screven (1744–1778) and the Georgia State Line and Militia arrived on its north bank. The force included Colonel John Stewart's (ca. 1719–1777) battalion of about 200 men, Colonel Samuel Jack's battalion of about 500 men and five field pieces, and Colonel George Walton's (1749–1804) detachment from the 1st Regiment Georgia Militia.

The whole army waited for hours while Governor Houstoun argued with Major General Robert Howe (1732–1786) over command of the expedition and whether they should attack the East Florida Rangers at Fort Tonyn, 10 miles downstream, or Major General Augustine Prevost's (1723–1786) Regulars posted 15 or 20 miles away on the St. Augustine highway. The two could not agree, so the governor persuaded George Mills, the only reliable guide available and owner of Mills' Ferry, located on the north side of the St. Marys River across from Fort Tonyn, to guide the militia. The Continentals began their march toward Fort Tonyn at 4 PM Sunday afternoon, June 28.

In the meantime, Loyalist Lieutenant Colonel Thomas Alexander Brown's (1744–1814) East Florida Rangers camped in nearby Cabbage Swamp. The Rangers took advantage of the Congressional forces' delay to secure their supplies and equipment and burn Fort Tonyn before fleeing into Cabbage Swamp. The Rangers emerged from the swamp to harass General Howe's forces as much as possible.

★ A picket of the Georgia brigade saw three horsemen reconnoitering the Congressional camp and fired at them on Monday, June 29, 1778. One of the Georgia light horsemen pursued one of the Loyalists so closely that the scout had to drop his baggage, including his green coat, to escape into Cabbage Swamp. The contents of the baggage revealed that it belonged to Lieutenant Colonel Thomas Alexander Brown (1744–1814), commander of the East Florida Rangers.

Major General Robert Howe (1732–1786) sent Brigadier General James Screven (1744–1778) and 900 troops to dislodge the Rangers, but they were unsuccessful after some time. Lieutenant Colonel James Mark Prevost (1736–1781) sent 200 Regulars, under Major Graham, to rescue Lieutenant Colonel Thomas Alexander Brown (1744–1814) and his Rangers from the swamp.

Brown withdrew his forces to Alligator Creek Bridge where they joined Colonel Prevost, but many of them had lost their weapons in the swamp. They departed so hastily that they buried, burned and hid provisions to prevent their capture. General Howe had his engineers examine the remains of Fort Tonyn to determine if it could be easily restored.

Meanwhile, the Continentals entered the Amelia Narrows, near the present site of Fernandina, and joined with Commodore Oliver Bowen's (1742–1800) fleet. This brought the force to about 800 men, including the naval force, which consisted of five galleys, two flats, two pettiaugers (see Photo FL-5) and several sloops and schooners.

While the Regulars were rescuing the Rangers, Colonel Prevost sent another detachment of British to disperse a party of Congressional troops encamped at Nassau Bluff, on the north side of the Nassau River near its mouth. The party accomplished its mission and returned to the camp at Alligator Bridge. They arrived about the same time as the rescued Rangers did.[8]

★ Georgia Governor John Houstoun (1744–1796) ordered Brigadier General James Screven's (1744–1778) 300 Georgia militiamen to pursue the Loyalists to Alligator Creek, to reconnoiter their position and to attack them if they had not received reinforcements. Brigadier General James Screven (1744–1778) sent a detachment of just over 100 mounted state line troops and militiamen under Lieutenant Colonel Elijah Clarke (1733–1799) to attack the position.

FL-5. Pettiauger Mercury *(replica). Courtesy of Gene Tozzi, Sailing Master, Pettiauger* Mercury.

Major John Faucheraud Grimké (1752–1819), who was with Major General Robert Howe (1732–1786), kept an interesting account of what transpired with the Continentals and what they heard of the militia. He ascribed the leadership of the Congressional forces at Alligator Creek to Brigadier General James Screven, but this is inconsistent with the actual charge being led by Colonel Elijah Clarke, whom Grimké does not mention.

Lieutenant Colonel James Mark Prevost (1736–1781), brother of Major General Augustine Prevost (1723–1786), was at Alligator Creek Bridge, some 18 miles due north of Cowford. He commanded 500 Crown troops inside the fort at Alligator Creek Bridge and 200 Regulars outside. Lieutenant Colonel Thomas Alexander Brown (1744–1814) and Colonel Daniel McGirth (d. ca. 1789) had about 900 East Florida Rangers. A deserter gave the following account of the Crown forces in East Florida: 800 regular troops, 100 Florida Rangers, 150 provincial militiamen, 350 Loyalists from the Carolinas and Georgia and 200 Native Americans, making a total of 1,600 troops.

The newly formed South Carolina Royalists and a detachment of grenadiers of the 2nd Battalion and light companies of the 60th Regiment and 4th Battalion 60th Regiment, manned a small redoubt (see Photo FL-6) surrounded by a trench and entanglements of log and brush. It guarded the Alligator Creek Bridge over that tributary of the Nassau River, about 14 miles from Fort Tonyn.

Colonel Clarke led 300 mounted Georgia militiamen against the weakest flank of the redoubt on Tuesday, June 30, 1778. They attacked about noon, just as the Rangers were crossing the bridge into camp, hoping to throw the Crown forces into confusion so the main attack could advance quickly on the Crown front. Clarke expected about 900

FL-6. Redoubt. Exterior of reconstructed Redoubt Number 9 at Yorktown, VA.

militiamen in the vicinity to act as reserves and assist in the initial attack. An even larger body of Continental troops near the St. Marys was too far away to help in this battle.

Captain Patrick Murray of the 60th Regiment light infantry saw the grenadiers (see Photo GA-15) marching into their camp, their drummer beating the "Grenadier's March," when the Congressional troops attacked suddenly, shouting "Down with the Tories." The drummer immediately beat "To arms" as the surprised grenadiers ran for their weapons.

The Congressional forces advanced but the horses got entangled in the logs and brush and had great difficulty getting through. When they reached the ditch, they found it was too wide to leap over. When the Loyalists heard the Georgia militiamen, they hastily lined the road and fired on the militia's flanks. The Regulars, who were probably cleaning their arms or bathing in the creek, had time to get under arms. Lieutenant Colonel Thomas Alexander Brown (1744–1814) and 200 British Regulars together with Colonel Daniel McGirth (d. ca. 1789) and about 100 Florida Rangers met them at the ditch. The horses, unaccustomed to the musket fire, would not advance. The Crown troops put up a steady fire that forced the militiamen to mount their horses and retreat. Colonel Clarke was shot in the thigh and barely escaped.[9]

As the diversionary action failed, the main body did not attempt to attack the front of the fort. A retreat was ordered. The militia lost 13 killed, including an African American, nine wounded, including Clarke and Brigadier General James Screven, and one captured. The Rangers attacked Clarke's left flank and the entire Georgia militia abandoned the assault after a brisk fight and retreated northward. The Crown troops lost one soldier killed and seven Rangers wounded, two seriously, and withdrew southward. Captain Murray's memoirs contain the following chronicle of events:

> At day break a large decked boat full of men appeared under sail in the Nassau passage, and made a signal for the Bluff, which not being answered, she put about and hastened down the rivers with oars. Captain Murray had notice of this by one of the Loyalists whom he had left there as a decoy and joined Major Prevost at 10 o'clock. At about mid-day when the men from the detachment were cleaning their arms and others washing in the creek in front of the camp the Grenadiers constructing a breastwork,—Major Graham's detachment had joined on the evening before—while Colonel Brown encamped at a swamp in front about 10 miles to collect his men.

At mid-day a mounted Sergeant came to Major Prevost's tent to announce the Colonel being at hand with his Corps. The Major, by the Sergeant, desired Colonel Brown to come to his tent; presently we heard Whitfield the Drummer beating the Grenadiers' March, and the rangers filing over a bridge where he had a sub-guard. Soon after entering when the Ranger drum beat to arms, and the Rangers many of whom had lost their arms in the cabbage swamp, were seen flying into that in front of our camp Captain Muller of the Grenadiers and his men running to the Camp for their arms, musket balls whistling over our tents while the enemy with sabres and rifles were shouting, 'down with the Tories.' Captains Smith and Johnston with a few of their Rangers bravely defended the Aligator bridge, till the regulars having got under arms and relieved them.

Murray reported the Loyalist losses in this battle as "One man of the 2nd. Battalion was killed and one of the 4th. wounded; Captains Johnston and Smith with five of Brown's rangers wounded." Colonel Brown sent his account of the battle of Alligator Creek Bridge to Governor Tonyn in a letter dated June 30:

Sir

I have the honour to inform your Excellency that the day before yesterday, on being informed that the Rebels had crossed the river St. Mary's in three different places high up—I immediately marched from Fort Tonyn within half a mile of their Camp and dispatched a party to reconnoitre the position of the rebels.

The party in a few minutes returned and informed me that a considerable body of horse was encamped at McGirtts with near Sixty Tents; from this information, and as I found the Rebels were attempting every pass of the river were it was fordable, and indefensible I thought proper to return to Fort Tonyn and secure our baggage, and Provisions; on our march the Rebels fired twice upon our scouts—In the evening I took post at little St. Mary's and on receiving information that Major Graham with a party refugees and regulars were on their march, I immediately crossed the woods and effected a junction with him.

Major Graham in a few minutes after our conjunction received orders to retreat, and returned to Camp before night.

As I was determined to harrass and annoy the Rebels as much as was in our power, when they presumed to advance, I took post at a Bridge Six Miles in his rear—after halting until morning I marched towards the Camp and received information from our rear guard, that the Rebel horse was in our rear charging full speed—and him I immediately formed on each side of the road about Sixty or Eighty yards from Major Prevost's Camp in expectation the regulars or refugees would have advanced to our support as the Rebels were in appearance very numerous.

The Regulars from a redoubt (for the defence of the pass of the swamp) fired very briskly; with two Companies of Rangers I immediately obtained the left flank of the rebels—the rebels struck with consternation at an attack in Front and flank fled in great disorder.

A number of the Rebels were killed, nine have been found, many of the wounded I observed the rebels packing on their horses, which have been driven off.

Six Indians joined me this day, this Check which the Rebels have received perhaps will tend to discourage them.

Major Prevost I believe purposes to retreat shortly—One of the regulars is killed, and five of the rangers wounded—Capt. Smith and Lieutenant Johnston I am apprehensive are mortally wounded— Johnston in the head and Smith in the breast.

A person from Georgia informs me that Moore, and nine of his Company are killed—this report wants confirmation.

I have the honor to be Sir,

(Signed) Thos. Brown[10]

★ As Major James Mark Prevost (1736–1781) moved his advance corps back from Alligator Creek to Six Mile Creek on July 1, he had his men cut trees to block the road through the swamps. Two frigates patrolled the coast. The Georgia militiamen and the Continentals were camped about 8 miles apart on opposite sides of the St. Marys River.

Governor John Houstoun (1744–1796) wanted Major General Robert Howe (1732–1786) and the Continentals ready to join the militia for another attack at Alligator Creek the following day, Wednesday, July 2. The Continentals were out of rice, as a supply galley had failed to arrive as expected; so General Howe agreed, on condition that Houstoun give them some rice. Houstoun declined, saying that he did not have enough provisions for the next day's rations. When the supply galley arrived on July 2nd, the Continentals had been without bread for three days. Houstoun's attack never occurred.

★ Lieutenant Colonel John McIntosh (1755–1826) led a raid on Fort Tonyn on, July 2, 1778. The fort was garrisoned by an estimated 300 Regulars. McIntosh killed one man and captured nine others before burning the fort. The destruction of Fort Tonyn was one of the principal goals of the third Florida expedition as it was a base for raids into Georgia by Lieutenant Colonel Thomas Alexander Brown's (1744–1814) East Florida Rangers and a haven for fleeing Loyalists.[11]

★ Colonel Elbert began marching out of East Florida with his men on Tuesday, July 14. His sick and wounded retreated in boats and ships through the waterways and returned to Savannah. The militia forces had no choice but to follow them.

The third and final attempt to capture St. Augustine ended in failure, as the previous two, mainly because of the inability of the commanders to cooperate with each other. The hot weather, inadequate transportation and supplies, sickness, and unrest along the Georgia frontier because of the Native Americans were other factors.[12]

See also **Georgia, Ogeechee River** pp. 13–16.

Proposed Fourth Invasion of Florida

The Marquis de Brétigny presented another plan to attack St. Augustine to the Continental Congress in Philadelphia on Wednesday, August 26, 1778. He informed them of Fort St. Mark's weak points and succeeded in persuading Congress to undertake another invasion of East Florida. The capture of St. Augustine and Pensacola was expected to end Native American raids along the frontiers and raids by East Florida Rangers in Georgia and South Carolina. This campaign would take place in the early winter, probably November, a more favorable season for military operations in the South.

The attacking force would include 3,000 men, a small artillery train and some siege cannons to reduce Fort St. Mark. Bateaux (see Photo FL-7) would land the troops, provisions, artillery and camp equipment at the St. Johns River, about 30 miles north of St. Augustine, under the protection of galleys. Mounted troops and light infantrymen would drive a herd of cattle there to be ready for the expedition.

Governor Patrick Tonyn (1725–1804) learned of these plans and had Captain James Moncrieff (1744–1793), the army engineer, construct additional armed boats for East Florida's defense. Congress appointed Major General Benjamin Lincoln (1733–1810) to replace Major General Robert Howe (1732–1786) as commander of the Southern Department on September 25. Howe received the official message from Congress in November, after he had also received an urgent message from Georgia for assistance. He wrote Congress that he was delaying his return northward to assist Georgia. He was defeated at Savannah.[13]

FL-7. Bateaux. Reenactors in reconstructed bateaux, a light flat-bottomed riverboat with sharply tapering stern and bow.

St. Marys River (Sept. 1775; May 29–31, 1776; June 1, 1776; June 7, 8, 9, 10, 1776; July 11, 1776; late summer, 1776; May 15, 1777; July 14, 1777)

Jermyn Wright (b. ca. 1708) had two plantations on the St. Marys River. One comprised 300 acres, about 12 miles from the mouth of the river. The larger plantation (500 acres) was about 80 miles farther upstream and about 100 miles west of St. Augustine. Jermyn and Charles Wright (b. ca. 1710), brothers of James Wright (1714–1785), governor of Georgia, built a fort on their land on the St. Marys River in 1776 or 1777 to protect their land during the war. The fort, named Wright's Fort became a rendezvous for the Georgia and North Florida Loyalists. The latter, called "Florida Rangers," robbed many south Georgians and stored their loot at Wright's Fort.

A 1953 state historical marker located on Point Peter Road near the intersection with Osborne Street (SR 40) in Saint Marys City, Georgia says that the fort was just east of there, at the junction of Peter Creek and St. Marys River and that it was called Fort Tonyn (see **Fort Tonyn** pp. 113–120).

Some believe Wright's Fort was at Scrubby Bluff, near where Interstate 95 crosses the St. Marys River. Others place it on the south side of the river in what is now Yulee, about 2 miles northeast of the junction of routes I-95 S (FL 9) and US 17 (FL 5).

Jermyn Wright (b. ca. 1708), brother of Sir James Wright (1714–1785), Georgia's Royal governor, was reputedly the wealthiest man in the country. He owned six plantations that included 13,000 acres in South Carolina, six tracts of land in Georgia, and 800 acres in Florida. Georgia Whigs came across the border and raided both plantations along the St. Marys River in September 1775.

Daniel McGirth (d. ca. 1789) had been a scout for the Rebels in Georgia early in the war. An officer at St. Illa, Georgia coveted McGirth's mare, "Gray Goose," and managed to have McGirth court-martialed. McGirth was imprisoned and whipped but managed to escape on "Gray Goose."

Daniel and his brother James rode with Captain John Baker's (1750–1830) party of 70 mounted men to attack Jermyn Wright's fort, a stockaded house, on the St. Marys River about 100 miles west of St. Augustine. The schooner *St. John* was at anchor 2 miles downstream from the fort and sent three armed boats to reinforce the garrison. Some of Baker's men fired on the lead boat and killed or wounded several of the crew. Baker's force then withdrew and camped about 8 or 9 miles from the fort. During the night, the McGirths, who were on guard duty, stole the horses of Baker's men and deserted to the enemy. Baker's forces advanced on the fort, burned buildings, destroyed the dams and pillaged the property.

Mr. Wright brought his slaves back to Georgia and abandoned his Florida plantations a few months later. The McGirths later joined Lieutenant Colonel Thomas Alexander Brown's (1744–1814) corps of Carolina King's Rangers in East Florida. Daniel was made lieutenant colonel and James a captain in that corps.[14]

★ In late May 1776, a band of Rebels raided the plantation of William Chapman, a Loyalist who lived on the St. Marys River. Lieutenant William Grant's HM Schooner *St. John* went up the river at 1 PM on Wednesday, May 29, to intercept some Rebels. The schooner sent her cutter, manned and armed with a midshipman, at 2 PM to assist in the landing. The following day, the *St. John* fired two swivel guns (see Photo GA-11) and subdued a boat along shore. Lieutenant Grant sent a boat to bring her on board and learned his prey was a canoe from Jacket Island with two barrels of indigo. He then sent an officer on shore to seize the cargo.

The *St. John* fired two 3-pounders at 7 AM on Friday, May 31 to bring to a small sloop from Georgia which had been forced to carry ammunition for the Rebels. That afternoon about 200 Whigs came down the river and seized a planter by the name of Jollie. They also intended to board the *St. John,* but Lieutenant Grant sent an express to Captain Colin(?) Graham, hoping that he would intercept the Rebels at the ferry crossing when they returned.[15]

★ Lieutenant William Grant received information on Saturday morning, June 1, 1776, that Captain Colin(?) Graham and his party had an engagement with the Whigs and that he lost one private. The Whigs then fled into the bushes and up trees. Lieutenant Grant sent a cutter, manned and armed with a midshipman, from the HM Schooner *St. John*, anchored in the St. Marys River, to ascertain whether Captain Graham wanted any assistance. The cutter returned the following morning and confirmed the report of Captain Graham's engagement.

★ The same day, the *St. John* fired two swivels to bring to a boat coming from Wright's Landing. Lieutenant William Grant saw a snow off the entrance of the St. Marys River, so he manned and armed a boat with an officer and sent her out to speak with the master of the snow which turned out to be from Bristol headed to St. Augustine with provisions.[16]

★ The HM Schooner *St. John*, anchored in the St. Marys River, fired two half pounders to bring to a schooner coming down the North River on Friday, June 7, 1776. Lieutenant William Grant fired the two half pounders again the following day to bring to a sailing boat coming down the river. On Sunday, he fired two 3-pounders to bring to a snow crossing the river and on Monday, he fired and brought to a canoe rowing across an inlet.[17]

★ A group of Rebels at Wright's Fort and Landing fired two guns to signal that the fort was being attacked about 4 PM on Thursday, July 11, 1776. The HM Schooner *St. John* answered with one gun and sent Captain Peter Beachop and six men aboard a cutter with orders to gain intelligence and to bring off the sick men if possible. They were not to allow the boat to go on shore.

The cutter and a canoe with soldiers set off about 4:30. The signal was repeated at 6, and the *St. John* answered with another gun. The fort fired several volleys of small arms at 6:30. When the canoe returned at 10 PM, the soldiers reported seeing the cutter fired upon from the marshes below the landing place. They thought the cutter and some of her crew were captured and some killed. The following morning, it was confirmed that the Rebels killed one to three crewmen and captured the others, including Captain Peter Beachop.[18]

★ Captain Benjamin Dodd, a Loyalist, purchased two plantations in the spring of 1776, one on the south side of St. Marys and the other on Trout Creek. Colonel Lachlan McIntosh (1727–1806) and his Georgia troops raided Loyalist Captain Benjamin Dodd's two plantations late in the summer. The raiding party overran Dodd's plantation on the St. Marys River, burned the buildings and left them in ruins. They captured six men and drove the garrison, recently reinforced to 100 men, to the south side of the St. Johns River. Both sides probably had a number of casualties, but the reports only mention the capture of six Crown troops before the crossing. The others probably took refuge in Fort San Nicholas.[19]

Lieutenant Colonel James Mark Prevost (1736–1781) and Governor Patrick Tonyn (1725–1804) joined forces to fill an armed shallop and the tender *Otter* with a force of regulars, rangers and Native Americans to go to the support of the outpost and the armed schooner already there. They also wanted to keep the settlers from abandoning their plantations and harvests and bringing their slaves to St. Augustine.[20]

★ Lieutenant Colonel Francis Henry Harris commanded a detachment of Continentals overland from the St. Marys to the Satilla in April and May 1777. It consisted of two captains, four subalterns, six sergeants, a drum and fife and 100 privates. His orders were to cut off any East Florida Rangers who were hunting cattle between those two rivers. His detachment destroyed everything along the Loyalists' line of march, but they found no East Florida Rangers.[21]

★ Colonel John Baker (1750–1830) and his 109 volunteers skirmished with a party of East Florida Rangers and Native Americans on the Florida side of the St. Marys River on Thursday, May 15, 1777. Baker had about five men wounded and his men killed one of the Native Americans.[22]

★ The brigantine *Dunvegan* arrived in London on Thursday, July 31, 1777. Captain John Smith reported that, when he left St. Augustine 17 days earlier (Monday, July 14, 1777), Lieutenant Colonel Thomas Alexander Brown (1744–1814) with about 138 East Florida Rangers and 200 Creeks left the St. Johns River and took a new position on the St. Marys River in Georgia. They expected reinforcements of 500 Regulars from St. Augustine, under the command of Major Glazier of the 60th Regiment, in order to join the people of St. Andrew parish in that province, who were determined to take arms against the rebel government upon that support. A few days before, some Native Americans had arrived at St. Augustine with several scalps from Georgia.[23]

Pensacola (March 10–May 9, 1781)

Pensacola is on the Gulf of Mexico on the western edge of the state near the Alabama border.

West Florida included portions of what are now Florida, Alabama, Mississippi, and Louisiana. The Chattahoochee and Appalachicola Rivers marked its eastern boundary while Lake Pontchartrain, Lake Maurepas, the Iberville River and the Mississippi River denoted the western boundary. The northern boundary line was approximately 32 degrees 28 minutes north and ran east to the Chattahoochee River from the confluence of the Yazoo and the Mississippi Rivers. The Gulf of Mexico formed the southern boundary.[24]

See the map of Alabama, Mississippi, Louisiana and Arkansas.

When Spain entered the war in 1779, her main area of activity was at sea and along the shores of the Gulf of Mexico. She did not want to appear as supporting the American War of Independence because she saw it as one of ideology and as a threat to her own empire in the New World. When she declared war, it was out of alliance with France, as the kings of the two countries were uncle and nephew. Yet, the forces of Bernardo de Gálvez (1746–1786), the young governor of Louisiana and an experienced soldier, probably helped relieve the pressure on the frontiers of Georgia and South Carolina in 1780 and brought indirect benefits to the Congressional cause in the south. Unlike France, Spain refused to sign a treaty with the United States, but she wanted to recover the possessions which she lost in the Seven Years War (French and Indian).

Bernardo de Gálvez planned to capture Pensacola, Mobile and other smaller Crown posts on the Gulf coast of West Florida. Brigadier General John Campbell (d. 1806) garrisoned the fortified city of Pensacola with 900 worn-out veterans, Irish deserters from the Continental army, ill-equipped Hessian mercenaries and untrained Loyalist troops.

The authorities in Havana gave Gálvez considerable opposition as they wanted a primarily naval campaign against Pensacola while Gálvez wanted to take Mobile first to cut Pensacola's supply source and to control the Native Americans in the area. Gálvez also needed more troops, artillery, supplies and ships which Havana refused to give him. Despite these obstacles, he proceeded with his attack on Mobile.

Gálvez's first fleet sailed from Havana on Monday, October 16, 1780 but was dispersed by a hurricane two days later. Some of the ships sank in the Gulf of Mexico and the rest returned badly damaged. Gálvez put together another expedition of between 8,000 and 10,000 troops with a large train of artillery.

A force of 1,315 men boarded transports and sailed from Havana on Tuesday, February 13, 1781. The convoy of 21 major vessels, including some vessels of war, 35 ships and several gunboats headed for Pensacola to defend Spanish positions on the mainland. They arrived at Santa Rosa Island, which shielded the Bay of Pensacola, on March 9 and occupied the island. The fleet could not enter Pensacola Bay, however, because of the danger of running aground on the sand bars and because of the British guns. Although Gálvez commanded the expedition, he did not have the authority to countermand an order from the commander of the fleet, Admiral José Calbo de Irazabal.

Gálvez landed on Santa Rosa Island at the mouth of Pensacola harbor at 3 AM on Saturday, March 10, 1781. He found the British battery there abandoned. A fort on Barrancas Coloradas (the red cliffs) guarded the harbor opposite Santa Rosa. The fort had 11 guns, including five 32-pounders.

José Calbo de Irazabal almost ran his 74-gun flagship *San Ramón* aground trying to negotiate the tricky bar at the mouth of the harbor. He found it impossible to bring the fleet into the harbor under the fire of Fort Barrancas Coloradas. General Gálvez realized the delay of the squadron and convoy in entering the harbor and feared that a strong

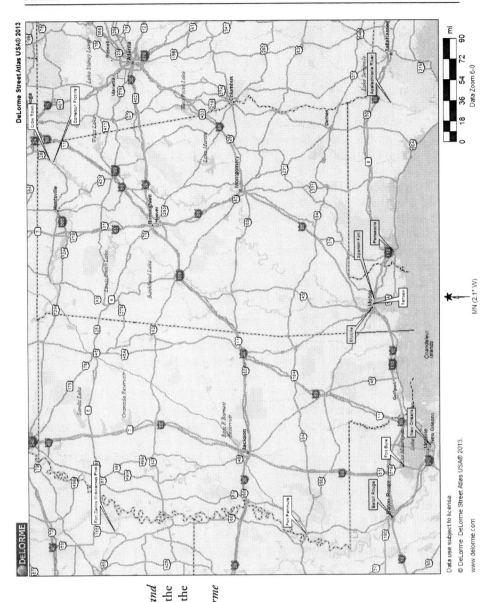

Alabama, Mississippi, Louisiana and Arkansas: Map for The Guide to the American Revolutionary War in the Deep South and on the Frontier © 2013 DeLorme (www.delorme.com) Street Atlas USA®

wind might force the warships (see Photo GA-17) and cargo vessels to set sail to avoid being wrecked upon the shore, thereby abandoning the troops on the island without means of subsistence. He decided to enter the harbor first, convinced that the others would follow him.

★ The next morning, Gálvez sent Admiral Calbo a 32-pound ball fired by Fort Barrancas Coloradas at his camp on Santa Rosa Island. He also sent a message with the cannonball: "whoever has honor and valour will follow me." The fleet included four ships from Louisiana which Gálvez had the right to command.

★ At 11 AM on Monday, March 17, Don Juan Riano's sloop *Valenzuela* positioned herself at the entrance of Pensacola harbor, accompanied by the brig *Galveztown* and two small gunboats. Sub-lieutenant D. Miguel Herrera arrived at 4 PM with letters from Colonel José Manuel Ignacio Timoteo de Ezpeleta Galdeano Dicastillo y del Prado, conde de Ezpeleta de Beire (1740–1823) to General Gálvez, advising him that he was marching with his troops to join him.

Gálvez embarked in an open boat at 2:30 PM on Sunday, March 18, to go on board the *Galveztown*, formerly William Pickles's *West Florida*, anchored at the mouth of Pensacola harbor. He ordered the captain to hoist the rear admiral's pennant, and the crew fired a salute of 15 guns to further clarify Gálvez's intentions. The *Galveztown* then set sail followed by two armed launches and the sloop *Valenzuela*, commanded by Don Juan Riano— Louisiana's entire navy—into Pensacola's harbor.

Fort Barrancas Coloradas had 11 guns and was garrisoned by approximately 140 officers and men. She fired her five 32-pounders on the fleet. Any round shot could have sunk the *Gálveztown*, but Gálvez and his staff stood on the quarterdeck as the shots whizzed above and around the ship. Although the British fired 140 cannon shots, they inflicted no casualties and only minor damage to the ships, piercing the *Gálveztown's* sails and shrouds. The next day, Calbo, shamed by Gálvez's success, led the rest of the fleet into the harbor.[25]

The Spaniards began landing 15,000 troops on Rowe's Island. They then advanced within a mile of Fort George, where they began a subterranean work while their batteries fired incessantly on the fort. The British garrison refused to surrender until a man deserted and instructed the Spaniards to shell the magazine. One shell (see Photo GA-7) blew it up, killing about 100 men.

★ A small British naval squadron arrived from Jamaica but did not dare to challenge the large fleet. Spanish infantry captured nine British seamen despite firing from the 18-gun sloop of war HMS *Port Royal* and the privateer *Mentor*. The Spanish captured the *Port Royal* and destroyed the *Mentor* in the harbor.[26]

Other troops came overland from Mobile (Alabama) and New Orleans (Louisiana), arriving a week later with 2,300 men to help in the siege of Pensacola, the last major British post in the area in early 1781. The French provided an additional 725 soldiers. The Chickasaws and Loyalists sniped at the Spanish camp from cover. They ambushed any soldier foolish enough to wander into the woods alone. The Spanish casualties at this time were caused by the Choctaws, Creeks, Seminoles, and Chickasaws, allied with the British, who raided Spanish outposts and attacked stragglers day and night.[27]

★ The convoy set sail at 2 PM on Monday, March 19, 1781, preceded by the King's frigates. General Gálvez decided to go to the Perdido River in a boat, at 5 PM, to instruct Colonel Ezpeleta personally about his plans. However, the winds and currents both forced him to return to the camp at 11 PM.[28]

★ That same day, near Pensacola, a party of Native Americans under British Captain Stevens attacked a Spanish boat, killing 10 and capturing one.[29]

★ The following morning, Gálvez sent an officer to Pensacola with a letter requesting General Campbell not to burn or destroy any of the ships or buildings of the King and private parties. That afternoon, the general went in a boat to examine the beach opposite the harbor in order to select a suitable landing place for the troops. At 8 PM, the Crown forces set fire to a guard-house on the beach where the general had made his examination that afternoon. When Gálvez saw this, he ordered Don Juan Riano's sloop and the armed launch from the *Galveztown* to approach land and fire grape shot at any enemies who might be there.

Early in the morning of the 21st, an officer arrived from Pensacola with the following letter from General Campbell:

> Most Excellent sir: My dear sir: The threats of the enemy who assail us are not considered under any other aspect than as an artifice or stratagem of war, which he makes use of to further his own purpose. I trust that in my defense of Pensacola (seeing that I am attacked) I will do nothing contrary to rules and customs of war; for I consider myself under obligations to your Excellency for your frank intimation, although I assure you that my conduct will depend rather on your own, in reply to the propositions Governor Chester will send you tomorrow regarding prisoners, and mine relative to the City of Pensacola, than upon your threats. In the meantime I remain your Excellency's most obedient servant, John Campbell.
>
> Headquarters Pensacola, March 20, 1781.

★ Both parties exchanged letters regarding the treatment of civilians and prisoners of war. Then, at 3 PM on Wednesday, March 21, 1781, Gálvez ordered the grenadiers encamped on that part of the island facing the harbor to prepare for battle. The other troops, also opposite the harbor, were ordered to occupy a small hill that would make them clearly visible to the enemy who could then realize the class and number of troops that Gálvez commanded. Several houses near Fort Barrancas were seen burning during the night. This displeased General Gálvez who had warned General Campbell about this in his letters.[30]

★ Colonel Ezpeleta and his troops marched inside the harbor on the opposite shore at 9:30 AM on March 22. General Gálvez went to reinforce him with 500 men, including the grenadiers, allowing Ezpeleta's troops to rest. After communicating his orders to camp, Gálvez returned to the island after dispatching a flag of truce to Pensacola with the following letter which he also sent to Governor Peter Chester:

> Most Excellent Sir, My dear sir: At the time we are reciprocally making one another the same propositions, for both of us aimed at the conservation of the goods and property of the individuals of Pensacola, at the same time, I say, the insult of burning the houses facing my Camp on the other side of the bay is committed before my very eyes. This fact tells of the bad faith with which you work and write, as also the conduct observed with the people from Mobile, a great many of whom have been victims of the horrible cruelties protected by your Excellency; all proves that your expressions are not sincere, that humanity is a phrase that although you repeat it on paper, your heart does not know, that your intentions are to gain time to complete the destruction of Western Florida; and I, who am indignant at my own credulity and the noble manner in which it is pretended to halucinate me, must not, nor do I wish to hear, other propositions than those of surrender, assuring your Excellency, that as it will not be my fault, I shall see Pensacola burn with the same indifference, that I shall see its cruel incendiaries perish upon its ashes. God keep your Excellency many years.[31]

Island of Sta. Rosa, March 22, 1781. Most Excellent Sir, Your most attentive servitor kisses your Excellency's hand, Bernardo de Gálvez.

The King's packet, the *S. Pio*, that had just returned from the vicinity of the "de los Perdidos" River to protect the launches in which the people from Mobile were destined to cross from one shore to another, entered the harbor Thursday afternoon, March 22. Fort Barrancas fired as briskly as possible but without causing it, or any of the four boats that followed, any damage whatever. All the troops camped on the shore facing the harbor that night to be ready to cross to the opposite side more quickly.

The following morning, the troops prepared rafts to transport the artillery, tents and ammunition to the opposite shore. Sails appeared on the horizon at 9 o'clock. They were believed to be the convoy from New Orleans which entered the harbor at 4 PM without suffering any loss, except for insignificant damage to the sails, despite the fire from Barrancas. The convoy consisted of 16 vessels with 1,400 men, cannons and ammunition. However, three other vessels had become separated the night before and were missing.

General Gálvez ordered both the troops on the ships and those on Santa Rosa Island to be ready to cross to the mainland on the following morning to join the troops already there. Colonel Ezpeleta explored the outer harbor with the quartermaster that same day to prepare for moving the camp nearer the city.[32]

Except for 200 men who were left there to occupy the island, the troops who were encamped on Santa Rosa Island embarked on the merchant ships at 4 PM on the 24th to be transported to the place selected for the camp on the mainland, to besiege Fort George and other adjacent fortifications.

★ Two British sailors who deserted from Barrancas arrived at the Spanish camp Saturday morning, the 25th, and informed the general of the condition of the fort and its forces. A party of Native Americans surprised the soldiers who had gone beyond the lines of the outposts that same morning. They killed two and wounded a few others, scalping the bodies of their victims.

★ The army began their march on the 26th to cut off the point of the outer harbor and come out on the beach. They also planned to surprise some Native Americans to avenge the killings of the previous day. The march went through five leagues of deep woods, with Native Americans scattered throughout, making the trek very difficult. Two parties of soldiers traveling to a given point by different roads both mistook each other for enemies in the darkness and thick woods. They both fired on each other and lost several men killed and wounded.

General Gálvez had the inner harbor explored on the 27th, despite fire from parties of Native Americans. The troops occupied a suitable spot and camped. The camp fires attracted a few parties of Native Americans around 10 PM. The warriors fired suddenly on the soldiers, killing some and wounding others. Gálvez then ordered the camp entrenched and a few battalion cannons disembarked for use with grape shot against any Native Americans who approached.[33]

★ Captain Henry Byrd and about 400 Native Americans attacked the camp and opened a brisk fire on the advanced guards about 3 PM on Wednesday, March 28, 1781. Gálvez turned out the light troops and the militia from New Orleans and brought up a few cannon to disperse the attackers. However, the Native Americans attacked the camp again from different points around midnight. They were repulsed again but not before the soldiers suffered a few losses in killed and wounded.[34]

General Gálvez decided to move the camp closer to Pensacola and ordered the reshipment of all the field artillery, supplies and materiel, as their transportation by land was very difficult. A launch was sent to Mobile (Alabama) on the 29th, with orders for the ships there to set sail immediately with artillery and ammunition destined for the expedition. He also ordered the companies of grenadiers, infantrymen and other light troops to prepare themselves to march at daybreak. After they occupied the beach of the inner harbor, the rest of the army would disembark in launches without fear of being attacked.[35]

★ General Gálvez led a column of 1100 men with two field pieces about 5 AM on Friday, March 30th. As they passed through a defile, the scouting parties advised him that Native Americans lay in ambush nearby; so he ordered a halt and a cannon brought up to fire on the Native Americans, causing them to flee.

The column arrived at the beach about 10:30 AM and occupied it. They were now within cannon shot of Fort George, without interference from the enemy. The troops posted outposts and sentinels in all the avenues and took all other precautions to insure safety. Gálvez also sent a message to Colonel Ezpeleta to embark with the rest of the troops and come to the new camp. He then boarded the frigate *Clara* to discuss the establishment of hospitals. He also instructed the ships to advance as near as possible to the camp of the troops.

The rest of the army began to arrive around 1 PM. Firing from the outposts began shortly afterward when a party of Native Americans approached. Gálvez sent the light troops to support the outposts and ordered the others to advance to occupy a plain where they could move more easily, should the enemy attempt a sortie.

Colonel Ezpeleta noticed that the troops were coming out of Fort George a short time later and that the fire from the Native Americans had increased greatly. He ordered the wings of the army to extend themselves to a certain distance in order to cut off the enemies' retreat should they abandon the field. However, the troops only came out to support the Native Americans and to attack the Spaniards with two field pieces with solid shot.

General Gálvez arrived at this time and decided to attack the Native Americans with a few companies of light infantry supported by two field pieces. This action forced the Native Americans and the British troops who supported them to retire quickly. The skirmish left three killed and 28 wounded, including the Colonel of the King's Regiment, who died the following day, and two subaltern officers.

The army was already entrenching itself at 7 PM, with its right wing resting on a house near the beach and its left on the point of the inner harbor. Six cannons were immediately placed on the left and two others on the right in case the enemy attacked during the night.[36]

General Gálvez went to the house to observe the city and the land in its vicinity on Saturday, March 31st. The troops spent the day finishing the trench and erecting tents. A deserter from the Maryland Regiment arrived at 7 PM with a report that General Campbell planned another sortie like the one of the day before and that there were 600 equipped troops, 300 sailors, many armed African Americans in the city and a large number of Native Americans encamped under the shelter of Fort George.

The quartermaster set out at 8 AM on Sunday, April 1, with a detachment of 500 men, to explore a height near the enemy forts. A contingent of about 250 Crown troops appeared a little while later and continued to observe the Spaniards until the detachment retired.

General Gálvez boarded his gig to explore the fort and vicinity of the town of Pensacola at 3 PM. Three deserters from the Waldeck Regiment arrived a little while later, but they had no additional information to add to that of the previous deserter. The troops spent the day clearing the woods around the camp to eliminate any shelter for the Native Americans.

Eight deserters from various regiments arrived at 2 AM with reports similar to the others. The quartermaster set out at 10 AM to mark the spot of the new camp, closer to the place the general had selected for his batteries.

Two more deserters arrived at 1 PM and reported that General Campbell had decided to open fire on the camp at 3 PM. General Gálvez ordered two thirds of the army to join the quartermaster with their arms and accoutrements to help finish the trench. He left all the tents up to conceal his intentions from the enemy.

The rest of the army retired about 6 PM. The tents were folded and the cannons were brought to the new camp while 110 men occupied the house until further orders.

The troops spent a quiet night. A British schooner set sail in the interior of the harbor at 7 AM. This attracted two launches from the warships (see Photo GA-17) and one from the brig *Galveztown* which captured it without opposition.

General Gálvez ordered the 110 men who had been left at the house to retire on Tuesday, April 3rd and two companies of light infantry to patrol near there daily to protect against desertion. He also ordered the launches with provisions and other military property to always come by the creek of the inner harbor which protected his rear because there was sufficient water to facilitate transportation.

General Gálvez ordered the navy to take four abandoned British ships anchored near the town in the afternoon. They included a frigate of war called *Port Royal* with 60 Spanish prisoners on board. He also ordered the brig *Galveztown* to go to the Scambier River to capture several abandoned schooners which deserters had reported.

Colonel Ezpeleta again went out with the quartermaster at 4 AM to examine the hill from which Gálvez planned to attack Fort George. Several workmen were laying out the camp there.

★ The chiefs of the Talapuz Nation arrived at the camp on Thursday, April 5. General Gálvez listened to their mission and it was agreed that they should supply the camp with fresh meat.

The troops continued clearing the woods during the morning and afternoon. They were also instructed to construct two redoubts (see Photo FL-6) on the creek of the inner harbor to protect the launches from attacks by the Native Americans who fired on them from various places. That night, around midnight, they approached the camp and fired, wounding an officer in his tent.

General Gálvez went with the quartermaster and several engineers at 6 AM to examine the hill and to select another closer place for the camp. The troops continued to clear the woods during the day and began to haul the ammunition which was being landed.

At 7 AM, the general learned that the brig *Galveztown* had captured a polacre and three schooners near the Scambier River. A lieutenant from the Maryland Regiment came to ask permission to serve under the general's command. After leaving the British service, he was walking toward Georgia when he learned of the arrival of the Spaniards. This officer and several deserters informed the general that the Native Americans were retiring and that they occupied themselves in robbing and burning the houses of the inhabitants and that several terrified families had asked permission to embark in the brig *Galveztown*. They also reported that Mr. Deans, captain of the British Royal Navy's frigate *Mentor*, had burned his ship to avoid its capture by the Spaniards.

That same morning, General Gálvez dispatched the Talapuz chiefs to the Native Americans who supported the Crown forces, to persuade them to remain neutral during the war and to bring all the cattle they could.

That afternoon, the troops began work on the two redoubts of the inner harbor in such a way that they could have flanking fire to keep the Native Americans as far away as possible.[37]

★ Lieutenant George Pinhorn (d. 1781) led a sortie against the Spanish lines on Tuesday, April 12, 1781. His men killed one and wounded nine but Pinhorn was killed in the action. Don Josef Solano's fleet of 20 ships arrived from Havana with 1,600 Spanish and four French frigates carrying 725 French soldiers on Friday, April 19. The Spanish forces included a regiment of the famed Irish Brigade under the command of Lieutenant Colonel Arturo O'Neil. These reinforcements brought Gálvez's army to more than 7,000 men. He was now ready to begin the final phase of the operation.

The Crown forces, which included two battalions of Pennsylvania and Maryland Loyalists, bloodied the Irish Regiment in one sortie and their 149 cannon and howitzers fought deadly duels with Gálvez's batteries.

★ Field Marshall Don Juan Manuel Cagigal, the commandant of artillery, the quartermaster general, the major general of the army and his aides-de-camp went on horseback accompanied by a party of light infantrymen, to reconnoiter the terrain and the distance for opening the trench and to establish the first one at 9:30 AM on Sunday, April 22. The Crown forces discovered them and fired cannon at them, forcing them to retire with one man wounded.

Two companies of French light infantry and the artillery companies arrived in camp that same morning and were assigned a camping place. The troops began disembarking; and, although they came under enemy fire passing before Barrancas Coloradas, they suffered no harm. The troops finished disembarking the next day.[38]

The encampment for the recently-arrived troops had also been laid out, with the order that it should be immediately protected by bulwarks because it was in the midst of woods and surrounded by Native Americans who hid in the forest and harassed the troops at all hours.

★ Brigadier Don Geronimo Giron and two engineers went, at 6 AM on Tuesday, the 24th, to the place where the two new batteries were to be established. The Crown forces soon discovered the companies of light infantry accompanying them and began to fire their artillery at them. A band of Native Americans had already begun annoying the scouting party with their musketry, and a force came out to support them when the artillery began to fire. The light infantry returned fire, advancing and retiring according to the circumstances. The firing continued for quite a while when the general ordered two more companies to go out the camp to support the others. The skirmish lasted until 9 AM, and 15 Spanish soldiers and two officers were wounded. The losses of the Crown forces are unknown, but several Native Americans remained dead on the field, besides one who deserted that same morning.

The Native Americans and some troops annoyed the outposts again during the afternoon. They fired for some time and wounded three soldiers before retiring.

The troops continued working on the trenches which were almost completed. The entrenchment was made of heavy pines and stakes filled with a sandy clay to a thickness of about seven feet.

★ A few companies of light infantry accompanied the Commandant of Artillery and a few Spanish officers who went to inspect the point of attack at 6 AM on the 25th. Shortly after their arrival there, two parties of Native Americans and two companies of enemy infantry fired on them. The light infantrymen and five companies returned fire until 7:30 when they retreated with five wounded.

The fort had a crescent shaped section jutting out close to another hill. The Spanish decided to extend their tunnel to this second hill and to convert it into another battery. Seeing this, the Crown forces concentrated their artillery fire on the hill. They followed with an infantry charge that forced the Spanish to retreat.

★ The engineers set out with five companies of grenadiers and light infantrymen with two field pieces between 2:30 and 4 PM on the 26th to trace the trench that was to be dug that night and to examine the crescent for the last time. Before they were half finished their task, many parties of Native Americans, supported by three or four companies, began to fire on them, compelling them to stop. The Spaniards replied and attacked them with the two field pieces they carried, forcing them to retire to the crescent in a hurry. However, the battery there began to fire with heavy artillery and several howitzers, preventing the conclusion of the exploration. The Spaniards returned to camp at 6:30 without having accomplished what they intended. However, they had already clearly marked where the trench should begin to be dug during the night. The Crown forces fired 16 cannonades and two bombs (see Photo GA-7) from the fort which produced no results whatever.

Brigadier Giron and 700 laborers with 300 fascines (see Photo GA-18), supported by 800 grenadiers and light infantrymen and four field pieces, set out between 9:30 and 10 PM to begin digging the trench. They had to cross a thick wood to get there. The great number of trees that had been cut and the pits that had been dug in various places made the way more difficult. The troops were also ordered to maintain strict silence so the march moved very slowly.

★ All the troops had not yet been posted at the avenues by 1 AM on the 27th. The night was dark, with some showers, thunder and much lightning, causing the work to be suspended for the time being because the troops would not have time to take cover before daybreak. The troops returned to camp at 3 AM, leaving two companies of grenadiers posted there for observation. Two companies of light infantry were sent to relieve them after dawn. They had orders to prevent the enemy from exploring the ground or removing the signals left for the opening of the trench.

Shots were heard in the direction where the light infantry was posted at 9 AM. The general was informed, at the same time, that the enemy was cutting trees in front of the crescent. Fearing they might entrench themselves there and frustrate his plans, he ordered four companies with two field pieces to go out immediately to join the light infantry in protecting the engineers who were again surveying the line. After accomplishing this, they were to prevent the enemy from cutting trees.

After the engineers had finished their operations without being discovered by the Crown forces, the four companies went to the place where the trees were being cut and found that work had already been started on a small parapet, and that two field pieces were already emplaced near the siege trenches.

The Crown forces fired their field pieces after a while, and the Spaniards replied briskly with the two they carried and with muskets. The battery at the crescent began to throw bombs (see Photo GA-7) and grenades until 1 PM. The Spanish troops were relieved by four other companies around noon, having lost four dead and 12 wounded. The relief troops were placed at a respectable distance, out of artillery range, and were to prevent the enemy cutting down the trees. These companies retired at 6 PM and the enemy remained in the woods, apparently constructing a redoubt which enfiladed the parallel line marked out by the engineers.

Orders had been given to dig the trench that night; but, as two soldiers from the Louisiana Regiment deserted that afternoon, the order was countermanded. A deserter who arrived at the camp at 11 PM told General Gálvez, upon examination, that there were more than 600 regular troops excluding the sailors, African Americans and armed civilians at the crescent along with about 400 Native Americans and that a new battery was being installed to the right of the crescent to increase the defense.

The engineers went out with 200 laborers, supported by three companies of grenadiers and infantrymen, at 9:30 AM on the 28th to open a street in the woods to allow the troops to get to the place where the trench had to be opened. They began to construct a covered road that afternoon to enable them to go to a small hill where a battery would be established to divert the fire of Fort George. Meanwhile, another one was constructed against the crescent.

At 6:30 PM, two or three companies of grenadiers occupied the post laid out in the morning. All the rest of the detachment composed of 700 laborers with 350 fascines and supported by 800 men left the camp between 7:30 and 8 PM to open the trench. The enemy waited for them at the other place marked out earlier, which was about 1,000 meters away. The workers quickly finished the task, and all the troops were under cover at daybreak. The trench was about 800 meters long and about 600 meters from the enemy fortifications on one side and 400 on the other.

General Gálvez was informed, at 11 PM, that the digging of the trench had begun undiscovered by the enemy. A little later, the quartermaster and the engineer of the detail informed the general that all the troops were under cover and that the work advanced rapidly.

★ The laborers were relieved to finish the trench and continue the opening of the covered road at 4 AM on the 29th. The Crown forces saw the work the Spaniards had accomplished during the night and began to fire cannons and mortars (see Photo GA-13) from 6 AM until 11 AM. The barrage began lively, at first, and proceeded slower later, leaving two dead and one wounded. Several parties who approached to explore the trench with two field pieces were vigorously repulsed with two others—4- and 8-pounders— that were placed at the head and tail of the trench. The Crown forces stopped firing at 11:30 AM, probably to cool their artillery.

At 8 PM, 800 soldiers left the camp to relieve those in the trench, and 600 began to construct a battery of six 24-pound cannons and several mortars on a height to divert enemy fire. Another battery was being constructed closer at the same time. The 600 men were also to continue the trench and to construct two redoubts to the right and left of it for its defense.

★ The Crown forces resumed intermittent fire from cannons, howitzers and mortars at 9 PM. The fire continued until 1 AM on the 30th and resumed with great intensity at daybreak, delaying the work on the trenches considerably. The Spaniards only built a fascine, widened the trench a little through its widest part and raised half of the parapet of the mortar and cannon battery outlined the previous day. The guards and workers were happily relieved, at 7 PM, by the same number of troops less 200 soldiers.

Some parties of Native Americans came through the nearby woods toward the camp and fired on the advanced positions which responded immediately with field pieces and rifles. After mortally wounding a soldier who was resting in his tent, and seriously wounding one officer and one soldier, the braves retreated, under cover of the woods, to the shores of the bay where the Spanish launches came through to unload their cargo. The warriors surprised six sailors who were fishing on the opposite side of the swamp and either killed them or carried them away as prisoners.

The French frigate *Andromanche* entered the port at noon to fire on the enemy fortifications from the sea at the same time as the Spanish trench batteries. The French and Crown forces fired on one another as the *Andromanche* passed before Barrancas Coloradas. She received only two or three hits which did not cause much damage.

A deserter arrived at 7 AM and reported that the Crown forces began constructing a battery of small caliber cannons in the glacis of Fort George. The Spaniards spent the entire day widening the trench, perfecting the batteries of cannons and mortars and in finishing the two redoubts without the enemy firing any more. The soldiers and laborers were relieved at 8 PM, and the four mortars were brought to the battery.

★ The Crown forces began to fire with several cannons, three mortars and four howitzers at daybreak on Tuesday, May 1, 1781. The fire continued without interruption until 10 AM when it was reduced to a slow pace. When they noticed that work was proceeding on the road that led from the trench to the battery, the Crown forces resumed heavy fire, to such an extent that General Gálvez wanted to suspend the work. However, the work continued through the night in spite of the bombs and grenades. A battery of six 24-pound cannons was in place by the following morning. They began to bombard the Crown fortifications.[39]

★ Crown forces artillery began to fire on the large Spanish working parties on Thursday, May 3, 1781. The Spanish batteries soon returned fire. Both sides suffered slight casualties. Robert Farmar (1718–1804) records in his journal that the besiegers fired 534 shots and 186 shells (see Photo GA-7) during the day and that the garrison lost one man killed and two wounded.[40]

★ Lieutenant Colonel DeHorn led Loyalists and German troops in a bayonet attack (see Photo GA-3) on the Spanish entrenchments. He lost one killed and one wounded but caused the Spaniards to lose 21 killed, 15 wounded and four captured.

★ The Spanish dug trenches to get the heavy artillery near the fortifications which Lieutenant General John Campbell (d. 1806) had constructed in anticipation of Gálvez's arrival. Early Tuesday morning, May 8, the Crown forces resumed their bombardment. The Spanish replied with a howitzer set up in one of the redoubts. The artillery accomplished little until a deserter revealed to Gálvez the location of the powder magazine in the fort's advanced redoubt. A shell struck and penetrated the magazine door on Tuesday, May 8, as its supply of gunpowder was being replenished. When the shell exploded, it completely destroyed the main redoubt, killing or wounding about 100 men. Farmar reported:

> About 9 o'clock, AM, a shell from the enemy's front battery was thrown in at the door of the magazine, at the advanced redoubt, as the men were receiving powder, which blew it up and killed forty seamen belonging to H.M. ships the *Mentor* and *Port Royal*; and forty-five men of the Pennsylvania Loyalists were killed by the same explosion; there were a number of men wounded, besides, Capt. Byrd, with seventy men of the 60th Regiment, immediately went up to the advanced redoubt and brought off 2 field-pieces and one howitzer, and a number of the wounded men; but was obliged to retire, as a great quantity of shell was lying about filled.[41]

Charles Stedman (1753–1812) records the event in his history of the war:

> Notwithstanding the great disparity of force between the besiegers and the garrison, the Spanish general thought fit to send for a reinforcement. In the mean time the troops that he had with him were landed, and the British works at Pensacola regularly invested. After some time the expected succours arrived, part of the Spanish

garrison of Mobile having marched across the country to join in the siege, and a fleet of fifteen ships of the line, under the command of Don Solano, having arrived from the Havannah, with an additional land force of three thousand men. Although the defence made by the garrison was brave and spirited, and the progress of the besiegers hitherto proportionably slow, it was apparent, from the force with which it was invested, that the place must ultimately fall: But its fate was unexpectedly precipitated by the baseness and perfidy of a traitor. A man of the name of Cannon, formerly an officer in one of the provincial regiments in garrison at Pensacola, had been broke the year before by a court-martial for ungentlemanlike behaviour, and retired to the Creek country among the Indians, whence he returned as soon as he heard of the landing of the Spaniards, and joined them on the fifth of April. By him they were made minutely acquainted with the state and situation of all the British works, and were thus enabled to direct their fire towards those quarters where it was likely to produce the greatest effect.

Indefatigable in his traitorous purpose, he used to climb to the top of a tall pine-tree, commanding a view of the British works, from whence he was enabled to inform the Spanish bombardiers where the shells discharged from their mortars took effect, and whether near or at a distance from the British magazines. Thus instructed, and improved by repeated trials, they acquired such a knowledge as at length enabled them to do fatal execution. On the morning of the eighth of May, a shell bursting at the door of a magazine in one of the advanced works, set fire to the powder within, which in an instant reduced the whole redoubt to a heap of rubbish. By the explosion seventy-six of the garrison lost their lives, and twenty-four were badly wounded. The enemy immediately advanced to take advantage of the confusion; but were repulsed in their first attempt by the fire from two flank works, which had been added to the redoubt after the commencement of the siege, and which fortunately were not injured by the blowing-up of the magazine. This repulse procured a short respite to the garrison, during which those who had been wounded by the explosion were carried off, some of the cannon removed from the flank works, which it was now judged necessary to evacuate, and the rest spiked up. The enemy, however, again advanced in greater force, and under cover of the flank works, which had been abandoned, kept up so hot a fire of musquetry upon another redoubt, that the men could no longer stand to their guns. There was also, it seems, a scarcity of ordnance shot in the garrison, from the great number that had been already expended. Under these circumstances, general Campbell thought fit to capitulate; and thus the province of West Florida was once more re-annexed to the Spanish dominions.[42]

General Gálvez's light troops attacked immediately, advancing through the smoking ruins with fixed bayonets (see Photo GA-3). They encountered no opposition and captured howitzers and cannon which were used in a steady shelling of Fort George. Some of the infantrymen occupied the ruins of the outer fortifications. These positions allowed them to fire freely on the fort's occupants at point-blank range, forcing General Campbell to surrender the following day. General Campbell had a white flag raised at 3 o'clock that afternoon and formally surrendered on May 10.

The Crown forces marched out from their several posts with all the honors of war (see Photo FL-8). They proceeded some hundred yards distance where they piled their arms. The officers kept their swords and delivered their colors to a body of Spanish grenadiers appointed to receive them. Lieutenant General John Campbell (d. 1806) surrendered Pensacola and the province of West Florida. The English prisoners were put on transports that took them to Havana and then to New York where they arrived on Wednesday, July 4, 1781. The capture of the city later provided Spain a pretext for claiming all of East and West Florida in the treaty that officially ended the war.[43]

FL-8. British surrender. Reenactors march to surrender. Yorktown, VA 225th anniversary commemoration.

The siege involved 23,200 Spanish troops, including seamen; 50 pieces of brass cannon; six 13- and six 9 ½-inch mortars (see Photo GA-13); an immense field train; and a naval force of 11 Spanish and four French ships of the line, four Spanish and four French frigates, transports, victuallers and row galleys.[44]

When Galvez reported the surrender a few days later, he listed 1,708 men captured (1051 men, including 595 seamen, and 62, including seamen, at Barrancas Coloradas). This figure did not include African Americans or the 56 men who deserted to the Spanish during the siege. He also listed 224 women and children dependents of the garrison. The Native Americans who had helped in the defense of Pensacola left during the negotiations for the surrender.[45]

The number of Native Americans involved in the defense of Pensacola is difficult to determine. Robert Farmar's journal for March 26 mentions 250 Native Americans were sent out to oppose a Spanish landing at Pensacola Bay. He notes that 70 Creeks arrived on April 9, about 90 Choctaws on April 15, and 54 Chickasaws on April 27. These forces harassed the Spanish throughout the siege and probably inflicted about one third of their casualties.[46]

The garrison suffered more than 100 killed and scores of wounded during the nine-week siege. The dead included Lieutenant Carrol, 16th; Lieutenant Pinhorn, Loyal Forresters; Ensign Ussal, of the Waldeckers; six sergeants; six corporals; one drummer; 45 privates; two midshipmen and 28 seamen. Among the wounded were Captain Anthony Foster who later recovered; Lieutenant Charles Ward, 3rd Battalion 60th Regiment; three corporals; one drummer and 17 privates. The Royal Artillery lost one corporal, two bombardiers, three gunners and two matrosses wounded. The Royal Navy reported

15 seamen wounded. Most of the casualties came from the explosion in the advanced redoubt. The Spanish army lost between 75 and 124 men killed and 198 to 247 wounded, while the navy had 21 killed and four wounded. In a letter dated May 26, 1781, Gálvez reported capturing 143 cannon, six howitzers, four mortars, and 40 swivel guns (see Photo GA-2) as well as more than 2,000 muskets and many other weapons and tons of military supplies.[47]

Gálvez immediately began to prepare for an expedition to Jamaica, but General Charles Cornwallis's (1738–1805) surrender at Yorktown forced him to abandon the project.[48]

3
ALABAMA

Alabama was part of West Florida and Georgia during the American War of Independence. The Cherokees and Creeks sided with the British. After Spain entered the war, in May 1779, Bernardo de Gálvez (1746–1786), governor of Louisiana, captured Mobile in 1780. The Treaty of Paris, which ended the war, returned both East and West Florida to Spain. Georgia claimed most of the interior of Alabama as part of its original grant.

> The Alabama Bureau of Tourism and Travel (401 Adams Avenue, Suite 126, P.O. Box 4927, Montgomery AL 36103; phone: 334-242-4169, website: **www.touralabama .org**) provides tourist information. The Alabama Department of Archives and History (624 Washington Avenue, Montgomery, AL 36310; phone: 334-242-4435) is a source for historical information.

See the map of Alabama, Mississippi, Louisiana and Arkansas.

Mobile (Feb. 9–March 14, 1780)
Fort Charlotte

> Mobile was located on the west bank of the Mobile River at the head of a large bay, approximately 30 miles long and 6 miles wide. Fort Charlotte occupied the lower end of the town near the bay, near the intersection of South Royal Street and Theatre Street. It was a square structure of solid masonry with four bastions (see Photo GA-21) 300 feet apart and embrasures (see Photo-GA-5) for 38 guns. The French built it in 1717 from locally-made brick and oyster-shell lime and named it Fort Conde de la Mobile. When the British took it over in 1763, after the Seven Years War, they renamed it Fort Charlotte in honor of young King George III's queen. By 1779, it had fallen into disrepair. It had a garrison of more than 300 men made up of the 4th Battalion of the 60th Regiment, the Royal Artillery, engineers, small detachments from the Pennsylvania and Maryland Loyalists, volunteers from the local inhabitants and artificers. They also had several African-Americans. The fort was the source of supplies for Pensacola and a strategic center for the control of the Native American tribes in the area.

After his victories at Baton Rouge (Louisiana) and Natchez (Mississippi), Colonel Bernardo de Gálvez (1746–1786) was able to regroup at New Orleans before setting off to conquer Mobile, the closest major British military post to Spanish Louisiana. In early 1780, several hundred Choctaws abandoned their station at Mobile because they were disappointed in the supplies provided by the British. This enabled Gálvez to sail into Mobile Bay on Wednesday, February 9, 1780 with a force of 754 Spanish regulars, militiamen, 139 free African Americans, 139 free mulattoes, slaves, Native Americans and Whigs from New Orleans to attack the British garrison of Fort Charlotte, a crumbling brick fortification.

Gálvez's force began boarding the transports at New Orleans on Sunday, January 2, 1780. After a difficult voyage of almost a month, half of Gálvez's fleet of 12 ships of assorted types ran aground on the treacherous sand bar at the mouth of the harbor, in a storm, on February 10. His troops soon had three of the vessels afloat, but the bad weather hampered Gálvez's efforts to land his troops and supplies and to refloat three other vessels. They unloaded the men and the supplies from the grounded vessels and managed to refloat two of the smaller ones. They destroyed one of the grounded frigates before landing south of Mobile. Gálvez received reinforcements of 567 men from the Regiment of Navarra from Havana on February 20. A week later, on the 28th, he began to move his troops to Mobile where he made camp at 4 PM. The *Valenzuela* bombarded the fort while the launches brought the baggage and provisions to shore.

The following morning, Tuesday, February 29, Gálvez sent four companies of soldiers to scout the fort. Captain Elias Durnford (1739–1794) of the Corps of Engineers and lieutenant governor of the colony, decided to hold his position. He fired cannons loaded with ball and grape shot (see Photo GA-7) at the troops and returned the fire of the *Valenzuela,* but the shots passed through the ship's rigging without causing any damage. Durnford successfully repelled the initial attack. He hoped for relief from the British garrison at Pensacola while Gálvez's army began digging trenches 2,000 yards from Fort Charlotte in preparation for a siege. Also that day, two leaders of the Crown forces and 20 Native Americans went to the Spanish camp asking for amnesty and protection. Gálvez granted it to them after the usual speeches, provided they remained neutral. According to Captain Joseph Calvert, some 20 chiefs and 250 braves of the Alabama nation offered their services to Gálvez at Mobile. Gálvez thanked them but declined the offer, saying that his fleet and army could accomplish the task.[1]

★ Brigadier General John Campbell (d. 1806) set out from the garrison at Pensacola with the 60th Foot on Sunday, March 5, 1780. The next day, the remaining Waldeckers followed him on the 72-mile march to Mobile. Campbell and his men arrived at Tensa, on the eastern channel of the Mobile River about 30 miles north of Mobile, on the 10th, but they lost valuable time building rafts to transport the men and their equipment downstream.

Meanwhile, Bernardo de Gálvez (1746–1786) led 300 men, protected by 200 soldiers, in constructing a battery near the fort on Friday, March 10, 1780. They worked so quickly that they were under cover by 10 PM. A shoulder of fascines (see Photo GA-18) hid the portion of the battery yet to be completed. Captain Elias Durnford (1739–1794) opened a heavy fire from the fort with cannon, carbines and muskets. The firing lasted until 11 AM, killing six and wounding five. Work stopped until dark but the heavy rain that night impeded further progress.[2]

The next day, scouts reported a force of more than 600 men were advancing from Pensacola. On the 12th, Gálvez moved nine of his heavy cannons into position on his forward battery and began a heavy bombardment of the fort at 10 AM. Captain William Pickles commanding the ship *West Florida,* also ordered his men to fire on the fort. The cannonade continued throughout the day, killing three and wounding nine. The attackers lost eight killed and 12 wounded. As the fort walls began to collapse, Captain Elias Durnford (1739–1794) surrendered his garrison of 300 at sunset. The formal surrender (see Photo FL-8) occurred on the 14th. Gálvez reported capturing 307: 13 officers, 113 soldiers, 56 sailors, 70 militiamen and 55 armed African Americans. They also captured 35 cannons and eight mortars (see Photo GA-13). General John Campbell (d. 1806) and 1,100 Regulars and Native Americans were only a few hours away.

Charles Stedman (1753–1812) records the event in his history of the war:

> The Spanish made a fresh incursion into West Florida, and succeeded in reducing the town and fort of Mobille, with the adjoining country. In the month of January

Don Bernardo de Galves sailed from New Orleans, with a fleet consisting of sixteen armed vessels, and a number of transports, having on board one thousand five hundred regular troops, and five hundred people of colour. On his passage he was overtaken by a storm, in which several of his vessels were lost, with a number of his troops, and great part of his provisions, artillery, and ammunition. With the rest he arrived off the entrance into Mobille Bay, and landed upon the point of land forming the eastern extremity of that inlet, where he remained until he obtained a reinforcement of men, and a fresh supply of provisions, artillery, and ammunition. When these arrived, Don Bernardo de Galves again embarked his troops, and, sailing up the Bay, landed at Dog River, about four miles from Mobille, on the twenty-fifth of February (1780). From thence he advanced against the fort, and proceeded to make regular approaches, a waste of labour and time that seemed unnecessary against a place so totally unprovided for defence. The fort had been originally built only as a protection against the Indians; and, after it came into the possession of Great Britain, had been suffered to go to decay, until the beginning of the present year, when captain Durnford, the chief engineer at Pensacola, was sent to put it in a state of defence. But this, it seems, was impossible, without an immense expence of money, and a greater length of time than intervened between his taking the command, and the arrival of the Spaniards. It was garrisoned by a company of the sixtieth regiment, amounting to eighty-two men, including officers; and to these were added, upon the approach of the Spaniards, thirty-six sailors, forty-five militia, and sixty people of colour. On the fourteenth of March the Spaniards opened a battery upon the fort, of eleven pieces of heavy cannon, which, in twelve hours, damaged its defences so entirely, and rendered it so untenable, that the commanding officer thought fit to capitulate. Honourable terms were obtained; and, although it was scarcely possible for the garrison to hold out longer, their surrender at this critical moment was, afterwards, a cause of regret, when they were informed that general Campbell, with seven hundred men, was then on his march from Pensacola to their relief, and at no great distance when the capitulation was signed.[3]

When he learned that Durnford had surrendered to Gálvez, Major General John Campbell and the relief column of 700 men from Pensacola returned to their base 100 miles away. Campbell could only be supplied by sea, and the Spanish now controlled most of the waters between Cuba and the Gulf Coast. British authorities later reported that had a British naval squadron been available to prevent the Spanish troop landings, Mobile would not have fallen.[4]

Tensaw or Tensa (March 17, 1780; early Nov. 1780)
Spanish Fort (Jan. 7, 1781)

The city of Mobile received much of its fresh water and food from Mobile Village, known as La Aldea, after the Spanish victory. The village was a palisaded (see Photo GA-14) outpost protected by a blockhouse (see Photo GA-1). It was located on the east bank of the Mobile River, about 8 miles northeast of the fortified town of Mobile, about 0.6 miles north of route US 31 (Spanish Fort Boulevard) and about 100 yards east of Cannonade Boulevard.

The outpost was garrisoned by 190 men from the Principe, España, Navarra and Havana regiments. They were supported by the Royal Artillery Corps and two 4-pounders and several fusiliers as well as the New Orleans Colored Militia Companies. Governor Bernardo de Gálvez (1746–1786) had created the Company of Free Mulatto Militia at New Orleans on March 26, 1778.[5]

British raids from Pensacola attacked the village on several occasions.

Some of Governor Bernardo de Gálvez's (1746–1786) scouts reported, on Wednesday, March 15, 1780, that Major General John Campbell (d. 1806) and a relief column of 700 men from Pensacola were coming to reinforce Fort Charlotte. When they learned of the fort's surrender, they decided to return to their base 100 miles away. Campbell could only be supplied by sea; and the Spanish now controlled most of the waters between Cuba and the Gulf Coast. British authorities later reported that had a British naval squadron been available to prevent the Spanish troop landings, Mobile would not have fallen. Campbell left Captain Patrick Strachan and his company of West Florida Royal Foresters behind to protect the loyal settlers in the area and to gather and drive the cattle to Pensacola.

On Friday, March 17, 1780, Gálvez's force surprised and captured Captain Strachan and 16 of his West Florida Royal Foresters in the Tensaw region, about 30 miles around the bay from Mobile. Early in November 1780, Native Americans and Loyalists attacked the post and killed at least four Spaniards before being driven off. The raids resulted in the scalping of Spanish soldiers and French farmers caught outside the blockhouse.[6]

★ The Crown forces sent a larger expedition against Mobile Village or Frenchtown on Wednesday, January 3, 1781. Colonel Johann Ludwig Wilhelm von Hanxleden (d. 1781) led 60 of his Waldeckers (3rd Waldeck Regiment), 100 British Regulars from the 60th (Royal American) Regiment of Foot which had seen service already at Baton Rouge and Mobile, and about 250 Pennsylvania and Maryland Loyalists, a few militia cavalrymen and 300 Native Americans against the Village while two British frigates (the HMS *Mentor* and another frigate) sailed from Pensacola to cut the communications with the Spanish Fort. The Spanish Fort was held by Lieutenant Ramon del Castro and 190 men of the Principe, España, Navarra and Havana regiments, across the bay from Tensaw.

The frigates hid their British colors behind some Spanish banners they had captured and easily sailed past the eight Spanish guns on Dauphin Island on January 5, 1781. The commanding officer mistook the British ships for part of a Spanish convoy from Havana that he had been expecting for several weeks. When the Spanish officer rowed out to greet the ships in a long-boat (see Photo AL-1) with five soldiers, the boat master and six sailors, he realized he had been tricked when they hailed the frigate's officer of the day and were immediately taken prisoners. The British learned from them that the defenses of Dauphin Island were weak and that the Mobile garrison got their rations of fresh meat from the royal herds grazing on Dauphin Island. They decided to "liberate" the cattle there and sent a landing party ashore to gather provisions. Sergeant Second-Class Jose Manuel Rodriguez (1759–1846) and his 18 men put up a stout defense which caught the landing party unprepared. They fired withering volleys of musketry, but the British troops managed to take three young beeves back to their boats.

★ An estimated 200 white soldiers with two 4-pounders and 200 to 500 Native Americans advanced under cover of a dense fog before sunrise on Sunday, January 7, 1781. They moved stealthily in a single column through the camp of the New Orleans Black militiamen who were in the trenches along the outer perimeter. Sublieutenant Manuel de Cordoba (d. 1781) of the España Regiment saw the troops moving toward the Spanish positions but thought they were militiamen returning to the outer trenches, so he did not give the order to fire until the attackers were upon his exposed position.

The Crown troops had reached the trenches without a shot being fired and halted momentarily, somewhat puzzled at the lack of any defense. The Spanish troops suddenly opened fire and the two forces advanced toward each other with fixed bayonets and knives drawn. Colonel Johann Ludwig Wilhelm von Hanxleden (d. 1781) halted

AL-1. Long boat of HMS Victory. Long boats were used to ferry troops to and from shore.

his troops and sent out scouting parties to find a weak spot in the Spanish palisade (see Photo GA-14). Spanish marksmen "opened a general volley against the enemy." The Waldeck sergeant major ordered his troops to charge the Spanish grenadiers but he was bayoneted and killed. The Spanish maintained such a withering fire that the Crown forces retreated. Most of the Waldeckers were killed in the trenches.

The initial onslaught caused some Spanish militiamen to break ranks and flee, hoping to find a boat near the shore which had brought rations to the Spanish troops the previous afternoon. However, the boat had been withdrawn to prevent any attempt to retreat. The Native Americans killed some of these troops fleeing toward the water. The rest took refuge in the blockhouse (see Photo GA-1) and offered stiff resistance. The defenders rallied and repulsed the attackers in hand-to-hand combat.

When Colonel von Hanxleden fell, the Crown forces ceased the attack and returned to Pensacola. Von Hanxleden died during the engagement along with two officers and 13 men, all found in the trenches and beneath the palisade. The wounded numbered 13 officers and 19 men. The defenders lost 14 killed, 23 wounded and one taken prisoner. Each army suffered about 20% casualties. The capture of Mobile allowed the Spanish to proceed with plans to attack Pensacola. However, 2,000 Creeks in the area prevented them from doing so.[7]

Hollywood
Donelson Flotilla (March 8, 1780)

The Donelson Flotilla incident occurred on the northeastern shore of Guntersville Lake west of the Tennessee River in Hollywood.

Richard Henderson (1734–1785) selected Colonel John Donelson (1718–1785) and James Robertson (1742–1814) to lead settlers into the Cumberland River region. Robertson made plans for an overland voyage while Donelson led another group along a water route. Donelson and approximately 30 families boarded the *Adventure* at Fort Patrick Henry on December 22, 1779. The *Adventure* accommodated several families, household goods and supplies necessary to sustain a settlement in a new land.

Another group joined Donelson's party at the mouth of the Clinch River. The group consisted of a large number of women and children, including Donelson's own large family and approximately 30 African American slaves. One of Donelson's children was his 13-year-old daughter Rachel (b. 1763), who would become the wife of Andrew Jackson (1767–1845). Others in the party included James Robertson's wife, Charlotte, and five of their 11 children. The flotilla of 30 or more canoes, flat boats and dugouts traversed the Holston, Tennessee, Ohio and Cumberland rivers.

John Donelson's flotilla came to the first inhabited Chickamauga town on the Tennessee River near Chattanooga (Tennessee) on Wednesday, March 8, 1780. The Chickamaugas saw the boats and hurried to the river and insisted that the party come ashore. They gave signs of friendship, calling the whites brothers and addressing them in other familiar terms. The boats anchored on the opposite shore. John Donelson, Jr., and John Caffrey (Caffery), Jr. (1756–1811) took a canoe and paddled toward the Chickamaugas. Archie Coody, a half-breed, and several other Native Americans met them midstream and warned them to return to the fleet, which they did, followed by Coody and his companions who seemed friendly. Colonel Donelson gave the Native Americans presents which pleased them very much.

As they looked across toward the village, the men saw a large party of Chickamaugas, armed and painted in red and black, embarking in canoes on the other side. Coody immediately ordered his companions to leave the fleet while he remained with the whites, urging them to depart immediately. The boats had barely left the shore when they discovered the Chickamaugas coming down the river, apparently intending to intercept them, but they did not do so.

Coody paddled alongside the fleet in his canoe for some time. After assuring Colonel Donelson that he had passed all the Chickamauga towns and was free from danger, Coody turned around and paddled back toward the first village. Donelson's party soon spotted another mud-cabin town similarly situated on the south side of the river and nearly opposite a small island. The Chickamaugas again invited them to come ashore, calling them brothers, as on the previous occasion. Colonel Donelson, sensing a trap, headed the boats to the opposite channel around the island.

The Chickamaugas called to them through one of their men who could speak English, telling them that the channel chosen was unsafe and that their side of the river was much better for passage. A band of Chickamaugas, concealed near the bank on the northern shore, fired at one of the boats when it came too near, killing one of the men.

One of the boats in the flotilla carried 28 passengers, among whom an epidemic of smallpox had broken out. That boat kept well to the rear of the others to prevent the spread of the disease to other members of the fleet. This party was far behind the rest of the fleet while these events were taking place. When they came down opposite the Chickamauga towns, the inhabitants were on the shore in large numbers. Seeing the boat cut off from the rest of the fleet, the Chickamaugas swarmed out in canoes, captured and killed the entire crew. Those in the boats ahead heard the cries of their comrades, but were unable to return to their aid.

The Chickamaugas suffered a swift retribution for their cruelty, as they became infected with their victims' smallpox which raged through their tribe and the tribes of their neighbors, the Creeks and Cherokees, for many months thereafter. Donelson's party reached the end of their 1,000-mile journey on Monday, April 24, 1780 and were finally reunited with family and friends at the Big Salt Lick (now Nashville, Tennessee).[8]

Stevenson
Crow Town (1780)

Crow Town (translation of Kâgûnyĭ, 'crow place', from kâgû 'crow', yĭ'locative') was in northeast Alabama about 12 miles south of the current Tennessee border. It was east of the John T. Reid Parkway (US 72|AL 2) in Stevenson and is now under Cow Creek. There's a historical marker on route US 72 at the intersection of US 72 and Kentucky Avenue in Stevenson.

Crow Town was the lowest of the five Cherokee Lower Towns established by Dragging Canoe (ca. 1730–1792), leader of the Chickamauga Cherokees, who supported the British during the American War of Independence. The other towns included Running Water (Amogayunyi), at the current Whiteside in Marion County, Tennessee, where Dragging Canoe made his headquarters; Nickajack (Ani-Kusati-yi, or Koasati place), 5 miles down the Tennessee River in the same county; Long Island (Amoyeligunahita), on the Tennessee just above the Great Creek Crossing; and Stecoyee (Utsutigwayi, also known as Lookout Mountain Town), at the current site of Trenton, Georgia.

The Chickamaugas from the Five Lower Towns launched raids on backcountry settlements from middle Tennessee to southwestern Virginia. One of these raids, in October 1780, struck the settlements along the Nolichucky and Watauga rivers to eliminate the Watauga militia. Nancy Ward (1735–1824), whose daughter was married to Joseph Martin (1740–1808), a Virginia agent to the Cherokees, warned Colonel John Sevier (1745–1815) of the impending attack. Sevier, who had just returned from Kings Mountain, mustered 300 Overmountain men and engaged the Cherokees at Boyd's Creek. Two weeks later, they proceeded to the Cherokee capital town of Chota and burned it. They also destroyed several Cherokee towns up the Tennessee River and probably also burned Crow Town.[9]

John Watts (or Kunokeski), also known as Young Tassel, (ca. 1760–1802), Dragging Canoe's nephew, became the leading war chief after his uncle's death in 1792. Tennessee militia leader James Ore launched a military expedition to punish the Chickamaugas for their raids in 1794. The devastating assault resulted in the Cherokees suing for peace.[10]

See **Tennessee, Cherokee Campaign of 1780** pp. 246–249.

4
MISSISSIPPI

The Treaty of Paris (1763) which ended the Seven Years War [French and Indian War (1756–1763)] gave Great Britain all of the former French territory east of the Mississippi River, including all of the present state of Mississippi. In the late 18th century, it was part of the province of West Florida. During the American War of Independence, the Native Americans, trappers and scouts supported the other colonies in their struggle for independence. Loyalists fled from the rebelling colonies and migrated to the districts of Natchez and Manchac, attracted particularly to the rich virgin bluffs around Natchez. The population of Natchez more than doubled during the war.

Spain now governed the remainder of Louisiana across the Mississippi River from West Florida. When Spain declared war on Great Britain, the governor of Louisiana, Bernardo de Gálvez (1746–1786), captured major settlements in West Florida and took over the administration of the region in 1781. Great Britain ceded West Florida to Spain in the peace treaty of 1783.

The Mississippi State Department of Archives and History [200 North Street, Jackson, MS 39201; (phone: 601-576-6850)] is a source of historical information about the state. The Mississippi Development Authority (Division of Tourism) [P.O. Box 849, Jackson, MS 39205; (phone: 601-359-3297, 800-733-6477; website: **www .visitmississippi.org**)] offers maps and tourist brochures.

See the map of Alabama, Mississippi, Louisiana and Arkansas.

Natchez
Fort Panmure (Feb. 18, 1778; April 15, 1778; Oct. 5, 1779; April 22, 1781)

The French built Fort Rosalie in 1716 on the bluffs above the Mississippi River on the site of the Grand Village of the Natchez tribe. The fort was repaired and rechristened Fort Panmure and was first occupied by the Spanish garrison in 1764. It was probably near the intersection of Franklin and North Pearl streets in Natchez.

The Spanish governor of Louisiana, 31-year-old Colonel Bernardo de Gálvez (1746–1786) continued to provide financial aid to the Rebels after he assumed office in 1777. He sent money, gunpowder and supplies to Colonel George Rogers Clark (1752–1818) in Illinois and provided services to Captain James Willing for his raid on Fort Panmure at Natchez on Wednesday, February 18, 1778.

Colonel George Rogers Clark led one military expedition that surprised and captured the British posts in the Illinois Country. Captain James Willing led another to conquer the British settlements in the "old Southwest." Willing and his band of 30 men boarded an armed sloop, the *Rattletrap*, at Fort Pitt on Sunday, January 11, 1778, and descended the Ohio and Mississippi rivers to Natchez. They intended to bring back five boat-loads of supplies from Louisiana. It seems that Willing was also unofficially authorized to plunder Loyalist property along the way and to dispose of it at public auction at New Orleans, Louisiana. Along the way, Willing recruited additional men, increasing his force to some 100 men. Willing's party reached the mouth of the Arkansas River by early February. They rested briefly before continuing. Willing divided his force in two, sending an advance contingent ahead while he and the rest of the men followed in close pursuit.

The advance party, under the command of Lieutenant Thomas McIntyre (McIntire), surprised and captured four British Indian agents after dark, on Wednesday evening, February 18, as they relaxed at the home of John Watkins, a Walnut Hill (Vicksburg) planter. McIntyre's men secured their prisoners and proceeded downstream to Natchez where they landed unopposed on the evening of February 19. Captain Willing had previously instructed McIntyre to send out two small detachments to seize the persons and property of Anthony Hutchins and William McIntosh (d. ca. 1799), two of the settlement's leading Loyalists. McIntyre caught the Natchez settlers completely by surprise and apprehended them relatively easily. Willing arrived the next day and immediately raised the American flag over the fort at Natchez. He then ordered the settlers to assemble in town, declaring them prisoners of the United States "on parole."

The inhabitants of Natchez, frightened by the unexpected appearance of an armed force, authorized four prominent planters to arrange favorable terms of capitulation. On February 21, the inhabitants swore to remain neutral if Willing promised to keep their lands and slaves safe. He apparently kept his promise in the Natchez area; but, south of it, he terrorized the British east bank of the river, seizing slaves and property and burning houses.[1]

Willing persuaded some of the sympathetic settlers of Natchez to join his force and increased the sense of terror by portraying his men as the advance guard of a large army. The advance group under McIntyre proceeded down the Mississippi with Anthony Hutchins and most of his slaves in custody.

Under cover of a dense early morning fog, McIntyre and his men surprised and captured the armed sloop *Rebecca*, anchored to the river bank at Manchac. Small detachments of men searched the countryside for slaves and property of known Loyalists, as McIntyre awaited Willing's arrival from Natchez and Oliver Pollock's (1737–1823) nephew Thomas from New Orleans.

Willing's larger force plundered the property of Loyalists in the Baton Rouge, Louisiana area further north. A few settlers were alerted of Willing's approach and managed to escape into Spanish territory, but most of the inhabitants were taken by surprise. When they departed, Willing and his men left a trail of devastation that one inhabitant described as "nothing to be seen but Destruction and Desolation."

This caused many citizens to flee across the river to seek the protection of the Spanish at Manchac. Colonel Bernardo de Gálvez ordered his people to receive them as refugees. He also permitted them to purchase supplies in New Orleans, including weapons. He let Willing use several public buildings as barracks for his troops and allowed Willing to dispose of the booty at public auction. These sales brought in more than $62,000.

Willing and his men soon needed Gálvez's protection as badly as the refugees, as two sloops of war headed up the river and another, with 100 soldiers, crossed the lakes to demand Willing's surrender. Governor Gálvez became alarmed at Willing's continued invasions of British territory and feared Great Britain might use them as an excuse to seize Louisiana. He persuaded Pollock to help him encourage Willing and his men to leave the province. Willing was in no hurry to return to Fort Pitt. He made one excuse after another to delay his departure, annoying Gálvez and infuriating Pollock, who feared Willing's stay would jeopardize his close relations with the Spanish governor.

The inhabitants of Natchez and the other settlements along the Mississippi had complained to Peter Chester (1717/18–1799), the British governor of West Florida, who sent two 32-gun frigates to New Orleans. The captains of these two ships had orders to demand the restoration of all property seized by Willing and the punishment of all those responsible for offenses against British citizens. The two British ship captains and the Spanish governor traded insults for more than two months, but Gálvez refused to surrender Willing and his men, keeping his commitment to Pollock, despite the two British war ships off the port of New Orleans.

The frigates blockaded the mouth of the Mississippi River and prevented Willing and his men from leaving by sea. The British also planned to cut off Willing's escape route to the north. Governor Chester sent a small force of Rangers and militiamen to Manchac where they surprised and captured a large number of people who were asleep.

★ About the same time, Loyalist Anthony Hutchins broke his parole in New Orleans and headed for Natchez with news that the Whigs intended to plunder the property of planters there as they had done in Baton Rouge. He rallied a few of his old friends and planned to ambush Captain Reuben Harrison (d. 1778) and his force at White Cliffs, about 15 miles south of Natchez. John Tally, a resident in the area and one of Hutchins's enemies, discovered the plot and warned Harrison. Harrison sent Tally back to inform Hutchins and the other inhabitants of Natchez that he was coming in peace and not to plunder and rob them. Hutchins and a few supporters remained unconvinced of Harrison's peaceful intentions. When the two parties reached the White Cliffs on Wednesday, April 15, 1778, they were each wary of the other. Someone fired; and, when the shooting ended, Harrison and three or four of his men were dead. The three wounded and remaining 10 surrendered. The British regained control of Natchez while Willing and his men remained trapped in New Orleans with both ends of the Mississippi River closed to them.

Governor Bernardo de Gálvez (1746–1786), to placate the British, had to order Willing to return some of the booty his men captured on Spanish soil. Willing haggled over each item as the neutral citizens of West Florida gradually became hostile. Willing's raid induced more than 300 to volunteer for military service with the Crown forces. Along with recruits from Jamaica and detachments from New York, the Crown forces received more than 1,000 reinforcements. Willing and his men obtained, from Governor Gálvez, a promise of safe conduct through Spanish territory, but they remained in the area until August 1778, when most of them left New Orleans and marched overland through Louisiana to Fort Kaskaskia in the Illinois country. There, they joined Colonel George Rogers Clark's western army. Willing left for Philadelphia in October on board a private sloop which the British captured at sea. He was eventually sent to New York where he remained a prisoner until exchanged for a British officer in September 1781.[2]

★ Major General John Campbell (d. 1806) arrived in West Florida from Jamaica in early 1779. He came with 1,200 fresh troops, mostly Germans from the province of Waldeck and American Loyalists from Maryland and Pennsylvania. He assigned most of these troops to protect the two valuable ports of Pensacola and Mobile from attack, but he dispatched about 400 of them to the Mississippi frontier. He advised Lieutenant Colonel Alexander Dickson, commander of the western forces, to erect a fort at or near Manchac, Louisiana and to repair Fort Panmure at Natchez.

When Governor Bernardo de Gálvez (1746–1786) learned, in early August 1779, that Spain signed a formal declaration of war against England in June, he acted before the British received the news. He assembled a mixed force of 2,000 from the lower Mississippi settlements and made preparations to seize British possessions along the Mississippi River before General Campbell was ready to attack New Orleans. This force consisted of veterans, Mexican recruits, African Americans (200 of whom were armed), Native Americans and militiamen of every class and color. On Friday morning, August 27, Gálvez led his army of 667 men toward Manchac. Along the way, an equal number of civilian volunteers and a detachment of Native Americans joined them, bringing their strength up to more than 1,400 men. They quickly captured Fort Bute at Manchac on Tuesday, September 7, 1779 and Baton Rouge five days later. The terms of surrender included the surrender of Fort Panmure whose high walls would have made its conquest very difficult.

See also **Louisiana, Manchac** and **Fort Bute** pp. 149–151.

Governor Bernardo de Gálvez (1746–1786) sent Captain Juan de Villebreuve with 50 men to occupy Fort Panmure on Tuesday, October 5, 1779. Captain de Villebreuve brought a letter for the inhabitants of Natchez that read:

> Colonel Dickson has capitulated to Governor Gálvez and surrendered his garrison; he has ordered the withdrawal of your forces and has delivered the fort to the Spanish officer commissioned for that purpose. The spirit of liberty, the protection which every American has received on this river from His Excellency Governor Gálvez, his generous conduct towards all the inhabitants, with the advantages which should now arise from uninterrupted trade with New Orleans, where you will find a good market for your products and the necessary supplies for your families, I hope will be more than sufficient encouragement for you to render all services within your means to the arms of His Catholic Majesty.[3]

A few days later, a messenger arrived from Pensacola, Florida with a letter from Brigadier General John Campbell (d. 1806), commander there, notifying the citizens of Natchez that Spain had entered the war against England and urging them to join in an attack on New Orleans. The news of the declaration of war arrived at Pensacola about a month after Gálvez received the news.[4]

★ A man by the name of Stille, who resided with Captain John McIntosh (1755–1826) on St. Catherine Creek, was captured carrying a letter from Captain McIntosh to Captain Juan Delavillebeuvre the commandant of the Spanish garrison at Fort Panmure "advising him to hold on, and that the revolt would soon die out." Captain John Blommart, commanding a force of between 100 and 200 Loyalists and Native Americans, got John Alston, a skilled forger, to write a letter to the commandant over the signature of his friend McIntosh. The letter stated that "further resistance was useless; that the insurgents had secretly undermined the fort, and deposited therein a large supply of powder brought by Indian pack-horses from Pensacola, and that that very night had been fixed on for the explosion." Blommart threatened to murder Stille, compelling him to deliver the forged letter.[5]

The trick succeeded. Delavillebeuvre agreed to the terms of capitulation after one man was killed on Sunday, April 22, 1781 when the Loyalists began firing on the fort. Shortly after the fort surrendered, the Crown forces disagreed over the fate of the 76 prisoners. Some wanted to send the prisoners to Pensacola, but Anthony Hutchins convinced Blommart that the guards who volunteered for the detail planned to kill them as soon as they got away from Blommart's control. Instead, Blommart sent Delavillebeuvre and his 76 men to Baton Rouge under a reliable guard. They made the journey unmolested.

Another cause of disagreement was the question of raising the American flag instead of the British. One faction planned to plunder the stores of supplies at Natchez and divide them. They had already broken into Delavillebeuvre's baggage; but Blommart, who had received sufficient warning, appointed a commissary and demanded careful records be kept. He only permitted supplies and ammunition to be issued as actually needed.[6]

5
LOUISIANA

France transferred its colony of Louisiana to Spain in 1762, in the secret Treaty of Fontainebleau, to induce Spain to enter the Seven Years War [French and Indian War (1756–1763)] as a French ally. When Great Britain won the war in 1763, she acquired nearly all of Louisiana east of the Mississippi River. Spain kept the larger western part which lay across the Mississippi from West Florida and retained the name Louisiana.

The predominantly French people were surprised and angry to now have a Spanish government. As Spain considered Great Britain her main rival in colonial North America, the Spanish, mostly in New Orleans, supplied the revolting colonies with arms, ammunition and provisions during the American War of Independence, as early as September 1776, hoping to eliminate the British presence. When Bernardo de Gálvez (1746–1786) was appointed governor-general of Louisiana in 1777, he accelerated the flow of supplies up the Mississippi and strengthened the defenses of his province. Meanwhile, the Crown forces reinforced their posts in West Florida and were prepared and waiting when Captain James Willing resumed his raids.

When Spain formally declared war on Great Britain in June 1779, her troops captured all the major British settlements in West Florida (Baton Rouge, Natchez and Pensacola) which covered the Gulf Coast area between the Perdido and Mississippi rivers. The Treaty of Paris, which ended the war, returned both East and West Florida to Spain.

> The Louisiana Office of Tourism offers free travel brochures and road maps through its website: **www.louisianatravel.com** or by phone: 225-342-8100. The Louisiana Historical Association in Lafayette (phone: 337-482-6027) is a source for historical information.

See the map of Alabama, Mississippi, Louisiana and Arkansas.

Manchac
Fort Bute (Feb. 23, 1778, March 14, 1778, Sept. 7, 1779)

> Fort Bute was on the shore of Lake Maurepas in Manchac on the north side of the confluence of Bayou Manchac and the Mississippi River below Baton Rouge, about 40 miles northwest of New Orleans. It was the main British post on the Mississippi until late July 1779 when the British realized it was indefensible against artillery. They condemned the six-gun star-shaped earthwork fort and decided to build another at Baton Rouge which then became the strongest post on the Mississippi. It was rebuilt in 1778 on a nearby site and captured by the Spanish in 1779.[1]

See also **Mississippi** pp. 145–148.

Lieutenant Thomas McIntyre (McIntire) and 18 men from Captain James Willing's force captured the armed sloop *Rebecca* and another ship near Fort Bute on Tuesday, February 23, 1778 and took them to New Orleans. Loyalists retaliated less than three weeks later by attacking the fort's guardhouse on Saturday, March 14, killing about two soldiers and wounding about three others. They captured 13 men and took possession of the fort. This action isolated Willing and his people in New Orleans. The British demanded that Colonel Bernardo de Gálvez (1746–1786) surrender Willing and his men but Gálvez refused. He arranged for Willing to return to Fort Pitt by way of Natchitoches and Arkansas Post to escape from an embarrassing situation and thus avoiding another confrontation with His Majesty forces.[2]

★ Major General John Campbell (d. 1806) arrived in West Florida from Jamaica in early 1779. He brought 1,200 fresh troops, mostly Germans from the province of Waldeck and American Loyalists from Maryland and Pennsylvania. Most of these troops were assigned to protect the two valuable ports of Pensacola and Mobile, but about 400 of them were dispatched to the Mississippi frontier. Under the command of Lieutenant Colonel Alexander Dickson, commander of the western forces, they erected a fort at or near Manchac and repaired Fort Panmure at Natchez.

Dickson encountered one problem after another, so progress on the fort proceeded very slowly. The Germans did not adjust well to the hot, humid climate of the southwest. Sickness and death took its toll. The Spanish took advantage of the situation by encouraging desertion from the British Army. Dickson was also short of funds and provisions. Heavy rains during the late spring and early summer also caused the Mississippi River to overflow its banks and to flood his camp at Manchac.

When the governor of Louisiana, Bernardo de Gálvez (1746–1786) learned, in early August 1779, that Spain signed a formal declaration of war against England on Monday, June 21, he kept the news a secret. He acted before the Crown forces received the news, assembling a mixed force of 2,000 men from the lower Mississippi settlements. This force consisted of 1,000 Spanish regulars, Mexican recruits, African Americans (200 of whom were armed), Native Americans and militiamen of every class and color. Gálvez was determined to capture Fort Bute at Manchac and then Baton Rouge.

Fort Bute was reinforced by 400 Hessians and there were rumors of an imminent British expedition down the Mississippi from Canada which intended to join forces with a seaborne thrust from Pensacola. Gálvez convened a council of war that advised him to protect New Orleans at all costs. Instead of following their advice, Gálvez went on the offensive.

On Wednesday, August 18, 1779, a few days before the motley army was to march, a hurricane in the Gulf of Mexico sank Gálvez's fleet in the Mississippi along with all their supplies and weapons. Only one ship survived. The storm did much damage to New Orleans, demolishing dozens of buildings and destroying crops and cattle for 40 miles along the river. Gálvez wrote about the furious storm in a letter to his uncle, Jose, the Minister of the Indies: ". . . for leagues around all is in ruins, the crops lost, the trees uprooted, the men overwhelmed, their wives and children scattered through the desert fields exposed to the weather, the land flooded and all sunk in the river, together with my resources, assistance and hopes. . . ." He ordered his men to raise the sunken ships and started collecting supplies again.[3]

Gálvez gathered the Creoles at the Place d'Armes in New Orleans, notified them of an impending attack by the Crown forces and appealed to the people for their support. On August 27, only four days later than he had planned, he led 500 Spanish regulars, 60 Creole militiamen, 80 African American and mulatto volunteers, and nine volunteers from New Orleans. The African Americans and Choctaws led the column, followed by the regulars and the militiamen in the rear. They headed upriver toward Baton Rouge. Along the way, they recruited another 600 Acadian and German militiamen and 60 Choctaws.

The August heat overcame a third of the army during the 11-day march of 115 miles. Gálvez and his army arrived at Manchac on Monday, September 6, 1779 and camped within a mile of the fort. Only then did he tell his men that Spain had declared war against England and that they were not just defending Louisiana. They were going to attack Fort Bute the next day. The Acadians were particularly anxious to get back at "those who had . . . driven them into exile like miserable outlaws." The defenders were still unaware of the declaration of war.

Gálvez placed his regulars north of the fort to cut off any avenue of retreat. The militia began the assault at 8:30 AM, advancing in heavy ground fog. They killed a sentry and wounded two others, ending the battle. Instead of the 450 man garrison they expected to find, they only found about two dozen men. Dickson had decided that the stockade at Manchac was indefensible, abandoned the work and moved his troops to higher ground at Baton Rouge in early September 1779, a move that saved his forces from being completely surprised. Twenty of the defenders surrendered immediately and six escaped in the fog.[4]

Baton Rouge (Sept. 12–22, 1779)
Fort New Richmond

Located on the Mississippi River in West Florida (now Louisiana), Baton Rouge was garrisoned by 500 men from the 16th Regiment of Foot, 110 grenadiers (see Photo LA-1) from the 3rd Waldeck Regiment, under Captain von Hacke, Loyalists of the 60th Royal Americans, and a miscellaneous group of regular troops, settlers and African American slaves all commanded by Lieutenant Colonel Alexander Dickson. They constructed a redoubt (see Photo FL-6) with 13 cannon, a moat 18 feet wide and 9 feet deep, and chevaux-de-frise (see Photo LA-2).

Governor Bernardo de Gálvez's (1746–1786) camp was situated between North Boulevard and Convention Street. He supposedly used a Native American mound located there as a breastwork and erected his batteries on its brow.

After Colonel Bernardo de Gálvez (1746–1786) captured Fort Bute on Tuesday, September 7, 1779, he rested his men for six days before proceeding to Baton Rouge, 15 miles away. He arrived at Baton Rouge on September 19th, only a day or so before the Crown forces had finished the fortifications. Having lost the element of surprise, Gálvez sent his Choctaw, African Americans and Creole militiamen to what seemed the logical point to begin an attack—a triangular grove of trees near the fort's north wall. They had orders to cut down the trees that evening and to make as much noise as possible to attract the attention of the enemy. The occupants of the fort fired round and grape shot (see Photo GA-7) into the woods all night while a larger detachment of regulars dug siege trenches on the other side of the fort and set up the heavy cannons.

The trenches were deep enough to protect the artillery from enemy fire by dawn on September 21. The guns, which were within musket range, battered the chevaux-de-frise, the barracks and other buildings in the fort. With their forces now down to about 700 men, Gálvez's officers wanted to attack immediately, afraid that dwindling supplies and the summer heat would further shrink the army. Gálvez reminded his officers that most of the men were heads of families and that a frontal charge against 13 cannon and 650 muskets would "fill the whole Province with grief and mourning."

The Crown forces had wasted much of their ammunition and most of their energy on the decoys without inflicting any casualties. Now their cannons pointed in the wrong direction. The Spanish began an incessant firing that tore gaping holes in the fort's embankments. One cannon ball supposedly landed on Lieutenant Colonel Alexander

LA-1. Hessian grenadiers. Re-enactors portraying Hessian grenadiers wearing blue regimental coats with buff facings, buff waistcoats and breeches, full gaiters with 21 buttons, and miter helmets with brass face plates.

LA-2. Chevaux-de-frise: obstacles consisting of horizontal poles with projecting spikes. They were used on land to block a passageway and modified to block rivers to enemy ships.

Dickson's breakfast table and interrupted his meal. By mid-afternoon, Dickson had had enough. He asked for a truce while the two sides arranged the terms of capitulation.

Dickson tried to delay the surrender because he expected reinforcements of other Waldeck troops from Pensacola. Dickson asked for the terms of surrender at 3 PM, after he had four men killed and two wounded. Gálvez drove a hard bargain. He demanded the surrender of all the forts on the Mississippi, particularly Fort Panmure at Natchez in what is now Mississippi. Even though Dickson knew that Fort Panmure was far more defensible than the hastily-built fortifications at Baton Rouge, he had no choice, under the circumstances, but to accept Gálvez's terms.

Gálvez sent an officer and 50 men to take possession of Fort Panmure on October 5. A number of Natchez settlers were bitterly unhappy with the turn of events. Although a few disgruntled inhabitants complained that Dickson had sacrificed their interests to gain more favorable terms for himself, a larger number publicly thanked him for his heroic exertions in defending the Mississippi settlements against overwhelming odds.[5]

Gálvez wrote to his uncle Jose about this battle on Saturday, October 16, 1779: "After a truce to bury the dead, the survivors left the fort with full military honors; 375 regular troops laid down their arms, hauled down their flags and were made prisoners. The civilians and blacks were left at liberty to return to their homes with the promise of remaining neutral. The regular troops, now prisoners, were left under the guard of four cadets, while the main body of the troops entered and took possession of the fort. At the same time, a Captain, Juan de Villebreuve, with 50 men, was sent to occupy Pan Mure and Natchez, a victory which was very satisfying, as the high walls around this outpost would have made its conquest very difficult." The report is preserved in the Archive of Simancas.[6]

With the fall of Fort Bute, Baton Rouge and Fort Panmure at Natchez, British control of the lower Mississippi valley ended. Gálvez gave Don Vizente Rillieux (1736–1800) of New Orleans command of a sloop of war to cruise the lakes to intercept British reinforcements from Pensacola. He went up the Amite River as far as Bayou Manchac, planning an ambush at Pass Manchac, between Lake Pontchartrain and Lake Maurepas. The 14-man crew constructed a masked battery and positioned their light cannon at the pass. When the first British ship appeared, Rillieux's men fired and started to yell, convincing the sailors they faced a large army. When the sailors went below deck, Rillieux and his men boarded the ship and sealed the hatches, capturing 56 Waldeckers and 12 sailors—a force that outnumbered Rillieux's crew by almost five to one.[7]

Gálvez's Mississippi campaign cost him only one man killed and two wounded. He and his motley army had captured over 1,000 enemy troops, three forts, eight large ships, and 1,300 miles of prime farm land on the east bank of the Mississippi.[8]

South of New Orleans (late Feb. 1778)

New Orleans, founded in 1718 on the east bank of the Mississippi River and south of Lake Pontchartrain, was named for Philippe II, Duc d'Orléans, regent of France under King Louis XV. It was a major commercial center of the Louisiana Territory.

Shortly after the capture of the ships at Fort Bute, some of Captain James Willing's troops and others under Captain Joseph Calvert seized two more British ships south of New Orleans, in late February 1778, probably around Chalmette: the HM Brig *Neptune,* loaded with lumber bound for Jamaica, and the HM Schooner *Dispatch,* with its cargo of 50 "Picked Negroes" and 100 barrels of flour. Willing's raiding parties also seized more slaves, the property and personal effects of planters they overlooked during the trip downstream and several barges and other vessels owned by Loyalists.[9]

Governor Bernardo de Gálvez (1746–1786) reported to his military council on some messages that had been intercepted on their way to the English garrisons. He also reported on information received from other sources. This intelligence confirmed his suspicions that the Crown forces were preparing for an immediate outbreak of hostilities. Moreover, 400 Walloon Guards had reinforced Fort Bute at Manchac. The Crown forces were mobilizing all their troops, as well as their Iroquois and Sioux allies, from Montreal, Canada to Pensacola, Florida, for a full offensive against New Orleans.

Gálvez's military council wanted to begin preparations immediately to defend the city. They concentrated their available soldiers and defenses there, leaving the forts ungarrisoned. They also sent an urgent request to Havana for help.

THE FRONTIER

6
MICHIGAN

The British used Detroit as a rallying point during the American War of Independence. Raiding parties left from here to attack the Whigs. The commander at Detroit was Lieutenant Governor Henry Hamilton (1734?–1796), known as the "Hair Buyer" because he was believed to have paid the Native Americans a bounty for each scalp they brought in—an allegation he denied. Hamilton sent out a series of expeditions to Kentucky and the upper Ohio in 1777 that made it a year of horror that the frontiersmen never forgot. The following year, a raid resulted in capturing Daniel Boone (1734–1820) who was taken to Detroit as a prisoner. He escaped later. Colonel Alexander McKee (ca. 1735–1799) succeeded Hamilton at Detroit. McKee sent out raiding parties against Whig settlements from 1780 to 1782. These raiding parties, made up mostly of Native Americans and some small contingents of the King's 8th Regiment, in garrison at Fort Lernault (i.e. Fort Detroit), along with a company of Butler's Rangers operated as far south as Kentucky.

George Rogers Clark (1752–1818) retaliated by leading troops into the Illinois country to capture three British posts which induced the British commandant at Fort Michilimackinac (see Photo MI-1) (now Mackinaw City) to move his defenses to Mackinac Island, where it was called simply Fort Mackinac. Clark planned to capture Detroit to stop the raids on the northern frontier from Fort Pitt (Pittsburgh, Pennsylvania) southward. Without aid from Hamilton, the Native Americans, who depended on the British for their arms, clothing, blankets and liquor, would not act.

Major General Charles Lee (1731–1782), commander of the Continental forces in the South and General George Washington's (1732–1799) senior officer, proposed attacking Detroit. Although Washington approved the idea, Congress ignored it because such a major campaign would require men and supplies that the country could not provide at a time when Washington prepared to defend New York against the main British army.

Neither the Continental Congress nor the states had undertaken an expedition against Detroit, even though urged to do so. George Morgan (1743–1810), a veteran Indian Agent who served the Whigs in that capacity in the Ohio Valley ardently supported the plan and finally resigned his office in disgust."[1]

The Historical Society of Michigan [1305 Abbott Road, East Lansing, MI 48823 (phone: 517-324-1828)], the Department of History, Arts and Libraries (phone: 517-373-2486) and the Michigan Historical Center (702 West Kalamazoo Street, Lansing, MI 48909 (phone: 517-373-0510) are sources of historical information. The Michigan Economic Development Corporation [300 North Washington Square, Lansing, MI 48913 (phone: 800-644-2489)] is a source for tourist information. **www.michigan.org** and **www.michigan.gov** are two helpful websites.

See the map of Michigan.

MI-1. Fort Michilimackinac. Exterior (top) courtesy Todd Harburn and interior (bottom) courtesy Dan O'Connell. Soldiers can use the elevated platform both to move around the fort's defenses and to fire their weapons through the palisades or loopholes.

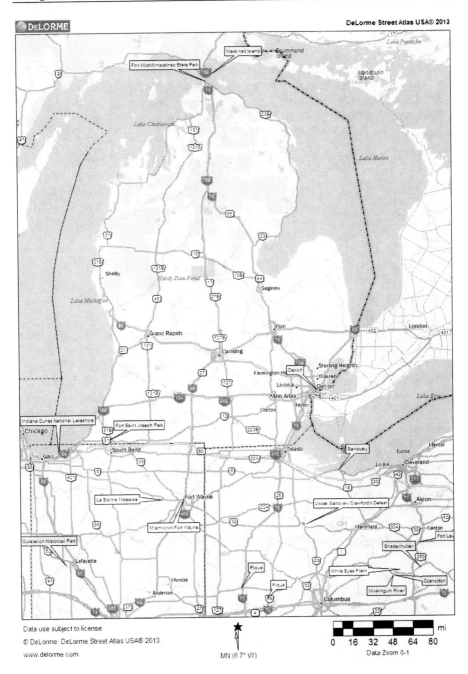

Michigan: Map for The Guide to the American Revolutionary War in the Deep South and on the Frontier
© *2013 DeLorme (www.delorme.com) Street Atlas USA®*

Niles

Fort St. Joseph (Feb. 12, 1781)

> Fort St. Joseph Park is on Bond Street, near the intersection with Fort Street, south of Niles. The Fort St. Joseph Historical Museum [508 East Main Street, Niles] has artifacts from the fort, most on display but many in storage. The items in storage can be viewed by calling 616-683-4702, ext. 236 to schedule an appointment.

After the attack on St. Louis, Missouri, the campaign of 1781 west of the Alleghenies began with a surprise attack on the British Fort St. Joseph (see Photo MI-2). Spain, which had joined the war against the British, sent Captain Don Eugenio Pourré (or Poure) with a force of 65 Spaniards and French militiamen from St. Louis and Cahokia and 60 Potawatomies to capture the British post and its fur traders. Fort Saint Joseph was the closest British post to St. Louis.[2] Historians give four major reasons for the attack:

1. to establish a Spanish claim east of the Mississippi,
2. to plunder and gain revenge for the British attack on St. Louis,
3. to provide defense against an expected British counterattack on St. Louis the next spring, or
4. to assist tribes friendly to Spain to fight the Crown forces.

Most documentary evidence seems to support the last view, especially a letter from Francisco Cruzat (1739–1790), lieutenant governor of Spanish Illinois, that describes an appeal for assistance from two Milwaukee chiefs hostile to the British, El Hetumo and Naquiguen.

The attackers left St. Louis on Tuesday, January 2, 1781 and arrived at Fort Saint Joseph on Monday, February 12. They caught the British unprepared, quickly surrounded

MI-2. Fort St. Joseph. This is the site of Fort St. Joseph. Western Michigan University continues to do excavations there each summer since 2002. The pipeline is used to suction off the water that seeps into the excavation pits during the night, since the fort site is on the bank of the St. Joseph River and partly below the river water level. Courtesy Todd Harburn.

the fort, and captured it easily, having struck a deal with a group of 200 nearby Potawatomies to give them half of the goods taken at the fort in exchange for their neutrality.

However, Pourré's force withdrew the following day and returned to Saint Louis, staying only long enough to permit Spain to claim, by right of conquest, the valleys of the St. Joseph and Illinois rivers at the end of the war. Some historians say that Spain wanted to lay claim to the region during future peace negotiations. The claim later created problems between Spain and the United States.

George Rogers Clark (1752–1818) went to Richmond, Virginia before the end of 1780 to consult with Governor Thomas Jefferson (1743–1826). They made arrangements for Clark to lead 2,000 men against the British stronghold early in the spring in hopes of adding "an extensive and fertile country" to the "Empire of Liberty." Jefferson made Clark a brigadier general and appointed him to lead the expedition which was to be largely a Virginia affair supported by Congress. Clark encountered many difficulties in obtaining both supplies and men and had to resort to a draft. He mustered 400 men at Pittsburgh, Pennsylvania and proceeded down the Ohio in August.[3]

★ The British and their Native American allies were heading toward the Ohio River, making it apparent that a march on Detroit could not succeed. George Rogers Clark (1752–1818) changed his plans and decided to attack the Native Americans and then to move against Detroit, if possible.

Captain Joseph Brant (1742–1807), Mohawk Chief Thayendanagea, intercepted a messenger from Colonel Archibald Lochry (d. 1781) who was coming to join Clark. Aware of Lochry's plans, Brant and 100 Loyalists and Native Americans surprised Lochry's force of 107 Pennsylvania militiamen near the mouth of the Big Miami River at a small creek now called Laughery Creek near what is now Aurora, Indiana, on Friday, August 24, 1781. The attack slew a third of Lochry's force immediately, including Lochry himself. The rest were captured.

Brant then joined Captain Andrew Thompson (1756–1782) and Alexander McKee (ca. 1735–1799) and their force of 100 British rangers and 300 Native Americans. They followed Clark toward the Ohio hoping to capture him. When they got within 25 miles of the Falls of the Ohio, the Native Americans refused to attack and the rangers were reluctant to fight with Clark. The warriors broke into small bands and most returned to their villages. The rangers, short on food, returned to Detroit.

The Treaty of Paris that ended the American War of Independence in 1783 set the Mississippi River as the western boundary of the United States, but Spain did not recognize this boundary until Pinckney's Treaty in 1795. The boundary between the United States and Canada was a line drawn through the middle of each of the Great Lakes and their connecting rivers. While Isle Royale in Lake Superior went to the United States, the ownership of the islands in the Detroit and Saint Marys rivers did not get determined until almost 50 years later.

The British continued to occupy Detroit and Fort Mackinac (see Photo MI-1), even after the treaty ceding present-day Michigan to the United States, because they did not think the new nation would survive and they wanted to maintain their profitable fur trade. To ensure this, British officials encouraged Native Americans to fight against any white settlement in the region. When Major General "Mad Anthony" Wayne's (1745–1796) army defeated Native American forces at the Battle of Fallen Timbers, near present-day Toledo, Ohio, in 1794, the British withdrew from their northwest outposts, according to the terms of Jay's Treaty.

7
OHIO

The territory north and west of the Ohio River, known as the Northwest Territory or Old Northwest, was strategically important in the 18th century. France and Great Britain struggled for domination of the area in the Seven Years War [French and Indian War (1756–1763)]. France ceded to Great Britain most of her territory and forts in North America, including all of the Ohio country, in the Treaty of Paris which ended the Seven Years War.

Ottawa chief Pontiac (1720?–1769) revolted [Pontiac's Rebellion (1763–1766)] and tried to expel the British and restore autonomy to the native people. His braves captured most of the forts in the large area north and west of the Ohio River, including Fort Sandusky on Lake Erie. When the French refused to help the Ottawas, Pontiac signed a treaty ending the war. The Ohio Native American tribes sided with the British during the War of American Independence.

The area was contested throughout the war and in subsequent campaigns against the Native Americans. The Peace of Ghent (1814) ended the War of 1812 and the conflicts with the Native Americans and set the Ohio boundary.

> The Ohio Historical Society [1982 Velma Avenue, Columbus, OH 43211, website: **www.ohiohistory.org**; phone: 614-297-2300] is the state's major historical agency. It publishes a visitor's guide which includes information about the state's Revolutionary War history.
>
> The Ohio Development Department's Division of Travel and Tourism (website: **www.discoverohio.com**; phone: 614-466-8844) provides tourism information. The Ohio Division of Parks and Recreation is another helpful source of tourist information.

See the map of Ohio.

Hockingport
Mouth of the Hocking River at the Ohio River (Oct. 11, 1776)

> The Hocking River meets the Ohio River at Hockingport at the state boundary with West Virginia.

Native Americans surprised a party of seven militiamen at the mouth of the Hocking River at the Ohio River on Friday, October 11, 1776. They killed two militiamen and wounded three.[1]

Raid on Sandusky
Squaw Campaign (Feb. 1778)

> The Squaw Campaign is also known as the Raid on Sandusky, which should not be confused with the Battle of Sandusky in 1782.

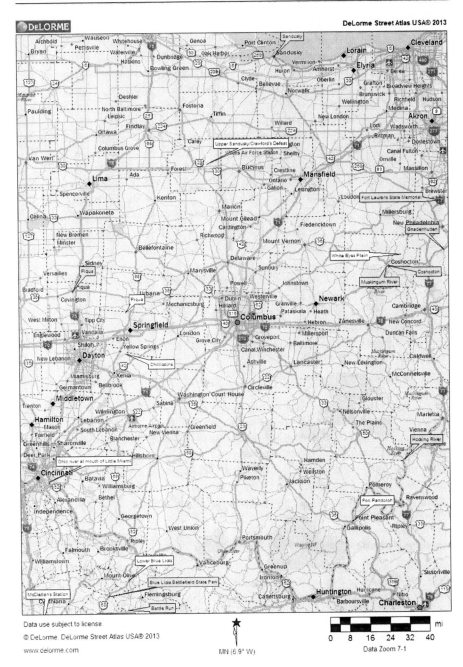

MN (6.9° W)

Data Zoom 7-1

Ohio: Map for The Guide to the American Revolutionary War in the Deep South and on the Frontier

© 2013 DeLorme (www.delorme.com) Street Atlas USA®

Brigadier General Edward Hand (1744–1802) met with officers of Virginia and Pennsylvania during October and November 1777 and concluded that he could not muster enough men to attack the Native Americans in the Ohio Valley. Moreover, the weather became too cold for the inadequately clothed troops to go on the offensive. Because he was unable to enlist and equip enough men for a campaign and because of his inability to get the Virginians and Pennsylvanians to agree on a course of action, Hand requested to be recalled, but, before Congress could act on his request, Virginia Governor Patrick Henry (1736–1799) asked Hand to create a diversion for Colonel George Rogers Clark's (1752–1818) campaign.

Hand crossed the Ohio in February 1778 with a large force comprised mostly of Pennsylvania militiamen. They marched north toward the Cayahoga and found some small Native American towns near present New Castle, Pennsylvania. They were almost deserted except for a small group of women and children and one man at one town. Hand's men, out of control, attacked them but most of the Native Americans escaped. At another village, they killed three women and a boy. The mother of Captain Pipe (Hopocan) (1725?–1818?), a friendly Delaware, was among the wounded and Pipe's brother was killed. This campaign of a disproportionately large force against defenseless women and children became known as the "Squaw Campaign" and undid any progress the Native American councils had achieved at Pittsburgh. Congress appointed a new commander for Fort Pitt in May 1778.[2]

Bolivar (Coshocton)

Fort Laurens (Jan. 23, 1779; Feb. 23, 1779; early March, 1779; March 28, 1779; mid-June, 1779; Aug. 1, 1779)

> The remains of Fort Laurens are west of route I-77 on the west bank of the Tuscarawas River, half a mile south of Bolivar, near the north line of the county. The area was also known as Coshocton which should not be confused with modern-day Coshocton 32 miles southwest of the site of Fort Laurens, east of the junction of the Tuscarawas and Walhonding rivers to form the Muskingum (see **Coshocton** below). Fort Pitt was about 80 miles east and Fort McIntosh 70 miles east.
>
> Fort Laurens was erected in the fall of 1778 (see Photo OH-1) by a detachment of 1,000 men from Fort Pitt under the command of General Lachlan McIntosh (1727–1806). Colonel John Gibson (1740–1822) garrisoned it with 150 men of the 13th Virginia Regiment. The rest of the army returned to Fort Pitt. The parapet walls were once crowned with pickets made of the split trunks of trees. They enclosed about an acre of land. A canal passed through the earthen walls in the 19th century.

OH-1. *Drawing of the original Fort Laurens, yet to be reconstructed. Courtesy Bob Kashary.*

Captain John Clark (d. 1819), of the 8th Pennsylvania Regiment, commanded an escort of a sergeant and 14 men bringing supplies for Colonel John Gibson (1740–1822). They reached Fort Laurens on Friday, January 1, 1779. As Clark and his men returned to Fort McIntosh, Simon Girty (1741–1818) and 17 Native Americans, mostly Mingoes, attacked them about 3 miles from Fort Laurens on Friday, January 23, 1779, killing two men (see Photo OH-2), wounding four and

OH-2. Site of the archeological dig outside the museum at Fort Laurens, showing the remains of two of the 14 soldiers who died there between January and August 1779 (left). There is also one unknown soldier buried outside the museum in a granite tomb. Every year the Northwest Department of the Brigade of the American Revolution remembers and honors this unknown soldier's sacrifice with a "trooping of the colours" and a "3 volley salute" (right). Courtesy Bob Kashary.

capturing one. The rest of the men, including Captain Clark, fought their way back to Fort Laurens. Girty also captured letters written by Colonel Gibson and other soldiers from Fort Laurens containing valuable information. He hurried back to Detroit with his prisoner and captured correspondence. (These letters are part of the Haldimand Collection in the British Museum.) Girty arrived at Detroit early in February and reported to Captain Richard Lernoult that the Wyandots on the Sandusky and other Native Americans were ready and willing to attack Fort Laurens and that he had come for ammunition.[3]

Henry Jolly (1757–1842), one of the men in the garrison and one of the last to leave it when the fort was evacuated in August 1779, notes:

> When the main army left the fort to return to Fort Pitt, Capt. Clark remained behind with a small detachment of United States troops, for the purpose of marching in the invalids and artificers who had tarried to finish the fort, or were too unwell to march with the main army. He endeavored to take the advantage of very cold weather, and had marched three or four miles (for I traveled over the ground three or four times soon after), when he was fired upon by a small party of Indians very close at hand, I think twenty or thirty paces. The discharge wounded two of his men slightly. [Other accounts of the affair state that 10 of Captain Clark's men were killed.] Knowing as he did that his men were unfit to fight the Indians in their own fashion, he ordered them to reserve their fire and to charge bayonet, which being promptly executed put the Indians to flight, and after pursuing a short distance, he called off his men and retreated to the fort bringing in the wounded.

Captain Lernoult sent Captain Henry Bird (1764–1858) and a few volunteers from Detroit to Upper Sandusky to encourage the Native Americans to attack Fort Laurens. He also furnished them with "a large supply of ammunition and clothing, also presents to the chief warriors." The Delawares, who supported the British and threatened with death any of their tribesmen who associated with the enemy, planned to strike the fort and drive off or destroy the cattle as well as to attack the main army under McIntosh at night if they attempted to assist the garrison.

★ A combined force of British Regulars and Delawares was able to surround Fort Laurens at Coshocton on the three land sides without being detected on Monday, February

22, 1779. The following morning, Colonel John Gibson (1740–1822), totally unaware that he was besieged, sent a wagoner and a party of 18 men to gather the firewood which the army had cut before they left the place. The soldiers had gone out for wood in the morning on several preceding days without incident. As the weather was very cold in the morning of the 23rd, they did not anticipate any Native Americans to be watching the fort, but the Delawares concealed themselves behind an ancient mound near the bank of the river about 220 to 275 yards from the fort.

The soldiers came under fire as they crossed an open field to get to the wood behind the mound. As they passed around on one side of the mound, some of the Delawares went around the other side, surrounding the wood party. The Delawares killed and scalped 17 of the soldiers within sight of the garrison. The other two were taken prisoners. One of them was released at the end of the war, but the other one was never heard of again.

The garrison was on alert that evening, bracing for another attack. Only about 100 of the 172 soldiers inside were fit for duty. After dusk, the Delawares paraded, in full war dress, in a large circle through the prairie where the ambush had occurred. Part of the circle was hidden by the mound, deceiving one of the soldiers who thought he counted 847 of them. Tension mounted inside the fort. However, the attackers probably did not have many more troops than the defenders, probably totaling less than 200.

After the morning ambush, the men immediately received full rations for two weeks, but spoilage and waste rapidly reduced those supplies more than should have occurred. When a relief expedition failed to arrive, morale waned. Rations of meat and flour were cut to four ounces a day at the beginning of the third week. Five days later, the rations were entirely depleted and there was no possibility of resupply. If the troops could not provide their own food, they faced starvation.[4]

However, the Delawares were also nearly starving. They proposed to Colonel Gibson that if he would give them a barrel of flour and some meat they would raise the siege. They thought that if the garrison did not have this quantity, they must surrender soon. If they had that quantity, they probably would not part with it. Colonel Gibson provided the flour and meat promptly and told them he had enough to spare, as he had plenty more. The assailants raised the siege soon afterward, finally compelled to return home, as they had exhausted their provisions.[5]

★ Before the Delawares left, a soldier crossed through enemy lines and reached Fort Pitt on Wednesday, March 3, informing General Lachlan McIntosh (1727–1806) of Colonel John Gibson's (1740–1822) critical situation and requesting reinforcements and provisions immediately. McIntosh knew that he needed to act soon, but he was short of supplies himself. A new expedition would have to take the original trail to reach Fort Laurens, but there were few packhorses and they were in poor condition with inadequate forage. His supply of flour was already low and he did not expect any more arriving any time soon. He had just received a large supply of cloth but had no tailors or thread to make clothing, rendering it useless. Shoes and stockings were so scarce that McIntosh allowed his men to hunt for deer whenever possible to make moccasins.[6]

★ General Lachlan McIntosh (1727–1806) ordered the lieutenants of several Virginia counties to gather all available men, horses, provisions and forage and report with them to Fort McIntosh on Monday, March 15, 1779. He then ordered Major Frederick Vernon (d. 1797) of the 8th Pennsylvania to lead a relief expedition of 150 privates and 18 officers to the Tuscarawas on Tuesday the 16th. The remainder of the regiment, 200 militiamen and 300 Continentals taken from Fort Pitt and Fort McIntosh, would escort them. However, the expedition did not leave until March 19, due to the late arrival of provisions and pack horses.

Although they had enough provisions for the march out and back and for the maintenance of the garrison for a time, the expedition could not transport all the supplies to the Tuscarawas because they did not have enough pack horses. As Major Richard Taylor's (d. 1826) detachment approached the Muskingum River, they came under fire from a band of Native Americans. Taylor lost two men killed. The expedition arrived at Fort Laurens four days later. However, with relief in sight, some of the soldiers inside the fort fired their muskets into the air as a *feu de joie,* frightening the pack horses. Many of them, unaccustomed to sudden explosions, ran into the woods, dropping their loads on the ground and scattering their contents. The soldiers of both the garrison and the relief party spent most of the day searching the surrounding woods, hoping to find the lost supplies. They only recovered a small amount.[7]

★ When General Lachlan McIntosh (1727–1806) set out from Fort McIntosh to relieve Fort Laurens, he also planned to attack the Sandusky towns. He thought that George Rogers Clark's (1752–1818) success in the West had demoralized the Native Americans enough to permit his own advance westward to succeed. If McIntosh could establish a new post on the Sandusky, he could advance on Detroit. However, the fiasco at Fort Laurens put an end to those plans. When McIntosh convened his officers to propose the attack on Sandusky, they rejected it unanimously as impracticable. They noted that

1. most of the road to Sandusky was under water and even the high ground was still very wet,
2. most of the forage brought by the relief party was depleted before they could rely on spring grass along the way, and
3. they had less than two weeks' supply of provisions for all the troops.[8]

McIntosh had to give up his dream of attacking Detroit. He requested and received a transfer to a command in the Southern colonies in the spring. As he prepared to return to Fort Pitt, the remains of the ambushed wood party were brought in for burial. The bodies, badly mutilated by wolves, were placed in a deep pit and covered with thin strips of bark and twigs. The burial party placed a piece of meat on top to entice wolves. The next day, they found seven wolves in the pit and shot them to avenge the disfigurement of the corpses. They then filled the pit with earth.

After the burial, General McIntosh left enough provisions at Fort Laurens for about two months before returning to his base. Major Vernon and 106 men and officers of the 8th Pennsylvania relieved Colonel John Gibson (1740–1822) and his garrison and waited for more supplies. When McIntosh arrived at Fort Laurens, he ordered that all the men who were not to remain at the fort receive their rations in bulk rather than daily. The rations should have sustained the soldiers until they reached Fort Pitt, but many of the men considered them as back-rations and consumed them immediately. About 40 men became sick on the first day's march and many more had to go without food throughout the six day journey.[9]

★ Later in the month, on Sunday, March 28, 1779, Native Americans attacked a 40-man wood-cutting party, killing Ensign John Clark (d.1779) and another soldier of Major Frederick Vernon's (d. 1797) unit outside Fort Laurens. By the middle of May, most of the garrison had to be sent away for lack of provisions.[10]

★ On Thursday, May 25, 1779, a Delaware named Big Cat (Hyngapushes) wrote to Colonel Daniel Brodhead (1736–1809), who had succeeded General Lachlan McIntosh (1727–1806) as commander of the Western Department, that British, Wyandots, Shawnees and Mingoes would lay siege to Fort Laurens in four days and completely destroy it with artillery. Brodhead ordered Major Frederick Vernon (d. 1797) "to throw up inner works of earth sufficient to resist light artillery." The earthworks were only a temporary measure as the fort could not withstand cannonading by heavy artillery. Brodhead also proposed cutting a road through the wilderness to connect Fort Laurens with Fort Pitt, but it was never cut because it could not have been done in time. On May 31, Brodhead wrote to Colonel Archibald Lochry (1733–1781) requesting recruits and horses to save the fort.

Meanwhile, the Native Americans gathered at the Sandusky towns and were preparing to attack Fort Laurens. It is still not known whether they had the cannons they threatened to use against the fort. Colonel John Bowman, county lieutenant of the Kentucky militia, learned of the movement. He mustered 300 volunteers from Harrodsburg, Kentucky and marched across the Ohio and up the Little Miami to the Shawnee town of Chillicothe. The Shawnees were divided over war policies and most of the tribe moved west by the time Bowman arrived. He plundered and burned the town, but the Shawnees quickly rebuilt it. As the Native Americans in the Ohio country rushed to protect their homes, they completely forgot about Fort Laurens, thereby saving it from possible disaster.

★ Major Frederick Vernon (d. 1797) received intelligence, around mid-June 1779, that a party was on their way to attack the settlements. Captain Brady (1756–1795), of the 8th Pennsylvania Regiment, set out to meet them with a young Delaware chief and 20 white men painted like Native Americans. However, the Native Americans had passed them and killed a soldier between Fort Crawford and Fort Hand. They killed a woman and four children and took two children prisoners at the Sawickly settlements. Captain Brady drove his party forward and met a band of seven Native Americans about 15 miles north of Kittanning, Pennsylvania. He attacked immediately, killing their captain and badly wounding several others. He recovered the two children prisoners and captured six horses, all the enemy's guns and tomahawks, the scalps they had taken and all their plunder.[11]

On Friday, July 16, 1779, Lieutenant-Colonel Richard Campbell (d. 1781) arrived at Fort Laurens with a party of officers and men from his 13th Virginia Regiment and some fresh troops from a Maryland regiment which had arrived at Fort Pitt at the end of May. Campbell intended to relieve the garrison with his 75 men and resupply the fort. Major Vernon was ordered to return all unnecessary supplies to Fort McIntosh. However, his pack horses were unable to carry the heavy loads, so Colonel Daniel Brodhead (1736–1809) could not salvage much from the fort.

The fort now had more provisions per man than it ever held. As Campbell could use the surplus for trading with the Native Americans, Brodhead had to warn him against trading abuses. Campbell could trade food for food, such as flour for venison, but he should not use provisions as money to acquire skins for clothing. Brodhead also asked him how 75 men could draw 101 rations daily if Campbell was following orders. Campbell offered no explanation but the overdraft apparently stopped.

★ Colonel Daniel Brodhead (1736–1809) wrote to Ensign John Beck (1762–1824) at Fort Laurens on Sunday, August 1, 1779 to inform him that two parties of about 20 hostile Native Americans had been seen moving from the Ohio toward the Tuscarawas. He hoped that troops coming back from Fort Laurens would meet and attack them. However, the raiders arrived at the fort before the warning. The troops were forming for battle when two soldiers, who were outside, were killed within sight of their comrades. Brodhead reported these two deaths (see Photo OH-2) to General George Washington (1732–1799) on August 4. The fort was considered untenable at such a distance from the frontiers and finally evacuated and its garrison brought safely back to Fort Pitt.[12]

Cincinnati
Ohio River at the mouth of the Little Miami (Oct. 4, 1779)

> The mouth of the Little Miami River is about 5 miles southeast of Cincinnati.

Native Americans under Simon Girty (1741–1818) ambushed some boats bound for New Orleans on the Ohio River at the mouth of the Little Miami River on Monday, October 4, 1779. Colonel David Rogers (1741–ca. 1800) and a guard of about 50 men were aboard along with some civilians. The warriors killed about 35 and captured 14 along with 600,000 Spanish dollars and much needed blankets and other supplies being transported from New Orleans to Fort Pitt.

★ Lieutenant Isaac Bowman (1757–1826) set out from Kaskaskia with seven or eight men around December 1779. The Chickasaws captured his boat in the Middle Mississippi River and killed most of the men.[13]

Chillicothe (June 1779; Oct. 1779; Aug. 6, 1780; Nov. 10, 1782)
Piqua (Aug. 8, 1780)
Brodhead's Expedition (summer 1780)
Coshocton Campaign

> The Shawnee, who were the Native Americans most hostile to the settlement of whites in the Ohio Valley, called their principal town Chillicothe. They were the objective of several punitive expeditions and had their towns destroyed frequently. Hence, in the 18th century, there were three separate places called Chillicothe at various times. One was on Paint Creek, in 1774, near its junction with the Scioto River. It was near the site of the modern town by the same name. Lord John Murray, 4th Earl of Dunmore (1732–1809) attacked it during Dunmore's War, but it endured until 1787 when Kentuckians destroyed it. Another was situated on the Little Miami River, near modern Xenia (east of Dayton), probably near what is now John Bryan State Park about 10 miles south of Springfield and about 12 miles southeast of Piqua. George Rogers Clark destroyed this town on August 6, 1780. The third one was originally called Piqua and was burned by Clark on November 10, 1782. Some authorities place it on the Great Miami River where route W US 36 (Covington Avenue) passes through it about a mile west of route I-75. Others say it was situated on the north side of the Mad River about 5 miles west of Springfield on the site where West Boston was later built. It was mostly on a plain, rising 15 or 20 feet above the river.[14]
>
> The Piqua division of the Shawnees also occupied several towns in Ohio which they called Piqua. The one destroyed by George Rogers Clark (1752–1818) in August 1780 was on the north side of the Mad River about 5 miles west of present Springfield. It was never rebuilt. The Shawnees then settled the Upper and Lower Piqua on the Great Miami River. Lower Piqua is now Piqua and Upper Piqua, the larger village, was 3 miles north on the site of the former town of Pickawillany at the

mouth of Loramie Creek. Lower Piqua was one of several places called Chillicothe in the 18th century.

The Piqua Historical Area (**www.ohiohistory.org/museums-and-historic-sites/ museum--historic-sites-by-name/johnston-farm--indian-agency**), 3 miles northwest of Piqua on route 66 (I-75, US 36 exit westbound) is a 200-acre park built on the former farm of John Johnston (1775–1861), United States Indian agent from 1812 to 1829. It recreates the Old Johnston Trading Post, a prerevolutionary trading post, and has an Indian mound. The trading post and the Clark Monument are believed to be on the site of the village destroyed in 1780. The Piqua Historic Indian Museum (phone: 800-852-2619) was built to resemble General Anthony Wayne's Fort Piqua. It offers displays of 18th century Shawnee culture and a restored mile-long section of the Miami and Erie Canal.

Congress sent Brigadier General Edward Hand (1744–1802) to assume command at Fort Pitt (now Pittsburgh, Pennsylvania) in the spring of 1777. He was to lead a punitive expedition into the Ohio country, but the Shawnee Chief Cornstalk (Keigh-tugh-qua, Hokoleskwa) (ca. 1720–1777), his son, Elinipsico (d. 1777), and a noted young warrior, Red Hawk (d. 1777), were murdered on their way to Point Pleasant, West Virginia to make peace in the summer of 1777. Hundreds of Native Americans swept across Ohio to avenge the murders, forcing Hand to delay his plans for several months.

The Shawnees defeated several parties of frontiersmen on the south shore of the Ohio River near Fort Henry, at the mouth of Wheeling Creek, in August and September 1777, killing more than 40 whites (see **Wheeling, West Virginia** pp. 190–195). Hand set out with 500 men, mostly militiamen, to attack Sandusky in February 1778, after receiving orders from Congress permitting him to take the offensive, even against Detroit, if the opportunity presented itself. However, rain and melting snow swelled the rivers, forcing him to abandon his expedition. Discouraged, Hand resigned his command.

Later in 1778, the Continental Congress sent General Lachlan McIntosh (1727–1806) with 500 Continentals and money to mount an expedition from Pittsburgh to Detroit to quell the Native American tribes. The expedition traveled 100 miles before being forced to halt due to lack of supplies and the expiration of the enlistment period of some of the accompanying militiamen. McIntosh accomplished relatively little and asked to be relieved of command.

Colonel Daniel Brodhead (1736–1809), an experienced frontier fighter, was appointed to succeed McIntosh early in 1779. Before Brodhead could take the offensive, Colonel George Rogers Clark (1752–1818) had captured Fort Sackville (Illinois) which alarmed both the British and their Native American allies.

★ Colonel John Bowman gathered 296 Kentucky militiamen at the mouth of the Licking River in May 1779. Captains William Harrod (1737–1801), Levi Todd (1758–1807), John Holder (1744–1797) and Benjamin Logan (1743–1802) commanded them. They crossed the Ohio in June 1779 and attacked Chillicothe, killing Red Hawk (d. 1779) and Chief Blackfish (Cot-ta-wa-ma-go or Mkah-day-way-may-qua) (ca. 1729–1779) who had "adopted" Daniel Boone (1734–1820) after he captured him. When the militiamen learned that Simon Girty (1741–1818) and a large band of reinforcements were approaching, they retreated. Bowman's men captured enough ponies to retreat quickly. The Shawnees pursued and attacked them until they recrossed the Ohio. The Kentuckians managed to escape with a large amount of plunder and over a hundred horses, but they lost nine men in the expedition.[15]

★ Colonel David Rogers (1741–ca. 1800) and Captain Robert Benham traveled down the Ohio River with 100 men in two keel boats in October 1779. Colonel Rogers noticed some Shawnees on the shores and landed 50 men to attack them. About 500 Shawnees ambushed them and a fierce battle ensued. Outnumbered five to one, Rogers and most of his men were tomahawked and scalped. Captain Benham escaped with a few survivors. Severely wounded, Benham lay in the woods for two days before a passing boat rescued him.[16]

Captain Richard Lernoult feared for the safety of Detroit. Although Clark had neither the men nor the supplies to undertake an expedition against the main British base in the Old Northwest at this time, he continued to make plans to do so in 1779 and 1780, but the plans were not executed. When Spain entered the war in 1779, Britain sent money and goods to Detroit to strengthen their alliances with the Native American tribes. The Crown forces assaulted the Spanish post at St. Louis on Friday, May 26, 1780 but were repulsed.

★ General George Rogers Clark (1752–1818) led an expedition of 1,000 men that marched from what is now Cincinnati on Wednesday, August 2, 1780 and headed for the Shawnee towns of Piqua and Chillicothe. He commanded the first division in the front. The artillery, military stores and baggage were placed in the center and Colonel Benjamin Logan (1743–1802) led the division in the rear. The men marched in four lines about 40 yards apart from each other. A line of flankers was placed on each side about the same distance from the right and left line. In the event of an enemy attack in the front or rear, the front was ordered to stand fast. The two right lines would wheel to the left and the two left lines to the right to form a complete line. The artillery would advance forward to the centre of the line. In case of an attack on either of the flanks, the lines and the artillery were ordered to stand fast while the opposite lines wheeled and formed on the two extremes of those lines.

The army proceeded without encountering anything unusual until they arrived at Chillicothe about 2 PM on Sunday, August 6. The Shawnees and other Ohio tribesmen, assisted by Simon Girty (1741–1818), were ready for Clark's arrival. Clark found the town abandoned and most of the houses burned down and burning, having been set on fire that morning. The army camped there for the night. They cut down several hundred acres of corn the next day. When they finished, they resumed their march about 4 PM and headed for the Piqua towns about 12 miles away. They got caught in a very heavy rain along the way. There was thunder and lightning and high winds. They had no tents or any other shelter from the torrential rain and could not keep their muskets dry. The rain stopped just before dark.

The men were ordered to make camp in a hollow square, with the baggage and horses in the center. They were to dry their clothes and belongings as soon as they could make fires. They were ordered to examine their muskets and to make sure they were in good order. They were then ordered to discharge them in the following manner: one company would fire and reload while a company at the opposite end of the camp would fire. The discharge would alternate until all the weapons had fired.

★ By sunrise on the morning of August 8th, the army marched to Piqua, on the west side of the Mad River, arriving about 2 PM. The road they took crossed the Mad River about a quarter of a mile below the town. As soon as the advanced guard crossed into a prairie of high weeds, the Shawnees who had concealed themselves in the weeds attacked them. The nature of the ground and the manner of the attack left no doubt that the attackers intended a general engagement.

Brigadier General George Rogers Clark (1752–1818) ordered Colonel Benjamin Logan (1743–1802) to file off to the right with about 400 men. They were to march up the river on the east side and to position themselves north of the town to prevent the warriors from escaping in that direction. Colonels William Linn (Lynn) (1734–1780), John Floyd (1751–1783) and James Harrod (1742–1793) took the rest of the men across the river to surround the town on the west side. General Clark took Colonel David Slaughter's troops and those attached to the artillery and marched directly toward the town.

The prairie of high weeds, where the attack began, was about 200 yards across. Colonels Lynn, Floyd and Harrod and their men, who were supposed to surround the town on the west side, had to cross that prairie to avoid the fire of the enemy hidden in the woods around the prairie. The Shawnees made a strong effort to turn the Kentuckians' left wing to prevent them from executing their assigned duties. Floyd and Lynn discovered the maneuver and extended the line of battle west, more than 1 mile from the town, to prevent being outflanked.

The battle continued until about 5 PM when the Shawnees disappeared unnoticed, except for a few in the town. The cannon, which had been entirely useless until now, fired on the houses. The first few shots drove the Shawnees outside. General Clark's nephew had been a prisoner among the tribes for many years. When he tried to come to the whites, toward the end of the action, he was mistaken for a Native American and mortally wounded. He died several hours later. Clark inflicted about 70 casualties and lost 14 men killed and 13 wounded.

The morning after the battle, a Frenchman who had been captured by the Shawnees on the Wabash, a short time before, was found in the loft of one of the cabins. He reported that the Shawnees did not expect that the Kentuckians would reach their town on that day. They intended to attack the Kentuckians in their camp during the night with the tomahawk and knife the night before, but the rain prevented it, as did the firing of the muskets. However, when they heard the firing, they understood the reason for it.

The Kentuckians apparently surprised the Shawnees. When they entered the town, which was built in the manner of the French villages, they found a considerable quantity of provisions cooked in large kettles and other vessels, almost untouched, indicating that the warriors had not dined.

The town extended along the edge of the river for more than 3 miles, with the houses more than 100 yards apart in many places. As Colonel Logan was ordered to surround the town on the east, he had to march the full 3 miles, leaving the Shawnees to concentrate their whole force against those on the opposite side of the town. Logan's party never saw any action.

The engagement was so intense, just before the end, that Simon Girty (1741–1818), a white man who had joined the Mingoes and been made a chief, withdrew with 300 of his men. He told them it was extremely foolish to continue the action against men who acted so much like madmen, as General Clark's men. He said they rushed in the extreme of danger with a seeming disregard of the consequences. The withdrawal of the 300 Mingoes so disconcerted the others that they soon dispersed.

The troops cut down the growing corn and destroyed the cabins and fort and collected horses the day after the battle, the 9th. They destroyed more than 500 acres of corn and every species of edible vegetables in the two Shawnee towns, Chillicothe and Piqua. This forced the Shawnees to spend their whole time hunting to support their wives and children, thereby leaving the Kentucky area quiet for a considerable time.

The army began their march homeward on Thursday, August 10th. They camped in Chillicothe that night and, the following day, cut a field of corn which had been left for the men and horses on their return. At the mouth of the Licking River, the army dispersed and each man made his best way home.[17]

★ Colonel Daniel Brodhead (1736–1809), in command of the western military department headquartered at Fort Pitt, led a second expedition of about 800 regulars and militiamen against the towns of the Delaware Indians in the forks of the Muskingum in the summer of 1780 to avenge the depredations and outrages committed upon settlers in western Pennsylvania, Virginia and eastern Ohio. The Delawares were also reported to be breaking their pledges and joining the British.

The expedition mustered at Wheeling, in what is now West Virginia, and made a rapid march to their destination. When they reached the river, a little below the lower Moravian town of Salem, Colonel Brodhead sent an express to the Rev. John Gottlieb Ernestus Heckewelder (1743–1823), the missionary there, informing him of his arrival in the neighborhood with his army. He requested a small supply of provisions and a visit from him in his camp. When Rev. Heckewelder arrived at the camp, the general informed him of the purpose of his expedition and inquired whether any of the Christian Native Americans were hunting or engaged in business in the direction of his march. Rev. Heckewelder answered in the negative and Colonel Brodhead stated that nothing would give him greater pain than to hear that any of the Moravians had been molested by his troops, as these Native Americans had always conducted themselves in a manner that did them honor.

★ As Colonel David Rogers was moving up the Ohio River with 70 men in October 1780, Simon Girty (1741–1818) and a band of Native Americans surprised him and slaughtered all but 13 who escaped.

★ Brigadier General George Rogers Clark (1752–1818) returned to Chillicothe after the Battle of Blue Licks in present-day Kentucky (see pp. 205–208). He was bitterly criticized as he was still in command of the Virginia territory west of the Appalachian Mountains. He arranged with Brigadier General William Irvine (1741–1804) for a simultaneous attack upon the Native Americans in Ohio. Irvine would lead a force into the Sandusky Valley while Clark would attack the Shawnees again. Having received word from General George Washington (1732–1799) that General Charles Cornwallis (1738–1805) had surrendered at Yorktown, Irvine did not move. However, fear of Irvine's forces prevented the Native Americans from concentrating all their forces against Clark.

Clark and 1,050 mounted riflemen and some artillery departed from the mouth of the Licking River on Monday, November 4, 1782, to raid Chillicothe. As they approached the town six days later, some of the Shawnees learned of their approach and fled. Clark retook two whites held prisoners, killed 10 Shawnees and wounded 10 others. He lost one killed and two wounded. They then burned the settlement and five surrounding villages and destroyed large quantities of corn and other provisions, leaving the Shawnees with little or no food for the coming winter.[18]

Lichtenau, near Coshocton
Forks of the Muskingum (April 19, 1781)

The village of Goschachgunk, or Lichtenau (" Pasture of Light") also called the "Forks of the Muskingum," was situated about 2 miles south of Coshocton on the east side of the Muskingum River, just below the junction of the Tuscarawas and Walhonding Rivers. It was the second capital of the Delaware nation in Ohio.

Marauding parties of hostile warriors crossed the Ohio River at various points to plunder and murder during the early spring of 1781. Colonel Daniel Brodhead (1736–1809), now Commander of the Western Military Department with headquarters at Fort Pitt, (now Pittsburgh), crossed the Ohio River with 300 Continentals and militiamen in early April to march against the Native Americans on the Muskingum. Some of the militiamen wanted to go up the river to destroy the Moravian villages (Salem, Gnadenhutten and Schonbrunn), but General Brodhead and Colonel David Shepherd, his second in command, prevented them from doing so. Brodhead's men captured a Native American prisoner at White Eyes' Plain, about 7 miles northeast of Coshocton. They soon found two more, one of whom was wounded. They both managed to escape. Brodhead knew they would hurry into town to notify the others of the army's approach.

Brodhead ordered a rapid march through a heavy rain to surprise the Delaware base of Lichtenau on Saturday, April 19, 1781, in an attempt to reach the town and take it by surprise before the escaped prisoners got there. The plan succeeded. The army reached the place in three divisions. The right and left wings approached the river a little above and below the town, while the center marched directly upon it.

They attacked the town, burned it, took about 30 prisoners and carried off a fortune in plunder. They captured all the inhabitants of the village on the east side of the river and 10 or 12 from a little village north of it without firing a single shot. As the recent rainfall made the river impassable, the villages on the west side of the river escaped destruction.

Pekillon, a friendly Delaware chief with Brodhead's army, identified 16 warriors among the prisoners. Shortly after dark, a council of war (see cover photo) condemned these 16 prisoners to death. They were bound and taken a short distance south of the town where they were executed with tomahawks and spears and scalped. Colonel Brodhead put about 20 militiamen in charge of the remaining prisoners.

When the army began its retreat from Coshocton, about 11 or 12 o'clock the next morning, April 20, the men marched about half a mile and began killing 15 male prisoners. They took the women and children, along with some friendly Moravian Christian Delawares found in the town, to Fort Pitt. They were later exchanged for an equal number of white prisoners.

Earlier in the next morning of the 20th, a Shawnee came to the opposite bank of the river and asked for the big captain. Brodhead presented himself and asked what he wanted. The man replied, "I want peace." Brodhead told him to "send over some of your chiefs." "Maybe you kill," said the Shawnee. Brodhead assured him they would not be killed.

One of the chiefs crossed the river and met Brodhead in the street. During the conversation, a man named Lewis Wetzel (1763–1808) came up behind the chief, took out a tomahawk concealed in his hunting-shirt and struck the chief on the back of the head, killing him instantly. Some authorities think that Lewis Wetzel's older brother committed this murder.[19]

Colonel Brodhead sent his official report of his expedition to the Muskingum to President Reed, of the Executive Council of Pennsylvania:

PHILADELPHIA, May 22, 1781. SIR:-In the last letter I had the honor to address to your Excellency, I mentioned my intention to carry an expedition against the revolted Delaware towns. I have now the pleasure to inform you that with about 300 men, (nearly half the number volunteers from the county), surprised the towns of Cooshasking and Indaochaie, killed fifteen warriors, and took upwards of twenty old men, women and children. About four miles above the town detached a party to cross the river Muskingum and destroy a party of about forty warriors, who had just before (as I learned by an Indian whom the advance guard took prisoner) crossed over with some prisoners and scalps, and were drunk, but excessive hard rains having swelled the river bank high, it was found impracticable. After destroying the towns, with great quantities of poultry and other stores, and killing about forty head of cattle, I marched up the river about seven miles, with a view to send for some craft from the Moravian towns, and cross the river to pursue the Indians; but when I proposed my plan to the volunteers found they conceived they had done enough, and were determined to return, wherefore I marched to Newcomerstown, where a few Indians, who remained in our interest, had withdrawn themselves, not exceeding thirty men. The troops experienced great kindness from the Moravian Indians and those at Newcomerstown, and obtained a sufficient supply of meat and corn to subsist the men and horses to the Ohio river. Captain Killbuck and Captain Luzerne, upon hearing of our troops being on the Muskingum, immediately pursued the warriors, killed one of their greatest villains and brought his scalp to me. The plunder brought in by the troops sold for about eighty pounds at Fort Henry. I had upon this expedition Captain Montour and Wilson, and three other faithful Indians who contributed greatly to success.

The troops behaved with great spirit, and although there was considerable firing between them and the Indians, I had not a man killed or wounded, and only one horse shot.

I have the honor to be with great respect and attachment, your Excellency's most obedient, most humble servant. DANIEL BRODHEAD, Col. 1st P. R.

Directed
His Excellency,
JOSEPH REED, Esq.

Gnadenhutten
Gnadenhutten Massacre (March 7, 1782)

Gnadenhutten is about 11 miles south of New Philadelphia on the Tuscarawas River.

Before he left the Tuscarawas Valley (then called Muskingum) on April 20, 1781, Colonel Daniel Brodhead (1736–1809) spoke with the Rev. John Gottlieb Ernestus Heckewelder (1743–1823) and possibly other Moravian missionaries who had been friendly to the settlers on the frontier. He described their dangerous position as "between two fires" and advised them to accompany him to Fort Pitt for protection. They declined the request.

Colonel David Williamson (1752–1809) and 300 men from western Pennsylvania and the Monongahela set out against the peaceful Christian Delawares at Gnadenhutten in March 1782. Williamson suspected that hostile Delawares, siding with the British, had taken over the village. When he arrived on Monday, March 4, he found 90 defenseless men, women and children. The frontiersmen stayed in the village peacefully for three days, after which Williamson placed the villagers under arrest. The militiamen took a vote whether to take the prisoners back to Fort Pitt or kill them. The decision was to execute them. The Moravians were given the night to prepare.

In the morning, the militiamen selected two slaughter houses and took the 29 men, 27 women and 34 children inside in small groups and beat them to death with wooden mallets. The troops then burned Gnadenhutten and the other Moravian missions before returning home to Pennsylvania with the plunder taken from their victims. This "Gnadenhutten Massacre" brought retaliation against another expedition led by Colonel William Crawford (1732–1782) at Sandusky in the early summer (see **Battle of Sandusky** below).[20]

Upper Sandusky
Battle of Sandusky (June 4–5, 1782)
Crawford's Defeat (also known as the Battle of the Olentangy)

> The site of the Battle of Sandusky or Crawford's Defeat was about 3.5 miles northeast of the town of Upper Sandusky.
> The war on the western frontier did not end with the British surrender at Yorktown. The massacre of 90 peaceful Delawares at the Gnaddenhutten mission in the Moravian towns of Ohio incited the need for vengeance. Word of the massacre spread to the other Delawares and, in June 1782, they joined the Wyandots to defeat a large force of Pennsylvania militiamen sent to attack the Sandusky villages.

Colonel William Crawford (1732–1782) had narrowly won election over the popular Colonel David Williamson (1752–1809) for command of the Pittsburgh militia. He led a force of 480 volunteers, including his son, son-in-law, and nephew, but only about 100 of his men were experienced fighters. They left Fort Pitt planning to surprise the Wyandots and Shawnees along the upper Sandusky River 150 miles away. Reports of Crawford's plan reached Detroit before he even set out. Colonel Arent Schuyler De Peyster (1736–1832), commandant at Detroit, sent reinforcements to his allies.

Captain William Caldwell (1763–1849) with 100 of Butler's Rangers and between 200 and 500 Mingo, Delaware, Munsee and Wyandot warriors met Crawford and his men in Sandusky Valley on Tuesday, June 4, 1782 and engaged them in battle early in the afternoon. The first day of fighting seemed to end in a draw.

When Crawford learned that Caldwell would receive reinforcements of 140 Shawnees and a unit of Loyalists with field artillery, he decided to retreat late in the evening. Crawford's troops tried to break through the ring of Native Americans. They broke into disorderly retreat when the reinforcements arrived. Some men got separated from their units and were killed. Others fled to Olentangy Creek, 5 miles away. Williamson restored some order and formed his men for battle the next day. Colonel Crawford and Dr. John Knight (1748–1838), a surgeon, were missing and 50 men killed or captured. Crawford and a small group of officers stayed behind to look for Crawford's missing son when they were captured by the Delawares on June 7.

The prisoners were taken to Sandusky. Most of them were tomahawked. Delaware Captain Pipe (Hopocan) (1725?–1818?) requested that Crawford be turned over to him. In revenge for Gnadenhutten, the Delaware stripped Crawford and tied him to a stake over red-hot coals. They poked and beat him with burning sticks and scalped him alive. After two hours, Crawford begged Simon Girty (1741–1818) to shoot him to end his sufferings. When Crawford fell into the fire, squaws shoveled the coals over him and his exposed skull.

The Shawnees, Delawares and Wyandots then headed for the next town where they planned to torture Dr. Knight in the same manner. However, only one brave guarded the prisoner. When he ordered Dr. Knight to gather wood for a fire, the doctor used a piece to club his guard and escape. He eventually arrived at Fort Pitt where he recounted the episode. The Shawnees, Delawares and Wyandots extended their exploits east of Pittsburgh following the Crawford disaster. General William Irvine (1741–1804) started organizing a second force at Pittsburgh to attack the Sandusky towns but the expedition never materialized.[21]

8
INDIANA

Indiana was part of the colony of Virginia during the American War of Independence. The fur trade was the main source of the economy. The Native Americans favored the French who treated them as equals, but the British slowly won them over because they paid higher prices for the furs and traded firearms. The French and the British fought over the fur trade for many years. With the defeat of the French in the Seven Years War [French and Indian War (1756–1763)], the British claimed Indiana and other regions. They began to occupy the Indiana region in 1777.

Lieutenant Colonel George Rogers Clark (1752–1818) planned to take control of the Ohio Valley away from the British in 1777. He captured Fort Kaskaskia in Illinois on Saturday, July 4, 1778, followed shortly afterward by Fort Massac. He then turned his attention to Vincennes, Indiana, which he captured that same summer, but he had to surrender it back to the Crown forces in December. Because of the importance of this post, Clark set out from Kaskaskia with about 130 American and French soldiers to recapture it, which he did on Thursday, February 25, 1779, after an arduous trek.

The Indiana Department of Tourism [1 North Capitol, Suite 700, Indianapolis, IN 46204 (phone: 317-232-8860) website: **www.in.gov/core/tourism.html**] provides tourism information. The Indiana Historical Bureau [State Library and Historical Building, 140 North Senate Avenue, Indianapolis, IN 46204 (phone: 317-232-2535) website: **www.in.gov/history/**] and the Indiana Historical Society [450 West Ohio Street, Indianapolis, IN 46204 (phone: 317-232-1882) website: **www.indianahistory.org**] are sources of historical information. The Tippecanoe County Historical Association [1001 South Street, Lafayette, IN 47901 (phone: 765-476-8411) website: **www.tcha.mus.in.us/**] maintains both Vincennes and Ouiatenon.

See the map of Illinois, Indiana and Missouri.

Vincennes (Feb. 25, 1779)

The George Rogers Clark National Historical Park is located on Barnett Street within the city of Vincennes along the Wabash River in the southwestern part of Indiana. From route US 50 east and west or from route US 41 from the north, use the 6th Street exit. Stay on 6th Street to the intersection with Barnett Street (approximately 2.5 miles). Turn right on Barnett and follow it to the park. On route US 41 from the south, use the Willow Street exit. Turn right on Willow Street for approximately 2 miles to the intersections with South 6th Street. Turn right and travel four blocks. Turn left on Barnett Street which will lead to the park. Website: **www.nps.gov/gero/index.htm.**

The George Rogers Clark Memorial, built in 1931–1932, is a Doric temple surrounded by a 20-acre plaza. The memorial contains seven large murals which depict Clark's life and the conquest of the Old Northwest. The rotunda houses a bronze statue of Clark. The memorial commemorates the capture of Fort Sackville

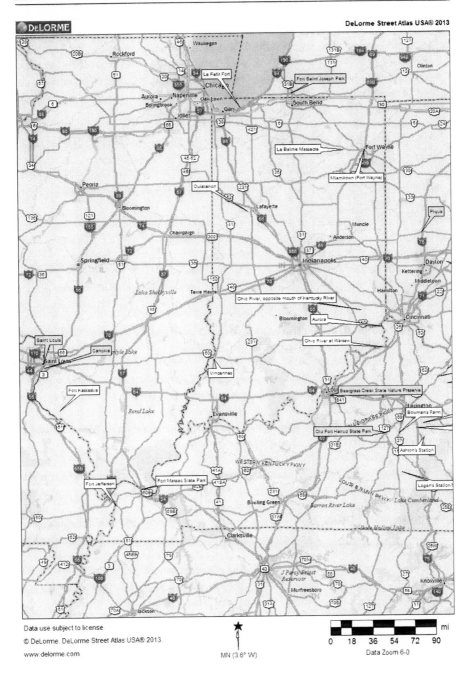

Illinois, Indiana and Missouri: Map for The Guide to the American Revolutionary War in
the Deep South and on the Frontier
© *2013 DeLorme (www.delorme.com) Street Atlas USA®*

from British Lieutenant Governor Henry Hamilton (1734?–1796) (The "Hair Buyer") and his soldiers by Lieutenant Colonel George Rogers Clark and his frontiersmen on February 25, 1779. The heroic march of Clark's men from Kaskaskia on the Mississippi in mid-winter and the subsequent victory over the British remains one of the great feats of the American Revolution. Adjacent to the memorial there is a visitor center where one can see interpretive programs and displays.

The exact location of Fort Sackville is not known, but it is believed it was located in the present-day George Rogers Clark National Historical Park. Archaeological evidence suggests that the fort's front wall was roughly between the Clark Memorial and the Lincoln Memorial Bridge in Vincennes. Fort Sackville was renamed for Patrick Henry (1736–1799) and Vincennes served as the capital of the Indiana Territory from 1800 to 1813.

The French built a series of military posts between the Great Lakes and the Louisiana territory. The one built in Vincennes was constructed in 1731 and named for the builder and first commander, François Marie Bissot, Sieur de Vincennes (1700–1736). A permanent settlement grew up around the post in the next few years. The British acquired the post from France after the Seven Years War [French and Indian War (1756–1763)] and renamed it Fort Sackville for a British government official.

The British dominated a large portion of the Trans-Appalachian frontier. The Proclamation of 1763 which officially ended the Seven Years War forbade the settlement of lands west of the Appalachian Mountains. There were many Native American tribes located between the Appalachian Mountains and the Mississippi River. Although never unified, the warriors from these tribes greatly outnumbered both the British and the Americans and constituted a strong military force on the western frontier. American settlement west of the Appalachian Mountains posed a threat to Native American tribes' way of life and caused most of them to favor the British.

British officials actively encouraged the Native Americans to attack the frontiersmen beginning in 1777. The British supplied the warriors with weapons and ammunition and rewarded them with gifts when successful war parties returned with scalps and prisoners. From their posts north of the Ohio River, the British sent Native American war parties against those settlers who ignored the proclamation line, including those in Kentucky (also a part of Virginia at that time).

Colonel George Rogers Clark (1752–1818) organized the Kentucky militia to defend against these raids. Not content to wait for the attacks, he took his plan to Patrick Henry (1736–1799), governor of Virginia, and gained approval for a major offensive campaign. He planned to lead a force of frontiersmen into the Illinois country and strike at the source of Native American raids.

Clark proceeded down the Ohio River with fewer than 200 men, called the Kentucky Long Knives, during the summer of 1778. He then marched overland, covering approximately 120 miles in five days. He captured the British posts at Kaskaskia and Cahokia along the Mississippi River, near St. Louis. French settlers occupied these posts after the Seven Years War. They disliked living under British rule, so Clark quickly gained their support. Father Pierre Gibault (1737–1814) and Dr. Jean Laffont volunteered to travel to Vincennes on Clark's behalf. That settlement also gave its support to Clark, but the French at Detroit, Michigan and other northern posts continued to support the British.

British Lieutenant Governor Henry Hamilton (1734?–1796) (The "Hair Buyer") received news about the fall of the three outposts by August 6. He left Detroit in early

October 1778, with a mixed force of English soldiers, French volunteers and militiamen, and Native American warriors, intending to retake Fort Sackville in Vincennes. Picking up Native American allies along the way, his force numbered about 500 when he arrived at Vincennes 71 days later (Thursday, December 17, 1778).

Clark left Captain Leonard Helm (ca. 1720–ca. 1782) in charge at Vincennes. With only a few men on whom he could depend, Helm had no hopes of defending the fort against Hamilton's force. Hamilton recaptured the fort on Thursday, December 17th, and the French settlers, faced with overwhelming force, returned to British allegiance.

Hamilton allowed most of his force to return home for the winter, as was customary in 18th-century warfare, postponing his intended invasion of the Illinois country. He planned to muster his forces in the spring for an attack on Clark's posts on the Mississippi River. Victories there would pave the way for a joint effort with tribes from south of the Ohio River to drive all American settlers from the Trans-Appalachian frontier.

Francis Vigo [Joseph Maria Francesco Vigo) (1747–1836)], a merchant and supporter of the Whig cause, left his home in St. Louis and headed for Vincennes, unaware that the fort was in British hands. He was taken prisoner near the settlement, held for several days and released, his captors not realizing Vigo's involvement with the Congressional forces. Vigo returned to St. Louis and then went to Kaskaskia, 50 miles south, where he provided Clark with valuable information concerning the military situation in Vincennes and Hamilton's intent to attack in the spring.

Clark, determined to capture Hamilton, set out from Kaskaskia on February 6, 1779, with his force of approximately 170 Whigs and Frenchmen. They covered the distance in 18 days. About 10 miles from Vincennes, they found themselves in country flooded with icy water which they had to wade through—sometimes shoulder-deep. They arrived in Vincennes after nightfall on Tuesday, February 23, 1779.

The French citizens greeted Clark's men warmly and provided them food and dry gunpowder. Clark's men surrounded the fort which was now defended by approximately 40 British soldiers and a similar number of French volunteers and militiamen from Detroit and Vincennes. The French troops were not inclined to fire on the enemy when they realized that the French inhabitants of the town again sided with the Whigs.

Clark brought, from Kaskaskia, flags sufficient for an army of 500. He had them unfurled and carried within view of the fort, giving the impression he had a much larger army. His soldiers, experienced woodsmen, armed with the famed long rifle which was accurate at longer ranges than the defenders' muskets, could maintain a rate of fire that convinced the British that they indeed faced a large army.

Clark ordered the construction of tunnels, from behind the river bank a short distance from the fort, to plant explosive charges under the fort walls or beneath the powder magazines. His men also built barricades and entrenchments to provide additional cover.

Hamilton considered surrendering and requested that Clark meet with him at the nearby church, St. Francis Xavier Catholic Church. He tried to get liberal conditions, but Clark insisted on unconditional surrender. After a long and heated discussion, they failed to agree upon acceptable terms and each commander returned to his respective post.

A Native American raiding party which Hamilton sent out to attack the settlers along the Ohio River returned to Vincennes at this time, during a lull in the battle. They saw the British flag flying as usual from the fort and began yelling and firing their weapons in the air. They realized their mistake too late, when the frontiersmen killed or wounded several of them and captured others.

Clark ordered five of the captured warriors to be tomahawked in full view of the fort in retaliation for the raids in which numerous men, women and children had been slaughtered. The executions were intended to demonstrate to Native American observers that the redcoats could no longer protect those tribes who made war on the settlers and to put pressure on the British who sensed they could suffer the same fate.

Hamilton reluctantly agreed to Clark's final terms which were just short of unconditional surrender. He described his thoughts at having to surrender: "The mortification, disappointment and indignation I felt, may possibly be conceived. . . ." The defeated British army marched out of Fort Sackville (see Photo FL-8) and laid down their arms at 10 AM on Thursday, February 25, 1779. Clark had the American flag raised above the fort and 13 cannon shots fired in celebration. An accident during the firings severely burned several men, including Captain Joseph Bowman (d. 1779) who died six months later and was buried in the church cemetery adjacent to the fort. The surrender of Fort Sackville marked the beginning of the end of British occupation and control of the western frontier of America.

Even though he was unable to achieve his ultimate objective of capturing Detroit, Clark successfully prevented the British from achieving their goal of driving the Whigs from the Trans-Appalachian frontier. His brilliant military activities caused the British to cede to the United States a vast area of land west of the Appalachian Mountains. That territory now includes the states of Ohio, Indiana, Illinois, Michigan, Wisconsin and the eastern portion of Minnesota.[1]

Ouiatenon, near Lafayette (Feb. 26, 1779)

Fort Ouiatenon Historical Park (**www.tcha.mus.in.us/ouiatenon.htm**) is on South River Road, about 3 miles southwest of West Lafayette. It has a reconstructed blockhouse, built in the 1930s, about a mile from the original fort site which is now private property (see Photo IN-1). The site of the fort was excavated by Indiana University in 1968 and by Michigan State University in the early 1970s. The Tippecanoe Historical Society has most of the archaeological collections and runs the annual 18th century event, Feast of the Hunter's Moon, at Fort Ouiatenon Historical Park. A marker on River Road commemorates the fort.

After Colonel George Rogers Clark (1752–1818) recaptured Vincennes, he learned that the British were sending supplies from Detroit to Vincennes. He sent Captain Leonard Helm (ca. 1720–ca. 1782) and 50 men up the Wabash River to intercept the convoy which he did on Friday, February 26, 1779. Helm returned on March 5th with the provisions and 40 British and French prisoners.[2]

Ohio River, opposite the mouth of the Kentucky River (Aug. 19, 1780)

This action occurred in what is now Vevey, Indiana, across the Ohio River from Carrollton, Kentucky.

Colonel Daniel Boone (1734–1820), Colonel John Todd (1750–1782), and Lieutenant Colonel Stephen Trigg (1742–1782) crossed the Ohio River on Saturday, August 19, 1780, and organized their men into three ragged formations. Trigg commanded the right, Todd the center and Boone the left. Some of the officers remained mounted, but most of them left their horses at the river's edge.

IN-1. Site of Fort Ouiatenon is now private property. The river is to the left behind the trees. Courtesy Todd Harburn.

The men loaded their weapons and began the half-mile march. Captain Hugh Mc-Gary (1744–1806) and two dozen rangers led the expedition along the trace to the crest of the hill. When they reached the summit, "a terrific war whoop was heard, which was caught up all along the ravines on both sides" recalled Peter Houston (1761–1855), one of the Boonesborough rangers. The Shawnees suddenly sprang from their hiding places and fired a deadly volley that brought down all but three of the rangers, "shot down like pigeons." McGary was one of the survivors.

Boone urged his men forward and rushed up the hill. When a Shawnee brave emerged from behind a stump, Boone fired and killed him, running forward over the body. His men followed and charged, pushing the Shawnees back.

McGary galloped to Boone's right to ask why he wasn't retreating, as Todd's and Trigg's lines had. Trigg's column had been cut to pieces within the first minute on a ridge to the right. Trigg himself had been shot from his horse and lay bleeding. The warriors fought from rock to stump, pressing the attack against Trigg's column.

The rangers shifted behind Boone's advancing column. Boone looked down the hill to see a band of Shawnees rushing to capture the unguarded horses along the river. They were soon on Boone's back, forcing him to retreat.

The battle had been under way for only about four or five minutes at this point, with constant firing and the sounds of explosions mixed with whooping and agonized screams. The Kentuckians had no bayonets for the hand-to-hand fighting. The smoke and dust added to the confusion.

They had already lost 40 dead or dying. The two dozen mounted officers made particularly good targets. Fifteen of them had been mortally wounded. Major Levi Todd (1756–1807), of the Fayette militia and one of the few to survive, saw his brother, Colonel John Todd (1750–1780), slump over in his saddle with a bullet in his chest. His horse ran off, and it was the last time Levi ever saw his brother.

When ordered to retreat, the men turned and ran down the hill, directly into the Shawnees who seemed to be seven or eight deep. Desperate fighting with knives and tomahawks ensued. Boone rallied his men in the confusion, ordered them to remain together and sent them into the woods on their left. Here, they found cover for a better river crossing. Boone remained behind with several others to guard their retreat.

When he saw his son Israel Boone (1759–1780) still fighting at his side, Daniel mounted a riderless horse and ordered him to mount and flee. Daniel turned away as Israel looked for a second horse to join him. At that moment, Daniel heard the sound of fighting on the ground behind him. He turned around to see Israel laying on his back in the dust, his arms outstretched, his body quaking and blood gushing from his open mouth. Daniel bent over his son "shot through the neck" and realized he was dead, so he rushed into the woods on his left and down to the river.

Many of the men were killed as they struggled across the river. They reassembled on the bank a little downriver from the ford. Many were wounded and six were missing. Boone's nephew, Squire Boone (1760–1817), had been shot in the hip—a wound that would cripple him for life. The dead included Thomas Boone (ca. 1748–1780), another of Daniel's nephews.

A day or two later, Boone was helping to bury the dead who still lay on the ground at the Blue Licks. Flocks of vultures circled above as they approached the Licking River on August 24. Five days in the August heat turned the bodies black and bloated. They were so mangled that it was difficult to identify them positively. Most of them had been scalped.

Nathan Boone (1781–1856) believed that his father found Israel and buried him separately from the others. Other members of the family thought that Israel was buried with the others in the mass grave at the crest of the hill.[3]

See also **Kentucky** p. 208.

Near Miamitown (Fort Wayne) (Nov. 5, 1780; Nov. 11, 1782)
The La Balme Massacre

The La Balme Massacre occurred on the little northern Indiana river called the Eel River, near the present Whitley County community of Columbia City. A large stone marker on county road 200 South (East 200 South), on the banks of the Eel River a few miles southeast of Columbia City, bears the inscription: "In memory of Colonel Auguste B. La Balme and his soldiers who were killed in battle with the Miami Indians under Little Turtle (Mishikinakwa) (ca. 1747–1812) at this place, November 5, 1780."

Colonel Auguste La Mottin de La Balme (1736–1780), a French soldier of fortune, led more than 100 French militiamen toward Detroit to invade Canada in 1780. They traveled across the plains of southern Illinois by horseback and arrived at Vincennes in August. There, La Balme found young Creoles interested in his plan, but when they delayed in forming themselves into a company, La Balme grew impatient and marched north up the Wabash River with his volunteers. They camped at Fort Ouiatenon (see Photo IN-1) for about three weeks to drill and await the new company of Creole volunteers from Vincennes. When they still failed to arrive, La Balme and his men resumed their trek up the Wabash. They arrived at Post Miami (now the city of Fort Wayne) where they were not received well by the inhabitants who were loyal to the Crown.

The troops raided the Miami capitol of Kekionga (at Fort Wayne) and learned about the Eel River Post, a rich fur trading post near the Miami village of Little Turtle, located about 7 miles southeast of the present community of Columbia City. La Balme left 20 of his troops at Kekionga while he and the rest of his men marched about 18 miles west to the Eel River Post.

A couple of disgruntled French traders who had lost all of their furs in the raid on Kekionga, incited the Miami in the neighboring villages and alerted the village of Little Turtle about La Balme's expedition shortly after their departure. The Miami annihilated the troops left at Kekionga and then hurried to Little Turtle to attack the rest of La Balme's force.

Little Turtle (Mishikinakwa) (ca. 1747–1812) was eager for a fight. He mustered more than 100 warriors even though he had not yet become a chief. Little Turtle and his warriors attacked La Balme's soldiers on Sunday, November 5, 1780, killing about 30, including the colonel himself, capturing one and scattering the rest.[4]

This victory made Little Turtle the principal war chief of the Miamis. When he presented La Balme's scalp, watch, spurs, sword and official papers to the British commander at Detroit, Little Turtle was rewarded with a gift of military supplies. The Miami tribe, which had been fairly neutral, now sided with the Crown forces. This presented a serious obstacle to Colonel George Rogers Clark's (1752–1818) plan to capture Detroit.[5]

★ On Monday, November 11, 1782, Colonel Benjamin Logan (1743–1802) and 150 mounted troops destroyed the British trading post at Miamitown. Logan lost one man killed and another wounded.[6]

Near Tremont
Le Petit Fort (Dec. 5, 1780)
"Battle of the Dunes" (sometimes referred to as the "Battle of Trail Creek")

Indiana Dunes State Park (**www.indianadunes.com**) is near Tremont some 11 miles west of where Michigan City now stands. A historical marker near the auxiliary parking lot in the park reads: "At Le Petit Fort, near this site, a battle was fought on December 5, 1780 between American forces under command of Lt. Thomas Brady and Jean Baptiste Hamelin and British forces under command of Dahreau de Quindre." Le Petit Fort was probably a simple cabin with gardens for growing vegetables surrounded by a palisade (see Photo GA-14). It may have been built by the *coureurs de bois* or illegal traders and most likely served as a warehouse for the furs of traveling merchant-voyageurs and as a trading post.

Fort St. Joseph Park is on Bond Street, near the intersection with Fort Street south of Niles, Michigan.

Colonel George Rogers Clark (1752–1818) might have been able to capture Detroit with little opposition had he done so in 1779 after his victories at Fort Sackville at Vincennes when Lieutenant Governor Henry Hamilton (1734?–1796) (The "Hair Buyer") was held prisoner. However, he waited for large reinforcements which never came. Moreover, obstacles and delays beyond his control, such as the so-called "Battle of the Dunes," further thwarted his plans.

Jean Baptiste Hamelin (1733–1804), a half-breed, led a group of 16 Americans and Creoles from Kaskaskia, Cahokia and other French settlements to raid Fort St. Joseph, near present-day Niles, Michigan in December 1780. They chose to attack the British fort on the east bank of the St. Joseph River, less than 10 miles north of the present city of South Bend, Indiana, while the Native American warriors were away hunting for their winter sustenance. The fort did not maintain a regular garrison at that time and was little more than a fur-trading post. The Creoles captured the fort and many bales of valuable furs from the nearby area villages that were stored there.

As the Creoles returned quickly with their captured pelts, a strong force of Potawatomis, probably under Chief Anaquiba (ca. 1720–1790) and his son, Topinabee or Topenebee "Quiet Sitting Bear" (1758–1826), who lived just south of the fort, pursued them down Trail Creek in northwestern Indiana. A running fight ensued for several miles along Trail Creek on Tuesday, December 5, 1780, according to one account. Major Arent Schuyler De Peyster (1736–1832), British commander at Michilimackinac, Michigan, in his report to Brigadier General Henry Watson Powell on January 8, 1781, presents another account. He says that Lieutenant Dagreaux Du Quindre (or Dagneau De Quindre) and a band of natives and Loyalist traders encountered the Creoles at the Indiana Dunes and recovered all of the furs by defeating Hamelin's forces, killing four, wounding two and capturing seven near Le Petit Fort which is near Aberconk Village, located inside Indiana Dunes State Park. The report read:

> Since the affair at the Miamis something similar happened at St. Joseph's. A Detachment from the Cahokias, consisting of sixteen men only, commanded by a half Indian named Jean Baptiste Hammelain, timed it so as to arrive at St. Joseph's with Pack Horses, when the Indians were out on their first Hunt, an old Chief and his family excepted. They took the Traders Prisoners, and carried off all the goods, consisting of at least Fifty Bales, and took the Route of Chicagou. Lieut. Dagreaux Du Quindre, who I had stationed near St. Josephs, upon being informed of it, immediately assembled the Indians, and pursued them as far as the petite Fort, a days Journey beyond the Riviere Du Chemin where on the 5th December, he summoned them to surrender, on their refusing to do it he ordered the Indians to attack them. Without a loss of a man on his side, killed four, wounded two, and took seven Prisoners, the other Three escaped in the thick Wood. Three of the Prisoners were brought in here amongst whom is Brady a Superintendent of Indian affairs. The rest he suffered the Indians to take to M. Makina. I look upon these Gentry as Robbers and not Prisoners of war, having no commission, that I can learn, other than a verbal order from Mons. Trottier an Inhabitant of the Cahoes. . . .[7]

This small incident increased Native American support for the Crown forces throughout the northern region and created another obstacle to Clark's plans to capture Detroit.

Aurora
Below the mouth of Laughery Creek on the Ohio River (near Aurora) (Aug. 24, 1781)

There are two markers commemorating the tragedy at the mouth of Laughery Creek, about 2 miles south and west of the present city of Aurora. One marker, erected by the Lochry Chapter of the Daughters of the American Revolution, is located at the east end of Lochry Bridge, in Riverview Cemetery, at Aurora. The bronze tablet lists the names of the known victims in Colonel Archibald Lochry's company. The Sons of the American Revolution dedicated a monument at the west end of Laughery Creek Bridge on route IN 56, 2 miles west of Aurora, in 1961.

George Rogers Clark (1752–1818) had gone to Richmond, Virginia before the end of 1780 to consult with Governor Thomas Jefferson (1743–1826). He was appointed brigadier general and received authorization to lead 2,000 men against the British stronghold of Detroit early in the spring of 1781. As he proceeded down the Ohio River in August, the British and their Native American allies were heading toward the Ohio to block him.

Clark changed his plans and decided to attack the Native Americans and then to move against Detroit, Michigan, if possible. He waited several days for Colonel Archibald Lochry's (1733–1781) company of 107 Pennsylvania militiamen to join him at what is now Wheeling, West Virginia, for the trip down the Ohio River. When they didn't arrive, Clark departed, around August 3, after leaving behind boats, supplies and instructions for Lochry's company to join him as soon as possible.

Lochry left Wheeling on Wednesday, August 8, 1781 while Clark waited again at the mouth of the Kanawha River. Meanwhile, many of Clark's militiamen began to desert and return to their homes in Virginia and Kentucky. Clark moved farther down-stream, away from the settlements, in an attempt to stop the desertions. He left the Kanawha three days before Lochry's troops arrived at the mouth of the river. After a brief pause to rest, Lochry headed down river where he encountered problems that delayed him further.

Lochry and his men had no river pilots and were inexperienced in river travel. Several of the boats struck bottom in the shallow river and were damaged. Most of the supplies Clark left them were almost gone because they had not rationed their food and supplies wisely. Lochry wrote a message to Clark, explaining his situation and sent Captain Samuel Shannon (1746–1781) and seven of his men to deliver it. One of Captain Joseph Brant's (1742–1807) (Mohawk Chief Thayendanagea) hunting parties captured Captain Shannon, his men and the dispatch on the second day of their voyage.

Aware of Lochry's plans, Brant and a force of between 100 and 200 Loyalists and Native Americans set out to intercept and ambush Lochry's militiamen before they reached the Falls of the Ohio (Louisville, Kentucky). Brant surprised them near the mouth of a small creek, now called Laughery Creek, where it flows from the north bank of the Ohio, about 2 miles south and west of the present city of Aurora, on Friday, August 24, 1781. Lochry made camp near this stream, unaware that Brant and his warriors had been following him for several days. Brant waited for Clark at the same location several days before, but when he saw more than 400 armed militiamen and several small swivel guns (see Photo GA-2), he decided to wait for Lochry.

Brant's forces surprised Lochry's troops as they prepared breakfast, attacking them suddenly from the north bank. Gunfire from the south bank and from several canoes full of warriors felled several of Lochry's men as they tried to get to their boats. The brief battle slew 36 militiamen immediately—a third of Lochry's force, including Lochry himself who was tomahawked as he sat on a log with the other prisoners. The remaining 64 were captured.

A guard took the militia prisoners to Detroit, while Brant advanced on Clark at the Falls of the Ohio, where he had constructed Fort Nelson. However, the warriors refused to assault the well-armed fort and began to desert with the booty they captured in the Lochry massacre. The Lochry massacre ended any attempt to organize an expedition against Detroit.[8]

9
ILLINOIS

Illinois became part of the French colony of Louisiana in 1717. With the defeat of the French in the Seven Years War [French and Indian War (1756–1763)], the French ceded the Illinois region to Great Britain. The British failed to make friends with the French settlers, many of whom moved west across the Mississippi River.

George Rogers Clark (1752–1818), of Virginia, planned to establish several settlements in the area north of the Ohio River during the American War of Independence. He and a small band of men captured the military post at Kaskaskia by surprise on Saturday, July 4, 1778. He then proceeded to capture Cahokia and other British forts which allowed Virginia to claim jurisdiction over the Illinois territory north of the Ohio River.

> The Abraham Lincoln Presidential Library, formerly the Illinois State Historical Library, [112 North Sixth Street, Springfield, IL 62701 (phone: 217-524-7216) website: **www.alplm.org/**] has collections of materials about the colonial and Revolutionary War periods. It also administers several sites and important state agencies dealing with the state's early history, including the Illinois Historic Preservation Agency and the Illinois Association of Museums. The Illinois State Historical Society [210 ½ South Sixth Street, Springfield, IL 62701 (phone: 217-525-2781)] publishes *Illinois Heritage* and the *Journal of the Illinois State Historical Society*.

See the map of Illinois, Indiana and Missouri.

Ellis Grove
Fort Kaskaskia (July 4, 1778)

> Fort Kaskaskia State Historic Site (website: **www.state.il.us/hpa/hs/Kaskaskia .htm**) is off Route IL 3, 10 miles north of town on the Mississippi River.
> The original site of Fort Kaskaskia has been obliterated by the Mississippi River, but a 275-acre park, which contains the Garrison Hill Cemetery, preserves the history of the area. Fort Kaskaskia was built by the French along the Kaskaskia River in 1736 before the French and Indian War. The settlement of 80 stone houses became the largest French colonial settlement in the Illinois region. The townspeople partially destroyed the fort to keep it out of British hands. The British took it over in 1763 and fortified a Jesuit mission in the village which they called Fort Gage.

The British left many of the former French outposts lightly defended during the War of American Independence, for they had gathered their western forces in Detroit, Michigan. Twenty-three-year-old George Rogers Clark (1752–1818), an explorer of the Ohio Valley, had secret orders from Patrick Henry (1736–1799), governor of Virginia, to capture the town of Kaskaskia and nearby Fort Gage. They expected that this might lead to the capture of the entire Northwest and open the Mississippi and Ohio rivers to Spanish supplies from New Orleans. Spain was an American ally at the time.

Clark sailed down the Ohio River with fewer than 200 men, called the Kentucky Long Knives, in the summer of 1778. He covered 120 miles in five days, landing at the site of where he planned a surprise overland attack on Kaskaskia. After a night crossing of the Kaskaskia River, Clark surrounded the town. When the French commander learned of Clark's approach, he mustered the militia, but he surrendered on Saturday, July 4, 1778 without firing a single shot.

Although the British were fairly tolerant of the inhabitants and their cultural and religious beliefs, the former French citizens disliked living under British rule. They much preferred Clark's benevolent leadership which won their allegiance to the state of Virginia. These new allies would become valuable in Clark's conquest of the region.[1]

Metropolis (summer 1778)
Fort Massac

Fort Massac State Park (Website: **www.free-attractions.com/sg/illinois/fort%20 massac%20state%20park.htm**) is at 1757 Fort Massac, west off route I-24 via US 45, 2 miles east of Metropolis. A reconstructed fort of 1796 and a statue of George Rogers Clark mark the site. A plaque near the monument reads: "In memory of George Rogers Clark—and his faithful companions in arms who by their enterprise and courage won the Illinois country for the Commonwealth of Virginia and so for the American Union."

The French built Fort Massac in 1757 but abandoned it long before George Rogers Clark (1752–1818) arrived in the summer of 1778. Clark and his Kentucky Long Knives rested at the site before the arduous overland march to capture Fort Kaskaskia.

Cahokia (May 26, 1780)

Cahokia is less than 4 miles south of St. Louis, Missouri near the junction of routes IL 3 (Mississippi Avenue) and IL 157 (Camp Jackson Road) west of I-255.

Spanish Illinois was a buffer between the British in Canada and in the Ohio Valley and the Spanish colony of New Spain. Britain also recognized the importance of Spanish Illinois. General Sir Frederick Haldimand (1718–1791), governor of Canada, authorized Emmanuel Hesse to lead a large force of traders, Loyalists, mercenaries and several hundred Fox, Sauk and Winnebago warriors from Detroit to St. Louis. The force left Prairie du Chien on Tuesday, May 2, 1780 under the command of Lieutenant Governor Patrick Sinclair (1736–1820) of Fort Michilimackinac(see Photo MI-1). Their objective was to raid the Spanish and French settlement of St. Louis (see **Missouri** pp. 227–229) and to capture the outposts beginning with Cahokia. Colonel George Rogers Clark (1752–1818) set out on May 13 with a small body of troops. He repulsed the attack on Cahokia on Friday, May 26, 1780, with the loss of four killed and five wounded.[2]

10
WEST VIRGINIA

West Virginia was part of Virginia in the 18th century. Virginia tried to provide protection for the area by constructing Fort Henry at Wheeling and Fort Randolph at Point Pleasant. These forts were complemented by Fort Pitt at Pittsburgh, Pennsylvania and many small private forts which formed the western perimeter of Virginia's frontier defenses. The present boundary between West Virginia and Pennsylvania was set in 1779.

The Crown forces instigated the Native American tribes to harass the settlers along the frontier. There were three major Native American expeditions in the area during the period of 1777 to 1782. Raids continued even after the American War of Independence until Brigadier General "Mad Anthony" Wayne's (1745–1796) decisive victory at the Battle of Fallen Timbers, in Ohio, in 1794.

The West Virginia Department of Archives and History (website: **www.wvculture .org**; phone: 304-558-0220) is part of West Virginia's Division of Culture and History. It encompasses almost every aspect of history and landmark preservation in the state, including the State Historical Society. It publishes *Marking Our Past* (2002), a 210-page guidebook to the state's nearly 1000 historical highway markers. The book is arranged by county and gives locations, full inscriptions of the markers, photographs and a history of the state's highway marker program.

See the map of West Virginia.

Summersville
Powell's Valley (late March 1777; late Dec. 1780)

Powell's Valley is near Powell's Mountain in Summersville.

Native Americans attacked a detachment of Virginia militiamen in Powell's Valley, the colony's westernmost valley in late March 1777. They killed two militiamen and wounded one.

★ Colonel Arthur Campbell (1743–1811) reported another incident of a Cherokee attack in Powell's Valley in late December 1780:

> The enemy in my absence, did some mischief in Powell's Valley, and on the Kentucky path near Cumberland Gap, besides three children that they scalped on Holstein; one of the perpetrators of which we killed on our return, and retook a number of horses. The Botetourt and Montgomery militia were too slow in their movements to do any service.[1]

Wheeling
Fort Henry (April 6, 1777; June 6, 1777; Sept. 1, 1777, Sept. 8, 1781; Sept. 11–13, 1782)

Fort Henry was located on an elevated point on the left (eastern bank) of the Ohio River, about a quarter mile above Wheeling Creek. Originally called Fort Fincastle,

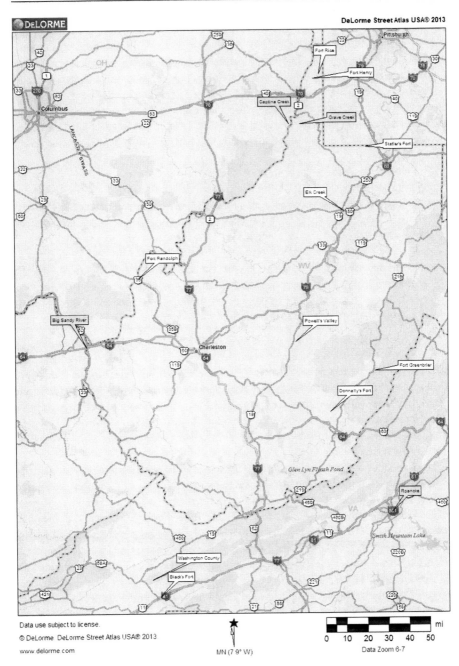

MN (7 9° W)

West Virginia: Map for The Guide to the American Revolutionary War in the Deep South and on the Frontier
© 2013 DeLorme (www.delorme.com) Street Atlas USA®

it was strengthened and refitted in 1776 and its name changed to "Fort Henry" in honor of Patrick Henry (1736–1799), then governor of Virginia. It stood on open ground and enclosed more than half an acre. There was a hill a short distance to the east with a gradual ascent on its western side but a precipice on its eastern side. It joined with another hill, nearly at right angles, at its northern end. There was room for a path over the brow of the first hill and along the side of the second to Wheeling Creek at the bottom. There was a considerable space of level land between the southern end of the hill and the creek. The site is now in Wheeling's downtown business district.

Fort Henry was a parallelogram built of white-oak pickets about 17 feet high with bastions (see Photo GA-21) at the angles. It contained several cabins along its western side. A two-story house for the commandant, a storehouse and other public buildings occupied the center of the enclosed area. The main entrance was on the eastern side of the fort and its longest side faced the river. Nothing remains of the fort. A bronze plaque on a stone on Main Street between 11th and Ohio Streets marks the site of the fort. Another marker on the northwest of Oglebay Park at Greggsville, Clinton and Potomac Road identifies the site of Fort Van Metre. Another marker on route WV 88 (Bethany Pike), near the intersection of Short Creek, near Wheeling, commemorates the death of Major Samuel McCulloch.

An express arrived at Fort Henry, in early April 1777, with news of a Jersey man, by the name of Ogden, who was found murdered and scalped near the mouth of Raccoon Creek. Another express brought news that some Cherokees killed and scalped three men of the Muchmore family at their house opposite the mouth of Yellow Creek on the Ohio River near the mouth of the Cheat River. Mrs. Muchmore and her three children were found almost burned to cinders. Lieutenant William Mason (1748–1793) and 10 militiamen pursued the murderers for 25 miles before overtaking them near Wheeling on Sunday, April 6, 1777.

They fought for some time before the Cherokees withdrew. Lieutenant Mason's party followed them several miles further. However, as they were out of provisions and feared falling into an ambuscade, they returned to the battlefield where they found one dead Cherokee, whom they scalped, some horses and other booty which the attackers had taken from some white people. Lieutenant Mason believed his men either killed or desperately wounded more Cherokees, judging by the quantity of blood on the ground.[2]

★ Native Americans, probably members of Captain Pluggy's (Tecanyaterighto, Plukkemehnotee) (d. 1776) gang, surprised a fishing party from Captain Johannes Van Metre's (1735–1818) Virginia militia company at Wheeling on Friday, June 6, 1777. They killed Thomas McCleary (1750–1777).[3]

★ Reports began to circulate, in early August 1777, that the Cherokees were planning to attack the whites. Scouts constantly observed their movements. The settlers at the mouth of Wheeling Creek—about 30 families—took shelter at Fort Henry and prepared to defend themselves. Between 400 and 500 militiamen assembled at the fort; but, because the attack did not occur at the time indicated in the reports, some began to think the reports were a false alarm and began to return home. Two companies left the fort on August 31st, the day before the attack.

About 350 Mingo, Shawnee and Wyandot tribesmen approached the Ohio River in small parties on August 31st and rendezvoused about 2 miles below Wheeling Creek. (Some accounts say they were led by Simon Girty (1741–1818), but none of the Girty family were actively fighting in this area at the time.) Lieutenant Governor Henry Hamilton (1734?–1796) (The "Hair Buyer") presumably supplied them with arms, ammunition and provisions. They crossed the river during the night and occupied the creek bottom which was cleared and mostly planted with corn. They formed two lines across it from the river to the creek and hid themselves in the corn. Six braves were concealed near the center of these lines, close to a path, as a decoy. The fort's garrison of 42 men and boys was totally unaware of their presence. (W. H. Hunter mentions only 30 defenders, noting the other 12 were women and young children.)[4]

Shortly after daybreak the next day, Monday, September 1st, Mr. Andrew Zane (1751–1811), an African American boy named Loudon and another man left the fort to go about a mile up Wheeling Creek to get some horses to move Dr. James McMechen's family from the fort to the Monongahela. When they reached the top of the hill in front of the fort, they discovered the six decoys stationed on the path. They turned and tried to reach the fort. One man was overtaken and tomahawked after running about 80 yards. Zane was pursued closely and escaped by jumping over a cliff. He was badly bruised by the fall, but he recovered. Loudon escaped unhurt to sound the alarm which the attackers hoped would draw the garrison into an ambuscade at the southern end of the hill near the creek.

Colonel David Shepherd (1734–1795), commander of the fort, thinking there were only a few attackers, ordered Captain Samuel Mason (1739–1803) and 14 men to go out to dislodge them. They soon located and fired at the six decoys, on the attackers' right flank, when the main body of warriors arose from their ambuscade and rushed upon Captain Mason and his men with horrible yells. Captain Mason ordered an immediate retreat. He and only two others escaped.

A heavy fog prevented the defenders from seeing what was happening and determining the number of assailants. A dozen veteran scouts left the fort to cover the retreat of Captain Mason's party. Only three of them escaped. The garrison, now reduced to nearly one-third its original strength, realized the nature and strength of the enemy who approached the fort in two columns preceded by a fife, drum and a British flag. They carried the bloody scalps of the fort's victims and completely surrounded the fort. Their leader demanded the fort's surrender, to which Colonel Shepherd responded: "Sir, we have consulted our wives and children, and all have resolved—men, women, and children—sooner to perish at their posts than place themselves under the protection of a savage army, with you at its head; or abjure the cause of liberty and the colonies." As their leader began to reply, a boy in one of the bastions (see Photo GA-21) fired a rifle at him, and the man retired.[5]

The Native Americans began their siege early in the morning, by discharging their weapons at the fort and continuing an indiscriminate fire against the walls, gate and other parts of the fort, until about 1 PM when they withdrew. They approached the fort a second time around 2:30 or 3 PM. Some of them took possession of the houses in the little village around the fort; others took shelter behind Colonel Ebenezer Zane's (1747–1812) fence, about 60 yards away, while others occupied a blacksmith's shop and stable opposite the north side of the fort. The others, probably the largest number, positioned themselves on the southern side of the fort, behind a rail fence and several piles of timber.

The Mingoes, Shawnees and Wyandots then began a furious attack on the southern side which drew the whole garrison to that side, inflicting heavy losses on the attackers. Meanwhile, their leader took 18 or 20 warriors from Colonel Zane's yard to assault the gate of the fort with rails and wooden sticks. The defenders repulsed the attack, killing several braves. The assault on the northern and eastern sides of the fort raged furiously until night when the tribesmen withdrew to the foot of the hill to rest. Irregular and scattered fire continued through the night.

When the besiegers found themselves compelled to withdraw from Fort Henry without having captured it as expected, the larger part of their force, together with Captain Pratt's British Rangers, crossed the Ohio with their plunder and marched through the wilderness toward the Sandusky. The remaining 60 or 70 braves went in the opposite direction, eastward toward the interior settlements. They headed toward Fort Rice to massacre and devastate in revenge for their disappointment at Fort Henry.[6]

See **Fort Rice** pp. 202–203.

Captain Andrew Van Swearingen (1747–1824) and 14 men arrived from Holliday's Fort, at Cross Creek, 24 miles above Wheeling, about 4 AM on Sunday, September 14 and entered the fort safely. Major Samuel McCulloch (1752–1782) and 40 mounted men from Short Creek arrived about daybreak. The Native Americans immediately rushed to the gate to cut off the reinforcements and to try to enter themselves. All the reinforcements entered the fort except for the major who was left outside. He turned his horse and galloped up the hill, hoping to reach Captain Johannes Van Metre's (1735–1818) fort. When he reached the point on the hill near where the Cumberland road crosses, he encountered another large body of Native Americans returning from a plundering expedition among the settlements. He galloped to the edge of the precipice (about 150 feet high and almost perpendicular) on the bank of Wheeling Creek. He coaxed his horse down the slope, crossed the creek and escaped.

A party of tribesmen, assembled at the foot of the hill near the fort, set fire to all the houses, buildings and fences in the vicinity, killed nearly 300 head of cattle belonging to the settlers and broke camp. They lost between 40 and 50 killed and wounded in the attack. The garrison lost 15 men killed and nine wounded.[7]

★ A second attack on Fort Henry occurred on Saturday, September 8, 1781, when chief Pekillon and a band of Delawares attempted to take the fort. They approached, carrying the British flag, and demanded the fort's surrender. Colonel David Shepherd (1734–1795) refused. A few men, who had come down in a boat from Pittsburgh, arrived during the night to re-enforce the garrison. The defenders had fashioned a wooden cannon out of a log to deceive the attackers. The reinforcements brought a cannon and some cannonballs. Some of the balls were used in the real cannon which was substituted for the wooden one, but the Delawares captured the rest.

Chief Pekillon began the assault about midnight. The Delawares rushed hard on the pickets and tried to destroy the fort by battering it in every way possible. An African American boy arrived about 8 AM and informed Colonel Shepherd that the attacking force consisted of a British captain and 40 regular soldiers and 260 Delawares. They kept a continual fire the whole day. During the night, they made many attempts to burn both the fort and Colonel Ebenezer Zane's (1747–1812) house. The African American slave saw a Delaware approach and killed him as he prepared to set fire to the residence.

The garrison then began firing the cannon which they fired 16 times during the attack. The attackers tried making one of their own out of a hollow tree which they wrapped with chains found in a blacksmith shop. They loaded it with a ball taken from the party from Pittsburgh. When they fired it, the explosion killed and injured several people around it but did no damage to the fort.

The attackers killed a young boy, took another prisoner, wounded a man in the wrist and shot a number of horses and cattle. When they left the fort, the Delawares went up

Wheeling Creek and took a blockhouse (see Photo GA-1) belonging to Mr. Link. They killed three men and took four prisoners, three of whom were murdered the next day. The only surviving prisoner escaped the following night.[8]

★ The third and last attack on Fort Henry occurred on Wednesday, September 11, 1782 when 250 Native American warriors and a company of 40 British Rangers from Detroit approached. A scout discovered the attackers' trail that morning and hastened to the fort. The alarm gun was fired and the drum beat to alert the families in the area.

The attackers arrived within view of the fort about 5 PM and posted their colors, the British Union Jack, about 400 yards away. The garrison saluted the flag with a shot from a 6-pound swivel (see Photo GA-2) brought from Fort Pitt after the previous attacks. The Native Americans kept out of range during the day; but, soon after dark, they came close to the stockade, yelling. They kept up an incessant fire of musketry and rifles for some time. They repeated this activity several times through the night and threw stones into the fort which the garrison threw back at them.

The siege continued the next day with little firing, except at horses and cattle. The attackers approached the fort and fired at it during the night, as they did the previous night. They also placed hemp and flax in some ravines near the stockade in an unsuccessful attempt to set the fort on fire.

The fort's supply of gunpowder was running low and there was a keg in Colonel Ebenezer Zane's (1747–1812) house, about 60 yards from the fort. None of the men wanted to risk their lives to go get it; and Colonel Shepherd didn't want to order anybody on such a dangerous mission, so he called for volunteers. Three or four young men stepped forward and it was decided to select one of them by lot when Colonel Zane's 16-year old sister Elizabeth Zane (1766–1826) asked to be permitted to go get the powder so as not to risk the loss of another man to defend the fort. Despite efforts to prevent her from doing so, she was finally allowed to go.

Several tribesmen, wandering around near the gate, saw Elizabeth leave the fort but paid no attention until she returned with the keg in her arms. (Some accounts say she carried the powder loose in her apron.) They then fired at her, but she entered the fort unharmed despite the musket balls flying all around her. The attackers withdrew from Fort Henry on Friday, the 13th.[9]

Some authorities say this event occurred during the first attack in 1777. Others think there may have been two similar incidents. In November 1849, 67 years after the event, 83-year-old Lydia Boggs Shepherd Cruger (1766–1867) signed an affidavit naming Molly Scott as the heroine of the gunpowder incident. She said that Betty Zane had not even been at the fort during the third siege. However, Molly Scott's grandson, James F. Scott, in a written statement, related how he had heard numerous times "from her own lips" to members of her immediate family, as well as to friends and neighbors, that she watched Betty Zane run to Colonel Zane's cabin for powder and return with it to the fort during the siege of 1782. Molly Scott never claimed credit for the act of bravery and Lydia Cruger's memory may have been failing.[10]

Donnally's Fort (May 29, 1777 or May 28, 1778)

Andrew Donnally built his house sometime before 1771 and fortified it. Donnally's Fort was a large, two-story, hewn-log dwelling protected by pickets or a palisade wall (see Photo GA-14). It was situated at the intersection of Raders Valley Road|County

Route 60/28 and Fort Donally Road| County Route 17/2|Culbertson Creek in Williamsburg. De Hass dates this event in June 1778.

Captain Alexander McKee (ca. 1735–1799) dispatched two soldiers to warn the people of the approach of Native Americans at Fort Randolph. They had attacked Colonel Andrew Donnally, Sr.'s (1755–1839) fort, guarded by only 25 men, on Thursday, May 29, 1777. The defenders of Donnally's fort put up a brave defense from sunrise until 3 AM when Colonel Samuel Lewis and Captain Mathew Arbuckle arrived with a party of 66 men. The reinforcements fired at the Native Americans, killing 17. The attackers continued their siege until night when they hauled nine of their men away. The militiamen scalped the dead tribesmen the following morning. The militiamen lost three men killed by their imprudence and one was shot through a port hole (see Photo GA-1) in the fort.[11]

★ About 200 Wyandots and Mingoes under Dunquat (Petawontakas, Dunquad, Daunghquat; Delaware name, Pomoacan), known as the "Half-King" attempted to avenge the death of Chief Cornstalk (Keigh-tugh-qua, Hokoleskwa) (ca. 1720–1777) at **Point Pleasant** (see pp. 196–197) on Wednesday, May 20, 1778. They surrounded Fort Randolph (see cover photo and Photo GA-3) and began a week-long siege. Unable to make the fort surrender, they then moved up the Kanawha to attack Fort Donnally. Messengers from Fort Randolph warned them of the impending attack. The neighboring settlers gathered at the fort and sent a call for help to Fort Savannah (Lewisburg). Colonel John Stuart (ca. 1710–1779) and 68 men arrived on the second day of the siege and routed the Wyandots and Mingoes. The Native Americans killed only four men.[12]

Elk Creek, Harrison County (July 31, 1777)

Elk Creek runs along route US 50 in Clarksburg.

A band of Native Americans killed and scalped Charles Grigsby's (1755–1814) wife and child at their home on a branch of Elk Creek in Harrison County on Thursday, July 31, 1777. One person was missing. A party of 13 or 14 pursued the raiders.[13]

Frankford, Lewisburg, Point Pleasant
Battle of the Great Kanawha/Battle of Point Pleasant (Oct. 10, 1774)

Fort Randolph (Aug. 31, 1777; late Dec. 1777; May 16, 1778; May 20, 1778)

Fort Randolph (see cover photo) was at Point Pleasant in what is now Tu-Endie-Wei State Park and Point Pleasant Battle Monument State Park (**www.tu-endie -weistatepark.com/**) at the mouth of the Kanawha River at the junction with the Ohio River. "The History of Mason County West Virginia," in *Hardesty's Historical Encyclopedia* (1883) page 3, provides the first recorded indication of a fort here. This fort, which served to guard the "backdoor" of Virginia, was garrisoned with 100 men under the command of Captain Mathew Arbuckle (1734–1790) and remained in operation throughout the American Revolution. It was named Fort Randolph for Peyton Randolph (ca. 1721–1775), a Virginia aristocrat who was unanimously elected as President of the First Continental Congress on September 4, 1774.

Chief Cornstalk's gravesite is in Tu-Endie-Wei State Park, near where Fort Randolph stood.

There's a reconstructed fort (P.O. Box 86, Point Pleasant, WV 25550) located in Krodel Park (phone: 304 675-1068) on route WV 2 North, just east of Point Pleasant. The fort is located approximately 1 mile from the sites of the original two forts that shared its name. The 44-acre park has a playground, clubhouse and picnic shelters and a 22-acre lake for fishing. Recreational vehicle camping is permitted.

Chief Cornstalk (Keigh-tugh-qua, Hokoleskwa) (ca. 1720–1777) and about 300 to 500 Shawnee and Mingo warriors attacked Colonel Andrew Lewis (1720–1781) and about 1,100 Virginia militiamen at Point Pleasant on October 10, 1774. They engaged in the Battle of the Great Kanawha, more generally known as the Battle of Point Pleasant, one of the bloodiest and fiercest battles of the Indian wars, hoping to halt Lewis's advance into the Ohio Country. The Shawnees and Mingoes retreated, were decisively defeated, after a long and furious battle, and driven across the Ohio. Many of their villages were destroyed. This engagement, the only major battle of Dunmore's War, probably occurred about 0.4 miles north of Fort Randolph, near the intersection of routes WV 2 (Viand Street) and WV 62 (6th Street). Lord John Murray, 4th Earl of Dunmore (1732–1809), the Royal Governor of Virginia, then led a second force into the Ohio country and compelled Cornstalk to agree to a treaty, ending the war.

★ The Virginia Assembly, alarmed at the defenseless state of their western border, ordered a new fort built at the mouth of the Kanawha River at the junction with the Ohio River in 1776. Captain Mathew Arbuckle's (1734–1790) Virginia militiamen built Fort Randolph in May 1776, naming it after Peyton Randolph, the first president of the Continental Congress, who had died the previous year. The fort, along with Fort Pitt and Fort Henry, was intended to prevent Native American raids into western Virginia and Pennsylvania.

The forts failed to deter raids, and the Virginians prepared for an offensive expedition into the Ohio country in 1777. A band of Native Americans attacked a scouting party from Captain Arbuckle's (1734–1790) garrison at Fort Randolph on Sunday, August 31, 1777, killing two.

★ The friendly Shawnee chief Cornstalk (Keigh-tugh-qua, Hokoleskwa) (ca. 1720–1777) came to Fort Randolph, in October 1777, accompanied by two other chiefs, Red Hawk (d. 1777) and Old Yie to discuss the rumored expedition. The Shawnees who followed Cornstalk wanted to stay out of the war, but Cornstalk warned the Virginians that he would not be able to keep all of the tribes neutral as British pressure was forcing the tribes to side with them and that the other chiefs would have to comply.

Expecting to be killed, Cornstalk offered Captain Arbuckle to kill him immediately, but Arbuckle declined to hurt the faithful chief and offered to hold him and the others as hostages to ensure that the Shawnees stayed neutral. When Cornstalk's son Elinipsico (d. 1777) arrived, looking for his father, he too was taken.

★ When one of the militiamen was killed outside the fort on Monday, November 10, 1777, his enraged companions charged into the fort and murdered Cornstalk and the other three Shawnee hostages. Virginia's governor Patrick Henry (1736–1799) brought the killers to trial, but they were acquitted because no one would testify against them.[14]

★ About 20 Native Americans ambushed Lieutenant William Moore's (d. 1777) reconnoitering party within about 100 yards of the turnip field at Fort Randolph in late December 1777. They killed Lieutenant Moore and one private. Captain William McKee's (1758–1824) Virginia militia company pursued the attackers who fled in different directions. The militiamen only got one blanket and a tomahawk.[15]

★ Some Native Americans outside Fort Randolph shot at two militiamen on Saturday, May 16, 1778. They killed one and wounded the other.

★ About 200 Wyandots and Mingoes under Dunquat (Petawontakas, Dunquad, Daunghquat; Delaware name, Pomoacan), known as the "Half-King", surrounded Fort Randolph and began a week-long siege on Wednesday, May 20, 1778. Unable to make the fort surrender, the Wyandots then moved up the Kanawha to attack Fort Donnally, which also withstood attack. The Virginians abandoned Fort Randolph in 1779, apparently because resources were needed elsewhere, and the Wyandots then burned it.[16]

See also **Fort Greenbrier,** below.

Marlinton
Fort Greenbrier (Sept. 11, 1777; May 21, 1778)

Fort Greenbrier was about in what is now Marlinton. It was in the area bounded by Judge Street, Jury Street and 10th Avenue.

A band of Shawnees attacked the family of Colonel James Graham outside Fort Greenbrier on Thursday, September 11, 1777. They killed Walter Caldwell (d. 1777) as he was shutting the door to keep them out. They also killed or captured several other people and wounded another person.[17]

★ A band of 200 to 300 Native Americans, mostly Shawnees, appeared near Fort Randolph (see cover photo) to avenge the death of Cornstalk (Keigh-tugh-qua, Hokolesk-wa) (ca. 1720–1777) about Wednesday, May 20, 1778. A small party approached to draw an attacking party out of the fort. They departed in great terror before the garrison was aware of their presence. At that time, the whole band rose up and began firing on the garrison for several hours but with little effect. Their line extended from the banks of the Ohio to the banks of the Kanawha. After a while, one of them advanced to the fort and requested to enter. Captain William McKee (1758–1824) approved. (Captain Mathew Arbuckle (1734–1790) was in Greenbrier visiting his family.) A short while after the Shawnee was admitted, a gun went off by accident. The Shawnees outside raised a hideous yell, but the man immediately mounted one of the bastions (see Photo GA-21) and signaled to his friends that all was well.

The Shawnee demanded the fort's surrender. Captain McKee asked to consider the matter until morning. He kept his men busy during the night bringing in water from the river, as he prepared for a long siege. The following morning, Captain McKee sent Cornstalk's sister Katherine Grenadier Squaw, Nonhelema (1740–1785), with his answer. Despite the murder of her brother and nephew, she was still attached to the whites and remained at the fort as an interpreter. She reported that the garrison would not surrender.

The Shawnees began the attack immediately and besieged the garrison for one week. Finding they could not take the garrison, the Shawnees decided to go to Fort Greenbrier. They rounded up all the cattle near the garrison for provision on their march and headed up the Kanawha. Captain McKee discovered their route and surmised their intentions, so he dispatched General Philip Hammon and Major John Prior (1735–1785) to pursue them with orders to pass them undiscovered, if possible, and give the people notice of their approach. The Shawnees had marched two days before them, but they pursued with such speed that they overtook the tribesmen and passed them one evening at William McClung's meadows, within 20 miles of Lewisburg (known as Camp Union). The braves were enjoying themselves and walking about on rising ground near McClung's house, giving Hammon and Prior a good view of their whole army, undiscovered. Hammon and Prior hurried to Colonel Andrew Donnally, Sr.'s (1755–1839) to alert them to the approach of about 200 warriors. Colonel Donnally brought in all his neighbors that night. Some 20 men, including Hammon and Prior, and about 60 women and children gathered at the fort before daybreak.

The garrison kept a good lookout, expecting an attack at any time. Very early in the morning of the following day, two scouts arrived within about a mile of Donnally's and heard brisk firing. They soon returned to report to Captain John Stewart (1749–1823) that the Shawnees had attacked the fort. Stewart mustered about 68 men and went to relieve the garrison. As they approached Donnally's house about 2 PM, they heard no firing. They left the road and took a path to the back of the house to avoid an ambuscade along the road.

They soon discovered a brave in a rye field looking at the house. When they fired at him, other warriors ran in the rye near where he stood. The reinforcements ran straight to the fort. The garrison, hearing the guns at the back of the house, thought another party of Shawnees was attacking. They all took posts at the port holes (see Photo GA-1), ready to fire. When some realized that they were reinforcements, they opened the gates and let them in. Only one man was shot through a fold of his hunting shirt. Once inside, the reinforcements found four men killed, two of whom were coming to the fort when they came upon the Shawnees and were killed. One of Donnally's servants was killed in front of the door in the first attack. Another was shot in a bastion of the fort.

The attack began about dawn when everyone in the fort was asleep except the sentry, Philip Hammon, and an African American boy named Dick. The warriors laid down three guns at a stable about 50 yards from the house and attacked at the kitchen door with their tomahawks and war clubs. Hammon opened the door and killed a brave on the threshold as he was splitting the door. Dick had a musket loaded with swanshot (heavy slugs) and fired into the yard with good effect. The Shawnees fell back and the door was secured.[18]

The firing awakened the people in the other end of the house and upstairs where most of the men were lying. They fired out of the windows upon the enemy so briskly that when Captain John Stewart (1749–1823) and his men got into the fort, 17 lay dead in the yard. As some of the Shawnees crawled under the floor and tried to force their way up, Hammon and Dick and one or two men from the loft waited for them. When one of them poked his head through the opening, Hammon struck him with his tomahawk. After a second was killed in the same way, the rest escaped. The attack continued most of the day, but at such a distance as to do little harm. One man was killed by a ball passing through a separation in the wall.

A warrior approached the fort after dark and called out in the English language that he wanted to make peace. He was invited in to discuss the terms but declined. The Shawnees departed that night, dragging their dead from the yard. They returned to Greenbrier only once or twice after that in small parties.[19]

Grave Creek (Sept. 27, 1777)

Grave Creek is in Moundsville, about 5 miles east-northeast of Powhattan Point and the Ohio River. A monument erected to Captain William Foreman (1751–1777) and the other victims bears this inscription:

This humble stone is erected to the memory of Captain Foreman and twenty of his brave men, who were slain by a band of ruthless savages—the allies of a civilized nation of Europe—on the 28th [27th] of September, 1777.

So sleep the brave who sink to rest,
By all their country's wishes blest.

Erosion by the river removed the soil on which this stone was placed. The Marshall County court ordered it removed to Moundsville Cemetery in 1875.[20]

The Grave Creek Mound (9th Street between Jefferson and Tomlinson Avenues) is one of the largest Native American burial mounds in America. It is 79 feet high, 900 feet in circumference at the base and 50 feet across the top.[21]

Captain William Foreman (1751–1777) raised a company of citizens east of the mountains to go help the settlers in the west. He arrived at Wheeling by the middle of September 1777. Some people there noticed some smoke in the direction of Grave Creek on Friday morning, September 26, 1777. Afraid that the Shawnees might be burning Mr. Tomlinson's stockade and houses, Captain Foreman, totally unfamiliar with Native American warfare, set out with his company of 46 Virginia militiamen (Foreman's 24 men, Captain William Linn's (Lynn) (1757–1837) 9, Captain Joseph Ogle's (1741–1821) 10 and 3 experienced scouts) to determine whether the stockade was burning and to offer any protection if necessary. However, the fort at Grave Creek had been abandoned before the siege of Wheeling and the only remaining building had been burned by the Native American raiders.

The militiamen went as far as Captina Creek, 18 miles below Wheeling, to reconnoiter the site of the abandoned fort at Grave Creek which they found safe. They remained overnight because there were no canoes available. They started back early the following morning. When they reached the lower end of Grave Creek narrows, some of the more experienced scouts suggested leaving the river bottom and returning by way of the ridge. Captain Foreman ridiculed the suggestion and ordered his party forward. His own men and several volunteer scouts obeyed the order, but some refused to go with him, including Linn, an experienced scout, who thought that if their movements had been observed, the Shawnees would most likely attack them at some point on the river. He thought that the Shawnees had been on the opposite side of the river observing them, that they had crossed during the night and were probably lying in ambush for their return.

During the heated interchange of opinions, Foreman refused to take the suggestions of a rough backwoodsman. Linn, convinced the plan could prove fatal, could only disagree with all the power of persuasion at his command. When Foreman ordered the march, Linn took six or eight others up the hillside while Foreman and his company followed the path along the base.

At the upper end of McMechen's Narrows (now called Grave Creek), where the bottom begins to widen, the men in front noticed some trinkets, beads and bands strewn along the path. Some of the men began to pick up the articles while the others gathered about in a compact group looking at the items. Meanwhile, the Shawnees stretched across the path in two lines, one above, the other below them. A large band arose from beneath the bank and opened fire on the company, killing Captain Foreman and most of his party, including his two sons. Those who escaped the first volley tried to rush up the steep hill that is an almost insurmountable barrier at this point. One of the men pulled himself up by a sapling but had the bark knocked into his face when a musket ball struck the sapling. The Shawnees pursued and killed several others. One who escaped said the tomahawks sounded "as if the Indians were cutting up beef."

When Linn and his party heard the guns, they rushed down the side of the hill, yelling, to give the impression they were much more numerous. The Shawnees ceased their pursuit, probably saving the lives of many. The total number of casualties was about 21 killed and four wounded. The survivors escaped to Wheeling. Colonel Shepherd led a party, two days later, to bury the dead in a common grave. Some suppose that the Shawnees were the same body that attacked Fort Henry at Wheeling, three weeks earlier, but there is no evidence to substantiate that conclusion.[22]

Statler's Fort (Stradler) (July 14, 1777)
Dunkard Creek (March 1778)

> Statler's Fort was a blockhouse located on the waters of Dunkard Creek, a western tributary of the Monongahela River, in the present Monongalia County, just south of the Pennsylvania border. The creek runs between Mount Morris, Pennsylvania through Blacksville, West Virginia. There's a historical marker commemorating the fort on route WV 7 (CR 52/1), about 0.22 miles east of Dunkard Creek in Maidsville, about 0.38 miles west of route CR 3/1 (Mooresville-Price Station).
>
> Statler's Fort was erected in 1770 and served as a safe haven for settlers in this region until 1794. The stockade stood until 1850 and was used as a church and a schoolhouse for many years.

A party of at least 20 Shawnees burned Jacob Farmer's (d. 1777) house and killed him and one of his daughters, Nathan Worley (d. 1777) and two of Jacob Jones's children on Monday, July 14, 1777. A young woman and two children were missing and presumed dead. Three men escaped to Statler's Fort. Colonel Zackwell or Zacquill Morgan (1735–1795) set out in pursuit.[23]

★ A band of Native Americans raided outlying posts along Dunkard Creek in March 1778. They killed six, wounded two and captured four.

Western Virginia (Nov. 6, 1778)

> General Lachlan McIntosh's route followed the Beaver River and then along the Mahoning River.[24]

General George Washington (1732–1799) appointed General Lachlan McIntosh (1727–1806) as commander of the Western Department in May 1778. His army of approximately 1,200 men, more than half from the northwest counties of Virginia, began to march west in early November 1778 to establish a second fort in a chain, this one in the heart of the Delaware nation. They began marching on Wednesday, November 4, 1777, despite insufficient quantities of salt, flour, whiskey and forage for the entire distance and the approach of winter.

General McIntosh ordered purchasing agents to buy the necessary provisions and stockpile them at Fort McIntosh to be forwarded as needed. He left Lieutenant-Colonel Richard Campbell (d. 1781) at Fort McIntosh with 150 men to forward supplies as they arrived, but they never saw the supplies. Nonetheless, McIntosh's column plodded on. The lack of forage eventually slowed the advance to about 4 miles a day, as the horses had to rest frequently. As the party slowly moved deeper into Shawnee territory, the danger of raids increased. Despite McIntosh's prohibition of unauthorized hunting and his orders to stay close to camp, some independent-minded frontiersmen, who made up a large segment of the force, paid little attention.

Two men, hunting against his orders, were killed and scalped a short distance from camp on Friday, November 6, 1778. McIntosh then began to enforce strict discipline court-martialing men who fired guns, hunted or strayed from camp without permission. He also strictly forbade any trading with Native Americans. He set punishments from fines to flogging with a hickory switch. On at least one occasion, General McIntosh overturned a court's decision because he found it too lenient and he reprimanded the officers in charge.

Snow and freezing rain slowed the expedition even more than the lack of supplies. The delays consumed more supplies. The army reached its destination, the headquarters of the Delaware nation on the Tuscarawas River, on November 8. Their rations were reduced to "4 oz. of injured flour and 8 oz. very poor beef" per man, per day.

McIntosh convened the Delawares and explained that he had come to build a fort as one of a chain along his path to Detroit. He ended his speech by telling them to send word to the neighboring tribes that they had 14 days to come to camp and treat with him. Otherwise, he would consider them enemies and hunt them down. The Delawares saw McIntosh's ragged army and began to laugh after he threatened them.

The troops completed the fort in December. McIntosh named it Fort Laurens (see **Ohio** pp. 164–169) and garrisoned it with 150 men under Colonel John Gibson (1740–1822). The army then began its return to Fort McIntosh where it arrived in a snowstorm on Christmas eve.[25]

Big Sandy River (Big Sandy Junction) (Sept. 15 1782)

> The Big Sandy Junction is at the northwest corner of West Virginia, at a fork in the Ohio River which forms the boundaries of Kentucky, Ohio and West Virginia.

Virginia militiamen pursued a band of marauding Native Americans on Sunday, September 15, 1782. They recovered two captives near Big Sandy Junction and wounded several Native Americans.

Bethany

Fort Rice (Sept. 6, 1780; ca. Sept. 15, 1782; Oct. 24, 1782)

> Fort Rice was a rectangular stockade with a blockhouse (see Photo GA-1) at one corner and several cabins within the enclosure. It was situated on the Dutch Fork of Buffalo Creek about 12 or 15 miles from its junction with the Ohio River, near where Bethany College now stands in Bethany, Brooke County. Constructed by Abraham and Daniel Rice, the fort provided protection for 12 families.

A large body of Native Americans appeared at Fort Rice near sundown on Wednesday, September 6, 1780. They attacked the fort, but the militiamen inside put up such a stiff resistance that the attackers withdrew. The garrison lost one man killed and another wounded.

The occupants of the fort saw multiple fires during the night as the Native Americans burned houses, barns and haystacks in the area. The full militia mustered the following day, reinforced by some volunteers from Cumberland County. They pursued the Native Americans who outran them. They called off the chase after 10 days.

★ Meanwhile, another party of Native Americans advanced down the North Branch and forced the evacuation of Fort Jenkins. They then destroyed the fort.[26]

★ A band of 100 Native Americans on their way home from their unsuccessful siege of Fort Henry (Wheeling September 11–13, 1782) tried to surprise Fort Rice around Sunday, September 15, 1782. The post was garrisoned by only six men who received advance warning about half an hour before the Native Americans' arrival. The attackers tried to storm the fort, but the defenders killed three and wounded one in the first volley. About 10 PM, the attackers set fire to a large barn filled with grain and hay, about 30 or 40 yards from the blockhouse. The flames threatened the fort for a while, but the current of air flowing in the opposite direction prevented the fort from igniting.

The attackers took advantage of the light from the flames and gathered on the opposite side of the fort from the fire and renewed their attack which lasted until about 2 AM, when they departed, after a 12-hour siege. The attackers lost four warriors—three of them in the first volley, the other about sundown. George Felebaum (d. 1782) was shot in the forehead through a porthole at the second fire; the other five defenders were unhurt. Sixty frontiersmen assembled the next morning and pursued the Native Americans for 2 or 3 miles before they discovered the tribesmen had separated into small parties. They then gave up the pursuit.

★ Soon after the Native Americans left Rice's fort, they moved across the hills in different directions and in detached parties. One of these parties saw four men heading toward Rice's fort, ambushed them and killed two of them on the first fire. The other two fled hastily. One escaped. The other, not so fast a runner and closely pursued by one of the braves, was in danger of being captured. He turned around to fire. His rifle flashed in the pan and he resumed running. He tried to shoot again but misfired. His pursuer hurled a tomahawk at his head but missed. The chase resumed. The Native American soon caught up and grabbed hold of his prey's belt. Tied in a bow-knot, the belt came loose. The white man tried his gun again. It fired. The warrior fell dead at his feet.[27]

★ Sergeant Edward Lee (d. 1782) and Private Robert Caruthers were on a scouting mission out of Fort Rice on Thursday, October 24, 1782, when a party of concealed Native Americans fired upon them about 2 miles away from the fort. Sergeant Lee was killed on the spot and Private Caruthers was taken prisoner.[28]

Westmoreland County see the Pennsylvania chapter in *The Guide to the American Revolutionary War in Pennsylvania, Delaware, Maryland, Virginia and North Carolina.*

11
KENTUCKY

Kentucky was part of the colony of Virginia during the American War of Independence. After the defeat of the French in the Seven Years War [French and Indian War (1756–1763)], the French ceded to Great Britain their land claims east of the Mississippi River. With the French no longer a threat, some pioneers began settling west of the Allegheny Mountains on lands claimed by Virginia. These lands later became part of West Virginia and Kentucky.

The Proclamation of 1763 forbade all new settlement west of the Appalachian Mountains to avoid provoking a war with the Native Americans in the Ohio Valley. The Iroquois transferred to the colonists all their land claims in northern and eastern Kentucky in the Treaty of Fort Stanwix (November 1768). The Cherokees gave up their claims to the same region in the Hard Labor Treaty later the same year. The people of Virginia and Pennsylvania now thought that these treaties eliminated all restrictions to westward expansion.

Land speculators in North Carolina formed a group called the Transylvania Company in August 1774 and appointed Judge Richard Henderson (1734–1785) to head it. The Transylvania Company bought a large area of present-day Tennessee and Kentucky from the Cherokees on March 17, 1775 in the Treaty of Sycamore Shoals. Daniel Boone (1734–1820), working for the Transylvania Company, blazed a trail from Virginia to the Kentucky River, across the mountains at Cumberland Gap, to open this land to settlement. This Wilderness Road became the main route for the new settlements and remained a portion of the major link between settlements in East and Middle Tennessee.

The Virginia General Assembly met in Williamsburg in October 1776 to discuss its jurisdiction over the region. Richard Henderson (1742–1814) and George Rogers Clark (1752–1818) argued in favor of granting Kentucky its independence, but Thomas Jefferson (1743–1826) and other delegates proposed to incorporate Kentucky into Virginia. The General Assembly created Kentucky County on December 7, 1776 and established Harrodsburg as the seat of government. (Kentucky became a state only in 1792.) The General Assembly also authorized the shipment of several hundred pounds of gunpowder and lead. George Rogers Clark was appointed major in command of the Kentucky Militia on March 5, 1777 with John Todd (1750–1782), James Harrod (1742–1793), Benjamin Logan (1743–1802) and Daniel Boone (1734–1820) captains at the forts at Harrodsburg, Logan's and Boonesborough (see Photo KY-1).

The settlements had a total of 121 men available to bear arms to protect 280 settlers. Harrodsburg was the largest with 40 families and 84 men at arms. Logan's Station was the smallest with a force of 15. Boonesborough had 22 men to defend 10 to 15 families, including about a dozen adult women, 30 children and 10 to 15 slaves. The terms "fort" and "station" were used synonymously in the 18th century.[1]

British officials planned an offensive against Kentucky in the spring of 1777 and formed various alliances with the northwestern tribes to combat the pioneers. Lieutenant Governor of Canada, Henry Hamilton (1734?–1796) (The "Hair Buyer"), asserting that the British forces needed to defeat the settlers in this region before they could assist the eastern armies, encouraged the Mingoes, Wyandots and Shawnees to attack the Kentucky settlements.[2]

KY-1 Boonesborough was constructed by Daniel Boone in 1775. This illustration is drawn from Pioneer Life in the West Comprising the Adventures of Boone Kenton Brady, Clarke the Whetzels, and others, in their Fierce Encounters with the Indians. *Philadelphia: John E. Potter & Company, [1858].*

The Kentucky Historical Society [100 West Broadway, Frankfort, KY 40601 (phone: 502-564-1792) website: **history.ky.gov/**] administers the Kentucky Historical Highway Marker Program and sells the guide, *Roadside History: A Guide to Kentucky Highway Markers* (University Press of Kentucky, 2002) and other books. The Kentucky Department of Tourism [Capitol Plaza Tower, 22nd floor, 500 Mero Street, Frankfort, KY 40601 (phone: 502-564-4930) website: **www.kentuckytourism .com**] provides tourism information by phone and online.

See the map of Kentucky.

Mount Olivet

Blue Licks (Dec. 25, 1776; Feb. 8, 1778; August 19, 1782)

The 100-acre Blue Licks Battlefield State Park (website: **parks.ky.gov/parks/ resortparks/blue_licks/**) is near Mount Olivet, Kentucky, on route US 68 at the crossing of the Licking River near the village of Blue Lick Springs in Nicholas County. It is the site of the first and last Revolutionary War engagements fought in Kentucky. The park covers most of the battlefield and offers beautiful scenery and marked landmarks of the battle. A granite obelisk commemorates those who died in the conflict and are interred in the burial grounds. It was dedicated on August 19,

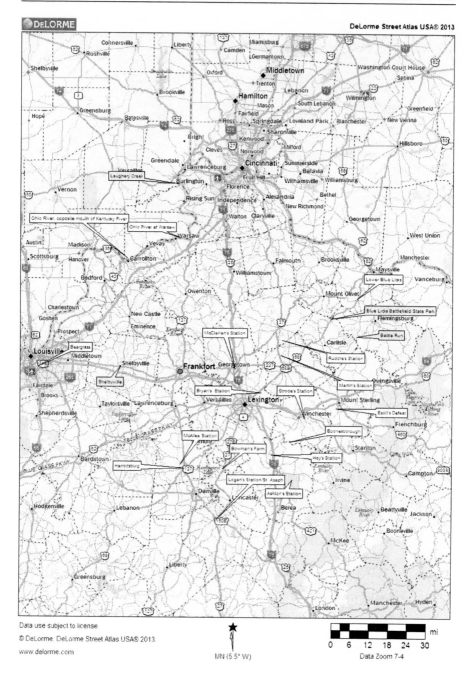

Kentucky: Map for The Guide to the American Revolutionary War in the Deep South and on the Frontier

© *2013 DeLorme (www.delorme.com) Street Atlas USA*®

1928 and bears a statement by Daniel Boone: "So valiantly did our small party fight, that, to the memory of those who unfortunately fell in the battle, enough of honor cannot be paid." A museum displays Native American and pioneer relics, bones of prehistoric animals found nearby, old gun and glassware collections and a small relief model of the field. It also shows a 10-minute audiovisual program. Recreational facilities include campsites, picnic areas, a playground and a community pool.

Lower Blue Licks is the present town of Mays Lick about 11 miles northeast of the Blue Licks Battlefield State Park.

Mingoes under their chief, Captain Pluggy (Tecanyaterighto, Plukkemehnotee) (d. 1776), attacked Colonel John Todd (1750–1782) and his militia at the Lower Blue Licks on Wednesday, December 25, 1776, as they sought gunpowder brought to Kentucky. Todd lost two men killed and two wounded.[3]

★ On Thursday, January 1, 1778, Daniel Boone (1734–1820) and a party of 30 men from Boonesborough went to the Blue Licks on the Licking River to make salt for the different garrisons in the country to preserve any game brought in by hunters or the little available pork and beef. A band of two Frenchmen and more than 100 Shawnees under Chief Blackfish (Cot-ta-wa-ma-go or Mkah-day-way-may-qua) (ca. 1729–1779), on their way to Boonesborough, captured Boone and 27 of his men as they made salt on Sunday, February 8, 1778. The other three men had already returned home with a supply of salt. Knowing it was impossible for them to escape, Boone ordered his men not to resist and to surrender themselves. They were taken to Chillicothe, the principal Indian town, on the Little Miami River, where they arrived on February 18, after an uncomfortable journey in very bad weather. The Shawnees were well equipped, indicating that they were supplied by the British who probably also encouraged or organized them. They treated Boone and his men well.[4]

On Tuesday, March 10, 40 Shawnees took Boone and 10 of his men to Detroit where they arrived on March 30. The Shawnees exhibited their great prize but refused to turn him over to Governor Henry Hamilton (d. 1796) (The "Hair Buyer") who offered them £100. Boone was eventually trusted to hunt on his own and gained the complete confidence of his captors.[5]

★ British captain William Caldwell (1763–1849) and Simon Girty (1741–1818) led a band of Loyalists and Native Americans against Wheeling, in what is now West Virginia, in July 1782. They then attempted a surprise raid on the unprotected outpost settlement of Bryan's Station, 6 miles northeast of modern Lexington, Kentucky, on the Elkhorn River, on Friday, August 16. After two days of futile fighting, Caldwell began a slow retreat northeast to the Ohio border. He and his men made it easy for the Kentuckians to follow their trail.

Daniel Boone (1734–1820), Benjamin Logan (1743–1802) and about 180 frontiersmen started converging on Bryan's Station a few hours after Caldwell had left. The Kentucky volunteers rode in pursuit of Caldwell's and Girty's force until dawn Monday, August 19, 1782. They stopped to rest 4 miles from the lower Blue Licks, about 40 miles from Bryan's Station, when they saw about 30 Native Americans in plain view. The remaining force of 50 Butler's Rangers [a Loyalist regiment recruited and commanded by John Butler (1728–1796)], and more than 300 Wyandot, Ottawa, Ojibwa, Shawnee, Mingo and Delaware warriors hid in the dense ravines, ready for an ambush. Lieutenant

Colonel John Todd (1750–1782) asked Daniel Boone his opinion. Boone knew the area well and sensed an ambush. He replied:

> You see the Indians have shown themselves on the hill beyond the river, loitering, as if to invite pursuit—there are two ravines there, filled with brush and timber for their protection; it is not wise to heedlessly run into the trap set for us.

Boone advocated waiting until Logan arrived with a large force, but if the men insisted on fighting, he suggested that half of them should cross the Licking River several miles north as high as a small creek called Elk and cross over to a ridge outside a ravine on the right. The other half of the troops would occupy the high ground north of the Licks, ready to co-operate with the right wing to flank the enemy and to prevent a possible ambush. The ford was narrow, but the water was deep and fast. Ravines and cliffs surrounded the north and sides, making it the worst possible place to launch an attack.

At a council of war (see cover photo), some of the men were convinced the Native Americans were on the run and could be defeated. If they waited, they might be attacked. Some accused Boone of cowardice. Major Hugh McGary (1744–1806) called out, "Those who are not cowards follow me; I will show them where the Indians are." He spurred his horse into the river, leading an advance party of about 25 men.

Boone commanded the left with about 70 men, including his son Israel Boone (1759–1782), Todd took the center and Lieutenant Colonel Stephen Trigg (1742–1782) commanded the right. The three divisions advanced about a mile and came within 60 yards of the enemy before the first shot was fired about 7:30 AM. The blistering volley from the woods left only McGary and two other men in the vanguard alive. Trigg and his men were annihilated. A few minutes later, the middle line collapsed.

Todd wrote later: "Several efforts were made to rally, but all in vain. . . . Our men suffered much in the retreat, many Indians having mounted our men's horses, having open woods to pass through to the river, and several were killed in the river."

The 15-minute battle cost the frontiersmen about 70 men killed and seven captured, including Daniel Boone's son, Israel. Logan's force had proceeded 6 miles beyond Bryan's Station when it encountered the first band of men fleeing from the battle. Logan and his men prepared to fight, but they only encountered more survivors.

Logan returned to the Lower Blue Licks on August 24, 1782 with 470 men. Boone recalled the event to his biographer, John Filson (ca. 1747–1788), the following year:

> Being reinforced, we returned to bury the dead, and found their bodies strewed every where, cut and mangled in a dreadful manner. This mournful scene exhibited a horror almost unparalleled: Some torn and eaten by wild beasts; those in the river eaten by fishes; all in such a putrefied condition that none could be distinguished from another.

Many settlers returned East after the battle. Boone wrote to the governor of Virginia on August 30 for an additional 500 militiamen to defend the frontier.[6]

Battle Run, below Blue Licks (ca. March 10, 1782)

Battle Run is about 10 miles southeast of Blue Licks Battlefield State Park and east of the Clay Wildlife Management Area.

A party of Native Americans raided Hoy's Station as a trick to draw the men away from other forts and settlements. They ambushed Captain John Holder (1744–1797) and 63 militiamen at Battle Run. The skirmish left one militiaman dead and three wounded.[7]

Upper Blue Licks (August 14, 1782)

A highway marker at the junction of routes KY 36 & 57 in Moorefield, in Nicholas County, Kentucky, about 7 miles southwest of Battle Run, tells the story of the event that occurred about 6 miles northeast.

Captain John Holder (1744–1797) and 17–20 militiamen pursued some Wyandots who had captured two boys, Jones Hoy and Jack Calloway, at Major Hoy's station near Boonesborough on Monday, August 12, 1782. The party overtook the Native Americans on Great Salt Creek (Licking River) on August 14, 1782. The Wyandots outnumbered Holder and defeated him, killing four of his men and wounding another. He withdrew without the boys. Hoy was held captive for seven years, Calloway not so long.

Georgetown
McClellan's (McClelland's) Station (Dec. 29, 1776)

McClellan's Station was in Georgetown in the area bounded by Dudley Avenue, Jackson Street, Military Street and Clayton Avenue.

Hinkston's Station was abandoned in July 1776. Its inhabitants moved closer to Harrodsburg and erected a small fort, known as McClellan's Station, on Elk Horn. The fortress was built and occupied by John McClelland (d. 1776) and his family; Colonel Robert Patterson (1753–1827); William (1750–1823), (1750–1807), (1751–1831), or (1755–1793); Francis (1754–1833) and Andrew McConnell (1730–1782); David Perry (1752–1789); Stephen Lowry (1760–1796) and others from Pennsylvania. Logan's Station was not completed and occupied as a fort until February 1777, some time after McClellan's had been abandoned.[8]

George Rogers Clark (1752–1818) had planned to go to Kentucky by way of the Wilderness Road until he learned that the gunpowder procured from Virginia was still stored at Fort Pitt. He retrieved the powder and proceeded down the Ohio River with his party of eight, despite information that Britain's Native American allies intended to ambush them. When they saw signs of Native American presence, they feared an ambush and buried the gunpowder on the Three Islands, a well-known landmark on the river near the mouth of Limestone Creek, near the present site of Maysville.

They brought their boats ashore further down river and took the buffalo road toward Harrodsburg to organize a rescue expedition. They passed through the Lower Blue Licks and camped at Hinkston's deserted settlement on the South Fork of Licking River (in modern Harrison County). Here, Simon Kenton also known as "Simon Butler" (1755–1836) and three other scouts informed Clark that John Todd's (1750–1782) hunting party was in the area. Kenton suggested that, if the two parties joined forces, they would be strong enough to return for the gunpowder and carry it to Fort Harrod.[9]

With a war party on his trail, Clark doubted that he and Todd could join forces in time to retrieve the gunpowder before the Native Americans found it. Several of his men were tired from the journey downriver and he feared that the Native Americans would overwhelm his small force. He left several men at Hinkston's Station to alert Todd's party while Clark and Kenton went to Harrodsburg for more men.

Todd's hunting party arrived at Hinkson's shortly after Clark's departure. When he learned about the hidden gunpowder, Todd led his and Clark's men—a combined party of 10 men—to retrieve it. They proceeded north along the buffalo road on Christmas Day 1776, crossed the Licking River and went on to Limestone Creek.

Near the Lower Blue Licks, they encountered a small group of 40 to 50 Wyandots, Mingoes (western Senecas living on the Scioto River) and renegades from the Shawnees. They were led by a Captain Pluggy (Tecanyaterighto, Plukkemehnotee) (d. 1776), a noted warrior, who was an enemy of the Virginians since Lord Dunmore's War. He was also the one who had ambushed Daniel Boone's party in 1773 and killed his son James. Chief Pluggy wanted the gunpowder badly. He followed Todd to McClellan's Station and attacked it on December 29, 1776. The assault against the 20 defenders continued for several hours until Chief Pluggy was killed and his party retreated. McClelland and two other white men were killed and several wounded. Joseph Rogers (1741–1834), Clark's young cousin, and Josiah Dixon (1750–1834) were captured. Todd escaped with his remaining men and hurried to inform Clark.

After this attack, Colonel James Harrod (1742–1793) and 30 men from Fort Harrod went for the gunpowder. Most of them had come to Harrodsburg by traveling down the Ohio River to Limestone Creek, so they were familiar with the wide buffalo trail that led across the forks of the Licking River into Kentucky. Harrod's party set out for Limestone Creek on Thursday, January 2, 1777. They marched along the buffalo road, passed Mc-Clellan's Station and the Lower Blue Licks (the present town of Mays Lick), turned off the road to the right and reached the Ohio River near the mouth of Cabin Creek.

Harrod's men dug up the kegs of gunpowder and loaded them on the horses. Harrod planned to return by way of the Shawnee war road which ran roughly parallel to the buffalo road from the mouth of Cabin Creek to the Licking River and the Upper Blue Licks. However, Kenton had scouted the area while the others loaded the gunpowder He noticed danger signs along the war road and suggested going several miles down the Ohio, cutting through the woods and taking the buffalo trace farther inland. In so doing, they avoided a possible attack by Pluggy's retreating warriors and arrived at Fort Harrod safely with the gunpowder where, Clark relates, they were greeted with "universal joy".

After moving the wounded, the settlers abandoned McClellan's Station, the last outpost north of the Kentucky River, and fled to Harrodsburg.[10]

Harrodsburg, Mercer County and vicinity

Harrodsburg (March 5, 1777; March 7, 1777; summer 1777; late summer 1777; late May 1778)

> Harrodsburg is about 28 miles southwest of Lexington. The location of the fort is at Old Fort Harrod State Park (website:**parks.ky.gov/parks/recreationparks/fort-harrod/**), West Lexington and Fort Streets in Harrodsburg. The fort, which consists of blockhouses (see Photo GA-1) and cabins connected by a 12-foot-high palisade (see Photo GA-14), has been reconstructed on a slightly reduced scale. The enclosure contains the original spring which still flows.

Chief Blackfish (Cot-ta-wa-ma-go or Mkah-day-way-may-qua) (ca. 1729–1779) and a party of 47 Shawnees attacked 17-year old James Ray (1760–1835), his younger brother, and another man as they surveyed and cleared some land 4 miles from Harrodsburg on Wednesday March 5, 1777. They killed the younger Ray and took the third man prisoner. James Ray escaped by running away. His running skill was so remarkable that

Blackfish mentioned to Boone the following year, after taking him prisoner at the Blue Licks, that some boy had outrun all his warriors at Harrodsburg.

Ray alerted the settlers at Harrodsburg who strengthened the fort and prepared for an attack. The Shawnees waited until the morning of March 7, 1777 to attack the fort. They set fire to an out cabin on the east side of the town. The settlers, not believing this to be the act of the enemy, rushed out of the fort to extinguish the flames. The Shawnees tried to ambush them as they returned, but the settlers retreated to the woods covering a hill. Each man took to a tree ("treed" as it was termed in the language of the times).

Hugh McGary (1744–1806) noticed a Shawnee wearing the hunting shirt of his dead stepson whose mutilated body he found a few days earlier. McGary hacked the man's body to pieces in a mad rage and fed the pieces to his dogs. McGary was wounded in the confrontation. They settlers lost one man killed, one captured and four wounded, one of whom died. They retreated to the fort, and the Shawnees withdrew.

★ During the summer of 1777, James Ray (1760–1835) and a friend by the name of McConnel (d. 1777) were target shooting when McConnel was suddenly shot dead. Ray spotted the enemy and tried to avenge his friend's death when he suddenly found himself attacked by a large body of Shawnees who had crept up unseen. Ray was exposed to their fire for a distance of 150 yards as he ran back to the fort. When he reached the stockade, the inhabitants did not dare to open the gate to let him in. Ray's only alternative was to throw himself flat on the ground behind a stump which was just large enough to protect his body. He lay in this position for four hours, under fire which occasionally sprayed him with dirt. Yet, the Shawnees did not attempt to move closer where they might come in firing range of the fort. Ray hollered out, "for God's sake dig a hole under the cabin wall, and take me in." The suggestion was adopted immediately and Ray managed to enter the fort.[11]

★ While Squire Boone (1760–1817), Daniel's nephew, was at Harrodsburg in the late summer of 1777, the fort came under sniper fire. Squire and a small company went out "to hunt Indians." Boone stooped to examine some tracks in the dust when he heard someone call "Boone come up!" When he turned in the direction of the voice, he heard another voice from the opposite direction. When he turned back, he got shot. The ball shattered one of his ribs.

A while later, when he had not yet fully recovered from his wound, Squire Boone and a small group were ambushed in a cornfield. Boone squatted in the grass to return fire when the man aside of him fell over upon him, dead. The sniper who fired the fatal shot rushed to claim the scalp. He did not see Squire lying beneath the body. When the killer came within a few feet, Squire jumped up and drew his sword, catching the attacker by surprise. The Shawnee swung his club, cutting a deep gash across Squire's forehead. Squire grabbed the Shawnee's belt with one hand and ran his sword completely through the man's abdomen with the other. The Shawnee tried to draw the knife from Squire's belt but could not get a firm grip on the handle because of the blood gushing from both of their wounds. They held on to each other until the Shawnee finally collapsed backward and fell on the point of the sword, snapping it. Squire declared it was "the best little Indian fight he ever was in . . . both men stood and fought so well."

★ Squire Boone was still recovering from his wound when Chief Blackfish (Cot-ta-wa-ma-go or Mkah-day-way-may-qua) (ca. 1729–1779) launched a second series of attacks on all of the forts in late May 1778.[12]

A party from Harrodburg went out to hunt for horses that had strayed when they spotted fresh signs of Native American presence. They took shelter in a nearby abandoned cabin. Despite the cold and damp, they did not build a fire in the fireplace so as not to reveal their position. They climbed into the loft for greater warmth and safety. There, they stretched out on the floor with their weapons aside of them to wait for nightfall.

A short while later, they heard somebody approaching the cabin. Six well-armed Native Americans entered, placed their weapons in a corner and built a fire. When one of the white men in the loft rolled over to see how many men were below, his two companions each grabbed an arm and tried to keep him quiet. One of the poles broke in the struggle and the men fell among the Native Americans who were so surprised and terrified that they ran from the house yelling, without stopping to pick up their weapons.

The equally astonished white men gathered their trophies and returned home. The incident has since been called "The Battle of the Boards."[13]

Stanford

Logan's Station (May 20, 1777; Sept. 1777)

Logan's Station or Fort (website: **www.logansfort.org**), also known as St. Asaph was in Stanford, about 19 miles southeast of Harrodsburg. It was in the area bounded by Portman Avenue, Lancaster Street and Maxwell Street, about 0.25 miles north of Saint Asaph Creek. Logan's Station protected 34 people, 13 of them men. They had a small supply of ammunition with little hope of getting more from the surrounding settlements.

The log fort was 90 by 150 feet set on a slight elevation about 50 yards west of the smaller spring at St. Asaph. Gates were located at each end and were raised and lowered by leather thongs. The main gate faced east. There were two blockhouses (see Photo GA-1), one on each end of the south side with three cabins between. The north side had only one blockhouse (on the northwest corner) with four adjoining cabins. The northeast corner was the only corner without a blockhouse.

About 100 Native Americans surrounded Logan's Fort on May 20, 1777. Some of them may have been among those who had recently attacked Boonesborough (see Photo KY-1). They hid in the thick cane which surrounded the fort and waited until the end of the day when the women went outside the fort to milk their cows, guarded by some of the men. The attackers suddenly fired on the settlers, killing one and wounding two others, one of them mortally. All the women and the rest of the men got back into the fort safely. They left one of the wounded outside, thinking he was dead. Benjamin Logan (1743–1802) immediately tried to form a small party to take him into the fort, but nobody was willing to accompany him. Logan rushed outside, took the wounded man into his arms and carried him into the fort under heavy fire which struck the palisades (see Photo GA-14) near his head as he entered the gate.

The Native Americans continued to besiege the little fort until the supply of ammunition was almost exhausted. The defenders met (see cover Photo) to decide whether to surrender or send to Holston for a fresh supply of powder and lead. Logan and two others volunteered to go to Holston to procure supplies. They left the fort at night and took unusual paths through the woods to avoid detection. They reached Holston safely and procured the necessary powder and lead. Logan returned to the fort alone after an absence of less than 10 days. His companions brought the ammunition and reached the fort safely a short while later.

The Native Americans lacked both the skill to carry on a regular siege and the discipline to assault the fort. They observed it closely for more than three months which distressed the occupants.

★ Colonel John Bowman (d. 1780) and 100 Virginia militiamen headed toward Logan's Fort in the beginning of September. He sent a detachment ahead of the main body. A band of Native Americans attacked the detachment and killed several of them. The rest arrived at the fort safely. Their arrival dispersed the besiegers to the great relief of the garrison.

Benjamin Logan (1743–1802), William Whitley (1749–1813) and other members of the settlement at St. Asaph's brought their wives and children to Fort Harrod in September 1777 for protection while they completed the stockade which became known as Logan's Station.[14]

Bowman's Farm (Sept. 11, 1777)

Bowman's Farm was along the west bank of the Kentucky River about 12 miles east of Harrodsburg.

The harvest in the autumn of 1777 produced little food. One of the rangers in Captain Joseph Bowman's (1740–1818) company testified that "he was allowed but one single pint of Corn per day, and that he had to grind himself of a hand mill. The balance of the time he had nothing furnished him but meat, [for] there was nothing else." Most of the cattle had been destroyed and the settlers had few dairy products to supplement their meager supply of corn. By the end of the year, the situation had become so desperate that some of the women followed the cattle around to observe what they ate. They would then boil the same greens with a piece of salt pork.

On Thursday, September 11, 1777, as a company of Captain Joseph Bowman's Virginia militia was shelling corn, they were attacked by a band of Native Americans that killed one and wounded six.[15]

Captain Bowman wrote his superiors at Fort Pitt, alerting them to his plight and begging for a shipment of corn. He told them the people were surviving on provisions taken from the woods, and that they could not get meat because they had almost no salt "for curing the provisions of the garrison." Without salt to preserve their food, they had to hunt constantly which depleted the supply of game, wasted ammunition and increased exposure to attack.

He also wrote that although "bountiful Nature hath plentifully furnished this country with salt springs, by reason of the incursions of the different nations of Indians this year past, we have been prevented from making what quantities would be necessary for ourselves and families." As the situation approached the point of crisis, Daniel Boone (1734–1820) agreed to lead a party of men to the lower salt springs on the Licking River, during the first week of January 1778, to make salt for the Kentucky settlements.[16]

McAfee Station (May 4, 1781)

McAfee Station was about 1.5 miles northwest of Harrodsburg along the west shore of the Salt River, at the mouth of Town Creek.

A band of Native Americans attacked McAfee Station about a half hour or an hour after sunrise on Friday, May 4, 1781 (some accounts put it on May 9). There were fewer than 20 men in the station at the time. About 150 warriors spent the previous night at a cabin and corn crib built by James McCoun, Jr. (1745–1790), near a spring on the west side of the Salt River about three quarters of a mile south of the station. The next morning, they surrounded McAfee Station, concentrating mostly on the east and south sides and expected an easy victory.

Samuel McAfee (1748–1801) and a man by the name of Isaac Clunendike (d. 1781) took a horse and a bag to go get some corn three quarters of a mile south. Meanwhile, Robert (1745–1795) and James McAfee (1736–1811) went to clear some ground for a turnip patch about 150 yards from the station. They set their weapons against a tree near where they worked.

About a quarter of a mile down the road, Samuel McAfee and Clunendike went down into a hollow where they came under fire. Clunendike fell dead. His horse ran to the station. Samuel McAfee tried to escape, but a huge Native American blocked his path before he had taken 10 or 15 steps. The two ran toward each other with their muskets level. Within a few feet of each other, both attempted to fire at the same time. The Native American's weapon flashed as he fell. McAfee jumped over his body and escaped.

Robert and James McAfee heard the gunfire, grabbed their weapons and started toward it. James McAfee saw seven warriors emerge from behind a brush heap and fire at him. He sought shelter behind a tree, but he soon faced six or seven other muskets from another direction that shot up the dirt near his feet. He then ran into the station.

Meanwhile, Robert met his brother Samuel who told him that Clunendike had been shot. He continued until he saw some Native Americans scalping him. He looked around and found the warriors had blocked his path, so he ran into the woods with a brave in hot pursuit.

He returned to the station where the Native Americans approached from every direction. Finding that they had little effect on the station, the Native Americans began killing the horses and cattle running round the houses.

Only one man was slightly wounded in the almost incessant firing. The firing began to slacken about 10 AM when Hugh McGary (1744–1806) arrived. He heard firing in the distance and gathered a party of about 45 riflemen in Harrodsburg. They raced to McAfee's, yelling and whooping louder than the Native Americans who fled with McGary's and McAfee's men in pursuit.[17]

★ The Native Americans crossed the ford of the river south of the station and killed one man and wounded another. The pursuers overtook the main body of Native Americans at James McCoun, Jr.'s (1745–1790) cabins on the west side of Salt River, about a mile below the station, where they had camped the night before.

The conflict resumed. The warriors fired from behind trees as they retreated. Two of them were killed. The others were pursued for several miles, as far as Lyons Run, where they dispersed and could be followed no farther. McAfee's station suffered little violence after this attack.

Boonesborough (March 6, 1777; April 15, 1777; April 24–27, 1777; May 23–25, 1777; early June, 1777; July 4, 1777; Aug. 11–20, 1777; Sept. 7, 1778; March 8, 1780; summer 1780)

Daniel Boone (1734–1820) began constructing a stockade and fort in 1775 at what would become known as Boonesborough (He completed it in April 1775. The settlement is located in Fort Boonesborough State Park (website: **parks.ky.gov/parks/ recreationparks/fort-boonesborough/**) which is accessible from route KY 627

(Boonesborough Road) in Richmond, about 16 miles southeast of Lexington (see Photo KY-1). Boonesborough was the site of repeated attacks by Native Americans during the American War of Independence in 1777 and 1780, but the most notable attack was a two-week siege in September 1778.

On Thursday, March 6, 1777, the day after Daniel Boone (1734–1820) had been appointed to command the fort and less than a week after the organization of the feeble militia of Kentucky County, Chief Blackfish (Cot-ta-wa-ma-go or Mkah-day-way-may-qua) (ca. 1729–1779) and 200 Shawnee warriors began harassing the settlement and lurking around the fort. Simon Kenton (1755–1836), known then by his assumed name of "Simon Butler," was also hiding near the fort at this time. The six-feet tall, 21-year old adventurer tried to warn the occupants of their danger. Rather than attempt to enter the station in the daytime, he waited until nightfall. He got in safely but not in time to avert a tragedy. The defenders made the frequent mistake of confusing a small band for the entire force. They rushed out of the fort to attack the Shawnees only to find a much larger group hidden nearby. Two of the occupants were ambushed and killed as they went toward the stockade.[18]

★ The Shawnees, who had shortly before retired from Harrodstown, tried unsuccessfully to destroy the fort at Boonesborough on Tuesday, April 15, 1777. The fort had only 22 guns compared with Chief Blackfish's (Cot-ta-wa-ma-go or Mkah-day-way-may-qua) (ca. 1729–1779) 100. The Native Americans fought for two days before withdrawing, but they remained in the forest cutting off all stragglers and keeping the settlers confined to the fort.[19]

★ Less than 10 days later, between April 24 and 27, 40 to 50 Shawnees besieged the Boonesborough stockade again. They attacked and tomahawked a man working near the gate and feigned a retreat. Boone pursued them with 10 men and suddenly found himself cut off from the fort. Boone and his men were overwhelmed and had to charge back to the gate. Seven of them were wounded, including Boone who broke his ankle leading the charge. He had to be carried inside by Simon Kenton (1755–1836), also known as "Simon Butler," who was struck down twice by Shawnees who tried to kill Boone.[20]

★ As the men worked in the cornfields at Boonesborough on Friday, May 23, 1777, a guard noticed sunlight flashing on a musket barrel in the woods on Hackberry Ridge. He alerted the others who fled into the fort. The Shawnees besieged the fort for two days, wounding three men and butchering most of the cattle before departing. The loss of the cattle was felt severely.[21]

★ A party of 18 men went from Boonesborough to the Ohio River in pursuit of a band of Native Americans in early June 1777. They killed one of the Native Americans and headed home. Along the way, they surprised and scattered another party of 30 Native Americans. They arrived safely back at Boonesborough with only one man wounded. A little later, the 200 Native Americans took revenge and besieged the fort for the fourth time in a year. They kept up the siege for two days and nights. They made a lot of noise but were unsuccessful in taking the fort.[22]

★ A party of Native Americans set out for the Scioto salt licks early in June 1777, taking Daniel Boone (1734–1820) with them. They went to make salt; but, when they finished and headed back, the Shawnees prevented Boone from escaping. Four hundred and fifty armed warriors were waiting at Chillicothe ready to march against Boonesborough. Held captive, Captain Boone acquired information of great importance to his garrison. He was determined to convey that information to save the garrison from destruction.

Boone watched for his chance to escape and managed to do so one day in mid-June. When he arose at his usual time in the morning of June 16, he went out, apparently to hunt, but he grabbed a horse and headed for Boonesborough instead. He rode as fast as he could until the horse collapsed. He then continued on foot, covering 160 miles in four days. He stopped only once to shoot and roast some buffalo meat.

He arrived at Boonesborough on Friday, June 20, and brought word of the impending attack. The inhabitants set to work repairing the fort which was in a bad state of defense. They gathered supplies and recruited more men from the already thin forces at nearby Harrodsburg and Logan's Station and waited impatiently for the enemy.

A few days later, another prisoner escaped from the Shawnees and brought news "that the Indians had, on account of Boone's elopement, postponed their march for three weeks." Chief Blackfish (Cot-ta-wa-ma-go or Mkah-day-way-may-qua) (ca. 1729–1779) had spies in the country, observing the activities at the different garrisons which had been strengthened since the last attacks. Most of the garrisons, particularly Boonesborough, had also increased in numbers.

Chief Blackfish and his warriors struck the garrisons through the summer, alternating between Boonesborough, Harrodsburg and Logan's. As they had no artillery, they could not breach the defenses of the forts. They usually stayed for only a day or two at a time, killing or capturing scouts and hunters and destroying the settlers' crops and killing or scattering their livestock. They also tomahawked or scalped people leaving the fort to gather corn or cattle. Food became scarce, and the number of able-bodied fighting men dwindled.

★ Encouraged by British officials, some 200 Native Americans besieged Fort Boonesborough on Friday, July 4, 1777. They hid in the tall corn growing in front of the fort. Daniel Boone (1734–1820), still recovering from his wound, was on a crutch, directing his men behind the stockade wall. The attackers kept up their fire for two days, killing one man and wounding two others. They burned the cornfields and the cabins in the hollow before withdrawing. Although this attack was the last of Blackfish's 1777 campaign, the settlers remained on their guard through the fall.[23]

★ As the settlers of Boonesborough anxiously awaited another attack, Captain Daniel Boone (1734–1820) and a company of 19 men left the fort on Friday, August 1, 1777, and headed north, intending to surprise the town of Paitcrek on the Scioto. About 4 miles from the town, they met a party of 30 warriors marching to join the army heading toward Boonesborough from Chillicothe. The two parties clashed. Boone and his men put the Native American warriors to flight, killing one and wounding two. Boone had only one man wounded. He captured three horses and all the enemy plunder. He then sent out two spies who reported that the town was evacuated.

Boone returned hastily to Boonesborough, hoping to arrive before the Shawnees. He passed their main force on the sixth day and arrived safely the following day. On the eighth day, Wednesday, September 7, 1778, Captain Duquesne, 11 French Canadians, Chief Blackfish (Cot-ta-wa-ma-go or Mkah-day-way-may-qua) (ca. 1729–1779), Chief Black Hoot and Chief Blackbird (Wash-ing-guhsah-ba) (ca. 1750–1800) of the Chippewas, Chief Moluntha or Malunthy (ca. 1692–1786) and 400 warriors and an interpreter, an African American named Pompey, appeared around Boonesborough. This was the largest force ever to besiege Boonesborough and was intended to alarm the garrison.

Chief Blackfish requested a council and chided Captain Boone for running away. He tried to persuade Boone to return and to bring the people of Boonesborough to live with the British. Captain Duquesne demanded that Boone surrender the fort in the name of his Britannic Majesty. Boone maintained his composure and requested two days' consideration which was granted. He called the garrison to council (see cover photo), but less than 50 men attended.

After their deliberations, the men unanimously decided: "We are determined to defend our fort as long as a man of us lives." When they adjourned, each man gathered his cattle and horses and secured them inside the fort walls. When the two days had expired, Captain Boone announced, from one of the bastions (see Photo GA-21) of the fort, the determination of his men to defend the garrison.

Disappointed, Captain Duquesne declared that Governor Henry Hamilton's (d. 1796) (The "Hair Buyer") orders were to take the garrison captives, to treat them as prisoners of war and not to rob or destroy them. He requested that nine of the principal persons in the garrison come out to treat with him. He promised to do no violence but to return home with the prisoners. If they swore allegiance to, and accepted the protection of, his Britannic Majesty, he would liberate them.

The apparent ease with which Boone got along with the Shawnees raised some suspicions among the Kentuckians, but Boone realized the value of stalling. While the two sides negotiated in a glade within 60 yards of the fort gate, the people inside the stockade busied themselves trying to give the impression of a large body of defenders. The negotiations continued for several days. The few articles, which required the Kentuckians to acknowledge British rule rather than to move away, were soon drawn up and signed in the presence of many Native Americans. Neither side was sincere.

Boone and his men were told that Native American custom was to shake hands to show their sincerity and seal the bargain. The Native Americans approached each of the nine white men, took his hand and immediately grappled him, intending to drag him off a prisoner. Each man tried to extricate himself and sought safety in the fort. The Native Americans discharged a heavy fire on them, wounding one. The others all escaped unhurt.

The attackers then began to assault the fort. The attack continued for nine days with little intermission. The garrison returned a brisk fire. The exhausted and tense occupants of the stockade began to quarrel among themselves. As water ran low, there was not enough to use for extinguishing fires set by blazing arrows. Courageous men climbed up on the roofs to douse the flames. Pompey, perched at the top of a tall tree, taunted the Kentuckians and sniped at soldiers within the fort. Daniel Boone put an end to that with a well-aimed shot.

Meanwhile, the Shawnees, most likely directed by the Frenchmen who were with them, began to tunnel under the fort. They began to dig a mine in the bank of the river about 60 yards from the river's edge. The defenders discovered the plot when new earth appeared in the stream below the fort. The Kentuckians began to dig an intercepting counter trench deep inside the fort. As they dug the soil, they threw the earth over the fort wall, alerting the attackers that their plan was discovered and would be defeated.

The besiegers stopped work on the mine. Now convinced that they could not take the fort either by force or by stealth, they raised the siege, as their provisions were nearly exhausted. Only two men were killed and four wounded in the fort during the siege. The Native Americans lost 37 killed and many wounded.[24] Nine days after the siege began, a downpour caused the tunnel to cave in and the attackers left during the night.[25]

★ The Shawnees left Boonesborough and its 22 men alone for a while, concentrating their attacks against Harrodsburg (65 men) and Logan's fort or St. Asaphs (15 men). They returned on Wednesday, March 8, 1780, when a band of them attacked Captain

Richard Calloway (1719–1780) near Boonesborough as he, Pemberton Rawlings (or Rollins) (d. 1780), and three African American men constructed a ferry boat on Canoe Ridge, about a mile north of Boonesborough. Shortly after a volley of gunshots, one of the African Americans arrived at the settlement with news of the Shawnee attack that killed Calloway and Captain John Kennedy, Jr. (1753–1780).[26]

Captain John Holder (1744–1797) immediately formed a party of riflemen and galloped to the rescue. They were too late. Calloway was already scalped and robbed of most of his clothing. Rawlings had been shot, tomahawked in the back of the neck and scalped. Although mortally wounded, he was still alive and died before sunset. The other two African Americans were taken prisoners and probably sold into slavery. The Shawnees eluded pursuit.[27]

★ In the summer of 1780, a band of Native Americans surprised Captain James Welch's scouting party northwest of Boone's Station, in what is now Fayette County, as they returned from a scouting expedition. They lost one man killed.[28]

Colonel George Rogers Clark's (1752–1818) preparations for an attack on Detroit, Michigan, spared the Kentucky forts from major attack during the summer of 1781. "But many people had moved away to escape military service, enormous quantities of meat stored for the campaign had spoiled, and the chronic shortage of money, credit and food was everywhere evident. Kentucky had lost almost 50 men killed by Indians in the first four months of the year, including Clark's reliable former officer, William Linn."[29]

Cynthiana, Bourbon County
Ruddle's Station (June 22, 1780)
Martin's Station (June 28, 1780)
Bird's Kentucky Raid

Ruddle's Station (website: **ramsha1780.org/**) was on the east bank of the Licking River, about 4 miles south of modern Cynthiana in Bourbon County. From Cynthiana, take route US 27 (Paris Pike) or TN 982 (New Lair Pike) south. About 0.3 miles before both routes meet south of Lair, Old Lair Pike intersects with New Lair Pike on the west side of the Licking River. Take Old Lair Pike east for about 1.1 miles and turn right (south) on the rural road. Follow it to the end. Ruddle's Station was about 0.3 miles farther, on the east bank of the Licking River.

Martin's Station (website: **ramsha1780.org/**) was about 4.75 miles south of Ruddle's Station. It was on Stoner Creek about 4.3 miles north of Paris. To get there from route US 68 (Millersburg Road) northeast of Paris, take Ruddles Mill Road (TN 1940) north for 2.8 miles and turn left (west) on Peacock Road. Proceed about 1.8 miles where the road forks to the right. Martin's Station was near the end of that fork.

The Crown forces planned a large operation against the Illinois country and Kentucky early in June 1780. The commander at Detroit sent 100 Native Americans and 150 whites under Captain Henry Bird (1764–1858) to take the Falls of the Ohio (Louisville). As they proceeded down the Maumee (Miami) River to the Ohio and up the Licking River to its fork near modern Falmouth, Kentucky, they recruited many more Native Americans increasing their force to 700 warriors.

Instead of going directly to the Falls, they first attacked Ruddle's and Martin's stations, two small forts at the forks of the Licking River. Despite their slow progress and their cutting a trail as they went, the Crown forces still managed to surprise the settlers. When they fired their six cannons at the fort on Tuesday, June 22, 1780, Captain Ruddle surrendered if the attackers promised to protect the prisoners. The Native Americans rushed through the gates and each grabbed a man, woman or child and began to plunder them and their cabins. Captain Bird could no longer control them. They tomahawked one man and two women. They loaded all the others with heavy baggage and forced them to march toward their towns. They tomahawked the weak and those unable to keep up.[30]

★ After the surrender of Ruddle's Station, Captain Henry Bird (1764–1858) headed to Martin's station, about 5 miles south, and captured that fort without resistance on Wednesday, June 28, 1780. Captain Bird lost one officer killed and one warrior wounded. He captured about 350 prisoners, most of them women and children. Here, he managed to keep his prisoners while he allowed the warriors to divide the spoils. He then ordered a retreat, but the Native Americans wanted to attack Lexington and Bryan's station because they had such easy victories. Bird had difficulty dissuading them.

The settlers lived in daily terror of further assaults for weeks afterward. General George Rogers Clark (1752–1818), the commandant at the Falls of the Ohio (Louisville), immediately planned a counterattack. He and his regiment and the armed force of the country headed for Pecaway or Piqua, the principal Shawnee town on a branch of the Great Miami. They arrived about 8 the next morning. They crossed the knee-deep river and had to pass through a dense nettle patch. When they emerged, they faced a body of Native Americans crouched behind a fence of brush surrounding a patch of woods. A brief skirmish ensued but neither side suffered much damage. When the Native Americans ran into the woods, Clark and his men paused to assess the situation.

Clark took his men up an adjacent hill to attack the retreating warriors while Colonel James Harrod (1742–1793) took his company to the side where they hid in the woods to protect the flanks. This was a dangerous position as everyone thought the Native Americans were reorganizing in the woods to prepare for more fighting. One man in Benjamin Logan's (1743–1802) regiment later remarked that he had been "mightily pleased" that the orders had not included his company.

When Harrod's men reached the edge of the woods, a warrior fired, killing one of his men. A general fire ensued from many directions. The Native Americans controlled an area full of ridges which gave them the advantage. Harrod's men advanced up one ridge. The enemy fired briefly and retreated to the next ridge. Harrod's men pushed the Native Americans from tree to tree, and "stand to stand, first in one direction two miles from town, and then in another one."

About 3 PM, the Native Americans ceased firing and retreated to their fort which was a triangular stockade covering about half an acre in the lower part of the town. This was a new structure evidently built for this attack. The men formed a hollow square, while a detachment hurried to bring up an old brass 6-pounder which the Illinois regiment captured at Vincennes. They fired a dozen balls into the fort, splitting the stockade. Then everything became quiet.

As the white men waited for signs of surrender, the Native Americans attacked them from the rear, breaking up their formation and forcing them "to tree." Logan and his men quickly recrossed the river to assist Clark. The Native Americans fled.

As it was getting dark, the Kentuckians camped around the fort. Almost half of them stood guard duty to watch for more surprise attacks. They lost 20 men killed and 40 wounded that day and took 73 scalps and 20 horses.[31]

The following morning, they tended the wounded and buried their dead which occupied them for two days. One of the most seriously wounded was Captain William McAfee (1750–1780). His men carried him to the mouth of the Licking River on a litter and took him by water to friends at Beargrass south of Louisville. He grew weaker by the hour. His wife arrived by his side two days before he died.

The Native Americans had left little behind so provisions were scarce. The weather was hot and sticky, so the men abandoned their objective of attacking Detroit. They burned the town to ashes, destroyed the crops and started home. Their food was so scarce on the return trip that some of them said later that they thought they would all starve.[32]

Carrollton
Ohio River, opposite the mouth of the Kentucky River (Aug. 19, 1780)

> This action occurred in what is now Vevey, Indiana, across the Ohio River from Carrollton, Kentucky.

See the **Indiana** chapter pp. 182–184.

Warsaw
Ohio River at Warsaw
Ohio River, 75 miles upstream from Louisville (July 11, 1781)

> This incident probably occurred just east of the city of Warsaw, Kentucky.

A band of Native Americans attacked Captain Coulson (or Colson) and a band of Virginia militiamen in a boat on the Ohio River on Wednesday, July 11, 1781. They killed four militiamen.[33]

Near Louisville
Beargrass (March 5, 1781)

> Beargrass is about 4 miles south of Louisville.

A band of Shawnees ambushed and killed Colonel William Linn (Lynn) (1734–1781) and captains Abraham Tipton (d. 1781) and John Chapman (d. 1781) at different places at Beargrass, about 4 miles south of Louisville, on Monday, March 5, 1781. Captain Aquilla Whitaker (1755–1824) along with 15 men pursued one of these marauding parties, trailing them to the Ohio River at the foot of the rapids. Supposing the Shawnees had crossed the river, Whitaker and his men embarked in a few canoes to follow them. He was astonished when the Shawnees fired on his company from the rear, killing and wounding nine. The rest of the party landed, attacked and defeated the enemy.[34]

Between Shelbyville and Louisville (April 1781)

Shelbyville is about 27 miles east of Louisville. (Some accounts place this event in September.)

A station settled by Squire Boone (1760–1817) near where Shelbyville now stands, became alarmed by the appearance of Native Americans in April 1781. The inhabitants decided to seek shelter at the stronger settlements on Beargrass. As the men, women and children carted their household goods and drove their cattle to these settlements, a large party of Native Americans overtook them on the road near Long Run, attacked them and inflicted many casualties.[35]

Colonel John Floyd (1751–1783) learned of this disaster and immediately mustered 25 men to punish the Native Americans. He divided his men into two parties and advanced cautiously. However, a party of 200 Native Americans ambushed and defeated him, killing half of his men. The Native Americans only lost nine or 10 killed. As Colonel Floyd retreated on foot, nearly exhausted and closely pursued by the enemy, Captain Samuel Wells (1727–1800), who retained his horse, dismounted and gave it to Floyd, and ran by his side to support him. This action cancelled forever the previous hostility between these officers and "they lived and died friends."[36]

Wickliffe
Fort Jefferson (July 25, 1780–Aug. 1780)

Fort Jefferson was established in 1780 on the Mississippi River 5 miles south of the junction with the Ohio River. It was a wooden structure about 100 yards from the bank of Mayfield Creek south of Wickliffe. It was about 100 feet square with two bastions (see Photo GA-21), one in the northeast corner and the other in the southwest.

See the map of Illinois, Indiana and Missouri.

Fort Jefferson was built on the lands of the Chickasaws and Choctaws without their consent. Despite instructions from the Governor of Virginia, the purchase was never made. The Chickasaws and Choctaws made a full scale attack on Fort Jefferson at daybreak on Tuesday, July 25, 1780 while settlers were at work in the fields. When the 300 warriors emerged from the forests, the settlers raced toward the fort. The guards fired their muskets at the Chickasaws and Choctaws as the settlers rushed to the fort, but many of the settlers were killed by arrows, hatchet and war club. The garrison, under the command of Captain Robert George (1756–1837), consisted of less than 30 men, two-thirds of whom were sick with the ague (malaria) and fever.

The attack lasted two weeks before the main army of Chickasaws arrived under the command of James Whitehead, of the British Southern Indian Department. [Most accounts say the commander was Captain James Logan Colbert (1720–1784), a Scot.] The Chickasaws camped on the island opposite the fort, just above Mayfield's Creek, and blockaded the fort without approaching within cannon-shot. They burned crops and cabins near the fort and destroyed livestock to starve out the fort's occupants. Unable to sustain themselves, a number of soldiers and settlers began to die from malnutrition. Seventeen victims were buried inside the fort.

Private Jack Ashe and a friendly Native American slipped out of the fort one night and made their way up the Mississippi River to Kaskaskia, over the next four days, hoping to get reinforcements. Captain George met with James Whitehead, under a flag of truce, on the sixth day. They agreed upon the terms of surrender in which the settlers acknowledged that the Chickasaws and Choctaws believed the pioneers had occupied the land without permission. They offered to leave the fort and move to another area if the Chickasaws and Choctaws would retreat. However, a shot was fired from the fort before the parley ended. It struck Whitehead in the arm. The Chickasaws and Choctaws, angry about the shooting under a white flag, gathered all their forces that night and made a furious assault upon the fort.

Captain George Owen, who commanded the artillery in one of the blockhouses (see Photo GA-1), had the swivel guns (see Photo GA-2) loaded with grape shot (see Photo GA-7)made with nails, rocks and musket balls. When the Chickasaws and Choctaws advanced, Owen had waited until they were on the wall before firing the swivel guns. The grape shot tore into the attackers who retreated, dragging the dead and wounded behind them. The Chickasaws withdrew on September 1, 1780. They had killed six people and taken one prisoner, burned the corn crop and killed most of the livestock.

Meanwhile, General George Rogers Clark (1752–1818) arrived from Kaskaskia (Illinois) with provisions and reinforcements, effectively raising the siege. This fort was abandoned on June 8, 1781, due to sickness and a lack of supplies. The troops arrived at "The Falls" on July 12, 1781.[37]

Near Winchester
Strode's Station (March 1–2, 1782)

Strode's Station was 2 miles east of Winchester.

About 25 Huron or Wyandot warriors attacked Strode's Station about 20 miles from Boonesborough on Friday and Saturday, March 1–2, 1782, killing two settlers [Patrick Donnalson (Donaldson) (d. 1782) and Jacob Spahr (d. 1782)] and wounding another. Captain James Estill (1750–1782) and a party of 25 men set out in pursuit and caught up with them at Little Mountain, near the future site of Mt. Sterling on March 22nd.[38]

See **Mt. Sterling** below for the story of Estill's defeat.

Near Mt. Sterling
Estill's Defeat (March 22, 1782)
Battle of Little Mountain

Mt. Sterling is about 30 miles east of Lexington.

Settlers began moving out of the stockades and into the open countryside after the Native American raids of 1780. This alarmed the Native Americans whom the British incited even further.[39]

On March 19, 1782, someone spotted an empty raft floating down the Kentucky River past Boonesborough. This was a sure sign Native Americans were in the area. The surrounding stations were all put on alert. Captain James Estill (1750–1782) mustered about 25 militiamen from the nearby stations and set out to find the Native Americans, leaving the stations weakly defended. A band of 25 Hurons or Wyandots appeared at

Estill's Station the following morning and captured a young girl and a slave named Monk. They immediately killed and scalped the girl. Monk told the warriors that there was a strong force of men inside the station, hoping to save the women and children. The attackers withdrew in a hurry.

Two young boys went to find the search party to inform them of the raid. They found Estill's party on the 21st near the mouth of Drowning Creek and relayed the bad news. The trackers found the Wyandots' trail and began pursuit, catching up with them on Friday, March 22, 1782, at the Little Round Mountain near present day Mt. Sterling. They surprised three Wyandots, at Hinkston Creek, skinning a buffalo 2 miles southwest of present Mt. Sterling. The three fled to the other side of the creek to join the main body. Heavy gunfire began immediately and both sides sought cover behind trees.

While both sides began with about 25 men, Lieutenant William Miller (1717–1811) along with six men said they would flank the Wyandots from the rear. They fled the scene instead, leaving Estill at a numerical disadvantage. The thickly wooded terrain also favored the Wyandots' type of warfare.

The Wyandots took advantage of their numerical strength and rushed across the creek to engage Estill's force in hand-to-hand combat with knives and tomahawks. They killed seven to nine men in the charge and wounded Captain Estill, who was recuperating from a broken arm incurred in a previous battle. His weak arm gave way in a knife fight with a much larger Wyandot. The man plunged his knife into Estill's heart.

When Estill fell, Joseph Proctor (ca. 1755–1844) managed to get a clear shot and killed the Wyandot. William Irvine (1763–1819) was also wounded in the battle, shot in the groin. When a Wyandot warrior noticed his condition, he moved in for the kill, but Irvine pointed his unloaded rifle at him as a bluff. Joseph Proctor was unable to help his fallen comrade and advised him to ride James Estill's horse to safety. It took several attempts for Irvine to mount the horse. He eventually managed to do so and rode to a designated spot where Proctor could help him and escort him to Bryan's Station, about 20 miles away, at great risk to his own personal safety. Irvine recovered and lived nearly 40 more years. The brief battle that covered an area of only a few acres left seven militiamen and 17 Wyandots dead.[40]

Richmond, Madison County
Estill's Station
Ashton's Station (May 1782)
Hoy's Station (ca. August 10, 1782)

> Ashton's Station, also known as Estill's Station, was on Muddy Creek, 5 miles south of Richmond in Madison County.
> William Hoy's Station was 6 miles north of Richmond.

The Native Americans attacked Ashton's station in May 1782, killing one man and taking another, an African American, prisoner. Captain Ashton (d. 1782) and 25 men pursued the attackers and overtook them, but the Native Americans outnumbered him and forced Captain Ashton to retreat after a two-hour skirmish which claimed eight men killed, including Captain Ashton, and four men mortally wounded.[41]

★ Native American warriors, incited by Captain Alexander McKee (ca. 1735–1799) and Simon Girty (1741–1818), attacked several stations in the countryside during the summer of 1782, stealing horses and killing the men. They captured two boys from Major Hoy's station around August 10, 1782. Captain John Holder (1744–1797) pursued them with 17 men but was defeated, losing four men killed and one wounded.[42]

Georgetown
Bryan's Station (August 15–17, 1782)

> Bryan's Station was located about 5 miles south of Georgetown, about 20 miles east of Frankfort and 6 miles northeast of Lexington on the Elkhorn River.

Simon Girty (1741–1818) fueled the fears of Native Americans, emphasizing the loss of their lands to settlers, the destruction of their crops and supply of game. He mustered about 500 Native Americans (mostly Wyandots, Chippewas, and Ottawas)—the greatest number of warriors ever assembled during the war. They headed toward Wheeling (West Virginia) in July. But when scouts returning from the Ohio River reported that General George Rogers Clark (1752–1818) was miles away, many of the Ohio Valley warriors left in disgust or fear of Clark. This left about 300 warriors with a few Loyalists under captains William Caldwell (1763–1849), Alexander McKee (ca. 1735–1799) and the Girty brothers.

The band crossed the Ohio near present-day Maysville, took the south fork of the Licking River and arrived unobserved at Bryan's Station, near Lexington, Thursday night, August 15, 1782. Bryan's Station (fort and station were synonymous in the 18th century) was a palisaded (see Photo GA-14) log fort shaped like a parallelogram 200 yards long and 50 yards wide. It housed 90 men, women and children in 20 to 40 cabins whose roofs sloped inward on each side behind the 600-foot-long walls. Blockhouses (see Photo GA-1) on the corners extended over the 12-foot palisades. The 44 men in the garrison could use the gun ports to fire along the front, rear and sides of the fort in a cross fire.

The Crown forces tried to surprise the fort by quietly surrounding it on the night of August 15. As the defenders were still awake, the attempt failed. As Native Americans had attacked Hoy's Station, in Madison County, the men from Bryan's were preparing to leave to help the settlers there. Captain Caldwell tried to trick the defenders by placing a few Wyandots at the rear of the station, just beyond firing range at dawn on August 16. These warriors were to fire their muskets and make a lot of noise to lure the fort's occupants into chasing the decoys and falling into an ambush. Their shots would signal Simon Girty and his force of 300 Native Americans and Loyalist Rangers, hidden on the opposite side of the fort, to storm this undefended side with flaming torches of flax and hickory bark and burn it to the ground.

However, the defenders, watching the warriors' strange behavior from the fort's ramparts, became suspicious and did not attack, suspecting a much larger war party might be hidden in the woods across the field from the front wall.

As the Crown forces waited for Captain Elijah Craig's (1738–1808) reaction, the gates opened and two horsemen—Nicholas Tomlinson and Thomas Bell (1753–1798)—galloped to Lexington for help. Craig thought he could hold out until help arrived unless the enemy had artillery. However, as the Wyandots distracted the fort's occupants that morning, the settlers had not done their morning chores or drawn the day's water from the spring which was 60 yards from the corner of the fort and within close firing range of the Wyandots' hiding place.

Girty believed that the fort's defenders were unaware of the large force of Wyandots and Rangers hidden a short distance away and that his scheme was working. However, Craig and his men suspected the trick, but they needed water to drink and to put out the fires that the attackers were expected to set with torches and flaming arrows.

To keep the Crown forces from realizing that they had discovered their plan, the defenders decided to send the women to the spring to draw water as they did every day. Some refused, saying they were not bullet-proof and that the Wyandots made no distinction between male and female scalps. However, the women and girls soon left the stockade and seemed to walk casually to the spring carrying every receptacle that could hold water. Fifteen-year-old Hetty Tomlinson (b. 1767) recalled later that "while we were dipping up the water I chanced to see under the bushes the feet of one Indian and the hand of another grasping a tomahawk; they were not twenty steps from me, and I trembled so I could hardly stand." The women returned safely and the gates were shut.

After several hours had passed, the Wyandot decoy party reappeared at the back of the fort. The men inside the garrison made as much noise as they could and ran far enough out of the rear of the fort to draw their fire before running back to safety. Girty heard the gunfire and thought the entire garrison had left. He then led his force of over 300 in a charge against the northeast wall with burning torches. The defenders let them get about 50 yards from the palisades before they fired a blistering volley that felled 30 Wyandots and forced Girty to retreat. As he withdrew, Girty set fire to a few cabins close to the station, but the east wind blew the flames away from the fort, thwarting Girty's efforts.

The Crown forces continued irregular firing throughout the 17th, sniping at the fort, killing two settlers and wounding two others. They fired flaming arrows over the walls into the dry timbers. The defenders hoisted young boys onto the cabin roofs to remove the smoldering shingles and douse the embers. Then the shooting stopped.

★ Colonel Levi Todd (1756–1807) and Captain William Ellis (1730–1785) were marching from Lexington and nearby Boone's Station with 17 mounted militiamen and 30 more on foot, coming to Bryan's aid. They arrived about 2 PM and noticed nothing unusual. However, the Crown forces were hidden, waiting "within pistol shot of the road," a buffalo path through the woods leading to the fort. Todd divided his men. Captain Ellis's horsemen took the road while Todd and the men on foot swung behind the enemy and through a 100-acre cornfield to the fort's entrance.

Ellis charged under musket fire. The galloping horses kicked up such a cloud of dust from the dry buffalo path that the riders could hardly be seen. The 17 riders reached Bryan's Station unharmed. Todd's men heard the shots as they crossed the corn field and rushed back to help. They ran into the Wyandots at that point, most of whom had fired and had not reloaded. After two Kentuckians were killed and two others wounded, the rest retreated to Lexington.

The Crown forces now faced 60 men inside Bryan's Station. The news of the attack was spreading and would certainly bring more relief. Girty moved behind a large stump near the fort and called to the defenders. He warned them that he expected cannons to arrive that evening. If they surrendered immediately, he promised leniency. If they resisted, they would all be tomahawked and scalped after the attackers breached the log walls. Aaron Reynolds (1753–1842) responded:

> We all know you have a good-for-nothing dog named Simon Girty because he looks
> so much like you. Bring on your artillery if you've got any, and be damned to you!

We, too, are expecting reinforcements, the whole country is marching to us, and if you and your gang of murderers stay here another day we will have your scalps drying in the sun.

Girty sternly rebuked Reynolds, saying that it "was no time for Joking." Reynolds howled back that Kentuckians did not need powder and lead "to beat such a son of a bitch as Girty," that switches for him and for the "yellow hides" of his Indian consorts would do. Cheers went up from the fort. Simon Girty, furious and "grossly insulted" by the exchange, cursed and swore vengeance, but his tirades were greeted with laughter.[43]

The Crown forces withdrew in the morning of the 18th, after killing four men and wounding three during the attack and losing about 30 of their own. They stole the settlers' horses, cut down the corn, set the hemp ablaze, and slaughtered 300 hogs, 150 cattle and all the sheep. They made no effort to hide their movements. The next day, 182 men from Bryan's Station and the surrounding forts pursued the Crown forces who seemed to invite an engagement. The pursuers found them at the Lower Blue Licks on the southern bank of the Licking River where they were ambushed on Monday, August 19.

See **Blue Licks** pp. 205–208.

12
MISSOURI

France ceded to Spain all the territory west of the Mississippi River in a secret treaty signed in 1762. Spain encouraged pioneers to come from the east, and settlers poured into the territory. The Spanish government encouraged immigration to the Missouri area to make the territory self-supporting. They even offered settlers Spanish citizenship and free land. One of these pioneers, Daniel Boone (1734–1820), received 850 acres and moved to what is now St. Charles County in 1799.

> The State Historical Society of Missouri is located at 1020 Lowry Street, Columbia, MO 65201 (phone: 573-882-7083; website: **shs.umsystem.edu/index.shtml**). The Missouri Division of Tourism (phone: 573-751-4133; website: **www.visitmo.com**) publishes an annual free travel guide which can be obtained on the website or by calling 800-519-4133. While there are no extant historic structures of the American War of Independence in Missouri, there are several architecturally important buildings associated with the periods before and after the war.

See the map of Illinois, Indiana and Missouri.

St. Louis (May 26, 1780)

> A small marker at 4th and Walnut streets in downtown St. Louis commemorates the action that occurred on May 26, 1780.

The region west of the Mississippi River and south of the Missouri River which was known as Spanish Illinois was important to Spain both economically and militarily. Britain and Spain competed for trade with the Native Americans in the Mississippi and Missouri valleys, as well as along the Ohio and Illinois rivers and in the Great Lakes region. St. Louis became the commercial center.

During the American War of Independence, the French and Spanish in St. Louis openly sympathized with the Rebels against Great Britain. They helped Lieutenant Colonel George Rogers Clark (1733–1799) who fought the Crown forces nearby in present-day Indiana. This led to a British and Native American force attacking St. Louis in 1780.

The Spanish government's restrictive trade policies with the Native Americans hampered the traders, most of whom were French or French Canadians who had remained in the region after the Spanish gained control. The cheaper prices and superior quality products sold by British traders at Prairie du Chien in present-day Wisconsin and Michilimackinac (see Photo MI-1) in present-day Michigan also affected their commerce.

Militarily, Spanish Illinois was a buffer between the British in Canada and in the Ohio Valley and the Spanish colony of New Spain. Britain also recognized the importance of Spanish Illinois and launched an unsuccessful attack on St. Louis from Prairie du Chien in May 1780.

General Sir Frederick Haldimand (1718–1791), governor of Canada, authorized Emmanuel Hesse to lead a large force of traders, Loyalists, mercenaries and several hundred Fox, Sauk and Winnebago warriors from Detroit to St. Louis. The force left Prairie du Chien on Tuesday, May 2, 1780 under the command of Lieutenant Governor Patrick Sinclair (1736–1820) of Fort Michilimackinac. Their objective was to raid the Spanish and French settlement of St. Louis.

Capitan Fernando de Leyba (d. 1780), Lieutenant Governor of Spanish Illinois and commander of the Spanish military at San Luis (St. Louis) had expected such an attack from the time he learned of Spain's involvement in the war against Britain. There was a small post at the mouth of the Missouri River, but no fort was deemed necessary because there were no Native Americans in the area. Spanish policy controlled the Native Americans with annual presents and cut off trade when problems developed.

The fighting at Vincennes (see **Indiana** pp. 178–182) in late 1778 and early 1779 brought the war closer to St. Louis. Rumors of a Native American attack from the north in early 1780 accentuated the need for defenses. Leyba wanted to build four stone towers, one at each corner of the town, that could serve as artillery emplacements and watchtowers. The settlers saw no need for a fort and refused to help Leyba construct defenses for the town. Leyba could only raise enough money to build one tower. He also brought five small cannons from an abandoned fort down the Mississippi, and the people of San Luis dug musket entrenchments at different approaches to the town.

Leyba's "army" consisted of 29 men of the Spanish Louisiana Regiment and a lieutenant and 12 reinforcements from the military outpost of Ste. Genevieve further down the river. In July 1779, his militia consisted of 175 infantrymen and about 50 dragoons. By December 1780, he had 220 men divided into two companies, but the militiamen were undisciplined and the cavalry had no horses. Rivalry and jealousy divided the officers.

Emmanuel Hesse's force of 750 men approached San Luis on Tuesday, May 23, 1780. (Estimates of the number of attackers vary greatly, but they did not exceed 950 and may have been considerably fewer.) They waited until May 26 to begin the attack on what was called Fort San Carlos. The tower puzzled the attackers who sent the Menominee and Winnebago warriors to discover its purpose. Despite his illness, Leyba had had himself carried to the artillery emplacement in the tower to direct the defenses. When the Menominees and Winnebagoes came into range, the artillery atop Fort San Carlos opened fire on them, and the Spanish forces in the trenches soon followed.

The attackers had not expected to find the city fortified and were surprised by the cannon volleys. Many of the Menominees and Winnebagoes fled when they saw the town could not be taken easily. The attackers retreated at the end of the day, ending the threat to San Luis and its neighboring Spanish outposts.

The retreating forces killed a number of civilians, both whites and slaves, who had refused to take seriously the rumors of the impending attack and had remained in the unprotected areas outside the city. Hesse's forces also killed or stole all the livestock and horses they could find.

Leyba decided not to pursue Hesse, whose force greatly outnumbered the Spaniards. Hesse withdrew to the Illinois River, destroying farms and taking prisoners along the way.

The defensive preparations in St. Louis minimized the casualties, and the town remained on alert for about two weeks afterward in fear of another attack coming down the Illinois from Chicago. When the attack failed to materialize, a 200-man Spanish and American expedition left St. Louis in mid-June to meet the Crown forces on the Illinois River. They found the Native American villages there abandoned. The attackers burned the structures and destroyed the crops.

The official report listed 79 people killed, wounded, or captured—a heavy loss for a village of only 700. King Carlos III (1716–1788) of Spain sent a dispatch congratulating Leyba and promoting him to the rank of lieutenant-colonel. Unfortunately, Leyba died of his illness before receiving the king's response to his report of the battle. The Spanish forces retaliated by launching their own offensive which resulted in the battle of Fort Saint Joseph (see **Michigan** pp. 160–164) on February 12, 1781.[1]

The Treaty of Paris, that ended the war in 1783, ceded the Illinois country on the west side of the Mississippi River to the United States, and many of the French settlers of the region moved into Upper Louisiana.

13
TENNESSEE

France, Spain and Great Britain all claimed the Tennessee region in the early 18th century, and all three countries competed for trade and friendship with the Native Americans. However, in the Treaty of Paris, which ended the Seven Years War [French and Indian War (1756–1763)], France gave the British all the lands east of the Mississippi.

Tennessee was part of North Carolina during the American War of Independence, but the rugged mountains separated the region from the mother colony. Permanent settlers lived in the Tennessee region by 1769, and new settlers continued to come from Virginia and North Carolina. They formed their own government in 1772, called the Watauga Association, and drew up one of the first written constitutions in North America.

The Transylvania Company bought a large area of present-day Tennessee and Kentucky from the Cherokees in 1775 and hired Daniel Boone (1734–1820) to blaze a trail to open this land to settlement. The trail, which became known as the Wilderness Road, began in Virginia and crossed the mountains at Cumberland Gap.

During the American War of Independence, both the settlers and the Native Americans tried to drive each other out of the Tennessee region. The conflicts here resulted from those tensions. Colonel John Sevier (1745–1815) led a group of Tennessee pioneers across the Great Smoky Mountain into South Carolina in 1780. They helped win the victory at the Battle of Kings Mountain, South Carolina (October 7, 1780). When the settlers' appeal for help from North Carolina proved unsuccessful in 1784, three counties in East Tennessee revolted against North Carolina and formed the independent state of Franklin and elected John Sevier as their governor.

North Carolina regained control of the Tennessee region in 1788 but gave it to the United States the following year. The federal government made the region a new territory and called it the Territory of the United States South of the River Ohio. Tennessee became the 16th state in 1796.

The Tennessee Historical Commission, in the Clover Bottom Mansion (2941 Lebanon Road, Nashville, TN 37243; phone: 615-532-1550 website: **www.tn.gov/ environment/hist/**) published *Tennessee Historical Markers*. The Tennessee Department of Tourist Development (312 Rosa L. Parks Avenue, Nashville, TN 37243; phone: 617-741-2159 website: **www.tn.gov/tourdev/**) publishes a free travel guide obtainable by calling 800-GO2-TENN.

See the map of Tennessee and west North Carolina.

Cherokee Campaign of 1776 (July 1, 1776–May 20, 1777)

The Cherokee towns are usually designated as Overhill Towns, Valley Towns, Middle Settlements and Lower Towns. The following list of towns and divisions was compiled during South Carolina Governor James Glen's (1701–1777) administration.

Overhill Towns: Great Tellico, Chatooga, Settico, Tallassee, Tennessee, Chote, and Toqua.

Valley Towns: Euforsee, Conastee, Little Tellico, Cotocanahut, Nayowee, Tomatly, and Chewohee.

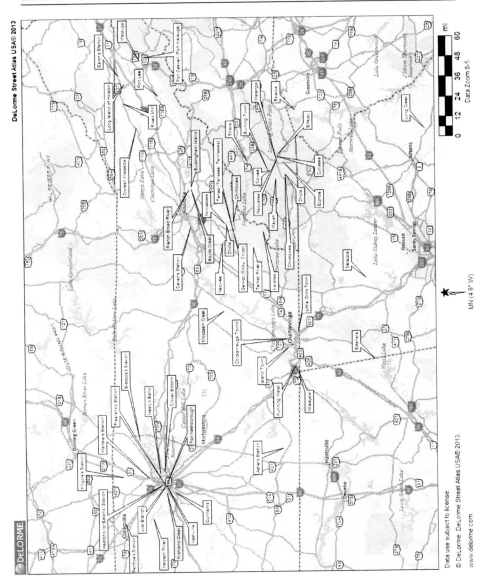

Tennessee and west North Carolina: Map for The Guide to the American Revolutionary War in the Deep South and on the Frontier *© 2013 DeLorme (www.delorme. com) Street Atlas USA®*

Middle Settlements: Joree, Watoga, Nukasee, Kewohee, Tiacentee, Echoee, Torsee, Cowee, Tarsalla, Coweechee, Elejay.

Lower Towns: Tomassee, Oustestee, Cheowee, Estatoee, Toxawa, Keowee, Oustanalle.

Out Towns: Tuckareechee, Kittowa, Conoustory, Stecoy, Oustanale, Tuckasegee. There is also a little town called Nuntiale and a village or two which brings the total to about 39 or 40 towns.[1]

The Cherokee Campaign of 1776 occurred in what are now the states of North and South Carolina, Tennessee, Georgia and Alabama. The towns involved include: Burning Town, Cowee, Cullasae (Cullasaja), Ellajoy (Ellajay), Etchoe, Nequasee, Sticoe, Watanga, and Wayah (Topton) in North Carolina; Estatoa in South Carolina; Island Town, Neowee, Noocassee, Sauta and Watauga in Tennessee; Long Creek and Selacoa in Georgia and Estanala in Alabama.

North Carolina:

Burning Town was on the east shore of Burningtown Creek, about midway between Wayah and Cowee.

Cowee (Kawi'yi) was located about 5.5 miles north of Franklin.

Cullasae (Cullasaja) was located about 3.5 miles southeast of Franklin near where route US 64 (TN 28|Highlands Road) crosses the Cullasaja River.

Ellajoy (Ellajay) was in the Nantahala National Forest about a mile east of Cullasae (Cullasaja) and about 4.25 miles southeast of Franklin.

Etchoe (Echoee or Etchoe Pass) was located about 4.5 miles south of Franklin.

Nequasee, (also spelled Nequassee, Nikwasi, Nucassee, Noucassih, etc.) was about a mile east of Franklin, in the Nantahala National Forest.

Sticoe was on the Tuckaseegee River in what is now Whittier.

Watanga was located about 1.5 miles southeast of Franklin west of the intersection of routes US 23 (US 64|US 441|Sylva Road) and TN 28 (Highlands Road.)

Wayah (Topton) was located about 10 miles west of Franklin.

South Carolina:

Estatoa was west of the confluence of Laurel Creek and Eastatoe Creek north of Sunset, South Carolina.

Tennessee:

Island Town was on Williams Island in the Tennessee River north of Chattanooga.

Neowee was on the peninsula near the end of Bay Point Road in Vonore.

Noocassee was 0.5 miles north of Chota in what is now Maryville.

The Hiwassee town of Watauga is on the Watauga River about 5 miles west-northwest of Elizabethton.

Georgia:

Long Creek was in Wilkes County, about 21 miles south-southeast of Athens.

Selacoa was west of where Salacoa Road crosses Salacoa Creek in Waleska.

Alabama:

Estanala was about 0.5 miles east of the intersection of routes AL 68 and County Road 140 in Gaylesville.

Sauta may have been in the northwestern part of the Fort Rucker Military Reservation, east of New Brockton.

General Griffith Rutherford's (ca. 1731–1800) expedition against the Cherokees proceeded as far as their Middle Towns (present-day Chattanooga) and drove the

Cherokees from their villages on the Little Tennessee River, destroyed their houses and crops and drove away their cattle. The route of his march was long known as Rutherford's Trace. It passed along Hominy Creek east of Canton, North Carolina, through Pigeon Gap and Balsam Gap, along Savannah Creek and through Cowee Gap. There are historical markers in North Carolina, commemorating the expedition at routes:

US 19/23/74 at Hominy Creek east of Canton

US 276 at Pigeon Gap east of Waynesville

NC 1243 (Old US 19 Alternate/23) at Balsam Gap southwest of Waynesville

US 23/441 at NC 116 southwest of Webster

US 23/441 southwest of Dillsboro, North Carolina at the Jackson/Macon County line.[2]

The Treaty of Paris, which ended the Seven Years War (1756–1763), also known as the French and Indian War, was followed by the Proclamation of 1763 which prohibited land sales and settlements west of the Appalachian Mountains. This stipulation rewarded the Native American tribes for siding with Britain in that war. However, that did not stop the westward migration.

Another treaty between Virginia and the Cherokees in 1772 set the top of the Blue Ridge Mountains as the eastern boundary, and a line running due west from the White Top mountain (where North Carolina, Virginia and Tennessee meet) as the northern boundary. The general impression at that time was that this line included the Watauga Settlement near what is now Jonesboro, Tennessee. The western boundary ran from 6 miles above Long Island of the Holston, south to the dividing ridge between the Watauga and the Toe rivers, thence in a southeasterly direction to the Blue Ridge, thence along the Blue Ridge to the Virginia line. This included the whole of Watauga, Ashe and Alleghany counties.

The proclamation was widely ignored as the first settlers came in fairly large numbers. The "long hunters," who hunted and trapped for several months at a time before returning home, were eager to take advantage of the absence of the French threat and were willing to contend with the Native American tribes for control of the rich lands. By 1769 hundreds of people had built log cabins in the valleys of the Watauga, Nolichucky and Holston rivers with the intention of making permanent homes. They encroached on the Cherokee towns where about 22,000 people lived and, by 1772, had formed the Watauga Association to govern themselves.

The frontiersmen, known as Wataugans, still considered themselves North Carolinians. They viewed the Cherokees as hostile and exaggerated any incident. The Cherokees viewed the frontiersmen as a threat to their lands, as the whites always demanded land cession and the release of any prisoners before the signing of a treaty, such as the Treaty of Sycamore Shoals in March 1775. Most of the Cherokees believed that supporting the British Army would be their best option to protect their lands. King George III (1738–1820) also had more resources than the colonists with which to bribe tribal leaders and to reward them for their support. Every year, British agents would bring the "king's presents" of food, supplies, guns and ammunition to the loyal tribes. Yet, the army never took full advantage of their numerous and powerful Native American allies.

Although the Cherokees insisted that the line of settlements be controlled according to the stipulations of the Proclamation of 1763 and subsequent treaties, their demands went largely unheeded. Killings and cheating in trade also caused the Cherokees to resent the whites. The white man also brought smallpox and alcoholism to the Native Americans. The Cherokees traded deerskins for rum. They insisted that the settlers leave; but the frontiersmen made it clear, in the spring of 1776, that they had no intention of leaving and they continued to build blockhouses (see Photo GA-1).

Alexander Cameron (ca. 1720–1781) served the royal government as an official agent to the Native Americans. He was deputy to John Stuart (ca. 1710–1779), the British superintendent for the Southern Indian Department. When the troubles began, Cameron fled from his residence to take refuge among the Cherokees who were already angry because the settlers had cheated the tribe out of 50,000 square miles of land in the Watauga area in the Treaty of Sycamore Shoals in March 1775.

The Whigs sent commissioners to the Cherokees who promised to give them gifts of ammunition and trade goods if they agreed not to help the Loyalists. The Whigs then shipped 1,000 pounds of gunpowder and lead to them from Charleston in October. However, some of the settlers delayed the shipment which was then seized by Loyalists who spread rumors that the ammunition was sent to the Cherokees for use against the Loyalists on the frontier.

In November, the Whigs requested that the Creek and Cherokee chiefs attend a parley the following spring, hoping to prevent an uprising that would be disastrous for everyone along the frontier. At the same time, John Stuart, in Florida, tried to persuade the tribes to join the British or to remain neutral.

The Great Council of Cherokees met in Chota on May 2, 1776 to try to resolve the problem. John Stuart came from Charleston, South Carolina to attend. He tried to negotiate a peaceful settlement and opposed the young and vicious Dragging Canoe (ca. 1730–1792) (Tsi'ui-Gunsin'n, Cui Canacina) who wanted to attack the Wataugan settlements and regain the land he believed was sold to the whites illegally in the Treaty of Sycamore Shoals. He threatened to turn the territory into a "dark and bloody ground." Some Iroquois, Delawares and Shawnees from the north sided with Dragging Canoe as did the Loyalists among the Creeks farther south. Stuart negotiated for a petition that the Wataugans leave their farms within 20 days and move elsewhere. The Wataugans ignored the petition. Having exhausted all their avenues to maintain peace, the Cherokees began to prepare for war in May and June 1776 to fight for their tribal society. John Stuart's brother Henry (1766–1790) and Alexander Cameron (ca. 1720–1781) managed to keep the Creeks and Choctaws pacified, leaving the Cherokees to fight alone.

★ The Cherokees planned a three-pronged attack. Warriors from the Lower Towns would advance against the South Carolina frontier and Georgia, while Dragging Canoe (ca. 1730–1792) (Tsi'ui-Gunsin'n, Cui Canacina) would lead the warriors from the Middle and Valley towns to attack the Holston settlements and move eastward into North Carolina. The Overhill tribes, under Abraham of Chilhowee, would destroy Watauga and Nolichucky and be responsible for keeping intruders out of the Upper Cherokee River area [Tennessee], alarming the settlers along the North Carolina and Virginia frontier and cutting off westward expansion through the Cumberland Gap into Kentucky.

Hostilities began in June 1776 with an attack on the settlements of Upper South Carolina and Georgia. Alexander Cameron (ca. 1720–1781) led the Cherokees in an attack on the white settlements along the frontiers from North Carolina to Georgia on July 1, 1776. They massacred men, women and children, without distinction of age or gender, sparing only the Loyalists' cabins with peeled poles wrapped with white cloth erected in front. These poles were called Passovers. The Cherokees did not surprise the settlers, as Colonel John Stuart (ca. 1710–1779), Superintendent of the Southern Indian

Department, and Alexander Cameron tried to persuade the people of Watauga and No-lichucky to leave and pro-Whig Cherokee traders revealed their plans.[3]

★ Abraham of Chilhowee and the Overhill tribes attacked around mid-July and be-sieged **Fort Caswell** (see pp. 240–141) on the Watauga River for two weeks. They retreated when Colonel William Russel (1735–1793) arrived with a relief expedition. Dragging Canoe (ca. 1730–1792) (Tsi'ui-Gunsin'n, Cui Canacina) and his warriors were forced to retreat near Eaton's Station after losing 14 men. The chief himself was wounded in both legs.

The attack occurred about the same time as the attack on Charleston by the joint expedition of General Henry Clinton (1730–1795) and Admiral Sir Peter Parker (1721–1811), causing the southerners to conclude there was a conspiracy between the Native Americans and the British military. They feared further attacks on the settlements unless something was done to stop them.

The Cherokees plundered houses and destroyed a great deal of property but killed rel-atively few people. Those who could took refuge in the hastily constructed blockhouses (see Photo GA-1); others gathered their most precious belongings and retreated across the mountains to areas of greater safety. The proprietors of the Transylvania Company placed the following notice in the *Virginia Gazette* on June 20, 1776:

> And as it is unsafe at this Time to settle the Country in small detached Parties, and the alarming Reports with Respect to the hostile Intention of the Cherokee Indians on the Frontier will no Doubt prevent Emigration for some Time to that Country, Care will be taken to cause those Lands to be laid off as soon as conveniently may be. . . .

★ The Cherokees raided the North Carolina settlements along the Catawba River in early July, killing 37 settlers and taking several prisoners. On July 12, General Griffith Rutherford (ca. 1731–1800) wrote:

> I am Under the Nessety of sending you by Express, the Allerming Condition, this Country is in, the Indins is making Grate Prograce, in Distroying and Murdering, in the frunteers of the County, 37 I am informed was killed Last Wednesday & Thurs-day on the Cuttaba River, I am also informed that Colo McDowel 10 men more & 120 women & children is Beshaged, in some kind of a fort, & the Indins Round them, no help to them before yesterday, & they were surrounded on Wednesday. I expect the next account to hear is that they are all destroyed . . . three off our Captains is kild & one Wounded. This day I set out with what men I can Raise for the Relefe of the Distrest. Pray, gentlemen, Consider our Distress; send us plenty of powder, and I hope under God we of Salisbury district are able to stand them.[4]

★ On Monday, July 15, 1776, the Cherokees attacked Lyndley's (Lindley's) Fort (see *The Guide to the American Revolutionary War in South Carolina*: Fort Lindley (Lyndley's) p. 266). Colonel Andrew Williamson (ca. 1730–1786) of South Carolina retaliated two weeks later by attacking and destroying the Cherokee "capitol" of Seneca (Esseneca) (see *The Guide to the American Revolutionary War in South Carolina*: Seneca pp. 272–273). He and a party of 25 militiamen on a scouting mission were later ambushed at Tamas-see (Tomassy) on August 11, 1776 (see *The Guide to the American Revolutionary War in South Carolina*: Tamassee (Tomassy, Ring Fight) pp. 273–275).

Major General Charles Lee (1731–1782), commander of the Continental forces in the south, urged Congress to send a major punitive expedition against the Cherokees before the British could invade the south and draw Continental troops away from the frontier. Within a few weeks of the Cherokee invasion, the Continental Congress autho-rized the expedition.

★ Colonel David Williamson (1752–1809) retaliated immediately on Friday, August 2nd. He led 1,800 militiamen into the Lower Towns whose inhabitants withdrew over the mountains to their brethren in the Middle, Valley and Overhill towns. The militiamen burned several villages and destroyed the corn fields which would have sustained the Cherokees in the coming winter, but they neither killed any Cherokees nor captured any prisoners. They then moved northwest to join the North Carolinians in destroying the Middle and Valley towns. General William Christian (ca. 1743–1786), Virginia Governor Patrick Henry's (1736–1799) brother-in-law, and his Virginia militia attacked the Overhill towns but found that the Cherokees learned of his expedition and withdrew. They found Neowee deserted and destroyed it.[5]

Williamson proposed that he and General Griffith Rutherford conduct a joint expedition. With 2,000 men from each colony (Virginia and the two Carolinas), they would strike the Cherokees from the north, east and south. General Griffith Rutherford (ca. 1731–1800) was assigned to the Cherokee expedition in North Carolina. He had little trouble in gathering troops, but he found supplies of everything from horses and salt to tent material and grain very scarce, so he could not set out until Sunday, September 1, 1776.

Rutherford led his 2,500 North Carolinians through the Swannanoa Gap in the Blue Ridge Mountains en route to the Cherokee Middle Towns about 80 miles away. They reached Watanga (present-day Franklin, North Carolina) on September 8 to find the town deserted. Disappointed in not finding General Williamson's South Carolina army which was supposed to meet him at Cowee on September 9th but was delayed, General Rutherford sent a detachment to locate Williamson as he destroyed the food caches and Cherokee towns of Nequasee, Etchoe, Cowee, Cullasae and Watanga on the Little Tennessee. They burned at least 36 towns. Rutherford left a force at Cowee and took a detachment of 900 men and 10 days' provisions and hurried along the Little Tennessee and headed toward Valley River and the Hiwassee. Around Monday, September 16, Rutherford crossed the Nantahala Mountains and destroyed the Valley Towns on the Valley and Hiwassee Rivers.

Meanwhile Williamson's 1,800 South Carolinians were moving northwest toward the planned rendezvous with Rutherford's army when they fell into a trap at Wayah, a mountain cove known as the Black Hole (about 9 miles west of the present town of Franklin, North Carolina) on September 19th (see *The Guide to the American Revolutionary War in Pennsylvania, Delaware, Maryland, Virginia and North Carolina*: Wayah pp. 256–257).

About 1,000 Middle and Overhill Cherokees were waiting to ambush Rutherford and his North Carolinians. Captain Edward Hampton (1740–1781), one of the brothers whose family had been nearly wiped out during the July massacre, and 30 Continentals attacked the Cherokees in the rear, catching them by surprise. The only avenue of escape was over the part of the mountain that jutted into the river.

At one point, Hampton, in his excitement, rammed in his bullet without powder. He sat down, unbreached his musket, withdrew the load and resumed firing. In contrast, a certain great bully at fist and skull fighting was frightened out of his wits and crawled under a shelving bank across a little stream flowing into the river and hid. William Hammon (1742–1817) was shot through the thigh. He ran but the bone broke, and he fell near the bully's hiding place. The bully watched as Hammon and another man were scalped and he never fired a shot.

The Cherokees were finally forced to retire after being flanked by Williamson's troops in a close fight that lasted about two hours. They later claimed they ran out of ammunition. Williamson lost 13 killed and 18 wounded. The Cherokee casualties are not known, but they supposedly sustained heavy losses, probably about 12 killed and nine captured.[6]

★ The South Carolinians regrouped, rested and then proceeded toward the Valley Towns through present-day Nantahala Gorge. The first town they destroyed was near Topton, North Carolina. They then destroyed five others before joining Rutherford and the North Carolinians at the Hiwassee River (lower Keowee River) near Murphy on September 23 or 26. The combined armies burned the Middle settlements over the next two weeks—a total of 36 villages—leaving no habitations or food. They then returned home in early October, considering it impracticable to cross the Smokies to assist Colonel William Christian (ca. 1743–1786). (Because of an unseasonable snowfall, this was known as the "Snow Campaign.")

Colonel David Williamson (1752–1809) arrived at Cowee two days after General Griffith Rutherford (ca. 1731–1800) had left. He sent men to look for Rutherford. They found him about 3 miles from where he had started two days before. They set out again and encountered a party of Cherokees who put up a stiff fight. Rutherford lost several men and the Cherokees eventually fled. Rutherford and Williamson proceeded to the Hiwassee towns, Watauga, Estatoa and Ellajay and burned them. Along the way, Rutherford ran into a foraging party that he himself had sent to Burning Town for provisions. Mistaking his own commander's force for the enemy, someone shouted: "The Indians! The Indians!" The party fled in a rush, leaving their officer in charge trailing behind and in danger of being deserted.

Williamson headed home by the route up the Hiwassee. Rutherford's forces returned by the same trail they came. The route has since been called Rutherford's Trace. As he had failed to destroy the towns on the Tuckasegee River, Rutherford sent Colonel William Moore (1751–1823 or 1730–1800) to do the job. Moore burned Sticoe (near Whittier, North Carolina) and at least one other town on the Oconaluftee River. The campaign cost 99 lives but inflicted 2,000 casualties on the Cherokees.

★ Colonel William Christian's (ca. 1743–1786) army of 2,000 Virginians and "over-the-mountain" men from Watauga crossed the Holston River on Tuesday, October 1, 1776, and proceeded to destroy the villages of the Overhill Cherokees from the Valley of the Holston southwest into what is now East Tennessee. They paused for several days to gather additional troops, then followed a path that brought them to the French Broad two days ahead of the projected arrival date, October 15. Shortly before Colonel Christian's troops arrived at the French Broad, he received a peace emissary from the Raven of Chota, Savanukah (or "Savanooka"), but he refused to consider the proposal until the Cherokees laid down their arms, released their prisoners and surrendered Alexander Cameron (ca. 1720–1781).

As Colonel Christian and the Raven of Chota could not come to an agreement, Christian and his men proceeded across the French Broad and the Little Tennessee to Island Town, Dragging Canoe's (ca. 1730–1792) settlement. They expected the Cherokees to take a stand at the French Broad to defend their territory, but the Cherokees withdrew into the mountains, leaving behind in their villages, "horses, cattle, dogs, hogs, and fowels," as well as "between forty and fifty thousand bushels of corn and ten or fifteen thousand bushels of potatoes" which were destroyed.[7]

During their campaign, Colonel David Williamson's (1752–1809) force burned 32 Cherokee villages, destroyed hundreds of acres of corn and defeated the Cherokees in five separate battles. Williamson dismissed the troops on October 11 and sent them home.[8]

Within a few weeks, the Cherokees began returning to their villages where some of the few standing houses had been plundered. They could erect shelters rather quickly, but, as their food supplies had been ruined, their survival in the approaching winter was a major problem.

Dragging Canoe (ca. 1730–1792), adamantly opposed to any concessions to the white man, separated from the Cherokees in 1777. He and his followers built a cluster of new towns farther south on the Tennessee River at Chickamauga Creek which would come to be called the Chickamaugas. They intended to continue fighting while, by late October, the rest of the Cherokees laid down their arms, released their captives and agreed to peace talks the following spring.

Colonel John Stuart (ca. 1710–1779), Superintendent of the Southern Indian Department, had hoped to use the Cherokees in a joint offensive against the southern states. Now, he had to look to the Creeks. However, the news of the Cherokee disaster spread quickly and most of the southern tribes decided to remain neutral. This caused the British Army to delay its invasion of the south.

★ In May 1777, delegates from the Lower, Middle and Valley towns traveled to DeWitt's Corner (Due West, South Carolina) (see *The Guide to the American Revolutionary War in South Carolina* pp. 275–276) to negotiate with the representatives of South Carolina and Georgia. North Carolina could not commission representatives in time for the meeting, so the other two states represented her interests. The terms of the agreement included peace, an exchange of prisoners and a land cession of all the remaining land in South Carolina except for a narrow strip along the Chatooga in present Oconee County along the western border.

Shortly after their return, the delegates soon found themselves at another conference with the representatives of North Carolina and Virginia. This time, they were joined by the Overhill Cherokees and met at the Long Island of the Holston River in July (see *The Guide to the American Revolutionary War in Pennsylvania, Delaware, Maryland, Virginia and North Carolina* p. 257). The signing of the Treaty of Long Island of the Holston on Sunday, July 20, 1777, in which the Overhill Cherokees ceded all their lands east of the Unicoi (Blue Ridge) Mountains and north of the Nolichucky River, officially ended the Cherokee Campaign of 1776. The Cherokees ceded to the state of South Carolina the present-day counties of Anderson, Pickens, Oconee and Greenville. The treaty expelled the Cherokees from Virginia and cut their possessions in Tennessee and North Carolina in half.[9]

Dragging Canoe (ca. 1730–1792) and several other chiefs moved west, rallied some Cherokees and continued intermittent fighting for several years. Their numbers were reduced and there were divisions among the tribes as to their plan of action, so they were no longer as much of a threat to the colonists as they had been. North Carolina and Virginia sent Colonel Evan Shelby (1720–1794) and 900 men to exterminate these warriors. These troops attacked the Chickamaugas, defeated them, and burned their villages, but they did not catch Dragging Canoe.

The borders remained calm until 1780. The campaign probably persuaded the Cherokees to side with the British after the surrender of Charleston, South Carolina on May 12, 1780.

Long Island Flats
Eaton's Station, Battle of Island Flats (July 20, 1776)

> Eaton's Station was near present day Kingsport. Long Island of the Holston is on the south edge of Kingsport in the South Fork of the Holston River.

The Cherokees drove the inhabitants of the Watauga and Nolichucky settlements back to the older and safer settlements in Virginia by mid-1776. Nancy Ward (1735–1824), a Cherokee princess who did not approve of their attacks, gave information about an impending attack to four traders who, in turn, warned the settlers. The Cherokees advanced in three columns. Old Abraham went after Nolichucky and Watauga while the Raven of Chota, Savanukah (or "Savanooka") struck into Carter's Valley to the west. Dragging Canoe (ca. 1730–1792) led the main force of about 170–200 warriors in the center. The Raven drove into Virginia as far as Seven Mile Ford on the South Fork of the Holston.

Scouts spotted Dragging Canoe's party heading toward Eaton's Station. Captain James Thompson (1742–1803 or 1749–1811) gathered five companies of militia, about 170 men, at Island Flats near Long Island of the Holston on Saturday morning, July 20, 1776. They decided to meet the Cherokees in the open before they could do much damage. They marched in two divisions, with flankers on each side and scouts in front. The scouts encountered Dragging Canoe's advance guard of 20 warriors and exchanged fire. The militiamen then rushed at them very forcefully, causing them to retreat. The militiamen laid an ambush in the trees and long cane. When the Cherokees entered the ambush site, the frontiersmen opened fire and wounded several of them.

As the Cherokees fled back to their main body, Captain Thompson decided to return to Eaton's Station with his main force, as it was getting late in the afternoon. They marched about a mile before they encountered Dragging Canoe's main force of equal size. Placed as an ambush, they attacked the militiamen from the rear as they passed by. The militiamen formed a line and Captain James Shelby took possession of a hill, preventing the Cherokees from surrounding them. The militiamen killed about 13 on the spot, in the 10-minute skirmish, and shot Dragging Canoe in the leg, breaking his thigh bone; but he survived. Dragging Canoe's brother, Little Owl (d. 1776), fell with a dozen bullet holes in his body. The Cherokees retreated, attacking outlaying settlements and killing 18 more people. They burned cabins and crops, slaughtered livestock and killed and scalped those who did not get away fast enough. The militiamen decided to return to the fort, fearing that a large party of Cherokees might be nearby. The battle lasted about an hour and left four militiamen wounded, one of whom was shot through the back of the neck with an arrow. A total of about 40 Cherokees were either slain outright or mortally wounded.[10]

Chuckey
Fort Lee (July 1776)

> Militiamen built Fort Lee near the confluence of the Big Limestone Creek and the Nolichucky River in 1776. The site is in Chuckey, about 0.37 miles from the Nolichucky River, across from the Davy Crockett Birthplace State Historic Park (website: **www.tn.gov/environment/parks/DavyCrockettSHP/**).

Isaac Thomas (1735–1810) and four white traders slipped out of Chota sometime on Monday, July 8, 1776, carrying Nancy Ward's (1735–1824) warning of an imminent Cherokee attack on the Holston, Watauga and Nolichucky people to the Overmountain settlements. They reached Fort Lee on July 11, 10 days before Abraham of Chilhowee attacked Fort Caswell (Fort Watauga) and nine days before Dragging Canoe's (ca. 1730–1792) battle at Island Flats (Kingsport). The settlers had anticipated Cherokee attacks for some time and made special efforts to strengthen the forts and stockades. The timely warning did give women and children ample time to reach the nearest fort for protection. The Cherokees burned Fort Lee in July 1776.[11]

Elizabethton
Fort Caswell (Fort Watauga) (July 21, 1776; Aug. 2, 1776)

Fort Caswell (Fort Watauga) was located on the strategic Sycamore Shoals about 3 miles southwest of Elizabethton. It was about 300 feet west of the Sycamore Shoals Monument (West G Street and Monument Place). There's a replica of the fort about 4.4 miles northeast in Sycamore Shoals Historic Park (website: **www.tn.gov/ environment/parks/SycamoreShoals/**), between route US 321 (TN 91|West Elk Avenue) and the Watauga River. Fort Caswell was the administrative center of the Watauga settlements.

The 1974 excavations revealed that the fort had an irregular shape and that it probably consisted of a group of cabins connected by a stockade. The shape of the reconstructed fort was based largely on the formations uncovered in these excavations and its design was based on contemporary Appalachian frontier forts, which typically consisted of log structures (some with overhanging second stories) and a stockade of sharpened poles (see Photo GA-14) surrounding a 1-acre courtyard.[12]

The Cherokee traders who passed Nancy Ward's (1735–1824) warning to the inhabitants of the Watauga and Nolichucky settlements also warned Fort Caswell of the impending Cherokee attack. About 150 to 200 settlers crowded into the fort. Colonel John Carter (1737–1781), the Committee of Safety commissioner, commanded the fort with Lieutenant James Robertson (1742–1814). Lieutenant John Sevier (1745–1815) and the garrison of the former Fort Lee on the Nolichucky brought the number of defenders up to 75. Chief Abraham of Chilhowee attacked Fort Caswell with 300 Cherokee warriors early Sunday morning, July 21, 1776.

Women working outside the fort discovered the Cherokees and fled to the safety of the stockade. The attackers fired at the men on the fort walls who quickly returned their fire. Catherine Sherrell or Sherrill, caught outside the fort milking cows, ran around to the other side where Lieutenant Sevier reached over the palisades as arrows and bullets flew around him. Catherine clung to his arm as he pulled her up to safety. (They married four years later.) The attack lasted about three hours. Unable to take the fort, the Cherokees halted the assault and settled in for a lengthy siege.

★ After almost two weeks, the Cherokees became impatient and launched a second assault on Friday, August 2, 1776. About 25 warriors ran toward an unprotected section of the wall that the defenders could not protect with their rifles and tried to set the fort walls on fire. James Robertson's (1742–1814) wife or sister, Ann (1757–1821), carried a bucket of boiling wash water to the parapet and poured it on them. The other women continued to pass buckets of water to her. She was wounded once in the arm but ignored the pain and continued scalding the Cherokees until they withdrew to the safety of the forest. Colonel William Russel, Sr. (or Russell) (1741–1793) arrived from Shelby's Fort with 100 men to end the two-week siege. The settlers lost 25 killed and wounded during the siege. The Cherokees captured a teenager named Tom or Samuel Moore (d. 1776) outside the fort and took him to Tuskegee where he was burned at the stake. Another captive, Lydia Russell Bean (1726–1788), was about to meet the same fate when Nancy Ward (1735–1824) intervened and used her authority as a Beloved Woman to spare her. The Cherokees lifted the siege and retreated after approximately two weeks. The arrival of the Virginia militia under Colonel William Christian (ca. 1743–1786) later that year largely ended the threat to the fort.[13]

Church Hill
Rice's Mill (April 10, 1777)
Cavett's Station (April 10, 1777; Sept. 25, 1793)

Rice's Mill was about 100 yards north of Lee Highway (US 11W | TN 1 | TN 346) where it crosses Hord Creek in Church Hill, about 10 miles due west-southwest of Kingsport.

Cavett's Station was about 8 miles southwest of Knoxville in the area bounded by Alexander Cavet Drive and Doublehead Lane. From exit 379A off route I-40 E (I-75 N), take Walker Springs Road for 0.36 miles then turn right on Broome Road NW and go 0.2 miles to Alexander Cavet Drive.

A historical marker at the intersection of Kingston Pike (US 11|70) and Gallaher View Road, on the right when traveling east on Kingston Pike, commemorates the 1793 engagement. It reads: "Here on Sept. 25, 1793, Alexander Cavett and 12 other settlers were massacred by a Cherokee war party under Doublehead, one of the more savage chiefs of the tribe."

Henry Rice (1728–1818) built and fortified a mill on Hord Creek, north of the Holston River, in 1775. The settlers took refuge from warring Cherokees there in 1776. Captain James Robertson (1742–1814) and eight other pioneers had a fight with 30 or 40 Cherokees near here on Thursday, April 10, 1777.

Dragging Canoe (ca. 1730–1792) (Tsi'ui-Gunsin'n, Cui Canacina) stole 10 horses from Captain James Robertson (1742–1814) and shot and scalped Frederick Calvitt (or Cavett) (d. 1777) 1.5 miles from his home, Cavett's Station, in April 1777. Thirteen members of Calvitt's family were killed here in a later attack on September 25, 1793 and the station was destroyed.

★ Captain James Robertson (1742–1814) pursued Dragging Canoe with nine men the following day. They killed one Cherokee and retook the 10 horses stolen the previous day. A party of Creeks and Cherokees attacked Captain Robertson's troops on their return in the evening and wounded two of his men. Robertson returned fire but was obliged to retreat as he was outnumbered. He still kept the horses and brought them in.[14]

Rogersville, Hawkins County
Crockett Massacre (ca. Aug. 1777)

The Crockett Massacre occurred near the intersection of Clay Street and East Main Road in Rogersville. The Crocketts are buried in the Rogersville Cemetery at South Rogen Road and West Crockett Street.

David Crockett (1727–1777) and his wife Elizabeth (1730–1777), pioneers and grandparents of Davy Crockett (1786–1836), left North Carolina and crossed the mountains to settle near Rogersville in present-day East Tennessee. The grandfather and his wife were two of about a dozen settlers living near Rogersville who were massacred by the Creeks and Cherokees while his older sons were with the Congressional forces at King's Mountain, South Carolina in 1777. They were buried near where they were killed.

Chattanooga and vicinity
Chickamauga towns (April 10–20, 1779; Aug. 1779)
Little Owl's Town (1779)

> There were several Chickamauga towns, all in the vicinity of modern Chattanooga and Lookout Mountain.[15] Little Owl's Town was about 8.75 miles southeast of Chattanooga on the South Chickahominy Creek.

Dragging Canoe (ca. 1730–1792) (Tsi'ui-Gunsin'n, Cui Canacina) withdrew from the Cherokee Nation in March 1777 and settled on Chickamauga Creek, just north of modern Chattanooga, with about 500 of his followers and their families. He called his people Ani-Yun'wiya—the Real People. The whites called them Chickamauga. The Chickamaugas were the only tribe not subdued by the North Carolinians in 1776. James Robertson (1742–1814), the first Indian Agent to the Cherokees, was posted at Chota (Echota). He learned that the Chickamaugas planned to attack the settlers at Holston.

Virginia Governor Patrick Henry (1736–1799) authorized Colonel Evan Shelby (1720–1794) to lead an expedition of 500 North Carolina and Virginia troops, including 100 Virginia Continentals on their way to join Colonel George Rogers Clark (1752–1818) in the Illinois country, to destroy the Cherokee villages. They left Big Creek Fort on Long Island of the Holston River on Saturday, April 10, 1779 and reached the Chickamauga towns by boat on April 20th to find that most of the warriors had gone to Savannah, Georgia. They killed six Cherokees and burned 11 towns and 20,000 bushels of corn, crops, food stores and supplies provided by the British. They also took goods which they sold for £25,000.[16]

★ British Indian agent Alexander Cameron (ca. 1720–1781) arrived in the Chickamauga towns with a company of Loyalists after Colonel Evan Shelby's (1720–1794) raid in April 1779. He encouraged the Chickamaugas to join him in an attack on the South Carolinian settlements. A force of 350 Chickamaugas and Loyalists soon headed toward the South Carolina frontier. The garrison at Fort Rutledge learned of the expedition and informed General Andrew Williamson (ca. 1730–1786) who mustered 750 mounted militiamen for a counter-attack.

General Williamson expected the Chickamaugas to return to defend their homes. He sent an advance party of 16 Cherokees from Seneca Town to offer peace and protection if the other tribes did not oppose his troops. He took one of the chiefs and several young men as hostages and marched toward the easternmost Chickamauga towns. Cameron's force came within a few miles of Williamson on Wednesday, August 25th. He was told that if he attacked, Williamson would kill all the prisoners and cut Cameron's army to pieces.

Williamson promised the chiefs safe passage home if they would surrender Cameron and other British leaders. He also threatened to destroy their villages if they refused.

The chiefs refused to turn over Cameron, and Williamson marched to the easternmost Chickamauga towns and burned them.

As the Chickamauga scouts reported Williamson's force as 1,500 men, Cameron withdrew his forces. He then sent agents to purchase 300 bushels of corn from the "neutral Indians" for the Chickamaugas.[17]

Colonel Evan Shelby (1720–1794) commanded 350 men and Colonel John Montgomery (ca. 1750–1794) 150 men on the Chickamauga expedition. Hudson, their pilot, guided the boats up the Chickamauga Creek. They captured a Chickamauga near the mouth of a branch and forced him to guide the troops through an inundated canebreak to Chickamauga, a town nearly 1 mile long. Dragging Canoe (ca. 1730–1792) (Tsi'ui-Gunsin'n, Cui Canacina) and Big Fool were its chiefs. The 500 Chickamaugas were astonished at the sudden invasion of their towns and fled into the mountains. Colonels Shelby and Montgomery burned the town while John McCrosky took a party to pursue the fleeing Chickamaugas across the river. McCrosky dispersed a camp of Chickamaugas which he found on Laurel Creek. Another party took and burned Little Owl's Town and other towns in a similar manner. Shelby took 150 horses, 100 cattle and great quantities of deer skins, owned in part by a trader named McDonald, and other spoils which were all sold at auction.[18]

Renfroe's Station (July 1780)

> Renfroe's Station was established in 1780 as the first settlement in Montgomery County. It was located near where route TN 76 crosses Parson's [Passenger] Creek. Moses Renfroe's (1728–1824) party separated from Colonel John Donaldson's (1718–1785) flotilla (see pp. 142–144) which later settled in Nashville. The Renfroe settlement lasted only three months before it was destroyed by a combined force of Choctaws and Chickasaws.
>
> The battle site is on the north side of the Red River at the mouth of Parson's (Passenger) Creek about 1.3 miles northwest of Renfroe's Station.

A combined force of Choctaws and Chickasaws attacked Renfroe's Station in July 1780. They killed and scalped Nathan Turpin (d. 1780) and another man. The fort was then abandoned. The Turpin family, relatives of the Freelands, headed to Freeland's Station (see *The Guide to the American Revolutionary War in Pennsylvania, Delaware, Maryland, Virginia and North Carolina* p. 10) while the others stopped on the east side of the river at Eaton's Station. They brought with them only a few necessary articles, hiding the remainder of their household goods and personal effects as securely as possible around the deserted fort.

The refugees camped by the roadside about dusk after a day of hard travel. Some of the party began to express regret at their hasty flight after they had eaten supper. They decided to return to the fort that night to get more of their property. They reached the deserted fort early the following morning and had gathered up all they could carry away before daylight. They then started the voyage toward Eaton's Station and the Bluff a second time. They camped 2 miles north of Sycamore Creek in what is now Cheatham County that evening.

A party of Choctaws and Chickasaws surprised them during the night with sudden and destructive fire. The settlers scattered and fled through the darkness in every direction. The Choctaws and Chickasaws pursued them and killed about 20 of them with the tomahawk. A Mrs. Jones was the only one to escape. Henry Ramsey rescued her the next day and brought her safely to Eaton's Station. The dead included Joseph Renfroe (d. 1780), Mr. Johns (d. 1780) and his entire family of 12.

Those who had not turned back but had continued their journey arrived at their destination in safety. When news of this incident reached Eaton's Station and the Bluff, both locations immediately sent a rescue party to assist the mortally wounded and to bury the dead. They found that the Choctaws and Chickasaws had captured and taken away all the horses and much of the plunder and that they destroyed and scattered over the ground whatever they could not carry.[19]

Kelso
Asher's Station (late summer 1780)

Asher's Station was about 300 yards south of Champ Road, about 3 miles east of Kelso.

A party of hunters was spending the night in a cabin at Asher's Station, in Sumner County, about 2.5 miles southeast of the place where the town of Gallatin now stands, in the late summer of 1780. A band of Native Americans learned of their presence and surrounded the cabin during the night. They attacked the following morning at daybreak, poking their muskets through the cracks and firing at the sleeping hunters. They killed a man named Payne (d. 1780) and wounded another by the name of Phillips. They scalped Payne and captured all the horses at the station. As the Native Americans rode single file in the buffalo path which led toward Bledsoe's Lick, they suddenly encountered a company of settlers composed of Alexander Buchanan (1752–1824), William Ellis, James Manifee, Alexander Thompson (1760–1794) and others, who were returning to the Bluff from a hunting expedition in Trousdale County. Buchanan, who was leading his party, fired and killed the first Native American and wounded the second. The other Native Americans fled, leaving the captured horses behind. This incident so much alarmed the settlers at Asher's that they broke up the station and went to Mansker's Lick (Casper Mansker's Lick).[20]

Castalian Springs
Bledsoe's Station (late summer 1780)

Bledsoe's Station was about 0.27 miles northwest of the intersection of route TN 25 (Hartsville Pike) and Rock Springs Road in Castalian Springs.

The same band of Native Americans that attacked Asher's Station headed up the river to Bledsoe's Station where they killed and scalped William Johnston (d. 1780) and Daniel Mungle (d. 1780) who were hunting together on the Barren River at Bledsoe's Lick or on the creek near it. The Native Americans then shot all the cattle they could find near the fort and set fire to some out houses and fencing. The Native Americans then headed up the river toward Hartsville. They met Thomas Sharp Spencer along the way. He was returning alone from a hunting trip and was leading two horses laden with bear meat and pelts. The Native Americans fired at Spencer, wounding him slightly. Greatly outnumbered, Spencer dismounted promptly and fled to Bledsoe's Station, leaving the horses and cargo behind.[21]

Madison
Neely's Lick/Neely's Bend (fall 1780)

> Neely's Lick, later called Larkin Sulphur Spring was on the Cumberland River in Madison. It was on Menees Lane about 0.4 miles east of Neely's Bend Road.

Native Americans, believed to be Creeks or Delawares, killed William Neely (1730–1780) at Neely's Lick, afterwards known as Neely's Bend, in the fall of 1780, a day or two after killing Ned Carver (d. 1780). They also captured Neely's daughter Mary (b. ca. 1764) and took her to Michigan. She managed to escape after two years and made her way to New York State and eventually back to her home.[22]

Goodlettsville
Mansker's Station (1780)

> Mansker's Station was on Memorial Drive east of French Street in Goodlettsville. A historical marker is located on the opposite corner.
>   Gasper Mansker (Casper, Kasper or Kaspar Mansco) established a station of the Cumberland Settlements near Mansker's Lick near Goodlettsville in 1780. Colonel John Donaldson (1718–1785) and his family moved here after abandoning his Clover Bottom Station, following the 1780 massacre. The road connecting with Nashboro was built in 1781. A great game trail ran northeast from the Lick.

Gasper Mansker (Casper, Kasper or Kaspar Mansco) took William Neely (1730–1780), James Franklin, Daniel Frazier and others with him in 1780. They traveled 12 miles north of the Bluff to the region of the twin licks he had discovered while hunting eight years before. They built a fort on the west side of Mansker's Creek, and 300 or 400 yards from what was later known as Walton's camp ground. They named the fort Mansker's Station.

The Native Americans attacked Mansker's Station sometime in 1780 and killed Patrick Quigley (d. 1780), John Stuckley (d. 1780), James Lumsley (d. 1780) and Betsy Kennedy (d. 1780).[23]

Williamsport
Gordon Ferry (1780)

> Gordon Ferry crossed the Duck River in Williamsport about 100 yards east of the Natchez Trace Parkway.

The Chickasaws attacked Freeland's Station in May 1780 and killed one man, D. Lariman (d. 1780), and cut his head off. About 20 whites, including Alexander Buchanan (1752–1824), John Brock (1751–1792), William Mann and Captain James Robertson (1742–1814), pursued the Chickasaws to the Duck River, near Gordon's Ferry. When they approached the Chickasaw camp, the white men dismounted and marched to the camp, which was deserted. A short time later, the Chickasaws killed Isaac Lefevre (d. 1780) near the fort on the Bluff.[24]

Ashland
Harpeth River (1780)

> The Harpeth River incident occurred about where route TN 49 (Ashland City Highway) crosses the river in Ashland.

A party of Native Americans approached the Bluff Station one night in the autumn of 1780 and stole a number of horses. They loaded the horses with whatever goods and plunder they could seize and escaped.

Captain James Leeper (1755–1781) and 15 men pursued the Native Americans the next morning and overtook them at the Harpeth River. The Native Americans heard the whites as they came "with a rush through the cane," and for some time "attempted to escape with the horses and plunder." However, Captain Leeper pursued them so closely that they burned the horses along with the various stolen articles which often got entangled in the bushes and cane. The Native Americans did not take the time and precaution to cut the ropes and thongs which fastened the loads on the animals. Every Native American fled to the bush at the first musket shot, abandoning all the horses and whatever was on them. Captain Leeper was certain he wounded the Native American at whom he fired as "the fellow dropped his gun and ran."[25]

Cherokee Campaign of 1780
French Broad River (Dec. 8, 1780)
Boyd's Creek (Dec. 16, 1780)
Chota Town, Chilhowee and Telassee (Dec. 22–26, 1780)
Chota Town, Settico (Sitiku, Citico, Sietego, Sietego, Sattoga), Little Tuskeego and Kaiatee (Dec. 27–28, 1780)
Tellico River (Dec. 28, 1780)
Nickajack (1780)
Running Water (1780)
Christowee (Dec. 31, 1780)
Tanasi (Tenasee, Tennessee) (1780)

> The French Broad River runs east/west from Douglas Lake. Boyd's Creek flows into the French Broad at Sevierville.
>
> Chota Town (also spelled Chote, Echota, Itsati and other similar variations), Sietego, Little Tuskeego and Kaiatee were all in what is now the western part of Cherokee National Forest and probably along the Tellico River. Chota was near the intersection of Allegheny Loop Road and Chota Road about 300 yards south of route TN 326 (Six Mile Road) in Maryville. Settico (Sitiku, Citico, Sietego, Sietego, Sattoga) was just north of where Howards Chapel Road crosses Little Toqua Creek in Vonore. The site of Little Tuskeego is unknown.
>
> Kaiatee is Katie on the Tellico River in Tellico Plains.
>
> Nickajack was along route TN 156 (Old Ladds Road|Shellmound Road) in South Pittsburg on the shore of Nickajack Lake|Bennett Lake.

> Running Water was on the southwest bank of the Tennessee River, 4 miles above Nickajack. The site is now under Nickajack Lake|Bennett Lake north of where route I-24 crosses the lake.[26]
> Christowee is the same as Chota.
> Tanasi (Tenasee, Tennessee) was about 1.5 miles east of Settico (Sitiku, Citico). The site is now under the waters of Tellico Lake|Little Tennessee River. Tanasi attained political prominence in 1721 when its civil chief was elected the first "Emperor of the Cherokee Nation." About the same time, the town name was also applied to the river on which it was located. During the mid-18th century, Tanasi became overshadowed and eventually absorbed by the adjacent town of Chota, which was to the immediate north. The first recorded spelling of Tennessee as it is today occurred on Lieutenant Henry Timberlake's map of 1762. In 1796, the name Tennessee was selected from among several as most appropriate for the 16th state.

The British encouraged the Cherokees on the South Carolina frontier to raid the settlements after the battle of Kings Mountain, expecting that the victors of the battle would return home to protect their homes. The plan worked, but the Cherokees did not expect any resistance, since the men were away fighting. Lieutenant Colonel John Sevier (1745–1815) and about 170 frontier militiamen marched toward Chota Town on Friday, December 8, 1780. (Colonel Arthur Campbell (1743–1811) says this event occurred on December 16th.) A party of 70 Chickamaugas set an ambush in a field of tall grass along the French Broad River, also known as Boyd's Creek.

The scouts discovered the ambush, and the mounted frontiersmen attacked immediately. Their intense fire caused the Chickamaugas to flee into a canebrake for cover. The militiamen killed 28 Chickamaugas and suffered only three wounded. They found General Henry Clinton's (1730–1795) proclamation and other documents expressive of their hostile intent among the baggage. Colonel Sevier and his men returned to Buckingham's Island on the Broad River to await reinforcements from Virginia.[27]

★ After Lieutenant Colonel John Sevier's (1745–1815) victory at Boyd Creek, he and his men withdrew to Buckingham Island to await the arrival of reinforcements. Colonel Arthur Campbell (1743–1811) arrived on Friday, December 22, 1780 with 300 to 400 Virginia and North Carolina militiamen. The combined forces crossed the French Broad River at Tomotley Ford and headed to the Tennessee River. They learned that the Cherokees were aware of their approach and had blocked all the normal fording places.

Colonel Campbell made a feint against the island town while the main body crossed the river on the 24th. The Cherokees seemed to be fleeing in consternation. Colonel Campbell divided his force, sending a part to destroy the Lower Towns while the main division proceeded to Chota. Just as he passed a defile above Toque, Colonel Campbell observed the Cherokees on the hills below the town who seemed ready to attack his van but he could not entice them to attack because they saw his main body coming. They let him pass quietly. There were only a few scattered shots exchanged at a great distance. The militiamen killed one Cherokee in the town and captured the provisions and 17 horses loaded with clothing, skins and household furniture. Campbell then burned the town. He discovered the fugitives were heading toward Tellico and Hiwassee.

Major Joseph Martin (1740–1808) discovered an escape path that led toward the towns of Tellico and Hiwassee. Colonel Campbell sent Captain James Crabtree (1750–1823) and a detachment of 60 men from the Virginia Regiment to burn the town of

Chilhowee the same day. They burned part of the town but were attacked by a superior force of Cherokees, forcing them back to the main force without any losses.

★ Colonel Arthur Campbell (1743–1811) sent Major Jonathan Tipton III (1734–1833), of the Carolina corps, with another detachment of 150 mounted militiamen across the river on Tuesday, December 26, 1780 to dislodge the Cherokees at Telassee. However, they were not able to cross the river. Another detachment of 150 infantrymen burned the rest of Chilhowee, killed three Cherokees and captured nine others.[28]

★ Nancy Ward (1735–1824), the Cherokee princess who alerted the Watauga and Nolichucky settlers about impending Cherokee attacks in 1776, was sent to Colonel Arthur Campbell's (1743–1811) camp at Chota Town on behalf of some of the chiefs to make an overture for peace. Campbell refused to consider peace because he still "wished first to visit the vindictive part of the nation, mostly settled at Hiwassee and Christowee, and to distress the whole as much as possible by destroying their habitations and provisions." The Virginia militiamen set fire to Chota, Sietego and Little Tuskeego, on Thursday, December 28, 1780, and moved to Kaiatee, a town on the Tellico River.

★ Major Joseph Martin (1740–1808), returning from a patrol on Thursday night, December 28, 1780, discovered a band of Cherokees. His men killed two of them and drove several others into the river. In another skirmish that same evening, some Cherokees gathering corn fired at some of the Virginia militiamen, one of whom wounded a Cherokee. When the commanding officer, Captain James Elliot (d. 1780), rode up to the wounded man, the Cherokee shot Captain Elliot in the head and grabbed his gun. The rest of the men in the patrol shot the Cherokee dead and killed three others in the skirmish. They buried Captain James Elliot beneath one of the cabins and then burned the cabin to prevent the mutilation of his corpse.[29]

★ Colonel Arthur Campbell (1743–1811) left a force of 150 men at Kaiatee on Friday, December 29, 1780 and marched 40 miles to Hiwassee Old Town. He found the town abandoned but captured a young warrior who reported that some Cherokees, together with the British Agent McDonald and some Loyalist militiamen, were at Christowee, 12 miles away, waiting to ambush them.

Campbell, aware that he was being observed, ordered the camp to be laid out and cooking fires kindled to give the impression that they were going to stay the night. He and 300 men (some refused to go) crossed the river after dark and discovered that the Cherokees had fled in a hurry, leaving behind almost all their corn and other provisions; many of their farming implements; all their heavy furniture; and part of their stocks of horses, cattle and hogs. The militiamen burned 1,000 cabins and 50,000 bushels of corn before returning to Kaiatee.

Major Joseph Martin (1740–1808) captured four prisoners on the return march. They reported that the Chickamauga chiefs wanted peace; so Major Martin sent the chiefs a message, saying that, if they wanted peace, they should send six of their chiefs to the Great Island to meet with him. The rest of the army headed home.

The militiamen killed 20 Cherokees and took 17 prisoners, mostly women and children during the campaign. They lost only one man killed and two wounded. Colonel Campbell reported the militiamen

> destroyed the towns of Chote, Seitego, Tuskeego, Chilhowee, Toque, Micliqua, Kai-a-tee, Sattoga, Telico, Hiwassee, and Chistowee, all the principal towns, besides some small ones, and several scattering settlements, in which were upwards of 1000 houses, and not less than 50,000 bushels of corn, and large quantities of other kinds of provisions, all of which after taking sufficient substance for the army, whilst in the

country and on its return, were committed to the flames, or otherwise destroyed. No place in the Over-Hill country remained unvisited, except the small town of Telassee, a scattering settlement in the neighbourhood of Chickamogga, and the town of Calogee, situated on the sources of the Mobile.[30]

The Chickamaugas moved farther down the Tennessee River to the foot of Lookout Mountain where they built the "Five Lower Towns:" Lookout Town (near Tiftonia, Tennessee), Crow Town (near Stevenson, Alabama), Long Island (near Bridgeport, Alabama), Runningwater (near Haletown, Tennessee), and Nickajack (near Shellmound, Tennessee). Discontented Creeks, Shawnees and Loyalists joined the Chickamaugas; and Dragging Canoe (ca. 1730–1792) (Tsi'ui-Gunsin'n, Cui Canacina) continued raiding white settlements.[31]

★ Nickajack was established as a Lower Town in 1774, near the Great Crossing of the Tennessee River, where the Creeks crossed into Tennessee just below Chattanooga. Colonel John Sevier (1745–1815) burned it in 1780.[32]

★ Running Water was established as a Lower Town in 1774 and served as a base for raids by Dragging Canoe (ca. 1730–1792) (Tsi'ui-Gunsin'n, Cui Canacina) and his nephew, John Watts (or Kunokeski), also known as Young Tassel, (ca. 1760–1802). Colonel John Sevier's (1745–1815) men burned the town in 1780.[33]

★ Colonel Arthur Campbell (1743–1811) found the Cherokee town of Settico (Sitiku, Citico) deserted in 1780 and his men probably burned it. In 1781, Nancy Ward (1735–1824) helped five white traders who were destined for execution to escape.[34]

★ Tanasi (also spelled Tanase, Tenasi, Tenassee, Tunissee, Tennessee and other such variations) was burned by Colonel John Sevier's (1745–1815) men in 1780.

Nashville and vicinity

Nashville (Oct. 1779)

Lick Branch (May 1780)

Richland Creek (May 1780)

Heaton's (or Eaton's) Station (July or Aug. 1780)

Clover Bottom (Nov. 1780)

Bernard killed (May 1780)

Dunham's (1780 or 1781)

Freeland's Station (Jan. 15, 1781)

Fort Nashborough (April 2, 1781)

Battle of the Bluffs

The stockade along First Avenue, North and Church Street, on the bluff a few blocks south of the actual site, contains a 6-foot high granite boulder with a Daughters of the American Revolution marker attached that reads: "Fort Nashborough. Named in memory of General Nash of North Carolina, who fell at Germantown, Pennsylvania, October 4, 1777, in the War of the Revolution. Erected on the bluff near this location, by the pioneers of the Cumberland settlement in the year 1780, as a central fort of defense against Indian attacks, was the scene of many noted historical events, especially the Indian attack of April 2, 1781, known as 'The Battle of the Bluffs.'"

A Tennessee historical marker outside the stockade notes the fort's significance: "Fort Nashborough. The original stockade fronted on the river slightly north of here, covering an area of about two acres. In that enclosure, on May 13, 1780, representatives of this and other settlements met and adopted the Cumberland Compact for the government of the new settlement. About 500 yards west, April 2, 1781, settlers assisted by dogs, drove off the Indians in the Battle of the Bluffs."[35]

Lick Creek (also known as Bledsoe's Lick Creek) is a tertiary stream feeding into the Cumberland River northeast of Nashville. It is also possible that the site could have been where Bledsoe Creek joins the Cumberland River about 2 miles farther south.

Richland Creek is in west Nashville near where Briley Parkway (TN 155) crosses James Avenue.

Heaton's (or Eaton's) Station was on the north shore of the Cumberland River in Nashville. It was near the intersection of Baptist World Center Drive and Haynes Mead Circle. There is a historical marker in the vicinity, but the location selected is at the highest location in the area, the most logical location for a fortified structure.

Clover Bottom was located northwest of route US 70 (TN 24|Lebanon Pike) about 0.38 miles west of where that route crosses the Stones River in Nashville. A historical marker is on the same road about 200 yards after the bridge.

Mr. Bernard was killed at the east end of Kellow Street near the intersection with 10th Avenue North in Nashville.

The Dunhams lived at what is now the northwest corner of the intersection of Bellemeade Boulevard and Harding Place in Nashville.

The site of Freeland's Station is marked at 1400 Eighth Avenue North in Nashville.

Several companies of men set out from the New Acquisition (York County, South Carolina) for guard duty in the "overmountain" settlements of eastern and middle Tennessee in October 1779. William Fleming was one of these men and he noted in his pension application that he

> volunteered as a private militiaman under Capt. [Robert] Leeper and marched to Cumberland in the State of Tennessee to guard the settlement against the Indians and was stationed at a place called the French Lick [the place where Nashville now stands]. Shortly after getting there Capt. Leeper was wounded in a skirmish with the Indians and was succeeded by Capt. Drake. We had several skirmishes with the Indians during this campaign in which I served eight months.[36]

★ A party of Creeks or Cherokees killed Joseph Hay (d. 1780) on the Lick Branch, between the Bluff and Freeland's Station, in May 1780. They then retreated quickly, taking his rifle, hunting knife, shot pouch and powder horn. His body was buried by the settlers in the open ground on a point of land east of Sulphur Spring.

★ A party of Creeks or Cherokees then invested Freeland's Station. They found an old man, named Bernard (d. 1780), clearing the land for his cabin near what was then called Denton's Lick and now Buena Vista Springs. They crept up but Bernard was so engaged in his work that he did not hear the warriors approach. They shot him dead, cut off his head and took it with them in triumph. The two small boys, Joseph and William Dunham, who were with the old man, escaped unhurt and gave the alarm to the people at Freeland's.[37]

★ John Milliken (d. 1780) and a hunter named Keywood had not heard the alarm and were heading toward a settlement between Freeland's Station and Denton's Lick in May

1780. They stopped at Richland Creek for a drink. A band of Creeks or Cherokees on the bank fired at them as they stooped down to drink. Milliken fell dead. The Native Americans cut off his head and took it with them. Keywood escaped uninjured and ran 5 or 6 miles to the fort at the Bluff with the news of Milliken's death.[38]

See also **Lick Branch** pp. 249–250.

★ A number of people determined to settle on the east side of the Cumberland River. They selected a station about 1.5 miles below the Bluffs, which was called Eaton's or Heaton's Station, as Amos Eaton was one of that party.

A party of Native Americans, believed to be Delawares, killed Jonathan Jennings (d. 1780) at the point of the first island above Nashville in July or August 1780. They then killed Ned Carver (d. 1780) higher up the Cumberland River on the bluff on the north side. His wife and two children escaped and went to Nashville.

★ The same party of Native Americans killed William Neely (d. 1780) at Neely's Lick, a day or two later, and took his daughter prisoner. They also killed James Mayfield (1722–1780) near Eaton's Station.[39]

See **Neely's Lick** p. 245.

★ John and Daniel Dunham had settled at Belle Meade near French Lick in the summer of 1780. They built a log house and made some other improvements but were obliged to move their families back to the fort at the Bluff for protection. Mrs. Dunham sent her little daughter to the woodpile, about 300 or 400 yards up the hill from the compound of Fort Nashborough, a few days later, to gather a basket of wood chips. Some Cherokees were hidden in a fallen treetop nearby. When the little girl came up the hill, they sprang out, seized her by the hair and scalped her. Her terrified mother heard her cries and ran up the hill toward her. A shot from the Native Americans wounded the mother.

The men from the fort had now armed themselves and came rushing to the rescue. The Native Americans saw them and fled into the surrounding thickets and escaped. Both mother and daughter recovered and lived for many years afterward but never completely recovered their health.[40]

★ Colonel John Donaldson (1718–1785) had gone up the river to the Clover Bottom with two boats in November 1780 to transport the corn that he and others had raised the previous summer. After loading the boats with the corn, they proceeded a short distance down the river when Colonel Donaldson remembered that he had forgotten to gather some cotton which he had planted at the lower end of the field. So, he asked his companions to go ashore to pick part of the crop. They thought that they should continue their journey as it was getting late. Colonel Donaldson insisted they go ashore.

A party of Native Americans lay in ambush to intercept the boats on their return. They attacked the people in the other boat shortly after they landed. The Native Americans killed everyone except a free African American and a white man. The white man swam to shore and wandered many days in the woods before he reached the bluff. The Native Americans captured Absalom Tatom's (1742–1802) slave, George, and wounded and captured the son of Jack Civil, a free mulatto. The slain included Abel Gower (1720–1780) and Abel Gower, Jr. (d. 1780) and John Robertson (d. 1780), the son of Captain James Robertson (1742–1814).

About dawn the following morning, a little dog began barking and warned the inhabitants of the station. They went out in a boat and retrieved the floating boat. They found it contained the body of an African American who had accompanied the party.

His chin had been eaten by the dog. The men concluded that the rest of the party were killed. Colonel Donaldson managed to escape to Mansker's Station.[41]

★ Colonel James Robertson (1742–1814) arrived at Freeland's Fort in early January 1781 with badly needed salt and ammunition. A short while later, a band of Chickasaws crept into the settlement at midnight on Monday, January 15th and tried to capture it. Robertson awoke, saw the Chickasaws and sounded the alarm to awake his 11 men and the neighbors who fired from inside their cabins. The firing of the swivel gun (see Photo GA-2) at Fort Nashborough signaled that help was on the way. The Chickasaws departed, leaving one dead. They killed two settlers, one white and one black, when rifle balls passed between the logs of their unchinked cabins.[42]

★ Colonel Samuel Barton (1749–1810) rode down to Wilson's Spring Branch in search of cattle around the end of March 1781. He was shot and wounded in the left wrist and escaped but was unable to take part in the imminent battle.

★ After the destruction of the Overhill and Valley towns, the Cherokees sued for peace. However, the Chickamaugas continued to strike the weaker settlements on the Cumberland River. Dragging Canoe (ca. 1730–1792) (Tsi'ui-Gunsin'n, Cui Canacina) led a party of about 200 Chickamaugas which arrived at the Bluff on Sunday, April 1, 1781. He positioned his warriors during the night for the engagement the following morning.

Three warriors approached the stockade, fired and retreated out of range. As they reloaded, Lieutenant James Robertson (1742–1814) and 20 mounted militiamen set out in pursuit but were ambushed when they reached Wilson's Spring Branch. Some Chickamaugas made a stand where the wings of their line hid in the creek bed and among the thick bushes on its banks. They fired at the militiamen who dismounted and quickly returned fire. The firing and yelling frightened the horses which ran away. A large detachment of Chickamaugas, concealed on the hillside to the west, emerged and cut off the avenue of retreat to the fort.

The panic stricken horses dashed through their lines at this moment and threw the Chickamaugas into confusion. When some of the warriors chased the horses, a gap opened in their ranks. Charlotte Reeves Robertson (1751–1843), observing the situation from the fort, opened the gate and turned loose the pack of hunting dogs. They headed straight for the Chickamaugas and attacked them with great ferocity, increasing the confusion. The militiamen took advantage of the confusion and retreated to the fort, taking their two wounded with them. The Chickamaugas pursued them closely. As they approached the fort, one man was shot in the leg and fell with a broken thigh bone. The others could not stop to help him. He primed his musket, which he had already charged as he ran, and shot his nearest pursuer dead.

A Chickamauga overtook another man within 20 yards of the gate and struck him on the shoulder, causing him to drop his musket. He seized his opponent's weapon. The Chickamauga took it away from him and knocked him to his knees. Another man, who had already reached the fort, fired and killed the Chickamauga.

As the militiamen had reached the stockade and were maintaining a brisk fire from its gate, the Chickamaugas began to withdraw. They reappeared at night, but a single discharge from the old swivel gun, loaded with broken stone and scraps of iron, followed by the discharge of a small piece at Eaton's Station, caused the Chickamaugas to disperse. The garrison, reinforced by a relief party from Eaton's, kept watch until daylight the next morning. The militiamen lost five men killed and two wounded in the affair.

The Chickasaw attacks decreased the following year when they made peace with the settlers. Their leader, Piomingo or Hopoi Mingo (d. 1795), considered the settlers less of a threat than the Spanish government. However, the Chickamaugas and their Creek allies continued attacking the settlements for the next 14 years.[43]

Waynesboro
Moccasin Creek (Sept. 11, 1781)

> Moccasin Creek runs north–south in Waynesboro, east of route TN 13 (Waynesboro Highway). The Coosa River is a tributary of the Alabama River in the states of Alabama and Georgia.

Colonel John Sevier (1745–1815) and 100 mounted riflemen conducted a series of attacks against the Cherokees in late June 1781. They killed 12 of Dragging Canoe's (ca. 1730–1792) warriors and the army soon increased to 200 men. When he learned of a family massacred on Moccasin Creek in September, Sevier and his army attacked deep into Native American territory, destroying several Chickamauga and Creek towns on the Coosa River.[44]

Cherokee Campaign of 1782

> Sauta may have been in the northwestern part of the Fort Rucker Military Reservation, east of New Brockton, Alabama.
>   Noocassee was 0.5 miles northeast of Chota on the north shore of Sixmile Creek and route TN 326 (Six Mile Road) in Maryville and east of Chota Road.
>   Selacoa was west of where Salacoa Road crosses Salacoa Creek in Waleska, Georgia.
>   Estanala was about 0.5 miles east of the intersection of routes AL 68 and County Road 140 in Gaylesville, Alabama.

The Raven of Chota, Savanukah (or "Savanooka") joined the Loyalist forces in the autumn of 1780. Colonel John Sevier (1745–1815) and 300 North Carolina militiamen invaded the French Broad region. They were joined by 400 Virginians under Colonel Arthur Campbell (1743–1811). Together, they destroyed Chota and proceeded toward Dragging Canoe (ca. 1730–1792) (Tsi'ui-Gunsin'n, Cui Canacina) towns on the Chickamauga River. However, they retired before reaching the Chickamaugas.

Minor raids and counterattacks continued through the spring of 1781, preventing any Cherokees from helping the British defend Augusta in May and June. As the British lost control of the South during the summer, the Cherokees made peace overtures. Meanwhile, The Raven of Chota and a few followers traveled to Savannah, Georgia to offer their services to the British defenders in exchange for the reopening of trade.

A final raid out of the Chickamauga territory occurred in December along the Tennessee River on the South Carolina frontier. A counterattack by the Georgia militia stopped a party of warriors trying to slip through to Savannah.

First Expedition

★ Brigadier General Andrew Pickens (1739–1817) and Colonel Elijah Clarke (1733–1799), each leading 150 men, joined forces to attack the Cherokees during the winter months early in 1782. They proceeded even though they failed to receive reinforcements from North Carolina, Virginia and Tennessee. The Cherokees left their villages and destroyed food supplies as they retreated, causing hunger for the pursuers and their horses. Pickens and Clarke retreated in a campaign that was a failure. They suffered two wounded and killed about 40 Cherokees. Believing that Pickens retreated because he feared a large engagement, the Cherokees continued attacking settlements.

Second Expedition

★ Brigadier General Andrew Pickens (1739–1817) requested South Carolina Governor John Matthews (Matthewes) (1744–1802) for permission to lead an expedition into the Cherokee country to stop their attacks and to wipe out the forces of Colonel Philemon Waters (1734–1796) and Dragging Canoe (ca. 1730–1792) (Tsi'ui-Gunsin'n, Cui Canacina). The governor approved the plan. General Pickens requested Colonel Elijah Clarke (1733–1799), of Georgia, for help on Thursday, September 5, 1782. He set September 16, at Long Creek in Wilkes County, Georgia, as the time and place of rendezvous.

Pickens set out on September 10 with 316 men and 30 days' provisions. He crossed Cherokee Ford and entered Georgia. Clarke's 98 Georgians brought his force to 414 men. Captain Robert Anderson (Andersen) (d. 1813) was in charge of the South Carolinians and Colonel John White led the North Carolinians. They rested a day to refresh the men and to plan their strategy.

★ On Thursday, September 19, 1782, they headed west toward the Chattahoochie River which they crossed at the ford of Beaver Shoal on September 24. Captain Robert Maxwell (1731–1792) and Captain John Mapp (1733–1789) would take turns leading the column with their companies of swordsmen. The whole column was to advance in silence as they marched through the woods, along a trail they had not explored, to avoid the usual trail which was guarded by the Cherokees. A traitor or a Loyalist spy alerted the Cherokees.

Some distance along a small trail, they encountered and captured two Cherokees who reported that there were several towns within 10 or 12 miles and that Colonel Thomas Waters (ca. 1738–after 1810) and his party were about 20 miles away. Pickens sent Captain Robert Anderson (Andersen) (d. 1813) up the river with 120 men, guided by one of the prisoners, to destroy the towns and villages on the river in that direction. He sent Colonel White downstream with similar orders. Clarke and Pickens took the more direct route to confront Waters.

The main purpose of the expedition was to destroy Waters and his force. Pickens introduced a new method of attack. His men used the rifle only while reconnoitering the enemy position. The soldiers attacked on horse, rushing toward the Cherokees with drawn swords and easily defeating the terrified warriors.

When Anderson and White arrived that afternoon, they reported the death of eight Cherokees and the destruction of several towns. Pickens headed to attack Sauta, about three days' march from the settlements. The night before the attack, they camped about half a mile out of the town. To keep from being discovered, Pickens ordered the troops to dismount at sundown, feed the horses from their meager supply of corn and refresh themselves. Each man was to sit with his back against a tree and hold his horse by the bridle and to keep awake so the horses would not escape. They were not to light any fires despite the cold, frosty night.

The men all mounted at daylight and attacked the town, using their swords and pistols if necessary. They had orders to kill anyone looking like a warrior, but they were to spare the old men, squaws and children. Pickens led his force to attack the upper part of the town while Clarke attacked the lower, intending to meet in the center. The rising sun glistened on the blades of the swords. The Cherokees, caught completely by surprise, fled in every direction. Some rushed to their cabins for their weapons; others fled across the savanna to the woods. The troops broke into squads and pursued, hacking the fleeing Cherokees with their swords. If a first blow failed, a succeeding trooper would strike a second or a third blow.

William Green (1740–1813), a large and powerful man, was long remembered for his skill in using his large sword to cleave the heads of fleeing Cherokees "like so many pumpkins." General Pickens himself, joined by 12 or 15 others, pursued a very dark young Cherokee who fled with his gun toward a deep ravine between two spurs skirting the town. As the horsemen could not enter the ravine, they surrounded it and shot down at the young man who taunted them with his dance. When they failed to kill him after some 20 shots, a man named Parata (possibly Prater) jumped from his horse and slid down the ravine carrying both his sword and rifle. Andrew Lee Pickens records that Parata, a fool-hardy fellow,

> came within twenty or thirty yards of the Indian, who was walking to and fro apparently unconcerned, and took aim. The red man then began dodging with the agility of a black snake, and when Parata fired he missed, and was immediately pursued by his intended victim. The white man closely pursued by the Indian with a poised gun, took shelter behind a large tree, and was pursued around the trunk, the red man seeking a sure shot. When the trigger was pulled, the ball merely grazed Parata's shoulder.
>
> "Now ---- damn ye," shouted the white man, "it's my turn!"
>
> Simultaneous blows from the white man's sword and the Indian's clubbed gun followed! The fascinated horsemen above, unable to render aid, could not tell who had the advantage! But fortune favored Parata! The sword struck the Indian's throat, his head fell upon his bosom, and his body sank to the ground, and his descending gun passed harmlessly over Parata's head. The nerves of the white man tense, he chopped the head of his fallen foe to pieces, punctuating each blow with a profane oath.[45]

Pickens, Clarke and their men also attacked Chota, less than three quarters of a mile away on the same creek. They found a few Cherokees there, killed some and dispersed the others. They also captured a few prisoners at another small town, perhaps Noocassee, a short distance above Chota. Around dusk, several parties were ordered out to scour the woods. They killed several more Cherokees, maybe as many as 79, according to one estimate, including one Loyalist and an African American. Pickens had no soldier killed and only four disabled. He also used less than three pounds of powder. He burned all of the towns and captured a quantity of skins and furs, some brass kettles, a large number of horses and some African Americans. They also took some cattle, some peas, beans and other provisions for the troops; but they destroyed the corn, some gathered and some standing.

Estimates of the enemy killed range from less than 40 to more than 80, 13 villages burned and many prisoners captured. However, Colonel Thomas Waters (ca. 1738–after 1810), the main objective of the expedition, managed to escape, helped by his many spies.

★ Colonel Elijah Clarke (1733–1799) marched from Selacoa on October 8, 1782 with 100 men in pursuit of Colonel Thomas Waters (ca. 1738–after 1810) who had stopped at Estanala about 60 miles west of Long Swamp. Waters, alerted to the danger, fled to St. Augustine, Florida. Captain Robert Maxwell's (1731–1792) company marched to Estanala on the same day and took 24 African Americans, most of whom had been stolen by Waters and his men in Georgia and South Carolina. They also took several horses and some furs and were back at their headquarters by the 15th.

Pickens released some of his prisoners and offered peace to the Cherokees, assuring them that he would not destroy any more towns if they would surrender the whites and

African Americans and enter into a peace treaty. He also told them that he blamed the white renegades among them rather than the Cherokees. He would stay two days in his present location awaiting their response to his peace offer. If the Cherokees did not accept the offer within two days, he would proceed with the destruction of towns and provisions.

As he waited, Pickens visited several towns in search of provisions and forage. He also brought his peace offering personally. Several chiefs had met in the mountains and appointed one of them, Chief Terrapin (1736–post 1796), to meet with Pickens. The Terrapin and a group of warriors brought six white prisoners, some of Waters's men, with them and promised to try to bring in the others, admitting that they were the cause of their recent trouble.

Several of the chiefs eventually came to Selacoa and proposed a council for a treaty at Long Swamp. Twelve chiefs and 200 warriors appeared on Thursday, October 17. They entered into temporary agreements which the whole nation would confirm at a time and place appointed by the governor of Georgia.

The Cherokees would surrender to Georgia all their lands south of the Savannah and east of the Chattahoochee rivers and trade would resume on similar terms to those previously held with the British. The treaty was signed on October 22, 1782 and the troops were dismissed. The Treaty of Augusta, a follow-up of the treaty of Long Swamp, was held at Augusta, Georgia, the following spring and consummated May 31, establishing the boundaries between Georgia and the Cherokees.[46]

Cross Plains
Kilgore Station (Mauldin's Station) (summer 1782)

Kilgore Station was located at the intersection of Main Street and Kilgore Trace in Cross Plains. A historical marker is on route TN 25 (Main Street), about 0.75 miles west.

Several people, including the Mauldins and Kilgore, had erected a fort on the north side of the Cumberland River on the head-waters of the Red River, near the Cross Plains, in Robertson County. The settlement became known as Mauldin's or Kilgore's Station. These "stationers" considered themselves so remote from the usual hunting-range of the Native Americans that they felt secure. However, the Native Americans discovered them in the summer of 1782 and killed two of their number, Philip Mason, Jr. (1764–1782) and Josiah Hoskins (d. 1782) in one day. They also captured Samuel Martin, a quarrelsome person and of such bad character that nobody mourned his loss. They also captured Isaac Johnston who later managed to escape.[47]

14
ARKANSAS

France ceded the Louisiana Territory, which included Arkansas, to Spain in 1762. Great Britain acquired the part east of the Mississippi River in the Treaty of Paris that ended the Seven Years War [French and Indian War (1756–1763)]. The Crown forces attacked Fort Carlos III, previously called Arkansas Post, in 1783, after the Spanish joined the French in the American War of Independence. The Spanish kept the territory until 1800 when it reverted to France in the Treaty of San Ildefonso. France sold all the land to the United States in the Louisiana Purchase three years later.

> The Arkansas Historical Association (416 Old Main, University of Arkansas, Fayetteville, AR 72701, phone: 479-575-5884; website: **www.uark.edu/depts/arkhist/home/**) publishes the *Arkansas Historical Quarterly* while the Arkansas Department of Parks and Tourism (**www.arkansas.com/**) is the official guide to the parks and recreational opportunities throughout the state. However, as there is only one site in this state related to the American War of Independence, visitors could address themselves directly to the Arkansas Post National Memorial (1741 Old Post Road, Gillett, AR 72055 (phone: 870-548-2207, website: **www.nps.gov/arpo/**).

See map of Alabama, Mississippi, Louisiana and Arkansas.

Gillett
Fort Carlos III (formerly the Arkansas Post) (April 17–24, 1783) "Colbert Incident"

> Fort Carlos III was on the Arkansas River a few miles above its juncture with the Mississippi River. The fort, about 75 miles southeast of Little Rock, protected the Arkansas, Cimarron and Canadian rivers. The site of Fort Carlos III and most of the battleground is flooded by the waters of Horseshoe Lake [Post Bend] which was created by the completion of Dam No. 2.
>
> Arkansas Post National Memorial, at 1741 Old Post Road, Gillett, AR 72055 (phone: 870-548-2207, website: **www.nps.gov/arpo/**) commemorates the site of the fort and the engagement which is sometimes referred to as the "Colbert Incident."
>
> The site of Red Bluffs, the location of Arkansas Post National Memorial, was the first high ground encountered within 30 miles of the mouth of the Arkansas River. The Arkansas River in the vicinity of Arkansas Post can fluctuate more than 30 feet between high and low water marks. The site, while above flood waters, was three days away from the Mississippi River, making it difficult to support convoys passing between St. Louis and New Orleans. Also, the river's swift current undermined the bank upon which the fort stood and eventually claimed it.[1]

The French government signed treaties of alliance and commerce with the Continental Congress in February 1778. The following summer, she entered the war against Great Britain. France persuaded her longtime ally, Spain, to enter the war the following year in April 1779. Spain hoped to embarrass her old enemy and to expand her colonial empire.

The stockade of Fort Carlos III consisted of "red oak stakes thirteen feet high, with diameters of 10 to 15 or 16 inches, split in two and reinforced inside by similar stakes to a height of six feet and a banquette of two feet" enclosed all "necessary places, including a house 45 feet long and 15 feet wide, and a storehouse, both serving to lodge my [Captain Balthazar de Villiers] troops, and around several smaller buildings." The embrasures (see Photo GA-5) for the cannons and swivel guns (see Photo GA-2) were "covered with sliding panels" which were "bullet proof."[2]

The fort and trading village of Arkansas Post were relocated from the south bank of the Arkansas River to a new location on the north side of the river, about 36 miles upstream, in 1779 because the spring floods inundated the lower Mississippi Valley. Post commandant Captain Balthazar de Villiers (ca. 1780–1832) and his men were busy relocating the post in August 1779, when New Orleans received the news that Spain had declared war on Great Britain.

Colonel Estevan Rodriguez Miró (1744–1795), acting-governor of Louisiana in the absence of Governor-General Bernardo de Gálvez (1746–1786), learned that the carriages of three of the four cannon at Fort Carlos III had rotted and that the stockade had not been pierced for embrasures. So, he shipped four naval carriages for the cannons from Natchez and sent Antonio Soler, second lieutenant of artillery, to cut embrasures in the stockade, mount the cannons and instruct the garrison in their use.[3]

Captain Jacobo DuBreuil arrived at Arkansas Post on January 5, 1783, and assumed command of the fort within 48 hours, after completing the necessary paperwork and inventories. On March 1, he sent Quapaw Chief Angaska up the Mississippi toward Chickasaw Bluffs to reconnoiter and to gather information on the activities of James Logan Colbert (1720–1784). Colbert, a Scot who had migrated to the American colonies to escape reprisals against suspected Jacobites, settled among the Chickasaws who were faithful allies of the British in the long struggle for control of the Mississippi Valley. Colbert had become one of their leaders and was planning to attack Fort Carlos III, formerly the Arkansas Post.

Angaska and his 23 Quapaw warriors, accompanied by 11 white hunters, had orders to locate Colbert's camp, determine the size of his forces and attack and destroy them if feasible. DuBreuil might have sent more volunteers with Angaska had he not had a critical shortage of food resulting from the previous year's poor harvest.

After talking about the attack for almost a year, Colbert was finally ready in early April 1783. Captain DuBreuil estimated Colbert's force at 100 whites and 14 Chickasaws and mixed-bloods. Malcom Clark, a participant, recalled they numbered "eleven Indians, sons and nephews of Colbert, five Negroes, one Frenchman, and enough English and Americans to make the number eighty-two."[4]

The party boarded a keelboat and bateau (see Photo FL-7) which had been converted into a sort of gunboat during the winter but it did not have any cannons. South of Chickasaw Bluffs, about 60 miles north of the mouth of the Arkansas, they captured 16 pirogues (pronounced as a pee-ro or pee-rog) from settlers traveling down the Mississippi to relocate in the Natchez District. Colbert's fleet turned into the south of the White River near which he captured a bercha (see Photo AR-1) headed upstream with a cargo of rum and sugar and a crew of eight or ten men. He also captured a bercha from New Orleans, with a cargo of powder, and two pirogues from Arkansas Post, loaded with beaver pelts and bear grease.

Skelch of a flat bottom Boat such as are used to descend the Ohio and the Mississipi.

AR-1. *Bercha is a flatboat used for transporting cargo, particularly on the Ohio and Mississippi rivers.*

The water at the lower ends of the White and Arkansas rivers was backing up for many miles because the Mississippi was flooding. Colbert led his forces up the White River with oars muffled with leather and then went up the Arkansas, as some of his Chickasaw relatives scouted the river ahead in a pirogue. Early in the evening of April 16, they stopped at Uzutluhi [Osotouy], a Quapaw village 10 miles south of Arkansas Post. Here, they met with Angaska, who had returned from his reconnaissance mission toward Chickasaw Bluffs, and told him that they were "coming with a dozen Americans to shake hands with Captain Dubreuil" in the morning.

The rest of Colbert's force passed the village after midnight on the 17th and entered the north bank of the Arkansas at Red Bluff and landed a short distance downstream from the habitants' fields. Colbert appointed seven men to guard the boats while the rest headed for the fort where they arrived at 2:30 AM on April 17, 1783.

Commandant DuBreuil was asleep. Sergeant Alexo Pastor and eight privates stood guard. Colbert and his men arrived without being noticed. They broke down the door of the dwelling in which Lieutenant Luis de Villars and his family slept about half a mile downstream from Fort Carlos III and captured them along with six other residents and their families. Four families escaped into the woods.

Sergeant Pastor and his men spotted Colbert's force and began firing in the darkness. Two of his men were killed, an African American settler was wounded and five other men captured in the 30 minute engagement. Only Sergeant Pastor escaped, fleeing to the fort, which he entered by crawling through an embrasure (see Photo-GA-5).[5]

Captain DuBreuil and his 40-man garrison took their stations as soon as they heard the first shots. Colbert's force managed to get within "pistol shot" of the stockade and took cover in a ravine from which they directed small-arms fire at the fort from 3 to 9 AM. The lead balls struck the "evergreen oak of which the palisades were made" and caused no damage.

Captain DuBreuil had his four 4-pounder cannons fired at the raiders to discourage them from rushing the fort, but the more than 300 shots fired at them inflicted no casualties. It did keep them from removing plunder they had taken from the residents' homes. Thinking that the raiders might have artillery to breach the stockade walls, Captain DuBreuil decided to drive them from the ravine by mid-morning. He ordered Sergeant Pastor to take nine privates of the Louisiana Regiment and four Quapaws to do so.

Just as Sergeant Pastor and his men were getting ready to charge, DuBreuil spotted Doña Marie Luisa de Villars and one of Colbert's officers, carrying a flag of truce. They approached by the road opposite the one Sergeant Pastor and his men were going to take. The officer fled in fear, leaving Doña Marie to deliver the message from Captain Colbert. The message, written in French, read:

> M. Le Capitain Colbert is sent by his superiors to take the post of the Arkansas and by this power Sir, he demands that you capitulate. It is his plan to take it with all his forces, having already taken all the inhabitants, together with the Lieut. Luis de Villars and his family.[6]

Doña Marie Luisa returned with Captain DuBreuil's refusal to surrender. The fort gate opened and Sergeant Pastor's detail charged the enemy with loud war whoops, taking them by surprise. Colbert's men panicked and fled toward the ravine and then toward the landing. Meanwhile, Captain DuBreuil spotted some of the raiders to his left. Fearing they might try to intercept Sergeant Pastor's patrol, DuBreuil called for them to proceed with caution. However, they hurried back to their boats moored at Red Bluff. One of Colbert's men was killed and a Chickasaw wounded during the skirmish and the retreat.

Colbert embarked his prisoners and sent some of the women and children to Captain DuBreuil with a message demanding his surrender by noon when he expected the arrival of 500 Chickasaws and two bateaux loaded with men armed with four swivels (see Photo GA-11) and a cannon. He then headed downstream after driving a tomahawk into the ground to signify his intention to return. Captain DuBreuil ignored Colbert's threat.

When Chief Angaska arrived at Fort Carlos III around noon, DuBreuil berated him for not alerting him about Colbert's movements. Angaska explained how the Chickasaws deceived him and that he gathered his warriors when he learned that the post was under attack. Many of them had gone into the woods to look for roots to feed their families who were without food because of the previous year's poor harvest.

DuBreuil decided to use Angaska to recover Colbert's prisoners. He sent Angaska in pursuit with 100 Quapaw warriors and 20 soldiers of the Louisiana Regiment. They overtook Colbert on April 24th and camped 6 miles below the mouth of the Arkansas River. Angaska visited Colbert's camp as his men took cover. Angaska told Captain Colbert that he came to free the prisoners. When asked how many men he had, Angaska told him 250 and invited Colbert to send someone to visit the camp if he wanted to verify.

Angaska's bluff was successful. Colbert released Lieutenant and Madame de Villars and their two servants and the rest of his prisoners, except four soldiers, a boy and three slaves.

His party then headed back to the Chickasaw Nation but reentered the Mississippi by way of the cutoff and the White River to avoid meeting the convoy they learned was going to Arkansas Post. They stayed opposite Concordia for two days and then proceeded up the Mississippi, traveling only about 6 miles per day, as they needed to stop to hunt for food. At one anchorage, they found two keelboats and recruited three men.

The convoy stopped at Arkansas Post and returned to the Mississippi to go upstream. It tied up some distance above the mouth of the St. Francis on May 11, 1783. When the commander learned that Colbert was coming upstream, he called for 100 volunteers. He embarked with them and 24 Quapaws and went 4.5 miles downriver where they engaged and defeated Colbert's flotilla—a bateau, a keelboat, a flatboat and three pirogues. They captured the flatboat and pirogues. Colbert's second-in-command, Captain William (d. 1783), was killed. A second man drowned, and a third had his arm broken. Three soldiers captured in the Arkansas Post raid were also released. Colbert's bateau and keelboat had escaped.

The former prisoners boarded a pirogue, taking 50 barrels of flour to Arkansas Post from the flatboat's cargo of 400 barrels. The men of the convoy then destroyed the flatboat and the two remaining pirogues and proceeded up the Mississippi, keeping a sharp lookout for Colbert.

Acting-Governor Miró wrote Captain Colbert on May 16, 1783, notifying him that the preliminary treaty of peace was signed on January 20, 1783. He also sent a copy of the *Jamaica Gazette* which contained the text of the treaty. Colbert released all his prisoners as soon as he learned of the peace treaty. Congress signed the treaty on Wednesday, September 3, 1783 and ratified it on Wednesday, January 14, 1784.[7]

NOTES

ABBREVIATION

NDAR: United States. Naval History Division. *Naval Documents of the American Revolution*. William Bell Clark, editor; with a foreword by President John F. Kennedy and an introd. by Ernest McNeill Eller. Washington: Naval History. Division, Dept. of the Navy: For sale by the Supt. of Docs., U.S. G.P.O., 1964–.

Preface

1. Desmarais, Norman. *Battlegrounds of Freedom: A Historical Guide to the Battlefields of the War of American Independence*. Ithaca, NY: Busca, 2005.

2. Heitman, Francis B. *Historical Register of Officers of the Continental Army during the War of the Revolution, April 1775 to December 1783*. Washington, DC.: The Rare Book Shop Publishing Company, 1914; Baltimore: Genealogical Publishing Company, 1967.

3. Peckham, Howard Henry. *The Toll of Independence: Engagements & Battle Casualties of the American Revolution*. Chicago: University of Chicago Press, 1974.

4. Boatner, Mark Mayo. *Encyclopedia of the American Revolution*. 3d ed. New York: McKay, 1980.

5. Boatner, Mark Mayo. *Landmarks of the American Revolution: A Guide to Locating and Knowing What Happened at the Sites of Independence*. Stackpole Books: Harrisburg, PA, 1973; 2nd ed. – Library of Military History. Detroit: Charles Scribner's Sons, 2007.

6. Selesky Harold E., editor in chief. *Encyclopedia of the American Revolution*, 2nd ed. Detroit: Charles Scribner's Sons, 2007.

7. Fremont-Barnes, Gregory, Richard Alan Ryerson, eds. *The Encyclopedia of the American Revolutionary War: A Political, Social, and Military History*. Santa Barbara, CA: ABC-CLIO, 2006.

8. Anderson, Fred. *A People's Army: Massachusetts Soldiers and Society in the Seven Years' War*. Chapel Hill, NC. 1984. pp. 84–85, 129.

9. Waller, George M. *The American Revolution in the West*. Chicago: Nelson Hall, 1976. pp. 30–31.

10. Adams, Charles F., ed. *The Works of John Adams*. Boston: Charles C. Little and James Brown, 1850. vol. 10 p. 110.

11. Adams, Charles F., ed. *The Works of John Adams*. Boston: Charles C. Little and James Brown, 1850, vol. 10 pp. 192–93.

12. Raphael, Ray. *A People's History of the American Revolution: How Common People Shaped the Fight for Independence*. New York: New Press, 2001. pp. 145, 342.

Georgia

1. *The Encyclopedia of the American Revolutionary War: a political, social, and military history*. Gregory Fremont-Barnes, Richard Alan Ryerson, editors. Santa Barbara, CA: ABC-CLIO, 2006. II: 493–494.

2. Brown to Tonyn Feb. 24, 1776. University of Michigan, William L. Clements Library. Sir Henry Clinton Papers. Cashin, Edward J. *The King's Ranger: Thomas Brown and the American Revolution on the southern frontier*. Athens: University of Georgia Press, c1989. p. 44.

3. *Encyclopedia of the American Revolution*. Harold E. Selesky, editor in chief. 2nd Ed. Detroit: Charles Scribner's Sons, 2007. Vol. 1 pp. 201–202. Rozema, Vicki. *Footsteps of the Cherokees: a guide to the Eastern homelands of the Cherokee Nation*. Winston-Salem, N.C.: John F. Blair, c1954. pp. 86–87, 143, 292, 305–306. Cherokee Prayer Site Guide: Including atrocity sites, death camps, missions, towns, battlefields, spiritual sites, etc. http://www.geocities.ws/gileadintl/atrocity-list.html.

4. Pension Application filed by Major Joseph McJunkin S18118 Transcribed and Annotated by William T. Graves. revwarapps.org/S18118.pdf. Pension application of William Kelly (Kelley) W7 Transcribed by Will Graves. revwarapps.org/w7.pdf. Pension application of Samuel Watson S17187 Transcribed by Susan K. Zimmerman and R. Neil Vance. revwarapps.org/s17187.pdf.

5. Ramsey, J. G. M. (James Gettys McGready). *The Annals of Tennessee to the end of the eighteenth century: comprising its settlement, as the Watauga association, from 1769 to 1777; a part of North Carolina, from 1777 to 1784; the state of Franklin, from 1784–1788; a part of North Carolina, from 1788–1790; the territory of the U. States, south of the Ohio, from 1790 to 1796; the state of Tennessee, from 1796 to 1800*. Charleston: J. Russell, 1853. Pension application of Matt Martin S2726 Transcribed by Will Graves. Rozema, Vicki. *Footsteps of the Cherokees: a guide to the Eastern homelands of the Cherokee Nation*. Winston-Salem, NC: John F. Blair, c1954. pp. 323–324.

6. Peckham, Howard Henry. *The Toll of Independence: engagements & battle casualties of the American Revolution*. Edited by Howard H. Peckham. Chicago: University of Chicago Press, 1974. p. 19.

7. Revolutionary War Pension Record of James Swords (Ga. S 32002) and David Haley (Va. R 4451).

8. O'Kelley, Patrick. *Nothing But Blood and Slaughter.* Booklocker.com, 2004. Vol. 1 pp. 185–187. Davis, Robert Scott, Jr. *Georgians in the Revolution: At Kettle Creek (Wilkes Co.) and Burke County.* Southern Historical Press, 1986. p. 125. Thomas Crawley Pension application. Moultrie, William, *Memoirs of the American Revolution so far as it related to the States of North and South Carolina and Georgia,* New York, 1802; (Eyewitness accounts of the American Revolution] vol. 1 pp. 206–207, 212–216. Harden, William, ed. *Order Book of Samuel Elbert, Colonel and Brigadier General in the Continental Army, Oct. 1776 to November 1778.* Georgia Historical Society Collections, 1902. pp. 54–55. White, George. *Historical Collections of Georgia.* New York: Pudney & Russell, 1855; Baltimore: Genealogical Pub. Co., 1969. p. 539. McCall, Hugh. *The History of Georgia, containing brief sketches of the most remarkable events up to the present day, 1784.* Savannah: Seymour & Williams, 1811; Atlanta: Cherokee Pub. Co., 1969, 1909. pp. 316–317. John Adam Treutlen to John Hancock, 5 August 1777. Item 73, "Georgia State Papers," in Papers of the Continental Congress, National Archives, Washington, DC. Smith, Gordon Burns. *Morningstars of Liberty: the Revolutionary War in Georgia, 1775–1783.* Milledgeville, GA: Boyd Publishing, 2006. Vol. 1 pp. 90–91.

9. Pension application of John Smith R9769.

10. McCall, Hugh. *The History of Georgia, containing brief sketches of the most remarkable events up to the present day, 1784.* Savannah: Seymour & Williams, 1811; Atlanta, Cherokee Pub. Co., 1969, 1909. p. 537. David H. Thurmond, Revolutionary War Pension Application S32010, in David W. Morgan. *Captain George Barber of Georgia.* Temple, OK: privately printed, 1975, p. 3. Peckham, Howard Henry. *The Toll of Independence: engagements & battle casualties of the American Revolution.* Edited by Howard H. Peckham. Chicago: University of Chicago Press, 1974. p. 95. Smith, Gordon Burns. *Morningstars of Liberty: the Revolutionary War in Georgia, 1775–1783.* Milledgeville, GA: Boyd Publishing, 2006. Vol. 1 pp. 276–277.

11. Davis, Robert Scott, Jr. *The Battle of Kettle Creek.* State of Georgia Department of Natural Resources, Office of Planning and Research, Historical Preservation Section, 1974. pp. 21–22. Davies, K. G. *Documents of the American Revolution 1770–1783* (Colonial Office Series) Volume XVII Transcripts 1779. Irish University Press, 1977. pp. 73–75. Davis, Robert Scott, Jr. *Georgia Citizens and Soldiers of the American Revolution.* Southern Historical Press, 1979. Davis, Robert Scott, Jr. *Georgians in the Revolution: At Kettle Creek (Wilkes Co.) and Burke County.* Southern Historical Press, 1986. pp. 163, 102–111, 143–144, 147–148. Campbell, Colin, ed. *Journal of an Expedition against the Rebels in Georgia in North America under the Orders of Archibald Campbell, Esquire, Lieutenant Colonel of His Majesty's 71st Regiment, 1778.* Darien, GA: Ahantilly, 1981. pp. 48, 59–60. Cashin, Edward J. *The King's Ranger: Thomas Brown and the American Revolution on the southern frontier.* Athens: University of Georgia Press, c1989. pp. 85–88. Butler, Lewis. *The Annals of the King's Royal Rifle Corps.* Volume 1. "The Royal Americans", John Murray, London, 1913. p. 313. Fanning, David, Col. *David Fanning's Narrative of his Exploits and Adventures as a Loyalist of North Carolina in the American Revolution, . . .* edited and annotated by John S. Barnes. New York: Printed For the Naval History Society by the De Vinne Press, 1912. p. 22. O'Kelley, Patrick. *Nothing But Blood and Slaughter.* Booklocker.com, 2004. Vol. 1 pp. 229–230. A Fragment of Rev. William Tennent's Journal in R. W. Gibbes, M. D. *Documentary History of the American Revolution, etc.* New York: D. Appleton & Co. 1855. p. 237. Campbell, Archibald. Journal of an Expedition against the Rebels of Georgia in North America Under the Orders of Archibald Campbell Esquire Lieut Colo of His Majesty's 71st Regiment 1778" (typescript in the State Archives of Georgia, Morrow, Georgia). pp. 59–60. Davis, Robert S., Jr. *Georgians in the Revolution: At Kettle Creek (Wilkes Co.) and Burke County.* Easley, SC: Southern Historical Press, 1996. pp. 100–104. Davis, Robert S., Jr. "Engagement at Burke County Jail, Georgia" in Richard L. Blanco, et al. eds. *The American Revolution, 1775–1783; An Encyclopedia.* New York, NY, 1993. Vol. 1 pp. 220–221. Letter from Camp at Fuzzel's (sic) place in Georgia, 27 January 1779. *The* (Charleston) *South-Carolina & American General Gazette.* February 18, 1779. Intelligence from camp at Boggy Gut in *The* (Charleston) *South-Carolina and American General Gazette.* February 25, 1779. Smith, Gordon Burns. *Morningstars of Liberty: the Revolutionary War in Georgia, 1775–1783.* Milledgeville, GA: Boyd Publishing, 2006. Vol. 1 pp. 135–138.

12. Fruth, Florence Knight. *Some Descendants of Richard Few of Chester County, Pennsylvania and Allied Lines, 1682–1976.* Parsons, WV: McClain Printing Company, 1977). p. 47. William Few Papers, MS Department, Perkins Library, Duke Library. Durham, NC. Smith, Gordon Burns. *Morningstars of Liberty: the Revolutionary War in Georgia, 1775–1783.* Milledgeville, GA: Boyd Publishing, 2006. Vol. 1 pp. 155–156.

13. *The* (Charleston) *South-Carolina & American General Gazette.* August 25, 1779. Jones, Charles C. Jr. *The History of Georgia.* Boston: Houghton, Mifflin and Company, 1883. Vol. II p. 363. O'Kelley, Patrick. *Nothing But Blood and Slaughter.* Booklocker.com, 2004. Vol. 1 pp. 308–309. Hayes, John T. *A Gentleman of Fortune, the Diary of Baylor Hill, First Continental Light Dragoons, 1777–1781.* The Saddlebag Press, 1995. Vol. II, pp. 89–92. Davis, Robert Scott, Jr. *Georgians in the Revolution: At Kettle Creek (Wilkes Co.) and Burke County.* Southern Historical Press, 1986. pp. 91, 104, 127. DeMond, Robert O. *The Loyalists in North Carolina During the Revolution.* Durham, NC: Duke University Press, 1940. p. 61. McCall, Hugh. *The History of Georgia, containing brief sketches of the most remarkable events up to the present day, 1784.* Savannah: Seymour & Williams, 1811; Atlanta, Cherokee Pub. Co., 1969, 1909. pp. 423–424. Thomas Crawley Pension File. *Pennsylvania Gazette.* September 29, 1779. Smith, Gordon Burns. *Morningstars of Liberty: the Revolutionary War in Georgia, 1775–1783.* Milledgeville, GA: Boyd Publishing, 2006. Vol. 1 p. 159.

14. *The Colonial Records of the State of Georgia.* compiled and published under authority of the legislature by Allen D. Candler. Atlanta, GA: C. P. Byrd, 1904. Vol. 12 p. 495. Robert Scott Davis Jr. *Georgia Citizens and Soldiers of the American Revolution.* Easley, SC: Southern Historical Press, 1979. pp. 66, 75. Smith, Gordon Burns. *Morningstars of Liberty: the Revolutionary War in Georgia, 1775–1783.* Milledgeville, GA: Boyd Publishing, 2006. Vol. 1 p. 182.

15. Hammett, L. B., compiler. *A List of the Most Probable Participants at the Battle of Kettle Creek, February 14, 1779, Wilkes County, Georgia that Took Place on the Land of James Hammett.* Cherith Creek Designs, Columbus, Georgia.

Columbus State University. Columbus, Georgia. 2008. p. 91. *Stirring Up a Hornet's Nest: The Kettle Creek Battlefield Survey.* LAMAR Institute Publication Series. Report Number 131. Washington, Georgia: The LAMAR Institute, 2008. pp. 46, 82, 86, 93. *The New Georgia Encyclopedia* www.georgiaencyclopedia.org/nge/Article.jsp?id=h-1088. Smith, Gordon Burns. *Morningstars of Liberty: the Revolutionary War in Georgia, 1775–1783.* Milledgeville, GA: Boyd Publishing, 2006. Vol. 1 pp. 141–143.

16. DeMond, Robert Orley. *The Loyalists of North Carolina During the Revolution.* Durham, NC, 1940. p. 105. Lossing, Benson John. *The Pictorial Field-Book of the Revolution: or, Illustrations, by pen and pencil, of the history, biography, scenery, relics, and traditions of the war for independence with eleven hundred engravings on wood,* by Lossing and Barritt, chiefly from original sketches by the author. New York: Harper Brothers, 1852. p. 711.

17. *Encyclopedia of the American Revolution.* Harold E. Selesky, editor in chief. 2nd Ed. Detroit: Charles Scribner's Sons, 2007. Vol. 1 p. 581. *The Encyclopedia of the American Revolutionary War: a political, social, and military history.* Gregory Fremont-Barnes, Richard Alan Ryerson, editors. Santa Barbara, CA: ABC-CLIO, 2006. Vol. II pp. 665–666. Coleman, Kenneth. *The American Revolution in Georgia.* Athens: University of Georgia Press, 1958. Davis, Robert Scott, Jr. *The Battle of Kettle Creek.* State of Georgia Department of Natural Resources, Office of Planning and Research, Historical Preservation Section, 1974. Davis, Robert Scott, Jr. *Kettle Creek Battle and Battlefield.* Washington, GA: Wilkes, 1978. Davis, Robert Scott, Jr. and Kenneth H. Thomas, Jr. *Kettle Creek: the Battle of the Cane Brakes, Wilkes County, Georgia. State of Georgia.* Atlanta: Department of Natural Resources, Historic Preservation Section, 1975. McCall, Hugh. *The History of Georgia, containing brief sketches of the most remarkable events up to the present day, 1784.* Savannah: Seymour & Williams, 1811; Atlanta, Cherokee Pub. Co., 1969, 1909. Smith, Gordon Burns. *Morningstars of Liberty: the Revolutionary War in Georgia, 1775–1783.* Milledgeville, GA: Boyd Publishing, 2006. Vol. 1 pp. 141–143.

18. Pension application of Benejah Nordyke R7691. Davis, Robert Scott. *The Kettle Creek Battlefield. Southern Campaigns of the American Revolution.* 3: 2.3 (February 2006): 36. Smith, Gordon Burns. *Morningstars of Liberty: the Revolutionary War in Georgia, 1775–1783.* Milledgeville, GA: Boyd Publishing, 2006. Vol. 1 pp. 141–143.

19. *Stirring Up a Hornet's Nest: The Kettle Creek Battlefield Survey.* Savannah: The LAMAR Institute, 2008. LAMAR Institute Publication Series, Report Number 131p. 85. Bonner, William. *Map of Georgia.* 1847. Pension application of John Smith R9769. Lindsay, Willis C. *A History of Washington, Wilkes County, Georgia.* Mary Willis Library, Washington, 1921. pp. 7, 23, 26. Revolutionary War Pension Statements of John G. Heard (GA. R 4822) and Evans Haines (GA W 8897). *The Colonial Records of the State of Georgia.* compiled and published under authority of the legislature by Allen D. Candler. Atlanta, GA: C. P. Byrd, 1904. Vol. 2 p. 212. Walter Scott to Alexander Cameron, March 27, 1779. British National Archives. Colonial Office Papers 5/80.

20. *The Colonial Records of the State of Georgia.* compiled and published under authority of the legislature by Allen D. Candler. Atlanta, GA: C. P. Byrd, 1904. Vol. 38 pt. 1 p. 163. Cashin, Edward J., and Robertson, Heard. *Augusta and the American Revolution: events in the Georgia back country, 1773–1783.* Darien, GA: Printed for Richmond County Historical Society by Ashantilly Press, 1975. pp. 3–5. Davidson, Grace Gillam, comp. *Wilkes County.* Vidalia, GA: S. H. Lucas, 1968. Vol. 1 p. 19.

21. *The Colonial Records of the State of Georgia.* compiled and published under authority of the legislature by Allen D. Candler. Atlanta, GA: C. P. Byrd, 1904. Vol. 38 pt. 1 p. 163. Cashin, Edward J., and Robertson, Heard. *Augusta and the American Revolution: events in the Georgia back country, 1773–1783.* Darien, GA: Printed for Richmond County Historical Society by Ashantilly Press, 1975. pp. 3–5. Davidson, Grace Gillam, comp. *Wilkes County.* Vidalia, GA: S. H. Lucas, 1968. Vol. 1 pp. 18, 21.

22. Revolutionary Pension Record of David H. Thurmond (Ga. S 32010) and Charles Gent (Ga. S 1903). Thurmond claimed that the militiamen wounded in Clarke's battle with the Indians were Job Hinton and James Smith and those killed were Giles Talbot, Jacob Patterson, and Peter Davis. See also. McCall, Hugh. *The History of Georgia, containing brief sketches of the most remarkable events up to the present day, 1784.* Savannah: Seymour & Williams, 1811; Atlanta, Cherokee Pub. Co., 1969, 1909. p. 317. Davis, Robert Scott, Jr. *Georgia Citizens and Soldiers of the American Revolution.* Southern Historical Press, 1979.

23. Revolutionary War Pension record of James Wood (Ga. W 4405). *South Carolina and American General Gazette.* April 9, 1779. Davis, Robert Scott, Jr. *Georgia Citizens and Soldiers of the American Revolution.* Southern Historical Press, 1979. p. 165. Davidson, Grace Gillam, comp. *Wilkes County.* Vidalia, GA S. H. Lucas, 1968. Vol. I p. 19.

24. Grace Gillam Davidson. *Early Records of Georgia, Wilkes County.* Macon, GA, 1933. Vol. I p. 19. Revolutionary War pension statement of James Wood (Ga. VV 4405). (Charleston) *South Carolina and American General Gazette.* 24 September 1778; 9 April 1779. "Fulsom's Fort," John H. Goff Collection on Georgia place names, State Archives of Georgia, Morrow, Georgia. Smith, Gordon Burns. *Morningstars of Liberty: the Revolutionary War in Georgia, 1775–1783.* Milledgeville, GA: Boyd Publishing, 2006. Vol. 1 p. 109.

25. Davidson, Grace Gillam. *Early Records of Georgia, Wilkes County.* Macon, GA, 1933. Vol. I p. 26. McCall, Hugh. *The History of Georgia, containing brief sketches of the most remarkable events up to the present day, 1784.* Savannah: Seymour & Williams, 1811; Atlanta, Cherokee Pub. Co., 1969, 1909. p. 395. Nail's fort. Goff Collection. Revolutionary War Pension Statements of Ezekiel Cloud (GA./S.C./NC. S 14004) and John Webb (GA. S 31055). Audited Account of William Pickens (AS 5936), South Carolina Department of Archives and History. Voucher of Thomas Johnston, January 28, 1780. Telamon Cuyler Collection, Special Collections, University of Georgia Libraries.

26. Davis, Robert Scott, Jr. *Georgia Citizens and Soldiers of the American Revolution.* Southern Historical Press, 1979. p. 162. Davis, Robert Scott, Jr. *Georgians in the Revolution: At Kettle Creek (Wilkes Co.) and Burke County.* Southern Historical Press, 1986. p. 162. O'Kelley, Patrick. *Nothing But Blood and Slaughter.* Booklocker.com, 2004. Vol. 1 p. 203.

27. O'Kelley, Patrick. *Nothing But Blood and Slaughter*. Booklocker.com, 2004. Vol. 1 p. 304. Davis, Robert Scott, Jr. *Georgians in the Revolution: At Kettle Creek (Wilkes Co.) and Burke County*. Southern Historical Press, 1986. p. 127. *Pennsylvania Gazette*. September 15, 1779.

28. David H. Corkran. *The Creek Indian Frontier*. University of Oklahoma, 1967. p. 318. Revolutionary War Pension Record of James Swords (Ga. S32002). Davis, Robert Scott, Jr. *Georgia Citizens and Soldiers of the American Revolution*. Southern Historical Press, 1979. p. 165. Davidson, Grace Gillam, comp. *Wilkes County*. Vidalia, GA: S. H. Lucas, 1968. Vol. I: 13.

29. Davis, Robert Scott, Jr. *Georgia Citizens and Soldiers of the American Revolution*. Southern Historical Press, 1979. p. 165.

30. Smith, Gordon Burns. *Morningstars of Liberty: the Revolutionary War in Georgia, 1775–1783*. Milledgeville, GA: Boyd Publishing, 2006. Vol. 1 p. 182.

31. Wright to Germain, Savannah, 5 March 1781, *Collections of the Georgia Historical Society*. Vol. 3 p. 335. *Royal Georgia Gazette*. 22 March 1781; 26 April 1781. Smith, Gordon Burns. *Morningstars of Liberty: the Revolutionary War in Georgia, 1775–1783*. Milledgeville, GA: Boyd Publishing, 2006. Vol. 1 p. 246.

32. Pension application of John Smith R9769.

33. *Royal Georgia Gazette*. 12 September 1781. Davis, Robert Scott, Jr. *Georgia Citizens and Soldiers of the American Revolution*. Southern Historical Press, 1979. p. 166. Smith, Gordon Burns. *Morningstars of Liberty: the Revolutionary War in Georgia, 1775–1783*. Milledgeville, GA: Boyd Publishing, 2006. Vol. 1 p. 254.

34. *Royal Gazette*. 12 September 1781. Davis, Robert Scott, Jr. *Georgia Citizens and Soldiers of the American Revolution*. Southern Historical Press, 1979. p. 166. McCall, Hugh. *The History of Georgia, containing brief sketches of the most remarkable events up to the present day, 1784*. Savannah: Seymour & Williams, 1811; Atlanta, Cherokee Pub. Co., 1969, 1909. p. 525, which states that this took place in July of 1781. Smith, Gordon Burns. *Morningstars of Liberty: the Revolutionary War in Georgia, 1775–1783*. Milledgeville, GA: Boyd Publishing, 2006. Vol. 1 p. 254.

35. Smith, Gordon Burns. *Morningstars of Liberty: the Revolutionary War in Georgia, 1775–1783*. Milledgeville, GA: Boyd Publishing, 2006. Vol. 1 p. 254.

36. *Royal Gazette* 24 October 1781. *Royal Georgia Gazette*. 27 September 1781. Smith, Gordon Burns. *Morningstars of Liberty: the Revolutionary War in Georgia, 1775–1783*. Milledgeville, GA: Boyd Publishing, 2006. Vol. 1 pp. 254–255.

37. Warren, Mary B. *Revolutionary Memoirs and Muster Rolls*. Heritage Papers, 1994. p. 130. O'Kelley, Patrick. *Nothing But Blood and Slaughter*. Booklocker.com, 2004. Vol. 3 p. 384.

38. Clarke to Martin, Water's Fort, 29 May 1782, in David W. Morgan. *Captain George Barber of Georgia*. Temple, OK: privately printed 1975. p. 2. Revolutionary War Pension Statements of Ezekiel Cloud (GA./S.C./NC. S 14004). Smith, Gordon Burns. *Morningstars of Liberty: the Revolutionary War in Georgia, 1775–1783*. Milledgeville, GA: Boyd Publishing, 2006. Vol. 1 pp. 277–278.

39. Fragment of Rev. William Tennent's Journal. R. W. Gibbes, M. D., *Documentary History of the American Revolution, etc.* New York: D. Appleton & Co., 1855. p. 236.

40. Davis, Robert Scott, Jr. *Georgians in the Revolution: At Kettle Creek (Wilkes Co.) and Burke County*. Southern Historical Press, 1986. p. 126. Davies, K. G. *Documents of the American Revolution 1770–1783* (Colonial Office Series) Volume XVII Transcripts 1779, Irish University Press, 1977. p. 75. Campbell, Archibald. Campbell, Colin, ed. *The Journal of Lieutenant Colonel Archibald Campbell During the Invasion of Georgia in 1778–1779*. Augusta, GA: Richmond County Historical Society, 1980. pp. 57–58. O'Kelley, Patrick. *Nothing But Blood and Slaughter*. Booklocker.com, 2004. Vol. 1 pp. 238–239. Smith, Gordon Burns. *Morningstars of Liberty: the Revolutionary War in Georgia, 1775–1783*. Milledgeville, GA: Boyd Publishing, 2006. Vol. 1 pp. 139–140.

41. Philadelphia, March 20. Extract of a letter from General Williamsons camp near Adams Ferry, South Carolina, February 16. *The New Jersey Gazette*. 2: 68 p. 2.

42. McCall, Hugh. *The History of Georgia, containing brief sketches of the most remarkable events up to the present day, 1784*. Savannah: Seymour & Williams, 1811; Atlanta, Cherokee Pub. Co., 1969, 1909. p. 483.

43. Lee, Henry. *Memoirs of the War in the Southern Department of the United States*. New York: University Publishing Co., 1869. pp. 162–165.

44. Robertson, Heard. "The Second British Occupation of Augusta, 1780–1781." *Georgia Historical Quarterly*. 58 (winter, 1974): 425. *The (Charleston) South-Carolina and American General Gazette*. 10 July 1780. Russell, David Lee. *The American Revolution in the Southern Colonies*. Jefferson, NC: McFarland, 2000. pp. 180–181 taken from McCall, Hugh. *The History of Georgia, containing brief sketches of the most remarkable events up to the present day, 1784*. Savannah: Seymour & Williams, 1811; Atlanta, Cherokee Pub. Co., 1969, 1909. pp. 480–485. Smith, Gordon Burns. *Morningstars of Liberty: the Revolutionary War in Georgia, 1775–1783*. Milledgeville, GA: Boyd Publishing, 2006. Vol. 1 pp. 199–200.

45. McCall, Hugh. *The History of Georgia, containing brief sketches of the most remarkable events up to the present day, 1784*. Savannah: Seymour & Williams, 1811; Atlanta, Cherokee Pub. Co., 1969, 1909. pp. 483–487. O'Kelley, Patrick. *Nothing But Blood and Slaughter*. Booklocker.com, 2004. Vol. 2 pp. 304–308. Smith, Gordon Burns. *Morningstars of Liberty: the Revolutionary War in Georgia, 1775–1783*. Milledgeville, GA: Boyd Publishing, 2006. Vol. 1 pp. 211–215.

46. O'Kelley, Patrick. *Nothing But Blood and Slaughter*. Booklocker.com, 2004. Vol. 3 pp. 258–261. Boatner, Mark M. *Encyclopedia of the American Revolution*. 3d ed., New York: McKay, 1980. pp. 50–51. Davis, Robert Scott, Jr. *Georgia Citizens and Soldiers of the American Revolution*. Southern Historical Press, 1979. p. 169. Cashin, Edward J. *The King's Ranger: Thomas Brown and the American Revolution on the southern frontier*. Athens: University of Georgia

Press, c1989. p. 132. DeMond, Robert O. *The Loyalists in North Carolina during the Revolution.* Durham, NC: Duke University Press, 1940. p. 119. Lee, Henry. *Memoirs of the War in the Southern Department of the United States.* New York: University Publishing Co., 1869. pp. 356–357. Sanford Berry Pension File S1638. Rankin, Hugh F. *The North Carolina Continentals.* Chapel Hill: University of North Carolina Press, 1971. pp. 331–333. Schenck, David. *North Carolina 1780–'81. Being a History of the Invasion of the Carolinas by the British Army under Lord Cornwallis in 1780–'81.* Edwards & Broughton, 1889. pp. 417–418. *Pennsylvania Gazette.* July 18, 1781. Draper, Lyman. Thomas Sumter Papers, Draper Manuscript Collection, State Historical Society of Wisconsin. Ward, Christopher. *The War of the Revolution.* New York: Macmillan, 1952. pp. 814–815. Smith, Gordon Burns. *Morningstars of Liberty: the Revolutionary War in Georgia, 1775–1783.* Milledgeville, GA: Boyd Publishing, 2006. Vol. 1 pp. 245–248.

47. Savannah, (in Georgia) March 14. *The Pennsylvania Packet or the General Advertiser.* 11: 877 (April 27, 1782): 3. Head-Quarters, April 21, 1782. *Connecticut Courant.* 904 (May 21, 1782): 3. Extract of a Letter from a Gentleman at Augusta, in Georgia, Dated March 12. *Continental Journal.* CCCXXVI (May 23, 1782): 3. *The Norwich Packet and the Weekly Advertiser.* 450(May 23, 1782): 3. *The Boston Evening-Post and the General Advertiser.* I: XXXII (May 25, 1782): 2. *The Providence Gazette and Country Journal.* XIX: 960 (May 25, 1782): 2. *The Boston Gazette, and the Country Journal.* 1448 (May 27, 1782): 2. *The Norwich Packet and the Weekly Advertiser.* 451 (May 30, 178): 3. Anthony Wayne to Nathanael Greene, Ebenezer, 22 February 1782, in Dennis M. Conrad et al., eds. *The Papers of General Nathanael Greene.* Chapel Hill and London: The University of North Carolina Press, 1998. Vol. 10 pp. 397–398. *Royal Georgia Gazette.* 14 March 1782. Smith, Gordon Burns. *Morningstars of Liberty: the Revolutionary War in Georgia, 1775–1783.* Milledgeville, GA: Boyd Publishing, 2006. Vol. 1 p. 272.

48. *A Map of South Carolina and a Part of Georgia. Containing the whole sea-coast; all the islands, inlets, rivers, creeks, parishes, townships, boroughs, roads, and bridges: As also, several plantations, with their proper boundary-lines, their names, and the names of their proprietors.* Composed from surveys taken by the Hon. William Bull . . . and William De Brahm . . . republished with considerable additions, from the surveys made & collected by John Stuart . . . by William Faden. Charing Cross, 1780. memory.loc.gov/cgi-bin/query/D?gmd: 7: . /temp/~ammem_6hRf: : @@@ mdb=gmd,klpmap,ww2map. southerncampaign.org/newsletter/v2n5.pdf p. 13.

49. southerncampaign.org/newsletter/v2n9.pdf p. 2.

50. Davies, K. G. *Documents of the American Revolution 1770–1783.* (Colonial Office Series). Irish University Press, 1977. XVII: 74–75. [Campbell, Archibald]. Campbell, Colin, ed. *The Journal of Lieutenant Colonel Archibald Campbell During the Invasion of Georgia in 1778–1779.* Augusta, GA: Richmond County Historical Society, 1980. pp. 50–56. Cashin, Edward J. *The King's Ranger: Thomas Brown and the American Revolution on the southern frontier.* Athens: University of Georgia Press, c1989. pp. 85–88. Fanning, David. *The Narrative of Col. David Fanning.* Edited with an introduction and notes by Lindley S. Butler. Davidson, NC: Briarpatch Press; Charleston, SC: Tradd Street Press, 1981. p. 22. Hayes, John T. *The Saddlebag Almanac.* January 1999 Vol. VII p. 74. British National Archives. War Office. *List of all the Officers of the Army* p. 302. Grimke, John Faucheraud. "Order Book of John Faucheraud Grimke, August 1778 to May 1780." *The South Carolina Historical and Genealogical Magazine.* XIV: 2 (April 1913): 103–106. Coakley, Robert W. and Conn, Stetson. *The War of the American Revolution.* Center of Military History, United States Army, 1975. p. 115. O'Kelley, Patrick. *Nothing But Blood and Slaughter.* Booklocker.com, 2004. Vol. 1 pp. 231–232. Doddridge, Joseph. *Notes on the Settlement and Indian Wars of the Western Parts of Virginia and Pennsylvania from 1763 to 1783.* Wellsburg, VA: Joseph Doddridge, 1824. pp. 279–280. *Royal Georgia Gazette.* 11 February 1779. Smith, Gordon Burns. *Morningstars of Liberty: the Revolutionary War in Georgia, 1775–1783.* Milledgeville, GA: Boyd Publishing, 2006. Vol. 1 pp. 138–139, 252.

51. News from Savannah, 20 September 1781, in *The* (Charleston) *Royal Gazette.* 20 October to 24 October 1781.

52. O'Donnell, James H. *Southern Indians in the American Revolution.* University of Tennessee Press, 1971. p. 119. *Pennsylvania Gazette.* March 13, 1782. *The Royal Georgia Gazette.* December 20, 1781. *Georgia Historical Society Collections.* Vol. X pp. 120–122. O'Kelley, Patrick. *Nothing But Blood and Slaughter.* Booklocker.com, 2004. Vol. 3 pp. 404–405.

52a. Davis, Robert Scott, Jr. *Georgians in the Revolution: At Kettle Creek (Wilkes Co.) and Burke County,* Southern Historical Press, 1986. p. 148. O'Kelley, Patrick. *Nothing But Blood and Slaughter.* Booklocker.com, 2004. Vol. 1 pp. 252–253.

53. McCall, Hugh. *The History of Georgia, containing brief sketches of the most remarkable events up to the present day, 1784.* Savannah: Seymour & Williams, 1811; Atlanta, Cherokee Pub. Co., 1969, 1909. pp. 399–400. *Pennsylvania Gazette.* March 17, 1779. Davis, Robert Scott, Jr. *The Battle of Kettle Creek.* State of Georgia Department of Natural Resources, Office of Planning and Research, Historical Preservation Section, 1974. p. 168. Davis, Robert Scott, Jr. *Georgians in the Revolution: At Kettle Creek (Wilkes Co.) and Burke County.* Southern Historical Press, 1986. pp. 90, 126, 147, 253. [Campbell, Archibald]. Campbell, Colin, ed. *The Journal of Lieutenant Colonel Archibald Campbell During the Invasion of Georgia in 1778–1779.* Augusta, GA: Richmond County Historical Society, 1980. pp. 60, 66, 122. O'Kelley, Patrick. *Nothing But Blood and Slaughter.* Booklocker.com, 2004. Vol. 1 pp. 243, 251. Smith, Gordon Burns. *Morningstars of Liberty: the Revolutionary War in Georgia, 1775–1783.* Milledgeville, GA: Boyd Publishing, 2006. Vol. 1 pp. 144–145.

54. Campbell, Colin, ed. *The Journal of Lieutenant Colonel Archibald Campbell During the Invasion of Georgia in 1778–1779.* Augusta, GA: Richmond County Historical Society, 1980. pp. 60, 122. O'Kelley, Patrick. *Nothing But Blood and Slaughter.* Booklocker.com, 2004. Vol. 1 pp. 243–244.

55. Extract of a letter from General Williamson, April 3, 1779" in *Virginia Gazette* (Dixon & Nicolson), 1 May 1779. "Logan Manuscript" in *Historical Collections of the Joseph Habersham Chapter, Daughters of the American Revolution.* Atlanta: Charles P. Byrd, State Printer, 1910. Vol. 3 p. 90. National Society of the Daughters of the American Revolution Centennial Administration, *DAR Patriot Index.* Centennial Edition, Part III. Washington,

DC: National Society of the Daughters of the American Revolution. 1994. p. 2517. David H. Corkran, *The Creek Frontier: 1540–1783.* Norman, OK: University of Oklahoma Press, 1967. pp. 318–319. O'Kelley, Patrick. *Nothing But Blood and Slaughter.* Booklocker.com, 2004. Vol. 1 p. 267–268. Smith, Gordon Burns. *Morningstars of Liberty: the Revolutionary War in Georgia, 1775–1783.* Milledgeville, GA: Boyd Publishing, 2006. Vol. 1 pp. 148–149.

56. Draper, Lyman. Thomas Sumter Papers, Draper Manuscript Collection, State Historical Society of Wisconsin. O'Kelley, Patrick. *Nothing But Blood and Slaughter.* Booklocker.com, 2004. Vol. 3 p. 164.

57. Pension application of Job Roundtree (South Carolina), S18187. Smith, Gordon Burns. *Morningstars of Liberty: the Revolutionary War in Georgia, 1775–1783.* Milledgeville, GA: Boyd Publishing, 2006. Vol. 1 p. 227.

58. Davis, Robert Scott, Jr. *Georgia Citizens and Soldiers of the American Revolution.* Southern Historical Press, 1979. p. 169. Davis, Robert Scott, Jr. *Georgians in the Revolution: At Kettle Creek (Wilkes Co.) and Burke County.* Southern Historical Press, 1986. pp. 93–94. Hay, Gertrude May (Sloan). *Roster of soldiers from North Carolina in the American Revolution: with an appendix containing a collection of miscellaneous records.* National Society Daughters of the American Revolution of North Carolina. Baltimore: Genealogical Pub. Co., 1967, 1932. p. 46. Pension Applications RG 15, Microcopy 804. O'Kelley, Patrick. *Nothing But Blood and Slaughter.* Booklocker.com, 2004. Vol. 3 p. 216.

59. Davis, Robert Scott, Jr. *The Battle of Kettle Creek.* State of Georgia Department of Natural Resources, Office of Planning and Research, Historical Preservation Section, 1974. pp. 26–27. Heitman, Francis B. *Historical Register of Officers of the Continental Army during the War of the Revolution. April 1775 to December 1783.* Washington, DC, 1914; Baltimore: Genealogical Publishing Company, 1967. p. 200. [Campbell, Archibald]. Campbell, Colin, ed. *The Journal of Lieutenant Colonel Archibald Campbell During the Invasion of Georgia in 1778–1779.* Augusta, GA: Richmond County Historical Society, 1980. pp. 59–60. Harden, William, ed. *Order Book of Samuel Elbert, Colonel and Brigadier General in the Continental Army, Oct. 1776 to November 1778.* Georgia Historical Society Collections, 1902. pp. 66–69. O'Kelley, Patrick. *Nothing But Blood and Slaughter.* Booklocker.com, 2004. Vol. 1 p. 240.

60. Boatner, Mark Mayo, *Landmarks of the American Revolution: A Guide to Locating and Knowing What Happened at the Sites of Independence.* Harrisburg, PA: Stackpole Books, 1992, p. 79. Davis, Robert Scott, Jr. *The Battle of Kettle Creek.* State of Georgia Department of Natural Resources, Office of Planning and Research, Historical Preservation Section, 1974. pp. 34–36. Davis, Robert Scott, Jr. *Georgia Citizens and Soldiers of the American Revolution.* Southern Historical Press, 1979. pp. 160–161. Davis, Robert Scott, Jr. *Georgians in the Revolution: At Kettle Creek (Wilkes Co.) and Burke County.* Southern Historical Press, 1986. p. 126. McCall, Hugh. *The History of Georgia, containing brief sketches of the most remarkable events up to the present day, 1784.* Savannah: Seymour & Williams, 1811; Atlanta, Cherokee Pub. Co., 1969, 1909. p. 394. Revolutionary War Pension records of John Verner (S.C. S 7793), John Harris (S.C. S 21808), Francis Carlisle (S.C. W 10576), Patrick Cain (S.C. S 1185), and Thomas Hamilton (S.C. S 30470). Smith, Gordon Burns. *Morningstars of Liberty: the Revolutionary War in Georgia, 1775–1783.* Milledgeville, GA: Boyd Publishing, 2006. Vol. 1 p. 142. O'Kelley, Patrick. *Nothing But Blood and Slaughter.* Booklocker.com, 2004. Vol. 1 p. 244. Petigru, James Louis. *James Petigru Carson, Life, Letters and Speeches of James Louis Petigru: The Union Man of South Carolina.* Washington: W. H. Lowdermilk & Co., 1920. p. 3. Mordecai Millar (Miller) pension application S16972. John Long pension application W5026. Jones, Charles Colcock. *The History of Georgia.* Houghton, Mifflin and Co., 1883. p. 338. www.carolana.com/SC/Revolution/revolution_cherokee_ford.html. Parker, John C. *Parker's Guide to the Revolutionary War in South Carolina: battles, skirmishes and murders.* Patrick, SC: Hem Branch Publishing, 2009. p. 2. Smith, Gordon Burns. *Morningstars of Liberty: the Revolutionary War in Georgia, 1775–1783.* Milledgeville, GA: Boyd Publishing, 2006. Vol. 1 p. 142.

61. Davis, Robert Scott, Jr. *Georgia Citizens and Soldiers of the American Revolution.* Southern Historical Press, 1979. pp. 164, 168.

62. Revolutionary War Pension Records of Asa Morgan (Ga. S 31870) and Benjamin Thompson (Ga. S 32016). Davis, Robert Scott, Jr. *Georgia Citizens and Soldiers of the American Revolution.* Southern Historical Press, 1979. p. 164. McCall, Hugh. *The History of Georgia, containing brief sketches of the most remarkable events up to the present day, 1784.* Savannah: Seymour & Williams, 1811; Atlanta, Cherokee Pub. Co., 1969, 1909. p. 392. Smith, Gordon Burns. *Morningstars of Liberty: the Revolutionary War in Georgia, 1775–1783.* Milledgeville, GA: Boyd Publishing, 2006. Vol. 1 p. 141.

63. Davis, Robert Scott, Jr. *The Battle of Kettle Creek.* State of Georgia Department of Natural Resources, Office of Planning and Research, Historical Preservation Section, 1974. p. 55. Davis, Robert Scott, Jr. *Georgians in the Revolution: At Kettle Creek (Wilkes Co.) and Burke County.* Southern Historical Press, 1986. pp. 91, 110–111, 127. *Pennsylvania Gazette.* May 12, 1779. *The (Charleston) Gazette of the State of South-Carolina.* 7 April 1779; and "Extract of a letter from General Williamson, April 3, 1779" in *Virginia Gazette* (Dixon & Nicolson). 1 May 1779. Davis, Robert Scott, Jr. and Kenneth H. Thomas, Jr. *Kettle Creek: the Battle of the Cane Brakes, Wilkes County, Georgia.* State of Georgia. Atlanta: Department of Natural Resources, Historic Preservation Section, 1975. pp. 64–65. O'Kelley, Patrick. *Nothing But Blood and Slaughter.* Booklocker.com, 2004. Vol. 1 p. 266–67. Smith, Gordon Burns. *Morningstars of Liberty: the Revolutionary War in Georgia, 1775–1783.* Milledgeville, GA: Boyd Publishing, 2006. Vol. 1 p. 149.

64. Davis, Robert Scott, Jr. *Georgia Citizens and Soldiers of the American Revolution.* Southern Historical Press, 1979. p. 169. Cashin, Edward J. *The King's Ranger: Thomas Brown and the American Revolution on the southern frontier.* Athens: University of Georgia Press, c1989. p. 131. O'Kelley, Patrick. *Nothing But Blood and Slaughter.* Booklocker. com, 2004. Vol. 3 p. 216.

65. Davis, Robert Scott, Jr. *Georgia Citizens and Soldiers of the American Revolution.* Southern Historical Press, 1979. p. 169. Cashin, Edward J. *The King's Ranger: Thomas Brown and the American Revolution on the southern frontier.* Athens: University of Georgia Press, c1989. p. 131. O'Kelley, Patrick. *Nothing But Blood and Slaughter.* Booklocker. com, 2004. Vol. 3 pp. 217–218.

66. Revolutionary War Pension Records of John Collins (Ga. R 2179), David H. Thurmond (Ga./S.C. R 9769), Moses Perkins (Ga. S 3677) and John Smith (Ga./S.C. R9769). Davis, Robert Scott, Jr. *The Battle of Kettle Creek.* State of Georgia Department of Natural Resources, Office of Planning and Research, Historical Preservation Section, 1974. p. 97. Davis, Robert Scott, Jr. *Georgia Citizens and Soldiers of the American Revolution.* Southern Historical Press, 1979. pp. 163, 168. O'Kelley, Patrick. *Nothing But Blood and Slaughter.* Booklocker.com, 2004. Vol. 2 p. 220.

67. Galphin to Henry Laurens, Silver Bluff, Georgia, 25 June 1778, Laurens Papers, 13: 513–5. The (Charleston) *South-Carolina and American General Gazette.* 16 October 1777. Searcy, Martha Condray. *The Georgia-Florida contest in the American Revolution, 1776–1778.* University, AL: University of Alabama Press, c1985. p113. Joseph Clay to Henry Laurens, Savannah, 29 September 1777. *Collections of the Georgia Historical Society.* Vol. 8 p. 40. Elbert, *Collections of the Georgia Historical Society.* Vol. 5, pt. 2 pp. 64–65, 76, 79. Smith, Gordon Burns. *Morningstars of Liberty: the Revolutionary War in Georgia, 1775–1783.* Milledgeville, GA: Boyd Publishing, 2006. Vol. 1 pp. 94–95.

68. O'Kelley, Patrick. *Nothing But Blood and Slaughter.* Booklocker.com, 2004. Vol. 4 p. 72. Peckham, Howard Henry. *The Toll of Independence: engagements & battle casualties of the American Revolution.* Edited by Howard H. Peckham. Chicago: University of Chicago Press, 1974. p. 95.

69. Peckham, Howard Henry. *The Toll of Independence: engagements & battle casualties of the American Revolution.* Edited by Howard H. Peckham. Chicago: University of Chicago Press, 1974. p. 96.

70. Peckham, Howard Henry. *The Toll of Independence: engagements & battle casualties of the American Revolution.* Edited by Howard H. Peckham. Chicago: University of Chicago Press, 1974. p. 98.

71. James Ownbey (Owenby) Pension application W3712.

72. Elliott, Daniel T. *Ebenezer Revolutionary War Headquarters: A Quest to Locate and Preserve.* LAMAR Institute Publication Series, Report Number 73, The LAMAR Institute, Box Springs, Georgia, 2003.

73. Wright to Dartmouth, 12 May 1775. *The Colonial Records of the State of Georgia.* Vol. 38, pt. 2 p. 439. Jones, Charles C. *History of Georgia.* Boston: Houghton, Mifflin and Company, 1883. Vol. 2 p. 175. Smith, Gordon Burns. *Morningstars of Liberty: the Revolutionary War in Georgia, 1775–1783.* Milledgeville, GA: Boyd Publishing, 2006. Vol. 1 p. 38.

74. Extract of a letter from Charleston, South Carolina, 10 June 1775, in *Virginia Gazette,* Dixon, 15 July 1775. Smith, Gordon B. "The Georgia Grenadiers." *Georgia Historical Quarterly.* 64 (winter, 1980): 405–15.

75. Sir James Wright, Governor of Georgia, to Lord Dartmouth July 8 and 10, 1775. *Collections of the Georgia Historical Society.* Vol. 3 pp. 191, 192, 194. NDAR 1: 845, 856. Governor Patrick Tonyn to Lord Dartmouth July 21, 1775. British National Archives, Colonial Office, Class 5/555, Library of Congress Transcript. NDAR 1: 949. Parker, John C. *Parker's Guide to the Revolutionary War in South Carolina: battles, skirmishes and murders.* Patrick, SC: Hem Branch Publishing, 2009. p. 25. "Brutus" (George Walton) to editor, 4 July 1784. *Georgia Gazette.* (July 8, 1784. Drayton, John. *Memoirs of the American Revolution, from its Commencement to the Year 1776, Inclusive; as Relating to the State of South Carolina: and Occasionally Refiring [sic] to the States of North Carolina and Georgia.* Charleston: A. E. Miller, 1821. Vol. 1 p. 268. Chesnutt, David R. et al., eds. *The Papers of Henry Laurens.* Columbia: University of South Carolina Press, 1985. Vol. 10 p. 220n. "Letters From Sir James Wright" in *Collections of the Georgia Historical Society.* Vol. 3 pp. 191, 194. Also see the report of Capt. Parry of the *Hope* in the (Savannah) *Georgia Gazette* and *The* (Savannah) *Gazette of the State of Georgia.* 25 October 1775. Letter from William Henry Drayton, 9 November 1775, in Hemphill and Watson. *Extracts from the Journals of the Provincial Congresses, 1776–1776.* Columbia, SC, 1960. p. 110. Henry Laurens to John Laurens, Charles Town, SC, 14 July 1775. *Laurens Papers.* Vol. 10 pp. 219–222, 220n. Barnwell, Stephen B. *The Story of An American Family.* Marquette, [MI] 1969. pp. 31–36. (Savannah) *Georgia Gazette* and *The* (Savannah) *Gazette of the State of Georgia.* 4 August 1763. Johnson, Joseph. *Traditions and Reminiscences of the American Revolution in the South* Charleston; 1851, reprinted, Spartanburg, SC: 1972, pp. 56–58. Council of Safety to Tunes (sic) Tebout, Charleston, 16 July 1775. *Laurens Papers.* Vol. 10 pp. 224–225. Mowat, Charles Loch. *East Florida as a British Province, 1763–1784.* (1943, reprinted, Gainesville: University of Florida Press, 1964) p. 107. Death announcement in The (Charleston) *South-Carolina and American General Gazette.* 26 March 1779. For an account of the capture of the *Betsy,* see Terry W. Lipscomb. *South Carolina Revolutionary War Battles, 1. The Carolina low country, April 1775–June 1776.* Columbia: South Carolina Department of Archives & History, 1994. pp. 8–10. Smith, Gordon Burns. *Morningstars of Liberty: the Revolutionary War in Georgia, 1775–1783.* Milledgeville, GA: Boyd Publishing, 2006. Vol. 1 pp. 25, 39.

76. Smith, Gordon Burns. *Morningstars of Liberty: the Revolutionary War in Georgia, 1775–1783.* Milledgeville, GA: Boyd Publishing, 2006. Vol. 1 p. 42. Sir James Wright to Lord Dartmouth, Savannah, 23 September 1775. *Collections of the Georgia Historical Society.* Vol. 3 pp. 212–213 and in NDAR 2: 191–2. (Savannah) *Georgia Gazette* and *The* (Savannah) *Gazette of the State of Georgia.* 5 July 1775. Samuel Rezneck, *Unrecognized Patriots.* London: 1975. p. 203. Joseph Habersham to William Henry Drayton, Savannah (GA), 9 February 1776, in Gibbes, Robert Wilson. *Documentary History of the American Revolution.* New York: D. Appleton & Co., 1855 (3 vols: 1764–1776, 1776–1782, 1781–1782). reprinted New York Times & Arno Press, 1971. Vol. 1 pp. 257–258.

77. Jackson, Harvey H. *Lachlan McIntosh and the Politics of Revolutionary Georgia.* Athens: University of Georgia Press, 1979. p. 36.

78. Peckham, Howard Henry. *The Toll of Independence: engagements & battle casualties of the American Revolution.* Edited by Howard H. Peckham. Chicago: University of Chicago Press, 1974. p. 12.

79. "Reminiscences of Dr. William Read, etc." in Gibbes, Robert Wilson. *Documentary History of the American Revolution.* New York: D. Appleton & Co., 1855 (3 vols: 1764–1776, 1776–1782, 1781–1782). reprinted New York Times & Arno Press, 1971. Vol. 2 pp. 248–293. Smith, Gordon Burns. *Morningstars of Liberty: the Revolutionary War in Georgia, 1775–1783.* Milledgeville, GA: Boyd Publishing, 2006. Vol. 1 pp. 53–54.

80. Captain Andrew Barkley, R. N. to Major General Henry Clinton, February 23, 1776. Sir Henry Clinton Papers, William L. Clements Library, University of Michigan, Ann Arbor. NDAR 4: 60.

81. O'Kelley, Patrick. *Nothing But Blood and Slaughter*. Booklocker.com, 2004. Vol. 1. p. 86. Boatner, Mark M. Encyclopedia of the American Revolution. 3d ed., New York: McKay, 1980. p. 537. NDAR vol. 4 pp. 59–61. www.lafayettesar.org/gamilitia.htm.

82. William Ewen to the South Carolina Council of Safety. *South-Carolina and American General Gazette*. February 23 to March 8, 1776. NDAR 4: 169.

83. Colonel Lachlan McIntosh to George Washington. Washington Papers, Library of Congress. NDAR 4: 246–249.

84. William Ewen to The South Carolina Council of Safety. *South-Carolina and American General Gazette*. February 23 to March 8, 1776. NDAR 4: 169.

85. *South-Carolina and American General Gazette*. February 23 to March 8, 1776; NDAR 5: 169–171.

86. Colonel Lachlan McIntosh to George Washington. Washington Papers, Library of Congress. NDAR 4: 246–249.

87. Jackson, Harvey H., "The Battle of the Rice Boats: Georgia Joins the Revolution." *Georgia Historical Quarterly.* 68 (Summer 1974): 235ss. Johnson, James M. *Militiamen, Rangers, and Redcoats; The Military in Georgia, 1754–1776.* Macon: Mercer University Press, 1992. pp. 141–155. Colonel Lachlan McIntosh to George Washington. Washington Papers, Library of Congress. NDAR 4: 246–249. Captain Andrew Barkley, R. N. to Major General Henry Clinton, February 23, 1776. Sir Henry Clinton Papers, William L. Clements Library, University of Michigan, Ann Arbor. NDAR 4: 60, 169, 172, 193–194, 246–9, 249, 279, 360–1, 371–2, 443. Letter from Savannah, 3 March 1776 in *American Archives*. Ed. Peter Force. Series 4, I. Washington, DC: M. St. Clair and Peter Force, 1837. pp. 110–111. Stevens, William B. *A History of Georgia: From its Discovery by Europeans to the Adoption of the Present Constitution.* Savannah: The Beehive Press, 1972 reprint of 1847 edition, p. 135. Coleman, Kenneth. *The American Revolution in Georgia*. Athens: University of Georgia Press, 1958. pp. 70ss. William Ewen to the South Carolina Council of Safety, March 4, 1776. Smith, Gordon Burns. *Morningstars of Liberty: the Revolutionary War in Georgia, 1775–1783.* Milledgeville, GA: Boyd Publishing, 2006. Vol. 1 p. 55.

88. Master's Log of HM Armed Vessel *Cherokee*. British National Archives. Admiralty 52/1662. NDAR 4: 167.

89. O'Kelley, Patrick. *Nothing But Blood and Slaughter*. Booklocker.com, 2004. Vol. 1 p. 92. Gibbes, Robert Wilson. *Documentary History of the American Revolution*. New York: D. Appleton & Co., 1855 (3 vols: 1764–1776, 1776–1782, 1781–1782). reprinted New York Times & Arno Press, 1971 (3 vols. in 1). v. 1 pp. 262–266. Smith, Gordon Burns. *Morningstars of Liberty: the Revolutionary War in Georgia, 1775–1783.* Milledgeville, GA: Boyd Publishing, 2006. Vol. 1 p. 55.

90. Shulham's Prize List, April 24, 1776. British National Archives. Admiralty 1/484. NDAR 4 p. 654.

91. Wright to Lord George Germain, p. s. of March 26 to a letter of March 20, 1776, *Collections of the Georgia Historical Society*. Vol. 3 pp. 239–241. Wright to Germain, April 26, 1776, ibid. Extract of a letter from the Council of Safety of Georgia to the Council of Safety of South Carolina, April 2, 1776. *The (Charleston) South-Carolina and American General Gazette*. April 10 to 17, 1776. Also see Davies, K. G. *Documents of the American Revolution 1770–1783*(Colonial Office Series), Volume 12 pp. 108–109. McIntosh to Washington, April 28, 1776, *American Archives*. Ed. Peter Force. Series 4, 5: 1106–7. NDAR 4: 515–516, 777. O'Kelley, Patrick. *Nothing But Blood and Slaughter*. Booklocker.com, 2004. Vol. 1 p. 97.

92. Journal of HM Sloop *Tamar*, Captain Edward Thornbrough; NDAR 4: 515. Master's Log of HM Armed Vessel *Cherokee*. British National Archives, Admiralty 52/1662; NDAR 4: 516. Letter from Georgetown, SC April 11, [1776]. *Pennsylvania Gazette*. May 29, 1776; NDAR 4: 777. Smith, Gordon Burns. *Morningstars of Liberty: the Revolutionary War in Georgia, 1775–1783.* Milledgeville, GA: Boyd Publishing, 2006. Vol. 1 pp. 56–57.

93. NDAR 5: 81–82. Captain Andrew Barkley, R. N. to Major General Henry Clinton, February 23, 1776. Sir Henry Clinton Papers, William L. Clements Library, University of Michigan, Ann Arbor. NDAR 4: 60. Sir James Wright's report in *The Colonial Records of the State of Georgia*. compiled and published under authority of the legislature by Allen D. Candler. Atlanta, GA: C. P. Byrd, 1904. Vol. 38, pt. 2 p. 120. Also see Capt. John Stanhope to Philip Stephens, 20 May 1776, in NDAR V: 176. Walton to McIntosh, Williamsburg, Virginia, 17 June 1776, from the papers of Octavia Celeste (Walton) LeVert. Published under the title "A Reflect of Our First Revolution" in *The Macon* (GA) *Daily Telegraph and Confederate*. 25 January 1865, republished in *The Valdosta* (GA) *Times*. 7 April 1877 with additional letters from George Walton under the title, "Geo. Walton, of Georgia" [from the *Augusta* (GA) *Chronicle and Constitutionalist*]. Smith, Gordon Burns. *Morningstars of Liberty: the Revolutionary War in Georgia, 1775–1783.* Milledgeville, GA: Boyd Publishing, 2006. Vol. 1 pp. 57–58.

94. Master's Log of HM Armed Vessel *Cherokee*. British National Archives. Admiralty 52/1662. NDAR, v6, p. 189.

95. "Historic Background of Camp Walleila" *Savannah Morning News*. 13 October 1937. The (Charleston) *South-Carolina and American General Gazette*. 25 September to 2 October 1776. Smith, Gordon Burns. *Morningstars of Liberty: the Revolutionary War in Georgia, 1775–1783.* Milledgeville, GA: Boyd Publishing, 2006. Vol. 1 pp. 62–63.

96. Jones, Charles C. Jr. *The History of Georgia*. Boston: Houghton, Mifflin and Company, 1883. Vol. II pp. 274–275. Mathew Nail's (Neal) pension application #S14004. Peckham, Howard Henry. *The Toll of Independence: engagements & battle casualties of the American Revolution*. Edited by Howard H. Peckham. Chicago: University of Chicago Press, 1974. p. 36. McCall, Hugh. *The History of Georgia, containing brief sketches of the most remarkable events up to the present day, 1784*. Savannah: Seymour & Williams, 1811; Atlanta, Cherokee Pub. Co., 1969, 1909. p. 348; account of the massacre in *Savannah Morning News*. 17 January 1897 (from the *Atlanta Journal*). Smith, Gordon Burns. *Morningstars of Liberty: the Revolutionary War in Georgia, 1775–1783.* Milledgeville, GA: Boyd Publishing, 2006. Vol. 1 pp. 91–92.

97. O'Kelley, Patrick. *Nothing But Blood and Slaughter*. Booklocker.com, 2004. Vol. 1 p. 198–199. Coulter, E. Merton. *Georgia: a Short History*. Chapel Hill: University of North Carolina Press, 1947. p. 136. George Galphin to Henry Laurens, Silver Bluff, Ga. (*sic*), 25 June 1778, in *Laurens Papers*. Vol. 13 pp. 513–515. report of James Moore's raid and death in *The* (Charleston) *Gazette of the State of South-Carolina*. 8 July 1778. Lewis Lanier (c1756–1839) served in the Virginia, North Carolina, and Georgia troops during the Revolutionary War, having moved from the former state to the latter during the course of the war. After the close of the Revolution. He resided in Greene, Camden (St. Mary's), Jefferson, Bulloch, and Screven Counties, Georgia. He served as a member of both the North Carolina and Georgia legislatures. He died on 12 February 1839. He married first Nancy, daughter of General Thomas Butler, of Essex County, Virginia. He married second in 1802/05 Esther Thorn. Among his children was Thomas B. Lanier, who was 54 years old in October 1846. Revolutionary War Pension File No, R6153. Virgil D. White, abs. *Genealogical Abstracts of Revolutionary War Pension Files*. Waynesboro, TN, 1990. Vol. 2 p. 2012. He was buried in the Little Ogeechee Baptist Church Cemetery in Oliver, Georgia. His wife Esther, who died 10 October 1855 at the age of 80 years, 5 months, and 23 days, was buried beside him. Smith, Gordon Burns. *Morningstars of Liberty: the Revolutionary War in Georgia, 1775–1783*. Milledgeville, Ga. Boyd Publishing, 2006. Vol. 1 pp. 109–111.

98. Rankin, Hugh F. *The North Carolina Continentals*. Chapel Hill, NC: University of North Carolina Press, 1971. pp. 184, 186. Lawrence, Alexander A. General Robert Howe and the British Capture of Savannah in 1778. *Georgia Historical Quarterly*. 36 (December 1952): 303, 305.

99. Order Book of John Faucheraud Grimke, August 1778 to May 1780. *South Carolina Historical and Genealogical Magazine*. 14 (January 1913): 45.

100. "Journal of the Garrison Regiment von Knoblauch, 1776–84," in *Hessian Documents of the American Revolution*. Morristown National Historical Park. Reuber, Johannes. *Diary of a Hessian Grenadier of Colonel Rail's Regiment*. trans. Bruce E. Burgoyne (privately printed, Johannes Schwalm Historical Association, s. l.: s. n.), (from a copy of the diary of Johannes Reuber in the possession of Kennery Jones, Worcester, MA). p. 35.

101. Campbell, Archibald. *Journal of an Expedition against the Rebels of Georgia in North America under the Orders of Archibald Campbell Esquire Lieut. Colol. of His Majesty's 71st Regiment, 1778*. Edited by Colin Campbell. Darien, GA.: Ashantilly Press, 1981. pp. 20–21. Campbell calls the plantation "Sheridoe's" in his account. Piecuch, Jim. *Three Peoples One King: Loyalists, Indians, and Slaves in the Revolutionary South, 1775–1782*. Columbia: University of South Carolina Press, 2008. p. 132.

102. *Encyclopedia of the American Revolution*. Harold E. Selesky, editor in chief. 2nd Ed. Detroit: Charles Scribner's Sons, 2007. Vol. II pp. 1035–1040. *The Encyclopedia of the American Revolutionary War: a political, social, and military history*. Gregory Fremont-Barnes, Richard Alan Ryerson, editors. Santa Barbara, CA: ABC-CLIO, 2006. Vol. IV pp. 1124–1130. Campbell, Colin, ed. *Journal of an Expedition against the Rebels in Georgia in North America under the Orders of Archibald Campbell, Esquire, Lieutenant Colonel of His Majesty's 71st Regiment, 1778*. Darien GA: Ashantilly, 1981. pp. 21–23, 108–109. Coleman, Kenneth. *The American Revolution in Georgia*. Athens: University of Georgia Press, 1958. Commager, Henry Steele. *The Spirit of Seventy Six: The Story of the American Revolution as Told by Participants*. New York, Harper & Row [1967]. Jones, Charles Colcock, Jr. *The siege of Savannah by the fleet of Count d'Estaing in 1779*. [New York]: New York Times [1968]. Kennedy, Benjamin, ed. *Muskets, Cannon Balls, and Bombs: Nine Narratives of the Siege of Savannah in 1779*. Savannah, GA: Beehive, 1974. Lawrence, Alexander A. *Storm Over Savannah, the Story of Count d'Estaing and the Siege of the Town in 1779*. University of Georgia Press, 1951. Searcy, Martha Condray. "General Robert Howe and the British Capture of Savannah in 1778." *Georgia Historical Quarterly*. 36 (December 1952): 303–327. Ward, Christopher. *The War of the Revolution*. New York: Macmillan, 1952. pp. 688–694. Wilson, David K. *The Southern Strategy: Britain's Conquest of South Carolina and Georgia, 1775–1780*. Columbia: University of South Carolina Press, 2005. O'Kelley, Patrick. *Nothing But Blood and Slaughter*. Booklocker.com, 2004. Vol. 1 p. 213. Bennett, Charles E., Lennon, Donald R. *A Quest for Glory: Major General Robert Howe and the American Revolution*. Chapel Hill: University of North Carolina Press, 1991. pp. 87–89.

103. McDaniel, Matthew F. K. *Georgia's forgotten battlefields a survey of and recommendations for selected revolutionary war battlefields and sites in the state*. Thesis (M. H. P.) University of Georgia, 2002. pp. 41–45. "Order Book of John Faucheraud Grimke, August 1778 to May 1780," *South Carolina Historical and Genealogical Magazine*. 14 (January 1913): 54–5. Capture of Mordecai Sheftall, Deputy Commissary-General of Issues to the Continental Troops for the State of Georgia, viz., 1778, December 29th in White, George. *Historical Collections of Georgia*. New York: Pudney & Russell, 1855; Baltimore: Genealogical Pub. Co., 1969. pp. 340–342. Smith, Gordon Burns. *Morningstars of Liberty: the Revolutionary War in Georgia, 1775–1783*. Milledgeville, GA: Boyd Publishing, 2006. Vol. 1 pp. 116–123.

104. *The Charlestown Gazette*. January 26, 1779. Smith, Gordon Burns. *Morningstars of Liberty: the Revolutionary War in Georgia, 1775–1783*. Milledgeville, GA: Boyd Publishing, 2006. Vol. 1 p. 136.

105. Davis, Robert Scott, Jr. *Georgia Citizens and Soldiers of the American Revolution*. Southern Historical Press, 1979. pp. 140–141. Moultrie, William, *Memoirs of the American Revolution so far as it related to the States of North and South Carolina and Georgia*. New York, 1802; (Eyewitness accounts of the American Revolution). [New York] New York Times [1968] vol. 1 p. 365. *Pennsylvania Gazette*. May 12, 1779. O'Kelley, Patrick. *Nothing But Blood and Slaughter*. Booklocker.com, 2004. Vol. 1 p. 265.

106. Davis, Robert Scott, Jr. *Georgians in the Revolution: At Kettle Creek (Wilkes Co.) and Burke County*. Southern Historical Press, 1986. p. 91. O'Kelley, Patrick. *Nothing But Blood and Slaughter*. Booklocker.com, 2004. Vol. 1 p. 262–63.

107. McCall, Hugh. *The History of Georgia, containing brief sketches of the most remarkable events up to the present day, 1784*. Savannah: Seymour & Williams, 1811; Atlanta, Cherokee Pub. Co., 1969, 1909. p. 418. Moultrie, William, *Memoirs of the American Revolution so far as it related to the States of North and South Carolina and Georgia*, New York, 1802; (Eyewitness accounts of the American Revolution). [New York]: New York Times [1968] vol. 1 pp. 379–382,

387–388. O'Kelley, Patrick. *Nothing But Blood and Slaughter*. Booklocker.com, 2004. Vol. 1 p. 270–71. Peckham, Howard Henry. *The Toll of Independence: engagements & battle casualties of the American Revolution*. Edited by Howard H. Peckham. Chicago: University of Chicago Press, 1974. p. 59. Lincoln Papers. South Carolina Archives. Moultrie, William. *Memoirs of the American Revolution so far as it related to the States of North and South Carolina and Georgia*, New York, 1802; (Eyewitness accounts of the American Revolution). [New York] New York Times [1968]. Vol. 1 pp. 379–382, 387–388. Heitman, Francis B. *Historical Register of Officers of the Continental Army during the War of the Revolution April 1775 to December 1783*. Washington, DC, 1914; Baltimore: Genealogical Publishing Company, 1967. pp. 74–89. Moss, Bobby Gilmer. *Roster of South Carolina Patriots in the American Revolution*. Baltimore: Genealogical Pub. Co., 1983. p. 423. O'Kelley, Patrick. *Nothing But Blood and Slaughter*. Booklocker.com, 2004. Vol. 1 p. 270–71. Parker, John C. *Parker's Guide to the Revolutionary War in South Carolina: battles, skirmishes and murders*. Patrick, SC: Hem Branch Publishing, 2009. p. 226, 227. Smith, Gordon Burns. *Morningstars of Liberty: the Revolutionary War in Georgia, 1775–1783*. Milledgeville, GA: Boyd Publishing, 2006. Vol. 1 pp. 153–154.

108. McCall stated that Muller's detachment consisted of 40 mounted grenadiers and three militia guides. McCall, Hugh. *The History of Georgia, containing brief sketches of the most remarkable events up to the present day, 1784*. Savannah: Seymour & Williams, 1811; Atlanta, Cherokee Pub. Co., 1969, 1909. Vol. III pp. 235, 421–22. Hudson Whitaker (1757–1817)had been commissioned captain in the 6th, Regiment North Carolina Continental Line. He resided in Baldwin County, Georgia, following the Revolutionary War. Extract of a letter from a gentleman in Augusta, dated July 5, 1779. *The Independent Chronicle and the Universal Advertiser*. XI: 571 p. 1. *The Pennsylvania Gazette*. August 18, 1779. Jones, Charles C. Jr. The History of Georgia. Boston: Houghton, Mifflin and Company, 1883. Vol. II pp. 361–362. *Collections of the Georgia Historical Society*. 11[Hawes, Lilla M., ed. "The Papers of James Jackson, 1781–1798" Savannah: The Georgia Historical Society, 1955] pp. 12–13. Lossing, Benson John. *The Pictorial Field-Book of the Revolution: or, Illustrations, by pen and pencil, of the history, biography, scenery, relics, and traditions of the war for independence with eleven hundred engravings on wood*, by Lossing and Barritt, chiefly from original sketches by the author. New York: Harper Brothers, 1852. p. 734n. O'Kelley, Patrick. *Nothing But Blood and Slaughter*. Booklocker. com, 2004. Vol. 1 p. 302–303. Smith, Gordon Burns. *Morningstars of Liberty: the Revolutionary War in Georgia, 1775–1783*. Milledgeville, GA: Boyd Publishing, 2006. Vol. 1 pp. 156–158.

109. Richard Head Pension application S13365. O'Kelley, Patrick. *Nothing But Blood and Slaughter*. Booklocker. com, 2004. Vol. 1 pp. 305–306. Simms, William Gilmore. *The Life of Francis Marion*. New York, 1844. pp. 15–17. Moultrie, William. *Memoirs of the American Revolution so far as it related to the States of North and South Carolina and Georgia*. New York, 1802; (Eyewitness accounts of the American Revolution). [New York] New York Times [1968] vol. II pp. 23–26. *Pennsylvania Gazette*. September 15, 1779. Hough, Franklin B. *The Siege of Savannah by the Combined American and French Forces under the command of Gen. Lincoln and the Count d'Estaing in the Autumn of 1779*. Albany: J. Munsell, 1806. p. 38.

110. O'Kelley, Patrick. *Nothing But Blood and Slaughter*. Booklocker.com, 2004. Vol. 1 p. 309. *Pennsylvania Gazette*. October 20, 1779; March 22, 1780.

111. Moultrie, William. *Memoirs of the American Revolution so far as it related to the States of North and South Carolina and Georgia*. New York, 1802; (Eyewitness accounts of the American Revolution). [New York] New York Times [1968] vol. 2 p. 34. Smith, Gordon Burns. *Morningstars of Liberty: the Revolutionary War in Georgia, 1775–1783*. Milledgeville, GA: Boyd Publishing, 2006. Vol. 1 pp. 166–167.

112. *The Pennsylvania Evening Post*. V: 635 (October 26, 1779): 243.

113. Journal of the Garrison Regiment von Knoblauch, 1776–84. *Hessian Documents of the American Revolution*. Morristown National Historical Park.

114. Boatner, Mark M. *Encyclopedia of the American Revolution*. 3d ed., New York: McKay, 1980. p. 192. Hough, Franklin Benjamin, ed. *The siege of Charleston by the British fleet and army, under the command of Admiral Arbuthnot and Sir Henry Clinton, which terminated with the surrender of that place on the 12th of May, 1780*. Albany, J. Munsell, 1867. P. 151. Hayes, John T. *The Saddlebag Almanac*. January 1997. Vol. V pp. 87, 91–92. Jones, Charles Colcock, ed. and tr. *The Siege of Savannah in 1779, as described in two contemporary journals of French officers in the fleet of Count d'Estaing*. Albany, N. Y., J. Munsell, 1874. P. 15. O'Kelley, Patrick. *Nothing But Blood and Slaughter*. Booklocker.com, 2004. Vol. 1 p. 310.

115. Jones, Charles Colcock. *The siege of Savannah by the fleet of Count d'Estaing in 1779*. (Eyewitness accounts of the American Revolution). [New York]: New York Times, [1968]. pp. 18–23, 28–29. Jones, Charles C. Jr. *The History of Georgia*. Boston: Houghton, Mifflin and Company, 1883. Vol. II p. 388. Lawrence, Alexander A. *Storm over Savannah: the story of Count d'Estaing and the siege of the town in 1779*. Athens: University of Georgia Press, 1951. p. 158. McCall, Hugh. *The History of Georgia, containing brief sketches of the most remarkable events up to the present day, 1784*. Savannah: Seymour & Williams, 1811; Atlanta, Cherokee Pub. Co., 1969, 1909. Vol. II, p. 255. *Rivington's Royal Gazette*. No. 334, Dec. 11, 1779. Dawson, Henry B. *Battles of the United States by Sea and Land*. New York: Johnson, Fry, & Company, 1858. pp. 562–569. *Connecticut Journal*. 631 (December 1, 1779): 3. *The Connecticut Gazette and The Universal Intelligencer*. XVII: 838, p. 3.

116. *Documents of the American Revolution 1770–1783* (Colonial Office Series), Edited by Davies, K. G. Irish University Press, 1979. XVII: 242–243. *Pennsylvania Gazette*. November 10, 1779; December 15, 1779; December 20, 1780. Hough, Franklin Benjamin, ed. *The siege of Charleston by the British fleet and army, under the command of Admiral Arbuthnot and Sir Henry Clinton, which terminated with the surrender of that place on the 12th of May, 1780*. Albany, J. Munsell, 1867. Spartanburg, SC: Reprint Company, 1975. pp. 151–152. Lawrence, Alexander A. *Storm Over Savannah, the Story of Count d'Estaing and the Siege of the Town in 1779*. Athens: University of Georgia Press, 1951. pp. 116–117. O'Kelley, Patrick. *Nothing But Blood and Slaughter*. Booklocker.com, 2004. Vol. 1 p. 353. Muster rolls of Capt. Thomas French's company in Clark, Murtie June. *Loyalists in the Southern Campaign of the Revolutionary War*. Baltimore: Genealogical Publishing Co., 1981. Vol. 3 pp. 10–14. Colonel John White to General Benjamin

Lincoln, 2 October 1779, in Albert Sidney Britt Jr. et al., eds. *Selected Eighteenth Century Manuscripts*. Savannah: The Society of Colonial Wars in the State of Georgia, 1980. pp. 53–54, taken from Collection No. 859 (1), Georgia Historical Society, Savannah, Georgia. Account of the Ogeechee capture in (Charleston) *Gazette of the State of South Carolina*, 6 October 1779; "Anecdote," *The (Fort Hawkins, GA) Messenger*, 2 June 1823; White, George. *Historical Collections of Georgia*. New York: Pudney & Russell, 1855; Baltimore: Genealogical Pub. Co., 1969. pp. 367–369. Lee, Henry. *Memoirs of the War in the Southern Department of the United States*. Ed. Robert E. Lee. New York: University Publishing Company, 1869. pp. 144–145. Thompson, Maurice. "A Boy's Strategy." *Atlanta Constitution Junior*. 17 November 1895. Smith, Gordon Burns. *Morningstars of Liberty: the Revolutionary War in Georgia, 1775–1783*. Milledgeville, GA: Boyd Publishing, 2006. Vol. 1 pp. 167–168.

117. *Encyclopedia of the American Revolution*. Harold E. Selesky, editor in chief. 2nd Ed. Detroit: Charles Scribner's Sons, 2007. Vol. II pp. 1035–1040. *The Encyclopedia of the American Revolutionary War: a political, social, and military history*. Gregory Fremont-Barnes, Richard Alan Ryerson, editors. Santa Barbara, CA: ABC-CLIO, 2006. Vol. IV pp. 1124–1130. Campbell, Colin, ed. *Journal of an Expedition against the Rebels in Georgia in North America under the Orders of Archibald Campbell, Esquire, Lieutenant Colonel of His Majesty's 71st Regiment, 1778*. Darien, GA: Ahantilly, 1981. Coleman, Kenneth. *The American Revolution in Georgia*. Athens: University of Georgia Press, 1958. Commager, Henry Steele. *The Spirit of Seventy Six: The Story of the American Revolution as Told by Participants*. New York, Harper & Row [1967]. Jones, Charles Colcock, Jr. *The siege of Savannah by the fleet of Count d'Estaing in 1779*. [New York]: New York Times [1968]. Kennedy, Benjamin, ed. *Muskets, Cannon Balls, and Bombs: Nine Narratives of the Siege of Savannah in 1779*. Savannah, GA: Beehive, 1974. Lawrence, Alexander A. *Storm Over Savannah, the Story of Count d'Estaing and the Siege of the Town in 1779*. University of Georgia Press, 1951. Searcy, Martha Condray. "General Robert Howe and the British Capture of Savannah in 1778." *Georgia Historical Quarterly*. 36 (December 1952): 303–327. Ward, Christopher. *The War of the Revolution*. New York: Macmillan, 1952. pp. 688–694. Wilson, David K. *The Southern Strategy: Britain's Conquest of South Carolina and Georgia, 1775–1780*. Columbia: University of South Carolina Press, 2005. Major Alexander MacDonald of Kinlochmoidart, 71st Highlanders, to his wife Susannah (Campbell of Airds) MacDonald, Savannah. November 6, 1779, in the Robertson MacDonald of Kinlochmoidart Papers, MS3945, folios (ff 58–59, National Library of Scotland. Edinburgh, Scotland. Duc De Castries, *Papiers De Famille* (Paris: Editions France-Empire, n. d.), 378. Benjamin Lincoln Collection 416 (September–October 1779) in the Domestic Collection of the Library of Congress, Washington, D. C. The Benjamin Lincoln Papers (13 reels of microfilm) Collection 488. Letter to the editor. (Savannah) *Daily Georgian*. August 8, 1835. Moses Buffington to Peter Buffington Sr., Savannah. December 8, 1779, in Albert Sidney Britt, Jr. et al., eds. *Selected Eighteenth Century Manuscripts*. Savannah: The Society of Colonial Wars in the State of Georgia, 1980): 54–5, taken from Collection No. 101(1). Georgia Historical Society. Savannah, Georgia. John Jones to Polly Jones. October 7, 1779, in *Muskets, Cannon Balls, &Bombs, Nine Narratives of the Siege of Savannah in 1779*, ed. and trans. Benjamin Kennedy. Savannah: Beehive Press, 1974. pp. 16, 19, 152. Jones, Charles C. Jr. *The Life and Services of the Honorable Maj. Gen. Samuel Elbert of Georgia*. Cambridge: The Riverside Press, 1887. p. 35. Journal of the Siege of Savannah from the *Royal Georgia Gazette*. November 18, 1779, in *The (Charleston) South-Carolina and American General Gazette*. December 10, 1779. Stevens, William Bacon. *A History of Georgia*. Philadelphia, PA, 1859. Vol. 2 p. 228. Lawrence, Alexander A. Storm Over Savannah, the Story of Count d'Estaing and the Siege of the Town in 1779. University of Georgia Press, 1951. p. 102. Testimony of John Were at the court-martial of General Robert Howe, *Proceedings of a General Court Martial, Held at Philadelphia for the Trial of Major General Howe, Dec. 7, 1781*. Philadelphia, 1782 reprinted in *Collections of the New York Historical Society 1879* (New York, 1880) p. 230. Orders for attack in Order Book of John Faucheraud Grimke. *South Carolina Historical And Genealogical Magazine*. 17 (January 1916): 85–6. Gordon, William. *The History of the Rise, Progress, and Establishment, of the Independence of the United States of America*. New York, NY, 1789. Vol. 3 p. 33. *The (Charleston) Gazette of the State of South-Carolina*. November 18, 1777. Duc De Castries. *Papiers De Famille*. Paris: Editions France-Empire, n. d. p. 378. Johnston, Elizabeth Lichtenstein. *Recollections of a Georgia Loyalist*. 1901 reprinted Spartanburg, SC: The Reprint Company, 1972). p. 62. *Connecticut Journal*. December 29, 1779. Reuber, Johannes. *Diary of a Hessian Grenadier of Colonel Rail's Regiment*. trans. Bruce E. Burgoyne (privately printed, Johannes Schwalm Historical Association, n. p. n. d.), (from a copy of the diary of Johannes Reuber in the possession of Kennery Jones, Worcester, MA). p. 39. Major Alexander MacDonald to his wife Susannah MacDonald, Savannah. November 6, 1779. Edinburgh, Scotland. National Library of Scotland. British Journal of the siege of Savannah, 3 September–25 October 1779, in the Francis Rush Clark papers, Collection No. 2338 (III) in the Sol Feinstone Collection of the David Library of the American Revolution. Washington Crossing, Pennsylvania. Smith, Gordon Burns. *Morningstars of Liberty: the Revolutionary War in Georgia, 1775–1783*. Milledgeville, GA: Boyd Publishing, 2006. Vol. 1 pp. 168–174.

118. "Account of the Siege of Savannah, from a British Source." Collections of the Georgia Historical Society. Savannah: Braid & Hutton, 1901. Vol. 5pt. 1 p. 138. Hough, Franklin Benjamin, ed. *The siege of Charleston by the British fleet and army, under the command of Admiral Arbuthnot and Sir Henry Clinton, which terminated with the surrender of that place on the 12th of May, 1780*. Albany, J. Munsell, 1867. Spartanburg, SC: Reprint Company, 1975. pp. 45, 78–79. O'Kelley, Patrick. *Nothing But Blood and Slaughter*. Booklocker.com, 2004. Vol. 1 p. 354.

119. Davies, K. G. *Documents of the American Revolution 1770–1783* (Colonial Office Series) Vol. XX Transcripts 1781. Irish University Press, 1979. p. 173. Smith, Charles R. *Marines in the Revolution*. History and Museums Division, Headquarters, U. S. Marine Corps, 1975. p. 246. *The Pennsylvania Gazette*. March 8, 1780. Hayes, John T. *The Saddlebag Almanac*. VI (January 1999): 3–4. O'Kelley, Patrick. *Nothing But Blood and Slaughter*. Booklocker. com, 2004. Vol. 2 p. 21–23.

120. Ibid.

121. Mays, Terry M. *Historical Dictionary of the American Revolution*. Scarecrow Press: Lanham, MD, 1999. McCall, Hugh. *The History of Georgia, containing brief sketches of the most remarkable events up to the present day, 1784*. Savannah: Seymour & Williams, 1811; Atlanta, Cherokee Pub. Co., 1969, 1909. p. 465. Smith, Gordon

Burns. *Morningstars of Liberty: the Revolutionary War in Georgia, 1775–1783*. Milledgeville, GA: Boyd Publishing, 2006. Vol. 1 p. 182.

122. Cashin, Edward J. *The King's Ranger: Thomas Brown and the American Revolution on the southern frontier*. Athens: University of Georgia Press, c1989. pp. 87, 99–108. Lee, Henry. *Memoirs of the War in the Southern Department of the United States*. New York: University Publishing Co., 1869. p. 175. Pancake, John S. *This Destructive War: The British Campaign in the Carolinas*. Tuscaloosa: University of Alabama Press, 1985. p. 62. Draper, Lyman. Thomas Sumter Papers, Draper Manuscript Collection, State Historical Society of Wisconsin. 11VV536–540. O'Kelley, Patrick. *Nothing But Blood and Slaughter*. Booklocker.com, 2004. Vol. 2 p. 128. Peckham, Howard Henry. *The Toll of Independence: engagements & battle casualties of the American Revolution*. Edited by Howard H. Peckham. Chicago: University of Chicago Press, 1974. p. 68. Wright to Germain, Savannah, 4 April 1780. Wright, Sir James. "Letters From Sir James Wright," *Collections of the Georgia Historical Society*. Savannah: The Morning News Office, 1873 vol. 3 pp. 281–282. Smith, Gordon Burns. *Morningstars of Liberty: the Revolutionary War in Georgia, 1775–1783*. Milledgeville, GA: Boyd Publishing, 2006. Vol. 1 p. 183.

123. McCall, Hugh. *The History of Georgia, containing brief sketches of the most remarkable events up to the present day, 1784*. Savannah: Seymour & Williams, 1811; Atlanta, Cherokee Pub. Co., 1969, 1909. pp. 465–466. O'Kelley, Patrick. *Nothing But Blood and Slaughter*. Booklocker.com, 2004. Vol. 2 pp. 135–136. *Pennsylvania Gazette*. May 24, 1780. British National Archives. Headquarters Papers of the British Army in America, folio 2482. *Royal American Gazette*. April 27, 1780. Peckham, Howard Henry. *The Toll of Independence: engagements & battle casualties of the American Revolution*. Edited by Howard H. Peckham. Chicago: University of Chicago Press, 1974. p. 69.

124. Jones, Charles Colcock, Jr. *The History of Georgia*. Boston: Houghton, Mifflin and Company, 1883. Vol. 2 pp. 499–501. O'Kelley, Patrick. *Nothing But Blood and Slaughter*. Booklocker.com, 2004. Vol. 3 p. 285.

125. Davis, Robert Scott, Jr. *Georgia Citizens and Soldiers of the American Revolution*. Southern Historical Press, 1979. p. 109. Draper, Lyman. *Kings Mountain and its Heroes: History of the Battle of King's Mountain, October 7th, 1780, and the Events Which Led to It*. The Overmountain Press, 1996. p. 341. Cashin, Edward J. *The King's Ranger: Thomas Brown and the American Revolution on the southern frontier*. Athens: University of Georgia Press, c1989. p. 146. Sanford Berry Pension File #S1638. Jones, Charles Colcock, Jr. *The History of Georgia*. Boston: Houghton, Mifflin and Company, 1883. Vol. II pp. 499–501. Hall, Leslie. *Land and Allegiance in Revolutionary Georgia*. University of Georgia Press, 2001. O'Kelley, Patrick. *Nothing But Blood and Slaughter*. Booklocker.com, 2004. Vol. 3 pp. 382–383. James Jackson to Nathan Brownson, Augusta, 7 November 1781 in Hawes, Lilla M., ed. "The Papers of James Jackson, 1781–1798" *Collections of the Georgia Historical Society*. Savannah: The Georgia Historical Society, 1955. Vol. 11 pp. 2–3. McCall, Hugh. *The History of Georgia, containing brief sketches of the most remarkable events up to the present day, 1784*. Savannah: Seymour & Williams, 1811; Atlanta, Cherokee Pub. Co., 1969, 1909. pp. 532–533. Smith, Gordon Burns. *Morningstars of Liberty: the Revolutionary War in Georgia, 1775–1783*. Milledgeville, GA: Boyd Publishing, 2006. Vol. 1 pp. 256–257.

126. Draper, Lyman. Thomas Sumter Papers, Draper Manuscript Collection, State Historical Society of Wisconsin. 17VV39. O'Kelley, Patrick. *Nothing But Blood and Slaughter*. Booklocker.com, 2004. Vol. 3 p. 368.

127. Friedrich de Porbeck to Landgraf (Frederick, Landgrave of Hesse), Savannah, Province of Georgia, January 1, 1781, in "Journal of the Hesse-Hanau Jaeger Corps, 1778–82," in *Hessian Documents of the American Revolution*. Morristown National Historical Park. Smith, Gordon Burns. *Morningstars of Liberty: the Revolutionary War in Georgia, 1775–1783*. Milledgeville, GA: Boyd Publishing, 2006. Vol. 1 p. 259.

128. Boyle, Joseph Lee. "The Revolutionary War Diaries of Captain Walter Finney," *South Carolina Historical Magazine*. 98 (April 1997): 136. Moultrie, William, *Memoirs of the American Revolution so far as it related to the States of North and South Carolina and Georgia*, New York, 1802; (Eyewitness accounts of the American Revolution]vol. 2 pp. 297–298. Wayne to Greene, 1 February 1782, from Old Saw Mill near Abercorn in Dennis M. Conrad et al., eds. *The Papers of General Nathanael Greene*. Chapel Hill and London: The University of North Carolina Press, 1998. Vol. 10 p. 379. Wayne to Greene, 11 February 1782, Ebenezer, ibid. p. 382. *Encyclopedia of the American Revolution*. Harold E. Selesky, editor in chief. 2nd Ed. Detroit: Charles Scribner's Sons, 2007. Vol. 419–420. Smith, Gordon Burns. *Morningstars of Liberty: the Revolutionary War in Georgia, 1775–1783*. Milledgeville, GA: Boyd Publishing, 2006. Vol. 1 pp. 264–265.

129. Wayne to Greene, 11 February 1782, Ebenezer in Dennis M. Conrad et al., eds. *The Papers of General Nathanael Greene*. Chapel Hill and London: The University of North Carolina Press, 1998. Vol. 10 p. 382. Cashin, Edward J. *The King's Ranger: Thomas Brown and the American Revolution on the southern frontier*. Athens: University of Georgia Press, c1989. p. 151, citing Habersham to Wayne, 8 February 1782. Smith, Gordon Burns. *Morningstars of Liberty: the Revolutionary War in Georgia, 1775–1783*. Milledgeville, GA: Boyd Publishing, 2006. Vol. 1 pp. 265–266.

130. "Notice to Invalids" in (Augusta, GA) *Southern Centinel and Gazette of the State*. 4 February 1796. Smith, Gordon Burns. *Morningstars of Liberty: the Revolutionary War in Georgia, 1775–1783*. Milledgeville, GA: Boyd Publishing, 2006. Vol. 1 p. 266.

131. Smith, Gordon Burns. *Morningstars of Liberty: the Revolutionary War in Georgia, 1775–1783*. Milledgeville, GA: Boyd Publishing, 2006. Vol. 1 p. 266.

132. Hawes, Lilla M., ed. "The Papers of James Jackson, 1781–1798," *Collections of the Georgia Historical Society*. Savannah: The Georgia Historical Society, 1955. Vol. 11 p. 25. Wright, Sir James. "Letters from Sir James Wright." *Collections of the Georgia Historical Society*. Savannah: The Georgia Historical Society, 1955. Vol. 3 p. 374. Wayne to Greene, 28 February 1782, Ebenezer in Dennis M. Conrad et al., eds. *The Papers of General Nathanael Greene*. Chapel Hill and London: The University of North Carolina Press, 1998. Vol. 10 p. 386; Greene to Wayne, 6 March 1782, ibid. p. 389. Parker, John C. *Parker's Guide to the Revolutionary War in South Carolina: battles, skirmishes and murders*.

Patrick, SC: Hem Branch Publishing, 2009. p. 225. Smith, Gordon Burns. *Morningstars of Liberty: the Revolutionary War in Georgia, 1775–1783*. Milledgeville, GA: Boyd Publishing, 2006. Vol. 1 pp. 266–267.

133. Captain Benjamin Fishbourne to Nathanael Greene, Ebenezer, 25 March 1782 in Dennis M. Conrad et al., eds. *The Papers of General Nathanael Greene*. Chapel Hill and London: The University of North Carolina Press, 1998. Vol. 10 pp. 536–537; and Anthony Wayne to Nathanael Greene, 25 March 1782, Ebenezer, Ibid. p. 539. Wayne to Greene, 25 March 1782, Ebenezer. Ibid. p. 394; Greene to Wayne, 6 April 1782. Ibid. p. 396. Jones, Charles C. Jr. *The History of Georgia*. Boston: Houghton, Mifflin and Company, 1883. Vol. 2 pp. 507–508. Smith, Gordon Burns. *Morningstars of Liberty: the Revolutionary War in Georgia, 1775–1783*. Milledgeville, GA: Boyd Publishing, 2006. Vol. 1 p. 273.

134. Petition of Captain James Swinney dated 14 May 1782 in Clark, Murtie June. *Loyalists in the Southern Campaign of the Revolutionary War*. Baltimore: Genealogical Publishing Co., 1981. Vol. 1 p. 222. Report from Johannes Hangleiter, Caspar Heik, Nicolaus Schubdrein, Johannes Michel, Jacob Gnann, Christopher Cramer, and Samuel Kraus, Ebenezer, 5 May 1783 to Henry Muhlenberg in Andrew W. Lewis, ed. "Henry Muhlenberg's Georgia Correspondence." *Georgia Historical Quarterly*. 49 (December 1965): 442. Public notice of loyalist petitions, Charleston, 3 July 1781, in *The* (Charleston) *Royal Gazette*, 7 July 1781 to 11 July 1781. Smith, Gordon Burns. *Morningstars of Liberty: the Revolutionary War in Georgia, 1775–1783*. Milledgeville, GA: Boyd Publishing, 2006. Vol. 1 pp. 270–271.

135. Searcy, Martha Condray. *The Georgia–Florida contest in the American Revolution, 1776–1778*. University, AL: University of Alabama Press, c1985. p. 158.

136. Smith, Gordon Burns. *Morningstars of Liberty: the Revolutionary War in Georgia, 1775–1783*. Milledgeville, GA: Boyd Publishing, 2006. Vol. 1 p. 273.

137. *Royal Georgia Gazette*. 25 April 1782. Smith, Gordon Burns. *Morningstars of Liberty: the Revolutionary War in Georgia, 1775–1783*. Milledgeville, GA: Boyd Publishing, 2006. Vol. 1 p. 273.

138. Extract from Wayne's General Orders, April 16, 1782, Colonel John Shey Eustace, Wayne's Deputy Adjutant General, Ebenezer HQ. Letters by Wayne, New York Public Library. "Another Revolutionary Soldier Gone." *Savannah Weekly Republican*. 19 December 1846. Strobel, Philip A. *The Salzburgers and Their Descendants*. 1855, reprinted, Athens: The University of Georgia Press, 1953. pp. 273–274. Smith, Gordon Burns. *Morningstars of Liberty: the Revolutionary War in Georgia, 1775–1783*. Milledgeville, GA: Boyd Publishing, 2006. Vol. 1 p. 273.

139. Wayne to Greene, 26 January 1782, dated Hampton Hall near Abercorn. in Dennis M. Conrad et al., eds. *The Papers of General Nathanael Greene*. Chapel Hill and London: The University of North Carolina Press, 1998. Vol. 10 p. 376. Greene to Wayne, 4 February 1782, ibid. p. 378. Smith, Gordon Burns. *Morningstars of Liberty: the Revolutionary War in Georgia, 1775–1783*. Milledgeville, GA: Boyd Publishing, 2006. Vol. 1 p. 278.

140. Wayne to Greene, 7 May 1782, Ebenezer, in Dennis M. Conrad et al., eds. *The Papers of General Nathanael Greene*. Chapel Hill and London: The University of North Carolina Press, 1998. Vol. 10 p. 405. Smith, Gordon Burns. *Morningstars of Liberty: the Revolutionary War in Georgia, 1775–1783*. Milledgeville, GA: Boyd Publishing, 2006. Vol. 1 p. 279.

141. Wayne to Greene, 18 May 1782, Ebenezer in Dennis M. Conrad et al., eds. *The Papers of General Nathanael Greene*. Chapel Hill and London: The University of North Carolina Press, 1998. Vol. 10 p. 408. Smith, Gordon Burns. *Morningstars of Liberty: the Revolutionary War in Georgia, 1775–1783*. Milledgeville, GA: Boyd Publishing, 2006. Vol. 1 p. 279.

142. McCall, Hugh. *The History of Georgia, containing brief sketches of the most remarkable events up to the present day, 1784*. Savannah: Seymour & Williams, 1811; Atlanta, Cherokee Pub. Co., 1969, 1909. pp. 541–543. Moultrie, William. *Memoirs of the American Revolution so far as it related to the States of North and South Carolina and Georgia*. New York, 1802; (Eyewitness accounts of the American Revolution). [New York]: New York Times, [1968]. p. 338. Nase, Henry. Diary of Henry Nase King's American Regiment. Nase Family Papers. The New Brunswick Museum, Archives Division, Transcribed by Todd Braisted. p. 22. (Savannah) *Royal Georgia Gazette*. 23 May 1782. Smith, Gordon Burns. *Morningstars of Liberty: the Revolutionary War in Georgia, 1775–1783*. Milledgeville, GA: Boyd Publishing, 2006. Vol. 1 pp. 279–281.

143. Smith, Gordon Burns. *Morningstars of Liberty: the Revolutionary War in Georgia, 1775–1783*. Milledgeville, GA: Boyd Publishing, 2006. Vol. 1 p. 280.

144. *The Pennsylvania Packet or the General Advertiser*. 11: 924 (August 15, 1782): 3. Garden, Alexander, *Anecdotes of the American Revolution, Illustrative of the Talents and Virtues of the Heroes and Patriots who Acted the Most Conspicuous Parts Therein*. Second series. Charleston, SC: A. E. Miller,1828. pp. 373–374. Lee, Henry. *Memoirs of the War in the Southern Department of the United States*. New York: University Publishing Co., 1869. pp. 555–560. Finney, Walter. "The Revolutionary War Diaries of Captain Walter Finney." Edited by Joseph Lee Boyle. *South Carolina Historical Magazine*. 98 (April 1997): 141, 145. Moultrie, William. *Memoirs of the American Revolution so far as it related to the States of North and South Carolina and Georgia*. New York, 1802; (Eyewitness accounts of the American Revolution). [New York]: New York Times, [1968]. II: 336, 338–339. *Pennsylvania Gazette*. August 21, 1782. Pension application of William Knight R6031. Savannah Unit, Georgia Writers' Project, Work Projects Administration in Georgia. Whitehall Plantation. *The Georgia Historical Quarterly*. Vol. 25, No. 4 (December 1941): 340-363; Vol. 26, No. 1 (March 1942): 40–64; Vol. 26, No. 2 (June 1942): 129–155. Elliott, Daniel T. *Ebenezer Revolutionary War Headquarters: A Quest to Locate and Preserve*. LAMAR Institute Publication Series, Report Number 73, The LAMAR Institute, Box Springs, Georgia, 2003. O'Kelley, Patrick. *Nothing But Blood and Slaughter*. Booklocker.com, 2004. Vol. 4 pp. 76–78. *Morningstars of Liberty: the Revolutionary War in Georgia, 1775–1783*. Milledgeville, GA: Boyd Publishing, 2006. Vol. 1 pp. 281–283.

145. (Savannah) *Georgia Gazette and The* (Savannah) *Gazette of the State of Georgia*. 13 March 1783. Smith, Gordon Burns. *Morningstars of Liberty: the Revolutionary War in Georgia, 1775–1783*. Milledgeville, GA: Boyd Publishing, 2006. Vol. 1 p. 287.

146. Peckham, Howard Henry. *The Toll of Independence: engagements & battle casualties of the American Revolution*. Edited by Howard H. Peckham. Chicago: University of Chicago Press, 1974. p. 13.

147. www.ourgeorgiahistory.com/wars/Revolution/revolution09.html.

148. Jones, Charles C. Jr. *The History of Georgia*. Boston: Houghton, Mifflin and Company, 1883. II pp. 274–275. McCall, Hugh. *The History of Georgia, containing brief sketches of the most remarkable events up to the present day, 1784*. Savannah: Seymour & Williams, 1811; Atlanta: Cherokee Pub. Co., 1969, 1909. p. 347. Pension Application of Shadrack Nolen, S4622. Smith, Gordon Burns. *Morningstars of Liberty: the Revolutionary War in Georgia, 1775–1783*. Milledgeville, GA: Boyd Publishing, 2006. Vol. 1 p. 93.

149. Searcy, Martha Condray. *The Georgia-Florida contest in the American Revolution, 1776–1778*. University, AL: University of Alabama Press, c1985. p. 130. Mowat, Charles Loch. *East Florida as a British Province 1763–1784*. Berkeley and Los Angeles: University of California Press, 1943; reprinted Gainesville, FL: University of Florida Press, 1964. p. 121. Siebert, Wilbur Henry. *Loyalists in East Florida, 1774 to 1785; the Most Important Documents Pertaining Thereto Edited with an Accompanying Narrative*. Deland: The Florida State Historical Society, 1929. American Revolutionary Series. Boston: Gregg Press, 1972. Vol. I p. 47, 51. Raab, James W. *Spain, Britain, and the American Revolution in Florida, 1763–1783*. Jefferson, NC and London: McFarland & Company, 2008. pp. 106–107.

150. Bennett, Charles E. and Lennon, Donald R. *A Quest for Glory: Major General Robert Howe and the American Revolution*. Chapel Hill & London: The University of North Carolina Press, 1991. p. 71. Governor Patrick Tonyn to Lord George Germain March 20, 1778. British National Archives. Colonial Office. 5/558, fols. 113–14. Addressed below close: "Right Honourable/Lord George Germain." Docketed: "St Augustine March 20 1778/Govr Tonyn/ (N°– 52)/R, June 6th (Inclosures 2)/Entd" NDAR 11: 744–745. Smith, Gordon Burns. *Morningstars of Liberty: the Revolutionary War in Georgia, 1775–1783*. Milledgeville, GA: Boyd Publishing, 2006. Vol. 1 pp. 102–103.

151. Searcy, Martha Condray. *The Georgia-Florida Contest in the American Revolution, 1776–1778*. University, AL: University of Alabama Press, c1985. p. 141.

152. www.ourgeorgiahistory.com/wars/Revolution/revolution09.html. Mowat, Charles Loch. *East Florida as a British Province 1763–1784*. Berkeley and Los Angeles: University of California Press, 1943; reprinted Gainesville, FL: University of Florida Press, 1964. p. 120.

153. *Encyclopedia of the American Revolution*. Harold E. Selesky, editor in chief. 2nd Ed. Detroit: Charles Scribner's Sons, 2007. Vol. 1: 373.

154. Raab, James W. *Spain, Britain, and the American Revolution in Florida, 1763–1783*. Jefferson, NC and London: McFarland & Company, 2008. p. 99.

155. O'Kelley, Patrick. *Nothing But Blood and Slaughter*. Booklocker.com, 2004. Vol. 1 pp. 173–175. O'Kelley, Patrick. *Unwaried Patience and Fortitude: Francis Marion's Orderly Book*. Infinity Publishing (PA), 2006. Davis, Robert Scott, Jr. *Georgia Citizens and Soldiers of the American Revolution*. Southern Historical Press, 1979. pp. 148–151. Davis, Robert Scott, Jr. *Georgians in the Revolution: At Kettle Creek (Wilkes Co.) and Burke County*. Southern Historical Press, 1986. p. 124. Butler, Lewis. *The Annals of the King's Royal Rifle Corps*; Volume 1. "The Royal Americans", John Murray, London, 1913. pp. 300–302. Moultrie, William, *Memoirs of the American Revolution so far as it related to the States of North and South Carolina and Georgia*. New York, 1802; (Eyewitness accounts of the American Revolution). [New York] New York Times [1968]. Vol. 1 pp. 188–189. *Pennsylvania Gazette*. April 2, 1777. Jackson, Harvey H. *Lachlan McIntosh and the Politics of Revolutionary Georgia*. Athens: University of Georgia Press, 1979. pp. 49–50. Searcy, Martha Condray. *The Georgia-Florida Contest in the American Revolution, 1776–1778*. [sl]: University of Alabama Press, 1985. pp. 84–88. Memoirs of Major Patrick Murray in Lewis Butler and Stewart Hare, eds. *The Annals of the King's Royal Rifle Corps*. London: Smith, Elder and Co. 1913. Vol. 1 p. 300. Milfort, Louis LeClerc. *Memoirs or, a Quick Glance at my Various Travels and my Sojourn in the Creek Nation*. trans. Ben C. McCary, 1959reprinted, Savannah: The Beehive Press, 1972. pp. 100–101. Lieutenant Colonel Thomas Brown's report of his capture of Fort Mcintosh in Robert Scott Davis Jr. *Georgia Citizens and Soldiers of the American Revolution*. Easley, SC: Southern Historical Press, 1979. pp. 148–150. Colonial Office Papers, 5/557, 249–54 (4c TSS) British Public Record Office. McCall, Hugh. *The History of Georgia, containing brief sketches of the most remarkable events up to the present day, 1784*. Savannah: Seymour & Williams, 1811; Atlanta, Cherokee Pub. Co., 1969, 1909. pp. 325–327. Butler et al. *The Annals of The King's Royal Rifle Corps*. Vol. 1 p. 301. Journal of the Garrison Regiment von Knoblauch, 1776–84. *Hessian Documents of the American Revolution*. Morristown National Historical Park. White, George. *Historical Collections of Georgia*. New York: Pudney & Russell, 1855; Baltimore: Genealogical Pub. Co., 1969. pp. 614–619. McIntosh to Washington, 13 April 1777.*Collections of the Georgia Historical Society*. Vol. 12 p. 46. Smith, Gordon Burns. *Morningstars of Liberty: the Revolutionary War in Georgia, 1775–1783*. Milledgeville, GA: Boyd Publishing, 2006. Vol. 1 pp. 73–75. Barss, Burton. *East Florida in the American Revolution*. Jacksonville: Guild Press, 1952. pp. 17–22.

156. Campbell, Colin, ed. *Journal of an Expedition against the Rebels in Georgia in North America under the Orders of Archibald Campbell, Esquire, Lieutenant Colonel of His Majesty's 71st Regiment, 1778*. Darien, GA: Ahantilly, 1981. pp. 33–34. O'Kelley, Patrick. *Nothing But Blood and Slaughter*. Booklocker.com, 2004. Vol. 1 p. 223.

157. *Encyclopedia of the American Revolution*. Harold E. Selesky, editor in chief. 2nd Ed. Detroit: Charles Scribner's Sons, 2007. Vol. 1 p. 109. *The Encyclopedia of the American Revolutionary War: a political, social, and military history*. Gregory Fremont-Barnes, Richard Alan Ryerson, editors. Santa Barbara, CA: ABC-CLIO, 2006. Vol. 1 pp. 134–135. Campbell, Colin, ed. *Journal of an Expedition against the Rebels in Georgia in North America under the Orders of Archibald Campbell, Esquire, Lieutenant Colonel of His Majesty's 71st Regiment, 1778*. Darien, GA: Ahantilly, 1981.

Cashin, Edward J. *The King's Ranger: Thomas Brown and the American Revolution on the southern frontier.* Athens: University of Georgia Press, c1989. Jones, Charles Colcock, Jr. *The History of Georgia.* Boston: Houghton, Mifflin and Company, 1883. Lumpkin, Henry. *From Savannah to Yorktown: the American Revolution in the South.* New York: Paragon, 1981. Smith, Page. *A New Age Now Begins.* New York: McGraw-Hill, 1976. Extract of a letter from camp, near Adam's ferry, Feb. 20" in *The (Charleston) South-Carolina and American General Gazette.* 4 March 1779. Charles C. Jones Jr. *The Life and Services of the Honorable Maj. Gen. Samuel Elbert of Georgia.* Cambridge: The Riverside Press, 1887. pp. 33–34. Colin Campbell, ed. *Journal of An Expedition against the Rebels of Georgia In North America Under the Orders of Archibald Campbell. Esquire Lieut. Colol. of His Majesty's 71ˢᵗ Regiment. 1778.* (Darien: The Ashantilly Press, 1981). p. 77. Charles C. Jones Jr. *The History of Georgia.* Boston: Houghton, Mifflin and Company, 1883. Vol. 2 p. 350. *Royal Georgia Gazette.* 11 March 1779. Collection of Lyman Copeland Draper, LL. D. in the Georgia, Alabama and South Carolina Papers, Draper Manuscripts, 13DD33. Rubert S. Davis Jr., "Colonel Dooly's Campaign of 1779," *Huntington Library Quarterly.* 46 (1984): 65–71. Lossing, Benson John. *The Pictorial Field-Book of the Revolution: or, Illustrations, by pen and pencil, of the history, biography, scenery, relics, and traditions of the war for independence with eleven hundred engravings on wood,* by Lossing and Barritt, chiefly from original sketches by the author. New York: Harper Brothers, 1852. Vol. 2 p. 713n. McCall, Hugh. *The History of Georgia, containing brief sketches of the most remarkable events up to the present day, 1784.* Savannah: Seymour & Williams, 1811; Atlanta, Cherokee Pub. Co. 1969, 1909. p. 413. *Virginia Gazette* (Dixon & Nicolson). 9 April 1779, 24 April 1779, 10 July 1779. *The (Charleston) Gazette of the State of South-Carolina.* 1 September 1779.Cote, Richard N. *Theodosia Burr Alston, Portrait of a Prodigy.* Mt. Pleasant, SC: Corinthian Books, 2003. Smith, Gordon Burns. *Morningstars of Liberty: the Revolutionary War in Georgia, 1775–1783.* Milledgeville, GA: Boyd Publishing, 2006. Vol. 1 pp. 144–147. Scoggins, Michael C; Edgar, Walter. *The Day It Rained Militia: Huck's Defeat and the Revolution in the South Carolina Backcountry, May–July 1780.* Charleston: the History Press, c2005. p. 36.

158. Doddridge, Joseph. *Notes on the Settlement and Indian Wars of the Western Parts of Virginia and Pennsylvania from 1763 to 1783.* Wellsburg, VA: Joseph Doddridge, 1824. pp. 276–277. O'Kelley, Patrick. *Nothing But Blood and Slaughter.* Booklocker.com, 2004. Vol. 1 pp. 230–231.

159. Brown, Tarleton. *Memoirs of Tarleton Brown, a Captain in the Revolutionary Army, Written by Himself,* with a Preface and Notes by Charles I. Bushnell. New York: Privately Printed, 1862. pp. 32–33. O'Kelley, Patrick. *Nothing But Blood and Slaughter.* Booklocker.com, 2004. Vol. 3 p. 54.

160. Smith, Gordon Burns. *Morningstars of Liberty: the Revolutionary War in Georgia, 1775–1783.* Milledgeville, GA: Boyd Publishing, 2006. Vol. 1 p. 279.

161. www.carolana.com/SC/Revolution/revolution_hudsons_ferry.html. Campbell, Archibald. *Sketch of the Northern Frontiers of Georgia.* Map Collection, Caroliniana Library, University of South Carolina, Columbia,1780. Campbell, Colin. *Expedition Against the Rebels of Georgia in North America Under Orders of Archibald Campbell Esquire Lieutenant Colonel of His Majesty's 71st Regiment 1778.* Reprint of 1780 edition, Chantilly Press, Darien, 1981. Cole, Nan, and Todd Braisted. South Carolina Royalists, Certification of Half Pay [1779]. 2003. www.royalprovincial. com/military/thist/scroyal/scrcert.htm. Elliott, Daniel T. *Archaeological Reconnaissance Survey at Hudson Ferry, Screven County, Georgia.* LAMAR Institute Publication Series, Number 57. Box Springs, Georgia: The LAMAR Institute, 2003.

162. Journal of H. M. Schooner *Hinchinbrook,* Lieutenant Alexander Ellis. British National Archives, Admiralty 51/4219. NDAR 4: 1243.

163. *Royal Georgia Gazette.* 25 April 1782. Smith, Gordon Burns. *Morningstars of Liberty: the Revolutionary War in Georgia, 1775–1783.* Milledgeville, GA: Boyd Publishing, 2006. Vol. 1 p. 275.

164. *South-Carolina and American General Gazette.* Thursday, January 2, 1777; NDAR 7: 850. O'Kelley, Patrick. *Nothing But Blood and Slaughter.* Booklocker.com, 2004. Vol. 1 p. 170.

165. Smith, Gordon Burns. *Morningstars of Liberty: the Revolutionary War in Georgia, 1775–1783.* Milledgeville, GA: Boyd Publishing, 2006. Vol. 1 pp. 66, 126.

166. Jones, Charles C. Jr. *The History of Georgia.* Boston: Houghton, Mifflin and Company, 1883. Vol. 2 p. 363. Smith, Gordon Burns. *Morningstars of Liberty: the Revolutionary War in Georgia, 1775–1783.* Milledgeville, GA: Boyd Publishing, 2006. Vol. 1 p. 159.

167. Jones, Charles C. Jr. *The History of Georgia.* Boston: Houghton, Mifflin and Company, 1883. Vol. 2 pp. 499–501. O'Kelley, Patrick. *Nothing But Blood and Slaughter.* Booklocker.com, 2004. Vol. 3 p. 197.

168. Siebert, Wilbur Henry. *Loyalists in East Florida, 1774 to 1785; the Most Important Documents Pertaining Thereto Edited with an Accompanying Narrative.* Deland: The Florida State Historical Society, 1929. (American Revolutionary Series). Boston: Gregg Press, 1972. Vol. 1 pp. 47–48.

169. Peckham, Howard Henry. *The Toll of Independence: engagements & battle casualties of the American Revolution.* Edited by Howard H. Peckham. Chicago: University of Chicago Press, 1974. p. 34.

170. Wayne to Greene, 1 April 1782, Ebenezer in Dennis M. Conrad et al., eds. *The Papers of General Nathanael Greene.* Chapel Hill and London: The University of North Carolina Press, 1998. Vol. 10 p. 395. Patrick Carr to unknown, McDonald's at the "Scotch Settlement," 12 April 1782, in the Historical Society of Pennsylvania, Philadelphia, Pennsylvania. *Royal Georgia Gazette.*25 April 1782. Extract of a Letter from Brigadier-General Wayne to Mr. Edward Moore, Brother to the Late Major Francis Moore, of the Georgia Line. *The Boston Evening-Post and the General Advertiser.* I: XXXVIII (July 6, 1782): 2. *Salem Gazette.* I: 39 (July 11, 1782): 2. Campbell, Colin, ed. *Journal of an Expedition against the Rebels in Georgia in North America under the Orders of Archibald Campbell, Esquire, Lieutenant Colonel of His Majesty's 71ˢᵗ Regiment, 1778.* Darien, GA: Ahantilly, 1981. pp. 39, 46. "Habersham's Indian Expedition." the *Historical Magazine.* IV (5)(May 1860)129–31. McCall, Hugh. *The History of Georgia, containing brief sketches of the most remarkable events up to the present day, 1784.* Savannah: Seymour & Williams, 1811; Atlanta,

Cherokee Pub. Co. 1969, 1909. p. 540. Chatham County Probate Court, Estate Files No. M–28 and M–51, and Minute Book (1783–1791), 259. Virgil D. White, abs. *Genealogical Abstracts of Revolutionary War Pension Files.* Waynesboro, TN, 1990. Vol. 2 p. 2399. Smith, Gordon Burns. *Morningstars of Liberty: the Revolutionary War in Georgia, 1775–1783.* Milledgeville, GA: Boyd Publishing, 2006. Vol. 1 pp. 274–275.

171. *Royal Georgia Gazette.* 25 April 1782.

172. McCall, Hugh. *The History of Georgia, containing brief sketches of the most remarkable events up to the present day, 1784.* Savannah: Seymour & Williams, 1811; Atlanta, Cherokee Pub. Co., 1969, 1909. Vol. I pp. 131–132. Jones, Charles C. Jr. *The History of Georgia.* Boston: Houghton, Mifflin and Company, 1883. Vol. 2 p. 275. Smith, Gordon Burns. *Morningstars of Liberty: the Revolutionary War in Georgia, 1775–1783.* Milledgeville, GA: Boyd Publishing, 2006. Vol. 1 pp. 93–94.

173. *Georgia Historical Quarterly.* 38: 167–8; 39: 60. *The Revolutionary Records of the State of Georgia.* 1: 330. (Savannah) *Georgia Gazette and The* (Savannah) *Gazette of the State of Georgia.* 20 September 1775. Smith, Gordon Burns. *Morningstars of Liberty: the Revolutionary War in Georgia, 1775–1783.* Milledgeville, GA: Boyd Publishing, 2006. Vol. 1 p. 65.

174. Letter from Col. Elbert to Major General Howe, at Savannah, April 19, 1778 in *South Carolina and American General Gazette.* April 23, 1778. Stevens, William B. *A History of Georgia: From its Discovery By Europeans to the Adoption of the Present Constitution.* Savannah: The Beehive Press, 1972 reprint of 1847 edition, p. 161. Searcy, Martha Condray. *The Georgia-Florida contest in the American Revolution, 1776–1778.* University, AL: University of Alabama Press, c1985. pp. 66–68, 134–135. Bennett, Charles E. and Lennon, Donald R. *A Quest for Glory: Major General Robert Howe and the American Revolution.* Chapel Hill & London: The University of North Carolina Press, 1991. p. 72.

175. Wayne to Greene, 7 May 1782, Ebenezer. Dennis M. Conrad et al., eds. *The Papers of General Nathanael Greene.* Chapel Hill and London: The University of North Carolina Press, 1998. Vol. 10 p. 405. Smith, Gordon Burns. *Morningstars of Liberty: the Revolutionary War in Georgia, 1775–1783.* Milledgeville, GA: Boyd Publishing, 2006. Vol. 1 p. 279.

176. Siebert, Wilbur Henry. *Loyalists in East Florida, 1774 to 1785; the Most Important Documents Pertaining Thereto Edited with an Accompanying Narrative.* Deland: The Florida State Historical Society, 1929. (American Revolutionary Series). Boston: Gregg Press, 1972. Vol. I pp. 66–67. Jones, Charles Colcock, Jr. *The History of Georgia.* Boston: Houghton, Mifflin and Company, 1883. Vol. II p. 298. Peckham, Howard Henry. *The Toll of Independence: engagements & battle casualties of the American Revolution.* Edited by Howard H. Peckham. Chicago: University of Chicago Press, 1974. p. 54.

177. Captain Henry Bryne, R. N. to Vice Admiral James Young, 21 May 1776, British National Archives. Admiralty 1/309 in NDAR 5: 197. Smith, Gordon Burns. *Morningstars of Liberty: the Revolutionary War in Georgia, 1775–1783.* Milledgeville, GA: Boyd Publishing, 2006. Vol. 1 p. 57.

178. Davis, Robert Scott, Jr. *Georgians in the Revolution: At Kettle Creek (Wilkes Co.) and Burke County.* Southern Historical Press, 1986. p. 125. Butler, Lewis. *The Annals of the King's Royal Rifle Corps.* Vol. 1: "The Royal Americans." London: John Murray, 1913. pp. 306–308. Houstoun to Laurens, 25 November 1778. *Laurens Papers.* Vol. 14 pp. 534–536. Heitman, Francis B. *Historical Register of Officers of the Continental Army during the War of the Revolution, April 1775. to December 1783.* Washington, DC, 1914; Baltimore: Genealogical Publishing Company, 1967. pp. 74–89. O'Kelley, Patrick. *Nothing But Blood and Slaughter.* Booklocker.com, 2004. Vol. 1 p. 205. Smith, Gordon Burns. *Morningstars of Liberty: the Revolutionary War in Georgia, 1775–1783.* Milledgeville, GA: Boyd Publishing, 2006. Vol. 1 p. 115.

179. McCall, Hugh. *The History of Georgia, containing brief sketches of the most remarkable events up to the present day, 1784.* Savannah: Seymour & Williams, 1811; Atlanta, Cherokee Pub. Co. 1969, 1909. pp. 365–366. Davis, Robert Scott, Jr. *Georgians in the Revolution: At Kettle Creek (Wilkes Co.) and Burke County.* Southern Historical Press, 1986. p. 125. Butler, Lewis. *The Annals of the King's Royal Rifle Corps.* Vol. 1: "The Royal Americans." London: John Murray, 1913. pp. 306–308. Heitman, Francis B. *Historical Register of Officers of the Continental Army during the War of the Revolution, April 1775 to December 1783.* Washington, DC. 1914; Baltimore: Genealogical Publishing Company, 1967. pp. 74–89. Moultrie, William, *Memoirs of the American Revolution so far as it related to the States of North and South Carolina and Georgia.* New York, 1802; (Eyewitness accounts of the American Revolution). [New York] New York Times [1968]. Vol. 1: p. 214. Harden, William, ed. *Order Book of Samuel Elbert, Colonel and Brigadier General in the Continental Army, Oct. 1776 to November 1778.* Georgia Historical Society Collections, 1902. p. 186. O'Kelley, Patrick. *Nothing But Blood and Slaughter.* Booklocker.com, 2004. Vol. 1 pp. 206, 208. Smith, Gordon Burns. *Morningstars of Liberty: the Revolutionary War in Georgia, 1775–1783.* Milledgeville, GA: Boyd Publishing, 2006. Vol. 1 p. 114.

180. *The (Charleston) South-Carolina and American General Gazette.* 26 November 1778. Smith, Gordon Burns. *Morningstars of Liberty: the Revolutionary War in Georgia, 1775–1783.* Milledgeville, GA: Boyd Publishing, 2006. Vol. 1 p. 114.

181. *The Massachusetts Spy: Or, American Oracle of Liberty.* 8: 407 (February 18, 1779): 3.

182. Smith, Gordon Burns. *Morningstars of Liberty: the Revolutionary War in Georgia, 1775–1783.* Milledgeville, GA: Boyd Publishing, 2006. Vol. 1 pp. 126–128. Murray, Major Patrick. *The Annals of the King's Royal Rifle Corps. Vol.* 1 p.310. White, George. *Historical Collections of Georgia.* New York: Pudney & Russell, 1855; Baltimore: Genealogical Pub. Co. 1969. pp. 472–473.

183. This account resembles that of Captain John Howell on June 4, 1781. Jones, Charles C. Jr. *The History of Georgia.* Boston: Houghton, Mifflin and Company, 1883. Vol. II p. 361. Peckham, Howard Henry. *The Toll of Independence: engagements & battle casualties of the American Revolution.* Edited by Howard H. Peckham. Chicago:

University of Chicago Press, 1974. p. 60. Searcy, Martha Condray. *The Georgia-Florida contest in the American Revolution, 1776–1778.* University, AL: University of Alabama Press, c1985. pp. 118, 163, 167. Smith, Gordon Burns. *Morningstars of Liberty: the Revolutionary War in Georgia, 1775–1783.* Milledgeville, GA: Boyd Publishing, 2006. Vol. 1 p. 203.

184. Extract of a letter from a gentleman in Augusta, dated July 5, 1779. *The Independent Chronicle and the Universal Advertiser.* XI: 571, page 1. White, George. *Historical Collections of Georgia.* New York: Pudney & Russell, 1855; Baltimore: Genealogical Pub. Co., 1969. p. 537. Jones, Charles C. Jr. The History of Georgia. Boston: Houghton, Mifflin and Company, 1883. Vol. II p. 362. McCall, Hugh. *The History of Georgia, containing brief sketches of the most remarkable events up to the present day, 1784.* Savannah: Seymour & Williams, 1811; Atlanta, Cherokee Pub. Co., 1969, 1909. p. 422.

185. McCall, Hugh. *The History of Georgia, containing brief sketches of the most remarkable events up to the present day, 1784.* Savannah: Seymour & Williams, 1811; Atlanta, Cherokee Pub. Co., 1969, 1909. p. 466.

186. *The Colonial Records of the State of Georgia.* compiled and published under authority of the legislature by Allen D. Candler. Atlanta, GA: C. P. Byrd, 1904. Vol. 12 p. 495. Davis, Robert Scott Jr. *Georgia Citizens and Soldiers of the American Revolution.* Easley, SC: Southern Historical Press, 1979. pp. 66, 75. Smith, Gordon Burns. *Morningstars of Liberty: the Revolutionary War in Georgia, 1775–1783.* Milledgeville, GA: Boyd Publishing, 2006. Vol. 1 p. 182.

187. Pancake, John S. *This Destructive War: The British Campaign in the Carolinas.* Tuscaloosa: University of Alabama Press, 1985. p. 62. Peckham, Howard Henry. *The Toll of Independence: engagements & battle casualties of the American Revolution.* Edited by Howard H. Peckham. Chicago: University of Chicago Press, 1974. p. 69. O'Kelley, Patrick. *Nothing But Blood and Slaughter.* Booklocker.com, 2004. Vol. 2 p. 130.

188. Jones, Charles Colcock, Jr. *The History of Georgia.* Boston: Houghton, Mifflin and Company, 1883. Vol. II pp. 499–501. O'Kelley, Patrick. *Nothing But Blood and Slaughter.* Booklocker.com, 2004. Vol. 3 pp. 272–273. Smith, Gordon Burns. *Morningstars of Liberty: the Revolutionary War in Georgia, 1775–1783.* Milledgeville, GA: Boyd Publishing, 2006. Vol. 1 p. 251.

189. *The (Charleston) Royal Gazette.*20 October to 24 October 1781. O'Kelley, Patrick. *Nothing But Blood and Slaughter.* Booklocker.com, 2004. Vol. 3 p. 367. Smith, Gordon Burns. *Morningstars of Liberty: the Revolutionary War in Georgia, 1775–1783.* Milledgeville, GA: Boyd Publishing, 2006. Vol. 1 p. 251.

190. Sullivan, Buddy. *Early Days on the Georgia Tidewater: the Story of McIntosh County & Sapelo, being a documented narrative account, with particular attention to the country's waterway and maritime heritage; plantation culture and uses of the land in the 19ᵗʰ century; and a detailed analysis of the history of Sapelo Island.* Researched & written by Buddy Sullivan. [Darien, GA]: McIntosh County Board of Commissioners, 1990. pp. 38, 71.

191. Searcy, Martha Condray. *The Georgia-Florida contest in the American Revolution, 1776–1778.* University, AL: University of Alabama Press, c1985. pp. 77–78. See McCall, Hugh. *The History of Georgia, containing brief sketches of the most remarkable events up to the present day, 1784.* Savannah: Seymour & Williams, 1811; Atlanta, Cherokee Pub. Co., 1969, 1909. Vol. II pp. 97, 324–325. Jones, Charles C. Jr. *The History of Georgia.* Boston: Houghton, Mifflin and Company, 1883. Vol. II p. 251. McIntosh to (Robert) Howe, 7 January 1777, in Hawes, Lilla M., ed. "The Papers of Lachlan McIntosh, 1774–1779," *Collections of the Georgia Historical Society.* Savannah: The Georgia Historical Society, 1957. Vol. 12 pp. 31–32. Smith, Gordon Burns. *Morningstars of Liberty: the Revolutionary War in Georgia, 1775–1783.* Milledgeville, GA: Boyd Publishing, 2006. Vol. 1 p. 66.

192. Davies, K. G. *Documents of the American Revolution, 1770–1783* (Colonial Office Series) XX Transcripts 1781. Irish University Press, 1979. p. 173. *Pennsylvania Gazette.* March 8, 1780; March 15, 1780. *The New Jersey Gazette.* 2: 102 (December 8, 1779): 3. O'Kelley, Patrick. *Nothing But Blood and Slaughter.* Booklocker.com, 2004. Vol. 1 p. 353–355.

193. Balch, Thomas. *The French in America during the war of independence of the United States, 1777–1783.* Thomas Balch; Thomas Willing Balch; Edwin Swift Balch, and others. Philadelphia, Porter & Coates, 1891–1895; Boston: Gregg Press, 1972. pp. 196–197. *Pennsylvania Gazette.* November 24, 1778. O'Kelley, Patrick. *Nothing But Blood and Slaughter.* Booklocker.com, 2004. Vol. 1 p. 356.

194. Nase, Henry. Diary of Henry Nase King's American Regiment. Nase Family Papers. The New Brunswick Museum, Archives Division, Transcribed by Todd Braisted. p. 23.

195. Hawes, Lilla M., ed. "The Papers of James Jackson, 1781–1798." *Collections of the Georgia Historical Society.* Savannah: The Georgia Historical Society, 1955. Vol. 11 p. 26. Anthony Wayne to Nathanael Greene, Headquarters, Savannah, 28 July 1782, in Dennis M. Conrad, ed. *The Papers of General Nathanael Greene.* Chapel Hill and London: The University of North Carolina Press, 2000. Vol. 11 pp. 470–471. Wayne to Greene, 28 February 1782, Ebenezer, ibid. p. 385.

Florida

1. Journal kept on board the South Carolina Sloop Commerce by Captain John Hatter, Sailing Master. "Hatter's Report." Drayton, John. *Memoirs of the American Revolution, From its Commencement to the Year 1776, Inclusive; as Relating to the State of South Carolina and Occasionally Referring to the States of North Carolina and Georgia.* Charleston, SC, 1821; (Eyewitness accounts of the American Revolution). [New York]: New York Times; Arno Press, c1969. NDAR 1: 1091–1092. Smith, Gordon Burns. *Morningstars of Liberty: the Revolutionary War in Georgia, 1775–1783.* Milledgeville, GA: Boyd Publishing, 2006. Vol. 1 p. 40.

2. Barss, Burton. *East Florida in the American Revolution.* Jacksonville: Guild Press, 1952. p. 14–15.

3. www.historicmarkers.com/Historical_Markers/Florida/Battle_of_Thomas_Creek_-_22/.

4. Mowat, Charles Loch. *East Florida as a British Province 1763–1784*. Berkeley and Los Angeles: University of California Press, 1943; reprinted Gainesville, FL: University of Florida Press, 1964. pp. 120–121. See Searcy, Martha Condray. *The Georgia-Florida contest in the American Revolution, 1776–1778*. University, AL: University of Alabama Press, c1985. p. 95 for the names. Governor Patrick Tonyn to Lord George Germain, St. Augustine 16ᵗʰ June 1777. British National Archives. Colonial Office. 5/557, 241–243. NDAR 9: 126–128. Boatner, Mark Mayo. *Landmarks of the American Revolution; A Guide to Locating and Knowing What Happened at the Sites of Independence.* Stackpole Books: [Harrisburg, PA], [1973]; 2nd ed. Library of Military History. Detroit: Charles Scribner's Sons, 2007. pp. 68, 73. Raab, James W. *Spain, Britain, and the American Revolution in Florida, 1763–1783.* Jefferson, NC and London: McFarland & Company. 2008. p. 102. Barss, Burton. *East Florida in the American Revolution.* Jacksonville: Guild Press, 1952. pp. 23–25. McCall, Hugh. *The History of Georgia, containing brief sketches of the most remarkable events up to the present day, 1784.* Savannah: Seymour & Williams, 1811; Atlanta, Cherokee Pub. Co., 1969, 1909. p. 340. Elbert, *Collections of the Georgia Historical Society.* 5, pt. 2: 25. For the derivation of the name Penholoway (or Finhalloway, etc.) Creek see Krakow, Kenneth K. *Georgia Place-names.* Macon: Winship Press, 1975. pp. 17–21. Bennett, Charles E. *Southernmost Battlefields of the Revolution.* Bailey's Crossroads, VA: Blair, 1970. pp. 8–23.Searcy, Martha Condray. *The Georgia-Florida contest in the American Revolution, 1776–1778.* University, AL: University of Alabama Press, c1985. p. 95; John Baker to Brigadier General McIntosh, Jericho, 22 May 1777, in the Peter Force Transcripts, Manuscript Collection No. 1601, Roll No. X-1601-01, in the Georgia Historical Society Library, Savannah, Georgia. Cashin, Edward J. *The King's Ranger: Thomas Brown and the American Revolution on the Southern Frontier.* Athens: University of Georgia Press, c1989. pp. 64–65. Charles Loch Mowat. *East Florida as a British Province, 1763–1784.* Gainesville, FL: University of Florida Press, 1964. pp. 107–124. Smith, Gordon Burns. *Morningstars of Liberty: the Revolutionary War in Georgia, 1775–1783.* Milledgeville, GA: Boyd Publishing, 2006. Vol. 1 pp. 76–78.

5. Searcy, Martha Condray. *The Georgia-Florida contest in the American Revolution, 1776–1778.* University, AL: University of Alabama Press, c1985. pp. 92–94.

6. Bennett, Charles E. *Southernmost Battlefields of the Revolution.* Bailey's Crossroads, VA: Blair, 1970. pp. 2–27. Searcy, Martha Condray. *The Georgia-Florida contest in the American Revolution, 1776–1778.* University, AL: University of Alabama Press, c1985. pp. 93–94.

7. Smith, Gordon Burns. *Morningstars of Liberty: the Revolutionary War in Georgia, 1775–1783.* Milledgeville, GA: Boyd Publishing, 2006. Vol. 1 pp. 78–80.

8. Barrs, Burton. *East Florida in the American Revolution.* Jacksonville: Guild Press, 1932. pp. 31–33. Raab, James W. *Spain, Britain, and the American Revolution in Florida, 1763–1783.* Jefferson, NC and London: McFarland & Company, 2008. p. 108. Mowat, Charles L. *History of East Florida: East Florida as a British Province, 1763–1784.* Berkeley: University of California Press, 1943. p. 122. Bennett, Charles E. and Lennon, Donald R. *A Quest for Glory: Major General Robert Howe and the American Revolution.* Chapel Hill & London: The University of North Carolina Press, 1991. p. 79.

9. Mowat, Charles Loch. *East Florida as a British Province 1763–1784.* Berkeley and Los Angeles: University of California Press, 1943; reprinted Gainesville, FL: University of Florida Press, 1964. p. 120.

10. Bennett, Charles E. *Southernmost Battlefields of the Revolution.* Bailey's Crossroads, VA: Blair, 1970. pp. 30–37. Bennett, Charles E., and Lennon, Donald R. *A Quest for Glory, Major General Robert Howe and the American Revolution.* Chapel Hill, NC: The University of North Carolina Press, 1991. McCall, Hugh. *The History of Georgia, containing brief sketches of the most remarkable events up to the present day, 1784.* Savannah: Seymour & Williams, 1811; Atlanta, Cherokee Pub. Co., 1969, 1909. p. 357. Murray's Memoir is in Butler, Lewis William George. *Royal Americans.* London: Smith, Elder & Co., 1913. pp. 304–305. Searcy, Martha Condray. *The Georgia-Florida contest in the American Revolution, 1776–1778.* University, AL: University of Alabama Press, c1985. pp. 144–145.

11. Bullen, Ripley P. Fort Tonyn and the Campaign of 1778. *The Florida Historical Quarterly.* 29: 4 (April, 1951): 253–260.

12. Letter from Elbert, Frederica, 19 April 1778, *The* (Charleston) *South-Carolina and American General Gazette.* 23 April 1778. Thomson, William. "Colonel Thomson's Order Book-June 24th, 1775, to November 3d, 1778," in A. S. Salley, the History of Orangeburg. County, South Carolina, etc. (Orangeburg, SC: R. Lewis Berry, Printer, 1898. pp. 455–456. James R. Ward, "Remains of Historic Fort Found on St. Marys River," (Jacksonville) *Florida Times Union.* 25 May 1975. Bennett, Charles E. *Southernmost Battlefields of the Revolution.* Bailey's Crossroads, VA: Blair, 1970. pp. 28–40. McCall, Hugh. *The History of Georgia, containing brief sketches of the most remarkable events up to the present day, 1784.* Savannah: Seymour & Williams, 1811; Atlanta: Cherokee Pub. Co., 1969, 1909. p. 359. Grimke, John Faucheraud. "Order Book of John Faucheraud Grimke, August 1778 to May 1780." *The South Carolina Historical and Genealogical Magazine.* XIV: 2 (April 1913): 190. Smith, Gordon Burns. *Morningstars of Liberty: the Revolutionary War in Georgia, 1775–1783.* Milledgeville, GA: Boyd Publishing, 2006. Vol. 1 pp. 104–106. Georgia in the American Revolution, 1775–1782 in Coleman, Kenneth. *A History of Georgia.* Athens: University of Georgia Press, 1977. pp. 77–80.

13. Memorial and particulars relative to Ft. St. Augustine with a plan of attack, by Marquis de Bretigny, 26 August 1778, U. S. Continental Congress. *Papers of the Continental Congress, 1774–1789.* National Archives and Records Service, microfilm. Smith, Gordon Burns. *Morningstars of Liberty: the Revolutionary War in Georgia, 1775–1783.* Milledgeville, GA: Boyd Publishing, 2006. Vol. 1 p. 112.

14. Siebert, Wilbur Henry. *Loyalists in East Florida, 1774 to 1785; the Most Important Documents Pertaining Thereto Edited with an Accompanying Narrative.* Deland: The Florida State Historical Society, 1929. (American Revolutionary Series). Boston: Gregg Press, 1972. Vol. I pp. 26, 37; vol. II pp. 329, 347–348. Peckham, Howard Henry. *The Toll of Independence: engagements & battle casualties of the American Revolution.* Edited by Howard H. Peckham. Chicago: University of Chicago Press, 1974. p. 6.

15. Journal of H. M. Schooner *St. John,* Lieutenant William Grant, British National Archives, Admiralty 51/4330. NDAR 5: 327–328.

16. Ibid. NDAR 5: 465.

17. Ibid. NDAR 5: 466.

18. Ibid. NDAR 5: 1031. *South Carolina and American General Gazette.* May 31 to August 2, 1776. NDAR 5: 1031.

19. Barss, Burton. *East Florida in the American Revolution.* Jacksonville: Guild Press, 1952. pp. 14–15.

20. Siebert, Wilbur Henry. *Loyalists in East Florida, 1774 to 1785; the Most Important Documents Pertaining Thereto Edited with an Accompanying Narrative.* Deland: The Florida State Historical Society, 1929. (American Revolutionary Series). Boston: Gregg Press, 1972. Vol. I p. 38.

21. Smith, Gordon Burns. *Morningstars of Liberty: the Revolutionary War in Georgia, 1775–1783.* Milledgeville, GA: Boyd Publishing, 2006. Vol. 1 p. 79.

22. Peckham, Howard Henry. *The Toll of Independence: engagements & battle casualties of the American Revolution.* Edited by Howard H. Peckham. Chicago: University of Chicago Press, 1974. p. 34. Fredriksen, John C. *Revolutionary War Almanac.* New York: Facts on File, c2006. p. 94. Mowat, Charles Loch. *East Florida as a British Province 1763–1784.* Berkeley and Los Angeles: University of California Press, 1943; reprinted Gainesville, FL: University of Florida Press, 1964. p. 120.

23. Extract of another letter from a gentleman in London, of the same date [August 6, 1777]. *Pennsylvania Evening Post.* October 21, 1777.

24. Haarmann, Albert W. The Spanish Conquest of British West Florida, 1779–1781. *The Florida Historical Quarterly.* 39: 2 (1960): 107.

25. Galvez Bernardo de. Diary of the Operations Against Pensacola, translated by Gaspar de Cusachs. New Orleans, LA. *The Louisiana Historical Quarterly.* 1 (January, 1917). 52.

26. *Royal Gazette.* 498 (July 7, 1781): 2.

27. Fleming, Thomas. Bernardo de Gálvez, the Forgotten Revolutionary Conquistador Who Saved Louisiana. *American Heritage.* 33: 3 (April/May), 1982. p. 38.

28. Rush, Nixon Orwin. *The Battle of Pensacola, March 9 to May 8, 1781; Spain's final triumph over Great Britain in the Gulf of Mexico.* Tallahassee, Florida: State University, 1966. pp. 57–58.

29. Peckham, Howard Henry. *The Toll of Independence: engagements & battle casualties of the American Revolution.* Edited by Howard H. Peckham. Chicago: University of Chicago Press, 1974. p. 82.

30. Galvez Bernardo de. Diary of the Operations Against Pensacola, translated by Gaspar de Cusachs. New Orleans, LA. *The Louisiana Historical Quarterly.* 1 (January, 1917): 52–56.

31. Galvez Bernardo de. Diary of the Operations Against Pensacola, translated by Gaspar de Cusachs. New Orleans, LA. *The Louisiana Historical Quarterly.* 1 (January, 1917): 56–58.

32. Galvez Bernardo de. Diary of the Operations Against Pensacola, translated by Gaspar de Cusachs. New Orleans, LA. *The Louisiana Historical Quarterly.* 1 (January, 1917): 56–58. Rush, Nixon Orwin. *The Battle of Pensacola, March 9 to May 8, 1781; Spain's final triumph over Great Britain in the Gulf of Mexico.* Tallahassee, Florida: State University, 1966. pp. 62–64. Peckham, Howard Henry. *The Toll of Independence: engagements & battle casualties of the American Revolution.* Edited by Howard H. Peckham. Chicago: University of Chicago Press, 1974. p. 82.

33. Galvez Bernardo de. Diary of the Operations Against Pensacola, translated by Gaspar de Cusachs. New Orleans, LA. *The Louisiana Historical Quarterly.* 1 (January, 1917): 58–59. Peckham, Howard Henry. *The Toll of Independence: engagements & battle casualties of the American Revolution.* Edited by Howard H. Peckham. Chicago: University of Chicago Press, 1974. p. 83. Rush, Nixon Orwin. *The Battle of Pensacola, March 9 to May 8, 1781; Spain's final triumph over Great Britain in the Gulf of Mexico.* Tallahassee, FL: State University, 1966. p. 65.

34. Bernardo de Gálvez's Combat Diary for the Battle of Pensacola, 1781. Edited by Maury Baker and Margaret Bissler Haas. *Florida Historical Quarterly.* 56: 2 (1977): 182. Peckham, Howard Henry. *The Toll of Independence: engagements & battle casualties of the American Revolution.* Edited by Howard H. Peckham. Chicago: University of Chicago Press, 1974. p. 83. Rush, Nixon Orwin. *The Battle of Pensacola, March 9 to May 8, 1781; Spain's final triumph over Great Britain in the Gulf of Mexico.* Tallahassee, FL: State University, 1966. pp. 65–66.

35. Galvez Bernardo de. Diary of the Operations Against Pensacola, translated by Gaspar de Cusachs. New Orleans, LA. *The Louisiana Historical Quarterly.* 1 (January, 1917): 59–60.

36. Bernardo de Gálvez's Combat Diary for the Battle of Pensacola, 1781. Edited by Maury Baker and Margaret Bissler Haas. *Florida Historical Quarterly.* 56: 2 (1977): 183. Peckham, Howard Henry. *The Toll of Independence: engagements & battle casualties of the American Revolution.* Edited by Howard H. Peckham. Chicago: University of Chicago Press, 1974. p. 83. Rush, Nixon Orwin. *The Battle of Pensacola, March 9 to May 8, 1781; Spain's final triumph over Great Britain in the Gulf of Mexico.* Tallahassee, FL: State University, 1966. pp. 66–67.

37. Galvez Bernardo de. Diary of the Operations Against Pensacola, translated by Gaspar de Cusachs. New Orleans, LA. *The Louisiana Historical Quarterly.* 1 (January, 1917): 61–63.

38. Peckham, Howard Henry. *The Toll of Independence: engagements & battle casualties of the American Revolution.* Edited by Howard H. Peckham. Chicago: University of Chicago Press, 1974. p. 84. Galvez Bernardo de. Diary of the Operations Against Pensacola, translated by Gaspar de Cusachs. New Orleans, LA. *The Louisiana Historical Quarterly.* 1 (January, 1917): 67. Worcester, Donald E. trans. Miranda's Diary of the Siege of Pensacola, 1781. *The Florida Historical Society Quarterly.* 29 (January, 1951): 176–177.

39. Galvez Bernardo de. Diary of the Operations Against Pensacola, translated by Gaspar de Cusachs. New Orleans, LA. *The Louisiana Historical Quarterly.* 1 (January, 1917): 67–71. Worcester, Donald E. trans.

Miranda's Diary of the Siege of Pensacola, 1781. *The Florida Historical Society.* Quarterly 29 (January, 1951): 177–183.

40. Smith, Buckingham, ed. Robert Farmar's Journal of the Siege of Pensacola, 1781. *Historical Magazine and Notes and Queries.* (June, 1860). p. 170. Caughey, John Walton. *Bernardo de Gálvez in Louisiana, 1776–1783.* Berkeley: University of California Press, 1934. pp. 187–214. Haarmann, Albert W. The Spanish Conquest of British West Florida, 1779–1781. *The Florida Historical Quarterly.* 39: 2, 1960. p. 130.

41. Smith, Buckingham, ed. Robert Farmar's Journal of the Siege of Pensacola, 1781. *Historical Magazine and Notes and Queries* (June, 1860). p. 171.

42. Stedman, C. *The History of the Origin, Progress and Termination of the American War.* London: printed for the author, 1794. Vol. II pp. 290–293.

43. Mora, Carl. Spain and the American Revolution: the campaigns of Bernardo de Gálvez. *Mankind.* 4: 8, 1974. p. 56. Bernardo de Gálvez's Combat Diary for the Battle of Pensacola, 1781. Edited by Maury Baker and Margaret Bissler Haas. *Florida Historical Quarterly.* 56: 2 (1977): 191–194. *The American Journal and General Advertiser.* III: 145 (July 18, 1781): 1. *The Providence Gazette and Country Journal.* XVIII: 916, p. 2.

44. *The American Journal and General Advertiser.* III: 145 (July 18, 1781): 1. *The Providence Gazette and Country Journal.* XVIII: 916, p. 2. Smith, Gordon Burns. *Morningstars of Liberty: the Revolutionary War in Georgia, 1775–1783.* Milledgeville, GA: Boyd Publishing, 2006. Vol. 1 p. 245.

45. *The American Journal and General Advertiser.* III: 145 (July 18, 1781): 1. *The Providence Gazette and Country Journal.* XVIII: 916, p. 2.

46. Smith, Buckingham, ed. "Robert Farmar's Journal of the Siege of Pensacola, 1781." *Historical Magazine and Notes and Queries.* (June 1860): 167–169. Haarmann, Albert W. The Siege of Pensacola, an order of battle. Tallahassee: *The Florida Historical Society Quarterly.* 44 (January, 1966): 193–199.

47. Haarmann, Albert W. The Spanish Conquest of British West Florida, 1779–1781. *The Florida Historical Quarterly.* 39: 2, 1960 p. 133. *The American Journal and General Advertiser.* III: 145 (July 18, 1781): 1. *The Providence Gazette and Country Journal.* XVIII: 916, p. 2.

48. Beerman, Eric, ed. and trans. *Yo Solo: The Battle Journal of Bernardo de Gálvez during the American Revolution.* New Orleans: Polyandros, 1978. Rush, Nixon Orwin. *The Battle of Pensacola, March 9 to May 8, 1781; Spain's final triumph over Great Britain in the Gulf of Mexico.* Tallahassee, FL: State University, 1966. Servies, James A., ed. *The Log of H.M.S. Mentor, 1780–1781: A New Account of the British Navy at Pensacola.* Pensacola: University Presses of Florida, 1982. Caughey, John Walton. *Bernardo de Gálvez in Louisiana, 1776–1783.* Berkeley: University of California Press, 1934. pp. 187–214. Cubberly, Fred. "Fort George (St. Michael), Pensacola." *Florida Historical Quarterly.* 6 (October 1928): 220–234. Farmar, Robert. "Bernardo de Galvez's Siege of Pensacola in 1781 (As related in Robert Farmar's Journal)." Edited by James A. Padgett. *Louisiana Historical Quarterly.* 26 (April 1943): 311–329. Faye, Stanley. "British and Spanish Fortifications of Pensacola, 1781–1821." *Florida Historical Quarterly.* 20 (January 1942): 277–292. Galvez, Bernardo de. "Bernardo de Galvez's Combat Diary for the Battle of Pensacola, 1781." Edited by Maury Baker and Margaret Bissler Haas. *Florida Historical Quarterly.* 56 (October 1977): 176–199. Galvez, Bernardo de. "Diary of the Operations at Pensacola." Translated by Gaspar de Cusachs. *Louisiana Historical Quarterly.* 1 (January 1917): 44–84. Haarmann, Albert W. "The Siege of Pensacola: An Order of Battle." *Florida Historical Quarterly.* 44 (January 1966): 193–199. Lackey, Robert J., ed. "The Siege of Pensacola in 1781." *Historical Magazine.* 4 (June 1976): 166–172. Rush, Nixon Orwin. *The Battle of Pensacola March 9 to May 8, 1781: Spain's Final Triumph Over Great Britain in the Gulf of Mexico.* Tallahassee, FL: Florida State University, 1966. Servies, James A., ed. *The Log of the H.M.S. Mentor, 1780–1781: A New Account of the British Navy at Pensacola.* Gainesville, FL: University Presses of Florida, 1982. Worcester, Donald E. translator. "Miranda's Diary of the Siege of Pensacola, 1781." *Florida Historical Quarterly.* 29 (January 1951): 163–196.

Alabama

1. Galvez Bernardo de. Diario, 28–29 February 1780, AGS GM 6912. Galvez Bernardo de. Bernardo De Galvez Diary of the Operations Against Pensacola, translated from a pamphlet belonging to Mr. Gaspar Cusachs New Orleans, La. "C" No. 1. *The Louisiana Historical Quarterly.* 47–84. Coker, William S. and Coker, Hazel P. *The Siege of Mobile 1780 in Maps with data on troops strength, military units, ships, casualties, and prisoners of war including a brief history of Fort Charlotte (Condé).* (Spanish Borderlands Series). Vol. IX. Pensacola: The Perdido Bay Press, 1982. p. 59. Calvert to Morris, Havana, 24 April 1780. *Papers of the Continental Congress.* Microcopy 274, Roll 64, p. 360.

2. Galvez Bernardo de. Diario, 9–10 March 1780, AGS GM 6912. Galvez Bernardo de. Bernardo De Galvez Diary of the Operations Against Pensacola, translated from a pamphlet belonging to Mr. Gaspar Cusachs New Orleans, La. "C" No. 1. *The Louisiana Historical Quarterly.* 47–84. Beer, William. "The Capture of Fort Charlotte, Mobile." *Publications of the Louisiana Historical Society.* 1 (1896): 31–34. Beer, William, ed. "The Surrender of Fort Charlotte, Mobile." *American Historical Review.* 1 (July 1896): 696–699. Coker, William S. and Coker, Hazel P. *The Siege of Mobile 1780 in Maps with data on troops strength, military units, ships, casualties, and prisoners of war including a brief history of Fort Charlotte (Condé).* (Spanish Borderlands Series) vol. IX. Pensacola: The Perdido Bay Press, 1982. p. 81.

3. Stedman, C. *The History of the Origin, Progress and Termination of the American War.* London: printed for the author, 1794. Vol. II pp. 188–189.

4. Beer, William. "The Capture of Fort Charlotte, Mobile." *Publications of the Louisiana Historical Society.* 1 (1896): 31–34. Beer, William, ed. "The Surrender of Fort Charlotte, Mobile." *American Historical Review.* 1 (July 1896): 696–699. Coker, William S. and Hazel P. Coker. T*he Siege of Mobile, 1780, in Maps: With Data on Troop Strength, Military Units, Ships, Casualties, and Prisoners of War including a Brief History of Fort Charlotte (Conde).* Pensacola, FL: Perdido Bay, 1982.

5. Galvez's appointment of Sergeant Juan Baptista Sarras, New Orleans, March 26, 1778, AGI, PC, legajo 184-A.

6. Peckham, Howard Henry. *The Toll of Independence: engagements & battle casualties of the American Revolution.* edited by Howard H. Peckham. Chicago: University of Chicago Press, 1974. p. 68. Galvez Bernardo de. Diario, 15–17 March 1780, AGS GM 6912. The reports of the number of men captured vary: 16, 20, and 37. Starr, J. Barton (Joseph Barton). *Tories, Dons, and Rebels: the American Revolution in British West Florida.* sponsored by the American Revolution Bicentennial Commission of Florida. Gainesville: University Presses of Florida, 1976. p. 174 n38. Caughey, John Walton. *Bernardo de Gálvez in Louisiana, 1776–1783.* Berkeley: University of California Press, 1934. p. 183. Galvez Bernardo de. Bernardo De Galvez Diary of the Operations Against Pensacola, translated from a pamphlet belonging to Mr. Gaspar Cusachs New Orleans, La. "C" No. 1. *The Louisiana Historical Quarterly.* 47–84. Coker, William S. and Coker, Hazel P. *The Siege of Mobile 1780 in Maps with data on troop strength, military units, ships, casualties, and prisoners of war including a brief history of Fort Charlotte (Condé).* (Spanish Borderlands Series). Vol. IX. Pensacola: The Perdido Bay Press, 1982. p. 95.

7. Caughey, John Walton. *Bernardo de Gálvez in Louisiana, 1776–1783.* Berkeley: University of California Press, 1934. pp. 171–186. Haarmann, Albert W. The Spanish Conquest of British West Florida, 1779–1781. *The Florida Historical Quarterly.* 39: 2, 1960. pp. 107–134. Holmes, Jack D. L. "Alabama's Bloodiest Day of the American Revolution: Counterattack at the Village, January 7, 1781."*Alabama Review.* 29 (July 1976): 208–219. "Dispatches of the Spanish Governors of Louisiana to the Captains-General of Cuba (11 vols. New Orleans Cabildo Museum). vol. X, book 2, pp. 21–23; *Ezpeleta to Piernas.* January 15, 1781, copy in ACS, CM, legajo 6912. The casualty list gives the following names of the dead: Sublieutenant Manuel Cordoba (España Regiment), Francisco Roca (España), Joseph Alvarez (España), Domingo Pardo (España), Pablo Britos (Principe), Geronimo Sanz (Principe), Jorge Ruano (Navarra), Pedro Yerro (Navarra), Manuel Blanco (Havana), Juan Santin (Havana), Alonso Martinez (Havana), Juan Fernandez (Havana), Simon Oficial (New Orleans Militia, Daniel Villars (New Orleans Militia).

8. Donelson, John. "Journal of a Voyage, intended by God's permission, in the good boat *Adventure*, from Fort Patrick Henry, on Holston river to the French Salt Springs on Cumberland River." Albright, Edward. *Early History of Middle Tennessee.* Nashville, TN: Brandon Printing Company, 1909. Ch. 14. Putnam, A. W. *The History of Middle Tennessee, or Life and Times of James Robertson.* Knoxville, University of Tennessee Press, 1971, 1859. Tennessee Historical Commission. *Three Tennessee Pioneer Documents.* [s. l.] : Univ. of Tennessee Press, 1964. John Donelson in the *Tennessee Encyclopedia of History and Culture* ver. 2.0. http://tennesseeencyclopedia.net/entry.php?rec=390. Finch, Jackie Sheckler. *Insiders' Guide to Nashville.* Guilford, CT: Insiders' Guide, 2011. pp. 23–24.

9. Rozema, Vicki. *Footsteps of the Cherokees: a guide to the Eastern homelands of the Cherokee Nation.* Winston-Salem, NC: John F. Blair, c1954. pp. 31, 394.

10. Cherokees in Alabama in *Encyclopedia of Alabama* http://www.encyclopediaofalabama.org/face/Article. jsp?id=h-1087. Chickamauga Wars (1776–1794) Wikipedia.com.

Mississippi

1. NDAR: 11, p. 680–682.

2. Fleming, Thomas. Bernardo de Gálvez, the Forgotten Revolutionary Conquistador Who Saved Louisiana. *American Heritage.* 33: 3 (April/May), 1982. p. 33. Haynes, Robert V. Mississippi and the American Revolution. http://www.vaiden.net/mississippi_highlights.html.

3. Boeta, Jose Rodulfo. *Bernardo de Galvez.* Madrid: Publicaciones Espanolas, 1977. p. 91. Delavillebeuvre, Juan. "Fort Panmure, 1779, as Related by Juan Delavillebeuvre to Bernardo de Galvez." Translated by Anna Lewis. *Mississippi Valley Historical Review.* 18 (March 1932): 541–548. Juan Delavillebeuvre to Bernardo de Galvez Dec. 12, 1779. Archivo General de las Indias. Papeles Procedentes de la Isla de Cuba. legajo 107. Scott, Kenneth, ed. "Britain Loses Natchez, 1779: An Unpublished Letter." *Journal of Mississippi History.* 26 (February 1964): 45–46. British National Archives. C. O. 5 vol. 397 p. 33.

4. Fleming, Thomas. Bernardo de Gálvez, the Forgotten Revolutionary Conquistador Who Saved Louisiana. *American Heritage.* 33: 3 (April/May), 1982. p. 36. Caughey, John Walton. *Bernardo de Gálvez in Louisiana, 1776–1783.* Berkeley: University of California Press, 1934.

5. Bearss, Edwin C. *Special History Report: The Colbert Raid Arkansas Post National Memorial Arkansas.* Denver, Colorado: Denver Service Center Historic Preservation Team National Park Service United States Department of the Interior, 1974. section II. B. 1. (http://www.nps.gov/arpo/colbert/).

6. Caughey, John Walton. *Bernardo de Gálvez in Louisiana, 1776–1783.* Berkeley: University of California Press, 1934. pp. 217–218. Bearss, Edwin C. *Special History Report: The Colbert Raid Arkansas Post National Memorial Arkansas.* Denver, Colorado: Denver Service Center Historic Preservation Team National Park Service United States Department of the Interior, 1974. Section II. B. 2. (http://www.nps.gov/arpo/colbert/). Peckham, Howard Henry. *The Toll of Independence: engagements & battle casualties of the American Revolution.* edited by Howard H. Peckham. Chicago: University of Chicago Press, 1974. p. 85. *Journal of Juan Delavillebeuvre April 21–May 4, 1781.* A. G. I. Cuba, p. 194.

Louisiana

1. Haarmann, Albert W. The Spanish Conquest of British West Florida, 1779–1781. *The Florida Historical Quarterly.* 39: 2, 1960. p. 111.

2. Peckham, Howard Henry. *The Toll of Independence: engagements & battle casualties of the American Revolution.* edited by Howard H. Peckham. Chicago: University of Chicago Press, 1974. pp. 47–48.

3. Boeta, Jose Rodulfo. *Bernardo de Galvez*. Madrid: Publicaciones Espanolas, 1977. p. 86.

4. Peckham, Howard Henry. *The Toll of Independence: engagements & battle casualties of the American Revolution.* edited by Howard H. Peckham. Chicago: University of Chicago Press, 1974. p. 64. Fleming, Thomas. Bernardo de Gálvez, the Forgotten Revolutionary Conquistador Who Saved Louisiana. *American Heritage.* 33: 3 (April/May), 1982. p. 34–36.

5. Haynes, Robert V. Mississippi and the American Revolution. http://www.vaiden.net/mississippi_highlights. html.

6. Boeta, Jose Rodulfo. *Bernardo de Galvez*. Madrid: Publicaciones Espanolas, 1977. p. 90–91.

7. Caughey, John Walton. *Bernardo de Gálvez in Louisiana, 1776–1783.* Berkeley: University of California Press, 1934. p. 161.

8. Fleming, Thomas. Bernardo de Gálvez, the Forgotten Revolutionary Conquistador Who Saved Louisiana. *American Heritage.* 33: 3 (April/May), 1982. p. 36.

9. Oliver Pollock to the Continental Commerce Committee. New Orleans 6th March 1778. NDAR 11: 535–536.

Michigan

1. Ward, Christopher. *The War of the Revolution*. New York: Macmillan, 1952. Vol. 2 p. 862.

2. Peckham, Howard Henry. *The Toll of Independence: engagements & battle casualties of the American Revolution.* edited by Howard H. Peckham. Chicago: University of Chicago Press, 1974. p. 80.

3. Boatner. Kinnaird, Lawrence. "The Spanish Expedition Against Fort St. Joseph in 1781, A New Interpretation." *Mississippi Valley Historical Review.* 19 (September 1932): 173–191.

Ohio

1. Peckham, Howard Henry. *The Toll of Independence: engagements & battle casualties of the American Revolution.* edited by Howard H. Peckham. Chicago: University of Chicago Press, 1974. p. 24.

2. Waller. George M. *The American Revolution in the West*. Chicago: Nelson Hall, 1976. p. 40.

3. Howe, Henry. *Historical Collections of Ohio.* Columbus: Henry Howe & Son, 1890. Vol. 3 pp. 378–380. Peckham, Howard Henry. *The Toll of Independence: engagements & battle casualties of the American Revolution.* Edited by Howard H. Peckham. Chicago: University of Chicago Press, 1974. p. 57.

4. Peckham, Howard Henry. *The Toll of Independence: engagements & battle casualties of the American Revolution.* Edited by Howard H. Peckham. Chicago: University of Chicago Press, 1974. p. 58. Pieper, Thomas I. and James B. Gidney. *Fort Laurens, 1778–1779: The Revolutionary War in Ohio.* [s. l.]: Kent State University Press, 1976. pp. 58–60.

5. Howe, Henry. *Historical Collections of Ohio.* Columbus: Henry Howe & Son, 1890. Vol. 3 pp. 378–380.

6. Pieper, Thomas I. and James B. Gidney. *Fort Laurens, 1778–1779: The Revolutionary War in Ohio.* [s. l.]: Kent State University Press, 1976. pp. 61–62.

7. Peckham, Howard Henry. *The Toll of Independence: engagements & battle casualties of the American Revolution.* Edited by Howard H. Peckham. Chicago: University of Chicago Press, 1974. p. 58.

8. Pieper, Thomas I. and James B. Gidney. *Fort Laurens, 1778–1779: The Revolutionary War in Ohio.* [s. l.]: Kent State University Press, 1976. pp. 63–64.

9. Pieper, Thomas I. and James B. Gidney. *Fort Laurens, 1778–1779: The Revolutionary War in Ohio.* [s. l.]: Kent State University Press, 1976. pp. 65–66.

10. Pieper, Thomas I. and James B. Gidney. *Fort Laurens, 1778–1779: The Revolutionary War in Ohio.* [s. l.]: Kent State University Press, 1976. Consul, Willshire Butterfield. *History of Fort Laurens.* Ohio State Archaeological and Historical Society, 1900. Peckham, Howard Henry. *The Toll of Independence: engagements & battle casualties of the American Revolution.* Edited by Howard H. Peckham. Chicago: University of Chicago Press, 1974. p. 58.

11. *The Pennsylvania Packet or the General Advertiser.* July 10, 1779. p. 1.

12. Pieper, Thomas I. and James B. Gidney. *Fort Laurens, 1778–1779: The Revolutionary War in Ohio.* [s. l.]: Kent State University Press, 1976. pp. 74–77.

13. Peckham, Howard Henry. *The Toll of Independence: engagements & battle casualties of the American Revolution.* edited by Howard H. Peckham. Chicago: University of Chicago Press, 1974. p. 66.

14. *Encyclopedia of the American Revolution.* 2nd ed. Harold E. Selesky, Editor in Chief. Detroit, New York, San Francisco: Charles Scribner's Sons. 2006. Vol. 1 p. 212.

15. Waller. George M. *The American Revolution in the West*. Chicago: Nelson Hall, 1976. p. 92.

16. http://www.heritagepursuit.com/Hardin/HarChapII.htm.

17. Bradford's Notes on Kentucky. In Howe, Henry. *Historical Collections of Ohio.* Columbus: Henry Howe & Son, 1890. Vol. 1 pp. 387–389. *The Pennsylvania Packet or the General Advertiser.* July 10, 1779. p. 1. Clark, George Rogers. *George Rogers Clark Papers 1771–1781.* James Alton James, ed. Springfield, Illinois Illinois State Historical Library, 1912. *Collections of the Illinois State Historical Library.* Vol. VIII. pp. cxxxix–cxli.

18. *The Freemen's Journal: or, The North-American Intelligencer.* II: XC (January 8, 1783): 3. *The New Jersey Gazette.* 6: 264 (January 15, 1783): 2.

19. Coshocton Campaign, derived from "Doddridge's Notes" in Howe, Henry. *Historical Collections of Ohio.* Columbus: Henry Howe & Son, 1890. Vol. 1 pp. 479–481. Waller. George M. *The American Revolution in the West.* Chicago: Nelson Hall, 1976. p. 112.

20. *Royal Gazette.* Issue 581 (April 24, 1782): 2. History of Coshocton County. Chapter XVII. http://www. heritagepursuit.com/Coshocton/cofile1.htm. http://www.tolatsga.org/dela.html. *Encyclopedia of the American Revolution.* Harold E. Selesky, editor in chief. 2nd ed. Detroit: Charles Scribner's Sons, 2007. Vol. I pp. 438–439. *The Encyclopedia of the American Revolutionary War: a political, social, and military history.* Gregory Fremont-Barnes, Richard Alan Ryerson, editors. Santa Barbara, CA: ABC-CLIO, 2006. Vol. II pp. 519–520. Hurt, R. Douglas. *The Ohio Frontier: Crucible of the Old Northwest, 1720–1830.* Bloomington and Indianapolis: Indiana University Press, 1996. Olmstead, Earl P. "A Day of Shame: The Gnadenhutten Story." *Timeline.* 8 (August–September 1991): 20–33.

21. Waller. George M. *The American Revolution in the West.* Chicago: Nelson Hall, 1976. p. 121. Butterfield, Consul Willshire. *An Historical Account of the Expedition against Sandusky under Col. William Crawford in 1782.* Cincinnati: R. Clarke, 1873. *Encyclopedia of the American Revolution.* Harold E. Selesky, editor in chief. 2nd Ed. Detroit: Charles Scribner's Sons, 2007. Vol. I pp. 286–288. *The Encyclopedia of the American Revolutionary War: a political, social, and military history.* Gregory Fremont-Barnes, Richard Alan Ryerson, editors. Santa Barbara, CA: ABC-CLIO, 2006. Vol. I pp. 11–315. Anderson, James H. *Ohio Archeological and Historical Publications.* 6 (1898): 14. Anderson, James H. "Col. William Crawford." *Ohio History.* 6 (1896): 1–34. Butterfield, Consul Willshire, ed. *The Washington–Crawford Letters: Being the Correspondence between George Washington and William Crawford from 1767 to 1781 Concerning Western Lands.* Cincinnati: Robert Clarke, 1877. Eckert, Allen. *The Frontiersmen: A Narrative.* Boston: Little, Brown, 1967. Knight, John. *Narrative of a Late Expedition Against the Indians.* New York: Garland, 1978. Brackenridge, Hugh Henry. *Narratives of a Late Expedition Against the Indians.* Philadelphia: Francis Bailey, 1783. Brown, Parker B. "The Battle of Sandusky: June 4–6, 1782." *Western Pennsylvania Historical Magazine.* 65 (April 1982): 115–151. Brown, Parker B. "Reconstructing Crawford's Army of 1782." *Western Pennsylvania Historical Magazine.* 65 (1982): 17–36. Brown, Parker B. "The Search for the Colonel William Crawford Burn Site: An Investigative Report." *Western Pennsylvania Historical Magazine.* 68 (1985): 43–66. Calloway, Colin G. *The American Revolution in Indian Country: Crisis and Diversity in Native American Communities.* Cambridge: Cambridge University Press, 1995. Pieper, Thomas I. and James B. Gidney. *Fort Laurens, 1778–1779: The Revolutionary War in Ohio.* [s. l.]: Kent State University Press, 1976. Rosenthal, Gustavus. "Journal of a Volunteer Expedition to Sandusky, from May 24 to June 13, 1782." *Pennsylvania Magazine of History and Biography.* 18 (1894): 120–157, 293–328.

Indiana

1. Burgan, Michael. *George Rogers Clark: American General.* (Revolutionary War Leaders). New York: Chelsea House, 2001. Gelbert, Doug. *American Revolutionary War Sites, Memorials, Museums, and Library Collections: A State-By-State Guidebook to Places Open to the Public.* McFarland: Jefferson, NC, c1998. Harding, Margery Herbling. *George Rogers Clark and his Men: military records, 1778–1784.* s. l.: Kentucky Historical Society, 1981. Lowell, Harrison H. *George Rogers Clark and the War in the West.* Lexington: University Press of Kentucky, 1976. Nester, William R. *Frontier War for American Independence.* Mechanicsburg, PA: Stackpole, 2004. Quaife, Milo Milton, ed. *The Conquest of the Illinois by George Rogers Clark.* Carbondale: Southern Illinois University Press, 2001. Scheer, George F. and Hugh F. Rankin. *Rebels and Redcoats.* Cleveland and New York: World Publishing Co., 1957. Starkey, Armstrong. *European and Native American Warfare, 1675–1815.* Oxford, UK: Routledge, 1998. Ward, Christopher. *The War of the Revolution.* New York: Macmillan, 1952. pp. 850–865.

2. Hamilton, Henry. *Henry Hamilton and George Rogers Clark in the American Revolution with the Unpublished Journal of Lieut. Gov. Henry Hamilton.* Edited by John D. Barnhart. Crawfordsville, IN: R. E. Banta, 1951. pp. 189–192.

3. Faragher, John Mack. *Daniel Boone: The Life and Legend of an American Pioneer.* New York: Henry Holt and Company, 1992. pp. 219–222.

4. Peckham, Howard Henry. *The Toll of Independence: engagements & battle casualties of the American Revolution.* Edited by Howard H. Peckham. Chicago: University of Chicago Press, 1974. p. 77.

5. Funk, Arville, L. *Revolutionary War Era in Indiana.* Corydon, IN: ALFCO Publications, 1975. pp. 17–20.

6. Clark, George Rogers. *George Rogers Clark Papers 1781–1784.* James, Alton James, ed. Springfield, Illinois State Historical Library, 1926. Collections of the Illinois State Historical Library Vol. XIX. p. 157. Peckham, Howard Henry. *The Toll of Independence: engagements & battle casualties of the American Revolution.* Edited by Howard H. Peckham. Chicago: University of Chicago Press, 1974. p. 97.

7. http://petite-fort.tripod.com/Fort_History.htm. Funk, Arville, L. *Revolutionary War Era in Indiana.* Corydon, IN: ALFCO Publications, 1975. pp. 21–22.

8. Funk, Arville, L. *Revolutionary War Era in Indiana.* Corydon, IN: ALFCO Publications, 1975. pp. 23–30.

Illinois

1. Alberts, Robert. *George Rogers Clark and the Winning of the Old Northwest.* Washington, DC: National Park Service, 1975. Ward, Christopher. *The War of the Revolution.* New York: Macmillan, 1952. pp. 850–865.

2. Clark, George Rogers. *George Rogers Clark Papers 1771–1781.* James, Alton James, ed. Springfield, Illinois State Historical Library, 1912. Collections of the Illinois State Historical Library Vol. VIII. pp. cxxxiii–cxxxiv.

West Virginia

1. Col. Arthur Campbell's Report of the Expedition Against the Cherokees, Dated Washington County, Jan. 15, 1781. *The Independent Ledger, and the American Advertiser*. III: 146 (March 19, 1781): 2.

2. *The Norwich Packet and the Connecticut, Massachusetts, New Hampshire, and Rhode Island Weekly Advertiser*. 4: 491 (from Monday, May 19 to Monday May 26, 1777): 3. *The Independent Chronicle and the Universal Advertiser*. 9: 460 (June 12, 1777): 2. *The Norwich Packet and the Connecticut, Massachusetts, New-Hampshire, and Rhode-Island Weekly Advertiser*. IV: 191 (May 26, 1777): 3.

3. Gen. Edward Hand to Jasper Yeates June 10, 1777. Original MS. in New York Public Library; Hand Papers A. L. S. *Pennsylvania archives*. Hazard, Samuel. Linn, John Blair and others. [s. l.: s. n.], 1852–?. 1ˢᵗ Series. Vol. V p. 445.

4. W. H. Hunter, "The Pathfinders of Jefferson County [Ohio]," *Ohio Archives and Historical Society Publications*. VI, 131.

5. De Hass, Wills. *History of the Early Settlement and Indian Wars of Western Virginia*. Wheeling: H. Hoblitzell; Philadelphia: King & Baird, 1851. p. 227.

6. Consul Willshire Butterfield; George Washington; William Irvine. *Washington-Irvine Correspondence: the official letters which passed between Washington and Brig.-Gen. William Irvine and between Irvine and others concerning military affairs in the West from 1781 to 1783; arranged and annotated, with an introduction containing an outline of events occurring previously in the Trans-Alleghany country*. Madison, WI: D. Atwood, 1882. p. 312.

7. Dawson, Henry B. *Battles of the United States by Sea and Land*. New York: Johnson, Fry, & Company, 1858. Vol. 1 pp. 266–270. De Hass, Wills. *History of the Early Settlement and Indian Wars of Western Virginia*. Wheeling: H. Hoblitzell; Philadelphia: King & Baird, 1851. pp. 223–230, 263–271. W. H. Hunter. "The Pathfinders of Jefferson County [Ohio]." *Ohio Archives and Historical Society Publications*. Vol. VI p. 131. *Chronicles of Border Warfare, or, A history of the settlement by the whites, of north-western Virginia, and of the Indian wars and massacres in that section of the state: with reflections, anecdotes, &c.* Withers, Alexander Scott; Powers, William; Hacker, William, and others. Cincinnati: R. Clarke Co., 1895 (7ᵗʰ Impression, 1920). pp. 356–360. Thwaites, Reuben Gold; Kellogg, Louise Phelps. *Frontier Defense on the Upper Ohio, 1777–1778*. Draper Series, Madison: Wisconsin Historical Society, 1912. Vol. III. p. 36.

8. Newton, J. H.; Nichols, G. G.; Sprankle, A. G. *History of the Pan-handle: being historical collections of the counties of Ohio, Brooke, Marshall and Hancock, West Virginia*. . . . Bowie, MD: Heritage Books, 1990, 1879. p. 127.

9. Norona, Delf. A Forgotten Account of the Sieges of Fort Henry. *West Virginia History*. 8 (April, 1947): 305–314. Dawson, Henry B. *Battles of the United States by Sea and Land*. New York: Johnson, Fry, & Company, 1858. Vol. 1 pp. 266–270. De Hass, Wills. *History of the Early Settlement and Indian Wars of Western Virginia*. Wheeling: H. Hoblitzell; Philadelphia: King & Baird, 1851. pp. 223–230, 263–271. W. H. Hunter, "The Pathfinders of Jefferson County [Ohio]." *Ohio Archives and Historical Society Publications*. Vol. VI p. 131. *Chronicles of Border Warfare, or, A history of the settlement by the whites, of north-western Virginia, and of the Indian wars and massacres in that section of the state: with reflections, anecdotes, &c.* Withers, Alexander Scott; Powers, William; Hacker, William, and others. Cincinnati: R. Clarke Co., 1895. 7ᵗʰImpression, 1920). pp. 219–228, 356–360. Thwaites, Reuben Gold; Kellogg, Louise Phelps. *Frontier Defense on the Upper Ohio, 1777–1778*. Draper Series, Madison: Wisconsin Historical Society, 1912. Boatner, Mark M. *Encyclopedia of the American Revolution*. McKay: New York, 3d ed., 1980, pp. 1196–1197. Massay, Glenn F. Fort Henry in the American Revolution. *West Virginia History*. 24 (1962–1963): 250–252, 256, 257. Clarke, Kenton Brady. *Pioneer Life in the West; comprising the adventures of Boone*. Philadelphia: The Keystone Publishing Co., 1890. p. 144–156. Hintzen, William. Betty Zane, Lydia Boggs, and Molly Scott: The Gunpowder Exploits at Fort Henry. *West Virginia History*. Vol. 55, pp. 95–109). Doddridge, Joseph. *Notes on the Settlement and Indian Wars of the Western Parts of Virginia and Pennsylvania from 1763 to 1783*. Wellsburg, VA: Joseph Doddridge, 1824. http://www.virtualology.com/virtualwarmuseum.com/revolutionarywarhall/forthenry.net/.

10. De Hass, Wills. *History of the Early Settlement and Indian Wars of Western Virginia*. Wheeling, VA: Hoblitzell, 1851. p. 280. Statement of J. F. Scott to W. C. Brockunier, Wheeling, August 1876, published in Newton, J. H.; Nichols, G. G.; Sprankle, A. G. *History of the Pan-handle: being historical collections of the counties of Ohio, Brooke, Marshall and Hancock, West Virginia*. . . . Bowie, MD: Heritage Books, 1990, 1879. p. 130.

11. Kellogg Louise Phelps. *Frontier Advance on the Upper Ohio 1778–1779*. Publications of the State Historical Society of Wisconsin Collections, Vol. XXIII; Draper Series, Vol. IV. Madison: Wisconsin Historical Society, 1916. p. 65. Peckham, Howard Henry. *The Toll of Independence: engagements & battle casualties of the American Revolution*. edited by Howard H. Peckham. Chicago: University of Chicago Press, 1974. p. 46.

12. Writers' Program (WV). *West Virginia; a guide to the mountain state*. compiled by workers of the Writers' Program of the Work Projects Administration in the State of West Virginia . . . Sponsored by the Conservation commission of West Virginia. New York: Oxford University Press [1941]. p. 435.

13. *Chronicles of Border Warfare, or, A history of the settlement by the whites, of north-western Virginia, and of the Indian wars and massacres in that section of the state: with reflections, anecdotes, &c.* Withers, Alexander Scott; Powers, William; Hacker, William, and others. Cincinnati: R. Clarke Co., 1895. pp. 217–218. Haymond, Henry. *History of Harrison County, West Virginia: from the early days of Northwestern Virginia to the present*. Morgantown, WV: Acme Pub. Co., 1973, 1910. p. 63. Calendar of letters. Wisconsin Historical Society. Draper Manuscript 1U74–79, 81, 82; 4ZZ10; 3NN146. Stember, Sol. *The Bicentennial Guide to the American Revolution*. Saturday Review Press: New York, [distributed by] Dutton, 1794; [s. l.]: New York Times and Arno Press, 1969. Vol. 3 pp. 76–78. Darlington's *Fort Pitt*, p. 226, August 2–13 in Thwaites, Reuben Gold; Kellogg, Louise Phelps. *Frontier Defense on the Upper Ohio, 1777–1778*. Draper Series, Vol. III. Madison: Wisconsin Historical Society, 1912. pp. 36–37.

14. Randolph C. Downes. *Council Fires on the Upper Ohio: A Narrative of Indian Affairs in the Upper Ohio Valley until 1795.* University of Pittsburgh Press, 1940; reprinted 1989, pp. 188, 205–207. Waller. George M. *The American Revolution in the West.* Chicago: Nelson Hall, 1976. pp. 35–39. *History of Fort Randolph: First Biennial Report of the Department of Archives and History.* West Virginia Department of Archives and History, 1906. pp. 236–39. http://www.wvculture.org/history/settlement/fortrandolph04.html.

15. Capt. William McKee to Gen. Edward Hand. Wisconsin Historical Society. Draper Manuscript 1U133 in Thwaites, Reuben Gold; Kellogg, Louise Phelps. *Frontier Defense on the Upper Ohio, 1777–1778.* Draper Series, Vol. III. Madison: Wisconsin Historical Society, 1912.

16. Nester, William. *The Frontier War for American Independence.* Mechanicsburg, PA: Stackpole, 2004. p. 195. *History of Fort Randolph: First Biennial Report of the Department of Archives and History.* West Virginia Department of Archives and History, 1906. pp. 236–239. http://www.wvculture.org/history/settlement/fortrandolph04.html

17. Peckham, Howard Henry. *The Toll of Independence: engagements & battle casualties of the American Revolution.* edited by Howard H. Peckham. Chicago: University of Chicago Press, 1974. p. 40. John Stewart (John Stuart) to Col° William Fleming Comm^d. of Botetourt. Septr. 12th 1777. 6NN112–18. A. D. S. in Thwaites, Reuben Gold; Kellogg, Louise Phelps. *Frontier Defense on the Upper Ohio, 1777–1778.* Draper Series, Vol. III. Madison: Wisconsin Historical Society, 1912. pp. 82,157 note 19.

18. Draper, Lyman. Draper Manuscript Collection. State Historical Society of Wisconsin. 2ZZ18.

19. Arthur Campbell to the Rev'd Charles Cummings. Col. William Christian to Col. William Fleming. 2ZZ81. A. L. S. Kellogg Louise Phelps. *Frontier Advance on the Upper Ohio 1778–1779.* Publications of the State Historical Society of Wisconsin Collections, Vol. XXIII; Draper Series, Vol. IV. Madison: Wisconsin Historical Society, 1916. pp. 70–73, 86–87, 405. De Hass, Wills. *History of the Early Settlement and Indian Wars of Western Virginia.* Wheeling: H. Hoblitzell; Philadelphia: King & Baird, 1851. pp. 240–253.

20. *Southern Historical Magazine.* (Charleston, WV). March 1809. p. 19.

21. Writers' Program (WV). *West Virginia; a guide to the mountain state.* compiled by workers of the Writers' Program of the Work Projects Administration in the State of West Virginia . . . Sponsored by the Conservation commission of West Virginia. New York: Oxford University Press, [1941]. p. 513.

22. De Hass, Wills. *History of the Early Settlement and Indian Wars of Western Virginia.* Wheeling: H. Hoblitzell; Philadelphia: King & Baird, 1851. pp. 231–234. Col. David Shepherd to Gen. Edward Hand. Draper, Lyman. Draper Manuscript Collection, State Historical Society of Wisconsin. 6ZZ9. Petition of John Cullins to Congress 2E67. 23d Cong., 1st sess., Reports of Committees, no. 268. Capt. John Van Metre to Col. Edward Cook. 75 6ZZ10—A. L. S. Kellogg Louise Phelps. *Frontier Advance on the Upper Ohio 1778–1779.* Publications of the State Historical Society of Wisconsin Collections, Vol. XXIII; Draper Series, Vol. IV. Madison: Wisconsin Historical Society, 1916. p. 112. Daniel McFarland to Gen. Edward Hand. 6ZZ11—A. L. S. Wisconsin Historical Society. Draper Manuscript in Thwaites, Reuben Gold; Kellogg, Louise Phelps. *Frontier Defense on the Upper Ohio, 1777–1778.* Draper Series, Vol. III. Madison: Wisconsin Historical Society, 1912. pp. 106–112. Waller. George M. *The American Revolution in the West.* Chicago: Nelson Hall, 1976. pp. 35–39. http://www.pointpleasantwv.org/Parks&Campgrounds/Local/Fort_Randolph/forts_randolph_blair.htm.

23. Calendar of letters. Wisconsin Historical Society. Draper Manuscript 1U64-67, 71, 72, July 14–20 in Thwaites, Reuben Gold; Kellogg, Louise Phelps. *Frontier Defense on the Upper Ohio, 1777–1778.* Draper Series, Vol. III. Madison: Wisconsin Historical Society, 1912. Peckham, Howard Henry. *The Toll of Independence: engagements & battle casualties of the American Revolution.* edited by Howard H. Peckham. Chicago: University of Chicago Press, 1974. p. 37. Writers' Program (WV). *West Virginia; a guide to the mountain state.* compiled by workers of the Writers' Program of the Work Projects Administration in the State of West Virginia . . . Sponsored by the Conservation commission of West Virginia. New York: Oxford University Press, [1941]. p. 205.

24. Kellogg Louise Phelps. *Frontier Advance on the Upper Ohio 1778–1779.* Publications of the State Historical Society of Wisconsin Collections, Vol. XXIII; Draper Series, Vol. IV. Madison: Wisconsin Historical Society, 1916. pp. 23, 185.

25. McIntosh to Col. Richard Campbell, November 3, 1778, p. 164. McIntosh to Col. Richard Campbell, November 7, 1778, pp. 167–168. McIntosh's Orders, November 2, 1778, pp. 439–444. McIntosh to Steel, November 3, 1778, pp. 165–166. McIntosh to Lackhart, November 4, 1778, p. 166; November 13, 1778, p. 444; November 16, 1778, pp. 444–445; November 17, 1778, p. 444. Richard Campbell to McIntosh, November 10, 1778, p. 169–170. McIntosh to Col. Richard Campbell, November 13, 1778, pp. 172–173. Steel to Col. Richard Campbell, 16 and 17 November, 1778, p. 173. Col. Richard Campbell to McIntosh, November 18, 1778, pp. 174–175. McIntosh's Orders, November 11, 1778, pp. 442–443. McIntosh's Orders, November 21, 1778. in Kellogg Louise Phelps. *Frontier Advance on the Upper Ohio 1778–1779.* Publications of the State Historical Society of Wisconsin Collections, Vol. XXIII; Draper Series, Vol. IV. Madison: Wisconsin Historical Society, 1916. Williams, Edward G., ed. "A Revolutionary Journal and Orderly Book of General Lachlan McIntosh's Expedition, 1778." *The Western Pennsylvania Historical Magazine.* XLIII (March, September, 1960), 12, 271. Jackson, Harvey H. *Lachlan McIntosh and the Politics of Revolutionary Georgia.* Athens: University of Georgia Press, 1979. pp. 84–85. Recollection of Capt. Jacob White, November. 1778, p. 163; Col. John Irving to McIntosh, November 8, 1778, Hawes, Lilla M., ed. *The Papers of James Jackson, 1781–1798.* Savannah: The Georgia Historical Society, 1955] pp. 32–33. Williams, Edward G. ed. "A Revolutionary Journal and Orderly Book of General Lachlan McIntosh's Expedition, 1778." *The Western Pennsylvania Historical Magazine.* XLIII (March, September, 1960). pp. 14–15, 16.

26. Hackenburg, Randy W. *Montour County and the American Revolution.* Boiling Springs, PA: Privately Published, 2009. p. 31. *Northumberland County in the American Revolution.* [Sunbury, PA]: Northumberland County Historical

Society (Pa.), 1976. pp. 236, 376–378. *Pennsylvania Archives.* Series 1, Vol. 9, p. 528. Meginness, John Franklin. *Otzinachson, or, A history of the West Branch Valley of the Susquehanna embracing a full account of its settlement, trials and privations endured by the early pioneers, full accounts of the Indian wars, predatory incursions, abductions, and massacres, &c., together with an account of the fair play system; and the trying scenes of the big runaway; interspersed with biographical sketches of some of the leading settlers, families, etc., together with pertinent anecdotes, statistics, and much valuable matter entirely new.* Philadelphia: H. B. Ashmead, 1857. pp. 260–263, 285. Meginness, John Franklin. *Otzinachson: a history of the West Branch Valley of the Susquehanna: its first settlement, privations endured by the early pioneers, Indian wars, predatory incursions, abductions and massacres, together with an account of the fair play system; and the trying scenes of the big run-away . . . biographical sketches of the leading settlers. . . .* Rev. ed. Williamsport, Pa. Gazette and Bulletin Printing House, 1889. pp. 623–625, 627,658.

27.   http://www.rootsweb.com/~wvbrooke/forts.htm.   http://www.rootsweb.com/~usgenweb/pa/1pa/1picts/frontierforts/ff33.html. Crumrine, Boyd; Ellis, Franklin. *History of Washington County, Pennsylvania: with biographical sketches of many of its pioneers and prominent men.* Philadelphia: H. L. Everts & Co., 1882. p. 134. *Chronicles of Border Warfare, or, A history of the settlement by the whites, of north-western Virginia, and of the Indian wars and massacres in that section of the state: with reflections, anecdotes, &c.* Withers, Alexander Scott; Powers, William; Hacker, William and others. Cincinnati: R. Clarke Co., 1895.

28. Hackenburg, Randy W. *Montour County and the American Revolution.* Boiling Springs, PA: Privately Published, 2009. p. 33. Meginness, John Franklin. *Otzinachson, or, A history of the West Branch Valley of the Susquehanna embracing a full account of its settlement, trials and privations endured by the early pioneers, full accounts of the Indian wars, predatory incursions, abductions, and massacres, &c., together with an account of the fair play system; and the trying scenes of the big runaway; interspersed with pertinent anecdotes, statistics, and much valuable matter entirely new.* Philadelphia: H. B. Ashmead, 1857, p. 271. Meginness, John Franklin. *Otzinachson: a history of the West Branch Valley of the Susquehanna: its first settlement, privations endured by the early pioneers, Indian wars, predatory incursions, abductions and massacres, together with an account of the fair play system; and the trying scenes of the big run-away . . . biographical sketches of the leading settlers . . .* Rev. ed. Williamsport, Pa. Gazette and Bulletin Printing House, 1889. p. 639.

Kentucky

1. Faragher, John Mack. *Daniel Boone: The Life and Legend of an American Pioneer.* New York: Henry Holt and Company, 1992. p. 145.

2. *The Encyclopedia of the American Revolutionary War: a political, social, and military history.* Gregory Fremont-Barnes, Richard Alan Ryerson, editors. Santa Barbara, CA: ABC-CLIO, 2006. Vol. II p. 663–665.

3. Peckham, Howard Henry. *The Toll of Independence: engagements & battle casualties of the American Revolution.* edited by Howard H. Peckham. Chicago: University of Chicago Press, 1974. p. 27.

4. Jillson, Willard Rouse; Boone, Daniel. *The Boone narrative; the story of the origin and discovery coupled with the reproduction in facsimile of a rare item of early Kentuckiana.* Louisville, KY: Standard Print. Co., 1932. p. 18. Butler, Mann. *A History of the Commonwealth of Kentucky.* Louisville: Wilcox, Dickerman and Co., 1834. p. 95.

5. Filson, John. *The Discovery and Settlement of Kentucke.* Wilmington [Kentucky]: James Adams, 1784; Ann Arbor: University Microfilms, 1966. p. 63. Butler, Mann. *A History of the Commonwealth of Kentucky.* Louisville: Wilcox, Dickerman and Co., 1834. p. 95.

6. Marshall, H. *History of Kentucky.* Frankfort: George S. Robinson, 1824. Vol. 1 p. 136. Butler, Mann. *A History of the Commonwealth of Kentucky.* Louisville: Wilcox, Dickerman and Co., 1834. pp. 124–127. *Encyclopedia of the American Revolution.* Harold E. Selesky, editor in chief. 2nd Ed. Detroit: Charles Scribner's Sons, 2007. Vol. I p. 78. *The Encyclopedia of the American Revolutionary War: a political, social, and military history.* Gregory Fremont-Barnes, Richard Alan Ryerson, editors. Santa Barbara, CA: ABC-CLIO, 2006. Vol. I p. 104. Adams, Michael C. C. "An Appraisal of the Blue Licks Battle." *Filson Club History Quarterly.* 75 (2001): 181–203. "Battle of Blue Licks." *Register of the Kentucky Historical Society.* 47 (July 1949): 247–249. Collins, Richard H. "The Siege of Bryan's Station." Edited by Willard Rouse Jillson. *Register of the Kentucky Historical Society.* 36 (January 1938): 15–25. Cotterill, Robert S. "Battle of Upper Blue Licks (1782)." *Historical Quarterly.* 2 (1927): 19–33. Wilson, Samuel M. *The Battle of the Blue Licks, August 19, 1782.* Lexington, KY: s. n., 1927.

7. http://www.mpcps.org/boone/danielb/dbtimeline.shtml.

8. Chinn, George Morgan. *Kentucky Settlement and Statehood 1750–1800.* Frankfort, KY: The Kentucky Historical Society, 1975. p. 125.

9. Chinn, George Morgan. *Kentucky Settlement and Statehood 1750–1800.* Frankfort, KY: The Kentucky Historical Society, 1975.

10. Ibid. pp. 125–127.

11. Butler, Mann. *A History of the Commonwealth of Kentucky.* Louisville: Wilcox, Dickerman and Co., 1834. p. 42–43. Faragher, John Mack. *Daniel Boone: The Life and Legend of an American Pioneer.* New York: Henry Holt and Company, 1992. pp. 145–147.

12. Faragher, John Mack. *Daniel Boone: The Life and Legend of an American Pioneer.* New York: Henry Holt and Company, 1992. pp. 149–150.

13. Story related by James Ray, as retold in J. J. Polk. *Autobiography of J. J. Polk.* Louisville. 1867 and in Collins, Lewis. *Historical sketches of Kentucky embracing its history, antiquities, and natural curiosities, geographical, statistical, and geological descriptions with anecdotes of pioneer life, and more than one hundred biographical sketches of distinguished pioneers, soldiers, statesmen, jurists, lawyers, divines, etc.* Maysville, Ky.: L. Collins, 1848. Vol. II p. 624 related in

Mason, Kathryn Harrod. *James Harrod of Kentucky*. Baton Rouge: Louisiana State University Press, 1951. pp. 176–177.

14. Dawson, Henry B. *Battles of the United States by Sea and Land*. New York: Johnson, Fry, & Company, 1858. Vol. 1 pp. 221–222. Butler, Mann. *A History of the Commonwealth of Kentucky*. Louisville: Wilcox, Dickerman and Co., 1834. p. 93.

15. Peckham, Howard Henry. *The Toll of Independence: engagements & battle casualties of the American Revolution.* edited by Howard H. Peckham. Chicago: University of Chicago Press, 1974. p. 40.

16. Faragher, John Mack. *Daniel Boone: The Life and Legend of an American Pioneer*. Henry Holt and Company New York, 1992. pp. 153–154.

17. Mason, Kathryn Harrod. *James Harrod of Kentucky*. Baton Rouge: Louisiana State University Press, 1951. p. 197.

18. Ranck, George W. *Boonesborough: Its Founding, Pioneer Struggles, Indian Experiences, Transylvania Days, and Revolutionary Annals*. Filson Club Publications No. 16. Louisville, Kentucky: John P. Morton & Company, 1901. p. 56.

19. Draper, Lyman. Draper Manuscript Collection, State Historical Society of Wisconsin. 12CC279. Cotterill, R. S. *History of Pioneer Kentucky*. Cincinnati: Johnson & Hardin, 1917. p. 115.

20. Ibid. Waller, George M. *The American Revolution in the West*. Chicago: Nelson Hall, 1976. pp. 41–42.

21. Faragher, John Mack. *Daniel Boone: The Life and Legend of an American Pioneer*. New York: Henry Holt and Company, 1992. pp. 149–150. Draper, Lyman. Draper Manuscript Collection, State Historical Society of Wisconsin. 12CC279. Cotterill, R. S. *History of Pioneer Kentucky*. Cincinnati: Johnson & Hardin, 1917. p. 115.

22. Cotterill, R. S. *History of Pioneer Kentucky*. Cincinnati: Johnson & Hardin, 1917. p. 118. Peckham, Howard Henry. *The Toll of Independence: engagements & battle casualties of the American Revolution*. Edited by Howard H. Peckham. Chicago: University of Chicago Press, 1974. p. 34.

23. Faragher, John Mack. *Daniel Boone: The Life and Legend of an American Pioneer*. New York: Henry Holt and Company, 1992. pp. 149–150.

24. Marshall, H. *History of Kentucky*. Frankfort: George S. Robinson, 1824. pp. 58–62. Waller, George M. *The American Revolution in the West*. Chicago: Nelson Hall, 1976. p. 80. Ranck, George W. *Boonesborough: Its Founding, Pioneer Struggles, Indian Experiences, Transylvania Days, and Revolutionary Annals*. Filson Club Publications No. 16. Louisville, Kentucky: John P. Morton & Company, 1901. p. 47.

25. Waller, George M. *The American Revolution in the West*. Chicago: Nelson Hall, 1976. pp. 79–81.

26. Faragher, John Mack. *Daniel Boone: The Life and Legend of an American Pioneer*. New York: Henry Holt and Company, 1992. p. 147.

27. Ranck, George W. *Boonesborough: Its Founding, Pioneer Struggles, Indian Experiences, Transylvania Days, and Revolutionary Annals*. Filson Club Publications No. 16. Louisville, KY: John P. Morton & Company, 1901. pp. 116–117.

28. Peckham, Howard Henry. *The Toll of Independence: engagements & battle casualties of the American Revolution.* edited by Howard H. Peckham. Chicago: University of Chicago Press, 1974. p. 73.

29. Waller, George M. *The American Revolution in the West*. Chicago: Nelson Hall, 1976. p. 116.

30. Filson, John. *The Discovery and Settlement of Kentucke*. Wilmington [Kentucky]: James Adams, 1784; Ann Arbor: University Microfilms, 1966. pp. 71–72.

31. Mason, Kathryn Harrod. *James Harrod of Kentucky*. Baton Rouge: Louisiana State University Press, 1951. pp. 190–192. Filson, John. *The Discovery and Settlement of Kentucke*. Wilmington [Kentucky]: James Adams, 1784; Ann Arbor: University Microfilms, 1966. pp. 71–72. Butler, Mann. *A History of the Commonwealth of Kentucky*. Louisville: Wilcox, Dickerman and Co., 1834. pp. 115–118. Lafferty, Maude Ward. "Destruction of Ruddle's and Martin's Fort's in the Revolutionary War." *Register of the Kentucky Historical Society*. 54 (October 1956): 297–338.

32. Mason, Kathryn Harrod. *James Harrod of Kentucky*. Baton Rouge: Louisiana State University Press, 1951, pp. 181–193.

33. Peckham, Howard Henry. *The Toll of Independence: engagements & battle casualties of the American Revolution.* edited by Howard H. Peckham. Chicago: University of Chicago Press, 1974. p. 88.

34. Marshall, H. *History of Kentucky*. Frankfort: George S. Robinson, 1824. p. 115. Cotterill, R. S. *History of Pioneer Kentucky*. Cincinnati: Johnson & Hardin, 1917. pp. 173–174. Peckham, Howard Henry. *The Toll of Independence: engagements & battle casualties of the American Revolution*. Edited by Howard H. Peckham. Chicago: University of Chicago Press, 1974. p. 81.

35. Marshall, H. *History of Kentucky*. Frankfort: George S. Robinson, 1824. pp. 115–116.

36. [Colonel Floyd's letters]. Butler, Mann. *A History of the Commonwealth of Kentucky*. Louisville: Wilcox, Dickerman and Co., 1834. pp. 15–117.

37. Butler, Mann. *A History of the Commonwealth of Kentucky*. Louisville: Wilcox, Dickerman and Co., 1834. pp. 112, 119. Kleber, John E. *The Kentucky Encyclopedia*. Lexington, KY: University Press of Kentucky, 1992. p. 345.

38. Bedford, A. Goff. *Land of Our Fathers: History of Clark County, Kentucky*. Mt. Sterling, KY: A. G. Bedford, 1958.

39. Ranck, George W. *Boonesborough: Its Founding, Pioneer Struggles, Indian Experiences, Transylvania Days, and Revolutionary Annals*. Filson Club Publications No. 16. Louisville, KY: John P. Morton & Company, 1901. p. 126.

40. Peckham, Howard Henry. *The Toll of Independence: engagements & battle casualties of the American Revolution*. Edited by Howard H. Peckham. Chicago: University of Chicago Press, 1974. p. 95.

41. Filson, John. *The Adventures of Colonel Daniel Boone: Containing a Narrative of the Wars of Kentucky: From the Discovery and Settlement of Kentucky.* Champaign, Ill. (P.O. Box 2782, Champaign 61825) Project Gutenberg. p. 8. http://authorsdirectory.com/b/1boon10.htm. http://www.earlyamerica.com/lives/boone/chapt3/index.html.

42. Filson, John. *The Adventures of Colonel Daniel Boone: Containing a Narrative of the Wars of Kentucky: From the Discovery and Settlement of Kentucky.* Champaign, Ill. (P. O. Box 2782, Champaign 61825) Project Gutenberg. p. 8. http://authorsdirectory.com/b/1boon10.htm. http://www.earlyamerica.com/lives/boone/chapt3/index.html.

43. Durrett, Reuben. *Bryant's Station and the Memorial Proceedings.* Filson Club Publications, No. 12. Louisville, KY: John P. Morton, 1897. pp. 115–116. Bradford, John. Historical Notes on Kentucky in Stipp, G. W. *Western Miscellany.* San Francisco: The Graborn Press, 1932. Section 13, pp. 129–130.

Missouri

1. Foley, William E. *A History of Missouri: Volume I 1673 to 1820.* Columbia: University of Missouri Press, 1971. p. 28. Blanco, Richard L., ed. *The War of the Revolution, 1775–1783: an encyclopedia.* New York: Garland Pub., 1993.

Tennessee

1. McDowell, William L. *Indian Books.* Columbia, SC: South Carolina Archives Dept., 1955–1970. (V. 1] Journals of the Commissioners of the Indian Trade, September 20, 1710–August 29, 1718. [v. 2] Documents relating to Indian affairs, May 21, 1750–August 7, 1754. [v. 3] Documents relating to Indian affairs, 1754–1765.).

2. Sketch of Henry Rutherford. *The American Historical Magazine.* V (1900): 225.

3. Saye, James Hodge. *Memoirs of Major Joseph McJunkin, Revolutionary Patriot.* [s. l.]: A Press, 1977. p. 6.

4. Ashe, Samuel A'Court. *History of North Carolina.* Greensboro: Charles L. Van Noppen, 1925. Vol. I pp. 548–549.

5. Ramsey, J. G. M. (James Gettys McGready). *The Annals of Tennessee to the end of the eighteenth century: comprising its settlement, as the Watauga association, from 1769 to 1777; a part of North Carolina, from 1777 to 1784; the state of Franklin, from 1784–1788; a part of North Carolina, from 1788-1790; the territory of the U. States, south of the Ohio, from 1790 to 1796; the state of Tennessee, from 1796 to 1800.* Charleston: J. Russell, 1853. Cherokee Prayer Site Guide: Including atrocity sites, death camps, missions, towns, battlefields, spiritual sites, etc. http://www.geocities. ws/gileadintl/atrocity-list.html.

6. Pickens, Andrew Lee. *Skyagunsta: the Border Wizard Owl, Major General Andrew Pickens (1739–1817).* Greenville, SC: Observer Printing Co., 1934. p. 29.

7. William Christian to Patrick Henry, October 27, 1776. *Virginia Magazine of History and Biography.* XVII (1909): 51–59.

8. Scoggins, Michael C; Edgar, Walter. *The Day It Rained Militia: Huck's Defeat and the Revolution in the South Carolina Backcountry, May–July 1780.* Charleston: the History Press, c2005. p. 34. Bass, Robert. *Gamecock: The life and campaigns of General Thomas Sumter.* Orangeburg, SC: Sandlapper, 2000. pp. 40–41.

9. Ashe, Samuel A'Court. *History of North Carolina.* Greensboro: Charles L. Van Noppen, 1925. Vol. I p. 553.

10. http://ftp.rootsweb.com/pub/roots-l/genealog/genealog.dentonj1. Kingsport-A Romance of Industry by Howard Long 1928. http://discoverkingsport.com/h-Battle-Island-Flats.shtml. O'Kelley, Patrick. *Nothing But Blood and Slaughter.* Booklocker.com, 2004. Vol. 1 pp. 151–152. Folmsbee, Stanley J.; Corlew, Robert E.; Mitchell, Enoch L. *Tennessee: A Short History.* Knoxville: The University of Tennessee Press, 1969. p. 68.

11. Alderman, Pat. *Nancy Ward/Dragging Canoe: Cherokee Chieftainess/Cherokee-Chickamauga War Chief.* The Overmountain Press, Jan 1, 1978. P. 44. *National Register of Historic Places Multiple Property Documentation Form, The Transformation of the Nolichucky Valley, 1776 –1960, 1. Settlement Patterns, 1776 –1960, March 1992.* National Park Service. P. 3.

12. Compton, Brian P. Revised History of Fort Watauga, A thesis presented to the faculty of the Department of History East Tennessee State University in partial fulfillment of the requirements for the degree Master of Arts in History. May 2005.

13. O'Kelley, Patrick. *Nothing But Blood and Slaughter.* Booklocker.com, 2004. Vol. 1 pp. 153–154. Folmsbee, Stanley J.; Corlew, Robert E.; Mitchell, Enoch L. *Tennessee: A Short History.* Knoxville: The University of Tennessee Press, 1969. p. 68. Ramsey, J. G. M. (James Gettys McGready). *The Annals of Tennessee to the end of the eighteenth century: comprising its settlement, as the Watauga association, from 1769 to 1777; a part of North Carolina, from 1777 to 1784; the state of Franklin, from 1784-1788; a part of North Carolina, from 1788-1790; the territory of the U. States, south of the Ohio, from 1790 to 1796; the state of Tennessee, from 1796 to 1800.* Charleston: J. Russell, 1853. Alderman, Pat. *The Overmountain Men.* The Overmountain Press, 1986. Woodward, Grace Steele. *The Cherokees.* Norman: University of Oklahoma Press, 1963.

14. "Letter from Charles Robertson to Richard Caswell, April 27, 1777. Cherokee Prayer Site Guide: Including atrocity sites, death camps, missions, towns, battlefields, spiritual sites, etc. http://www.geocities.ws/gileadintl/ atrocity-list.html. Ramsey, J. G. M. (James Gettys McGready). *The Annals of Tennessee to the end of the eighteenth century: comprising its settlement, as the Watauga association, from 1769 to 1777; a part of North Carolina, from 1777 to 1784; the state of Franklin, from 1784-1788; a part of North Carolina, from 1788-1790; the territory of the U. States, south of the Ohio, from 1790 to 1796; the state of Tennessee, from 1796 to 1800.* Charleston: J. Russell, 1853. p. 581. Fulmer, Linda. *Historical Notes on the Cherokee People.* Lindale, Texas: International Reconciliation Coalition Research, 2000. http://www.geocities.ws/gileadintl/cherokeehistory.html. Alderman, Pat. *The Overmountain Men: Battle of King's Mountain, Cumberland decade, State of Franklin, Southwest territory.* Johnson City, TN: Overmountain Press, 1986. Starr, Emmet. History of the Cherokee Indians and their Legends and Folk Lore. Baltimore, MD:

Genealogical Pub. Co., 2003, 1921. Woodward, Grace Steele. *The Cherokees*. Norman: University of Oklahoma Press, 1963. p. 98. *Encyclopedia of Tennessee*. New York: Somerset Publishers, 1993. Milling, Chapman James. *Red Carolinians*. Columbia, SC: University of South Carolina Press, 1969.

15. O'Kelley, Patrick. *Nothing But Blood and Slaughter*. Booklocker.com, 2004. Vol. 1 p. 269.

16. http://jrshelby.com/rfotw/genjames.htm. Extract of a letter from his Excellency Gov. Jefferson to the President of Congress, dated Williamsburg, June 19, 1779. *The Independent Ledger, and the American Advertiser*. II: 59 (July 26, 1779): 2. Letter of Evan Shelby to Gen. Washington, June 4, 1779. *The Independent Ledger, and the American Advertiser*. II: 59 (July 26, 1779): 2. O'Kelley, Patrick. *Nothing But Blood and Slaughter*. Booklocker.com, 2004. Vol. 1 p. 269. Robert L. English Pension File #R3354.

17. O'Kelley, Patrick. *Nothing But Blood and Slaughter*. Booklocker.com, 2004. Vol. 1 p. 307. Nichols, John L. Alexander Cameron, British Agent Among the Cherokee, 1764–1781. *South Carolina Historical Magazine*. 97: 2 (April 1996): 111. Davies, K. G. *Documents of the American Revolution 1770–1783* (Colonial Office Series) Vol. XVII Transcripts 1779. Irish University Press, 1977. pp. 232–233, 267–271. O'Donnell, James H. *Southern Indians in the American Revolution*. University of Tennessee Press, 1971. pp. 84–85.

18. Ramsey, J. G. M. (James Gettys McGready). *The Annals of Tennessee to the end of the eighteenth century: comprising its settlement, as the Watauga association, from 1769 to 1777; a part of North Carolina, from 1777 to 1784; the state of Franklin, from 1784-1788; a part of North Carolina, from 1788-1790; the territory of the U. States, south of the Ohio, from 1790 to 1796; the state of Tennessee, from 1796 to 1800*. Charleston: J. Russell, 1853. pp. 187–188. Parris, George. *Initial Phases of the War of Independence in the South (1775–1780)*, 1998. p. 61. http://donmchugh. tripod.com/paris/1775_1800.htm

19. Albright, Edward. *Early History of Middle Tennessee*. Brandon printing Company, 1909. Chapter 19, "Massacre At Renfroe's Station."

20. Alderman, Pat. *The Overmountain Men*. The Overmountain Press, 1986. p. 151. Albright, Edward. *Early History of Middle Tennessee*. Brandon printing Company, 1908. Chapter 19. Carr, John. *Early Times in Middle Tennessee*. Nashville, TN: Pub. for E. Carr, by E. Stevenson & F.A. Owen, 1857. Chapter 1. Pension application of Robert Hansley (Hensley) S4323, Transcribed by Will Graves.

21. Ramsey, J. G. M. (James Gettys McGready). *The Annals of Tennessee to the end of the eighteenth century: comprising its settlement, as the Watauga association, from 1769 to 1777; a part of North Carolina, from 1777 to 1784; the state of Franklin, from 1784-1788; a part of North Carolina, from 1788-1790; the territory of the U. States, south of the Ohio, from 1790 to 1796; the state of Tennessee, from 1796 to 1800*. Charleston: J. Russell, 1853. p. 447. Allbright, Edward. *Early History of Middle Tennessee*. Brandon Printing Company, 1909. p. 76. Carpenter, W. H. *History of Tennessee from Its Earliest Settlement to the Present time*. Philadelphia: Lippincott, Grambo & Co., 1854, p. 126. Putnam, A. W. *History of Middle Tennessee . . .*, Knoxville: University of Tennessee Press 1971, 1859. p. 89.

22. Ramsey, J. G. M. (James Gettys McGready). *The Annals of Tennessee to the end of the eighteenth century: comprising its settlement, as the Watauga association, from 1769 to 1777; a part of North Carolina, from 1777 to 1784; the state of Franklin, from 1784-1788; a part of North Carolina, from 1788-1790; the territory of the U. States, south of the Ohio, from 1790 to 1796; the state of Tennessee, from 1796 to 1800*. Charleston: J. Russell, 1853. p. 447. Allbright, Edward. *Early History of Middle Tennessee*. Brandon Printing Company, 1909. p. 80.

23. Allbright, Edward. *Early History of Middle Tennessee*. Brandon Printing Company, 1909. p. 51.

24. Ramsey, J. G. M. (James Gettys McGready). *The Annals of Tennessee to the end of the eighteenth century: comprising its settlement, as the Watauga association, from 1769 to 1777; a part of North Carolina, from 1777 to 1784; the state of Franklin, from 1784-1788; a part of North Carolina, from 1788-1790; the territory of the U. States, south of the Ohio, from 1790 to 1796; the state of Tennessee, from 1796 to 1800*. Charleston: J. Russell, 1853. p. 448.

25. Putnam, Albigence Waldo. *History of Middle Tennessee . . .* Knoxville: University of Tennessee Press, 1971, 1859. p. 116. Albright, Edward. *Early History of Middle Tennessee*. Nashville, TN: Brandon Printing Company, 1909.

26. Rozema, Vicki. *Footsteps of the Cherokees: a guide to the Eastern homelands of the Cherokee Nation*. Winston-Salem, NC: John F. Blair, c1954. p. 89.

27. Colonel Campbell's Report of the Expedition Against the Cherokees, Dated Washington County, Jan. 15, 1781. *The Independent Ledger, and the American Advertiser*. III: 146 (March 19, 1781): 2. *The New Jersey Gazette*. IV: 169 (March 21, 1781): 1. *The Norwich Packet and the Weekly Advertiser*. 390 (March 22,1781): 1. Thomas's *Massachusetts Spy Or, American Oracle of Liberty*. XI: 519 (April 19, 1781): 1. O'Kelley, Patrick. *Nothing But Blood and Slaughter*. Booklocker.com, 2004. Vol. 2 p. 380. White, Katherine Keogh. *The King's Mountain Men, The story of the Battle with Sketches of the American Soldiers who took part*. Genealogical Publishing Company, 1966. pp. 176, 182, 189, 206, 224. *Pennsylvania Gazette*. February 28, 1781. Dann, John C. *The Revolution Remembered, Eyewitness Account of the War for Independence*. University of Chicago Press, 1980. pp. 307–309. O'Donnell, James H. *Southern Indians in the American Revolution*. University of Tennessee Press, 1971. pp. 107–108.

28. Col. Campbell's Report of the Expedition Against the Cherokees, Dated Washington County, Jan. 15, 1781. *The Independent Ledger, and the American Advertiser*. III: 146 (March 19, 1781): 2. *The New Jersey Gazette*. IV: 169 (March 21, 1781): 1. *The Norwich Packet and the Weekly Advertiser*. 390 (March 22,1781): 1. Thomas's *Massachusetts Spy Or, American Oracle of Liberty*. XI: 519 (April 19, 1781): 1. O'Kelley, Patrick. *Nothing But Blood and Slaughter*. Booklocker.com, 2004. Vol. 2 pp. 388–389. *Pennsylvania Gazette*. February 28, 1781. Dann, John C. *The Revolution Remembered, Eyewitness Account of the War for Independence*. University of Chicago Press, 1980. pp. 308–309. O'Donnell, James H. *Southern Indians in the American Revolution*. University of Tennessee Press, 1971. pp. 107–108.

29. O'Kelley, Patrick. *Nothing But Blood and Slaughter*. Booklocker.com, 2004. Vol. 2 pp. 392–393. *Pennsylvania Gazette*. February 28, 1781. Dann, John C. *The Revolution Remembered, Eyewitness Account of the War for Independence*.

University of Chicago Press, 1980. pp. 308–309. O'Donnell, James H. *Southern Indians in the American Revolution.* University of Tennessee Press, 1971. pp. 107–108. http://donmchugh.tripod.com/paris/1775_1800.htm.

30. Col. Campbell's Report of the Expedition Against the Cherokees, Dated Washington County, Jan. 15, 1781. *The Independent Ledger, and the American Advertiser.* III: 146 (March 19, 1781): 2. *The New Jersey Gazette.* IV: 169 (March 21, 1781): 1. *The Norwich Packet and the Weekly Advertiser.* 390 (March 22,1781): 1. Thomas's *Massachusetts Spy Or, American Oracle of Liberty.* XI: 519 (April 19, 1781): 1.

31. O'Kelley, Patrick. *Nothing But Blood and Slaughter.* Booklocker.com, 2004. Vol. 2 pp. 398–399.

32. Swanton, John R. *The Indian Tribes of North America.* Washington: U.S. G.P.O., 1952. Starr, Emmett. *History of the Cherokee Indians and their Legends and Folk Lore.* Baltimore, MD: Genealogical Pub. Co., 2003, 1921. Ramsey, J. G. M. (James Gettys McGready). *The Annals of Tennessee to the end of the eighteenth century: comprising its settlement, as the Watauga association, from 1769 to 1777; a part of North Carolina, from 1777 to 1784; the state of Franklin, from 1784–1788; a part of North Carolina, from 1788–1790; the territory of the U. States, south of the Ohio, from 1790 to 1796; the state of Tennessee, from 1796 to 1800.* Charleston: J. Russell, 1853. Rozema, Vicki. *Footsteps of the Cherokees: a guide to the Eastern homelands of the Cherokee Nation.* Winston-Salem, NC: John F. Blair, c1954.

33. Ramsey, J. G. M. (James Gettys McGready). *The Annals of Tennessee to the end of the eighteenth century: comprising its settlement, as the Watauga association, from 1769 to 1777; a part of North Carolina, from 1777 to 1784; the state of Franklin, from 1784–1788; a part of North Carolina, from 1788–1790; the territory of the U. States, south of the Ohio, from 1790 to 1796; the state of Tennessee, from 1796 to 1800.* Charleston: J. Russell, 1853. Cherokee Prayer Site Guide: Including atrocity sites, death camps, missions, towns, battlefields, spiritual sites, etc. http://www.geocities.ws/gileadintl/atrocity-list.html. Rozema, Vicki. *Footsteps of the Cherokees: a guide to the Eastern homelands of the Cherokee Nation.* Winston-Salem, NC: John F. Blair, c1954. p. 89. Fulmer, Linda. *Historical Notes on the Cherokee People.* Lindale, TX: International Reconciliation Coalition Research, 2000. http://www.geocities.ws/gileadintl/cherokeehistory.html.

34. Ramsey, J. G. M. (James Gettys McGready). *The Annals of Tennessee to the end of the eighteenth century: comprising its settlement, as the Watauga association, from 1769 to 1777; a part of North Carolina, from 1777 to 1784; the state of Franklin, from 1784–1788; a part of North Carolina, from 1788–1790; the territory of the U. States, south of the Ohio, from 1790 to 1796; the state of Tennessee, from 1796 to 1800.* Charleston: J. Russell, 1853. Woodward, Grace Steele. *The Cherokees.* Norman: University of Oklahoma Press, 1963. Cherokee Prayer Site Guide: Including atrocity sites, death camps, missions, towns, battlefields, spiritual sites, etc. http://www.geocities.ws/gileadintl/atrocity-list.html.

35. http://www.wnfoundersmuseum.org/ftnash.htm.

36. William Fleming Pension Application S32250. Scoggins, Michael C; Edgar, Walter. *The Day It Rained Militia: Huck's Defeat and the Revolution in the South Carolina Backcountry, May–July 1780.* Charleston: the History Press, c2005. p. 37.

37. Ramsey, J. G. M. (James Gettys McGready). *The Annals of Tennessee to the end of the eighteenth century: comprising its settlement, as the Watauga association, from 1769 to 1777; a part of North Carolina, from 1777 to 1784; the state of Franklin, from 1784–1788; a part of North Carolina, from 1788–1790; the territory of the U. States, south of the Ohio, from 1790 to 1796; the state of Tennessee, from 1796 to 1800.* Charleston: J. Russell, 1853. p. 446. Albright, Edward. *Early History of Middle Tennessee.* Nashville, TN: Brandon Printing Company, 1909. p. 73.

38. Albright, Edward. *Early History of Middle Tennessee.* Nashville, TN: Brandon Printing Company, 1909. p. 73. Putnam, Albigence Waldo. *History of Middle Tennessee . . .* Knoxville: University of Tennessee Press, 1971, 1859. p. 83.

39. Putnam, Albigence Waldo. *History of Middle Tennessee . . .* Knoxville: University of Tennessee Press, 1971, 1859. p. 66. Ramsey, J. G. M. (James Gettys McGready). *The Annals of Tennessee to the end of the eighteenth century: comprising its settlement, as the Watauga association, from 1769 to 1777; a part of North Carolina, from 1777 to 1784; the state of Franklin, from 1784–1788; a part of North Carolina, from 1788–1790; the territory of the U. States, south of the Ohio, from 1790 to 1796; the state of Tennessee, from 1796 to 1800.* Charleston: J. Russell, 1853. p. 447.

40. Albright, Edward. *Early History of Middle Tennessee.* Nashville, TN: Brandon Printing Company, 1909. p. 94. Haywood, John. *The Civil and Political History of the State of Tennessee from its Earliest Settlement up to the Year 1796.* Nashville, TN: Publishing House of the Methodist Episcopal Church, South, 1891. p. 130 ff.

41. Haywood, John. op. cit. p. 128.

42. O'Kelley, Patrick. *Nothing But Blood and Slaughter.* Booklocker.com, 2004. Vol. 3 p. 26. Williams, Samuel Cole. *Tennessee During the Revolutionary War.* Nashville, TN: Tennessee Historical Commission, 1944.

43. http://en.wikipedia.org/wiki/Fort_Nashborough. http://victorian.fortunecity.com/rothko/420/aniyuntikwalaski/bluff.html. Henderson, Archibald. *The Conquest of the Old Southwest.* Chapter XIX. http://www.worldwideschool.org/library/books/lit/historical/TheConquestoftheOldSouthwest/chap19.html. O'Kelley, Patrick. *Nothing But Blood and Slaughter.* Booklocker.com, 2004. Vol. 3 pp. 175–176. Lipscomb, Terry W. *South Carolina Revolutionary Battles Part Ten, Names in South Carolina.* Volume XXX, Winter 1983, South Carolina Historical Society, 1983. p. 13. Draper, Lyman. Thomas Sumter Papers, Draper Manuscript Collection, State Historical Society of Wisconsin. Guild, Josephus Conn. *Old times in Tennessee: with historical, personal, and political scraps and sketches.* Nashville: Tavel, Eastman & Howell, 1878. pp. 300–304.

44. Revolutionary War Pension Applications, RG 15, Microcopy 804. O'Kelley, Patrick. *Nothing But Blood and Slaughter.* Booklocker.com, 2004. Vol. 3 p. 358.

45. Pickens, Andrew Lee. *Skyagunsta: the Border Wizard Owl, Major General Andrew Pickens (1739–1817).* Greenville, SC: Observer Printing Co., 1934. pp. 118–119.

46. Ibid. pp. 116–122.

47. Putnam, Albigence Waldo. *History of Middle Tennessee* . . . Knoxville: University of Tennessee Press, 1971, 1859. p. 156. Ramsey, J. G. M. (James Gettys McGready). *The Annals of Tennessee to the end of the eighteenth century: comprising its settlement, as the Watauga association, from 1769 to 1777; a part of North Carolina, from 1777 to 1784; the state of Franklin, from 1784–1788; a part of North Carolina, from 1788–1790; the territory of the U. States, south of the Ohio, from 1790 to 1796; the state of Tennessee, from 1796 to 1800.* Charleston: J. Russell, 1853. p. 456.

Arkansas

1. Coleman Roger E. *The Arkansas River and the Development of Arkansas Post.* Arkansas Historic Preservation Program, 1991. (Presented as a paper at Arkansas Post National Memorial on May 18, 1991 for the tenth annual Arkansas Heritage Week).

2. De Villiers to Gálvez, July 11, 1781, in Kinnaird, Lawrence. *Spain in the Mississippi Valley, 1765–1794.* Washington: U. S. Govt. Print. Off., 1949–. Vol. 1 pp. 429–431.

3. Faye, Stanley. "The Arkansas Post of Louisiana: Spanish Dominion," *The Louisiana Historical Quarterly.* 27, no. 3 [1944?]: 682.

4. Dubreuil to Miró, May 5, 1783, Papeles de Cuba, Legajo 107; Papeles de Cuba, Legajo 3, No. 8. Coleman Roger E. *The Arkansas River and the Development of Arkansas Post.* Arkansas Historic Preservation Program, 1991. (Presented as a paper at Arkansas Post National Memorial on May 18, 1991 for the tenth annual Arkansas Heritage Week) notes 63, 64, 102.

5. Corbitt, Duvon C. James Colbert and the Spanish claims to the east bank of the Mississippi. *Mississippi Valley Historical Review.* 24: 4 (Mar. 1938): 466–67. Faye, Stanley. "The Arkansas Post of Louisiana: Spanish Dominion." *The Louisiana Historical Quarterly.* 27, no. 3 [1944?]: 682–84. Dubreuil to Miró, May 5, 1783, Papeles de Cuba, Legajo 107.

6. Dubreuil to Miró, May 5, 1783, Papeles de Cuba, Legajo 107. Corbitt, Duvon C. James Colbert and the Spanish claims to the east bank of the Mississippi. *Mississippi Valley Historical Review.* 24: 4 (Mar. 1938): 467–68. Faye, Stanley. "The Arkansas Post of Louisiana: Spanish Dominion." *The Louisiana Historical Quarterly.*27, no. 3 [1944?]: 684–685.

7. Bearss, Edwin C. *Special History Report: the Colbert Raid Arkansas Post National Memorial Arkansas.* Denver, Colorado: Denver Service Center Historic Preservation Team National Park Service United States Department of the Interior, 1974. (http://www.nps.gov/arpo/colbert/). Faye, Stanley. "The Arkansas Post of Louisiana: Spanish Dominion." *The Louisiana Historical Quarterly.* 27, no. 3 [1944?]. Coleman Roger E. *The Arkansas River and the Development of Arkansas Post.* Arkansas Historic Preservation Program, 1991. (Presented as a paper at Arkansas Post National Memorial on May 18, 1991 for the tenth annual Arkansas Heritage Week).

Glossary

1. *Oxford English Dictionary.*

GLOSSARY

Abatis: Sharpened branches pointing out from a fortification at an angle toward the enemy to slow or disrupt an assault. (See Photo GA-16.)

Accoutrement: Piece of military equipment carried by soldiers in addition to their standard uniform and weapons.

Bar shot: A double shot consisting of two half cannon balls joined by an iron bar, used in sea-warfare to damage masts and rigging. (See Photo GA-7.)

Bastion: A fortification with a projecting part of a wall to protect the main walls of the fortification. (See Photo GA-21.)

Battalion: The basic organizational unit of a military force, generally 500 to 800 men. Most regiments consisted of a single battalion which was composed of ten companies.

Bateau: A light flat-bottomed riverboat with sharply tapering stern and bow. (See Photo FL-7.)

Battery: Two or more similar artillery pieces that function as a single tactical unit; a prepared position for artillery; an army artillery unit corresponding to a company in an infantry regiment.

Bayonet: A long, slender blade that can be attached to the end of a musket and used for stabbing. (See Photo GA-3.)

Bercha: A flatboat used for transporting cargo, particularly on the Ohio and Mississippi rivers. (See Photo AR-1.)

Best bower: The large anchor (about 4,000 pounds) on the starboard side of the bow of a vessel. The other is called the small-bower. Also the cable attached to this anchor. (See Photo SC-24.)

Blunderbuss: A short musket with a large bore and wide muzzle capable of holding a number of musket or pistol balls, used to fire shot with a scattering effect at close range. It is very effective for clearing a narrow passage, door of a house or staircase, or in boarding a ship. (See Photo GA-6.)

Bomb: An iron shell, or hollow ball, filled with gunpowder. It has a large touch-hole for a slow-burning fuse which is held in place by pieces of wood and fastened with a cement made of quicklime, ashes, brick dust, and steel filings worked together with glutinous water. A bomb is shot from a mortar mounted on a carriage. It is fired in a high arc over fortifications and often detonates in the air, raining metal fragments with high velocity on the fort's occupants. (See Photo GA-7.)

Bombproof: A structure built strong enough to protect the inhabitants from exploding bombs and shells.

Brig: A small two-masted sailing vessel with square-rigged sails on both masts.

Brigade: A military unit consisting of about 800 men.

Broadside: 1. The firing of all guns on one side of a vessel as nearly simultaneously as possible. 2. A large piece of paper printed on one side for advertisements or public notices.

Canister or **Cannister shot:** A kind of case-shot consisting of a number of small iron balls packed in sawdust in a cylindrical tin or canvas case. They were packed in four tiers between iron plates. (See Photo GA-7.)

Carronade: A short, stubby piece of artillery, usually of large caliber, having a chamber for the powder like a mortar. It is chiefly used on shipboard.

Chain shot: A kind of shot formed of two balls, or half-balls, connected by a chain, chiefly used in naval warfare to destroy masts, rigging, and sails. (See PhotoGA-7.)

Chandeliers: Large and strong wooden frames used instead of a parapet. Fascines are piled on top of each other against it to cover workmen digging trenches. Sometimes they are only strong planks with two pieces of wood perpendicular to hold the fascines.

Chevaux-de-frise: Obstacles consisting of horizontal poles with projecting spikes to block a passageway. They were used on land and modified to block rivers to enemy ships. (See Photo LA-2.)

Cohorn or **coehorn:** A short, small-barreled mortar for throwing grenades.

Company: The smallest military unit of the army consisting of about 45 to 110 men commanded by a captain, a lieutenant, and an ensign, and sometimes by a second lieutenant. A company usually has two sergeants, three or four corporals and two drums.

Crown forces: The allied forces supporting King George III. They consisted primarily of the British army, Hessian mercenaries, Loyalists, and Native Americans.

Cutter: 1. A single-masted sailing vessel similar to a sloop but having its mast positioned further aft. 2. A ship's boat, usually equipped with both sails and oars. In the eighteenth century, the terms sloop and cutter seem to have been used almost interchangeably.

Demilune: Fortification similar to a bastion but shaped as a crescent or half-moon rather than as an arrow.

Dragoon: A soldier who rode on horseback like cavalry. Dragoons generally fought dismounted in the 17th and 18th centuries.

Earthworks: A fortification made of earth. (See Photo FL-6.)

Embrasure: A slanted opening in the wall or parapet of a fortification designed for the defender to fire through it on attackers. (See Photo GA-5.)

Envelopment: An assault directed against an enemy's flank. An attack against two flanks is a double envelopment.

Espontoon: See **Spontoon.**

Fascine: A long bundle of sticks tied together, used in building earthworks and in strengthening ramparts. (See Photo GA-18.)

Fraise: Sharpened stakes built into the exterior wall of a fortification to deter attackers. (See Photo FL-6.)

Gabion: A cylindrical basket made of wicker and filled with earth for use in building fortifications.

Galley: A long boat propelled by oars. These boats had a shallow draft and were particularly useful in rivers, lakes, and other shallow bodies of water.

General engagement: An encounter, conflict, or battle in which the majority of a force is involved.

Glacis: A bank of earth in front of the conterscarp or covered way of a fort.

Grape shot: A number of small iron balls tied together to resemble a cluster of grapes. When fired simultaneously from a cannon, the balls separate into multiple projectiles. The shot usually consisted of nine balls placed between two iron plates. (See Photos GA-7.)

Grenadier: A soldier armed with grenades; a specially selected foot soldier in an elite unit selected on the basis of exceptional height and ability. (See Photos GA-15 and LA-1.)

Gun: A cannon. Guns were referred to by the size of the shot they fired. A 3-pounder fired a 3-pound ball, a 6-pounder fired a 6-pound ball.

Gundalow: An open, flat bottomed vessel about 53 feet long, 15 feet wide, and almost four feet deep in the center. It is equipped with both sails and oars, designed to carry heavy loads, usually armed with one gun at the bow and two mid-ship.

Hessian: A German soldier who fought with the British army. Most of the German soldiers came from the principality of Hesse-Cassel, hence the name. Other German states that sent soldiers include Brunswick, Hesse-Hanau, Waldeck, Ansbach-Bayreuth, and Anhalt-Zerbst. (See Photo LA-1.)

Howitzer: A cannon with a short barrel and a bore diameter greater than 30 mm and a maximum elevation of 60 degrees, used for firing shells at a high angle of elevation to reach a target behind cover or in a trench.

Hussars or **Huzzars:** Horse soldiers resembling Hungarian horsemen. They usually wore furred bonnets adorned with a cock's feather, a doublet with a pair of breeches, to which their stockings are fastened, and boots. They were armed with a saber, carbines, and pistols.

Jaeger: A hunter and gamekeeper who fought with the Hessians for the British army. They wore green uniforms, carried rifles, and were expert marksmen.

Jollyboat: A sailing vessel's small boat, such as a dinghy, usually carried on the stern. "A clincher-built ship's boat, smaller than a cutter, with a bluff bow and very wide transom, usually hoisted at the stern of the vessel, and used chiefly as a hack-boat for small work."[1]

Langrage: A particular kind of shot, formed of bolts, nails, bars, or other pieces of iron tied together, and forming a sort of cylinder, which corresponds with the bore of the cannon.

League: A unit of distance usually estimated at about three miles.

Letter of marque: A license granted by a monarch authorizing a subject to take reprisals on the subjects of a hostile state for alleged injuries. Later: Legal authority to fit out an armed vessel and use it in the capture of enemy merchant shipping and to commit acts which would otherwise have constituted piracy. See also **Privateer.**

Light infantry: Foot soldiers who carried lightweight weapons and minimal field equipment.

Loophole: Aperture or slot in defenses through which the barrels of small arms or cannon can be directed at an outside enemy. (See Photo GA-1.)

Loyalist: An American who supported the British during the American Revolution; also called Tory.

Magazine: A structure to store weapons, ammunition, explosives, and other military equipment or supplies.

Man-of-war: A warship. (See Photo GA-18.)

Matross: A private in an artillery unit who needed no specialized skills. Matrosses usually hauled cannon and positioned them. They assisted in the loading, firing, and sponging the guns.

Militia: Civilians who are part-time soldiers who take military training and can serve full-time for short periods during emergencies.

Minuteman: Member of a special militia unit, called a Minute Company. A minuteman pledged to be ready to fight at a minute's notice.

Mortar: A cannon with a relatively short and wide barrel, used for firing shells in a high arc over a short distance, particularly behind enemy defenses. They were not mounted on wheeled carriages. (See Photo GA-13.)

Musket: A firearm with a long barrel, large caliber, and smooth bore. It was used between the 16th and 18th centuries, before rifling was invented. (See Photo GA-3.)

Open order: A troop formation in which the distance between the individuals is greater than in close order (which is shoulder to shoulder). Also called extended order.

Palisade: A fence of pales or stakes, pointed at the top, and set firmly in the ground in a close row with others to form an enclosure or defense (See Photo GA-14).

Parapet: Earthen or stone defensive platform on the wall of a fort.

Parley: A talk or negotiation, under a truce, between opposing military forces.

Parole: A promise given by a prisoner of war, either not to escape, or not to take up arms again as a condition of release. Individuals on parole can remain at home and conduct their normal occupations. Breaking parole makes one subject to immediate arrest and often execution. From the French *parole* which means one's word of honor.

Pettiauger or **pettyauger:** 1. A long, narrow canoe hollowed from the trunk of a single tree or from the trunks of two trees fastened together. 2. An open flat-bottomed schooner-rigged vessel or two-masted sailing barge, of a type used in North America and the Caribbean. (See Photo FL-5.)

Pinnace: 1. A small light vessel, usually having two schooner-rigged (originally square-rigged) masts, often in attendance on a larger vessel and used as a tender or scout, to carry messages, etc. 2. A small boat, originally rowed with eight oars, later with sixteen, forming part of the equipment of a warship or other large vessel. It could also be navigated with a sail. (See Photo GA-12.)

Pirogue: A flat-bottomed boat six to 20 feet long with flaring sides and a sharp bow used for fishing and transportation in the Louisiana swamps and bayous. Propelled by paddles or poles.

Polacre: A three-masted vessel with square-rigged sails and pole masts without tops and crosstrees.

Portage: An overland route used to transport a boat or its cargo from one waterway to another; the act of carrying a boat or its cargo from one waterway to another.

Privateer: An armed vessel owned and crewed by private individuals and holding a government commission known as a letter of marque authorizing the capture of merchant shipping belonging to an enemy nation. See **Letter of marque.**

Rampart: An earthen fortification made of an embankment and often topped by a low protective wall.

Ravelin: A small outwork fortification shaped like an arrowhead or a V that points outward in front of a larger defense work to protect the sally port or entrance.

Redoubt: A temporary fortification built to defend a prominent position such as a hilltop. (See Photo GA-8 and FL-6.)

Regiment: A permanent military unit usually consisting of two or three companies. British regiments generally consisted of ten companies, one of which was grenadiers. Some German regiments consisted of 2,000 men.

Regular: Belonging to or constituting a full-time professional military or police force as opposed to, for example, the reserves or militia.

Ropewalk: A long, narrow building where rope is made.

Round shot: Spherical ball of cast-iron or steel for firing from smooth-bore cannon, a cannon ball. The shots were referred to by the weight of the ball: a 9-pound shot weighed 9 pounds; a 12-pound shot weighed 12 pounds. Round shot was used principally to batter fortifications. The balls could be heated ("hot shot") and fired at the hulls of ships or buildings to set them on fire. The largest balls (32- and 64-pounders) were sometimes called "big shot." (See Photo GA-7.)

Sapper: A soldier who specializes in making entrenchments and tunnels for siege operations.

Schooner: A fast sailing ship with at least two masts and with fore and aft sails on all lower masts.

Scow: A flat-bottomed sailboat with a rectangular hull.

Sedan chair: A chair or windowed cabin suitable for a single occupant. It is borne on poles or wooden rails that pass through brackets on the sides of the chair. The two or more porters who bear the chair are called "chairmen."

Shell: An explosive projectile fired from a large-bore gun such as a howitzer or mortar. See also **Bomb, Howitzer,** and **Mortar.** (See Photo GA-7.)

Ship of the line: A large warship with sufficient armament to enter combat with similar vessels in the line of battle. A ship of the line carried 60 to 100 guns.

Shot: A bullet or projectile fired from a weapon. See also: **Bar shot, Canister shot, Chain shot, Grape shot, Round shot, Sliding bar shot, Star shot.** (See Photo GA-7.)

Sliding bar shot: A projectile similar to a bar shot. A sliding bar shot has two interlocked bars that extend almost double the length of a bar shot, thereby increasing the potential damage to a ship's rigging and sails. (See Photo GA-7.)

Sloop: A small single-masted sailing vessel with sails rigged fore-and-aft and guns on only one deck. In the 18th century, the terms sloop and cutter seem to have been used almost interchangeably.

Sloop of war: A three-masted, square-rigged naval vessel with all her guns mounted on a single uncovered main deck.

Snow: A small sailing-vessel resembling a brig, carrying a main and fore mast and a supplementary trysail mast close behind the mainmast; formerly employed as a warship.

Sons of Liberty: Patriots who belonged to secret organizations to oppose British attempts at taxation after 1765. They often resorted to violence and coercion to achieve their purposes.

Spike [a gun]: To destroy a cannon by hammering a long spike into the touch hole or vent, thereby rendering it useless.

Spontoon: A type of half-pike or halberd carried by infantry officers in the 18th century (from about 1740). (See Photo GA-19.)

Stand of arms: A complete set of arms (musket, bayonet, cartridge box, and belt) for one soldier.

Star shot: A kind of chain-shot. (See Photo GA-7.)

Tory: A Loyalist, also called Refugee and Cow-Boy. The Whigs usually used the term in a derogatory manner.

Trunnions: Two pieces of metal sticking out of the sides of an artillery piece. They serve to hold the artillery piece on the carriage and allow it to be raised or lowered. The trunnions are generally as long as the diameter of the cannonball and have the same diameter.

Whig: Somebody who supported independence from Great Britain during the American Revolution. The name comes from the British liberal political party that favored reforms and opposed many of the policies of the King and Parliament related to the American War for Independence.

INDEX

Other titles in the

BATTLEGROUNDS OF FREEDOM series

by Norman Desmarais

Battlegrounds of Freedom: A Historical Guide to the Battlefields of the War of American Independence. 2005. This fascinating travelogue invites readers to re-enact each battle with maps and photos, well-written text, abundant notation of websites, and many other useful references. This work covers Maine to Georgia as well as western territories, listing all the major battles and many minor ones. 262 pages, 19 maps, 109 photos. Paperback. 0-9666196-7-6. $26.95.

The Guide to the American Revolutionary War in Canada and New England: Battles, Raids, and Skirmishes. 2009. Follow along as the author retraces every encounter of the Revolutionary War in Canada and New England along geographical lines. 262 pages, 8 maps, 49 photos. Paperback. 978-1-934934-01-2. $21.95.

The Guide to the American Revolutionary War in New York: Battles, Raids, and Skirmishes. 2010. Follow along as the author retraces every encounter of the Revolutionary War in New York along geographical lines. 284 pages, 4 maps, 37 photos. Paperback. 978-1-934934-02-9. $22.95.

The Guide to the American Revolutionary War in New Jersey: Battles, Raids, and Skirmishes. 2011. Follow along as the author retraces every encounter of the Revolutionary War in New Jersey along geographical lines. 286 pages, 3 maps, 44 photos. Paperback. 978-1-934934-04-3. $22.95.

The Guide to the American Revolutionary War in Pennsylvania, Delaware, Maryland, Virginia, and North Carolina: Battles, Raids, and Skirmishes. 2011. Follow along as the author retraces every encounter of the Revolutionary War in Pennsylvania and several South Atlantic states along geographical lines. 356 pages, 7 maps, 62 photos. Paperback. 978-1-934934-05-0. $29.95.

The Guide to the American Revolutionary War in South Carolina: Battles, Raids, and Skirmishes. 2012. Follow along as the author retraces every encounter of the Revolutionary War in South Carolina along geographical lines. 404 pages, 4 maps, 48 photos. Paperback. 978-1-934934-06-7. $37.95.

All titles available at www.buscainc.com or from book vendors everywhere

CPSIA information can be obtained at www.ICGtesting.com
Printed in the USA
LVOW12s2141070415

433704LV00001B/158/P